EVERYMAN, I will go with thee,

and be thy guide,

In thy most need to go by thy side

JOHN STOW

Born about 1525, the son of a London chandler.
Became a tailor; freeman of the Merchant
Taylors' Company, 1547. Charged with
Catholic sympathies, 1568–70, but acquitted.
Died 6th April 1605.

Stow's Survey of London

INTRODUCTION BY
H. B. WHEATLEY

Dent London Melbourne Toronto
EVERYMAN'S LIBRARY
Dutton New York

No 589 Hardback ISBN 0 460 00589 8
No 1589 Paperback ISBN 0 460 01589 3

INTRODUCTION

Stow's *Survey of London*, from its first publication in 1598, has taken rank as the first authority on the history of London, but this very fame has been the cause of some injury to the unity of the work, owing to the additions of successive editors, whose words have often been quoted as if they were written by the original author, although often referring to occurrences long after Stow's death.

What the reader of to-day wants, is the original work as it left the hands of the veteran antiquary, or as nearly as the change of spelling allows, because this gives him a vivid picture of Elizabethan London—the city in which Shakespeare lived and worked among a multitude of the men and women of those " spacious days," respecting whom we are all eager to learn something more. The *Survey* is a masterpiece of topographical literature written by a Londoner of ripe experience, who was interested in everything that occurred around him.

Stow founded his work upon documents of great value collected by himself, and also upon the splendid series of manuscripts belonging to the city of London, to which he had access as " fee'd chronicler " of the corporation.

The great charm of the book to the general reader is to be found in the personal touches by which we are informed of changes and incidents which occurred in Stow's own experience. Of this special feature several instances have been singled out, such as the boy fetching milk from the farm attached to the abbey of the minoresses, for which he paid one halfpenny for three pints; and the staking out by the tyrannical Thomas Cromwell of part of the gardens of Stow's father and others in Throgmorton Street to be added to his own garden, which after his execution came into the possession of the Drapers' Company, and are now covered by Throgmorton Avenue. Stow, in his description of the monuments of St. Paul's, alluding to the burial places of Sir Philip Sidney, Sir Francis Walsingham and Sir Christopher Hatton, says of

the latter "under a most sumptuous monument where a
merry poet writ thus—

> " Philip and Francis have no tombe,
>   For great Christopher takes all the roome."

Henry Holland, in his *Monumenta Sepulchralia Sancti Pauli*,
1614, tells us that there is " no doubt but the merry poet was
the merry old man Stow himself."

During the whole of his life Stow was indefatigable in his
work, but he kept the best wine for the last. The first edition
of the *Survey of London* was published in 1598, when he was
past seventy years of age, but there can be no doubt that the
whole of his previous life was a preparation for his great work.
He always lived in London, and he was interested in every
particular connected with his native city. Nothing of value
in its history ever escaped him, and what he did not personally
know, he often obtained information of from older men than
himself. Some of his informants could tell what their fathers
saw, so that their reminiscences often take us back to a long
past time. It is this mixture of the personal remembrances
of old men with his own memory of what he had seen, and
his careful examination of places himself, in corroboration of
tradition, which give such special value to his book.

Stow was always in search of information at first hand, and
other authors were glad to avail themselves of his wide experience. Sir George Buck, when writing the *History of
Richard III.*, availed himself of Stow's information that he
had talked to old men who remembered that maligned king
as " a comely prince." Stow's arrangement of his materials
is admirable, and many modern topographers might imitate
him with advantage. He himself acknowledged that the
model for his *Survey* was his friend William Lambarde's
excellent *Perambulation of Kent*, 1576. Some of his explana-
tions of the names of places, being grounded on historical
evidence, are often of great value, but others are little better
than crude guesses. This is not to the discredit of an author
writing in the sixteenth century, but some modern writers,
who ought to have a better knowledge of the origin of place
names, have been unwise enough to quote these as possible
etymologies. C. L. Kingsford, in his excellent edition of
the *Survey*, has corrected most of these from trustworthy
old documents. Stow improved his book in the second
edition, published in 1603, two years before his death, but he

omitted some passages in the first edition which are of interest to us, and which are noted in this edition.

Although it is chiefly the *Survey* which keeps Stow's memory green in popular esteem, his other literary productions were highly appreciated by many distinguished contemporaries. He found a valuable patron in Archbishop Parker, for whom he edited some old chronicles. Among his many friends must be named Camden, Lambarde, Savile, Dr. Dee, Robert Glover, Somerset Herald, and Fleetwood the Recorder, who hung in his study a portrait of Stow inscribed, " Johannes Stowe, Antiquarius Angliæ." The " antiquary " was very proud of this honour, and he told Massingham, who records the incident in his diary, that he thought himself " worthy of that title for his pains."

Stow was born about the year 1525, and came of a good London stock, his grandfather and father were tallow chandlers, and supplied the church of St. Michael, Cornhill, with lamp oil and candles. Thomas Stow, the grandfather, died in 1527, and directed his body " to be buried in the little green churchyard of St. Michael, Cornhill, nigh the wall as may be by my father and mother."

We have no particulars as to John Stow's schooling, and Kingsford points out that his remarks in the " chapter of Schools and other houses of Learning," respecting his seeing the scholars of divers grammar schools repair to the church-yard of St. Bartholomew, Smithfield, to a scholastic battle of disputation " hardly suggests that he took part in their exercises."

The general opinion seems to be that he was self-taught, but it is strange that the son of a fairly well-to-do citizen should not have been a scholar at one of these free grammar schools. He did not follow his father's business as a tallow chandler, but set up for himself as a tailor, in a house by the well within Aldgate, over which in later times a structure was erected widely known as Aldgate pump. Tailors have very generally had to put up with threadbare jokes on their trade, and Stow was no exception to the rule. Aubrey reports that Sir Henry Spelman said to Sir William Dugdale, " We are beholding to Mr. Speed and Stow for *stitching* up for us our English history," and Aubrey adds, " It seems they were both tailors." Stow was admitted to the freedom of the Merchant Taylors' Company, on 25th November 1547, but was never called to the livery or any office in the company. At the same

time he seems to have been highly esteemed, and was helpful
to the company. He became a pensioner about 1578, and
received four pounds a year until mid-summer 1600; this is
sometimes called his " fee " and sometimes his " pension."
At the latter date, when he had fallen upon evil days, his
pension was increased to ten pounds a year. This information
is given by C. M. Clode, under the heading of " the loving
brother of this mysterie, John Stowe," in his *Memorials of the
Fraternity*, 1875.

Stow's first literary work is one that does him great credit,
namely, the 1561 edition of Chaucer's works, and subse-
quently he helped his " loving friend " Speght with notes
from " divers records and monuments," which that friend used
in his edition of Chaucer published in 1597. He then turned
to the publication of the results of his historical studies. In
1565, he brought out *A Summarie of Englyshe Chronicles*,
which was frequently reprinted, also *The Summarie* abridged,
first in 1566, and often reprinted. *The Chronicles of England*
were published in 1580 and not reprinted. *The Annals of
England* appeared first in 1592, other editions issued by Stow
himself in 1601 and 1605. Editions continued by Edmond
Howes were published in 1615 and 1631.

The *Annals* are much of a compilation, but Stow has made
them interesting by the frequent insertion of his own opinions
and remarks. The bibliography of these works is somewhat
complicated, but Kingsford has set forth the dates and
distinctive characters of the different books with much
clearness.

Stow early fell into a discord with the chronicler Grafton,
and the two belaboured one another in print, sometimes having resort to bad puns. Grafton sneered at the " Memories
of superstitious foundations, fables foolishly *stowed* together,"
and Stow replied by alluding to empty *townes* and unfruitfull
grafts of Momus' offspring."

Stow's life was a stormy one, and he had much to endure,
both publicly and in his own family, but his friends helped
him through many of his difficulties. His younger brother
Thomas was ungrateful, and a thorn in his side for many
years.

In the early part of 1569 he was brought before the Lord
Mayor for having in his possession a copy of the manifesto
of the Spanish Ambassador on behalf of the Duke of Alva, but
he seems to have been able to clear himself. The same matter

was brought before the master and wardens of the Merchant Taylors' Company. Clode remarks respecting this occurrence: "It is curious to note from the depositions of the several examinants how very shy of knowing much about the matter they appear to have been. The knowledge or memory of the nine taylors examined was too frequently failing them to bring guilt home to any brother of the craft."

The trouble about the Alva manifesto drew the attention of the Queen's Council to Stow's library, and the Bishop of London (Grindal) was directed to have his house searched, and in reply the Bishop enclosed to Cecil a catalogue of "Stowe the taylour his unlawfull bookes," amongst these are "a great store of folishe fabulous bokes of old prynt as of Sir Degory, Sir Tryamore," etc., "old fantastical popish books printed in the old type." Thomas Stapleton's translation of Bede's *Ecclesiastical History* is among the objectionable books. Nothing, however, came of all this pother.

Stow appears to have been fairly well off for some years of his life, when he spent a considerable amount of money on the extensive collection of manuscripts which he gathered together. This library was well known to and much appreciated by his fellow antiquaries. Many of the important documents are now in the British Museum and other public libraries.

He gave up his business in order to devote himself uninterruptedly to his antiquarian labours. Although these labours were much appreciated they were not profitable, and in consequence his means were very limited in his later years. His poverty was brought under the notice of James I., who acknowledged his claims, but instead of giving substantial aid the king granted letters patent, dated 8th March 1604, authorising John Stow and his deputies to collect money—the "voluntary contribution and kind gratuities" of the king's subjects. This authority brought little money to the chronicler's wasted coffers, and it was indeed a pitiful reward for the well-directed labours of a life-time.

Stow did not long survive this remarkable instance of royal favour. He died on the 6th April 1605, and was buried in the Church of St. Andrew Undershaft, Leadenhall Street, where his widow erected a terra cotta monument to his memory, this, which shows the man as he lived, is one of the most interesting monuments in the city of a past London worthy.

Edmond Howes, his literary executor, and continuator of his

Annals, has left a vivid picture of the old chronicler, which completes this short notice of one of the most distinguished " Lovers of London."

" He was tall of stature, lean of body and face, his eyes small and crystalline, of a pleasant and cheerful countenance; his sight and memory very good; very sober, mild, and courteous to any that required his instructions; and retained the true use of all his senses unto the day of his death, being of an excellent memory. He always protested never to have written anything either for malice, fear, or favour, nor to seek his own particular gain or vain-glory ; and that his only pains and care was to write *truth*. He could never ride, but travelled on foot unto divers cathedral churches, and other chief places of the land to search records. He was very careless of scoffers, back-biters, and detractors. He lived peacefully, and died of the stone colic, being four-score years of age."

Stow is greatly to be commended for printing as an appendix to his *Survey*, William Fitzstephen's *Descriptio Londoniæ*, which originally formed an introduction to the same writer's *Life of Becket*. It is a remarkable relic, and unique in its interest as a vivid description of London in the twelfth century. The author is carried away by his enthusiasm, and probably exaggerates the beauties of the city. But he is not blind to evils, for he wisely says, " The city is delightful indeed, if it has a good governor," and we know that it did not always have that. The account of the sports of the citizens is particularly valuable, especially the early notice of the use of skates on the Moorfields during the winter time. We may be proud as Englishmen that no other city in Europe possesses so early a description of a mediæval town. It should be noted incidentally that " King Henry the Third " mentioned at the close of Fitzstephen's account is not the king usually known by that name; but Henry the second son of Henry II. This prince was crowned during his father's life-time; but died in 1182, seven years before his father. Matthew Paris also speaks of him as Henry III.

An enlarged edition of the *Survey* was prepared by Anthony Munday after Stow's death, and published in 1618. In 1633, four months after Munday's death, another edition, in folio, appeared " completely finished by the study of A. M., H. D., and others." John Strype took the matter in hand in the next century and made a new book of the *Survey* in two volumes, folio, 1720. The sixth edition, enlarged by John Strype, "brought down to the present time by careful hands," was published in the same form in 1754–5. Strype died in 1737. This edition of Stow is an excellent history of London, but most persons will agree with Thomas Hearne in his criticism, "Stow should have been simply reprinted as a venerable original, and the additions given in a different character."

It was not until 1842 that Stow's edition of 1603 was reprinted, when it was edited by W. J. Thoms, founder and first editor of *Notes and Queries*. C. L. Kingsford produced a critical edition of Stow's second edition (1603) which is of great value. It was published by the Clarendon Press, Oxford, in 1908. The editor gives an account of Stow's collections and MSS., tracing their present location.

HENRY B. WHEATLEY.

EDITORIAL NOTE

FOR this edition of the Survey the text has been revised and is reissued with misprints corrected and the following additions: (1) An enlarged Bibliography includes a list of ancient and medieval sources used by Stow, together with references to modern editions wherever possible. (2) Additional notes have been appended to correct the more glaring of Stow's errors. In the case of the sheriffs and mayors (pp. 444–73), Stow is so inaccurate that his list is quite useless for all practical purposes. It has therefore been corrected in the text. (3) A complete topographical index is supplied.

1956.

SELECT BIBLIOGRAPHY

I

The following authorities are mentioned in the text or footnotes of this edition:

Abbo of Fleury: *Passio Sancti Edmundi*, apud Migne CXXXIX.

Ammianus Marcellinus: *Rerum Gestarum Libri XXXI*, ed. C. U. Clarke, 1915.

Asser: *Aelfredi Regis Res Gestae*, ed. W. H. Stevenson, 1904.

Baldwin, William: *Beware of the Cat*, 1570, 1574 (a rare work, of which only ten copies are known to exist).

Bede: *Historia Ecclesiastica*, ed. E. Holder, 1890.

Beware of the Cat, see BALDWIN.

Caesar, C. Julius: *De Bello Gallico*, ed. T. Rice Holmes, 1914.

Calendar of the Close Rolls, 27 vols., 1892–1913 (continuing *Rotuli Clausarum in Turri Londiniensi Asservati*, 2 vols., ed. T. H. Hardy, 1833–4).

Calendars of Letter-Books of the City of London, 11 vols., ed. R. R. Sharpe, 1899–1912.

[C.P.R.] Calendars of the Patent Rolls, 49 vols., 1891–1914 (continuing *Calendar of Patent Rolls in the Tower*, ed. T. H. Hardy, 1935.

Capgrave, John: *Nova Ligenda Angliae* (a Catalogue of the English Saints, being a recension of Tinmouth's *Sanctilogium* (1366), which is itself based on the *Sanctilogium* by Guido, Abbot of Saint-Denis), 2 vols., ed. C. Horstmann, 1901.

Cartulary of the Hospital of St John, Cott. MS. Nero E. VI.

Commines, Philippe de, *Mémoires*, ed. C. Whiblen, 1897.

Dio Cassius: *Historiarum Romanarum quae supersunt*, ed. U. P. Boissevin, 5 vols., 1895–1931.

Fabian, Robert: *The Great Chronicle of London*, ed. A. H. Thomas, 1928.

Florence of Worcester: *Chronicon ex Chronicis*, ed. B. Thorpe, 2 vols., 1848–9.

Geoffrey of Monmouth: *Historia Regum Britanniae*, ed. J. A. Giles, 1844.

Gervase of Tilbury: *Otia Imperialia*, ed. G. Leibnitz, 1707–10.

Grafton, R., *An Abridgement of the Chronicles of England*, 1562.

Henry of Huntingdon: *Historia Anglorum*, ed. T. Arnold, 1879.

Higden, Ranulf: *Polychronicon*, ed. C. Babington and J. R. Lumbry, 9 vols., 1865–86.

Hoveden, Roger: *Chronica*, ed. W. Stubbs, 4 vols., 1872–3.

Knighton, H.: *Chronicon*, ed. J. R. Lumby, 2 vols., 1889–95.

Letter-Books, see CALENDARS OF LETTER-BOOKS.

Liber Bermondsey
Liber Burton ⎫ vols. i, ii, iii of *Annales Monastici*, 5 vols., ed.
Liber Dunstable ⎬ H. R. Luard, 1864–9.
Liber Waverley ⎭

Liber Clerkenwell, Cott. MS. Faustina B. ii.

Liber Custumarum, in *Munimenta Gildhallae Londiniensis*, vol. ii, i. ii, ed. H. T. Riley, 1861.

Liber de Antiquis Ligibus, ed. H. T. Riley, 1863.

Liber Dunmow, Cott. MS. Cleopatra C. iii: fos. 291–7.

Liber Dunthorn, MS. in the Corporation of London Records Office.

Liber Ely, MS. in Muniment Room at Ely Cathedral.

Liber Horn, MS. in the Corporation of London Records Office.

Liber Papie, Cott. MS. Vitellius F. xvi.

Liber St Albans, printed with Amundesham's *Annales* in vol. ix of *Chronica Monasterii Sancti Albani*, ed. H. T. Riley, 1863–76.

Liber St Bartholomew, Cott. MS. Vespasian ix.

Liber S. Mariae Eborum, ed. (as *An Anominalle Chronicle*) V. H. Galbraith, 1927.

Liber S. Mariae Overie, MS. lost.

Liber Trinitatis, MS. in the Hunterian Museum, Glasgow; modern copy Guildhall Records MS. 122; printed in the notes to T. Hearne's edition of William of Newburgh, 1719.

Liber Woodbridge, MS. lost.

London, John [of], *alias* Bever, John, once reputed author of *Flores Historiarum*, ed. H. R. Luard, 1890.

Lydgate, John: *Legend of St Edmund and St Fremund*, ed. Lord F. Harvey in *Corolla Sancti Edmundi*, 1907. For 'London Lick-penny' see Lydgate's *Minor Poems* (Percy Society).

Marianus Scotus: *Chronica*, apud Migne CXLVII.

Matthew Paris: *Chronica Majora*, ed. H. Luard, 7 vols., 1872–83.

Mountgomery, John: 'Order of the Marching Watch,' printed in Harrison's *England*, ed. Furnival, E.E.T.S., 1909.

Packington, William: Chronicle (written in French) of which translated fragments survive in Leland's *Collectanea*.

Paston Letters, The, ed. J. Gairdner, 6 vols., 1904.

Peter of Ickham: *Le Livere de Reis de Brittanie*, ed. S. Glover, 1865.

Pomponius Mela: *De Situ Orbis*, ed. C. H. Tzschucke, 1806–7.

Ranulph of Coggeshall: *Chronicon*, ed. J. Stevenson, 1875.

Roger of Wendover: *Flores Historiarum*, ed. H. O. Coke, 1841–4.

Rotuli Parliamentorum (Parliament Rolls), 6 vols., 1767–83; Index, 1832.

Simeon of Durham: *Opera*, ed. T. Arnold, 2 vols., 1882–5.

Strabo: *Geographia*, ed. H. L. Jones, 8 vols. (Loeb Library).

Sulcardus: *De Constitutione Ecclesiae Westmonasteriensis*, Cott. MS. Faustina A. iii.

Tacitus: P. Cornelius, *Annales*, ed. K. Nipperdey and G. Andresen, 11th edition, 1915.

Trivet, N.: *Annales Sex Regum Angliae*, ed. A. Hall, 1719.

Vita Arkenwaldi, ed. Sir I. Gollancz, 1922.

Walsingham, Thomas: *Historia Anglicana*, printed as vol. i of *Chronica Monasterii Sancti Albani*, ed. H. T. Riley, 12 vols., 1863–76.

Walter of Coventry: *Memoriale*, ed. W. Stubbs, 2 vols., 1872–3.

William of Malmesbury: *Gesta Regum*, ed. W. Stubbs, 1887–9.

Wittikind: *Res Gestae Saxonicae*, apud Migne CXXXVII.

II

STOW'S WORKS. *Woorkes of Geffrey Chaucer* (ed.), 1561; *Summarie of Englyshe Chronicles*, 1565; other editions, 1566, 1570, 1574, 1575, 1590; The Summary abridged, 1566, 1567, 1573, 1584, 1587, 1598, 1604, 1607, 1611, 1618; ed. Matthew of Westminster's *Flores Historiarum*, 1567; ed. Matthew Paris's *Chronica Majora*, 1571; ed. Thos. Walsingham's *Historia Anglicana*, 1574; *The Chronicles of England*, 1580; rearranged as *The Annales of England*, 1592; other editions, 1601, 1605; re-edited by Edmund Howse, 1615, 1631; *The Successions of the History of England*, 1638 (Lourdes); ed. second edition of Holinshed's *Chronicle*, 1585-7; *A Survey of London*, 1598, 1603; enlarged edition by Anthony Munday, 1618 and 1633; by J. Strype, 1720, 1754; modernized by Wm. J. Thoms, 1842, 1876; by Henry Morley, 1890, 1893 (with index), 1908; by C. L. Kingsford, 1908; *Selections from A Survey of London*, ed. by A. Barter, 1910.

BIOGRAPHIES. By Edmund Howe (in *Annales of England*), 1615; by J. Strype (in *Survey of London*), 1720; by Wm. J. Thoms (in *Survey of London*), 1876; by C. M. Clode (in *The Early History of the Guild of Merchant Taylors*), 1888; by C. L. Kingsford (in *Survey of London*), 1908.

AUTHORITIES. 'Stow's Survey of London' by G. R. B. Richards, *More Books*, xx, 1945; 'Stow's Continuation and the Defense of Brut', *Modern Language Review*, xlv, 1950.

CONTENTS

A

SVRVAY OF

LONDON.

Conteyning the Originall, Antiquity,

Increase, Moderne estate, and description of that
City, written in the yeare 1598, by Iohn Stow
Citizen of London.

Since by the same Author increased,

with diuers rare notes of Antiquity, **and**
published in the yeare,
1603.

Also an Apologie (or defence) against the

opinion of some men, concerning that Citie,
the greatnesse thereof.

VVith an Appendix, contayning in Latine

Libellum de situ & nobilitate Londini : Written by
William Fitzstephen, in the raigne of
Henry the second.

————

Imprinted by Iohn Windet, Printer to the hono-
rable Citie of London.
1603.

A

SVRVAY OF
LONDON

Contayning the Originall, Antiquity,
Increase, Moderne estate, and description of that
Citie, written in the yeare 1598. by Iohn Stow
Citizen of London.

Since by the same Author increased,
with divers rare notes of Antiquity, and
published in the yeare,
1603.

Also an Apologie (or defence) against the
opinion of some men, concerning that Citie,
the greatnesse thereof.

With an Appendix, contayning in Latine
... of William FitzStephen, in the raigne of
Henry the second.

Imprinted by Iohn Windet, Printer to the hono-
rable Citie of London.
1603

TO THE RIGHT HONOURABLE

ROBERT LEE

LORD MAYOR OF THE CITY OF LONDON

TO THE COMMONALTY AND CITIZENS OF THE SAME

JOHN STOW, CITIZEN, WISHETH LONG HEALTH AND FELICITY

SINCE the first publishing of the perambulation of Kent by that learned gentleman, William Lambert, Esq., I have heard of sundry other able persons to have (according to the desire of that author) essayed to do somewhat for the particular shires and counties where they were born or dwelt; of which none that I know (saving John Norden, for the counties of Middlesex and Hertford) have vouchsafed their labour to the common good in that behalf. And, therefore, concurring with the first, in the same desire to have drawn together such special descriptions of each place, as might not only make up a whole body of the English chorography amongst ourselves, but also might give occasion and courage to M. Camden to increase and beautify his singular work of the whole, to the view of the learned that be abroad, I have attempted the discovery of London, my native soil and country, at the desire and persuasion of some of my good friends, as well because I have seen sundry antiquities myself touching that place, as also for that through search of records to other purposes, divers written helps are come to my hands, which few others have fortuned to meet withall; it is a service that most agreeth with my professed travels; it is a duty that I willingly owe to my native mother and country, and an office that of right I hold myself bound in love to bestow upon the politic body and members of the same. What London hath been of ancient time men may here see, as what it is now every man doth behold. I know that the argument, being of the chief and principal city of the land, required the pen of some excellent artisan, but fearing that none would attempt and finish it, as few have essayed any, I chose rather (amongst other my labours)

to handle it after my plain manner, than to leave it unperformed.
Touching the dedication, I am not doubtful where to seek my
patron, since you be a politic estate of the city, as the walls and
buildings be the material parts of the same.   To you, therefore,
do I address this my whole labour, as well that by your authority
I may be protected, as warranted by your own skill and understanding of that which I have written.   I confess that I lacked
my desire to the accomplishment of some special parts,[1] which
some other of better ability promised to perform; but as I then
professed, have since out of mine old store-house added to this
work many rare notes of antiquity, as may appear to the reader,
which I do afford in all duty, and recommend to your view, my
labours to your consideration, and myself to you service, during
life, in this or any other.

---

[1] The Dedication of the first edition is precisely the same, except in the
concluding paragraph, which there stands as follows:—
  " I confess that I lacked my desire to the accomplishment of some
speciall partes: but I trust hereafter that shal be supplied, and I professe
(if more touching this worke come unto me) to afforde it, in all dutie.   In
the meantime I recommend this to your view, my laboures to your consideration, and myself to your service (as I have professed during life) in
this or any other."

THE AUTHOR TO THE READER

BECAUSE amongst others mine authors, I have oftentimes alleged Fitz-Stephens as one more choice than other, namely, for the ancient estate of this city, more than four hundred years since: and also the said author being rare, I have in this place thought good by impression to impart the same to my loving friends, the learned antiquaries, as the author wrote it in the Latin tongue; and first to note in effect what Master Bale, in commendation of the said author, writeth:

" William Stephanides, or Fitzstephen, a monk of Canterbury, born of worshipful parents in the city of London, well brought up at the first under good masters, did more and more increase in honest conditions and learning; for ever in his young years there appeared in him a certain light of a gentleman-like disposition, which promised many good things, afterwards by him performed. Such time as other spent in brawls and idle talk, he employed in wholesome exercises for the honour of his country, following therein the example of Plato, and was very studious both in humanity and divinity."

The city of London, his birth-place, the most noble of all other cities of this land, and the prince's seat, situated in the south part of this island, he loved above all the other, so that at length he wrote most elegantly in Latin of the site and rights of the same. Leland, in divers of his books, commendeth him for an excellent writer. He lived in the reign of King Stephen, wrote in the reign of Henry II., and deceased in the year of Christ 1191, in the reign of Richard I.

THE SURVEY OF LONDON

THE ORIGINAL, ANTIQUITY, INCREASE, MODERN ESTATE, AND DESCRIPTION OF THAT CITY

As the Roman writers,[1] to glorify the city of Rome, derive the original thereof from gods and demi-gods, by the Trojan progeny, so Geoffrey of Monmouth,[2] the Welsh historian, deduceth the foundation of this famous city of London, for the greater glory thereof, and emulation of Rome, from the very same original. For he reporteth that Brute, lineally descended from the demi-god Æneas, the son of Venus, daughter of Jupiter, about the year of the world 2855, and 1108 before the nativity of Christ, built this city near unto the river now called Thames, and named it Troynovant, or Trenovant. But herein, as Livy, the most famous historiographer of the Romans, writeth, antiquity is pardonable, and hath an especial privilege, by interlacing divine matters with human, to make the first foundation of cities more honourable, more sacred, and, as it were, of greater majesty.

King Lud (as the aforesaid Geoffrey of Monmouth noteth) afterwards not only repaired this city, but also increased the same with fair buildings, towers, and walls, and after his own name called it Caire-Lud, as Lud's town; and the strong gate which he built in the west part of the city he likewise, for his own honour, named Ludgate.

This Lud had issue two sons, Androgeus and Theomantius, who being not of age to govern at the death of their father, their uncle Cassibelan took upon him the crown; about the eighth

[1] "As Rome, the chiefe citie of the world, to glorifie it selfe, drew her originall from the gods, goddesses, and demy gods, by the Trojan progeny, so this famous citie of London for greater glorie, and in emulation of Rome, deriveth itselfe from the very same originall. For, as Jeffreye of Monmoth, the Welche historian, reporteth, Brute descended from the demy god Eneas, the sonne of Venus, daughter of Jupiter, aboute the yeare of the world 2855, the yeare before Christe's nativitie, 1108, builded a citie neare unto a river now called Thames, and named it Troynovant, or Trenovant."—*1st edition*, 1598.

[2] [*See* Bibliography.]

3

year of whose reign, Julius Cæsar arrived in this land with a
great power of Romans to conquer it; the manner of which
conquest I will summarily set down out of his own Commentaries
[*see* Bibliography], which are of far better credit than the
relations of Geoffrey Monmouth.

The chief government of the Britons, and ordering of the wars,
was then by common advice committed to Cassibelan, whose
seigniory was separated from the cities towards the sea-coast
by the river called Thames, about fourscore miles from the sea.
This Cassibelan, in times past, had made continual war upon the
cities adjoining; but the Britons being moved with the Roman
invasion, had resolved in that necessity to make him their
sovereign, and general of the wars (which continued hot between
the Romans and them); but in the meanwhile the Troynovants,
which was then the strongest city well near of all those countries
(and out of which city a young gentleman, called Mandubrace,
upon confidence of Cæsar's help, came unto him into the main-
land of Gallia, now called France, and thereby escaped death,
which he should have suffered at Cassibelan's hand), sent their
ambassadors to Cæsar, promising to yield unto him, and to do
what he should command them instantly, desiring him to
protect Mandubrace from the furious tyranny of Cassibelan,
and to send him into their city with authority to take the government thereof upon him. Cæsar accepted the offer, and appointed
them to give unto him forty hostages, and withal to find him
grain for his army; and so sent he Mandubrace unto them.

When others saw that Cæsar had not only defended the
Trinobants against Cassibelan, but had also saved them harmless from the pillage of his own soldiers, then did the Conimagues,
Segontians, Ancalits, Bibrokes, and Cassians, likewise submit
themselves unto him; and by them he learned that not far
thence was Cassibelan's town, fortified with woods and marsh
ground, into the which he had gathered a great number both of
men and cattle.

For the Britons call that a town (saith Cæsar), when they
have fortified a cumbersome wood with a ditch and rampart,
and thither they resort to abide the approach of their enemies;
to this place therefore marched Cæsar with his legions; he
found it excellently fortified, both of nature and by man's
advice; nevertheless, he resolved to assault it in two several
places at once, whereupon the Britons, being not able to endure
the force of the Romans, fled out at another part, and left the
town unto him: a great number of cattle he found there, and

many of the Britons he slew, and others he took in the chase.

Whilst these things were doing in these quarters, Cassibelan sent messengers into Kent, which lieth upon the sea, in which there reigned then four particular kings, named Cingetorex, Carvill, Taximagull, and Segonax, whom he commanded to raise all their forces, and suddenly to set upon and assault the Romans in their trenches by the sea-side; the which, when the Romans perceived, they sallied out upon them, slew a great sort of them, and taking Cingetorex their noble captain prisoner, retired themselves to their camp in good safety.

When Cassibelan heard of this, and had formerly taken many other losses, and found his country sore wasted, and himself left almost alone by the defection of the other cities, he sent ambassadors by Comius of Arras to Cæsar, to intreat with him concerning his own submission; the which Cæsar did accept, and taking hostages, assessed the realm of Britain to a yearly tribute, to be paid to the people of Rome, giving strait charge to Cassibelan that he should not seek any revenge upon Mandubrace or the Trinobantes, and so withdrew his army to the sea again.

Thus far out of Cæsar's Commentaries concerning this history, which happened in the year before Christ's nativity 54. In all which process there is for this purpose to be noted, that Cæsar nameth the city of Trinobantes, which hath a resemblance with Troynova, or Trinobantum, having no greater difference in the orthography than changing b into v, and yet maketh an error whereof I will not argue; only this I will note, that divers learned men do not think "*civitas Trinobantum*" to be well and truly translated, "the city of the Trinobantes;" but it should rather be the state, commonalty, or seigniory of the Trinobantes; for that Cæsar in his Commentaries useth the word *civitas*, only for a people living under one and the selfsame prince and law; but certain it is that the cities of the Britons were in those days neither artificially built with houses, nor strongly walled with stone, but were only thick and cumbersome woods, plashed within and trenched about. And the like in effect do other the Roman and Greek authors directly affirm, as Strabo, Pomponius Mela, and Dion [1] a senator of Rome, which flourished in the several reigns of the Roman emperors, Tiberius, Claudius, Domitian, and Severus; to wit, that before the arrival of the Romans the Britons had no towns, but called that a town which had a thick entangled wood, defended, as I said, with a ditch and bank,

[1] [*See* Bibliography.]

the like whereof, the Irishmen, our next neighbours, do at this day call Fastness.[1] But after that these hither parts of Britain were reduced into the form of a province by the Romans, who sowed the seeds of civility over all Europe; this city, whatsoever it was before, began to be renowned, and of fame. For Tacitus,[2] who first of all authors nameth it Londinum, saith, that in the 62nd year after Christ, it was, albeit no colony of the Romans, yet most famous for the great multitude of merchants, provision, and intercourse. At which time, in that notable revolt of the Britons from Nero, in which 70,000 Romans and their confederates were slain, this city, with Verulam, near St. Albans, and Maldon in Essex, then all famous, were ransacked and spoiled. For Suetonius Paulinus, then lieutenant for the Romans in this isle, abandoned it, as not then fortified, and left it to the spoil.

Shortly after, Julius Agricola, the Roman lieutenant, in the time of Domitian, was the first that by adhorting the Britons publicly, and helping them privately, won them to build houses for themselves, temples for the gods, and courts for justice, to bring up the noblemen's children in good letters and humanity, and to apparel themselves Roman-like, whereas before (for the most part) they went naked, painting their bodies, etc., as all the Roman writers have observed.

True it is, I confess, that afterwards many cities and towns in Britain, under the government of the Romans, were walled with stone and baked bricks or tiles, as Richborrow or Ryptacester,[3] in the Isle of Thanet, until the channel altered his course, beside Sandwich in Kent; Verulamium,[4] beside St. Albans, in Hertfordshire; Cilcester [5] in Hampshire; Wroxcester [6] in Shropshire; Kencester [7] in Herefordshire, three miles from Hereford town; Ribchester,[8] seven miles above Preston, on the water of Rible;

---

[1] " The like whereof the Irishmen, our next neighbours, doe at this day call *paces.*"—*1st edition*, p. 4.

[2] [*See* Bibliography.]

[3] Richborough, about 1½ m. from Sandwich, Rom. *Rutupiuac.*

[4] On the banks of the river Verulam, opposite to St. Alban's, which is supposed to have arisen out of its ruin.

[5] Silchester, in Hampshire, seven miles from Basingstoke; the *Caer Segont* of the Britons, and *Segontium* of the Romans, and *Silcester* of the Saxons. Leland states its walls to have been two miles in compass.

[6] Wroxeter, five miles from Shrewsbury. Its walls are stated to have been three yards in thickness, and to have extended for a circumference of three miles.

[7] Kenchester, three miles from Hereford, Rom. *Ariconium.*

[8] Ribchester, six miles from Blackburn, in Lancashire, supposed to be the *Rego-dunum* of the Romans.

Aldburgh, a mile from Boroughbridge, or Watling Street, on Ure river, and others; and no doubt but this city of London was also walled with stone, in the time of the Roman government here, but yet very lately, for it seemeth not to have been walled in the year of our Lord 296, because in that year, when Alectus the tyrant was slain in the field, the Franks easily entered London and had sacked the same, had not God, of his great favour, at the very instant, brought along the river of Thames, certain bands of Roman soldiers, who slew those Franks in every street of the city.

WALL ABOUT THE CITY OF LONDON

In a few years after, as Simeon of Durham,[1] an ancient writer, reporteth, Helen, the mother of Constantine the Great, was the first that inwalled this city, about the year of Christ 306; but however those walls of stone might have been built by Helen, yet the Britons, I know, had no skill of building with stone, as it may appear by that which followeth, about the year of Christ 399, when Arcadius and Honorius, the sons of Theodosius Magnus, governed the empire, the one in the east, the other in the west; for Honorius having received Britain, the city of Rome was invaded and destroyed by the Goths, after which time the Romans left to rule in Britain, as being employed in defence of their territories nearer home, whereupon the Britons not able to defend themselves against the invasions of their enemies, were many years together under the oppression of two most cruel nations, the Scots and Picts, and at the length were forced to send their ambassadors with letters and lamentable supplications to Rome, requiring aid and succour from thence, upon promise of their continual fealty, so that the Romans would rescue them out of the hands of their enemies. Hereupon the Romans sent unto them a legion of armed soldiers, which coming into this island, and encountering with the enemies, overthrew a great number of them, and drove the rest out of the frontiers of the country; and so setting the Britons at liberty, counselled them to make a wall, extending all along between the two seas, which might be of force to keep out their evil neighbours, and then returned home with great triumph. The Britons wanting masons built that wall, not of stone as they were advised, but made it of turf, and that so slender, that it served little or nothing at all for their defence, and the enemy

---

[1] The reference is not found in Simeon of Durham, but in Henry of Huntingdon. [*See* Bibliography.]

perceiving that the Roman legion was returned home, forthwith arrived out of their boats, invaded the borders, overcame the country, and, as it were, bore down all that was before them.

Whereupon ambassadors were eftsoon dispatched to Rome, lamentably beseeching that they would not suffer their miserable country to be utterly destroyed: then again another legion was sent, which coming upon a sudden, made a great slaughter of the enemy, and chased him home, even to his own country. These Romans at their departure, told the Britons plainly, that it was not for their ease or leisure to take upon them any more such long and laborious journeys for their defence, and therefore bade them practice the use of armour and weapons, and learn to withstand their enemies, whom nothing else did make so strong as their faint heart and cowardice; and for so much as they thought that it would be no small help and encouragement unto their tributary friends whom they were now forced to forsake,[1] they built for them a wall of hard stone from the west sea to the east sea, right between those two cities, which were there made to keep out the enemy, in the selfsame place where Severus before had cast his trench. The Britons also putting to their helping hands as labourers.

This wall they built eight feet thick in breadth, and twelve feet in height, right, as it were by a line, from east to west, as the ruins thereof remaining in many places until this day do make to appear. Which work, thus perfected, they give the people strait charge to look well to themselves, they teach them to handle their weapons, and they instruct them in warlike feats. And lest by the sea-side southwards, where their ships lay at harbour, the enemy should come on land, they made up sundry bulwarks, each somewhat distant from the other, and so bid them farewell, as minding no more to return. This happened in the days of the Emperor Theodosius the younger, almost 500 years after the first arrival of the Romans here, about the year after Christ's incarnation 434.

The Britons after this, continuing a lingering and doubtful war with the Scots and Picts, made choice of Vortigern to be their king and leader, which man (as saith Malmesbury [2]) was neither valorous of courage, nor wise of counsel, but wholly given over to the unlawful lusts of his flesh; the people likewise, in short

---

[1] Wittikind, a monk of Corbeil, who died about the year 1000. [See Bibliography.]
[2] [See Bibliography.] Bede [Hist. Eccl. See Bibliography].

time, being grown to some quietness, gave themselves to gluttony
and drunkenness, pride, contention, envy, and such other vices,
casting from them the yoke of Christ. In the mean season, a
bitter plague fell among them, consuming in short time such a
multitude that the quick were not sufficient to bury the dead;
and yet the remnant remained so hardened in sin, that neither
death of their friends, nor fear of their own danger, could cure the
mortality of their souls, whereupon a greater stroke of vengeance
ensued upon the whole sinful nation. For being now again
infested with their old neighbours the Scots and Picts, they
consult with their king Vortigern,[1] and send for the Saxons, who
shortly after arrived here in Britain, where, saith Bede, they
were received as friends; but as it proved, they minded to
destroy the country as enemies; for after that they had driven
out the Scots and Picts, they also drove the Britons, some over
the seas, some into the waste mountains of Wales and Cornwall,
and divided the country into divers kingdoms amongst themselves.

These Saxons were likewise ignorant of building with stone
until the year 680; for then it is affirmed that Benet, abbot of
Wirrall,[2] master to the reverend Bede, first brought artificers
of stone houses and glass windows into this island amongst the
Saxons, arts before that time unto them unknown, and therefore
used they but wooden buildings. And to this accordeth Policronicon, who says, "that then had ye wooden churches, nay
wooden chalices and golden priests, but since golden chalices and
wooden priests." And to knit up this argument, King Edgar in
his charter to the abbey of Malmesbury, dated the year of
Christ 974, hath words to this effect: "All the monasteries in
my realm, to the outward sight, are nothing but worm-eaten
and rotten timber and boards, and that worse is, within they are
almost empty, and void of Divine service."

Thus much be said for walling, not only in respect of this city,
but generally also of the first within the realm. Now to return
to our Trinobant (as Cæsar hath it), the same is since by Tacitus,
Ptolemæus, and Antoninus, called Londinium, Longidinium; of
Ammianus,[3] Lundinum, and Augusta, who calleth it an ancient
city; of our Britons, Lundayne; of the old Saxons, Lunden-
ceaster, Lundenbrig, Londennir; of strangers Londra and
Londres; of the inhabitants, London; whereof you may read a
more large and learned discourse, and how it took the name, in

[1] Wittikind, Bede [*Hist. Eccl.*].
[2] Benedict, abbot of Wearmouth.   [3] [*See* Bibliography.]

that work of my loving friend, Master Camden, now Clarencieux, which is called *Britannia*.

This city of London having been destroyed and burnt by the Danes and other Pagan enemies, about the year of Christ 839, was by Alfred, king of the West Saxons, in the year 886, repaired, honourably restored, and made again habitable. Who also committed the custody thereof unto his son-in-law, Ethelred, Earl of Mercia, unto whom before he had given his daughter, Ethelfled.

And that this city was then strongly walled may appear by divers accidents, whereof William of Malmesbury hath, that about the year of Christ 994, the Londoners shut up their gates, and defended their king Ethelred within their walls against the Danes.

In the year 1016,[1] Edmund Ironsides reigning over the West Saxons, Canute the Dane bringing his navy into the west part of the bridge, cast a trench about the city of London, and then attempted to have won it by assault, but the citizens repulsed him, and drove them from their walls.

Also, in the year 1052, Earl Goodwin, with his navy, sailed up by the south end of the bridge, and so assailed the walls of this city.

William Fitzstephen, in the reign of King Henry II., writing of the walls of this city, hath these words: " The wall is high and great, well towered on the north side, with due distances between the towers. On the south side also the city was walled and towered, but the fishful river of Thames, with his ebbing and flowing, hath long since subverted them."

By the north side, he meaneth from the river of Thames in the east to the river of Thames in the west, for so stretched the wall in his time, and the city being far more in length from east to west than in breadth from south to north, and also narrower at both ends than in the midst, is therefore compassed with the wall on the land side, in form of a bow, except denting in betwixt Cripplegate and Aldersgate; but the wall on the south side, along by the river of Thames, was straight as the string of a bow, and all furnished with towers or bulwarks (as we now term them) in due distance every one from other, as witnesseth our author, and ourselves may behold from the land side. This may suffice for proof of a wall, and form thereof, about this city, and the same to have been of great antiquity as any other within this realm.

[1] Asser, Marianus, Florentius. [*See* Bibliography.]

And now touching the maintenance and repairing the said wall. I read, that in the year 1215, the 16th of King John,[1] the barons, entering the city by Aldgate, first took assurance of the citizens, then brake into the Jews' houses, searched their coffers to fill their own purses, and after with great diligence repaired the walls and gates of the city with stone taken from the Jews' broken houses. In the year 1257,[2] Henry III. caused the walls of this city, which were sore decayed and destitute of towers, to be repaired in more seemly wise than before, at the common charges of the city. Also in the year 1282, King Edward I. having granted to Robert Kilwarby, archbishop of Canterbury, license for the enlarging of the Blackfriars' church, to break and take down a part of the wall of the city, from Ludgate to the river of Thames; he also granted to Henry Walleis, mayor, and the citizens of London, the favour to take, toward the making of the wall and enclosure of the city, certain customs or toll, as appeareth by his grant. This wall was then to be made from Ludgate west to Fleet bridge along behind the houses, and along by the water of the Fleet unto the river of Thames. Moreover, in the year 1310, Edward II. commanded the citizens to make up the wall already begun, and the tower at the end of the same wall, within the water of Thames near unto the Blackfriars, etc. 1328, the 2nd of Edward III., the walls of this city were repaired. It was also granted by King Richard II. in the tenth year of his reign, that a toll should be taken of the wares sold by land or by water for ten years, towards the repairing of the walls, and cleansing of the ditch about London.[3] In the 17th of Edward IV. Ralph Joceline, mayor, caused part of the wall about the city of London to be repaired; to wit, betwixt Aldgate and Aldersgate. He also caused Moorfield to be searched for clay, and brick thereof to be made and burnt; he likewise caused chalk to be brought out of Kent, and to be burnt into lime in the same Moorfield, for more furtherance of the work. Then the Skinners to begin in the east made that part of the wall betwixt Aldgate and Bevis Marks, towards Bishopsgate, as may appear by their arms in three places fixed there: the mayor, with his company of the Drapers, made all that part betwixt Bishopsgate and Allhallows church, and from Allhallows towards the postern called Moorgate. A great part of the same wall was repaired by the executors of Sir John Crosby, late alderman,

[1] Roger of Wendover, Matthew Paris, Ranul. Coggeshall. [See Bibliog.]
[2] Matthew Paris.
[3] Patent [C.P.R. See Bibliography.]

as may appear by his arms in two places there fixed: and other companies repaired the rest of the wall to the postern of Cripplegate. The Goldsmiths repaired from Cripplegate towards Aldersgate, and there the work ceased. The circuit of the wall of London on the land side, to wit, from the Tower of London in the east unto Aldgate, is 82 perches; from Aldgate to Bishopsgate, 86 perches; from Bishopsgate in the north to the postern of Cripplegate, 162 perches; from Cripplegate to Aldersgate, 75 perches; from Aldersgate to Newgate, 66 perches; from Newgate in the west to Ludgate, 42 perches; in all, 513 perches of assize. From Ludgate to the Fleet-dike west, about 60 perches; from Fleetbridge south to the river Thames, about 70 perches; and so the total of these perches amounteth to 643, every perch consisting of five yards and a half, which do yield 3536 yards and a half, containing 10,608 feet, which make up two English miles and more by 608 feet.

OF ANCIENT AND PRESENT RIVERS, BROOKS, BOURNS, POOLS, WELLS, AND CONDUITS OF FRESH WATER, SERVING THE CITY, AS ALSO OF THE DITCH COMPASSING THE WALL OF THE SAME FOR DEFENCE THEREOF.

Anciently, until the Conqueror's time, and two hundred years after, the city of London was watered, besides the famous river of Thames on the south part, with the river of the wells, as it was then called, on the west; with the water called Walbrooke running through the midst of the city into the river Thames, serving the heart thereof; and with a fourth water or bourn, which ran within the city through Langborne ward, watering that part in the east. In the west suburbs was also another great water, called Oldborne, which had its fall into the river of Wells; then were there three principal fountains, or wells, in the other suburbs; to wit, Holy well, Clement's well, and Clarkes' well. Near unto this last-named fountain were divers other wells, to wit, Skinners' well, Fags' well, Gode well, Loder's well, and Radwell. All which said wells, having the fall of their overflowing in the aforesaid river, much increased the stream, and in that place gave it the name of Well. In West Smithfield there was a pool, in records called Horsepoole, and one other pool near unto the parish church of St. Giles without Cripplegate. Besides all which, they had in every street and lane of the city divers fair wells and fresh springs; and after this manner was this city then served with sweet and fresh waters, which being since decayed, other means have been sought to supply the want, as shall be shown. But first of the aforenamed rivers and other waters is to be said, as following:

Thames, the most famous river of this island, beginneth a little above a village called Winchcombe, in Oxfordshire; and still increasing, passeth first by the University of Oxford, and so with a marvellous quiet course to London, and thence breaketh into the French ocean by main tides, which twice in twenty-four hours' space doth ebb and flow more than sixty miles in length, to the great commodity of travellers, by which all kind of merchandise be easily conveyed to London, the principal storehouse and staple of all commodities within this realm; so that, omitting to speak of great ships and other vessels of burthen, there pertaineth to the cities of London, Westminster, and borough of Southwark, above the number, as is supposed, of 2000 wherries and other small boats, whereby 3000 poor men, at the least, be set on work and maintained.

That the river of Wells, in the west part of the city, was of old so called of the wells, it may be proved thus:—William the Conqueror in his charter to the college of St. Marten le Grand, in London, hath these words: " I do give and grant to the same church all the land and the moor without the postern, which is called Cripplegate, on either part of the postern; that is to say, from the north corner of the wall, as the river of the Wells, there near running, departeth the same moor from the wall, unto the running water which entereth the city." [1] This water hath long since been called the river of the Wells, which name of river continued; and it was so called in the reign of Edward I., as shall be shown, with also the decay of the said river. In a fair book of parliament records, now lately restored to the Tower, it appeareth [2] that a parliament being holden at Carlile in the year 1307,[3] the 35th of Edward I., " Henry Lacy, earl of Lincoln, complained, that whereas in times past the course of water, running at London under Oldborne bridge and Fleete bridge into the Thames, had been of such breadth and depth, that ten or twelve ships navies at once, with merchandise, were wont to come to the foresaid bridge of Fleete, and some of them to Oldborne bridge: now the same course, by filth of the tanners and such others, was sore decayed; also by raising of wharfs; but especially, by a diversion of the water made by them of the new Temple,

---

[1] " This water hath been since that time called Turne mill brooke; yet then called the river of the Wells, which name of river," etc.—1st *edition*.
[2] Parliament record. [*Rot. Parl. See* Bibliography.]
[3] Date should read 1306.

for their mills standing without Baynardes Castle, in the first
year of King John,[1] and divers other impediments, so as the
said ships could not enter as they were wont, and as they ought:
wherefore he desired that the mayor of London with the sheriffs
and other discreet aldermen, might be appointed to view the
course of the said water; and that by the oaths of good men, all
the aforesaid hindrances might be removed, and it to be made
as it was wont of old. Whereupon Roger le Brabason, the
constable of the Tower, with the mayor and sheriffs, were
assigned to take with them honest and discreet men, and to make
diligent search and enquiry how the said river was in old time,
and that they leave nothing that may hurt or stop it, but keep
it in the same state that it was wont to be." So far the record.
Whereupon it followed that the said river was at that time
cleansed, these mills removed, and other things done for the
preservation of the course thereof, notwithstanding never
brought to the old depth and breadth; whereupon the name
of river ceased, and it was since called a brook, namely, Turnmill or Tremill brook, for that divers mills were erected upon
it, as appeareth by a fair register-book,[2]containing the foundation of the priory at Clarkenwell, and donation of the lands
thereunto belonging, as also divers other records.

This brook hath been divers times since cleansed, namely,
and last of all to any effect, in the year 1502, the 17th of Henry
VII., the whole course of Fleete dike, then so called, was
scowered, I say, down to the Thames, so that boats with fish
and fuel were rowed to Fleete bridge, and to Oldborne bridge,
as they of old time had been accustomed, which was a great
commodity to all the inhabitants in that part of the city.

In the year 1589 was granted a fifteenth, by a common council
of the city, for the cleansing of this brook or dike; the money
amounting to a thousand marks, was collected, and it was under-
taken, that by drawing divers springs about Hampstead heath
into one head and course, both the city should be served of fresh
water in all places of want; and also, that by such a follower, as
men call it, the channel of this brook should be scowered into the
river of Thames; but much money being therein spent, the
effect failed, so that the brook, by means of continual encroachments upon the banks getting over the water, and casting of
soilage into the stream, is now become worse cloyed and choken
than ever it was before.

The running water, so called by William the Conqueror in his

[1] Patent record. [C.P.R.]   [2] [See Bibliography.]

said charter, which entereth the city, etc. (before there was any ditch) between Bishopsgate and the late made postern called Moorgate, entered the wall, and was truly of the wall called Walbrooke, not of Gualo, as some have far fetched: it ran through the city with divers windings from the north towards the south into the river of Thames, and had over the same divers bridges along the streets and lanes through which it passed. I have read in a book [1] entitled the Customs of London,[2] that the prior of the Holy Trinity within Aldgate ought to make over Walbrooke in the ward of Brod street, against the stone wall of the city, viz., the same bridge that is next the Church of All Saints, at the wall. Also that the prior of the new hospital, St. Mary Spittle without Bishopsgate, ought to make the middle part of one other bridge next to the said bridge towards the north: and that in the twenty-eight year of Edward I. it was by inquisition found before the mayor of London, that the parish of St. Stephen upon Walbrooke ought of right to cover the course of the said brook, and therefore the sheriffs were commanded to distrain the said parishioners so to do, in the year 1300. The keepers of those bridges at that time were William Jordan and John de Bever. This water-course, having divers bridges, was afterwards vaulted over with brick, and paved level with the streets and lanes where through it passed; and since that, also houses have been built thereon, so that the course of Walbrooke is now hidden underground, and thereby hardly known.

Langborne water, so called of the length thereof, was a great stream breaking out of the ground in Fenchurch street, which ran down with a swift course, west, through that street, athwart Grastreet, and down Lumbard street, to the west end of St. Mary Wolnothes church, and then turning the course down Shareborne lane, so termed of sharing or dividing, it brake into divers rills or rillets to the river of Thames: of this bourn that ward took the name, and is till this day called Langborne ward. This bourn also is long since stopped up at the head, and the rest of the course filled up and paved over, so that no sign thereof remaineth more than the names aforesaid. [See Add. Notes.]

Oldborne, or Hilborne, was the like water, breaking out about the place where now the bars do stand, and it ran down the whole street till Oldborne bridge, and into the river of the Wells, or Turnemill brook. This bourn was likewise long since stopped up at the head, and in other places where the

---

[1] " In an old writing book."—*1st edition*, p. 14.   [2] Liber Custum.

same hath broken out, but yet till this day the said street is there called High Oldborne hill, and both the sides thereof, together with all the grounds adjoining, that lie betwixt it and the river of Thames, remain full of springs, so that water is there found at hand, and hard to be stopped in every house. [See Additional Notes.]

There are (saith Fitzstephen) near London, on the north side, special wells in the suburbs, sweet, wholesome, and clear; amongst which Holy well, Clarkes' well, and Clement's well, are most famous, and frequented by scholars and youths of the city in summer evenings, when they walk forth to take the air.

The first, to wit, Holy well, is much decayed and marred with filthiness purposely hid there, for the heightening of the ground for garden-plots.

The fountain called St. Clement's well, north from the parish church of St. Clement's and near unto an inn of Chancerie called Clement's Inn, is fair curbed square with hard stone, kept clean for common use, and is always full.

The third is called Clarkes' well, or Clarkenwell, and is curbed about square with hard stone, not far from the west end of Clarkenwell church, but close without the wall that incloseth it. The said church took the name of the well, and the well took the name of the parish clerks in London, who of old time were accustomed there yearly to assemble, and to play some large history of Holy Scripture.[1] And for example, of later time, to wit, in the year 1390, the 14th of Richard II., I read, the parish clerks of London, on the 18th of July, played interludes at Skinners' well, near unto Clarkes' well, which play continued three days together; the king, queen, and nobles being present. Also in the year 1409, the 10th of Henry IV., they played a play at the Skinners' well, which lasted eight days, and was of matter from the creation of the world. There were to see the same the most part of the nobles and gentles in England, etc.

Other smaller wells were many near unto Clarkes' well, namely Skinners' well, so called for that the skinners of London held there certain plays yearly, played of Holy Scripture, etc. In place whereof the wrestlings have of later years been kept, and is in part continued at Bartholomew tide.

Then there was Fagges well, near unto Smithfield by the Charterhouse, now lately damned up, Godewell, Loder's well,

---

[1] This precise definition of the nature of the performances of the parish clerks, " some large hystorie of Holy Scripture," does not occur in the first edition of the *Survey*.

and Radwell, all decayed, and so filled up, that their places are hardly now discerned.

Somewhat north from Holywell is one other well curbed square with stone, and is called Dame Annis the clear, and not far from it, but somewhat west, is also one other clear water called Perillous pond, because divers youths, by swimming therein, have been drowned; and thus much be said for fountains and wells.

Horsepoole, in West Smithfield, was some time a great water; and because the inhabitants in that part of the city did there water their horses, the same was in old records called Horsepoole; it is now much decayed, the springs being stopped up, and the land water falling into the small bottom, remaining inclosed with brick, is called Smithfield pond.[1]

By St. Giles' churchyard was a large water called a Pool. I read in the year 1244 that Anne of Lodburie was drowned therein; this pool is now for the most part stopped up, but the spring is preserved, and was coped about with stone by the executors of Richard Whittington.

The said river of the Wells, the running water of Walbrooke, the bourns aforenamed, and other the fresh waters that were in and about this city, being in process of time, by incroachment for buildings and heightenings of grounds, utterly decayed, and the number of citizens mightily increased, they were forced to seek sweet waters abroad; whereof some, at the request of King Henry III., in the twenty-first year of his reign,[2] were, for the profit of the city, and good of the whole realm, thither repairing, to wit, for the poor to drink, and the rich to dress their meat, granted to the citizens and their successors, by one Gilbert Sanforde, with liberty to convey water from the town of Teyborne by pipes of lead into their city.

The first cistern of lead, castellated with stone in the city of London, was called the great Conduit in West Cheape, which was begun to be built in the year 1285, Henry Wales being then mayor. The water-course from Paddington to James head hath 510 rods; from James head on the hill to the Mewsgate, 102 rods; from the Mewsgate to the Cross in Cheape, 484 rods.

The tun upon Cornhill was cisterned in the year 1401; John Shadworth then being mayor.

Bosses of water at Belinsgate, by Powle's wharf, and by St. Giles' church without Cripplegate, made about the year 1423.

---

[1] " Is but fowle, and is called Smithfield Pond."—*1st edition*, p. 15.
[2] Patent, 1236. [C.P.R.]

Water conveyed to the gaols of Newgate and Ludgate, 1432.

Water was first procured to the Standard in West Cheape about the year 1285, which Standard was again new built by the executors of John Welles, as shall be shown in another place. King Henry VI., in the year 1442, granted to John Hatherley, mayor, license to take up two hundred fodders of lead for the building of conduits, of a common garnery, and of a new cross in West Cheape, for the honour of the city.

The Conduit in West Cheape, by Powle's gate, was built about the year 1442; one thousand marks were granted by common council for the building thereof, and repairing of the other conduits.

The Conduit in Aldermanbury, and the Standard in Fleet street, were made and finished by the executors of Sir William Eastfield in the year 1471; a cistern was added to the Standard in Fleete street, and a cistern was made at Fleetbridge, and one other without Cripplegate, in the year 1478.

Conduit in Grastreet, in the year 1491.

Conduit at Oldbourne cross about 1498; again new made by William Lambe 1577.

Little conduit by the Stockes market, about 1500.

Conduit at Bishopsgate, about 1513.

Conduit at London wall, about 1528.

Conduit at Aldgate without, about 1535.

Conduit in Lothbury, and in Coleman street, 1546.

Conduit of Thames water at Dowgate, 1568.

Thames water, conveyed into men's houses by pipes of lead from a most artificial forcier standing near unto London bridge, and made by Peter Moris, Dutchman, in the year 1582, for service of the city, on the east part thereof.

Conduits of Thames water, by the parish churches of St. Mary Magdalen, and St. Nicolas Colde Abbey near unto old Fish street, in the year 1583.

One other new forcier was made near to Broken wharfe, to convey Thames water into men's houses of West Cheape, about Powle's, Fleete street, etc., by an English gentleman named Bevis Bulmer, in the year 1594. Thus much for waters serving this city; first by rivers, brooks, bourns, fountains, pools, etc.; and since by conduits, partly made by good and charitable citizens, and otherwise by charges of the commonalty, as shall be shown in description of wards wherein they be placed. And now some benefactors to these conduits shall be remembered.

In the year 1236 certain merchant strangers of cities beyond the seas, to wit, Amiens, Corby, and Nele, for privileges which they enjoyed in this city, gave one hundred pounds towards the charges of conveying water from the town of Teyborne. Robert Large, mayor, 1439, gave to the new water conduits then in hand forty marks, and towards the vaulting over of Walbrooke near to the parish church of St. Margaret in Lothbery, two hundred marks.

Sir William Eastfield, mayor, 1438, conveyed water from Teyborne to Fleete street, to Aldermanbury, and from Highbury to Cripplegate.

William Combes, sheriff, 1441, gave to the work of the conduits ten pounds.

Richard Rawson, one of the sheriffs, 1476, gave twenty pounds.

Robert Revell, one of the sheriffs, 1490, gave ten pounds.

John Mathew, mayor, 1490, gave twenty pounds.

William Bucke, tailor, in the year 1494, towards repairing of conduits, gave one hundred marks.

Dame Thomason, widow, late wife to John Percivall Taylor, mayor, in the year 1498 gave toward the conduit in Oldbourne twenty marks.

Richard Shore, one of the sheriffs, 1505, gave to the conduit in Oldbourne ten pounds.

The Lady Ascue, widow of Sir Christopher Ascue, 1543, gave towards the conduits one hundred pounds.

David Wodrooffe, sheriff, 1554, gave towards the conduit at Bishopsgate twenty pounds.

Edward Jackman, one of the sheriffs, 1564, gave towards the conduits one hundred pounds.

Barnard Randulph, common sergeant of the city, 1583, gave to the water conduits nine hundred pounds.[1]

Thus much for the conduits of fresh water to this city.

THE TOWN DITCH WITHOUT THE WALL OF THE CITY

The ditch, which partly now remaineth, and compassed the wall of the city, was begun to be made by the Londoners in the year 1211,[2] and was finished in the year 1213, the 15th of King John. This ditch being then made of 200 feet broad, caused no small hindrance to the canons of the Holy Trinity,[3] whose church stood near unto Aldgate; for that the said ditch passed

---

[1] In the first edition, Barnard Randulph's gift is stated to be £700 only.
[2] Liber Dunstable. [See Bibliography.]
[3] Liber Trinitat. [See Bibliography.]

through their ground from the Tower of London unto Bishopsgate. This ditch, being originally made for the defence of the
city, was also long together carefully cleansed and maintained,
as need required; but now of late neglected and forced either
to a very narrow, and the same a filthy channel, or altogether
stopped up for gardens planted, and houses built thereon; even
to the very wall, and in many places upon both ditch and wall
houses to be built; to what danger of the city, I leave to wiser
consideration, and can but wish that reformation might be had.

In the year of Christ 1354, the 28th of Edward III., the ditch
of this city flowing over the bank into the Tower ditch, the king
commanded the said ditch of the city to be cleansed, and so
ordered, that the overflowing thereof should not force any filth
into the Tower ditch.

Anno 1379, John Philpot, mayor of London, caused this
ditch to be cleansed, and every householder to pay five pence,
which was for a day's work towards the charges thereof.
Richard II., in the 10th of his reign, granted a toll to be taken of
wares sold by water or by land, for ten years, towards repairing
of the wall and cleansing of the ditch.

Thomas Falconer, mayor, 1414, caused the ditch to be cleansed.

Ralph Joceline, mayor, 1477, caused the whole ditch to be cast
and cleansed, and so from time to time it was cleansed, and
otherwise reformed, namely, in 1519, the 10th of Henry VIII.,
for cleansing and scowering the common ditch between Aldgate
and the postern next the Tower ditch. The chief ditcher had
by the day seven pence, the second ditcher six pence, the other
ditchers five pence. And every vagabond (for so were they
termed) one penny the day, meat and drink, at charges of the
city. £95 3s. 4d.

In my remembrance also the same was cleansed, namely the
Moore ditch, when Sir William Hollies was mayor, in the year
1540, and not long before, from the Tower of London to
Aldgate.

It was again cleansed in the year 1549, Henry Amcotes being
mayor, at the charges of the companies. And again, 1569, the
11th of Queen Elizabeth, for cleansing the same ditch between
Aldgate and the postern, and making a new sewer, and wharf of
timber, from the head of the postern into the town ditch,
£814 15s. 8d. Before the which time the said ditch lay open,
without wall or pale, having therein great store of very good
fish, of divers sorts, as many men yet living, who have taken and
tasted them, can well witness; but now no such matter: the

charge of cleansing is spared, and great profit made by letting out the banks, with the spoil of the whole ditch.

I am not ignorant of two fifteenths granted by a common council in the year 1595, for the reformation of this ditch, and that a small portion thereof, to wit, betwixt Bishopsgate and the postern called Mooregate, was cleansed, and made somewhat broader; but filling again very fast, by reason of overraising the ground near adjoining, therefore never the better: and I will so leave it, for I cannot help it.

BRIDGES OF THIS CITY

The original foundation of London bridge, by report of Bartholomew Linsted, alias Fowle, last prior of St. Mary Overies church in Southwark, was this: A ferry being kept in place where now the bridge is built, at length the ferryman and his wife deceasing, left the same ferry to their only daughter, a maiden named Mary, which with the goods left by her parents, and also with the profits arising of the said ferry, built a house of Sisters, in place where now standeth the east part of St. Mary Overies church, above the choir, where she was buried, unto which house she gave the oversight and profits of the ferry; but afterwards the said house of Sisters being converted into a college of priests, the priests built the bridge (of timber) as all the other great bridges of this land were, and from time to time kept the same in good reparations, till at length, considering the great charges of repairing the same, there was, by aid of the citizens of London, and others, a bridge built with arches of stone, as shall be shown. [*See* Additional Notes.]

But first of the timber bridge, the antiquity thereof being great, but uncertain; I remember to have read,[1] that in the year of Christ 994, Sweyn, king of Denmark, besieging the city of London, both by water and by land, the citizens manfully defended themselves, and their king Ethelred, so as part of their enemies were slain in battle, and part of them were drowned in the river of Thames, because in their hasty rage they took no heed of the bridge.

Moreover, in the year 1016, Canute the Dane, with a great navy, came up to London, and on the south of the Thames caused a trench to be cast, through the which his ships were towed into the west side of the bridge, and then with a deep trench, and straight siege, he compassed the city round about.

[1] Will. Malmesbury.

Also, in the year 1052, Earl Goodwin, with the like navy, taking his course up the river of Thames, and finding none that offered to resist on the bridge, he sailed up the south side of the said river. Furthermore, about the year 1067, William the Conqueror, in his charter to the church of St. Peter at Westminster, confirmed to the monks serving God there, a gate in London, then called Buttolph's gate, with a wharf which was at the head of London bridge.

We read likewise, that in the year 1114, the 14th of Henry I., the river of Thames was so dried up, and such want of water there, that between the Tower of London and the bridge, and under the bridge, not only with horse, but also a great number of men, women, and children, did wade over on foot.[1]

In the year 1122, the 22nd of Henry I., Thomas Arden gave the monks of Bermondsey the church of St. George, in Southward, and five shillings rent by the year, out of the land pertaining to London bridge.

I also have seen a charter under seal to the effect following:— " Henry king of England, to Ralfe B. of Chichester, and all the ministers of Sussex, sendeth greeting, know ye, etc. I command by my kingly authority, that the manor called Alcestone, which my father gave, with other lands, to the abbey of Battle, be free and quiet from shires and hundreds, and all other customs of earthly servitude, as my father held the same, most freely and quietly, and namely, from the work of London bridge, and the work of the castle at Pevensey: and this I command upon my forfeiture. Witness, William de Pontlearche, at Byrry." The which charter, with the seal very fair, remaineth in the custody of Joseph Holland, gentleman.

In the year 1136, the 1st of king Stephen,[2] a fire began in the house of one Ailewarde, near unto London stone, which consumed east to Aldgate, and west to St. Erkenwald's shrine, in Powle's church; the bridge of timber over the river of Thames was also burnt, etc., but afterwards again repaired. For Fitzstephen writes, that in the reign of King Stephen and of Henry II., when pastimes were showed on the river of Thames, men stood in great number on the bridge, wharfs, and houses, to behold.

Now in the year 1163, the same bridge was not only repaired, but newly made of timber as before, by Peter of Cole church, priest and chaplain.

Thus much for the old timber bridge, maintained partly by

[1] Liber Bermon. [See Biblio.], Lib. Trin.   [2] Liber Trinitat.

the proper lands thereof, partly by the liberality of divers persons, and partly by taxations in divers shires, have I proved for the space of 215 years before the bridge of stone was built.

Now touching the foundation of the stone bridge, it followeth: —About the year 1176, the stone bridge over the river of Thames, at London, was begun to be founded by the aforesaid Peter of Cole church, near unto the bridge of timber, but somewhat more towards the west, for I read, that Buttolfe wharf was, in the Conqueror's time, at the head of London bridge.[1] The king assisted this work: a cardinal then being legate here; and Richard, archbishop of Canterbury, gave one thousand marks towards the foundation; the course of the river, for the time, was turned another way about, by a trench cast for that purpose, beginning, as is supposed, east about Radriffe, and ending in the west about Patricksey, now termed Batersey. This work; to wit, the arches, chapel and stone bridge, over the river of Thames at London, having been thirty-three years in building, was in the year 1209 finished by the worthy merchants of London, Serle Mercer, William Almaine, and Benedict Botewrite, principal masters of that work, for Peter of Cole church deceased four years before, and was buried in the chapel on the bridge, in the year 1205.[2]

King John gave certain void places in London to build upon, the profits thereof to remain towards the charges of building and repairing the same bridge: a mason being master workman of the bridge, builded from the foundation the large chapel on that bridge of his own charges, which chapel was then endowed for two priests, four clerks, etc., besides chantries since founded for John Hatfield and other.[3] After the finishing of this chapel, which was the first building upon those arches, sundry houses at times were erected, and many charitable men gave lands, tenements, or sums of money, towards maintenance thereof, all which was sometimes noted and in a table fair written for posterity remaining in the chapel, until the same chapel was turned into a dwelling-house, and then removed to the bridge house, the effect of which table I was willing to have published in this book, if I could have obtained the sight thereof. But making the shorter work, I find by the account of William

[1] Liber Waverley. [*See* Bibliography.]
[2] " For Peter of Colechurch deceased foure years before this worke was finished, and was buried in the chappell builded on the same bridge, in the year 1205."—*1st edition*, p. 21.
[3] " So that in the yeare 23 of Henrie the 6 there was 4 chaplens in the said chappell."—*1st edition*, p. 21.

Mariner and Christopher Eliot, wardens of London bridge from Michaelmas, in the 22nd of Henry VII., unto Michaelmas next ensuing, by one whole year, that all the payments and allowances came to £815 17s. 2¼d., as there is shown by particulars, by which account then made, may be partly guessed the great charges and discharges of that bridge at this day, when things be stretched to so great a price. And now to actions on this bridge.

The first action to be noted was lamentable; for within four [1] years after the finishing thereof, to wit, in the year 1212, on the 10th of July, at night,[2] the borough of Southwark, upon the south side the river of Thames, as also the church of our Lady of the Canons there, being on fire, and an exceeding great multitude of people passing the bridge, either to extinguish and quench it, or else to gaze at and behold it, suddenly the north part, by blowing of the south wind was also set on fire, and the people which were even now passing the bridge, perceiving the same, would have returned, but were stopped by fire; and it came to pass, that as they stayed or protracted time, the other end of the bridge also, namely, the south end, was fired, so that the people thronging themselves between the two fires, did nothing else but expect present death; then came there to aid them many ships and vessels, into the which the multitude so unadvisedly rushed, that the ships being drowned, they all perished.[3]   It was said, that through the fire and shipwreck there were destroyed about three thousand persons, whose bodies were found in part, or half burnt, besides those that were wholly burnt to ashes, and could not be found.

About the year 1282, through a great frost and deep snow, five arches of London bridge were borne down and carried away.

In the year 1289, the bridge was so sore decayed for want of reparations that men were afraid to pass thereon, and a subsidy was granted towards the amendment thereof,[4] Sir John Britain being custos of London. 1381, a great collection or gathering was made of all archbishops, bishops, and other ecclesiastical persons, for the reparations of London bridge. 1381, Wat Tyler, and other rebels of Kent, by this bridge entered the city, as ye may read in my *Summary* and *Annals*.

In the year 1395,[5] on St. George's day, was a great justing on

---

[1] " Within 3 yeres."—*1st edition*.
[2] " A marvellous terrible chance happened for the citie of London, upon the south side of the river of Thames."—*Ibid*.
[5] Liber Dunmow, Walter Covent, W. Packenton. [*See* Bibliography.]
[4] Patent of Edward II. [C.P.R.]   [5] The date was 1390.

London bridge, betwixt David Earl of Crawford of Scotland, and the Lord Wells of England; in the which the Lord Wells was at the third course borne out of the saddle: which history proveth, that at that time the bridge being coped on either side, was not replenished with houses built thereupon, as it hath since been, and now is. The next year, on the 13th of November, the young Queen Isabell, commonly called the little, for she was but eight years old, was conveyed from Kenington besides Lamhith, through Southwarke to the Tower of London, and such a multitude of people went out to see her, that on London bridge nine persons were crowded to death, of whom the prior of Tiptre, a place in Essex, was one, and a matron on Cornhill was another.

The Tower on London bridge at the north end of the draw-bridge (for that bridge was then readily to be drawn up, as well to give passage for ships to Queenhithe, as for the resistance of any foreign force), was begun to be built in the year 1426, John Rainwell being mayor.

Another tower there is on the said bridge over the gate at the south end towards Southwarke, whereof in another place shall be spoken.

In the year 1450, Jack Cade, and other rebels of Kent, by this bridge entered the city: he struck his sword on London Stone, and said himself then to be lord of the city, but were by the citizens overcome on the same bridge, and put to flight, as in my *Annals*.

In the year 1471, Thomas, the bastard Fawconbridge, besieged this bridge, burnt the gate, and all the houses to the draw-bridge, that time thirteen in number.

In the year 1481, a house called the Common Siege on London bridge fell down into the Thames; through the fall whereof five men were drowned.

In the year 1553, the 3rd of February, Sir Thomas Wyat, and the Kentish men, marched from Depeford towards London; after knowledge whereof, forthwith the draw-bridge was cut down, and the bridge gates shut. Wyat and his people entered Southwarke, where they lay till the 6th of February, but could get no entry of the city by the bridge, the same was then so well defended by the citizens, the Lord William Howard assisting, wherefore he removed towards Kingstone, etc., as in my *Annals*.

To conclude of this bridge over the said river of Thames, I affirm, as in other my descriptions, that it is a work very rare, having with the draw-bridge twenty arches made of squared stone, of height sixty feet, and in breadth thirty feet, distant one from another twenty feet, compact and joined together with vaults and cellars; upon both sides be houses built, so that it seemeth rather a continual street than a bridge; for the fortifying whereof against the incessant assaults of the river, it hath overseers and officers, viz., wardens, as aforesaid, and others.

Fleete bridge in the west without Ludgate, a bridge of stone, fair coped on either side with iron pikes; on the which, towards the south, be also certain lanthorns of stone, for lights to be placed in the winter evenings, for commodity of travellers. Under the bridge runneth a water, sometimes called, as I have said, the river of the Wels, since Turnemill brooke, now Fleete dike, because it runneth by the Fleete, and sometimes about the Fleete, so under Fleete bridge into the river of Thames. This bridge hath been far greater in times past, but lessened, as the water course hath been narrowed. It seemeth this last bridge to be made or repaired at the charges of John Wels, mayor, in the year 1431, for on the coping is engraven Wels embraced by angels, like as on the standard in Cheape, which he also built. Thus much of the bridge: for of the water course, and decay thereof, I have spoken in another place.

Oldbourne bridge, over the said river of the Wels more towards the north, was so called, of a bourn that sometimes ran down Oldbourne hill into the said river. This bridge of stone, like as Fleet bridge from Ludgate west, serveth for passengers with carriage or otherwise, from Newgate toward the west and by north.

Cowbridge, more north, over the same water by Cowbridge street or Cowlane: this bridge being lately decayed, another of timber is made somewhat more north, by Chick lane, etc.

Bridges over the town ditch there are divers; to wit, without Aldgate, without Bishopsgate, the postern called Moorgate, the postern of Criplegate without Aldersgate, the postern of Christ's hospital, Newgate, and Ludgate; all these be over paved likewise, with stone level with the streets. But one other there is of timber over the river of Wels, or Fleet dike, between the precinct of the Black Friers, and the house of Bridewell.

There have been of old time also, divers bridges in sundry places over the course of Walbrooke, as before I have partly noted, besides Horseshew bridge, by the church of St. John Baptist, now called St. John's upon Walbrooke. I read, that of old time every person having lands on either side of the said brook, should cleanse [1] the same, and repair the bridges so far

---

[1] " Should vaulte, or bridge, and clense the same."—*1st edition*, p. 24.

as their lands extended. More, in the 11th of Edward III. the inhabitants upon the course of this brook were forced to pile and wall the sides thereof. Also, that in the 3rd of Henry V. this water-course had many bridges, since vaulted over with bricks, and the streets where through it passed so paved, that the same water-course is now hardly discerned. For order was taken in the 2nd of Edward IV., that such as had ground on either side of Walbrooke, should vault and pave it over, so far as his ground extended. And thus much for bridges in this city may suffice.

GATES IN THE WALL OF THIS CITY

Gates in the wall of this city of old time were four; to wit, Aeldgate for the east, Aldersgate for the north, Ludgate for the west, and the Bridgegate over the river of Thames for the south; but of later times, for the ease of citizens and passengers, divers other gates and posterns have been made, as shall be shown.

In the reign of Henry II. (saith Fitzstephen) there were seven double gates in the wall of this city, but he nameth them not. It may therefore be supposed, he meant for the first, the gate next the Tower of London,[1] now commonly called the Postern, the next be Aeldgate, the third Bishopsgate, the fourth Ealdersgate, the fifth Newgate, the sixth Ludgate, the seventh Bridgegate. Since the which time hath been builded the postern called Moorgate, a postern from Christ's hospital towards St. Bartholomew's hospital in Smithfield, etc. Now of every of these gates and posterns in the wall, and also of certain watergates on the river of Thames, severally somewhat may, and shall be noted, as I find authority, or reasonable conjecture to warrant me.

For the first, now called the postern by the Tower of London, it showeth by that part which yet remaineth, to have been a fair and strong arched gate, partly built of hard stone of Kent, and partly of stone brought from Caen in Normandy, since the Conquest, and foundation of the high tower, and served for passengers on foot out of the east, from thence through the city

---

[1] " Which then served as a posterne for passengers out of the east, from thence through Tower street, East cheape, and Candlewecke street to London Stone, the middle point of that highway, then through Budge row, Watheling street, and leaving Paul's church on the right hand, to Ludgate in the west; the next be Aldgate, Bishopsgate, Criplegate, Aldersgate, Ludgate, and the Bridgegate over the Thames. Since the which time hath been builded Newgate." etc.—*1st edition*, p. 25.

to Ludgate in the west.   The ruin and overthrow of this gate
and postern began in the year 1190, the 2nd of Richard I., when
William Longshampe, bishop of Ely, chancellor of England,
caused a part of the city wall, to wit, from the said gate towards
the river of Thames to the white tower, to be broken down, for
the enlarging of the said tower, which he then compassed far
wide about with a wall embattled, and is now the outer wall.
He also caused a broad and deep ditch to be made without the
same wall, intending to have derived the river of Thames with
her tides to have flowed about it, which would not be.   But the
southside of this gate, being then by undermining at the foundation loosened, and greatly weakened; at length, to wit, after
two hundred years and odd, the same fell down in the year 1440,
the 18th of Henry VI., and was never since by the citizens
re-edified.[1]   Such was their negligence then, and hath bred
some trouble to their successors, since they suffered a weak and
wooden building to be there made, inhabited by persons of lewd
life, oft times by inquest of Portsoken ward presented, but not
reformed; whereas of former times the said postern was accounted of as other gates of the city, and was appointed to men
of good credit.   Amongst other, I have read, that in the 49th
of Edward III., John Cobbe was admitted custos of the said
postern, and all the habitation thereof, for term of his life, by
William Walworth, then mayor of London, etc.   More, that
John Credy, Esq., in the 21st of Richard II., was admitted custos
of the said postern and appurtenances by Richard Whittington,
mayor, the aldermen, and commonalty, etc.

AELDGATE

The next gate in the east is called Aeldgate, of the antiquity
or age thereof.[2]   This is one and the first of the four principal
gates, and also one of the seven double gates, mentioned by
Fitzstephen.   It hath had two pair of gates, though now but
one; the hooks remaineth yet.   Also there hath been two port-
closes; the one of them remaineth, the other wanteth, but the
place of letting down is manifest.   For antiquity of the gate:
it appeareth by a charter of King Edgar to the knights of
Knighten Guild, that in his days the said port was called Aeldgate, as ye may read in the ward of Portsoken.   Also Matilda

---

[1] " Was never re-edified againe of stone, but an homely cottage, with
a narrow passage made of timber, lath and loame, hath beene in place
thereof set up, and so remaineth."—*1st edition*, p. 25.
[2] [*See* Additional Notes.]

the queen, wife to Henry I., having founded the priory of the
Holy Trinity within Aeldgate, gave unto the same church, to
Norman the first prior, and the canons that devoutly serve
God therein,[1] the port of Aeldgate, and the soke or franchises
thereunto belonging, with all customs as free as she held the
same; in the which charter she nameth the house Christ's
church, and reporteth Aeldgate to be of his domain.

More, I read [2] in the year 1215, that in the civil wars between
King John and his barons, the Londoners assisting the barons'
faction, who then besieged Northampton, and after came to
Bedford castle, where they were well received by William
Beauchampe, and captain of the same; having then also secret
intelligence that they might enter the city of London if they
would, they removed their camp to Ware, from thence in the
night coming to London, they entered Aeldgate, and placing
guardians or keepers of the gates, they disposed of all things in
the city at their pleasure. They spoiled the friars' houses, and
searched their coffers; [3] which being done, Robert Fitzwalter,
Geffry Magnavile Earl of Essex, and the Earl of Glocester, chief
leaders of the army, applied all diligence to repair the gates and
walls of this city with the stones taken from the Jews' broken
houses, namely, Aeldgate being then most ruinous (which had
given them an easy entry), they repaired, or rather newly built,
after the manner of the Normans, strongly arched with bulwarks
of stone from Caen in Normandy, and small brick, called Flanders tile, was brought from thence, such as hath been here used
since the Conquest, and not before.

In the year 1471,[4] the 11th of Edward IV., Thomas, the
bastard Fawconbridge, having assembled a riotous company of
shipmen and other in Essex and Kent, came to London with a
great navy of ships, near to the Tower; whereupon the mayor
and aldermen, by consent of a common council, fortified all
along the Thames side, from Baynard's castle to the Tower,
with armed men, guns, and other instruments of war, to resist
the invasion of the mariners, whereby the Thames side was
safely preserved and kept by the aldermen and other citizens
that assembled thither in great numbers. Whereupon the
rebels, being denied passage through the city that way, set upon
Aeldgate, Bishopsgate, Cripplegate, Aeldersgate, London bridge,
and along the river of Thames, shooting arrows and guns into
the city, fired the suburbs, and burnt more than threescore

[1] Liber Trinitat. [2] Matthew Paris.
[3] Ranul. Coggeshall. [4] Liber Dunthorn. [See Biblio.]

houses. And further, on Sunday the eleventh of May, five thousand of them assaulting Aeldgate, won the bulwarks, and entered the city; but the portclose being let down, such as had entered were slain, and Robert Basset, alderman of Aeldgate ward, with the recorder, commanded in the name of God to draw up the portclose; which being done, they issued out, and with sharp shot, and fierce fight, put their enemies back so far as St. Bottolph's church, by which time the Earl Rivers, and lieutenant of the Tower, was come with a fresh company, which joining together, discomfited the rebels, and put them to flight, whom the said Robert Basset, with the other citizens, chased to the Mile's End, and from thence, some to Popular, some to Stratford, slew many, and took many of them prisoners. In which space the Bastard having assayed other places upon the water side, and little prevailed, fled toward his ships. Thus much for Aeldgate.

BISHOPSGATE

The third, and next toward the north, is called Bishopsgate, for that, as it may be supposed, the same was first built by some Bishop of London, though now unknown when, or by whom; but true it is, that the first gate was first built for ease of passengers toward the east, and by north, as into Norfolk, Suffolk, Cambridgeshire, etc.; the travellers into which parts, before the building of this gate, were forced, passing out at Aeldgate, to go east till they came to the Mile's end, and then turning on the left hand to Blethenhall green [1] to Cambridge heath, and so north, or east, and by north, as their journey lay. If they took not this way, by the east out at Aeldgate, they must take their way by the north out at Aeldersgate, through Aeldersgate street and Goswel street towards Iseldon, and by a cross of stone on their right hand, set up for a mark by the north end of Golding lane, to turn eastward through a long street, until this day called Alder street, to another cross standing, where now a smith's forge is placed by Sewer's-ditch church, and then to turn again north towards Totenham, Endfield, Waltham, Ware, etc. The eldest note that I read of this Bishopsgate, is that William Blund, one of the sheriffs of London,[2] in the year 1210, sold to Serle Mercer, and William Almaine, procurators or wardens of London bridge, all his land, with the garden, in the

---

[1] " Now called Bednal Green."—*1st edition*, p. 26.
[2] Liber Trinitat.

parish of St. Buttolph without Bishopsgate, between the land of Richard Casiarin, towards the north, and the land of Robert Crispie towards the south, and the highway called Berewards lane on the east, etc.

Next I read in a charter,[1] dated the year 1235, that Walter Brune, citizen of London, and Rosia his wife, having founded the priory or new hospital of our blessed Lady, since called St. Mary Spittle without Bishopsgate, confirmed the same to the honour of God and our blessed Lady, for canons regular.

Also in the year 1247, Simon Fitzmarie, one of the sheriffs of London, the 29th of Henry III., founded the hospital of St. Mary, called Bethlem without Bishopsgate.[2] Thus much for the antiquity of this gate.[3]

And now for repairing the same,[3] I find that Henry III. confirmed to the merchants of the Haunce, that had a house in the city called Guildhalla Theutonicorum, certain liberties and privileges. Edward I. also confirmed the same; in the tenth year of whose reign it was found that the said merchants ought of right to repair the said gate called Bishopsgate; whereupon Gerard Marbod, alderman of the Haunce and other, then remaining in the city of London, for themselves, and all other merchants of the said Haunce, granted two hundred and ten marks sterling to the mayor and citizens; and covenanted that they and their successors should from time to time repair the same gate. This gate was again beautifully built in the year 1479, in the reign of Edward IV., by the said Haunce merchants.

Moreover, about the year 1551, these Haunce merchants, having prepared stone for that purpose, caused a new gate to be framed, there to have been set up, but then their liberties, through suit of our English merchants, were seized into the king's hand; and so that work was stayed, and the old gate yet remaineth.

POSTERN OF MOREGATE

Touching the next postern, called Moregate, I find that Thomas Falconer, mayor, about the year 1415, the third of Henry V., caused the wall of the city to be broken near unto Coleman street, and there built a postern, now called Moregate, upon the moor side where was never gate before. This gate he made for ease of the citizens, that way to pass upon causeys into the field for their recreation: for the same field was at that time a parish. This postern was re-edified by William Hampton, fishmonger, mayor, in the year 1472. In the year also, 1511, the third of Henry VIII., Roger Acheley, mayor, caused dikes and bridges to be made, and the ground to be levelled, and made more commodious for passage, since which time the same hath been heightened. So much that the ditches and bridges are covered, and seemeth to me that if it be made level with the battlements of the city wall, yet will it be little the drier, such is the moorish nature of that ground.

POSTERN OF CRIPPLEGATE

The next is the postern of Cripplegate, so called long before the Conquest. For I read in the history of Edmond, king of the East Angles, written by Abbo Floriacensis, and by Burchard, sometime secretary to Offa, king of Marcia,[1] but since by John Lidgate, monk of Bury, that in the year 1010, the Danes spoiling the kingdom of the East Angles, Alwyne, bishop of Helmeham, caused the body of King Edmond the Martyr to be brought from Bedrisworth (now called Bury St. Edmondes), through the kingdom of the East Saxons, and so to London in at Cripplegate; a place, saith mine author, so called of cripples begging there: at which gate, it was said, the body entering, miracles were wrought, as some of the lame to go upright, praising God. The body of King Edmond rested for the space of three years in the parish church of St. Gregorie, near unto the cathedral church of St. Paul. Moreover, the charter of William the Conqueror, confirming the foundation of the college in London, called St. Martin the Great, hath these words:[2] "I do give and grant to the same church and canons, serving God therein, all the land and the moore without the postern, which is called Cripplegate, on either side the postern." More I read, that Alfune built the parish church of St. Giles, nigh a gate of the city, called Porta Contractorum, or Cripplesgate, about the year 1099.

This postern was sometime a prison, whereunto such citizens and others, as were arrested for debt or common trespasses, were committed, as they be now, to the compters, which thing appeareth by a writ of Edward I. in these words: "*Rex vic. London. salutem : ex graui querela B. capt. & detent. in prisona nostra de Criples gate pro x. l. quas coram Radulpho de Sandwico tunc custod. ciuitatis nostræ London. & I. de Blackwell ciuis recognit. debit. etc.*"[3] This gate was new built by the brewers of

---

[1] Abbo Burchard. [*See* Addit. Notes.]   [2] Liber S. Barthol. [See Biblio.]
            [3] Record [C.P.R.].

London in the year 1244, as saith Fabian's manuscript.[1] Edmond Shaw, goldsmith, mayor in the year 1483, at his decease appointed by his testament his executors, with the cost of four hundred marks, and the stuff of the old gate, called Cripplesgate, to build the same gate of new, which was performed and done in the year 1491.

ALDERSGATE

The next is Ældresgate, or Aldersgate,[2] so called not of Aldrich or of Elders, that is to say, ancient men, builders thereof; not of Eldarne trees, growing there more abundantly than in other places, as some have fabled,[1] but for the very antiquity of the gate itself, as being one of the first four gates of the city, and serving for the northern parts, as Aldgate for the east; which two gates, being both old gates, are for difference sake called, the one Ealdgate, and the other Aldersgate. This is the fourth principal gate, and hath at sundry times been increased with buildings, namely, on the south, or inner side, a great frame of timber hath been added and set up, containing divers large rooms and lodgings; also on the east side is the addition of one great building of timber, with one large floor, paved with stone or tile, and a well therein curbed with stone, of a great depth, and rising into the said room, two stories high from the ground; which well is the only peculiar note belonging to that gate, for I have not seen the like in all this city to be raised so high. John Day, stationer, a late famous printer of many good books, in our time dwelt in this gate, and built much upon the wall of the city towards the parish church of St. Anne.

POSTERN OUT OF CHRIST'S HOSPITAL

Then is there also a postern gate, made out of the wall on the north side of the late dissolved cloister of Friers minors, commonly of their habit called Grey friars, now Christ's church and hospital. This postern was made in the first year of Edward VI to pass from the said hospital of Christ's church unto the hospital of St. Bartlemew in Smithfield.

NEWGATE

The next gate on the west, and by north, is termed Newgate. as latelier built than the rest, and is the fifth principal gate, This gate was first erected about the reign of Henry I. or of

[1] [See Bibliography.].
[2] In a book, called *Beware of the Cat*. [See Bibliography.]

King Stephen, upon this occasion.[1] The cathedral church of St. Paul, being burnt about the year 1086, in the reign of William the Conqueror, Mauritius, then bishop of London, repaired not the old church, as some have supposed, but began the foundation of a new work, such as men then judged would never have been performed; it was to them so wonderful for height, length, and breadth, as also in respect it was raised upon arches or vaults, a kind of workmanship brought in by the Normans, and never known to the artificers of this land before that time, etc. After Mauritius, Richard Beamore did wonderfully advance the work of the said church, purchasing the large streets and lanes round about, wherein were wont to dwell many lay people, which grounds he began to compass about with a strong wall of stone and gates. By means of this increase of the church territory, but more by inclosing of ground for so large a cemetery or churchyard, the high and large street stretching from Aldegate in the east until Ludgate in the west, was in this place so crossed and stopped up, that the carriage through the city westward was forced to pass without the said churchyard wall on the north side, through Pater noster row; and then south, down Ave Mary lane, and again west, through Bowyer row to Ludgate; or else out of Cheepe, or Watheling street, to turn south, through the old Exchange; then west through Carter lane, again north by Creede lane, and then west to Ludgate: which passage, by reason of so often turning, was very cumbersome and dangerous both for horse and man; for remedy whereof a new gate was made, and so called, by which men and cattle, with all manner of carriages, might pass more directly (as afore) from Aldegate, through West Cheape by Paules, on the north side; through St. Nicholas shambles and Newgate market to Newgate, and from thence to any part westward over Oldborne bridge, or turning without the gate into Smithfielde, and through Iseldon to any part north and by west.   This gate hath of long time been a gaol, or prison for felons and trespassers, as appeareth by records [2] in the reign of King John, and of other kings; amongst the which I find one testifying, that in the year 1218, the 3rd of King Henry III., the king writeth unto the sheriffs of London, commanding them to repair the gaol of Newgate for the safe keeping of his prisoners, promising that the charges laid out should be allowed unto them upon their account in the Exchequer.

[1] " About the raigne of Henry II. or Richard I."—1st edition, p 30.
[2] Close roll. [See Bibliography.]

Moreover, in the year 1241, the Jews of Norwich were hanged for circumcising a Christian child; their house called the Thor was pulled down and destroyed; Aron, the son of Abraham, a Jew, at London, and the other Jews, were constrained to pay twenty thousand marks at two terms in the year, or else to be kept perpetual prisoners in Newgate of London, and in other prisons. In 1255, King Henry III. lodging in the tower of London, upon displeasure conceived towards the city of London, for the escape of John Offrem, a prisoner, being a clerk convict, out of Newgate, which had killed a prior that was of alliance to the king, as cousin to the queen: he sent for the mayor and sheriffs to come before him to answer the matter; the mayor laid the fault from him to the sheriffs, forasmuch as to them belonged the keeping of all prisoners within the city; and so the mayor returned home, but the sheriffs remained there prisoners by the space of a month and more; and yet they excused themselves, in that the fault chiefly rested in the bishop's officers; for whereas the prisoner was under custody, they at his request had granted license to imprison the offender within the gaol of Newgate, but so as the bishop's officers were charged to see him safely kept. The king, notwithstanding all this, demanded of the city three thousand marks for a fine.

In the year 1326, Robert Baldoke, the king's chancellor, was put in Newgate, the 3rd of Edward III. In the year 1337, Sir John Poultney gave four marks by the year to the relief of prisoners in Newgate. In the year 1385, William Walworth gave somewhat to relieve the prisoners in Newgate, so have many others since. In the year 1414 [1419], the gaolers of Newgate and Ludgate died, and prisoners in Newgate to the number of sixty-four. In the year 1418, the parson of Wrotham, in Kent, was imprisoned in Newgate. In the year 1422, the first of Henry VI., license was granted to John Coventre, Jenken Carpenter, and William Grove, executors to Richard Whittington, to re-edify the gaol of Newgate, which they did with his goods.

Thomas Knowles, grocer, sometime mayor of London, by license of Reynold, prior of St. Bartholomew's in Smithfield, and also of John Wakering, master of the hospital of St. Bartholomew, and his brethren, conveyed the waste of water at the cistern near to the common fountain and chapel of St. Nicholas (situate by the said hospital) to the gaols of Newgate, and Ludgate, for the relief of the prisoners. Tuesday next after Palm Sunday 1431, all the prisoners of Ludgate were removed into Newgate by Walter Chartesey, and Robert Large, sheriffs of

London; and on the 13th of April the same sheriffs (through the false suggestion of John Kingesell, jailor of Newgate) set from thence eighteen persons free men, and these were let to the compters, pinioned as if they had been felons; but on the sixteenth of June, Ludgate was again appointed for free men, prisoners for debt; and the same day the said free men entered by ordinance of the mayor, aldermen, and commons, and by them Henry Deane, tailor, was made keeper of Ludgate prison. In the year 1457, a great fray was in the north country between Sir Thomas Percie, Lord Egremond, and the Earl of Salisbury's sons, whereby many were maimed and slain; but, in the end, the Lord Egremond being taken, was by the king's counsel found in great default, and therefore condemned in great sums of money, to be paid to the Earl of Salisbury, and in the meantime committed to Newgate. Not long after, Sir Thomas Percie, Lord Egremond, and Sir Richard Percie his brother, being in Newgate, broke out of prison by night, and went to the king; the other prisoners took the leads of the gate, and defended it a long while against the sheriffs and all their officers, insomuch that they were forced to call more aid of the citizens, whereby they lastly subdued them, and laid them in irons: and this may suffice for Newgate.

LUDGATE

In the west is the next, and sixth principal gate, and is called Ludgate, as first built (saith Geoffrey Monmouth) by King Lud, a Briton, about the year before Christ's nativity, 66. Of which building, and also of the name, as Ludsgate, or Fludsgate, hath been of late some question among the learned;[1] wherefore I overpass it, as not to my purpose, only referring the reader to that I have before written of Cæsar's Commentaries, and other Roman writers, concerning a town or city amongst the Britons. This gate I suppose to be one of the most ancient; and as Aldgate was built for the east, so was this Ludsgate for the west. I read,[2] as I told you, that in the year 1215, the 17th of King John, the barons of the realm, being in arms against the king, entered this city, and spoiled the Jews' houses; which being done, Robert Fitzwater and Geffrey de Magnavilla, Earl of Essex, and the Earl of Gloucester, chief leaders of the army, applied all diligence to repair the gates and walls of this city, with the stones of the Jews' broken houses, especially (as it seemeth) they then repaired, or rather new built Ludgate.

[1] [*See* Additional Notes.]   [2] Roger Wendover, Matthew Paris.

For in the year 1586, when the same gate was taken down to be newly built, there was found couched within the wall thereof a stone taken from one of the Jews' houses, wherein was graven in Hebrew characters these words following: *Hæc est statio Rabbi Mosis, filii insignis Rabbi Isaac:* which is to say, this is the station or ward of Rabbi Moyses, the son of the honourable Rabbi Isaac, and had been fixed upon the front of one of the Jews' houses, as a note or sign that such a one dwelt there. In the year 1260, this Ludgate was repaired, and beautified with images of Lud, and other kings, as appeareth by letters patent of license given to the citizens of London, to take up stone for that purpose, dated the 25th of Henry III. These images of kings in the reign of Edward VI. had their heads smitten off, and were otherwise defaced by [1] such as judged every image to be an idol; and in the reign of Queen Mary were repaired, as by setting new heads on their old bodies, etc. All which so remained until the year 1586, the 28th of Queen Elizabeth, when the same gate being sore decayed, was clean taken down; the prisoners in the meantime remaining in the large south-east quadrant to the same gate adjoining; and the same year the whole gate was newly and beautifully built, with the images of Lud and others, as afore, on the east side, and the picture of her majesty Queen Elizabeth on the west side: all which was done at the common charges of the citizens, amounting to fifteen hundred pounds or more.

This gate was made a free prison in the year 1378, the 1st of Richard II., Nicholas Brembar being mayor.[2] The same was confirmed in the year 1382, John Northampton being mayor, by a common council in the Guildhall; by which it was ordained that all freemen of this city should, for debt, trespasses, accounts, and contempts, be imprisoned in Ludgate, and for treasons, felonies, and other criminal offences, committed to Newgate, etc. In the year 1431, the 10th of King Henry VI., John Wells being mayor, a court of common council established ordinances (as William Standon and Robert Chicheley, late mayors, before had done), touching the guard and government of Ludgate and other prisons.

Also in the year 1463, the third of Edward IV., Mathew Philip, being mayor, in a common council, at the request of the well-disposed, blessed, and devout woman, Dame Agnes Forster, widow, late wife to Stephen Forster, fishmonger, sometime mayor, for the comfort and relief of all the poor prisoners, certain

[1] " By unadvised folkes."—*1st edition.*
[2] Record, Guildhall. [*Letter-Books. See* Bibliography.]

articles were established. Imprimis, that the new works then late edified by the same Dame Agnes, for the enlarging of the prison of Ludgate, from thenceforth should be had and taken as a part and parcel of the said prison of Ludgate; so that both the old and new work of Ludgate aforesaid be one prison, gaol keeping, and charge for evermore.

The said quadrant, strongly built of stone by the before-named Stephen Forster, and Agnes his wife, containeth a large walking-place by ground of thirty-eight feet and a half in length, besides the thickness of the walls, which are at the least six foot, makes altogether forty-four feet and a half; the breadth within the walls is twenty-nine feet and a half, so that the thickness of the walls maketh it thirty five feet and a half in breadth. The like room it hath over it for lodgings, and over it again fair leads to walk upon, well embattled, all for fresh air and ease of prisoners, to the end they should have lodging and water free without charge, as by certain verses graven in copper, and fixed on the said quadrant, I have read in form following:—

> " Devout souls that pass this way,
> For Stephen Forster, late mayor, heartily pray;
> And Dame Agnes his spouse to God consecrate,
> That of pity this house made for Londoners in Ludgate.
> So that for lodging and water prisoners here nought pay,
> As their keepers shall all answer at dreadful doomsday."

This place and one other of his arms, three broad arrow-heads, taken down with the old gate, I caused to be fixed over the entry of the said quadrant; but the verses being unhappily turned inward to the wall, procured the like in effect to be graven outward in prose, declaring him to be a fishmonger, because some upon a light occasion (as a maiden's head in a glass window) had fabled him to be a mercer, and to have begged there at Ludgate, etc. Thus much for Ludgate.

Next this is there a breach in the wall of the city, and a bridge of timber over the Fleet dike, betwixt Fleetebridge and Thames, directly over against the house of Bridewel. Thus much for gates in the wall.

Water-gates on the banks of the river Thames have been many, which being purchased by private men, are also put to private use, and the old names of them forgotten; but of such as remain, from the west towards the east, may be said as followeth:—

The Blacke-friers stairs, a free landing-place.

Then a water-gate at Puddle wharf, of one Puddle that kept

a wharf on the west side thereof, and now of Puddle water, by means of many horses watered there.

Then Powle's wharf, also a free landing-place with stairs, etc. Then Broken wharf, and other such like.

But, Ripa Regina, the Queene's bank, or Queene hithe may well be accounted the very chief and principal water-gate of this city, being a common strand or landing-place, yet equal with, and of old time far exceeding, Belins gate, as shall be shown in the ward of Queene hithe.

The next is Downe gate, so called of the sudden descending[1] or down-going of that way from St. John's church upon Walbrooke unto the river of Thames, whereby the water in the channel there hath such a swift course, that in the year 1574, on the fourth of September, after a strong shower of rain, a lad, of the age of eighteen years, minding to have leapt over the channel, was taken by the feet, and borne down with the violence of that narrow stream, and carried toward the Thames with such a violent swiftness, as no man could rescue or stay him, till he came against a cart-wheel that stood in the watergate, before which time he was drowned and stark dead.

This was sometimes a large water-gate, frequented of ships and other vessels, like as the Queene hithe, and was a part thereof, as doth appear by an inquisition made in the 28th year of Henry III., wherein was found, that as well corn as fish, and all other things coming to the port of Downegate, were to be ordered after the customs of the Queene's hithe, for the king's use; as also that the corn arriving between the gate of the Guild hall of the merchants of Cullen (the Styleyard), which is east from Downegate, and the house then pertaining to the Archbishop of Canterbury, west from Baynarde's Castle, was to be measured by the measure, and measurer of the Queene's soke, or Queene hithe. I read also, in the 19th of Edward III., that customs were then to be paid for ships and other vessels resting at Downegate, as if they rode at Queene hithe, and as they now do at Belingsgate. And thus much for Downegate may suffice.

The next was called Wolfes gate,[2] in the ropery in the parish of Allhallowes the Lesse, of later time called Wolfes lane, but now out of use; for the lower part was built on by the Earle of Shrewsburie, and the other part was stopped up and built on by the chamberlain of London.

The next is Ebgate,[3] a water-gate, so called of old time, as

[1] [See Additional Notes.]
[2] Liber Horne. Liber S. Alban. [See Biblio. and Add. Notes.]
[3] Liber Trinitat. Liber S. Alban. Record, E. 3. [C.P.R.]

appeareth by divers records of tenements near unto the same adjoining. It standeth near unto the church of St. Laurence Pountney, but is within the parish of St. Marten Ordegare. In place of this gate is now a narrow passage to the Thames, and is called Ebgate lane, but more commonly the Old Swan.

Then is there a water-gate at the bridge foot, called Oyster gate, of oysters that were there of old time, commonly to be sold, and was the chiefest market for them and for other shell-fishes. There standeth now an engine or forcier, for the winding up of water to serve the city, whereof I have already spoken.

BRIDGE GATE

The next is the Bridge gate, so called of London Bridge, whereon it standeth. This was one of the four first and principal gates of the city, long before the Conquest, when there stood a bridge of timber, and is the seventh and last principal gate mentioned by W. Fitzstephen; which gate being new [1] made, when the bridge was built was built of stone, hath been often-times since repaired. This gate, with the tower upon it, in the year 1436 fell down, and two of the farthest arches southwards also fell therewith, and no man perished or was hurt therewith. To the repairing whereof, divers wealthy citizens gave large sums of money; namely, Robert Large, sometime mayor, one hundred marks; Stephen Forster, twenty pounds; Sir John Crosbye, alderman, one hundred pounds, etc. But in the year 1471,[2] the Kentish mariners, under the conduct of bastard Fauconbridge, burned the said gate and thirteen houses on the bridge, besides the Beer houses at St. Katherine's, and many others in the suburbs.

The next is Buttolphe's gate, so called of the parish church of St. Buttolph, near adjoining. This gate was sometimes given or confirmed by William Conqueror to the monks of Westminster in these words: "W. rex Angliæ, etc., William, king of England, sendeth greeting to the sheriffes, and all his ministers, as also to all his loving subjects, French and English, of London: Know ye that I have granted to God and St. Peter of Westminster, and to the abbot Vitalis, the gift which Almundus of the port of S. Buttolph gave them, when he was there made monke: that is to say, his Lords court with the houses, and one wharf, which is at the head of London bridge, and all other his lands which he had in the same city, in such sort as King Edward more bene-ficially and amply granted the same; and I will and command

---

[1] " Weakly made."—1st *edition*, p. 36.   [2] W. Dunthorn.

that they shall enjoy the same well and quietly and honourably, with sake and soke, etc."

The next is Bellinsgate, used as an especial port, or harbour, for small ships and boats coming thereto, and is now [1] most frequented, the Queen's hithe being almost forsaken. How this gate took that name, or of what antiquity the same is, I must leave uncertain, as not having any ancient record thereof, more than that Geoffrey Monmouth writeth, that Belin, a king of the Britons, about four hundred years before Christ's nativity, built this gate, and named it Belin's gate, after his own calling; and that when he was dead, his body being burnt, the ashes, in a vessel of brass, were set upon a high pinnacle of stone over the same gate. But Cæsar and other Roman writers affirm, of cities, walls, and gates, as ye have before heard; and therefore it seemeth to me not to be so ancient, but rather to have taken that name of some later owner of the place, happily named Beling, or Biling, as Somar's key, Smart's key, Frosh wharf, and others, thereby took their names of their owners. Of this gate more shall be said when we come to Belin's gate ward.

Then have you a water-gate, on the west side of Wool wharf, or Customers' key,[2] which is commonly called the water-gate, at the south end of Water lane.

One other water-gate there is by the bulwark of the Tower, and this is the last and farthest water-gate eastward, on the river of Thames, so far as the city of London extendeth within the walls; both which last named water-gates be within the Tower ward.

Besides these common water-gates, were divers private wharfs and keys, all along from the east to the west of this city, on the bank of the river of Thames; merchants of all nations had landing-places, warehouses, cellars, and stowage of their goods and merchandises, as partly shall be touched in the wards adjoining to the said river. Now, for the ordering and keeping these gates of this city in the night time, it was appointed in the year of Christ 1258, by Henry III., the 42nd of his reign,[3] that the ports of England should be strongly kept, and that the gates of London should be new repaired, and diligently kept in the night, for fear of French deceits, whereof one writeth these verses:

> " Per noctem portæ clauduntur Londoniarum,
> Mœnia ne forte fraus frangat Francigenarum."

[1] " The largest water-gate on the river of Thames, and therefore most frequented."—*1st edition*, p. 36.

[2] " Which is now of late most beautifully enlarged and built."—*1st edition*, p. 37.　　　[3] Matthew Paris.

OF TOWERS AND CASTLES

" The city of London (saith Fitzstephen) hath in the east a
very great and a most strong palatine Tower, whose turrets and
walls do rise from a deep foundation, the mortar thereof being
tempered with the blood of beasts. In the west part are two
most strong castles, etc." To begin therefore with the most
famous Tower of London, situate in the east, near unto the
river of Thames: it hath been the common opinion, and some
have written (but of none assured ground), that Julius Cæsar,
the first conqueror of the Britons, was the original author and
founder, as well thereof as also of many other towers, castles,
and great buildings within this realm; but (as I have already
before noted) Cæsar remained not here so long, nor had he in his
head any such matter, but only to dispatch a conquest of this
barbarous country, and to proceed to greater matters. Neither
do the Roman writers make mention of any such buildings
created by him here; and therefore leaving this, and proceeding to more grounded authority, I find in a fair register-book,
containing the acts of the Bishops of Rochester, set down by
Edmond de Hadenham, that William I., surnamed Conqueror,
built the Tower of London; to wit, the great white and square
tower there, about the year of Christ 1078, appointing Gundulph,
then Bishop of Rochester, to be principal surveyor and overseer
of that work, who was for that time lodged in the house of
Edmere, a burgess of London; the very words of which mine
author are these: " *Gundulphus Episcopus mandato Willielmi
Regis magni præfuit operi magnæ Turris London. quo tempore
hospitatus est apud quendam Edmerum Burgensem London. qui
dedit unum* were *Ecclesiæ Rofen.*"
Ye have before heard that the wall of this city was all round
about furnished with towers and bulwarks, in due distance
every one from other; and also that the river Thames, with his
ebbing and flowing, on the south side, had subverted the said
wall and towers there. Wherefore King William, for defence of
this city, in place most dangerous, and open to the enemy,
having taken down the second bulwark in the east part of the
wall from the Thames, built this tower, which was the great
square tower, now called the White Tower, and hath been since
at divers times enlarged with other buildings adjoining, as shall
be shown. This tower was by tempest of wind [1] sore shaken in

[1] W. Malmesbury, Matthew Paris, John London. [*See* Bibliography.]

the year 1090, the 4th of William Rufus, and was again by the said Rufus and Henry I. repaired. They also caused a castle to be built under the said tower, namely, on the south side towards the Thames, and also incastellated the same round about.

Henry Huntingdon, libro sexto, hath these words: " William Rufus challenged the investure of prelates; he pilled and shaved the people with tribute, especially to spend about the Tower of London, and the great hall at Westminster."

Othowerus, Acolinillus, Otto, and Geffrey Magnaville, Earl of Essex, were four the first constables of this Tower of London, by succession; all which held by force a portion of land (that pertained to the priory of the Holy Trinitie within Aldgate); that is to say, East Smithfield, near unto the Tower, making thereof a vineyard, and would not depart from it till the 2nd year of King Stephen, when the same was abridged and restored to the church. This said Geffrey Magnaville was Earl of Essex, constable of the Tower, sheriff of London, Middlesex, Essex, and Hertfordshire,[1] as appeareth by a charter of Maud the empress, dated 1141. He also fortified the Tower of London against King Stephen; but the king took him in his court at St. Albones, and would not deliver him till he had rendered the Tower of London, with the castles of Walden and Plashey in Essex. In the year 1153 the Tower of London and the castle of Windsor were by the king delivered to Richard de Lucie, to be safely kept. In the year 1155, Thomas Becket being chancellor to Henry II., caused the Flemings to be banished out of England,[2] their castles lately built to be pulled down, and the Tower of London to be repaired.

About the year 1190, the 2nd of Richard I., William Long-shampe, Bishop of Elie, Chancellor of England, for cause of dissension betwixt him and Earl John, the king's brother that was rebel, inclosed the tower and castle of London, with an outward wall of stone embattled, and also caused a deep ditch to be cast about the same, thinking (as I have said before) to have environed it with the river of Thames. By the making of this inclosure and ditch in East Smithfield, the church of the Holy Trinitie in London lost half a mark rent by the year, and the mill was removed that belonged to the poor brethren of the hospital of St. Katherine,[3] and to the church of the Holy Trinitie

[1] Ex charta. [Trivet. *See* Bibliography.]
[2] Roger Wendover, John Bever. [See Bibliography.]
[3] " St. Katherine's mill stood where now is the Iron Gate of the Tower."
—*Stow.*

aforesaid, which was no small loss and discommodity to either part; and the garden which the king had hired of the brethren for six marks the year, for the most part was wasted and marred by the ditch. Recompense was often promised, but never performed, until King Edward coming after, gave to the brethren five marks and a half for that part which the ditch had devoured, and the other part thereof without he yielded to them again, which they hold: and of the said rent of five marks and a half, they have a deed, by virtue whereof they are well paid to this day.

It is also to be noted, and cannot be denied, but that the said inclosure and ditch took the like or greater quantity of ground from the city within the wall; namely, one of that part called the Tower Hill, besides breaking down of the city wall, from the White Tower to the first gate of the city, called the Postern; yet have I not read of any quarrel made by the citizens, or recompense demanded by them for that matter, because all was done for good of the city's defence thereof, and to their good likings. But Matthew Paris writeth, that in the year 1239, King Henry III. fortified the Tower of London to another end; wherefore the citizens, fearing lest that were done to their detriment, complained, and the king answered, that he had not done it to their hurt, but (saith he) I will from henceforth do as my brother doth, in building and fortifying castles, who beareth the name to be wiser than I am. It followed in the next year, saith mine author, the said noble buildings of the stone gate and bulwark, which the king had caused to be made by the Tower of London, on the west side thereof, were shaken as it had been with an earthquake, and fell down, which the king again commanded to be built in better sort than before, which was done; and yet again, in the year 1247, the said wall and bulwarks that were newly built, wherein the king had bestowed more than twelve thousand marks, were irrecoverably thrown down, as afore; for the which chance the citizens of London were nothing sorry, for they were threatened that the said wall and bulwarks were built, to the end that if any of them would contend for the liberties of the city, they might be imprisoned; and that many might be laid in divers prisons, many lodgings were made that no one should speak with another: thus much Matthew Paris for this building. More of Henry III., his dealings against the citizens of London, we may read in the said author, in 1245, 1248, 1249, 1253, 1255, 1256, etc. But, concerning the said wall and bulwark, the same was finished, though not in his time; for I read that Edward I., in the second of his reign, commanded the treasurer and chamberlain of the Exchequer to deliver out of his treasury unto Miles of Andwarp two hundred marks, of the fines taken out of divers merchants or usurers of London, for so be the words of the record, towards the work of the ditch then new made, about the said bulwark, now called the Lion Tower. I find also recorded, that Henry III., in the 46th of his reign, wrote to Edward of Westminster, commanding him that he should buy certain perie plants, and set the same in the place without his Tower of London. within the wall of the said city, which of late he had caused to be inclosed with a mud wall, as may appear by this that followeth: the mayor and commonalty of London were fined for throwing down the said earthen wall against the Tower of London, the 9th of Edward II. Edward IV. in place thereof built a wall of brick. But now for the Lion Tower and lions in England, the original, as I have read, was thus.

Henry I. built his manor of Wodstock, with a park, which he walled about with stone, seven miles in compass, destroying for the same divers villages, churches, and chapels; and this was the first park in England. He placed therein, besides great store of deer, divers strange beasts to be kept and nourished, such as were brought to him from far countries, as lions, leopards, linces, porpentines,[1] and such other. More I read, that in the year 1235, Frederick the emperor sent to Henry III. three leopards, in token of his regal shield of arms, wherein three leopards were pictured; since the which time those lions and others have been kept in a part of this bulwark, now called the Lion Tower, and their keepers there lodged. King Edward II., in the 12th of his reign, commanded the sheriffs of London to pay to the keepers of the king's leopard in the Tower of London sixpence the day for the sustenance of the leopard, and three-halfpence a day for diet for the said keeper, out of the fee farm of the said city. More, in the 16th of Edward III., one lion, one lioness, one leopard, and two cat lions, in the said Tower, were committed to the custody of Robert, the son of John Bowre.

Edward IV. fortified the Tower of London, and inclosed with brick, as is aforesaid, a certain piece of ground, taken out of the Tower Hill, west from the Lion Tower, now called the bulwark. His officers also, in the 5th of his reign, set upon the said hill both scaffold and gallows, for the execution of offenders; where-

---

[1] Lynxes, porcupines.

upon the mayor and his brethren complained to the king, and were answered that the same was not done in derogation of the city's liberties, and thereof caused proclamation to be made, etc., as shall be shown in Tower street.

Richard III., repaired and built in this tower somewhat. Henry VIII., in 1532, repaired the White Tower, and other parts thereof. In the year 1548, the 2nd of Edward VI., on the 22nd of November, in the night, a Frenchman lodged in the round bulwark, betwixt the west gate and the postern, or drawbridge, called the warders' gate, by setting fire on a barrel of gunpowder, blew up the said bulwark, burnt himself, and no more persons. This bulwark, was forthwith again new built.

And here, because I have by occasion spoken of the west gate of this tower the same, as the most principal, is used for the receipt and delivery of all kinds of carriages, without the which gate divers bulwarks and gates, towards the north, etc. Then near within this west gate, opening to the south, is a strong postern for passengers by the ward-house, over a drawbridge let down for that purpose. Next on the same south side, toward the east, is a large water-gate, for receipt of boats and small vessels, partly under a stone bridge from the river of Thames. Beyond it is a small postern, with a drawbridge, seldom let down but for the receipt of some great persons, prisoners. Then towards the east is a great and strong gate, commonly called the Iron gate, but not usually opened. And thus much for the foundation, building, and repairing of this tower, with the gates and posterns, may suffice. And now somewhat of accidents in the same shall be shown.

In the year 1196, William Fitzosbert, a citizen of London, seditiously moving the common people to seek liberty, and not to be subject to the rich and more mighty, at length was taken and brought before the Archbishop of Canterbury in the Tower, where he was by the judges condemned, and by the heels drawn thence to the Elms in Smithfield, and there hanged.

In 1214, King John[1] wrote to Geffrey Magnaville to deliver the Tower of London, with the prisoners, armour, and all other things found therein belonging to the king, to William, archdeacon of Huntingdon. In the year 1216, the 1st of Henry III., the said Tower was delivered to Lewis of France and the barons of England.[2]

In the year 1206 pleas of the crown were pleaded in the Tower; likewise in the year 1220, and likewise in the year 1224, and

[1] Patent, the 15th of King John.   [2] Matthew Paris.

again in the year 1243, before William of Yorke, Richard Passelew, Henry Brahe, Jerome of Saxton, justices.

In the year 1222, the citizens of London having made a tumult against the abbot of Westminster, Hubert of Burge, chief justice of England, came to the Tower of London, called before him the mayor and aldermen, of whom he inquired for the principal authors of that sedition; amongst whom one, named Constantine Fitz Aelulfe, avowed that he was the man, and had done much less than he ought to have done: whereupon the justice sent him with two other to Falks de Brent, who with armed men brought them to the gallows, where they were hanged.

In the year 1244, Griffith, the eldest son of Leoline, Prince of Wales, being kept prisoner in the Tower, devised means of escape, and having in the night made of the hangings, sheets, etc., a long line, he put himself down from the top of the Tower, but in the sliding, the weight of his body, being a very big and a fat man, brake the rope, and he fell and brake his neck withall.

In the year 1253, King Henry III. imprisoned the sheriffs of London in the Tower more than a month, for the escape of a prisoner out of Newgate, as you may read in the chapter of Gates.

In the year 1260, King Henry, with his queen (for fear of the barons), were lodged in the Tower. The next year he sent for his lords, and held his parliament there.

In the year 1263, when the queen would have removed from the Tower by water towards Windsor, sundry Londoners got them together to the bridge, under the which she was to pass, and not only cried out upon her with reproachful words, but also threw mire and stones at her, by which she was constrained to return for the time; but in the year 1265, the said citizens were fain to submit themselves to the king for it, and the mayor, aldermen, and sheriffs were sent to divers prisons, and a custos also was set over the city; to wit, Othon, constable of the Tower, etc.

In the year 1282, Leoline, prince of Wales, being taken at Bewlth castle, Roger Lestrange cut off his head, which Sir Roger Mortimer caused to be crowned with ivy, and set it upon the Tower of London.

In the year 1290, divers justices, as well of the bench as of the assizes, were sent prisoners to the Tower, which with great sums of money redeemed their liberty. Edward II., the 14th of his reign, appointed for prisoners in the Tower, a knight twopence the day, an esquire one penny the day, to serve for their diet.

In the year 1320, the king's justices sat in the Tower, for trial of matters; whereupon John Gifors, late mayor of London, and many others, fled the city, for fear to be charged of things they had presumptuously done.

In the year 1321, the Mortimers yielding themselves to the king, he sent them prisoners to the Tower, where they remained long, and were adjudged to be drawn and hanged. But at length Roger Mortimer, of Wigmore, by giving to his keepers a sleepy drink, escaped out of the Tower, and his uncle Roger, being still kept there, died about five years after.

In the year 1326, the citizens of London won the Tower, wresting the keys out of the constable's hands, delivered all the prisoners, and kept both city and Tower to the use of Isabel the queen, and Edward her son.

In the year 1330, Roger Mortimer, Earl of March, was taken and brought to the Tower, from whence he was brought to the Elms, and there hanged.

In the year 1344, King Edward III., in the 18th of his reign, commanded florences of gold to be made and coined in the Tower; that is to say, a penny piece of the value of five shillings and eight pence, the halfpenny piece of the value of three shillings and four pence, and a farthing piece worth twenty pence; Percevall de Port of Lake being then master of the coin. And this is the first coining of gold in the Tower, whereof I have read, and also the first coinage of gold in England. I find also recorded, that the said king in the same year ordained his exchange of money to be kept in Serne's Tower, a part of the king's house in Bucklesbury. And here to digress a little (by occasion offered), I find that, in times before passed, all great sums were paid by weight of gold or silver, as so many pounds or marks of silver, or so many pounds or marks of gold, cut into blanks, and not stamped, as I could prove by many good authorities which I overpass. The smaller sums also were paid in starlings, which were pence so called, for other coins they had none. The antiquity of this starling penny usual in this realm is from the reign of Henry II., notwithstanding the Saxon coins before the Conquest were pence of fine silver the full weight, and somewhat better than the latter starlings, as I have tried by conference of the pence of Burghrede, king of Mercia, Aelfred, Edward, and Edelred, kings of the West Saxons, Plegmond, Archbishop of Canterbury, and others. William the Conqueror's penny also was fine silver of the weight of the easterling, and had on the one side stamped an armed head, with a beardless face—for the Normans wore no beards—with a sceptre in his hand. The inscription in the circumference was this: " Le Rei Wilam; " [1] on the other side, a cross double to the ring, between four rowals of six points.

King Henry I. his penny was of the like weight, fineness, form of face, cross, etc.

This Henry, in the 8th year of his reign, ordained the penny, which was round, so to be quartered by the cross, that they might easily be broken into halfpence and farthings.[2] In the 1st, 2nd, 3rd, 4th, and 5th of King Richard I. his reign, and afterwards, I find commonly easterling money mentioned, and yet ofttimes the same is called argent, as afore, and not otherwise.

The first great sum that I read of to be paid in easterlings was in the reign of Richard I., when Robert, Earl of Leicester, being prisoner in France, proffered for his ransom a thousand marks easterlings, notwithstanding the easterling pence were long before. The weight of the easterling penny may appear by divers statutes, namely, of weights and measures, made in the 51st of Henry III. in these words: " Thirty-two graines of wheat, drie and round, taken in the middest of the eare, shoulde be the weight of a starling penie, 20 of those pence should waye one ounce, 12 ounces a pound Troy." It followeth in the statute eight pound to make a gallon of wine, and eight gallons a bushel of London measure, etc. Notwithstanding which statute, I find, in the 8th of Edward I., Gregorie Rokesley, mayor of London, being chief master or minister of the Kinge's Exchange, or mintes, a new coin being then appointed, the pound of easterling money should contain as afore twelve ounces; to wit, fine silver, such as was then made into foil, and was commonly called silver of Guthurons lane,[3] eleven ounces, two easterlings, and one ferling or farthing, and the other seventeen pence ob. q. [4] to be alloy. Also, the pound of money ought to weigh twenty shillings and three pence by account; so that no pound ought to be over twenty shillings and three pence, nor less than twenty shillings and two pence by account; the ounce to weigh twenty pence, the penny weight twenty-four grains (which twenty-four by weight then appointed were as much as the former thirty-two grains of wheat), a penny force twenty-five grains and a half, the penny deble or feeble twenty-two grains and a half, etc.[1]

Now for the penny easterling, how it took that name I think good briefly to touch. It hath been said, that Numa Pompilius, the second king of the Romans, commanded money first to be made, of whose name they were called *nummi;* and when copper pence, silver pence, and gold pence, were made, because every silver penny was worth ten copper pence, and every gold penny worth ten silver pence, the pence therefore were called in Latin, denarii, and oftentimes the pence are named of the matter and stuff of gold or silver. But the money of England was called of the workers and makers thereof; as the florin of gold is called of the Florentines, that were the workers thereof, and so the easterling pence took their name of the Easterlings which did first make this money in England, in the reign of Henry II.

Thus have I set down according to my reading in antiquity of money matters, omitting the imaginations of late writers, of whom some have said easterling money to take that name of a star, stamped in the border or ring of the penny; other some of a bird called a star or starling stamped in the circumference; and other (more unlikely) of being coined at Strivelin or Starling, a town in Scotland, etc.

Now concerning halfpence and farthings, the account of which is more subtle than the pence, I need not speak of them more than that they were only made in the Exchange at London, and nowhere else: first appointed to be made by Edward I. in the 8th of his reign; and also at the same time the said king coined some few groats of silver, but they were not usual. The king's Exchange as London was near unto the cathedral church of St. Paul, and is to this day commonly called the Old Change, but in evidences the Old Exchange.

The king's exchanger in this place was to deliver out to every other exchanger throughout England, or other the king's dominions, their coining irons, that is to say, one standard or staple, and two trussels or puncheons; and when the same was spent and worn, to receive them with an account what sum had been coined, and also their pix or bore of assay, and deliver other irons new graven, etc. I find that in the 9th of King John, there was besides the mint at London, other mints at Winchester, Excester, Chichester, Canterburie, Rochester, Ipswich, Norwich,

[1] By the terms *force* and *deble,* it is presumed the maximum and minimum weights are intended.

Linne, Lincolne, York, Carleil, Northampton, Oxford, St. Edmondsbury, and Durham. The exchanger, examiner, and trier, buyeth the silver for coinage, answering for every hundred pounds of silver bought in bullion or otherwise, ninety-eight pounds fifteen shillings, for he taketh twenty-five shillings for coinage.

King Edward I., in the 27th of his reign, held a parliament at Stebenheth, in the house of Henry Waleis, mayor of London, wherein amongst other things there handled, the transporting of sterling money was forbidden.

In the year 1351, William Edington, bishop of Winchester, and treasurer of England, a wise man, but loving the king's commodity more than the wealth of the whole realm, and common people (saith mine author [1]) caused a new coin, called a groat, and a half-groat, to be coined and stamped, the groat to be taken for four pence, and the half-groat for two pence, not containing in weight according to the pence called easterlings, but much less, to wit, by five shillings in the pound; by reason whereof, victuals and merchandises became the dearer through the whole realm. About the same time also, the old coin of gold was changed into a new; but the old florin or noble, then so called, was worth much above the taxed rate of the new, and therefore the merchants engrossed up the old, and conveyed them out of the realm, to the great loss of the kingdom. Wherefore a remedy was provided by changing of the stamp.

In the year 1411, King Henry IV. caused a new coin of nobles to be made, of less value than the old by four pence in the noble, so that fifty nobles should be a pound troy weight.

In the year 1421 was granted to Henry V. a fifteenth, to be paid at Candlemas and at Martinmas, of such money as was then current, gold or silver, not overmuch clipped or washed; to wit, that if the noble were worth five shillings and eight pence, then the king should take it for a full noble of six shillings and eight pence, and if it were less of value than five shillings and eight pence, then the person paying that gold to make it good to the value of five shillings and eight pence, the king always receiving it for a whole noble of six shillings and eight pence. And if the noble so paid be better than five shillings and eight pence, the king to pay again the surplusage that it was better than five shillings and eight pence. Also this year was such scarcity of white money, that though a noble were

---

[1] Thomas Walsingham. [*See* Bibliography.]

so good of gold and weight as six shillings and eight pence, men might get no white money for them.

In the year 1465, King Edward IV. caused a new coin both of gold and silver to be made, whereby he gained much; for he made of an old noble a royal, which he commanded to go for ten shillings. Nevertheless, to the same royal was put eight pence of alloy, and so weighed the more, being smitten with a new stamp, to wit, a rose. He likewise made half-angels of five shillings, and farthings of two shillings and six pence, angelets of six shillings and eight pence, and half-angels of three shillings and four pence. He made silver money of three pence, a groat, and so of other coins after that rate, to the great harm of the commons. W. Lord Hastings, the king's chamberlain, being master of the king's mints, undertook to make the monies under form following, to wit,—of gold, a piece of eight shillings and four pence sterling, which should be called a noble of gold, of the which there should be fifty such pieces in the pound weight of the Tower; another piece of gold of four shillings and two pence sterling, and to be of them an hundred such pieces in the pound; and a third piece of gold, of two shillings and one penny sterling, two hundred such pieces in the pound; every pound weight of the Tower to be worth twenty pounds, sixteen shillings, and eight pence, the which should be twenty-three carats, three grains and a half fine, etc., and for silver thirty-seven shillings and six pence; the piece of four pence to be one hundred and twelve groats and two pence in the pound weight.

In the year 1504, King Henry VII. appointed a new coin, to wit, a groat, and half-groat, which bare but half faces; the same time also was coined a groat, which was in value twelve pence, but of those but a few, after the rate of forty pence the ounce.

In the year 1526, the 18th of Henry VIII., the angel noble being then the sixth part of an ounce troy, so that six angels were just an ounce, which was forty shillings sterling, and the angel was also worth two ounces of silver, so that six angels were worth twelve ounces of silver, which was forty shillings. A proclamation was made on the sixth of September, that the angel should go for seven shillings and four pence, the royal for eleven shillings, and the crown for four shillings and four-pence. And on the fifth of November following, again by proclamation, the angel was enhanced to seven shillings and sixpence, and so every ounce of gold to be forty-five shillings, and the ounce of silver at three shillings and nine pence in value.

In the year 1544, the 35th of Henry VIII., on the 16th of May, proclamation was made for the enhancing of gold to forty-eight shillings, and silver to four shillings the ounce. Also the king caused to be coined base moneys, to wit, pieces of twelve pence, six pence, four pence, two pence, and a penny, in weight as the late sterling, in show good silver, but inwardly copper. These pieces had whole, or broad faces, and continued current after that rate till the 5th of Edward VI., when they were on the 9th of July called down, the shilling to nine pence, the groat to three pence, etc., and on the 17th of August from nine pence to six pence, etc. And on the 30th of October was published new coins of silver and gold to be made, a piece of silver five shillings sterling, a piece of two shillings and five pence, of twelve pence, of six pence, a penny with a double rose, half-penny a single rose, and a farthing with a portclose. Coins of fine gold: a whole sovereign of thirty shillings, an angel of ten shillings, an angelet of five shillings. Of crown gold: a sovereign twenty shillings, half-sovereign ten shillings, five shillings, two shillings and six pence, and base moneys to pass as before, which continued till the 2nd of Queen Elizabeth, then called to a lower rate, taken to the mint, and refined, the silver whereof being coined with a new stamp of her majesty, the dross was carried to foul highways, to heighten them. This base money, for the time, caused the old sterling moneys to be hoarded up, so that I have seen twenty-one shillings current given for one old angel to gild withal. Also rents of lands and tenements, with prices of victuals, were raised far beyond the former rates, hardly since to be brought down. Thus much for base moneys coined and current in England have I known. But for leather moneys, as many people have fondly talked, I find no such matter. I read,[1] that King John of France, being taken prisoner by Edward the Black Prince at the battle of Poictiers, paid a ransom of three millions of florences, whereby he brought the realm into such poverty, that many years after they used leather money, with a little stud or nail of silver in the middle thereof. Thus much for mint and coinage, by occasion of this Tower (under correction of others more skilful) may suffice. And now to other accidents there.

In the year 1360, the peace between England and France being confirmed, King Edward came over into England, and

[1] Philip Comines. [See Bibliography.]

straight to the Tower, to see the French king then prisoner there, whose ransom he assessed at three millions of florences, and so delivered him from prison, and brought him with honour to the sea.

In the year 1381, the rebels of Kent drew out of the Tower (where the king was then lodged) Simon Sudberie, archbishop of Canterbury, lord chancellor, Robert Hales, prior of St. John's, and treasurer of England, William Appleton, friar, the king's confessor, and John Legg, a sergeant of the king's, and beheaded them on the Tower hill, etc.

In the year 1387, King Richard held his feast of Christmas in the Tower. And in the year 1399, the same king was sent prisoner to the Tower.

In the year 1414 [1413], Sir John Oldcastell brake out of the Tower. And the same year, a parliament being holden at Ley-cester, a porter of the Tower was drawn, hanged, and headed, whose head was sent up, and set over the Tower gate, for consenting to one Whitlooke, that brake out of the Tower.

In the year 1419, Friar Randulph was sent to the Tower, and was there slain by the parson of St. Peter's in the Tower.

In the year 1428, there came to London, a lewd fellow, feigning himself to be sent from the Emperor to the young King Henry VI., calling himself Baron of Blakamoore, and that he should be the principal physician in this kingdom; but his subtlety being known, he was apprehended, condemned, drawn, hanged, headed, and quartered, his head set on the Tower of London, and his quarters on four gates of the city.

In the year 1458, in Whitsun week, the Duke of Somerset, with Anthonie Rivers, and other four, kept jousts before the queen in the Tower of London, against three esquires of the queen's, and others.

In the year 1465, King Henry VI. was brought prisoner to the Tower, where he remained long.

In the year 1470, the Tower was yielded to Sir Richard Lee, mayor of London, and his brethren the aldermen, who forth-with entered the same, delivered King Henry of his imprison-ment, and lodged him in the king's lodging there; but the next year he was again sent thither prisoner, and there murdered.

In the year 1478, George Duke of Clarence was drowned with malmsey in the Tower; and within five years after King Edward V., with his brother, were said to be murdered there.

In the year 1485, John Earl of Oxford was made constable of the Tower, and had custody of the lions granted him.[1]

In the year 1501, in the month of May, was a royal tourney of lords and knights in the Tower of London before the king.

In the year 1502, Queen Elizabeth, wife to Henry VII., died of childbirth in the Tower.

In the year 1512, the chapel in the high White Tower was burnt. In the year 1536 Queen Anne Bullein was beheaded in the Tower. 1541, Lady Katherine Howard, wife to King Henry VIII., was also beheaded there.

In the year 1546, the 27th of April, being Tuesday in Easter week, William Foxley, potmaker for the Mint in the Tower of London, fell asleep, and so continued sleeping, and could not be wakened with pricking, cramping, or otherwise burning whatsoever, until the first day of the term, which was full fourteen days and fifteen nights, or more, for that Easter term beginneth not before seventeen days after Easter. The cause of his thus sleeping could not be known, though the same was diligently searched after by the king's physicians, and other learned men; yea, the king himself examining the said William Foxley, who was in all points found at his awakening to be as if he had slept but one night. And he lived more than forty years after in the said Tower, to wit, until the year of Christ 1587, and then deceased on Wednesday in Easter week.

Thus much for these accidents: and now to conclude thereof in summary. This Tower is a citadel to defend or command the city; a royal palace for assemblies or treaties; a prison of state for the most dangerous offenders; the only place of coinage for all England at this time; the armoury for warlike provision; the treasury of the ornaments and jewels of the crown; and general conserver of the most records of the king's courts of justice at Westminster.

TOWER ON LONDON BRIDGE

The next tower on the river of Thames is on London bridge, at the north end of the drawbridge. This tower was newly begun to be built in the year 1426. John Reynwell, mayor of London, laid one of the first corner stones in the foundation of this work, the other three were laid by the sheriffs and bridge masters; upon every of these four stones was engraven in fair roman letters the name of " Ihesus." And these stones I have

[1] Patent, 1st of Henry VII.

seen laid in the bridge storehouse since they were taken up, when that tower was of late newly made of timber. This gate and tower was at the first strongly built up of stone, and so continued until the year 1577, in the month of April, when the same stone arched gate and tower being decayed, was begun to be taken down, and then were the heads of the traitors removed thence, and set on the tower over the gate at the bridge-foot towards Southwark. This said tower being taken down, a new foundation was drawn, and Sir John Langley, lord mayor, laid the first stone in the presence of the sheriffs and bridge masters, on the 28th of August; and in the month of September, in the year 1579, the same tower was finished—a beautiful and chargeable piece of work, all above the bridge being of timber.

TOWER ON THE SOUTH OF LONDON BRIDGE

Another tower there is on London bridge, to wit, over the gate at the south end of the same bridge towards Southwark. This gate, with the tower thereupon, and two arches of the bridge, fell down, and no man perished by the fall thereof, in the year 1436;[1] towards the new building whereof divers charitable citizens gave large sums of money; which gate, being then again newly built, was, with seventeen houses more on the bridge, in the year 1471, burnt by the mariners and sailors of Kent, Bastard Fauconbridge being their captain.

BAYNARD'S CASTLE

In the west of this city (saith Fitzstephen) are two most strong castles, etc. Also Gervasius Tilbury,[2] in the reign of Henry II., writing of these castles, hath to this effect:—"Two castels," saith he, "are built with walles and rampires, whereof one is, in right of possession, Baynardes; the other the Barons of Mountfichet." The first of these castles, banking on the river Thames, was called Baynard's Castle, of Baynard a nobleman, that came in with the Conqueror, and then built it, and deceased in the reign of William Rufus; after whose decease Geffrey Baynard succeeded, and then William Baynard, in the year 1111, who by forfeiture for felony, lost his barony of Little Dunmow, and King Henry gave it wholly to Robert, the son of Richard, the son of Gilbard of Clare, and to his heirs, together with the honour of Baynard's Castle. This Robert married

---

[1] W. Dunthorne.   [2] Fitzstephen, Gerv. Tilbury.

Maude de Sent Licio, lady of Bradham, and deceased 1134; was buried at St. Needes by Gilbert of Clare, his father. Walter his son succeeded him; he took to wife Matilde de Bocham, and after her decease, Matilde, the daughter and co-heir of Richard de Lucy, on whom he begat Robert and other: he deceased in the year 1198, and was buried at Dunmow; after whom succeeded Robert Fitzwater, a valiant knight.

About the year 1213 there arose a great discord between King John and his barons, because Matilda, surnamed the Fair, daughter to the said Robert Fitzwater, whom the king unlawfully loved, but could not obtain her, nor her father would consent thereunto, whereupon, and for other like causes, ensued war through the whole realm. The barons were received into London, where they greatly endamaged the king; but in the end the king did not only therefore banish the said Fitzwater, amongst other, out of the realm, but also caused his castle called Baynard, and other his houses, to be spoiled; which thing being done, a messenger being sent unto Matilda the Fair about the king's suit, whereunto she would not consent, she was poisoned;[1] Robert Fitzwater, and other, being then passed into France, and some into Scotland, etc.[2]

It happened in the year 1214, King John being then in France with a great army, that a truce was taken betwixt the two kings of England and France for the term of five years; and a river, or arm of the sea, being then between either host, there was a knight in the English host, that cried to them of the other side, willing some one of their knights to come and joust a course or twain with him; whereupon, without stay, Robert Fitzwater, being on the French part, made himself ready, ferried over, and got on horseback, without any man to help him, and showed himself ready to the face of his challenger, whom at the first course he struck so hard with his great spear, that horse and man fell to the ground; and when his spear was broken he went back to the King of France; which when the king had seen, " By God's tooth," quoth he (after his usual oath), " he were a king indeed that had such a knight." The friends of Robert, hearing these words, kneeled down, and said:—" O king, he is your knight; it is Robert Fitzwater." And thereupon, the next day he was sent for, and restored to the king's favour; by which means peace was concluded, and he received his livings,

---

[1] " Virginitie defended with the losse of worldly goods, and life of the bodie, for life of the soule."—*Stow*.

[2] Liber Dunmow.

and had license to repair his castle of Baynard, and other castles.

The year 1216, the 1st of Henry III., the castle of Hartford being delivered to Lewis the French prince, and the barons of England, Robert Fitzwater requiring to have the same, because the keeping thereof did by ancient right and title pertain to him, was answered by Lewis, "that Englishmen were not worthy to have such holds in keeping, because they did betray their own lord," etc. This Robert deceased in the year 1234, and was buried at Dunmow, and Walter his son that succeeded him, 1258. His barony of Baynard, was in the ward of King Henry, in the nonage of Robert Fitzwater. This Robert took to his second wife, Ælianor, daughter and heir to the Earl of Ferrars, in the year 1289; and in the year 1303, on the 12th of March, before John Blondon, mayor of London, he acknowledged his service to the same city, and sware upon the Evangelists, that he would be true to the liberties thereof, and maintain the same to his power, and the counsel of the same to keep, etc.

THE RIGHTS THAT BELONGED TO ROBERT FITZWALTER CHAS-
TALIAN OF LONDON, LORD OF WODEHAM, WERE THESE:—

The said Robert, and his heirs, ought to be, and are chief bannerers of London, in fee of the chastilarie, which he and his ancestors had by Castle Baynard, in the said city. In time of war the said Robert, and his heirs, ought to serve the city in manner as followeth: that is, The said Robert ought to come, he being the twentieth man of arms on horseback, covered with cloth, or armour, unto the great west door of St. Paul, with his banner displayed before him of his arms; and when he is come to the said door, mounted and apparelled, as before is said, the mayor with his aldermen and sheriffs armed in their arms, shall come out of the said church of St. Paul, unto the said door, with a banner in his hand, all on foot, which banner shall be gules, with the image of St. Paul, gold, the face, hands, feet, and sword, of silver; and as soon as the said Robert shall see the mayor, aldermen, and sheriffs, come on foot out of the church, armed with such a banner, he shall alight from his horse, and salute the mayor, and say to him,—"Sir mayor, I am come to do my service, which I owe to the city." And the mayor and aldermen shall answer,—"We give to you, as our bannerer of fee in this city, this banner of this city to bear, and govern to the honour and profit of the city to our power." And the said Robert and his heirs shall receive the banner in his hands, and shall go on foot out of the gate with the banner in his hands; and the mayor, aldermen, and sheriffs, shall follow to the door, and shall bring a horse to the said Robert worth twenty pounds, which horse shall be saddled with a saddle of the arms of the said Robert, and shall be covered with sandals of the said arms. Also they shall present to him twenty pounds sterling money, and deliver it to the chamberlain of the said Robert for his expenses that day. Then the said Robert shall mount upon the horse which the mayor presented to him, with the banner in his hand, and as soon as he is up, he shall say to the mayor, that he cause a marshal to be chosen for the host, one of the city; which marshal being chosen, the said Robert shall command the mayor and burgesses of the city to warn the commoners to assemble together, and they shall all go under the banner of St. Paul, and the said Robert shall bear it himself unto Aldgate, and there the said Robert and mayor shall deliver the said banner of St. Paul from thence, to whom they shall assent or think good. And if they must make any issue forth of the city, then the said Robert ought to choose two forth of every ward, the most sage personages, to foresee to the safe keeping of the city after they be gone forth. And this counsel shall be taken in the priory of the Trinity near unto Aldgate. And before every town or castle which the host of London besiege, if the siege continue a whole year, the said Robert shall have for every siege of the commonalty of London an hundred shillings for his travail, and no more. These be the rights that the said Robert hath in the time of war.—Rights belonging to Robert Fitzwalter, and to his heirs in the city of London, in the time of peace, are these: that is to say, the said Robert hath a soken or ward in the city, that is, a wall of the canonry of St. Paul, as a man goeth down the street before the brewhouse of St. Paul unto the Thames, and so to the side of the mill, which is in the water that cometh down from the Fleet bridge, and goeth so by London walls, betwixt the Friers preachers and Ludgate, and so returneth back by the house of the said Friars unto the said wall of the said canonry of St. Paul, that is, all the parish of St. Andrew, which is in the gift of his ancestors by the said seigniority. And so the said Robert hath appendant unto the said soken all these things under-written,—that he ought to have a soke man, and to place what sokeman he will, so he be of the sokemanry, or the same ward; and if any of the sokemanry be impleaded in the Guildhall, of any thing that toucheth not the body of the mayor that for the time is, or that toucheth the body of no sheriff, it is not lawful for the sokeman of the sokemanry of the said Robert Fitzwalter to demand a court of the said Robert, and the mayor, and his citizens of London, ought to grant him to have a court, and in his court he ought to bring his judgments, as it is assented and agreed upon in this Guildhall, that shall be given them. If any, therefore, be taken in his sokemanry, he ought to have his stocks and imprisonment in his soken; and he shall be brought from thence to the Guildhall before the mayor, and there they shall provide him his judgment that ought to be given of him; but his judgment shall not be published till he come into the court of the said Robert, and in his liberty.   And the judgment shall be such, that if he have deserved death by treason, he to be tied to a post in the Thames at a good wharf where boats are fastened, two ebbings and two flowings of the water.   And if he be condemned for a common thief, he ought to be led to the Elms, and there suffer his judgment as other thieves.   And so the said Robert and his heirs hath honour that he holdeth a great franchise within the city, that the mayor of the city and citizens are bound to do him of right, that is to say, that when the mayor will hold a great council, he ought to call the said Robert, and his heirs, to be with him in council of the city, and the said Robert ought to be sworn to be of council with the city against all people, saving the king and his heirs.   And when the said Robert cometh to the hustings in the Guildhall of the city, the mayor, or his lieutenant, ought to rise against him, and set him down near unto him; and so long as he is in the Guildhall, all the judgment ought to be given by his mouth, according to the record of the recorders of the said Guildhall; and so many waifes as come so long as he is there, he ought to give them to the bailiffs of the town, or to whom he will, by the counsel of the mayor of the city.   These be the franchises that belonged to Robert Fitzwalter in London, in time of peace; which for the antiquity thereof I have noted out of an old record.   [See Additional Notes.]

This Robert deceased in the year 1305, leaving issue Walter Fitzrobert, who had issue Robert Fitzwalter, unto whom, in the year 1320, the citizens of London acknowledged the right which they ought to him and his heirs for the Castle Baynard; he deceased 1325; unto whom succeeded Robert Fitzrobert, Fitzwalter, etc.   More of the Lord Fitzwalter may ye read in my Annals in 51st of Edward III.   But how this honour of Baynard's castle, with the appurtenances, fell from the possession of the Fitzwalters, I have not read; only I find, that in the year 1428, the 7th of Henry VI., a great fire was at Baynard's castle, and that same Humfrey, Duke of Gloucester, built it of new. By his death and attainder, in the year 1446, it came to the hands of Henry VI., and from him to Richard, Duke of York, of whom we read, that in the year 1457 he lodged there, as in his own house. In the year 1460, the 28th of February, the Earls of March and of Warwick, with a great power of men, but few of name, entered the city of London, where they were of the citizens joyously received; and upon the 3rd of March, being Sunday, the said earl caused to be mustered his people in St. John's field; whereunto that host was showed and proclaimed certain articles and points wherein King Henry, as they said, had offended; and thereupon, it was demanded of the said people, whether the said Henry was worthy to reign as king any longer or not: whereunto the people cried Nay. Then it was asked of them, whether they would have the Earl of March for their king; and they cried, Yea, Yea. Whereupon, certain captains were appointed to bear report thereof unto the said Earl of March, then being lodged at his castle of Baynard. Whereof when the earl was by them advertised, he thanked God, and them for their election; notwithstanding he showed some countenance of insufficiency in him to occupy so great a charge, till by exhortation of the Archbishop of Canterbury, the Bishop of Excester, and certain noblemen, he granted to their petition; and on the next morrow at Paul's he went on procession, offered, and had *Te Deum* sung. Then was he with great royalty conveyed to Westminster, and there, in the great hall, set in the king's seat, with St. Edward's sceptre in his hand.

Edward IV. being dead, leaving his eldest son Edward, and his second son Richard, both infants, Richard, Duke of Glocester,[1] being elected by the nobles and commons in the Guildhall of London, took on him the title of the realm and kingdom, as imposed upon him in this Baynard's castle, as ye may read penned by Sir Thomas More, and set down in my Annals.

Henry VII., about the year 1501, the 16th of his reign, repaired, or rather new built this house, not embattled, or so strongly fortified castle like, but far more beautiful and commodious for the entertainment of any prince or great estate.

---

[1] Stow in his first edition says, "there practised for the crown . . .;" and the admirable scene in *Richard the Third* (act III., sc. 7), in which Gloucester is by Buckingham, the mayor, and citizens of London, "enforced to a world of cares," is laid by Shakspeare with great historic truth in "the court of Baynard's castle."

In the 17th of his reign, he, with his queen were lodged there, and came from thence to Powles church, where they made their offering, dined in the bishop's palace, and so returned. The 18th of his reign he was lodged there, and the ambassadors from the king of the Romans, where thither brought to his presence, and from thence the king came to Powles, and was there sworn to the king of the Romans, as the said king had sworn to him.

The 20th of the said king, he with his knights of the order, all in their habits of the Garter, rode from the Tower of London, through the city, unto the cathedral church of St. Paul's, and there heard evensong, and from thence they rode to Baynard's castle, where the king lodged; and on the next morrow, in the same habit they rode from thence again to the said church of St. Paul's, went on procession, heard the divine service, offered, and returned. The same year the king of Castile was lodged there.

In the year 1553, the 19th of July, the council, partly moved with the right of the Lady Mary's cause, partly considering that the most of the realm were wholly bent on her side, changing their mind from Lady Jane, lately proclaimed queen, assembled themselves at this Baynard's castle, where they communed with the Earl of Pembroke, and the Earl of Shrewsbury, and Sir John Mason, clerk of the council, sent for the lord mayor, and then riding into Cheap to the cross, where Garter King at Arms, trumpet being sounded, proclaimed the Lady Mary, daughter of King Henry VIII., and Queen Katherine, queen of England, etc.

This castle now belongeth to the Earl of Pembroke.[1]

Next adjoining to this castle was sometime a tower, the name whereof I have not read; but that the same was built by Edward II. is manifest by this that followeth. King Edward III., in the second year of his reign, gave unto William de Ros, of Hamolake, in Yorkshire, a tower upon the water of Thames, by the castle of Baynard in the city of London, which tower his father had built; he gave the said tower and appurtenances to the said William Hamolake, and his heirs, for a rose yearly, to be paid for all service due, etc. This tower, as seemeth to me, was since called Legat's inn, the 7th of Edward IV.

---

[1] It was destroyed in the Great Fire, before which time it had become the residence of the Earls of Shrewsbury.

TOWER OF MOUNTFIQUIT

The next tower or castle, banking also on the river of Thames, was, as is afore showed, called Mountfiquit's castle, of a nobleman, Baron of Mountfiquit, the first builder thereof, who came in with William the Conqueror, and was since named Le Sir Mountfiquit. This castle he built in a place not far distant from Baynard's, towards the west. The same William Mountfiquit lived in the reign of Henry I., and was witness to a charter then granted to the city for the sheriffs of London. Richard Mountfiquit lived in King John's time; and in the year 1213, was by the same king banished the realm into France, when peradventure King John caused his castle of Mountfiquit, amongst other castles of the barons, to be overthrown; the which after his return, might be by him again re-edified; for the total destruction thereof was about the year 1276, when Robert Kiliwarble, archbishop of Canterbury, began the foundation of the Fryers Preachers church there, commonly called the Blacke Fryers, as appeareth by a charter the 4th of Edward I., wherein is declared that Gregorie de Rocksley, mayor of London, and the barons of the same city, granted and gave unto the said Archbishop Robert, two lanes or ways next the street of Baynard's castle, and the tower of Mountfiquit, to be applied for the enlargement of the said church and place.

One other tower there was also situate on the river of Thames near unto the said Blacke Fryers church, on the west part thereof built at the citizens' charges, but by license and commandment of Edward I. and of Edward II., as appeareth by their grants; which tower was then finished, and so stood for the space of three hundred years, and was at the last taken down by the commandment of John Shaw, mayor of London, in the year 1502.

Another tower, or castle, also was there in the west part of the city pertaining to the king. For I read, that in the year 1087, the 20th of William I., the city of London, with the church of St. Paul, being burned, Mauritius, then bishop of London, afterwards began the foundation of a new church, whereunto King William, saith mine author, gave the choice stones of this castle standing near to the bank of the river of Thames, at the west end of the city. After this Mauritius, Richard his successor purchased the streets about Paul's church,[1] compassing

[1] Vita Arkenwald. [See Bibliography.]

the same with a wall of stone and gates. King Henry I. gave to this Richard so much of the moat or wall of the castle, on the Thames side to the south, as should be needful to make the said wall of the churchyard, and so much more as should suffice to make a way without the wall on the north side, etc.

This tower or castle thus destroyed, stood, as it may seem, where now standeth the house called Bridewell. For notwithstanding the destruction of the said castle or tower, the house remained large, so that the kings of this realm long after were lodged there, and kept their courts; for until the 9th year of Henry III. the courts of law and justice were kept in the king's house, wheresoever he was lodged, and not elsewhere. And that the kings have been lodged, and kept their law courts in this place, I could show you many authors of record, but for plain proof this one may suffice. "*Hæc est finalis concordia, facta in Curia Domini regis apud Sanct. Bridgid. London. a die Sancti Michaelis in 15 dies, Anno regni regis Johannis 7. coram G. Fil. Petri. Eustachio de Fauconberg, Johanne de Gestlinge, Osbart filio Hervey, Walter De Crisping Justiciar. et aliis baronibus Domini regis.*" [1] More, as Matthew Paris hath, about the year 1210, King John, in the 12th of his reign, summoned a parliament at St. Bride's in London, where he exacted of the clergy and religious persons the sum of one hundred thousand pounds; and besides all this, the white monks were compelled to cancel their privileges, and to pay forty thousand pounds to the king, etc. This house of St. Bride's of latter time being left, and not used by the kings, fell to ruin, insomuch that the very platform thereof remained for great part waste, and, as it were, but a laystall of filth and rubbish; only a fair well remained there. A great part of this house, namely, on the west, as hath been said, was given to the Bishop of Salisbury; the other part towards the east remaining waste until King Henry VIII. built a stately and beautiful house thereupon, giving it to name Bridewell, of the parish and well there. This house he purposely built for the entertainment of the Emperor Charles V., who in the year 1522 came into this city, as I have showed in my Summary, Annals, and large Chronicles.

On the north-west side of the city, near unto Redcross street, there was a tower, commonly called Barbican, or Burhkenning; for that the same being placed on a high ground, and also built of some good height, was in old time as a watch-tower for the city, from whence a man might behold and view the whole

[1] Liber Burton, super Trent. [*See* Bibliography.]

city towards the south, and also into Kent, Sussex, and Surrey, and likewise every other way, east, north, or west.

Some other Burhkennings, or watch-towers, there were of old time in and about the city, all which were repaired, yea, and others new built, by Gilbart de Clare, Earl of Glocester, in the reign of King Henry III., when the barons were in arms, and held the city against the king; but the barons being reconciled to his favour in the year 1267, he caused all their burhkennings, watch-towers, and bulwarks, made and repaired by the said earl, to be plucked down, and the ditches to be filled up, so that nought of them might be seen to remain; and then was this burhkenning, amongst the rest, overthrown and destroyed; and although the ditch near thereunto, called Hound's ditch, was stopped up, yet the street of long time after was called Hound's ditch; and of late time more commonly called Barbican. The plot or seat of this burhkenning, or watch-tower, King Edward III., in the year 1336, and the 10th of his reign, gave unto Robert Ufford, Earl of Suffolk, by the name of his manor of Base court, in the parish of St. Giles without Cripplegate, of London, commonly called the Barbican.

Tower Royal was of old time the king's house. King Stephen was there lodged; but sithence called the Queen's Wardrobe. The princess, mother to King Richard II. in the 4th of his reign was lodged there; being forced to fly from the Tower of London when the rebels possessed it. But on the 15th of June (saith Froissart), Wat Tyler being slain, the king went to this lady princess his mother, then lodged in the Tower Royal, called the Queen's Wardrobe, where she had tarried two days and two nights; which tower (saith the record of Edward III., the 36th year [1]) was in the parish of St. Michel de Paternoster, etc. In the year 1386, King Richard, with Queen Anne his wife, kept their Christmas at Eltham, whither came to him Lion, king of Ermony,[2] under pretence to reform peace betwixt the kings of England and France; but what his coming profited he only understood; for besides innumerable gifts that he received of the king and his nobles, the king lying then in this Tower Royal, at the Queen's Wardrobe in London, granted to him a charter

[1] Liber Sanct. Mariæ Eborum. [See Bibliography.]

[2] Armenia. Ermony, from the Old French " Ermenie." See Roquefort's Glossaire, s. v.

Chaucer, too, in his Monke's Tale, line 14,343, etc., says:—

" Ne dorste never be so corageous
Ne non Ermin, ne non Egiptien,
Ne Surrien, ne non Arabien."

of a thousand pounds by year during his life. He was, as he affirmed, chased out of his kingdom by the Tartarians. More concerning this tower shall you read when you come to Vintry Ward, in which it standeth.

Sernes tower in Bucklesberie, was sometime the king's house. Edward III., in the 18th of his reign, appointed his exchange of moneys therein to be kept; and in the 32d, he gave the same tower to his free chapel of St. Stephen at Westminster.

OF SCHOOLS AND OTHER HOUSES OF LEARNING

" In the reign of King Stephen and of Henry II.," saith Fitzstephen, " there were in London three principal churches, which had famous schools, either by privilege and ancient dignity, or by favour of some particular persons, as of doctors which were accounted notable and renowned for knowledge in philosophy. And there were other inferior schools also. Upon festival days the masters made solemn meetings in the churches, where their scholars disputed logically and demonstratively; some bringing enthimems, other perfect syllogisms; some disputed for shew, other to trace out the truth; cunning sophisters were thought brave scholars when they flowed with words; others used fallacies; rhetoricians spake aptly to persuade, observing the precepts of art, and omitting nothing that might serve their purpose: the boys of diverse schools did cap or pot verses, and contended of the principles of grammar; there were some which on the other side with epigrams and rymes, nipping and quipping their fellowes, and the faults of others, though suppressing their names, moved thereby much laughter among their auditors." Hitherto Fitzstephen, for schools and scholars, and for their exercises in the city in his days; sithence the which time, as to me it seemeth, by the increase of colleges and students in the universities of Oxford and Cambridge, the frequenting of schools, and exercises of scholars in the city, as had been accustomed, hath much decreased.

The three principal churches which had these famous schools by privileges, must needs be the cathedral church of St. Paul for one; seeing that by a general council, holden in the year of Christ 1176, at Rome, in the patriarchy of Laterane, it was decreed, that every cathedral church should have his schoolmaster to teach poor scholars, and others as had been accustomed, and that no man should take any reward for license to teach. The second, as most ancient, may seem to have been the monastery of St. Peter's at Westminster, whereof Ingulphus, Abbot of Crowland, in the reign of William the Conqueror, writeth thus:—" I, Ingulphus, an humble servant of God, born of English parents, in the most beautiful city of London, for to attain to learning, was first put to Westminster, and after to study of Oxford," etc. And writing in praise of Queen Edgitha, wife to Edward the Confessor: " I have seen her," saith he, " often when being a boy, I came to see my father dwelling in the king's court, and often coming from school, when I met her, she would oppose me, touching my learning and lesson; and falling from grammar to logic, wherein she had some knowledge, she would subtilly conclude an argument with me, and by her handmaiden give me three or four pieces of money, and send me unto the palace where I should receive some victuals, and then be dismissed." [*See* Additional Notes.]

The third school seemeth to have been in the monastery of St. Saviour, at Bermondsey in Southwark; for other priories, as of St. John by Smithfield, St. Bartholomew in Smithfield, St. Mary Overie in Southwark, and that of the Holy Trinity by Aldgate, were all of later foundation, and the friaries, colleges, and hospitals, in this city, were raised since them in the reigns of Henry III., Edward I., II., and III., etc. All which houses had their schools, though not so famous as these first named.

But touching schools more lately advanced in this city, I read, that King Henry V., having suppressed the priories aliens, whereof some were about London; namely, one hospital, called Our Lady of Rouncivall, by Charing Cross; one other hospital in Oldborne; one other without Cripplegate; and the fourth without Aldersgate; besides other that are now worn out of memory, and whereof there is no monument remaining more than Rouncivall, converted to a brotherhood, which continued till the reign of Henry VIII. or Edward VI. This, I say, and other their schools being broken up and ceased, King Henry VI., in the 24th of his reign, by patent, appointed, that there should be in London grammar schools, besides St. Paul's, at St. Martin's le Grand, St. Mary le Bow in Cheap, St. Dunstan's in the west, and St. Anthony's. And in the next year, to wit, 1447, the said king ordained by parliament that four other grammar schools should be erected, to wit, in the parishes of St. Andrew in Oldborne, Allhallowes the Great in Thames street, St. Peter's upon Cornhill, and in the hospital of St. Thomas of Acons in West Cheap; since the which time as divers schools, by suppressing of religious houses, whereof they were members, in the reign of Henry VIII., have been decayed, so again have some others been newly erected, and founded for them; as namely Paul's school, in place of an old ruinea house, was built in most ample manner, and largely endowed, in the year 1512, by John Collet, Doctor of Divinity, Dean of Paul's, for one hundred and fifty-three poor men's children, for which there was ordained a master, surmaster, or usher, and a chaplain. Again, in the year 1553, after the erection of Christ's hospital, in the late dissolved house of the Gray Friars, a great number of poor children being taken in, a school was also ordained there at the citizen's charges. Also, in the year 1561, the Merchant Taylors of London founded one notable free grammar school, in the parish of St. Laurence Poultney by Candleweeke street, Richard Hils, late master of that company, having given five hundred pounds towards the purchase of a house, called the Mannor of the Rose, sometime the Duke of Buckingham's, wherein the school is kept. As for the meeting of the schoolmasters on festival days, at festival churches, and the disputing of their scholars logically, etc., whereof I have before spoken, the same was long since discontinued; but the arguing of the schoolboys about the principles of grammar hath been continued even till our time; for I myself, in my youth, have yearly seen, on the eve of St. Bartholomew the Apostle, the scholars of divers grammar schools repair unto the churchyard of St. Bartholomew, the priory in Smithfield, where upon a bank boarded about under a tree, some one scholar hath stepped up, and there hath opposed and answered, till he were by some better scholar overcome and put down; and then the overcomer taking the place, did like as the first; and in the end the best opposers and answerers had rewards, which I observed not but it made both good schoolmasters, and also good scholars, diligently against such times to prepare themselves for the obtaining of this garland. I remember there repaired to these exercises, amongst others, the masters and scholars of the free schools of St. Paul's in London, of St. Peter's at Westminster, of St. Thomas Acon's hospital, and of St. Anthonie's hospital; whereof the last-named commonly presented the best scholars, and had the prize in those days.

This priory of St. Bartholomew being surrendered to Henry VIII., those disputations of scholars in that place surceased; and was again, only for a year or twain, in the reign of Edward VI., revived in the cloister of Christ's hospital, where the best

scholars, then still of St. Anthonie's school,[1] were rewarded with
bows and arrows of silver, given to them by Sir Martin Bowes,
goldsmith. Nevertheless, however the encouragement failed,
the scholars of Paul's, meeting with them of St. Anthonie's,
would call them Anthonie pigs, and they again would call the
other pigeons of Paul's, because many pigeons were bred in
St. Paul's church, and St. Anthonie was always figured with a
pig following him; and mindful of the former usage, did for
a long season disorderly in the open street provoke one another
with, *Salve tu quoque, placet tibi mecum disputare ? Placet.*
And so proceeding from this to questions in grammar, they
usually fell from words to blows with their satchels full of books,
many times in great heaps, that they troubled the streets and
passengers; so that finally they were restrained with the decay
of St. Anthonie's school. Out of this school have sprung divers
famous persons, whereof although time hath buried the names
of many, yet in mine own remembrance may be numbered these
following:—Sir Thomas More, knight, lord chancellor of England, Dr. Nicholas Heath, sometime Bishop of Rochester, after
of Worcester, and lastly Archbishop of York and Lord Chancellor of England; Doctor John Whitgift, Bishop of Worcester,
and after Archbishop of Canterbury, etc.

Of later time, in the year of Christ 1582, there was founded
a public lecture in chirurgerie, to be read in the College of
Physicians in Knight riders street, to begin in the year 1584,
on the sixth of May, and so to be continued for ever, twice every
week, on Wednesday and Friday, by the honourable Baron,
John Lord Lombley, and the learned Richard Caldwell, doctor
in physic, the reader whereof to be Richard Forster, doctor of
physic, during his life.

Furthermore, about the same time there was also begun
a mathematical lecture, to be read in a fair old chapel, built by
Simon Eayre, within the Leaden hall; whereof a learned citizen
born, named Thomas Hood, was the first reader. But this
chapel, and other parts of that hall, being employed for stowage
of goods taken out of a great Spanish caracke, the said lecture
ceased any more to be read, and was then in the year 1588
read in the house of master Thomas Smith in Grasse street,
etc.

Last of all, Sir Thomas Gresham, knight, agent to the queen's
highness, by his last will and testament made in the year 1579,

---

[1] " Howsoever the same be now fallen, both in number and estimation."
—*1st edition*, p. 56.

gave the Royal Exchange, and all the buildings thereunto appertaining; that is to say, the one moiety to the mayor and commonalty of London and their successors, upon trust that they perform as shall be declared; and the other moiety to the mercers in like confidence. The mayor and commonalty are to find four to read lectures of divinity, astronomy, music, and geometry, within his dwelling-house in Bishopsgate street, and to bestow the sum of two hundred pounds; to wit, fifty pounds the piece, etc. The mercers likewise are to find three readers, that is, in civil law, physic, and rhetoric, within the same dwelling-house, the sum of one hundred and fifty pounds; to every reader, fifty pounds, etc.: which gift hath been since that time confirmed by parliament, to take effect and begin after the decease of the Lady Anne Gresham, which happened in the year 1596, and so to continue for ever. Whereupon the lecturers were accordingly chosen and appointed to have begun their readings in the month of June, 1597; whose names were, Anthony Wootton, for divinity; Doctor Mathew Guin, for physic; Doctor Henry Mountlow, for the civil law; Doctor John Bull, for music; Beerewood, for astronomy; Henry Brigges, for geometry; and Caleb Willis, for rhetoric. These lectures are read daily, Sundays excepted, in the term times, by every one upon his day, in the morning betwixt nine and ten, in Latin; in the afternoon, betwixt two and three, in English; save that Dr. Bull is dispensed with to read the music lecture in English only upon two several days, Thursday and Saturday, in the afternoons, betwixt three and four of the clock.

HOUSES OF STUDENTS IN THE COMMON LAW

But besides all this, there is in and about this city a whole university, as it were, of students, practicers or pleaders, and judges of the laws of this realm, not living of common stipends, as in other universities it is for the most part done, but of their own private maintenance, as being altogether fed either by their places or practice, or otherwise by their proper revenue, or exhibition of parents and friends; for that the younger sort are either gentlemen or the sons of gentlemen, or of other most wealthy persons. Of these houses there be at this day fourteen in all; whereof nine do stand within the liberties of this city, and five in the suburbs thereof; to wit:

Within the liberties

Serjeants' inn in Fleet Street, Serjeants' inn in Chancery lane; for judges and sergeants only.

The Inner temple, the Middle temple, in Fleet street; houses of court.

Clifford's inn in Fleet street, Thavies inn in Oldborne, Furnival's inn in Oldborne, Barnard's inn in Oldborne, Staple inn in Oldborne; houses of Chancery.

Without the liberties

Gray's inn in Oldborne, Lincoln's inn in Chancery lane by the old Temple; [1] houses of court.

Clement's inn, New inn, Lion's inn; houses of Chancery, without Temple bar, in the liberty of Westminster.

There was sometime an inn of sergeants in Oldborne, as you may read of Scrop's inn over against St. Andrew's church.

There was also one other inn of Chancery, called Chester's inn, for the nearness of the Bishop of Chester's house, but more commonly termed Strand inn, for that it stood in Strand street, and near unto Strand bridge without Temple bar, in the liberty of the duchy of Lancaster. This inn of Chancery, with other houses near adjoining, were pulled down in the reign of Edward VI. by Edward Duke of Sommerset, who in place thereof raised that large and beautiful house, but yet unfinished, called Sommerset house.

There was moreover, in the reign of King Henry I., a tenth house of Chancery, mentioned by Justice Fortescue in his book of the laws of England, but where it stood, or when it was abandoned, I cannot find, and therefore I will leave it, and return to the rest.

The houses of court be replenished partly with young students, and partly with graduates and practisers of the law; but the inns of Chancery being, as it were, provinces, severally subjected to the inns of court, be chiefly furnished with officers, attorneys, solicitors, and clerks, that follow the courts of the King's Bench or Common Pleas; and yet there want not some other being young students, that come thither sometimes from one of the Universities, and sometimes immediately from grammar schools; and these having spent some time in studying upon the first elements and grounds of the law, and having

[1] " In Oldborne."—1st *edition.*

performed the exercise of their own houses (called Boltas Mootes,[1] and putting of cases), they proceed to be admitted, and become students in some of these four houses or inns of court, where continuing by the space of seven years or thereabouts, they frequent readings, meetings, boltings, and other learned exercises, whereby growing ripe in the knowledge of the laws, and approved withal to be of honest conversation, they are either, by the general consent of the benchers or readers, being of the most ancient, grave, and judicial men of every inn of the court, or by the special privilege of the present reader there, selected and called to the degree of utter barristers, and so enabled to be common counsellors, and to practice the law, both in their chambers and at the bars.

Of these, after that they be called to a further step of preferment, called the Bench, there are twain every year chosen among the benchers of every inn of court to be readers there, who do make their readings at two times in the year also; that is, one in Lent, and the other at the beginning of August.

And for the help of young students in every of the inns of Chancery, they do likewise choose out of every one inn of court a reader, being no bencher, but an utter barrister there, of ten or twelve years' continuance, and of good profit in study. Now, from these of the said degree of counsellors, or utter barristers, having continued therein the space of fourteen or fifteen years at the least, the chiefest and best learned are by the benchers elected to increase the number, as I said, of the bench amongst them; and so in their time do become first single, and then double, readers to the students of those houses of court; after which last reading they be named apprentices at the law, and, in default, of a sufficient number of sergeants at law, these are, at the pleasure of the prince, to be advanced to the places of sergeants; out of which number of sergeants also the void places of judges are likewise ordinarily filled; albeit, now and then some be advanced, by the special favour of the prince, to the estate, dignity, and place, both of sergeant and judge, as it were in one instant. But from thenceforth they hold not any room in those inns of court, being translated to one of the said two inns, called Sergeante's inns, where none but the sergeants and judges do converse.

---

[1] Cowell, in his *Law Dictionary*, says, " Bolting is a term of art used in Gray's Inn, and applied to the bolting or arguing of *moot* cases." He endeavours to show that the bolting of cases is analogous to the *boulting* or sifting of meal through a bag. All readers of Shakspeare must be familiar with the use of the word in the latter sense.

OF ORDERS AND CUSTOMS

Of orders and customs in this city of old time, Fitzstephen saith as followeth: " Men of all trades, sellers of all sorts of wares, labourers in every work, every morning are in their distinct and several places: furthermore, in London, upon the river side, between the wine in ships and the wine to be sold in taverns, is a common cookery, or cooks' row; there daily, for the season of the year, men might have meat, roast, sod, or fried; fish, flesh, fowls, fit for rich and poor. If any come suddenly to any citizen from afar, weary, and not willing to tarry till the meat be bought and dressed, while the servant bringeth water for his master's hands, and fetcheth bread, he shall have immediately from the river's side all viands whatsoever he desireth: what multitude soever, either of soldiers or strangers, do come to the city, whatsoever hour, day or night, according to their pleasures may refresh themselves; and they which delight in delicateness may be satisfied with as delicate dishes there as may be found elsewhere. And this Cooke's row is very necessary to the city; and, according to Plato in Gorgias, next to physic, is the office of cooks, as part of a city.

" Without one of the gates is a plain field, both in name and deed, where every Friday, unless it be a solemn bidden holy day, is a notable show of horses to be sold; earls, barons, knights, and citizens repair thither to see or to buy; there may you of pleasure see amblers pacing it delicately; there may you see trotters fit for men of arms, sitting more hardly; there may you have notable young horses, not yet broken; there may you have strong steeds, well limbed geldings, whom the buyers do specially regard for pace and swiftness; the boys which ride these horses, sometimes two, sometimes three, do run races for wagers, with a desire of praise, or hope of victory. In another part of that field are to be sold all implements of husbandry, as also fat swine, milch kine, sheep, and oxen; there stand also mares and horses fit for ploughs and teams, with their young colts by them. At this city, merchant strangers of all nations had their keys and wharfs; the Arabians sent gold; the Sabians spice and frankincense; the Scythian armour, Babylon oil, India purple garments, Egypt precious stones, Norway and Russia amber-greece and sables, and the Frenchmen wine. According to the truth of Chronicles, this city is ancienter than Rome, built of the ancient Troyans and of Brute, before that was built by Romulus and Rhemus; and therefore useth the ancient customs of Rome. This city, even as Rome, is divided into wards; it hath yearly sheriffs instead of consuls; it hath the dignity of senators in aldermen. It hath under officers, common sewers, and conduits in streets; according to the quality of causes, it hath general courts and assembles upon appointed days. I do not think that there is any city wherein are better customs, in frequenting the churches, in serving God, in keeping holy days, in giving alms, in entertaining strangers, in solemnising marriages, in furnishing banquets, celebrating funerals, and burying dead bodies.

" The only plagues of London are immoderate quaffing among the foolish sort, and often casualties by fire. Most part of the bishops, abbots, and great lords of the land have houses there, whereunto they resort, and bestow much when they are called to parliament by the king, or to council by their metropolitan, or otherwise by their private business."

Thus far Fitzstephen, of the estate of things in his time, whereunto may be added the present, by conference whereof the alteration will easily appear.

Men of trades and sellers of wares in this city have oftentimes since changed their places, as they have found their best advantage. For whereas mercers and haberdashers used to keep their shops in West Cheape,[1] of later time they held them on London Bridge, where partly they yet remain. The goldsmiths of Gutheron's lane and Old Exchange are now for the most part removed into the south side of West Cheape, the peperers and grocers of Soper's lane are now in Bucklesberrie, and other places dispersed. The drapers of Lombard street and of Corne-hill are seated in Candlewick street and Watheling street; the skinners from St. Marie Pellipers, or at the Axe, into Budge row and Walbrooke; the stock fishmongers in Thames street; wet fishmongers in Knightriders street and Bridge street; the iron-mongers, of Ironmongers' lane and Old Jurie, into Thames street; the vintners from the Vinetree into divers places. But the brewers for the more part remain near to the friendly water of Thames; the butchers in Eastcheape, St. Nicholas shambles, and the Stockes market; the hosiers of old time in Hosier lane,

---

[1] Thus Lydgate, in his ballad of *London Lackpenny* :

" Then to the Chepe I began me drawne,
    Where much people I saw for to stande:
One offered me velvet, sylke and lawne,
    An other he taketh me by the hande,
    ' Here is Pary's thred the fynest in the lande,' " etc.

near unto Smithfield, are since removed into Cordwayner street, the upper part thereof by Bow church, and last of all into Birchoveris lane by Cornehill; the shoe-makers and curriers of Cordwayner street removed the one to St. Martin's le Grand, the other to London wall near unto Mooregate; the founders remain by themselves in Lothberie; cooks,[1] or pastelars, for the more part in Thames street, the other dispersed into divers parts; poulters of late removed out of the Poultrie, betwixt the Stockes and the great Conduit in Cheape, into Grasse street and St. Nicholas shambles; bowyers, from Bowyers' row by Ludgate into divers places, and almost worn out with the fletchers; pater noster makers of old time, or bead-makers, and text-writers, are gone out of Pater noster row, and are called stationers of Paule's churchyard;[2] patten-makers, of St. Margaret, Pattens' lane, clean worn out; labourers every work-day are to be found in Cheape, about Soper's lane end; horse-coursers and sellers of oxen, sheep, swine, and such like, remain in their old market of Smithfield, etc.

That merchants of all nations had their keys and wharfs at this city, whereunto they brought their merchandises before and in the reign of Henry II., mine author wrote of his own knowledge to be true, though for the antiquity of the city he took the common opinion. Also that this city was in his time and afore divided into wards, had yearly sheriffs, aldermen, general courts, and assemblies, and such like notes by him set down, in commendation of the citizens; whereof there is no question, he wrote likewise of his own experience, as being born and brought up amongst them.

And to confirm his opinion, concerning merchandises then hither transported, whereof happily may be some argument, Thomas Clifford[3] (before Fitzstephen's time), writing of Edward the Confessor, saith to this effect: " King Edward, intending to make his sepulchre at Westminster; for that it was near to the famous city of London, and the river of Thames, that brought in all kind of merchandises from all parts of the world, etc."

---

[1] The cooks in Lydgate's time, as we learn from the same ballad, resided chiefly in Eastcheap:

" Then I hyed me into East Chepe;
    One cryes ribbs of befe, and many a pye:
  Pewter pottes they clattered on a heape;
    There was harpe, pype and mynstrelsye," etc.

[2] " Pater noster beade-makers and text-writers are gone out of Paternoster rowe into stationers of Paule's churchyard."—1st edition, p. 63.

[3] Thomas Clifford. [See Additional Notes.]

And William of Malmesbury, that lived in the reign of William I.
and II., Henry I., and King Stephen, calleth this a noble city, full
of wealthy citizens, frequented with the trade of merchandises
from all parts of the world. Also I read, in divers records,
that of old time no woad was stowed or harboured in this city,
but all was presently sold in the ships, except by license purchased
of the sheriffs, till of more later time; to wit, in the year 1236,
Andrew Bokerell, being mayor, by assent of the principal citizens,
the merchants of Amiens, Nele, and Corby, purchased letters
insealed with the common seal of the city, that they when they
come might harbour their woads, and therefore should give the
mayor every year fifty marks sterling; and the same year they
gave one hundred pounds towards the conveying of water from
Tyborn to this city. Also the merchants of Normandie made
fine for license to harbour their woads till it was otherwise provided, in the year 1263, Thomas Fitz Thomas being mayor, etc.,
which proveth that then as afore, they were here amongst other
nations privileged.

It followeth in Fitzstephen, that the plagues of London in
that time were immoderate quaffing among fools, and often
casualties by fire. For the first — to wit, of quaffing — it
continueth as afore, or rather is mightily increased, though
greatly qualified among the poorer sort, not of any holy absti-
nence, but of mere necessity, ale and beer being small, and
wines in price above their reach. As for prevention of casualties
by fire, the houses in this city being then built all of timber, and
covered with thatch of straw or reed, it was long since thought
good policy in our forefathers wisely to provide, namely, in the
year of Christ 1189, the first of Richard I., Henry Fitzalwine [1]
being then mayor, that all men in this city should build their
houses of stone up to a certain height, and to cover them with
slate or baked tile; since which time, thanks be given to God,
there hath not happened the like often consuming fires in this
city as afore.

But now in our time, instead of these enormities, others are
come in place no less meet to be reformed; namely, purprestures,
or encroachments on the highways, lanes, and common grounds,
in and about this city; whereof a learned gentleman and grave
citizen [2] hath not many years since written and exhibited a book
to the mayor and commonalty; which book, whether the same
have been by them read and diligently considered upon, I know

[1] Liber Constitutions. [See Biblio.   Liber Horne.   Liber Clerkenwell.
[2] W. Patten. [See Additional Notes.]

not, but sure I am nothing is reformed since concerning this matter.

Then the number of cars, drays, carts, and coaches, more than hath been accustomed, the streets and lanes being straitened, must needs be dangerous, as daily experience proveth.

The coachman rides behind the horse tails, lasheth them, and looketh not behind him; the drayman sitteth and sleepeth on his dray, and letteth his horse lead him home. I know that, by the good laws and customs of this city,[1] shodde carts [2] are forbidden to enter the same, except upon reasonable cause, as service of the prince, or such like, they be tolerated. Also that the fore horse of every carriage should be lead by hand; but these good orders are not observed. Of old time coaches were not known in this island, but chariots or whirlicotes, then so called, and they only used of princes or great estates, such as had their footmen about them; and for example to note, I read that Richard II., being threatened by the rebels of Kent, rode from the Tower of London to the Myles end, and with him his mother, because she was sick and weak, in a whirlicote, the Earls of Buckingham, Kent, Warwicke, and Oxford, Sir Thomas Percie, Sir Robert Knowles, the Mayor of London, Sir Aubery de Vere, that bare the king's sword, with other knights and esquires attending on horseback. But in the next year, the said King Richard took to wife Anne, daughter to the King of Bohemia, that first brought hither the riding upon side-saddles; and so was the riding in wherlicoates and chariots forsaken, except at coronations and such like spectacles; but now of late years the use of coaches, brought out of Germany, is taken up, and made so common, as there is neither distinction of time nor difference of persons observed; for the world runs on wheels with many whose parents were glad to go on foot.

Last of all, mine author in this chapter hath these words: [3] " Most part of the bishops, abbots, and great lords of the land, as if they were citizens and freemen of London, had many fair houses to resort unto, and many rich and wealthy gentlemen spent their money there." And in another place he hath these words: " Every Sunday in Lent a fresh company of young men comes into the fields on horseback, and the best horsemen conducteth the rest; then march forth the citizens' sons, and other

---

[1] Liber S. Mariæ Eborum.
[2] Carts shod or bound with iron. *Carrectæ ferro ligatæ* are mentioned in the Liber Garderobæ, Edw. I.
[3] W. Fitzstephen.

young men, with disarmed lances and shields, and practise feats of war; many courtiers likewise and attendants of noblemen repair to this exercise, and whilst the hope of victory doth inflame their minds, they do show good proof how serviceable they would be in martial affairs, etc." Again he saith: "This city, in the troublesome time of King Stephen, showed at a muster twenty thousand armed horsemen and forty thousand footmen, serviceable for the wars, etc." All which sayings of the said author, well considered, do plainly prove that in those days the inhabitants and repairers to this city, of what estate soever, spiritual or temporal, having houses here, lived together in good amity with the citizens, every man observing the customs and orders of the city, and those to be contributary to charges here, rather than in any part of the land wheresoever. This city, being the heart of the realm, the king's chamber and prince's seat, whereunto they made repair, and showed their forces, both of horses and of men, which caused in troublesome time, as of King Stephen, the musters of this city to be so great in number.

And here, to touch somewhat of greater families and households kept in former times by noblemen, and great estates of this realm, according to their honours or dignities,[1] I have seen an account made by H. Leicester, cofferer to Thomas Earl of Lancaster, for one whole year's expenses in the Earl's house, from the day next after Michaelmas, in the seventh year of Edward II., until Michaelmass in the eight year of the same king, amounting to the sum of £7957 13s. 4½d. as followeth:[2]

To wit, in the pantry, buttery, and kitchen, £3405, etc.; for one hundred and eighty-four tons, one pipe of red or claret wine, and one ton of white wine bought for the house, £104 17s. 6d.

For grocery ware, £180 17s.

For six barrels of sturgeon, £19.

For six thousand eight hundred stock-fishes, so called for

[1] There are few documents calculated to throw greater light upon the social and domestic life of our ancestors than their Household Books. Stow has here set an example, which has of late years been followed to a great extent. The Liber Garderobæ, Edw. I., published by the Society of Antiquaries in 1787—*The Northumberland Household Book—The Privy Purse Expences of Henry VIII.—The Privy Purse Expences of the Princess Mary*, etc.; and lastly, the handsome volume, printed for the Roxburgh Club by Beriah Botfield, Esq., M.P., containing the *Household Book of the Countess of Leicester, wife of Simon de Montford*, and that of Sir John Howard, afterwards Duke of Norfolk, in the reign of Richard III., afford views of ancient manners and illustrations of olden customs, which would be sought for in vain in works of a graver character.

[2] Record of Pontefract, as I could obtain of M. Cudnor.—*Stow.*

dried fishes of all sorts, as lings, habardines, and other, £41 6s. 7d.

For one thousand seven hundred and fourteen pounds of waxe, with vermelion and turpentine to make red waxe, £314 7s. 4¼d.

For two thousand three hundred and nineteen pounds of tallow candles for the household, and one thousand eight hundred and seventy of lights for Paris candles, called perchers, £31 14s. 3d.

Expenses on the earl's great horses, and the keeper's wages, £486 4s. 3½d.

Linen cloth for the earl and his chaplains, and for the pantry, £43 17s.

For one hundred and twenty-nine dozen of parchment, with ink, £4 8s. 3½d.

Sum, £5230 17s. 7¼d.

Item, for two cloths of scarlet for the earl against Christmass, one cloth of russet for the Bishop of Angew, seventy cloths of blue for the knights (as they were then termed), fifteen cloths of medley for the lords' clerks, twenty-eight cloths for the esquires, fifteen cloths for officers, nineteen cloths for grooms, five cloths for archers, four cloths for minstrels and carpenters, with the sharing and carriage for the earl's liveries at Christmasse, £460 15s.

Item, for seven furs of variable miniver (or powdered ermine), seven hoods of purple, three hundred and ninety-five furs of budge for the liveries of barons, knights, and clerks, one hundred and twenty-three furs of lamb for esquires, bought at Christmas, £147 17s. 8d.

Item, sixty-five cloths, saffron colour, for the barons and knights in summer, twelve red cloths, mixed, for clerks, twenty-six cloths, ray, for esquires, one cloth, ray, for officers' coats in summer, and four cloths, ray, for carpets in the hall, for £345 13s. 8d.

Item, one hundred pieces of green silk for the knights, fourteen budge furs for surcoats, thirteen hoods of budge for clerks, and seventy-five furs of lambs for the lord's liveries in summer, with canvas and cords to truss them, £72 19s.

Item, saddles for the lord's liveries in summer, £51 6s. 8d.

Item, one saddle for the earl of the prince's arms, 40s.

Sum, £1079 18s. 3d.

Item, for things bought, whereof cannot be read in my note, £241 14s. 1¼d.

For horses lost in service of the earl, £8 6s. 8d.

Fees paid to earls, barons, knights, and esquires, £623 15s. 5d.

In gifts to knights of France, the Queen of England's nurses, to the Countess of Warren, esquires, minstrels, messengers, and riders, £92 14s.

Item, one hundred and sixty-eight yards of russet cloth,[1] and twenty-four coats for poor men, with money given to the poor on Maundy Thursday, £8 16s. 7d.

Item, twenty-four silver dishes, so many saucers and so many cups for the buttery, one pair of pater nosters, and one silver coffin, bought this year, £103 5s. 6d.

To divers messengers about the earl's business, £34 19s. 8d.

In the earl's chamber, £5.

To divers men for the earl's old debts, £88 16s. 0¾d.

Sum, £1207 7s. 11¾d.

The expences of the countess at Pickering for the time of this account, as in the pantry, buttery, kitchen, and other places, concerning these offices, £285 13s. 0½d.

In wine, wax, spices, cloths, furs, and other things for the countess' wardrobe, £154 7s. 4½d.

Sum, £439 8s. 6¼d.

Sum total of the whole expenses, £7957 13s. 4½d.

Thus much for this Earl of Lancaster.

More I read, that in the 14th of the same Edward II., Hugh Spencer the elder (condemned by the commonalty) was banished the realm; at which time it was found by inquisition that the said Spencer had in sundry shires, fifty-nine manors: he had twenty-eight thousand sheep, one thousand oxen and steers, one thousand two hundred kine, with their calves, forty mares with their colts, one hundred and sixty drawing horses, two thousand hogs, three hundred bullocks, forty tuns of wine, six hundred bacons, eighty carcases of Martilmasse beef, six hundred muttons in larder, ten tuns of cider; his armour, plate, jewels, and ready money, better than £10,000, thirty-six sacks of wool, and a library of books. Thus much the record, which provision for household showeth a great family there to be kept.

Nearer to our time, I read,[2] in the 36th of Henry VI., that the greater estates of the realm being called up to London,

The Earl of Salisbury came with five hundred men on horseback, and was lodged in the Herber.

---

[1] Northern russet, half a yard and half a quarter broad, I have seen sold for four pence the yard, and was good cloth of a mingled colour.—*Stow*.

[2] Rob. Fabian, manuscript. [*See* Bibliography.]

Richard, Duke of York, with four hundred men, lodged at Baynard's castle.

The Dukes of Excester and Sommerset, with eight hundred men.

The Earl of Northumberland, the Lord Egremont, and the Lord Clifford, with fifteen hundred men.

Richard Nevill, Earl of Warwick, with six hundred men, all in red jackets, embroidered with ragged staves before and behind, and was lodged in Warwicke lane; in whose house there was oftentimes six oxen eaten at a breakfast, and every tavern was full of his meat; for he that had any acquaintance in that house, might have there so much of sodden and roast meat as he could prick and carry upon a long dagger.

Richard Redman, Bishop of Ely, 1500, the 17th of Henry VII.,[1] besides his great family, housekeeping, alms dish, and relief to the poor, wheresoever he was lodged. In his travelling, when at his coming or going to or from any town, the bells being rung, all the poor would come together, to whom he gave every one six pence at the least.

And now to note of our own time somewhat. Omitting in this place Thomas Wolsey, Archbishop of Yorke, and cardinal, I refer the reader to my *Annals*, where I have set down the order of his house and household, passing all other subjects of his time. His servants, daily attending in his house, were near about four hundred, omitting his servants' servants, which were many.

Nicholas West, Bishop of Ely, in the year 1532, kept continually in his house an hundred servants, giving to the one half of them 53s. 4d. the piece yearly; to the other half each 40s. the piece; to every one for his winter gown four yards of broad cloth, and for his summer coat three yards and a half: he daily gave at his gates, besides bread and drink, warm meat to two hundred poor people.

The housekeeping of Edward, late Earl of Derby, is not to be forgotten, who had two hundred and twenty men in check roll: his feeding aged persons twice every day, sixty and odd, besides all comers, thrice a week, appointed for his dealing days, and every Good Friday two thousand seven hundred, with meat, drink, and money.

Thomas Audley, lord chancellor, his family of gentlemen before him, in coats garded with velvet, and chains of gold; his yeomen after him in the same livery, not garded.

William Powlet, lord great master, Marquis of Winchester,

---

[1] Liber Ely. [*See* Bibliography.]

kept the like number of gentlemen and yeomen in a livery [1] of Reading tawny, and great relief at his gate.

Thomas Lord Cromwell, Earl of Essex, kept the like or greater number in a livery of grey marble; the gentlemen garded with velvet, the yeomen with the same cloth, yet their skirts large enough for their friends to sit upon them.

Edward, Duke of Sommerset, was not inferior in keeping a number of tall and comely gentlemen and yeomen, though his house was then in building, and most of his men were lodged abroad.

The late Earl of Oxford, father to him that now liveth, hath been noted within these forty years to have ridden into this city, and so to his house by London stone, with eighty gentlemen in a livery of Reading tawny, and chains of gold about their necks, before him, and one hundred tall yeomen, in the like livery, to follow him without chains, but all having his cognisance of the blue boar embroidered on their left shoulder.

OF CHARITABLE ALMS IN OLD TIMES GIVEN

These, as all other of their times, gave great relief to the poor. I myself, in that declining time of charity, have oft seen at the Lord Cromwell's gate in London more than two hundred persons served twice every day with bread, meat, and drink sufficient; for he observed that ancient and charitable custom, as all prelates, noblemen, or men of honour and worship, his predecessors, had done before him; whereof somewhat to note for example, Venerable Bede writeth, that prelates of his time having peradventure but wooden churches, had notwithstanding on their board at their meals one alms dish, into the which was carved some good portion of meat out of every other dish brought to their table; all which was given to the poor, besides the fragments left, in so much as in a hard time, a poor prelate wanting victuals, hath caused his alms dish, being silver, to be divided among the poor, therewith to shift as they could, till God should send them better store.

Such a prelate was Ethelwald, Bishop of Winchester, in the reign of King Edgar, about the year of Christ 963: he in a great famine sold away all the sacred vessels of his church for to relieve the almost starved people, saying that there was no reason that the senseless temples of God should abound in riches, and lively temples of the Holy Ghost to lack it.

[1] Every livery coat had three yards of broad cloth.—*Stow.*

Walter de Suffilde, Bishop of Norwich, was of the like mind; about the year 1245, in a time of great dearth, he sold all his plate, and distributed it to the poor every pennyworth.

Robert Winchelsey, Archbishop of Canterbury, about the year 1293, besides the daily fragments of his house, gave every Friday and Sunday, unto every beggar that came to his gate, a loaf of bread sufficient for that day, and there more usually, every such alms day, in time of dearth, to the number of five thousand, and otherwise four thousand, at the least; more, he used every great festival day to give one hundred and fifty pence to so many poor people, to send daily meat, bread, and drink, to such as by age or sickness were not able to fetch his alms, and to send meat, money, and apparel to such as he thought needed it.

I read,[1] in 1171, that Henry II., after his return into England, did penance for the slaughter of Thomas Becket, of whom (a sore dearth increasing) ten thousand persons, from the first of April, till new corn was inned, were daily fed and sustained.

More, I find recorded,[2] that in the year 1236, the 20th of Henry III., William de Haverhull, the king's treasurer, was commanded, that upon the day of the Circumcision of our Lord, six thousand poor people should be fed at Westminster, for the state of the king, queen, and their children. The like commandment the said King Henry gave to Hugh Gifford and William Browne, that upon Friday next after the Epiphany, they should cause to be fed in the great hall at Windsore, at a good fire, all the poor and needy children that could be found, and the king's children being weighed and measured, their weight and measure to be distributed for their good estates. These few examples for charity of kings may suffice.

I read, in the reign of Edward III., that Richard de Berie, Bishop of Durham, did weekly bestow for the relief of the poor eight quarters of wheat made into bread, besides his alms dish, fragments of his house, and great sums of money given to the poor when he journeyed. And that these alms dishes were as well used at the tables of noblemen as of the prelates, one note may suffice in this place.

I read, in the year 1452, that Richard, Duke of York, then claiming the crown, the Lord Rivers should have passed the sea about the king's business, but staying at Plimmoth till his money was spent, and then sending for more, the Duke of Sommerset sent him the image of St. George in silver and gold, to be sold,

---

[1] Pater de Ickham. [See Biblio.]   [2] Record of the Tower. [C.P.R.]

with the alms dish of the Duke of Glocester, which was also of great price, for coin had they none.

To end of orders and customs in this city, also of great families kept by honourable persons thither repairing, and of charitable alms of old times given, I say, for conclusion, that all noble persons, and other of honour and worship, in former times lodging in this city, or liberties thereof, did without grudging bear their parts in charges with the citizens, according to their estimated estates, as I have before said, and could prove by examples; but let men call to mind Sir Thomas Cromwel, then lord privy seal and vicar-general, lying in the city of London; he bare his charges to the great muster there in A.D. 1539; he sent his men in great number to the Miles end, and after them their armour in cars, with their coats of white cloth, the arms of this city; to wit, a red cross, and a sword, on the breast and back; which armour and coats they ware amongst the citizens, without any difference, and marched through the city to Westminster.

SPORTS AND PASTIMES OF OLD TIME USED IN THIS CITY

" Let us now," saith Fitzstephen, " come to the sports and pastimes, seeing it is fit that a city should not only be commodious and serious, but also merry and sportful; whereupon in the seals of the popes, until the time of Pope Leo, on the one side was St. Peter fishing, with a key over him, reached as it were by the hand of God out of heaven, and about it this verse:

' Tu pro me navem liquisti, suscipe clavem.'

And on the other side was a city, and this inscription on it: ' *Aurea Roma*.' Likewise to the praise of Augustus Cæsar and the city, in respect of the shows and sports, was written:

' Nocte pluit tota, redeunt spectacula mane,' etc.

' All night it raines, and shews at morrow tide returne again,
And Cæsar with almighty Jove hath matcht an equal raign.'

" But London, for the shows upon theatres, and comical pastimes, hath holy plays, representations of miracles, which holy confessors have wrought, or representations of torments wherein the constancy of martyrs appeared. Every year also at Shrove Tuesday, that we may begin with children's sports, seeing we all have been children, the school-boys do bring cocks of the game to their master, and all the forenoon they delight themselves in cock-fighting: after dinner, all the youths go into the fields to play at the ball.

" The scholars of every school have their ball, or baston, in their hands; the ancient and wealthy men of the city come forth on horseback to see the sport of the young men, and to take part of the pleasure in beholding their agility. Every Friday in Lent a fresh company of young men comes into the field on horseback, and the best horseman conducteth the rest. Then march forth the citizens' sons, and other young men, with disarmed lances and shields, and there they practice feats of war. Many courtiers likewise, when the king lieth near, and attendants of noblemen, do repair to these exercises; and while the hope of victory doth inflame their minds, do show good proof how serviceable they would be in martial affairs.

" In Easter holidays they fight battles on the water; a shield is hung upon a pole, fixed in the midst of the stream, a boat is prepared without oars, to be carried by violence of the water, and in the fore part thereof standeth a young man, ready to give charge upon the shield with his lance; if so be he breaketh his lance against the shield, and doth not fall, he is thought to have performed a worthy deed; if so be, without breaking his lance, he runneth strongly against the shield, down he falleth into the water, for the boat is violently forced with the tide; but on each side of the shield ride two boats, furnished with young men, which recover him that falleth as soon as they may. Upon the bridge, wharfs, and houses, by the river's side, stand great numbers to see and laugh thereat.

" In the holidays all the summer the youths are exercised in leaping, dancing, shooting, wrestling, casting the stone, and practising their shields; the maidens trip in their timbrels, and dance as long as they can well see. In winter, every holiday before dinner, the boars prepared for brawn are set to fight, or else bulls and bears are baited.

" When the great fen, or moor, which watereth the walls of the city on the north side, is frozen, many young men play upon the ice; some, striding as wide as they may, do slide swiftly; others make themselves seats of ice, as great as millstones; one sits down, many hand in hand do draw him, and one slipping on a sudden, all fall together; some tie bones to their feet and under their heels; and shoving themselves by a little picked staff, do slide as swiftly as a bird flieth in the air, or an arrow out of a cross-bow. Sometime two run together with poles, and hitting one the other, either one or both do fall, not without hurt; some break their arms, some their legs, but youth desirous of glory in this sort exerciseth itself against the time of war.

Many of the citizens do delight themselves in hawks and hounds; for they have liberty of hunting in Middlesex, Hartfordshire, all Chiltron, and in Kent to the water of Cray." Thus far Fitzstephen of sports.

These, or the like exercises, have been continued till our time, namely, in stage plays, whereof ye may read in anno 1391, a play by the parish clerks of London at the Skinner's well besides Smithfield, which continued three days together, the king, queen, and nobles of the realm being present. And of another, in the year 1409, which lasted eight days, and was of matter from the creation of the world, whereat was present most part of the nobility and gentry of England. Of late time, in place of those stage plays, hath been used comedies, tragedies, interludes, and histories, both true and feigned; for the acting whereof certain public places [1] have been erected. Also cocks of the game are yet cherished by divers men for their pleasures, much money being laid on their heads, when they fight in pits, whereof some be costly made for that purpose. The ball is used by noblemen and gentlemen in tennis courts, and by people of meaner sort in the open fields and streets.

The marching forth of citizens' sons, and other young men on horseback, with disarmed lances and shields, there to practise feats of war, man against man, hath long since been left off, but in their stead they have used on horseback to run at a dead mark, called a quinten; for note whereof I read,[2] that in the year of Christ 1253, the 38th of Henry III., the youthful citizens, for an exercise of their activity, set forth a game to run at the quinten; and whoever did best should have a peacock, which they had prepared as a prize. Certain of the king's servants, because the court lay then at Westminster came, as it were, in spite of the citizens, to that game, and giving reproachful names to the Londoners, which for the dignity of the city, and ancient privilege which they ought to have enjoyed, were called barons, the said Londoners, not able to bear so to be misused, fell upon the king's servants, and beat them shrewdly, so that upon complaint to the king he fined the citizens to pay a thousand marks. This exercise of running at the quinten was practised by the youthful citizens as well in summer as in winter, namely, in the feast of Christmas, I have seen a quinten set upon Cornehill, by the Leaden hall, where the attendants on the lords of merry disports have run, and made great pastime; for he

[1] " As the Theater, the Curtine," etc.—*1st edition*.
[2] Matthew Paris.

that hit not the broad end of the quinten was of all men laughed
to scorn, and he that hit it full, if he rid not the faster, had a
sound blow in his neck with a bag full of sand hung on the other
end. I have also in the summer season seen some upon the
river of Thames rowed in wherries, with staves in their hands,
flat at the fore end, running one against another, and for the
most part, one or both overthrown, and well ducked.

On the holy days in summer the youths of this city have in the
field exercised themselves in leaping, dancing, shooting, wrestling, casting of the stone or ball, etc.

And for defence and use of the weapon, there is a special
profession of men that teach it. Ye may read in mine *Annals*
how that in the year 1222 the citizens kept games of defence,
and wrestlings, near unto the hospital of St. Giles in the field,
where they challenged, and had the mastery of the men in the
suburbs, and other commoners, etc. Also, in the year 1453,
of a tumult made against the mayor at the wrestling besides
Clearke's well, etc. Which is sufficient to prove that of old
time the exercising of wrestling, and such like, hath been much
more used than of later years. The youths of this city also
have used on holy days after evening prayer, at their masters'
doors, to exercise their wasters and bucklers; and the maidens,
one of them playing on a timbrel, in sight of their masters
and dames, to dance for garlands hung athwart the streets;
which open pastimes in my youth being now suppressed, worse
practices within doors are to be feared. As for the baiting of
bulls and bears, they are to this day much frequented, namely,
in Bear gardens,[1] on the Bank's side, wherein be prepared
scaffolds for beholders to stand upon. Sliding upon the ice
is now but children's play; but in hawking and hunting many
grave citizens at this present have great delight, and do rather
want leisure than goodwill to follow it.

Of triumphant shows made by the citizens of London, ye may
read,[2] in the year 1236, the 20th of Henry III., Andrew Bockwell
then being mayor, how Helianor, daughter to Reymond, Earl
of Provance, riding through the city towards Westminster, there
to be crowned queen of England, the city was adorned with
silks, and in the night with lamps, cressets, and other lights
without number, besides many pageants and strange devices
there presented; the citizens also rode to meet the king and
queen, clothed in long garments embroidered about with gold,

[1] The Bear garden on the Bankside is not mentioned in the first edition.
[2] Matthew Paris.

and silks of divers colours, their horses gallantly trapped to the number of three hundred and sixty, every man bearing a cup of gold or silver in his hand, and the king's trumpeters sounding before them. These citizens did minister wine, as bottelers, which is their service, at their coronation. More, in the year 1293, for victory obtained by Edward I. against the Scots, every citizen, according to their several trade, made their several show, but especially the fishmongers, which in a solemn procession passed through the city, having, amongst other pageants and shows, four sturgeons gilt, carried on four horses; then four salmons of silver on four horses; and after them six and forty armed knights riding on horses, made like luces of the sea; and then one representing St. Magnus, because it was upon St. Magnus' day, with a thousand horsemen, etc.

One other show, in the year 1377, made by the citizens for disport of the young prince, Richard, son to the Black Prince, in the feast of Christmas, in this manner:—On the Sunday before Candlemas, in the night, one hundred and thirty citizens, disguised, and well horsed, in a mummery, with sound of trumpets, sackbuts, cornets, shalmes, and other minstrels, and innumerable torch lights of wax, rode from Newgate, through Cheape, over the bridge, through Southwarke, and so to Kennington beside Lambhith, where the young prince remained with his mother and the Duke of Lancaster his uncle, the Earls of Cambridge, Hertford, Warwicke, and Suffolke, with divers other lords. In the first rank did ride forty-eight in the likeness and habit of esquires, two and two together, clothed in red coats and gowns of say or sandal, with comely visors on their faces; after them came riding forty-eight knights in the same livery of colour and stuff; then followed one richly arrayed like an emperor; and after him some distance, one stately attired like a pope, whom followed twenty-four cardinals, and after them eight or ten with black visors, not amiable, as if they had been legates from some foreign princes. These maskers, after they had entered Kennington, alighted from their horses, and entered the hall on foot; which done, the prince, his mother, and the lords, came out of the chamber into the hall, whom the said mummers did salute, showing by a pair of dice upon the table their desire to play with the prince, which they so handled that the prince did always win when he cast them. Then the mummers set to the prince three jewels, one after another, which were a bowl of gold, a cup of gold, and a ring of gold, which the prince won at three casts. Then they set to the prince's mother, the duke, the earls, and other lords, to every one a ring of gold, which they did also win. After which they were feasted, and the music sounded, the prince and lords danced on the one part with the mummers, which did also dance; which jollity being ended, they were again made to drink, and then departed in order as they came.

The like was in Henry IV., in the 2nd of his reign, he then keeping his Christmas at Eltham, twelve aldermen of London and their sons rode in a mumming, and had great thanks.

Thus much for sportful shows in triumphs may suffice. Now for sports and pastimes yearly used.

First, in the feast of Christmas, there was in the king's house, wheresoever he was lodged, a lord of misrule, or master of merry disports,[1] and the like had ye in the house of every nobleman of honour or good worship, were he spiritual or temporal. Amongst the which the mayor of London, and either of the sheriffs, had their several lords of misrule, ever contending, without quarrel or offence, who should make the rarest pastimes to delight the beholders. These lords beginning their rule on Alhollon eve, continued the same till the morrow after the Feast of the Purification, commonly called Candlemas day. In all which space there were fine and subtle disguisings, masks, and mummeries, with playing at cards for counters, nails, and points, in every house, more for pastime than for gain.

Against the feast of Christmas every man's house, as also the parish churches, were decked with holm, ivy, bays, and whatsoever the season of the year afforded to be green. The conduits and standards in the streets were likewise garnished; amongst the which I read, in the year 1444, that by tempest of thunder and lightning, on the 1st of February, at night, Powle's steeple was fired, but with great labour quenched; and towards the morning of Candlemas day, at the Leaden hall in Cornhill, a standard of tree being set up in midst of the pavement, fast in the ground, nailed full of holm and ivy, for disport of Christmas to the people, was torn up, and cast down by the malignant spirit (as was thought), and the stones of the pavement all about were cast in the streets, and into divers houses, so that the people were sore aghast of the great tempests.

In the week before Easter had ye great shows made for the

---

[1] In the edition of Brand's *Popular Antiquities*, edited by Sir Henry Ellis, vol. i. 272—278, will be found a very large and curious collection of materials illustrative of this ancient custom.

fetching in of a twisted tree, or with, as they termed it, out of the woods into the king's house; and the like into every man's house of honour or worship.

In the month of May, namely, on May-day in the morning, every man, except impediment, would walk into the sweet meadows and green woods, there to rejoice their spirits with the beauty and savour of sweet flowers, and with the harmony of birds, praising God in their kind; and for example hereof, Edward Hall hath noted, that King Henry VIII., as in the 3rd of his reign, and divers other years, so namely, in the 7th of his reign, on May-day in the morning, with Queen Katherine his wife, accompanied with many lords and ladies, rode a-maying from Greenwitch to the high ground of Shooter's hill, where, as they passed by the way, they espied a company of tall yeomen, clothed all in green, with green hoods, and bows and arrows, to the number of two hundred; one being their chieftain, was called Robin Hoode, who required the king and his company to stay and see his men shoot; whereunto the king granting, Robin Hoode whistled, and all the two hundred archers shot off, loosing all at once; and when he whistled again they likewise shot again; their arrows whistled by craft of the head, so that the noise was strange and loud, which greatly delighted the king, queen, and their company. Moreover, this Robin Hoode desired the king and queen, with their retinue, to enter the green wood, where, in harbours made of boughs, and decked with flowers, they were set and served plentifully with venison and wine by Robin Hoode and his men, to their great contentment, and had other pageants and pastimes, as ye may read in my said author.

I find also, that in the month of May, the citizens of London of all estates, lightly in every parish, or sometimes two or three parishes joining together, had their several mayings, and did fetch in May-poles, with divers warlike shows, with good archers, morris dancers, and other devices, for pastime all the day long; and toward the evening they had stage plays, and bonfires in the streets. Of these mayings we read, in the reign of Henry VI., that the aldermen and sheriffs of London, being on May-day at the Bishop of London's wood, in the parish of Stebunheath,[1] and having there a worshipful dinner for themselves and other commoners, Lydgate the poet, that was a monk of Bury, sent to them, by a pursuivant, a joyful commendation of that season, containing sixteen staves of metre royal, beginning thus:—

[1] Stepney.

> " Mightie Flora! goddess of fresh flowers,—
> Which clothed hath the soyle in lustie greene,
> Made buds spring, with her sweete showers,
> By the influence of the sunne shine.
> To doe pleasance of intent full cleane,
> Unto the States which now sit here,
> Hath Vere downe sent her owne daughter deare.
>
> Making the vertue, that dared in the roote,
> Called of clarkes the vertue vegitable,
> For to transcend, most holsome and most soote,
> Into the crop, this season so agreeable,
> The bawmy liquor is so commendable,
> That it rejoyceth with his fresh moysture,
> Man, beast, and fowle, and every creature," etc.

These great Mayings and May-games, made by the governors and masters of this city, with the triumphant setting up of the great shaft (a principal May-pole in Cornehill, before the parish church of St. Andrew), therefore called Undershaft, by means of an insurrection of youths against aliens on May-day, 1517, the 9th of Henry VIII., have not been so freely used as afore, and therefore I leave them, and will somewhat touch of watches, as also of shows in the night.[1]

OF WATCHES IN THIS CITY, AND OTHER MATTERS COMMANDED, AND THE CAUSE WHY

William Conqueror commanded that in every town and village, a bell should be nightly rung at eight o'clock, and that all people should then put out their fire and candle, and take their rest; which order was observed through this realm during his reign, and the reign of William Rufus. But Henry I., restoring to his subjects the use of fire and lights, as afore; it followeth, by reason of wars within the realm, that many men also gave themselves to robbery and murders in the night; for example whereof in this city Roger Hoveden writeth thus:—" In the year 1175 [1174], a council was kept at Nottingham; in time of which council a brother of the Earl Ferrers being in the night privily slain at London, and thrown out of his inn into the dirty street, when the king understood thereof, he swore that he would be avenged on the citizens. For it was then (saith mine author) a common practice in the city, that a hundred or more in a company, young and old, would make nightly invasions

---

[1] A paper by Mr. Saunders, in Knight's *London*, i. 169, entitled, " The Old Spring Time in London," forms a very agreeable commentary on this section of our author's work.

upon houses of the wealthy, to the intent to rob them; and if they found any man stirring in the city within the night that were not of their crew, they would presently murder him, insomuch that when night was come no man durst adventure to walk in the streets.   When this had continued long, it fortuned that as a crew of young and wealthy citizens, assembling together in the night, assaulted a stone house of a certain rich man, and breaking through the wall, the good man of that house, having prepared himself with others in a corner, when he perceived one of the thieves named Andrew Bucquint to lead the way, with a burning brand in the one hand, and a pot of coals in the other, which he essayed to kindle with the brand, he flew upon him, and smote off his right hand, and then with a loud voice cried ' Thieves! ' at the hearing whereof the thieves took their flight, all saving he that had lost his hand, whom the good man in the next morning delivered to Richard de Lucie, the king's justice.   This thief, upon warrant of his life, appeached his confederates, of whom many were taken, and many were fled.   Among the rest that were apprehended, a certain citizen of great countenance, credit, and wealth, named John Senex,[1] who forasmuch as he could not acquit himself by the water dome, as that law was then, he offered to the king five hundred pounds of silver for his life; but forasmuch as he was condemned by judgment of the water, the king would not take the offer, but commanded him to be hanged on the gallows, which was done, and then the city became more quiet for a long time after."   But for a full remedy of enormities in the night I read, that in the year 1253, Henry III. commanded watches in the cities and borough towns to be kept, for the better observing of peace and quietness amongst his people.

And further, by the advice of them of Savoy, he ordained, that if any man chanced to be robbed, or by any means damnified by any thief or robber, he to whom the charge of keeping that country, city, or borough, chiefly appertained, where the robbery was done, should competently restore the loss.   And this was after the use of Savoy, but yet thought more hard to be observed here than in those parts; and, therefore, leaving those laborious watches, I will speak of our pleasures and pastimes in watching by night.

In the months of June and July, on the vigils of festival days,

---

[1] Rich thieves most worthy to be hanged. The judgment of fire and water, called *ordalii*, was condemned by Pope Innocent III. 1203. Decretat, lib. 5.—*Stow*.

and on the same festival days in the evenings after the sun setting, there were usually made bonfires in the streets, every man bestowing wood or labour towards them; the wealthier sort also, before their doors near to the said bonfires, would set out tables on the vigils, furnished with sweet bread and good drink, and on the festival days with meats and drinks plentifully, whereunto they would invite their neighbours and passengers also to sit and be merry with them in great familiarity, praising God for his benefits bestowed on them. These were called bonfires as well of good amity amongst neighbours that being before at controversy, were there, by the labour of others, reconciled, and made of bitter enemies loving friends; and also for the virtue that a great fire hath to purge the infection of the air. On the vigil of St. John the Baptist, and on St. Peter and Paul the apostles, every man's door being shadowed with green birch, long fennel, St. John's wort, orpin, white lilies, and such like, garnished upon with garlands of beautiful flowers, had also lamps of glass, with oil burning in them all the night; some hung out branches of iron curiously wrought, containing hundreds of lamps alight at once, which made a goodly show, namely in New Fish street, Thames street, etc. Then had ye besides the standing watches all in bright harness, in every ward and street of this city and suburbs, a marching watch, that passed through the principal streets thereof, to wit, from the little conduit by Paule's gate to West Cheape, by the stocks through Cornhill, by Leaden hall to Aldgate, then back down Fenchurch street, by Grasse church, about Grasse church conduit, and up Grasse church street into Cornhill, and through it into West Cheape again. The whole way for this marching watch extendeth to three thousand two hundred tailor's yards of assize; for the furniture whereof with lights, there were appointed seven hundred cressets, five hundred of them being found by the companies, the other two hundred by the chamber of London. Besides the which lights every constable in London, in number more than two hundred and forty,[1] had his cresset: the charge of every cresset was in light two shillings and four pence, and every cresset had two men, one to bear or hold it, another to bear a bag with light, and to serve it, so that the poor men pertaining to the cressets, taking wages, besides that every one had a straw hat, with a badge painted, and his break-

---

[1] More than two hundred and forty constables in London, the one half of them each night went in the marching watch, the other half kept their standing watch in every street and lane.—*Stow*.

fast in the morning, amounted in number to almost two thousand. The marching watch contained in number about two thousand men, part of them being old soldiers of skill, to be captains, lieutenants, serjeants, corporals, etc., wiflers, drummers, and fifes, standard and ensign bearers, sword players, trumpeters on horseback, demilances on great horses, gunners with hand guns, or half hakes, archers in coats of white fustian, signed on the breast and back with the arms of the city, their bows bent in their hands, with sheaves of arrows by their sides, pikemen in bright corslets, burganets, etc., halberds, the like billmen in almaine rivets, and apernes of mail in great number; there were also divers pageants, morris dancers, constables, the one-half, which was one hundred and twenty, on St. John's eve, the other half on St. Peter's eve, in bright harness, some overgilt, and every one a jornet [1] of scarlet thereupon, and a chain of gold, his henchman following him, his minstrels before him, and his cresset light passing by him, the waits of the city, the mayor's officers for his guard before him, all in a livery of worsted, or say jackets party-coloured, the mayor himself well mounted on horseback, the swordbearer before him in fair armour well mounted also, the mayor's footmen, and the like torch bearers about him, henchmen twain upon great stirring horses, following him. The sheriffs' watches came one after the other in like order, but not so large in number as the mayor's; for where the mayor had besides his giant three pageants, each of the sheriffs had besides their giants but two pageants, each their morris dance, and one henchman, their officers in jackets of worsted or say, party-coloured, differing from the mayor's, and each from other, but having harnessed men a great many, etc.

This midsummer watch was thus accustomed yearly, time out of mind, until the year 1539, the 31st of Henry VIII., in which year, on the 8th of May, a great muster was made by the citizens at the Mile's end, all in bright harness, with coats of white silk, or cloth and chains of gold, in three great battles, to the number of fifteen thousand, which passed through London to Westminster, and so through the Sanctuary, and round about the park of St. James, and returned home through Oldborne. King Henry, then considering the great charges of the citizens for the furniture of this unusual muster, forbad the marching watch provided for at Midsummer for that year, which being once laid down, was not raised again till the year

---

[1] A large coat or cloak, from the French " journade."—See Roquefort's *Glossaire*, s. v.

1548, the 2nd of Edward VI., Sir John Gresham then being mayor, who caused the marching watch, both on the eve of St. John the Baptist and of St. Peter the Apostle, to be revived and set forth in as comely order as it hath been accustomed, which watch was also beautified by the number of more than three hundred demilances and light horsemen, prepared by the citizens to be sent into Scotland for the rescue of the town of Hadington, and others kept by the Englishmen. Since this mayor's time, the like marching watch in this city hath not been used, though some attempts have been made there-unto; as in the year 1585, a book was drawn by a grave citizen,[1] and by him dedicated to Sir Thomas Pullison, then lord mayor, and his brethren the aldermen, containing the manner and order of a marching watch in the city upon the evens accustomed; in commendation whereof, namely, in times of peace to be used, he hath words to this effect: " The artificers of sundry sorts were thereby well set a-work, none but rich men charged, poor men helped, old soldiers, trumpeters, drummers, fifes, and ensign-bearers, with such like men, meet for princes' service, kept in ure, wherein the safety and defence of every common weal consisteth. Armour and weapon being yearly occupied in this wise, the citizens had of their own readily prepared for any need; whereas by intermission hereof, armourers are out of work, soldiers out of pay, weapons overgrown with foulness, few or none good being provided," etc.

In the month of August, about the feast of St. Bartholomew the Apostle, before the Lord Mayor, aldermen, and sheriffs of London, placed in a large tent near unto Clarkenwell, of old time, were divers days spent in the pastime of wrestling, where the officers of the city, namely, the sheriffs, sergeants, and yeomen, the porters of the king's beam or weigh-house, now no such men, and other of the city, were challengers of all men in the suburbs, to wrestle for games appointed, and on other days, before the said mayor, aldermen, and sheriffs, in Fensburie field, to shoot the standard, broad arrow, and flight, for games; but now of late years the wrestling is only practised on Bartholomew's day in the afternoon, and the shooting some three or four days after, in one afternoon, and no more. What should I speak of the ancient daily exercises in the long bow by citizens of this city, now almost clean left off and forsaken?— I overpass it; for by the mean of closing in the common grounds, our archers, for want of room to shoot abroad, creep into bowling

[1] John Mountgomery. [*See* Bibliography.]

alleys, and ordinary dicing houses, nearer home, where they have room enough to hazard their money at unlawful games; and there I leave them to take their pleasures.

HONOUR OF CITIZENS, AND WORTHINESS OF MEN IN THE SAME

"This city," saith Fitzstephen, "is glorious in manhood: furnished with munitions, populous with inhabitants; insomuch, that in the troublesome time of King Stephen, it hath showed at a muster twenty thousand armed horsemen, and threescore thousand footmen, serviceable for the wars. Moreover (saith he), the citizens of London, wheresoever they become, are notable before all other citizens in civility of manners, attire, table, and talk. The matrons of this city are the very modest Sabine ladies of Italy. The Londoners, sometime called Trinobantes, repelled Cæsar, which always made his passage by shedding blood; whereupon Lucan sung:

'Territa quæsitis ostendit terga Britannis.'

"The city of London hath bred some which have subdued many kingdoms, and also the Roman empire. It hath also brought forth many others, whom virtue and valour hath highly advanced; according to Apollo, in his Oracle to Brute, 'Sub occasu solis,' etc. In the time of Christianity, it brought forth that noble emperor, Constantine, which gave the city of Rome and all the imperial ensigns to God, St. Peter, and Pope Silvester; choosing rather to be called a defender of the church than an emperor; and, lest peace might be violated, and their eyes troubled by his presence, he retired from Rome, and built the city of Constantinople. London also in late time hath brought forth famous kings: Maude the empress, King Henry, son to Henry II., and Thomas the Archbishop," etc.

This Thomas, surnamed Becket, born in London, brought up in the priory of Marton, student at Paris, became the sheriff's clerk of London for a time, then parson of St. Mary hill, had a prebend at London, another at Lincoln, studied the law at Bononie, etc., was made Chancellor of England, and Archbishop of Canterbury, etc. Unto this might be added innumerable persons of honour, wisdom, and virtue, born in London; but of actions done by worthy citizens I will only note a few, and so to other matters.

The citizens of London, time out of mind, founded an hospital of St. James in the fields for leprous women of their city.

In the year 1197, Walter Brune, a citizen of London, and Rosia, his wife, founded the hospital of our Lady, called Domus Dei, or St. Marie Spittle, without Bishopsgate of London; a house of such relief to the needy, that there was found standing at the surrender thereof nine score beds, well furnished for receipt of poor people.

In the year 1216, the Londoners sending out a navy, took ninety-five ships of pirates and sea-robbers; besides innumerable others that they drowned, which had robbed on the river of Thames.

In the year 1247, Simon Fitzmary, one of the sheriffs of London, founded the hospital of St. Mary called Bethlem, and without Bishopsgate.

In the year 1283, Henry Wallice, then mayor, built the Tun upon Cornhill, to be a prison for night-walkers, and a market-house called the Stocks, both for fish and flesh, standing in the midst of the city. He also built divers houses on the west and north side of Paule's churchyard; the profits of all which buildings are to the maintenance of London Bridge.

In the year 1332, William Elsing, mercer of London, founded Elsing Spittle within Cripplegate, for sustentation of an hundred poor blind men, and became himself the first prior of that hospital.

Sir John Poultney, draper, four times mayor, in 1337 built a fair chapel in Paule's church, wherein he was buried. He founded a college in the parish church of St. Laurence, called Poultney: he built the parish church called Little Alhallowes, in Thames street; the Carmelite friars church in Coventry: he gave relief to prisoners in Newgate and in the Fleet, and ten shillings a-year to St. Giles' hospital by Oldborne for ever, and other legacies long to rehearse.

John Stodie, vintner, mayor 1358, gave to the vintners all the quadrant wherein the Vintners' hall now standeth, with all the tenements round about, from Stodies lane, wherein is founded thirteen alms houses for so many poor people, etc.

Henry Picard, vintner, mayor 1357, in the year 1363, did in one day sumptuously feast Edward III., king of England, John, king of France, David, king of Scots, the king of Cyprus, then all in England, Edward, prince of Wales, with many other noblemen, and after kept his hall for all comers that were willing to play at dice and hazard. The Lady Margaret, his wife, kept her chamber to the same effect, etc.

John Lofken, fishmonger, four times mayor, 1367, built an

hospital called Magdalen's, in Kingstone upon Thames; gave thereunto nine tenements, ten shops, one mill, one hundred and twenty-five acres of land, ten acres of meadow, one hundred and twenty acres of pasture, etc.; more, in London, he built the fair parish church of St. Michael in Crooked lane, and was there buried.

John Barnes, mayor 1371, gave a chest with three locks, and one thousand marks therein, to be lent to young men upon sufficient pawn, and for the use thereof, to say *De profundis*, or *Pater noster*, and no more: he also was a great builder of St. Thomas Apostle's parish church, as appeareth by his arms there, both in stone and glass.

In the year 1378, John Filpot, sometime mayor, hired with his own money one thousand soldiers, and defended the realm from incursions of the enemy, so that in small time his hired men took John Mercer, a sea-rover, with all his ships, which he before had taken from Scarborrow, and fifteen Spanish ships, laden with great riches.

In the year 1380, Thomas of Woodstocke, Thomas Percie, Hugh Calverley, Robert Knoles, and others, being sent with a great power to aid the duke of Brytaine, the said John Filpot hired ships for them of his own charges, and released the armour, which the soldiers had pawned for their battles, more than a thousand in number. "This most noble citizen," saith Thomas Walsingham, "that had travailed for the commodity of the whole realm, more than all other of his time, had often relieved the king by lending him great sums of money and otherwise, deceased in A.D. 1384, after that he had assured lands to the city for the relief of thirteen poor people for ever."

In the year 1381, William Walworth, then mayor, a most provident, valiant, and learned citizen, did by his arrest of Wat Tyler (a presumptuous rebel, upon whom no man durst lay hands), deliver the king and kingdom from the danger of most wicked traitors, and was for his service knighted in the field.

Nicholas Brembar, John Filpot, Robert Laund, Nicholas Twiford, and Adam Francis, aldermen, were then for their service likewise knighted; and Sir Robert Knoles, for assisting of the mayor, was made free of this city.

This Sir Robert Knoles, thus worthily infranchised a citizen, founded a college with an hospital at Pontefract: he also built the great stone bridge at Rochester, over the river of Medway, etc.

John Churchman, grocer, one of the sheriffs, 1386, for the

quiet of merchants, built a certain house upon Wool wharf, in Tower ward, to serve for tronage or weighing of wools, and for the customer, comptroller, clerks, and other officers to sit, etc.

Adam Bamme, goldsmith, mayor 1391, in a great dearth, procured corn from parts beyond the seas, to be brought hither in such abundance as sufficed to serve the city, and the countries near adjoining; to the furtherance of which good work he took out of the orphans' chest in the Guildhall two thousand marks to buy the said corn, and each alderman laid out twenty pounds to the like purpose.

Thomas Knoles, grocer, mayor 1400, with his brethren the aldermen, began to new build the Guildhall in London, and instead of an old little cottage in Aldermanberie street, made a fair and goodly house, more near unto St. Laurence church in the Jurie: he re-edified St. Anthony's church, and gave to the grocers his house near unto the same, for relief of the poor for ever. More, he caused sweet water to be conveyed to the gates of Newgate and Ludgate, for relief of the prisoners there.

John Hinde, draper, mayor 1405, newly built his parish church of St. Swithen by London stone: his monument is defaced, save only his arms in the glass windows.

Thomas Falconar, mercer, mayor 1414, lent to King Henry V., towards maintenance of his wars in France, ten thousand marks upon jewels. More, he made the postern called Mooregate, caused the ditches of the city to be cleansed, and did many other things for good of the same city.

William Sevenoke, grocer, mayor 1419, founded in the town of Sevenoke, in Kent, a free school for poor men's children, and thirteen alms houses: his testament saith, twenty poor men and women.

Richard Whittington, mercer, three times mayor, in the year 1421 began the library of the grey friars in London, to the charge of four hundred pounds: his executors with his goods founded and built Whittington college, with alms houses for thirteen poor men, and divinity lectures to be read there for ever. They repaired St. Bartholomew's hospital in Smithfield; they bare some charges to the glazing and paving of the Guildhall; they bare half the charges of building the library there, and they built the west gate of London, of old time called Newgate, etc.

John Carpenter, town-clerk of London, in the reign of Henry V., caused with great expense to be curiously painted upon board, about the north cloister of Paule's, a monument of

Death leading all estates, with the speeches of Death, and answer of every state. This cloister was pulled down 1549. He also gave tenements to the city, for the finding and bringing up of four poor men's children with meat, drink, apparel, learning at the schools in the universities, etc., until they be preferred, and then other in their places for ever.

Robert Chichley, grocer, mayor 1422, appointed by his testament, that on his minde day, a competent dinner should be ordained for two thousand four hundred poor men, householders of this city, and every man to have two pence in money. More, he gave one large plot of ground, thereupon to build the new parish church of St. Stephen, near unto Walbrooke, etc.

John Rainwell, fishmonger, mayor 1427, gave tenements to discharge certain wards of London of fifteenths and other payments.

John Wells, grocer, mayor, 1433, a great builder of the chapel or college of the Guildhall, and was there buried. He caused fresh water to be conveyed from Tyborne to the standard in West Cheape for service of the city.

William Eastfield, mercer, 1438, appointed his executors of his goods to convey sweet water from Tyborne, and to build a fair conduit by Aldermanberie church, which they performed, as also made a standard in Fleet street by Shew lane end; they also conveyed water to Cripples gate, etc.

Stephen Browne, grocer, mayor 1439, sent into Prussia, causing corn to be brought from thence; [1] whereby he brought down the price of wheat from three shillings the bushel to less than half that money.

Philip Malpas, one of the sheriffs 1440, gave by his testament one hundred and twenty-five pounds, to relieve poor prisoners, and every year for five years, four hundred shirts and smocks, forty pairs of sheets, and one hundred and fifty gowns of frieze, to the poor; to five hundred poor people in London six shillings and eight pence; to poor maids' marriages one hundred marks; to highways one hundred marks; twenty marks the year to a graduate to preach; twenty pounds to preachers at the Spittle the three Easter holidays, etc.

Robert Large, mercer, mayor 1440, gave to his parish-church of St. Olave in Surry two hundred pounds; to St. Margaret's in Lothberie twenty-five pounds; to the poor twenty pounds; to London bridge one hundred marks; towards the vaulting over the water-course of Walbrooke two hundred marks; to

" To London in greater quantitie."—1st *edition*, p. 80.

poor maids' marriages one hundred marks; to poor householders one hundred pounds, etc.

Richard Rich, mercer, one of the sheriffs 1442, founded alms houses at Hodsdon in Hertfordshire.

Simon Eyre, draper, mayor 1446, built the Leaden hall for a common garner of corn for the use of this city, and left five thousand marks to charitable uses.

Godfrey Bollein, mayor of London, 1458, by his testament, gave liberally to the prisons, hospitals, and lazar houses, besides a thousand pounds to poor householders in London, and two hundred pounds to poor householders in Norfolke.[1]

Richard Rawson, one of the sheriffs 1477, gave by testament large legacies to the prisoners, hospitals, lazar houses, to other poor, to highways, to the water-conduits, besides to poor maids' marriages three hundred and forty pounds, and his executors to build a large house in the churchyard of St. Marie Spittle, wherein the mayor and his brethren do use to sit and hear the sermons in the Easter holidays.

Thomas Ilam, one of the sheriffs 1480, newly built the great conduit in Cheape, of his own charges.

Edward Shaw, goldsmith, mayor 1483, caused the Cripplegate of London to be newly built of his goods, etc.

Thomas Hill, grocer, mayor 1485, caused of his goods the conduit of Grasse street to be built.

Hugh Clopton, mercer, during his life a bachelor, mayor 1492, built the great stone-arched bridge at Stratford upon Avon in Warwickshire, and did many other things of great charity, as in my *Summary*.

Robert Fabian and one of the sheriffs, 1494, gathered out of divers good authors, as well Latin as French, a large Chronicle of England and of France, which he published in English, to his great charges, for the honour of this city, and common utility of the whole realm.

Sir John Percivall, merchant-taylor, mayor 1498, founded a grammar-school at Macklefield in Cheshire, where he was born; he endowed the same school with sufficient lands for the finding of a priest master there, to teach freely all children thither sent, without exception.

The Lady Thomasine his wife founded the like free school, together with fair lodgings for the schoolmasters, scholars, and

---

[1] " In the yeare 1471, John Stockton, mayor, and eleven aldermen of London, with the recorder, were all made knightes in the fielde by Edward IV., for their good service done to him."—*1st edition*, p. 81.

other, and added twenty pounds of yearly revenue for supporting the charges, at St. Mary Wike in Devonshire, where she was born.

Stephen Gennings, merchant-taylor, mayor 1509, founded a fair grammar-school at Ulfrimhampton [1] in Staffordshire, left good lands, and also built a great part of his parish church, called St. Andrew's Undershaft, in London.

Henry Keble, grocer, mayor 1511, in his life a great benefactor to the new building of old Mary church, and by his testament gave a thousand pounds towards the finishing thereof; he gave to highways two hundred pounds; to poor maids' marriages one hundred marks; to poor husbandmen in Oxford and Warwick shires one hundred and forty ploughshares, and one hundred and forty coulters of iron; and in London, to seven almsmen six pence the week for ever.

John Collet, a citizen of London by birth and dignity, dean of Paule's, doctor of divinity, erected and built one free school in Paule's churchyard, 1512, for one hundred and fifty-three poor men's children to be taught free in the same school, appointing a master, a surmaster, and a chaplain, with sufficient stipends to endure for ever, and committed the oversight thereof to the mercers in London, because himself was son to Henry Collet, mercer, mayor of London, and endowed the mercers with lands to the yearly value of one hundred and twenty pounds or better.

John Tate, brewer, then a mercer, mayor 1514, caused his brewhouse, called the Swan, near adjoining to the hospital of St. Anthonie in London, to be taken down for the enlarging of the said church, then newly built, a great part of his charge. This was a goodly foundation, with alms houses, free school, etc.

George Monox, draper, mayor 1515, re-edified the decayed parish church of Waltonstow, or Walthamstow, in Essex; he founded there a free school, and alms houses for thirteen alms people, made a causeway of timber over the marshes from Walthamstow to Lock bridge, etc.

Sir John Milborne, draper, mayor 1522, built alms houses, fourteen in number, by the Crossed Friers church in London, there to be placed fourteen poor people; and left to the Drapers certain messuages, tenements, and garden plots, in the parish of St. Olave in Hart street, for the performance of stipends to the said alms people, and other uses. Look more in Ealdgate ward.

Robert Thorne, merchant-taylor, deceased a bachelor in the

[1] Wolverhampton.

year 1532, gave by his testament to charitable actions more than four thousand four hundred and forty pounds, and legacies to his poor kindred more five thousand one hundred and forty-two pounds, besides his debts forgiven, etc.

Sir John Allen, mercer, mayor of London, and of council to King Henry VIII., deceased 1544, buried in St. Thomas of Acres in a fair chapel by him built. He gave to the city of London a rich collar of gold to be worn by the mayor, which was first worn by Sir W. Laxton. He gave five hundred marks to be a stock for sea-coal; his lands purchased of the king, the rent thereof to be distributed to the poor in the wards of London for ever. He gave besides to the prisons, hospitals, lazar houses, and all other poor in the city, or two miles without, very liberally, and long to be recited.

Sir William Laxton, grocer, mayor 1545, founded a fair free school at Owndale in Northamptonshire, with six alms houses for the poor.

Sir John Gresham, mercer, mayor 1548, founded a free school at Holt, a market-town in Norfolk.

Sir Rowland Hill, mercer, mayor 1550, caused to be made divers causeways both for horse and man; he made four bridges, two of stone, containing eighteen arches in them both; he built one notable free school at Drayton in Shropshire; he gave to Christ's hospital in London five hundred pounds, etc.

Sir Andrew Jud, skinner, mayor 1551, erected one notable free school at Tunbridge in Kent, and alms houses nigh St. Helen's church in London, and left to the Skinners lands to the value of sixty pounds three shillings and eight pence the year; for the which they be bound to pay twenty pounds to the schoolmaster, eight pounds to the usher, yearly, for ever, and four-shillings the week to the six alms people, and twenty-five shillings and four pence the year in coals for ever.

Sir Thomas White, merchant-taylor, mayor 1554, founded St. John's college, Oxford, and gave great sums of money to divers towns in England for relief of the poor, as in my *Summary*.

Edward Hall, gentleman, of Gray's inn, a citizen by birth and office, as common sergeant of London, and one of the judges in the Sheriffs' court; he wrote and published a famous and eloquent chronicle, entitled, " The Uniting of the Two noble Families, Lancaster and Yorke."

Richard Hils, merchant-taylor, 1560, gave five hundred pounds towards the purchase of a house called the manor of the Rose, wherein the merchant-taylors founded their free school in London; he also gave to the said merchant-taylors one plot of ground, with certain small cottages on the Tower hill, where he built fair alms houses for fourteen sole women.

About the same time William Lambert, Esq., born in London, a justice of the peace in Kent, founded a college for the poor which he named of Queen Elizabeth, in East Greenwich.

William Harper, merchant-taylor, mayor 1562, founded a free school in the town of Bedford, where he was born, and also buried.

Sir Thomas Gresham, mercer, 1566, built the Royal Exchange in London, and by his testament left his dwelling house in Bishopsgate street to be a place for readings, allowing large stipends to the readers, and certain alms houses for the poor.

William Patten, gentleman, a citizen by birth, a customer of London outward, justice of peace in Middlesex, the parish church of Stokenewenton being ruinous, he repaired, or rather new built.

Sir Thomas Roe, merchant-taylor, mayor 1568, gave to the merchant-taylors lands or tenements, out of them to be given to ten poor men, cloth-workers, carpenters, tilers, plasterers, and armourers, forty pounds yearly, namely, four pounds to each, also one hundred pounds to be lent to eight poor men; besides he enclosed with a wall of brick nigh one acre of ground, pertaining to the hospital of Bethlem, to be a burial for the dead.

Ambrose Nicholas, salter, mayor 1576, founded twelve alms houses in Monke's well street, near unto Creple's gate, wherein he placed twelve poor people, having each of them seven pence the week, and once every year five sacks of coals, and one quarter of a hundred faggots, all of his gift for ever.

William Lambe, gentleman and clothworker, in the year 1577, built a water-conduit at Oldborne cross to his charges of fifteen hundred pounds, and did many other charitable acts, as in my *Summary*.

Sir T. Offley, merchant-taylor, mayor, deceased 1580, appointed by his testament the one half of all his goods, and two hundred pounds deducted out of the other half given to his on Henry, to be given and bestowed in deeds of charity by his executors, according to his confidence and trust in them.

John Haydon, sheriff 1583, gave large legacies, more than three thousand pounds, for the relief of the poor, as in my *Summary*.

Barnard Randolph, common sergeant of London 1583, gave and delivered with his own hand, nine hundred pounds towards the building of water-conduits, which was performed. More, by testament he gave one thousand pounds to be employed in charitable actions; but that money being in hold fast hands, I have not heard how it was bestowed, more than of other good men's testaments—to be performed.

Sir Wolston Dixie, skinner, mayor 1586, founded a free school at Bosworth, and endowed it with twenty pounds land by year.

Richard May, merchant-taylor, gave three hundred pounds toward the new building of Blackwell hall in London, a market-place for woollen cloths.

John Fuller, Esq., one of the judges in the sheriffs' court of London, by his testament, dated 1592, appointed his wife, her heirs and assigns, after his decease, to erect one alms house in the parish of Stikoneth,[1] for twelve poor single men, aged fifty years or upwards, and one other alms house in Shoreditch, for twelve poor aged widow women of like age, she to endow them with one hundred pounds the year, to wit, fifty pounds to each for ever, out of his lands in Lincolne shire, assured ever unto certain fiefs in trust, by a deed of feoffment. Item: more, he gave his messuages, lands, and tenements, lying in the parishes of St. Benet and St. Peter, by Powle's wharf in London, to feoffees in trust, yearly for ever, to disburse all the issues and profits of the said lands and tenements, to the relieving and discharge of poor prisoners in the Hole, or two penny wards in the two compters in London, in equal portions to each compter, so that the prisoners exceed not the sum of twenty-six shillings and eight pence for every one prisoner at any one time.

Thus much for famous citizens have I noted their charitable actions, for the most part done by them in their lifetime. The residue left in trust to their executors, I have known some of them hardly (or never) performed; wherefore I wish men to make their own hands their executors, and their eyes their over-seers, not forgetting the old proverb:—

" Women be forgetfull, children be unkind,
    Executors be covetous, and take what they find.
    If any body aske where the dead's goods became,
    They answere, So God me help, and holy dome, he died a poore man."

One worthy citizen merchant-taylor, having many years considered this proverb foregoing, hath therefore established to twelve poor aged men, merchant-taylors, six pounds two shillings to each yearly for ever. He hath also given them gowns of good

[1] Stokenheath.

broad cloth, lined thoroughly with bays, and are to receive every three years' end the like new gowns for ever.

And now of some women, citizens' wives, deserving memory, for example to posterity shall be noted.

Dame Agnes Foster, widow, sometime wife to Stephen Foster, fishmonger, mayor 1455, having enlarged the prison of Ludgate in 1463, procured in a common council of this city, certain articles to be established for the ease, comfort, and relief of poor prisoners there, as in the chapter of gates I have set down.

Avise Gibson, wife unto Nicholas Gibson, grocer, one of the sheriffs 1539, by license of her husband, founded a free school at Radclyffe, near unto London, appointing to the same, for the instruction of sixty poor men's children, a schoolmaster and usher with fifty pounds; she also built alms houses for fourteen poor aged persons, each of them to receive quarterly six shillings and eight pence the piece for ever; the government of which free school and alms houses she left in confidence to the Coopers in London. This virtuous gentlewoman was after joined in marriage with Sir Anthony Knevet, knight, and so called the Lady Knevet; a fair painted table of her picture was placed in the chapel which she had built there, but of late removed thence, by the like reason as the Grocer's arms fixed on the outer wall of the schoolhouse are pulled down, and the Coopers set in place.[1]

Margaret Danne, widow to William Danne, ironmonger, one of the sheriffs of London, gave by her testament to the ironmongers, two thousand pounds, to be lent to young men of that company, paying after the rate of five pounds in the year for every hundred; which one hundred pounds so rising yearly, to be employed on charitable actions, as she then appointed, but not performed in more than thirty years after.

Dame Mary Ramsey, wife to Sir Thomas Ramsey, mayor about the year 1577, being seised of lands in fee simple of her inheritance to the yearly value of two hundred and forty-three pounds, by his consent gave the same to Christ's hospital in London towards the relief of poor children there, and other ways, as in my *Summary* and *Abridgment* I have long since expressed; which gift she in her widowhood confirmed and augmented, as is showed by monuments in Christ's hospital erected.

Thus much for the worthiness of citizens in this city, touching

[1] " Cursed is hee that removeth his neighbors mark, have I read."—*Stow.*

whom John Lidgate, a monk of Bury, in the reign of Henry VI.,
made (amongst other) these verses following:—

> " Of seaven things I prayse this citty.
> Of true meaning and faithful observance;
> Of righteousnes, truth, and equity;
> Of stablenes aye kept in legiance;
> And for of vertue thou hast suffisance,
> In this lond here, and other londs all,
> The kinges chamber of custome, men thee call."

Having thus in generality handled the original, the walls,
gates, ditches, and fresh waters, the bridges, towers, and castles,
the schools of learning and house of law, the orders and customs,
sports and pastimes, watchings and martial exercises, and lastly
the honour and worthiness of the citizens, I am now to set
down the distribution of this city into parts; and more especially
to declare the antiquities noteworthy in every of the same; and
how both the whole and parts have been from time to time
ruled and governed.

THE CITY DIVIDED INTO PARTS

The ancient division of this city was into wards or alder-
manries. And therefore I will begin at the east, and so proceed
through the high and most principal street of the city to the
west, after this manner.

First, Through Aldgate street to the west corner of St.
Andrewe's church, called Undershaft, on the right hand, and
Lyme street corner on the left; all which is of Aldgate ward;
from thence through Cornhill street to the west corner of Leaden
hall; all which is of Lyme street ward. From thence, leaving
the street that leadeth to Bishopsgate on the right hand, and the
way that leadeth into Grasse street on the left, still through
Cornhill street, by the conduit to the west corner against the
Stocks; all which is in Cornhill ward. Then by the said Stocks
(a market-place both of fish and flesh standing in the midst of
the city) through the Poultry (a street so called) to the great
conduit in West Cheape, and so through Cheape to the standard,
which is of Cheape ward, except on the south side from Bow-lane
to the said standard, which is of Cordwayner street ward. Then
by the standard to the great cross, which is in Cripplegate ward
on the north side, and in Bred street ward on the south side.
And to the little conduit by Paule's gate, from whence of old
time the said high street stretched straight to Ludgate, all in the
ward of Faringdon within, then divided truly from east to west,

but since by means of the burning of Paule's church, which was in the reign of William I., Mauricius, then bishop of London, laid the foundation of a new church, so far in largeness exceeding the old, that the way towards Ludgate was thereby greatly straitened, as before I have discoursed.

Now from the north to the south this city was of old time divided, not by a large highway or street, as from east to west, but by a fair brook of sweet water, which came from out the north fields through the wall, and midst of the city, into the river of Thames; which division is till this day constantly and without change maintained. This water was called (as I have said) Walbrooke, not Galus brook of a Roman captain slain by Asclepiodatus, and thrown therein, as some have fabled, but of running through, and from the wall of this city; the course whereof, to prosecute it particularly, was and is from the said wall to St. Margaret's church in Lothberrie; from thence beneath the lower part of the Grocers' hall, about the east part of their kitchen, under St. Mildred's church, somewhat west from the said Stockes' market; from thence through Buckles berry, by one great house built of stone and timber called the Old Barge, because barges out of the river of Thames were rowed up so far into this brook, on the backside of the houses in Walbrooke street (which street taketh the name of the said brook) by the west end of St. John's church upon Walbrooke, under Horse-shew bridge, by the west side of Tallowchandler's hall, and of the Skinner's hall, and so behind the other houses to Elbow lane, and by a part thereof down Greenewitch lane, into the river of Thames.

This is the course of Walbrooke, which was of old time bridged over in divers places, for passage of horses and men, as need required; but since, by means of encroachment on the banks thereof, the channel being greatly straitened, and other noyances done thereunto, at length the same by common consent was arched over with brick, and paved with stone, equal with the ground, where through it passed, and is now in most places built upon, that no man may by the eye discern it, and therefore the trace thereof is hardly known to the common people.

This city was divided from east to west, and from north to south. I am further to show how the same was of old time broken into divers parts called wards, whereof Fitzstephen, more than four hundred years since, writeth thus:—" This city, (saith he) even as Rome, is divided into wards; it hath yearly sheriffs instead of consuls. It hath the dignity of senators in aldermen," etc. The number of these wards in London was, both before and in the reign of Henry III., twenty-four in all; whereof thirteen lay on the east side of the said Walbrooke, and eleven on the west. Notwithstanding these eleven grew much more large than those of the east; and therefore in the year of Christ 1393, in the 17th of Richard II., Faringdon ward, which was then one entire ward, but mightily increased of buildings without the gates, was by act of parliament appointed to be divided into twain, and to have two aldermen, to wit, Faringdon within, and Faringdon without, which made up the number of twelve wards on the west side of Walbrooke, and so the whole number of twenty-five on both sides. Moreover, in the year 1550, the mayor, commonalty, and citizens of London, purchasing the liberties of the borough of Southwark, appointed the same to be a ward of London, and so became the number of thirteen wards on the east, twelve on the west, and one south of the river Thames, in the said borough of Southwark, in the county of Surrey, which in all arise to the number of twenty-six wards, and twenty-six aldermen of London.

Wards on the east part of Walbrooke are these:—

 1 Portsoken ward without the walls.
 2 Tower street ward.
 3 Ealdegate ward.
 4 Lime street ward.
 5 Bishopsgate ward, within the walls and without.
 6 Brod street ward.
 7 Cornehil ward.
 8 Langbourne ward.
 9 Billingsgate ward.
10 Bridge ward within.
11 Candlewick street ward.
12 Walbrooke ward.
13 Downgate ward.

Wards on the west side of Walbrooke are these:

14 Vintry ward.
15 Cordwainer street ward.
16 Cheape ward.
17 Colman street warde.
18 Basinghall warde.
19 Cripplegate ward, within and without.
20 Aldersgate ward, within and without.
21 Farringdon ward within.
22 Bread street ward.

23 Queenhithe ward.
24 Castle Baynard ward.
25 Farringdon ward without the walls.

One ward south the river Thames, in the borough of South-wark, by the name of

26 Bridge ward without.

OF PORTSOKEN WARD, THE FIRST IN THE EAST PART

Seeing that of every of these wards I have to say somewhat, I will begin with Portsoken ward without Aldgate.

This Portsoken, which soundeth [1] the franchise at the gate, was sometime a guild, and had beginning in the days of King Edgar, more than six hundred years since.[2] There were thirteen knights or soldiers, well-beloved to the king and realm, for service by them done, which requested to have a certain portion of land on the east part of the city, left desolate and forsaken by the inhabitants, by reason of too much servitude. They besought the king to have this land, with the liberty of a guild for ever. The king granted to their request, with con-ditions following : that is, that each of them should victoriously accomplish three combats, one above the ground, one under ground, and the third in the water; and after this, at a certain day in East Smithfield, they should run with spears against all comers; all which was gloriously performed; and the same day the king named it Knighten Guild, and so bounded it, from Aldgate to the place where the bars now are, toward the east, on both the sides of the street, and extended it towards Bishops-gate in the north, unto the house then of William Presbiter, after of Giffrey Tanner, and then of the heirs of Colver, after that of John Easeby, but since of the Lord Bourchier, etc. And again towards the south unto the river of Thames, and so far into the water, as a horseman, entering the same, may ride at a low water, and throw his spear; so that all East Smithfield, with the right part of the street that goeth to Dodding pond into the Thames, and also the hospital of St. Katherin's, with the mills that were founded in King Stephen's days, and the outward stone wall, and the new ditch of the Tower, are of the said fee and liberty; for the said wall and ditch of the Tower were made in the time of King Richard, when he was in the Holy Land, by William Longshampe, Bishop of Ely, as before I have noted unto you.

[1] " As much as "—*1st edition*, p. 85.   [2] Liber Trinitat.

These knights had as then none other charter by all the days of Edgar, Ethelred, and Cnutus, until the time of Edward the Confessor, whom the heirs of those knights humbly besought to confirm their liberties; whereunto he graciously granting,[1] gave them a deed thereof, as appeareth in the book of the late house of the Holy Trinity. The said charter is fair written in the Saxon letter and tongue. After this, King William, the son of William the Conqueror, made a confirmation of the same liberties, unto the heirs of those knights, in these words: " William, king of England, to Maurice Bishop, and Godffrey de Magum, and Richard de Parre, and to his faithfull people of London, greeting: Know ye me to have granted to the men of Knighten Guilde, the guilde that belonged to them, and the land that belonged there-unto, with all customes, as they had the same in the time of King Edward, and my father. Witnesse, Hugh de Buche, at Rething.''

After him, King Henry I. confirmed the same by his charter to the like effect, the recital whereof I pretermit for brevity. After which time, the church of the Holy Trinity, within Aldgate of London, being founded by Queen Matilda, wife to the said Henry, the multitude of brethren, praising God day and night therein, in short time so increased, that all the city was delighted in the beholding of them; insomuch, that in the year 1115,[2] certain burgesses of London, of the progeny of those noble English knights; to wit, Radulphus Fitalgod, Wilmarde le Deucreshe, Orgar le Prude, Edward Hupcornehill, Blackstanus, and Alwine his kinsman, and Robert his brother, the sons of Leafstanus the goldsmith, Wiso his son, Hugh Fitzvulgar, Algare Secusme, coming together into the chapter-house of the said church of the Holy Trinity, gave to the same church and canons serving God therein, all the lands and soke called in English Knighten Guilde, which lieth to the wall of the city, without the same gate, and stretcheth to the river of Thames; they gave it, I say, taking upon them the brotherhood and participation of the benefits of that house, by the hands of Prior Norman. And the better to confirm this their grant, they offered upon the altar there the charter of Edward, together with the other charters which they had thereof; and afterward they did put the foresaid prior in seisine thereof, by the church of St. Buttolphe's, which is built thereon, and is the head of that land. These things were thus done before Bernard, prior of Dunstable, John, prior of Derland, Geffrey Clinton, chamber-

---

[1] Liber Trinitat.   [2] The date should read 1125.

lain, and many other clerks and laymen, French and English.
Orgar le Prude (one of their company) was sent to King Henry,
beseeching him to confirm their gift, which the king gladly
granted by his deed: "Henrie, king of England, to Richard
Bishop of London, to the shireffes and provost, and to all his
barons and faithfull people, French and English, of London and
Middlesex, greeting: Know ye mee to have graunted and confirmed to the church and canons of the Holy Trinitie of London,
the soke of the English Knighten Guilde, and the land which
pertaineth thereunto, and the church of St. Buttolph, as the
men of the same guilde have given and granted unto them: and I
will and straightly commaund, that they may hold the same well
and honourably and freely, with sacke and soke, toll and thea,
infangthefe, and all customs belonging to it, as the men of the
same Guild in best sort had the same in the time of K. Edward,
and as King William, my father and brother, did grant it to them
by their writs. Witnesse, A. the queene, Geffrey the chauncellor,
Geoffrey of Clinton,[1] and William of Clinton, at Woodstocke." All
these prescribed writings (saith my book), which sometime belonged
to the priory of the Holy Trinity, are registered in the end of the
Book of Remembrances, in the Guildhall of London, marked with
the letter C, folio 134. The king sent also his sheriffs, to wit,
Aubrey de Vere, and Roger, nephew to Hubert, which upon his
behalf should invest this church with the possessions thereof,
which the said sheriffs accomplished coming upon the ground; Andrew Buchevite, and the forenamed witnesses, and other, standing
by; notwithstanding, Othowerus Acolivillus, Otto, and Geffrey,
Earl of Essex, constables of the Tower by succession, withheld by
force a portion of the said land, as I have before delivered.

The prior and canons of the Holy Trinity, being thus seised
of the said land and soke of Knighten Guilde, a part of the
suburb without the wall (but within the liberties of the city),
the same prior was, for him and his successors, admitted as one
of the aldermen of London, to govern the same land and soke:
according to the customs of the city, he did sit in court, and
rode with the mayor and his brethren the aldermen, as one of
them, in scarlet or other livery as they used, until the year 1531,
at the which time the said priory, by the last prior there, was
surrendered to King Henry VIII., in the 23rd of his reign, who
gave this priory to Sir Thomas Audley, knight, lord chancellor
of England, and he pulled down the church; since the which
dissolution of that house, the said ward of Portsoken hath been

[1] [*See* Additional Notes.]

governed by a temporal man, one of the aldermen of London, elected by the citizens, as the aldermen of other wards. Thus much for the out-bounds of Knighten guilde, or Portsoken ward, and for the antiquity and government thereof.

Now, of the parts therein, this is specially to be noted. First, the east part of the Tower standeth there, then an hospital of St. Katherine's, founded by Matilda the queen, wife to King Stephen, by license of the priory and convent of the Holy Trinity in London, on whose grounds he founded it. Helianor the queen, wife to King Edward I., a second foundress, appointed there to be a master, three brethren chaplains, and three sisters, ten poor women, and six poor clerks; she gave to them the manor of Carlton in Wiltshire, and Upchurch in Kent, etc. Queen Philippa, wife to King Edward III., 1351, founded a chantry there, and gave to that hospital ten pounds land by year; it was of late time called a free chapel, a college, and an hospital for poor sisters. The choir, which of late years was not much inferior to that of Paules, was dissolved by Dr. Wilson, a late master there, the brethren and sisters remaining: this house was valued at £315 14s. 2d., being now of late years inclosed about, or pestered with small tenements and homely cottages, having inhabitants, English and strangers, more in number than in some city in England. There lie buried in this church the countess of Huntingdon, countess of the March in her time, 1429; John Holland, Duke of Exeter and Earl of Huntingdon, 1447, and his two wives, in a fair tomb on the north side the choir; Thomas Walsingham, esquire, and Thomas Ballarde, esquire, by him, 1465; Thomas Flemming, knight, 1466, etc.[1]

On the east and by north of the Tower, lieth East Smithfield and Tower hill, two plots of ground so called, without the wall of the city; and east from them both was sometime a monastery, called New Abbey, founded by King Edward III. in the year 1359, upon occasion as followeth:

In the year 1348, the 23rd of Edward III., the first great pestilence in his time began, and increased so sore, that for want of room in churchyards to bury the dead of the city and of the suburbs, one John Corey, clerk, procured of Nicholas, prior of the Holy Trinity within Aldgate, one toft[2] of ground near

---

[1] The further history of this establishment will be found in Nichols' *History of the Hospital and Collegiate Church of St. Katherine, near the Tower of London.*

[2] The Danish *toft*, Swedish *tomt*, properly signifies the ground upon which a house stands. See Grimm's *Deutsche Rech. Altherthümer*, s. 539.

unto East Smithfield, for the burial of them that died, with condition that it might be called the churchyard of the Holy Trinity; which ground he caused, by the aid of divers devout citizens, to be inclosed with a wall of stone. Robert Elsing, son of William Elsing, gave five pounds thereunto; and the same was dedicated by Ralph Stratford, Bishop of London, where innumerable bodies of the dead were afterwards buried, and a chapel built in the same place to the honour of God: to the which King Edward setting his eye (having before, in a tempest on the sea, and peril of drowning, made a vow to build a monastery to the honour of God, and our lady of grace, if God would grant him grace to come safe to land), built there a monastery, placing an abbot, and monks of the Cistercian, or White order. The bounds of this plot of ground, together with a decree for tithes thereof, are expressed in the charter, the effect whereof I have set down in another place, and have to show. This house, at the late general suppression, was valued at £546 0s. 10d. yearly; it was surrendered in the year 1539, the 30th of Henry VIII.; since the which time, the said monastery being clean pulled down by Sir Arthur Darcie, knight, and others, of late time in place thereof is built a large storehouse for victuals; and convenient ovens are built there, for baking of biscuits to serve her majesty's ships. The grounds adjoining, belonging to the said abbey, are employed in building of small tenements.

For Tower hill, as the same is greatly diminished by building of tenements and garden-plots, etc. So it is of late, to wit, in the year of Christ 1593, on the north side thereof, and at the west end of Hog street, beautified by certain fair alms houses, strongly built of brick and timber, and covered with slate for the poor, by the merchant-tailors of London, in place of some small cottages given to them by Richard Hils, sometime a master of that company, one thousand loads of timber for that use, being also given by Anthonie Radcliffe, of the same society, alderman. In these alms houses, fourteen charitable brethren of the said merchant-tailors yet living, have placed fourteen poor sole women, which receive each of them of their founder sixteen pence, or better, weekly, besides £8 15s. yearly, paid out of the common treasury of the same corporation for fuel.

From the west part of this Tower hill, towards Aldgate, being a long continual street, amongst other smaller buildings in that row, there was sometime an abbey of nuns of the order of St. Clare, called the Minories, founded by Edmond, Earl of Lancaster,

Leycester, and Darbie, brother to King Edward I., in the year
1293; the length of which abbey contained fifteen perches and
seven feet, near unto the king's street or highway, etc., as
appeareth by a deed, dated 1303.

A plague of pestilence being in this city, in the year 1515,
there died in this house of nuns professed to the number of
twenty-seven, besides other lay people, servants in their house.
This house was valued to dispend £418 8s. 5d. yearly, and was
surrendered by Dame Elizabeth Salvage, the last abbess there,
unto King Henry VIII. in the 30th of his reign, the year of
Christ 1539.

In place of this house of nuns is now built divers fair and
large storehouses for armour and habiliments of war, with
divers workhouses, serving to the same purpose: there is a
small parish church for inhabitants of the close, called St.
Trinities.

Near adjoining to this abbey, on the south side thereof, was
sometime a farm belonging to the said nunnery; at the which
farm I myself in my youth have fetched many a halfpenny
worth of milk, and never had less than three ale pints for a
halfpenny in the summer, nor less than one ale quart for a
halfpenny in the winter, always hot from the kine, as the same
was milked and strained. One Trolop, and afterwards Goodman, were the farmers there, and had thirty or forty kine to the
pail. Goodman's son being heir to his father's purchase, let
out the ground first for grazing of horses, and then for garden-
plots, and lived like a gentleman thereby.

On the other side of that street lieth the ditch without the
walls of the city, which of old time was used to be open, always
from time to time cleansed from filth and mud, as need required;
of great breadth, and so deep, that divers, watering horses where
they thought it shallowest, were drowned, both horse and man.
But now of later time the same ditch is inclosed, and the banks
thereof let out for garden-plots, carpenters' yards, bowling
allies, and divers houses thereon built, whereby the city wall
is hidden, the ditch filled up, a small channel left, and that very
shallow.

From Aldgate, east, lieth a large street and highway, sometime replenished with few, but fair and comely buildings; on the
north side whereof, the first was the parish church of St. Buttolph,
in a large cemetery or churchyard. This church hath been
lately new built at the special charges of the priors of the Holy
Trinity; patrons thereof, as it appeareth by the arms of that

house, engraven on the stone work. The parishioners of this parish being of late years mightily increased, the church is pestered with lofts and seats for them. Monuments in this church are few: Henry Jorden founded a chauntry there; John Romany Ollarie, and Agnes his wife, were buried there about 1408; Richard Chester, alderman, one of the sheriffs, 1484; Thomas Lord Darcie of the north, knight of the garter, beheaded 1537; Sir Nicholas Carew, of Bedington, in Surrey, knight of the garter, beheaded 1538; Sir Arthur Darcie, youngest son to Thomas Lord Darcie, deceased at the new abbey on the Tower hill, was buried there. East from this parish church, there were certain fair inns for receipt of travellers repairing to the city, up towards Hog lane end, somewhat within the bars, a mark showing how far the liberties of the city do extend.

This Hog lane stretcheth north toward St. Mary Spitle without Bishopsgate, and within these forty years [1] had on both sides fair hedge rows of elm trees, with bridges and easy stiles to pass over into the pleasant fields, very commodious for citizens therein to walk, shoot, and otherwise to recreate and refresh their dull spirits in the sweet and wholesome air, which is now within a few years made a continual building throughout, of garden-houses and small cottages; and the fields on either sides be turned into garden-plots, tenter yards, bowling alleys, and such like, from Houndes ditch in the west, as far as White Chappell, and further towards the east.

On the south side of the highway from Aldgate were some few tenements, thinly scattered here and there, with many void spaces between them, up to the Bars; but now that street is not only fully replenished with buildings outward, and also pestered with divers alleys, on either side to the bars, but to White Chappell and beyond. Among the which late buildings, one memorable for the commodity of that east part of this city is a fair water conduit, hard without the gate; at the building whereof in the year 1535, Sir John Allen being mayor, two-fifteens were granted by the citizens for the making and laying of pipes, to convey water from Hackney to that place; and so that work was finished.

From Aldgate, north-west to Bishopsgate, lieth the ditch of the city called Houndes ditch; for that in old time, when the same lay open, much filth (conveyed forth of the city), especially dead dogs, were there laid or cast; wherefore of latter time a mud wall was made, inclosing the ditch, to keep out the laying

[1] " These fortie-four yeares last."—*1st edition*, p. 92.

of such filth as had been accustomed. Over against this mud wall, on the other side of the street, was a fair field, sometime belonging to the priory of the Trinity, and since by Sir Thomas Audley given to Magdalen college in Cambridge: this field (as all other about the city) was inclosed, reserving open passage thereinto, for such as were disposed. Towards the street were some small cottages, of two stories high, and little garden-plots backward, for poor bed-rid people, for in that street dwelt none other, built by some prior of the Holy Trinity, to whom that ground belonged.

In my youth, I remember, devout people, as well men as women of this city, were accustomed oftentimes, especially on Fridays, weekly to walk that way purposely there to bestow their charitable alms; every poor man or woman lying in their bed within their window, which was towards the street, open so low that every man might see them, a clean linen cloth lying in their window, and a pair of beads, to show that there lay a bed-rid body, unable but to pray only. This street was first paved in the year 1503.

About the latter reign of Henry VIII., three brethren that were gunfounders, surnamed Owens, got ground there to build upon, and to inclose for casting of brass ordinance. These occupied a good part of the street on the field side, and in a short time divers others also built there, so that the poor bed-rid people were worn out, and, in place of their homely cottages, such houses built as do rather want room than rent; which houses be for the most part possessed by brokers, sellers of old apparel, and such like. The residue of the field was for the most part made into a garden by a gardener named Cawsway, one that served the markets with herbs and roots; and in the last year of King Edward VI. the same was parcelled into gardens wherein are now many fair houses of pleasure built.

On the ditch side of this street the mud wall is also by little and little all taken down, the bank of the ditch being raised, made level ground, and turned into garden-plots and carpenters' yards, and many large houses are there built; the filth of which houses, as also the earth cast out of their vaults, is turned into the ditch, by which means the ditch is filled up, and both the ditch and wall so hidden that they cannot be seen of the passers by. This Portsoken ward hath an alderman and his deputy, common councillors six, constables four, scavengers four, for the wardemote inquest eighteen, and a beadle. To the fifteen it is cessed at four pounds ten shillings.

TOWER STREET WARD

The first ward in the east part of this city within the wall is called Tower street ward, and extendeth along the river of Thames from the said Tower in the east almost to Belinsgate in the west. One half of the Tower, the ditch on the west side, and bulwarks adjoining, do stand within that part where the wall of the city of old time went straight from the postern gate south to the river of Thames, before that the Tower was built. From and without the Tower ditch, west and by north, is the said Tower hill, sometime a large plot of ground, now greatly straitened by incroachments (unlawfully made and suffered) for gardens and houses; some on the bank of the Tower ditch, whereby the Tower ditch is marred, but more near unto the wall of the city from the postern north, till over against the principal fore-gate of the Lord Lumley's house, etc.; but the Tower ward goeth no further that way.

Upon this hill is always readily prepared, at the charges of the city, a large scaffold and gallows of timber, for the execution of such traitors or transgressors as are delivered out of the Tower, or otherwise, to the sheriffs of London by writ, there to be executed. I read, that in the fifth of King Edward IV.[1] a scaffold and gallows was there set up by other the king's officers, and not of the city's charges, whereupon the mayor and his brethren complained, but were answered by the king that the Tower hill was of the liberty of the city; and whatsoever was done in that point was not in derogation of the city's liberties, and therefore commanded proclamation [2] to be made, as well within the city as in the suburbs, as followeth: " Forasmuch as, the seventh day of this present month of November, gallows were erect and set up besides our Tower of London, within the liberties and franchises of our city of London, in derogation and prejudice of the liberties and franchises of this city, the king our sovereign lord would it be certainly understood that the erection and setting up of the said gallows was not done by his commandment; wherefore the king our sovereign lord willeth that the erection and setting up the said gallows be not any precedent or example thereby hereafter to be taken, in hurt, prejudice, or derogation of the franchises, liberties, and privileges of the said city, which he at all times hath had, and hath in his benevolence, tender favour, and good grace, etc.

[1] Liber L. folio 40. [Letter-Books.]   [2] Proclamation. W. Dunthorn.

Apud Westminst. 9 die Novemb. anno regni nostri quinto."
On the north side of this hill is the said Lord Lumley's house,
and on the west side divers houses lately built, and other
incroachments along south to Chick lane,[1] on the east of Barking
church, at the end whereof you have Tower street stretching
from the Tower hill, west to St. Margaret Patten's church
parsonage.

Now therefore, to begin at the east end of the street, on the
north side thereof, is the fair parish church called Allhallows
Barking, which standeth in a large, but sometime far larger,
cemetery or churchyard; on the north side whereof was sometime built a fair chapel, founded by King Richard I.; some
have written that his heart was buried there under the high
altar. This chapel was confirmed and augmented by King
Edward I. Edward IV. gave license to his cousin John, Earl
of Worcester, to found there a brotherhood for a master and
brethren; and he gave to the custos of that fraternity, which
was Sir John Scot, knight, Thomas Colte, John Tate, and John
Croke, the priory of Totingbecke, and advowson of the parish
church of Streatham, in the county of Surrey, with all the
members and appurtenances, and a part of the priory of Okeborn
in Wiltshire, both priors aliens, and appointed it to be called
the king's chapel or chantry, *In capella Beatæ Mariæ de Barking*.
King Richard III. new built and founded therein a college of
priests, etc. Hamond de Lega was buried in that chapel.
Robert Tate, mayor of London, 1488,[2] and other, were there
buried. This chapel and college were suppressed and pulled
down in the year 1548, the 2nd of King Edward VI. The
ground was employed as a garden-plot during the reigns of
King Edward, Queen Mary, and part of Queen Elizabeth, till
at length a large strong frame of timber and brick was set
thereon, and employed as a store-house of merchants' goods
brought from the sea by Sir William Winter, etc.

Monuments in the parish church of Allhallows Barking, not
defaced, are these:—Sir Thomas Studinham, of Norwich diocess,
knight, 1469; Thomas Gilbart, draper and merchant of the
staple, 1483; John Bolt, merchant of the staple, 1459; Sir John
Stile, knight, draper, 1500. William Thinne, esq., one of the
clerks of the Green cloth, and master of the household to King
Henry VIII., 1546; Humfrey Monmouth, draper, one of the
sheriffs, 1535; Henry Howard, Earl of Surrey, beheaded 1546;

---

[1] " And to Berewardes lane."—*1st edition*, p. 95.
[2] " When he deceased, 1501."—*Ibid.*

Sir Richard Devereux, son and heir to the Lord Ferrers of Chartley; Richard Browne, esq. 1546; Philip Dennis, esq. 1556; Andrew Evenger, salter; William Robinson, mercer, alderman, 1552; William Armorer, cloth-worker, esquire, governor of the pages of honour, or master of the heance men, servant to Henry VIII., Edward VI., and Queen Mary, buried 1560. Besides which there be divers tombs without inscription. John Crolys and Thomas Pike, citizens of London, founded a chantry there 1388. [See Additional Notes.]

By the west end of this parish church and chapel, lieth Sidon lane, now corruptly called Sything lane, from Tower street up north to Hart street. In this Sidon lane divers fair and large houses are built, namely, one by Sir John Allen, sometime mayor of London, and of council unto King Henry VIII.; Sir Francis Walsingham, knight, principal secretary to the queen's majesty that now is, was lodged there, and so was the Earl of Essex, etc. At the north-west corner of this lane standeth a proper parish church of St. Olave, which church, together with some houses adjoining, as also others over against it in Hart street, are of the said Tower street ward. Monuments in this parish church of St. Olave be these:—Richard Cely and Robert Cely, fellmongers, principal builders and benefactors of this church; Dame Johan, wife to Sir John Zouch, 1439; John Clarenciaulx, king of arms, 1427; Thomas Sawle; Sir Richard Haddon, mercer, mayor 1512; Thomas Burnell, mercer, 1548; Thomas Morley, gentleman, 1566; Sir John Radcliffe, knight, 1568; and Dame Anne his wife, 1585; Chapone, a Florentine gentleman, 1582; Sir Hamond Vaughan, knight; George Stoddard, merchant; etc.

Then have ye out of Tower street, also on the north side, one other lane, called Marte lane, which runneth up towards the north, and is for the most part of this Tower street ward; which lane is about the third quarter thereof divided from Aldgate ward, by a chain to be drawn athwart the said lane, above the west end of Hart street. Cokedon hall, sometime at the south-west end of Marte lane, I read of.[1]

A third lane out of Tower street, on the north side, is called Mincheon lane, so called of tenements there sometime pertaining to the Minchuns or nuns of St. Helen's in Bishopsgate street. This lane is all of the said ward, except the corner house towards Fenchurch street. In this lane of old time dwelt divers strangers

[1] " Woodroffe lane towardes the Tower in this parish."—1st edition p. 97.

born of Genoa and those parts; these were commonly called galley men, as men that came up in the galleys brought up wines and other merchandises, which they landed in Thames street, at a place called Galley key; they had a certain coin of silver amongst themselves, which were halfpence of Genoa, and were called Galley halfpence; these halfpence were forbidden in the 13th of Henry IV., and again by parliament in the 4th of Henry V. It was, that if any person bring into this realm halfpence, suskinges, or dodkins, he should be punished as a thief; and he that taketh or payeth such money shall leese a hundred shillings, whereof the king shall have the one half, and he that will sue the other half. Notwithstanding, in my youth, I have seen them pass current, but with some difficulty, for that the English halfpence were then, though not so broad, somewhat thicker and stronger.

The Clothworkers' hall is in this lane. Then at the west end of Tower street have ye a little turning towards the north to a fair house sometime belonging to one named Griste, for he dwelt there in the year 1449. And Jack Cade, captain of the rebels in Kent, being by him in this his house feasted, when he had dined, like an unkind guest, robbed him of all that was there to be found worth the carriage. Next to this is one other fair house, sometime built by Angell Dune, grocer, alderman of London, since possessed by Sir John Champneis, alderman, and mayor of London. He built in this house a high tower of brick, the first that I ever heard of in any private man's house, to overlook his neighbours in this city. But this delight of his eye was punished with blindness some years before his death. Since that time, Sir Percevall Hart, a jolly courtier, and knight-harbinger to the queen, was lodged there, etc. From this house, somewhat west, is the parish church of St. Margaret's Pattens; to the which church and house, on the north side, and as far over against on the south, stretcheth the farthest west part of this ward.

And, therefore, to begin again at the east end of Tower street, on the south side, have ye Beare lane, wherein are many fair houses, and runneth down to Thames street. The next is Sporiar lane, of old time so called, but since and of later time named Water lane, because it runneth down to the water gate by the Custom house in Thames street. Then is there Hart lane for Harpe lane, which likewise runneth down into Thames street. In this Hart lane is the Bakers' hall, sometime the dwelling-house of John Chichley, chamberlain of London, who

was son to William Chichley, alderman of London, brother to
William Chichley, archdeacon of Canterburie, nephew to Robert
Chichley, mayor of London, and to Henry Chichley, archbishop
of Canterburie. This John Chichley, saith John Leland, had
twenty-four children. Sir Thomas Kirrioll, of Kent, after he
had been long prisoner in France, married Elizabeth, one of the
daughters of this Chichley, by whom he had this Chichley's
house. This Elizabeth was secondly married to Sir Ralfe
Ashton, knight-marshal, and thirdly, to Sir John Burchier, uncle
to the late Burchier, Earl of Essex, but she never had child.
Edward Poynings made part with Burchier and Elizabeth, to
have Ostenhanger in Kent, after their death, and entered into
it, they living.

In Tower street, between Hart lane and Church lane, was a
quadrant called Galley row, because galley men dwelt there.
Then have ye two lanes out of Tower street, both called Church
lanes, because one runneth down by the east end of St. Dunstan's
church, and the other by the west end of the same; out of the
west lane turneth another lane west towards St. Marie Hill, and
is called Fowle lane, which is for the most part in Tower street
ward.

This church of St. Dunstone is called, in the east, for difference
from one other of the same name in the west; it is a fair and
large church of an ancient building, and within a large churchyard; it hath a great parish of many rich merchants, and other
occupiers of divers trades, namely salters and ironmongers.

The monuments in that church be these:—In the choir, John
Kenington, parson, there buried 1374; William Islip, parson,
1382; John Kryoll, esq., brother to Thomas Kryoll, 1400;
Nicholas Bond, Thomas Barry, merchant, 1445; Robert Shelly,
esq., 1420; Robert Pepper, grocer, 1445; John Norwich,
grocer, 1390; Alice Brome, wife to John Coventry, sometime
mayor of London, 1433; William Isaack, draper, alderman,
1508; Edward Skales, merchant, 1521; John Ricroft, esq.,
sergeant of the larder to Henry VII. and Henry VIII., 1532;
Edwaters, esq., sergeant-at-arms, 1558; Sir Bartholomew
James, draper, mayor 1479, buried under a fair monument
with his lady; Ralfe Greenway, grocer, alderman, put under the
stone of Robert Pepper, 1559; Thomas Bledlow, one of the
sheriffs 1472; James Bacon, fishmonger, sheriff, 1573; Sir
Richard Champion, draper, mayor 1568; Henry Herdson,
skinner, alderman, 1555; Sir James Garnado, knight; William
Hariot, draper, mayor 1481, buried in a fair chapel by him built,

1517; John Tate, son to Sir John Tate, in the same chapel in the north wall; Sir Christopher Draper, ironmonger, mayor 1566, buried 1580. And many other worshipful personages besides, whose monuments are altogether defaced.

Now for the two Church lanes, they meeting on the south side of this church and church yard, do join in one, and running down to the Thames street, the same is called St. Dunstan's hill, at the lower end whereof the said Thames street towards the west on both sides almost to Belin's gate, but towards the east up to the water gate, by the bulwark of the Tower, is all of Tower street ward. In this street, on the Thames side, are divers large landing-places called wharfs or keys, for craneage up of wares and merchandise, as also for shipping of wares from thence to be transported. These wharfs and keys commonly bear the names of their owners, and are therefore changeable. I read, in the 26th of Henry VI., that in the parish of St. Dunstone in the east, a tenement, called Passeke's wharf, and another called Horner's key, in Thames street, were granted to William Harindon, esq. I read also, that in the 6th of Richard II., John Churchman, grocer, for the quiet of merchants, did newly build a certain house upon the key, called Wool wharf, in the Tower street ward, in the parish of Allhallows Barking, betwixt the tenement of Paule Salisberrie on the east part, and the lane called the water gate on the west, to serve for tronage, or weighing of wools in the port of London; whereupon the king granted that during the life of the said John, the aforesaid tronage should be held and kept in the said house, with easements there for the balances and weights, and a counting place for the customer, controllers, clerks, and other officers of the said tronage, together with ingress and egress to and from the same, even as was had in other places, where the said tronage was wont to be kept, and that the king should pay yearly to the said John during his life forty shillings at the terms of St. Michael and Easter, by even portions, by the hands of his customer, without any other payment to the said John, as in the indenture thereof more at large appeareth.

Near unto this Customer's key towards the east, is the said water gate, and west from it Porter's key, then Galley key, where the gallies were used to unlade and land their merchandises and wares; and that part of Thames street was therefore of some called Galley row, but more commonly Petty Wales.

On the north side, as well as on the south of this Thames street, are many fair houses large for stowage, built for merchants; but towards the east end thereof, namely, over against Galley key, Wool key, and the Custom house, there have been of old time some large buildings of stone, the ruins whereof do yet remain, but the first builders and owners of them are worn out of memory, wherefore the common people affirm Julius Cæsar to be the builder thereof, as also of the Tower itself. But thereof I have spoken already. Some are of another opinion, and that a more likely, that this great stone building was sometime the lodging appointed for the princes of Wales, when they repaired to this city, and that, therefore, the street in that part is called Petty Wales, which name remaineth there most commonly until this day, even as where the kings of Scotland were used to be lodged betwixt Charing cross and White hall, it is likewise called Scotland, and where the earls of Briton were lodged without Aldersgate, the street is called Britain street, etc.

The said building might of old time pertain to the princes of Wales, as is aforesaid, but is since turned to other use.

It is before noted of Galley key, that the galleys of Italie, and other parts, did there discharge their wines and merchandises brought to this city. It is like, therefore, that the merchants and owners procured the place to build upon for their lodgings and storehouses, as the merchants of the Haunce of Almaine were licensed to have a house, called *Gilda Teutonicorum*, the Guild hall of the Germans. Also the merchants of Burdeaux were licensed to build at the Vintry, strongly with stone, as may be yet seen, and seemeth old, though often repaired; much more cause have these buildings in Petty Wales, though as lately built, and partly of the like stone brought from Caen in Normandie, to seem old, which for many years, to wit, since the galleys left their course of landing there,[1] hath fallen to ruin, and been let out for stabling of horses, to tipplers of beer, and such like; amongst others, one Mother Mampudding (as they termed her) for many years kept this house, or a great part thereof, for victualling; and it seemeth that the builders of the hall of this house were shipwrights, and not house carpenters; for the frame thereof (being but low) is raised of certain principal posts of main timber, fixed deep in the ground, without any groundsell, boarded close round about on the inside, having none other wall from the ground to the roof, those boards not exceeding the length of a clap board, about an inch thick, every board ledging over other as in a ship or galley, nailed with ship nails called rough and clench, to wit, rough nails with broad

[1] " No gallies landed here in memorie of men living."—*Stow*.

round heads, and clenched on the other side with square plates of iron. The roof of this hall is also wrought of the like board, and nailed with rough and clench, and seemeth as it were a galley, the keel turned upwards; and I observed that no worm or rottenness is seen to have entered either board or timber of that hall, and therefore, in mine opinion, of no great antiquity.[1]

I read, in 44th of Edward III., that a hospital in the parish of Barking church was founded by Robert Denton, chaplain, for the sustentation of poor priests, and other both men and women, that were sick of the frenzy, there to remain till they were perfectly whole, and restored to good memory. Also I read, that in the 6th of Henry V. there was in the Tower ward a messuage, or great house, called Cobham's inn; and in the 37th of Henry VI, a messuage in Thames street pertaining to Richard Longvile, etc. Some of the ruins before spoken of may seem to be of the foresaid hospital, belonging peradventure to some prior alien, and so suppressed among the rest in the reign of Edward III. or Henry V., who suppressed them all. Thus much for the bounds and antiquities of this ward, wherein is noted the Tower of London, three parish churches, the custom house, and two halls of companies, to wit, the clothworkers and the bakers. This ward hath an alderman, his deputy, common councillors eight, constables thirteen, scavengers twelve, wardmote men thirteen, and a beadle; it is taxed to the fifteenth at six and twenty pounds.[1]

ALDGATE WARD

The second ward within the wall, on the east part, is called Aldgate ward, as taking name of the same gate. The principal street of this ward beginneth at Aldgate, stretching west to sometime a fair well, where now a pump is placed; from thence the way being divided into twain, the first and principal street is called Aldgate street, runneth on the south side to Lime street corner, and half that street down on the left hand is also of that ward. In the mid way on that south side, betwixt Aldgate and Lime street, is Hart horn alley, a way that goeth through into Fenchurch street over against Northumberland house. Then have ye the Bricklayers' hall, and another alley called Sprinckle

---

[1] " But I leave every man to his own judgment, and pass to other matters."—*1st edition*, p. 101.

[1] " It is taxed to the fifteene at forty-six pounds, and accounted in the Exchequer at forty-five pounds ten shillings."—*1st edition*, p. 102.

alley, now named Sugarloafe alley, of the like sign.   Then is there
a fair house, with divers tenements near adjoining, sometimes
belonging to a late dissolved priory, since possessed by Mistress
Cornewallies, widow, and her heirs, by gift of Henry VIII., in
reward of fine puddings (as it was commonly said) by her made,
wherewith she had presented him.   Such was the princely liberality of those times.   Of later time Sir Nicholas Throgmorton,
knight, was lodged there.   Then, somewhat more west is Belzettar's lane, so called of the first builder and owner thereof, now
corruptly called Billitar lane.[1]   Betwixt this Belzettar lane and
Lime street was of later time a frame of three fair houses, set up
in the year 1590, in place where before was a large garden plot,
enclosed from the high street with a brick wall, which wall being
taken down, and the ground dug deep for cellarage, there was
found right under the said brick wall another wall of stone,
with a gate arched of stone, and gates of timber to be closed
in the midst towards the street; the timber of the gates was
consumed, but the hinges of iron still remained on their staples
on both the sides.   Moreover, in that wall were square windows,
with bars of iron on either side of the gate.   This wall was
under ground about two fathoms deep, as I then esteemed it,
and seemeth to be the ruins of some houses burned in the reign
of King Stephen, when the fire began in the house of one Ale-
warde, near London stone, and consumed east to Aldgate,
whereby it appeareth how greatly the ground of this city hath
been in that place raised.   On the north side this principal street
stretcheth to the west corner of St. Andrewe's church, and then
the ward turneth towards the north by St. Marie street, on the
east side to St. Augustine's church in the wall, and so by Buries
markes again, or about by the wall to Aldgate.   The second
way from Aldgate, more towards the south, from the pump
aforesaid, is called Fenchurch street, and is of Aldgate ward
till ye come to Culver alley, on the west side of Ironmongers
hall, where sometime was a lane which went out of Fenchurch
street to the middest of Lime street, but this lane was stopped
up for suspicion of thieves that lurked there by night.   Again
to Aldgate out of the principal street, even by the gate and
wall of the city, runneth a lane south to Crowched Friers,
and then Woodroffe lane to the Tower hill, and out of this
lane west a street called Hart street, which of that ward
stretched to Sydon lane by St. Olave's church.   One other lane
more west from Aldgate goeth by Northumberland house

[1] [*See* Additional Notes.]

toward the Crossed Friers; then have ye on the same side the
north end of Mart lane and Blanch Apleton, where that ward
endeth.

Thus much for the bounds; now for monuments, or places
most ancient and notable.

I am first to begin with the late dissolved priory of the Holy
Trinity, called Christ's church, on the right hand within Aldgate.
This priory was founded by Matilda, queen, wife to Henry I.,
in the same place where Siredus sometime began to erect a
church in honour of the Cross and of St. Marie Magdalen, of
which the Dean and Chapter of Waltham were wont to receive
thirty shillings. The queen was to acquit her church thereof,
and in exchange gave unto them a mill. King Henry confirmed
her gift. This church was given to Norman, first canon regular
in all England. The said queen also gave unto the same church,
and those that served God therein, the plot of Aldgate, and the
soke thereunto belonging, with all customs so free as she had
held the same, and twenty-five pound blankes, which she had
of the city of Excester, as appeareth by her deed, wherein she
nameth the house Christ's church, and reporteth Aldgate to
be of her domains, which she granteth with two parts of the rent
of the city of Excester. Norman took upon him to be prior
of Christ's church, in the year of Christ 1108, in the parishes of
St. Mary Magdalen, St. Michael, St. Katherine, and the Blessed
Trinity, which now was made but one parish of the Holy Trinity,
and was in old time of the Holy Cross or Holy Rood parish.
The priory was built on a piece of ground in the parish of St.
Katherine towards Aldgate, which lieth in length betwixt the
King's street, by the which men go towards Aldgate, near to the
chapel of St. Michael towards the north, and containeth in
length eighty-three ells, half, quarter, and half-quarter of the
king's iron eln, and lieth in breadth, etc. The soke and ward
of Aldgate was then bounded as I have before showed. The
queen was a means also that the land and English Knighten
Guild was given unto the prior Norman: the honourable man,
Geffrey de Clinton, was a great helper therein, and obtained
that the canons might enclose the way betwixt their church
and the wall of the city, etc. This priory, in process of time,
became a very fair and large church, rich in lands and ornaments, and passed all the priories in the city of London or shire
of Middlesex; the prior whereof was an alderman of London,
to wit, of Portsoken ward.

I read, that Eustacius, the eighth prior, about the year 1264, because he would not deal with temporal matters, instituted Theobald Fitz Ivonis, alderman of Portsoken ward under him, and that William Rising, prior of Christ's church, was sworn alderman of the said Portsoken ward in the 1st of Richard II. These priors have sitten and ridden amongst the aldermen of London, in livery like unto them, saving that his habit was in shape of a spiritual person, as I myself have seen in my childhood; at which time the prior kept a most bountiful house of meat and drink, both for rich and poor, as well within the house as at the gates, to all comers, according to their estates.

These were the monuments in this church:—Sir Robert Turke, and Dame Alice his wife; John Tirell, esquire; Simon Kempe, esquire; James Manthorpe, esquire; John Ascue, esquire; Thomas Fauset, of Scalset, esquire; John Kempe, gentleman; Robert Chirwide, esquire; Sir John Heningham, and Dame Isabel his wife; Dame Agnes, wife first to Sir William Bardolph, and then to Sir Thomas Mortimer; John Ashfield, esquire; Sir John Dedham, knight; Sir Ambrose Charcam; Joan, wife to Thomas Nuck, gentleman; John Husse, esquire; John Beringham, esquire; Thomas Goodwine, esquire; Ralph Walles, esquire; Dame Margaret, daughter to Sir Ralph Chevie, wife to Sir John Barkeley, to Sir Thomas Barnes, and to Sir W. Bursire; William Roofe; Simon Francis; John Breton, esquire; Helling, esquire; John Malwen and his wife; Anthonie Wels, son to John Wels; Nicholas de Avesey, and Margarie his wife; Anthonie, son to John Milles; Baldwine, son to King Stephen, and Mathilde, daughter to King Stephen, wife to the Earl of Meulan; Henry Fitzalwine, mayor of London, 1213; Geffrey Mandevile, 1215; and many other. But to conclude of this priory: King Henry VIII., minding to reward Sir Thomas Audley, speaker of the parliament against Cardinal Wolsey, as ye may read in Hall, sent for the prior, commending him for his hospitality, promised him preferment, as a man worthy of a far greater dignity, which promise surely he performed, and compounded with him, though in what sort I never heard, so that the prior surrendered all that priory, with the appurtenances, to the king, in the month of July, in the year 1531, the 23rd of the said king's reign. The canons were sent to other houses of the same order, and the priory, with the appurtenances, King Henry gave to Sir Thomas Audley, newly knighted, and after made lord chancellor.

Sir Thomas Audley offered the great church of this priory, with a ring of nine bells well tuned (whereof four the greatest

were since sold to the parish of Stebunhith, and the five lesser
to the parish of St. Stephen in Coleman street) to the parishioners
of St. Katherine Christ church, in exchange for their small parish
church, minding to have pulled it down, and to have built there
towards the street; but the parishioners having doubts in their
heads of after-claps, refused the offer. Then was the priory
church and steeple proffered to whomsoever would take it down,
and carry it from the ground, but no man would undertake the
offer; whereupon Sir Thomas Audley was fain to be at more
charges than could be made of the stones, timber, lead, iron, etc.
For the workmen, with great labour, beginning at the top,
loosed stone from stone, and threw them down, whereby the
most part of them were broken, and few remained whole; and
those were sold very cheap, for all the buildings then made
about the city were of brick and timber. At that time any man
in the city might have a cart-load of hard stone for paving
brought to his door for six pence or seven pence, with the
carriage. The said Thomas Lord Audley built and dwelt on this
priory during his life, and died there in the year 1544; since the
which time the said priory came by marriage of the Lord
Audley's daughter and heir unto Thomas, late Duke of Norfolk,
and was then called the Duke's place.

The parish church of St. Katherine standeth in the cemetery
of the late dissolved priory of the Holy Trinity, and is therefore
called St. Katherine Christ church. This church seemeth to be
very old; since the building whereof the high street hath been
so often raised by pavements, that now men are fain to descend
into the said church by divers steps, seven in number. But the
steeple, or bell-tower thereof, hath been lately built, to wit, about
the year 1504; for Sir John Percivall, merchant-tailor, then
deceasing, gave money towards the building thereof. There
be the monuments of Sir Thomas Fleming, knight of Rowles,
in Essex, and Margaret his wife, 1464; Roger Marshall, esquire;
Jane Horne, wife to Roger Marshall; William Multon, alias
Burdeaux, herald; John Goad, esquire, and Joan his wife;
Beatrix, daughter to William Browne; Thomas Multon, esquire,
son to Burdeaux, herald; John Chitcroft, esquire; John Wake-
fielde, esquire; William Criswicke; Anne and Sewch, daughters
to Ralph Shirley, esquire; Sir John Rainsford, knight of Essex;
Sir Nicholas Throkmorton, chief butler of England, one of the
chamberlains of the exchequer, ambassador, etc., 1570, and
other.

At the north-west corner of this ward, in the said high street,

standeth the fair and beautiful parish church of St. Andrew the
Apostle; with an addition, to be known from other churches
of that name, of the knape or undershaft; and so called St.
Andrew Undershaft, because that of old time, every year on
May-day in the morning, it was used, that an high or long shaft
or May-pole, was set up there, in the midst of the street, before
the south side of the said church; which shaft when it was
set on end and fixed in the ground, was higher than the church
steeple. Geffrey Chaucer, writing of a vain boaster, hath these
words, meaning of the said shaft:

> " Right well aloft, and high ye beare your heade,
> The weather cocke, with flying, as ye would kill,
> When ye be stuffed, bet of wine, then brede,
> Then looke ye, when your wombe doth fill,
> As ye would beare the great shaft of Cornehill,
> Lord, so merrily crowdeth then your croke,
> That all the streete may heare your body cloke." [1]

This shaft was not raised at any time since evil May-day (so
called of an insurrection made by apprentices and other young
persons against aliens in the year 1517); but the said shaft was
laid along over the doors, and under the pentises of one row
of houses and alley gate, called of the shaft Shaft alley (being
of the possessions of Rochester bridge), in the ward of Lime
street. It was there, I say, hung on iron hooks many years,
till the third of King Edward VI., that one Sir Stephen, curate
of St. Katherine Christ's church, preaching at Paules cross, said
there that this shaft was made an idol, by naming the church
of St. Andrew with the addition of " under that shaft: " he
persuaded therefore that the names of churches might be
altered; also that the names of days in the week might be
changed; the fish days to be kept any days except Friday and
Saturday, and the Lent any time, save only betwixt Shrovetide
and Easter. I have oft times seen this man, forsaking the
pulpit of his said parish church, preach out of a high elm-tree [2]
in the midst of the churchyard, and then entering the church,
forsaking the altar, to have sung his high mass in English upon
a tomb of the dead towards the north. I heard his sermon at
Paules cross, and I saw the effect that followed; for in the
afternoon of that present Sunday, the neighbours and tenants
to the said bridge, over whose doors the said shaft had lain,
after they had well dined, to make themselves strong, gathered
more help, and with great labour raising the shaft from the

---

[1] [*See* Additional Notes.]
[2] " The said elm-tree, his preaching place, is lately taken down."—*Stow.*

hooks, whereon it had rested two-and-thirty years, they sawed it in pieces, every man taking for his share so much as had lain over his door and stall, the length of his house; and they of the alley divided among them so much as had lain over their alley gate. Thus was this idol (as he [1] termed it) mangled, and after burned.

Soon after was there a commotion of the commons in Norfolk, Suffolk, Essex, and other shires; by means whereof, straight orders being taken for the suppression of rumours, divers persons were apprehended and executed by martial law; amongst the which the bailiff of Romfort, in Essex, was one, a man very well beloved: he was early in the morning of Mary Magdalen's day, then kept holiday, brought by the sheriffs of London and the knight-marshal to the well within Aldgate, there to be executed upon a gibbet set up that morning, where, being on the ladder, he had words to this effect: " Good people, I am come hither to die, but know not for what offence, except for words by me spoken yesternight to Sir Stephen, curate and preacher of this parish, which were these: He asked me, ' What news in the country? ' I answered, ' Heavy news.' ' Why? ' quoth he. ' It is said,' quoth I, ' that many men be up in Essex, but, thanks be to God, all is in good quiet about us: ' and this was all, as God be my judge," etc. Upon these words of the prisoner, Sir Stephen, to avoid reproach of the people, left the city, and was never heard of since amongst them to my knowledge. I heard the words of the prisoner, for he was executed upon the pavement of my door where I then kept house. Thus much by digression: now again to the parish church of St. Andrew Under-shaft, for it still retaineth the name, which hath been new built by the parishioners there since the year 1520; every man putting to his helping hand, some with their purses, other with their bodies. Steven Gennings, merchant-tailor, sometime mayor of London, caused at his charges to be built [2] the whole north side of the great middle aisle, both of the body and choir, as appeareth by his arms over every pillar graven, and also the north isle, which he roofed with timber and sealed; also the whole south side of the church was glazed, and the pews in the south chapel made of his costs, as appeareth in every window, and upon the said pews. He deceased in the year 1524, and was buried in the Grey friars church. John Kerkbie, merchant-tailor, sometime one of the sheriffs, John Garlande, merchant-

---

[1] " As he, poore man, tearmed it."—*1st edition*, p. 108.
[2] " The one halfe, to wit."—*1st edition*, p. 109.

tailor, and Nicholas Levison, mercer, executor to Garlande, were great benefactors to this work; which was finished to the glazing in the year 1529, and fully finished 1532. Buried in this church:[1] Philip Malpas, one of the sheriffs, 1439; Sir Robert Dennie, knight, and after him Thomas Dennie, his son, in the year 1421; Thomas Stokes, gentleman, grocer, 1496. In the new church: John Nichell, merchant-tailor, 1537; William Draper, esquire, 1537; Isabell and Margaret, his wives; Nicholas Levison, mercer, one of the sheriffs, 1534; John Gerrarde, woolman, merchant of the staple, 1456; Henry Man, doctor of divinity, bishop of Man, 1550; Stephen Kyrton, merchant-tailor, alderman, 1553; David Woodroffe, haberdasher, one of the sheriffs, 1554; Stephen Woodroffe, his son, gave one hundred pounds in money, for the which the poor of that parish receive two shillings in bread weekly for ever; Sir Thomas Offley, merchant-tailor, mayor, 1556; he bequeathed the one half of all his goods to charitable actions, but the parish received little benefit thereby; Thomas Starkey, skinner, one of the sheriffs, 1578; Hugh Offley, leatherseller, one of the sheriffs, 1588; William Hanbury, baker.

Now down St. Mary street, by the west end of the church towards the north, stand divers fair houses for merchants and other; namely, one fair great house, built by Sir William Pickering the father, possessed by Sir William his son, and since by Sir Edward Wootton of Kent. North from this place is the Fletchers' hall, and so down to the corner of that street, over against London wall, and again eastwards to a fair house lately new built, partly by Master Robert Beale, one of the clerks of the council.

Then come you to the Papey, a proper house, wherein sometime was kept a fraternity or brotherhood of St. Charity and St. John Evangelist, called the Papey, for poor impotent priests (for in some language priests are called papes), founded in the year 1430 by William Oliver,[2] William Barnabie, and John Stafford, chaplains or chantry priests in London, for a master, two wardens, etc., chaplains, chantry priests, conducts, and other brethren and sisters, that should be admitted into the church of St. Augustine Papey in the wall. The brethren of this house becoming lame, or otherwise into great poverty, were here relieved, as to have chambers, with certain allowance of bread, drink, and coal, and one old man and his wife to see

---

[1] "The monuments of the dead, buried in this church, are these."—1st edition, p. 109.   [2] [See Additional Notes.]

them served and to keep the house clean. This brotherhood, among others, was suppressed in the reign of Edward VI.; since the which time in this house hath been lodged Master Moris of Essex; Sir Francis Walsingham, principal secretary to her majesty; Master Barret of Essex, etc.

Then next is one great house, large of rooms, fair courts, and garden-plots; sometimes pertaining to the Bassets, since that to the abbots of Bury in Suffolk, and therefore called Buries markes, corruptly Bevis markes, and since the dissolution of the abbey of Bury, to Thomas Henage the father, and to Sir Thomas his son. Then next unto it is the before-spoken priory of the Holy Trinity; to wit, the west and north part thereof, which stretcheth up to Aldgate, where we first began.

Now in the second way from Aldgate, more toward the south from the well or pump aforesaid, lieth Fenne church street; on the right hand whereof, somewhat west from the south end of Belzetter's lane is the Ironmongers' hall; which company was incorporated in the 3rd of Edward IV. Richard Fleming was their first master; Nicholas Marshall and Richard Cox were custos, or wardens. And on the left hand, or south side, even by the gate and wall of the city, runneth down a lane to the Tower hill; the south part whereof is called Woodroffe lane, and out of this lane toward the west a street called Hart street. In this street, at the south-east corner thereof, sometime stood one house of Crouched (or crossed) friars, founded by Ralph Hosiar and William Sabernes about the year 1298. Stephen, the tenth prior of the Holy Trinity, in London granted there tenements for 13s. 8d. by the year unto the said Ralph Hosiar and William Sabernes, who afterwards became friars of St. Crosse; Adam was the first prior of that house. These friars founded their house in place of certain tenements purchased of Richard Wimbush, the twelfth prior of the Holy Trinity, in the year 1319, which was confirmed by Edward III. the 17th of his reign, valued at £52 13s. 4d., surrendered the twelfth of November, the 30th of Henry VIII. In this house was buried Master John Tirres; Nicholas, the son of William Kyriell, esquire; Sir Thomas Mellington, baron of Wemesse, and Dame Elizabeth his wife, daughter and heir of William Botelar, baron of Wome; Robert Mellington, esquire, and Elizabeth his wife, daughter to Ferreis of Ousley; Henry Lovell, son to William Lord Lovell; Dame Isabel, wife to William Edwarde, mayor of London, 1471; William Narborough, and Dame Elizabeth his wife; William Narborough, and Dame Beatrix his wife; William

Brosked, esquire; William Bowes; Lionel Mollington, esquire, son of Robert Mollington; Nicholas Couderow, and Elizabeth his wife; Sir John Stratford, knight; Sir Thomas Asseldy, knight, clerk of the crown, sub-marshal of England, and justice of the shire of Middlesex; John Rest, grocer, mayor of London, 1516; Sir John Skevington, knight, merchant-tailor, sheriff, 1520; Sir John Milborne, draper, mayor in the year 1520, was buried there, but removed since to St. Edmondes in Lombard street; Sir Rice Grifith, beheaded on the Tower hill, 1531.

In place of this church is now a carpenters' yard, a tennis court, and such like; the friars' hall was made a glass-house, or house wherein was made glass of divers sorts to drink in; which house in the year 1575, on the 4th of September, burst out into a terrible fire, where being practised all means possible to quench, notwithstanding as the same house in a small time before had consumed a great quantity of wood by making of glasses, now itself having within it about forty thousand billets of wood, was all consumed to the stone walls, which nevertheless greatly hindered the fire from spreading any further.

Adjoining unto this friars' church, by the east end thereof in Woodroffe lane towards the Tower hill, are certain proper alms houses, fourteen in number, built of brick and timber, founded by Sir John Milborne, draper, sometime mayor, 1521, wherein he placed thirteen aged poor men and their wives, if they have wives: these have their dwellings rent free, and 2s. 4d. the piece, the first day of every month, for ever. One also is to have his house over the gate, and 4s. every month: more, he appointed every Sunday for ever, thirteen penny loaves of white bread, to be given in the parish church of St. Edmonde in Lombard street, to thirteen poor people of that parish; and the like thirteen loaves to be given in the parish church of St. Michael upon Cornhill, and in either parish every year one load of chare coal, of thirty sacks in the load; and this gift to be continued for ever: for performance whereof, by the master and wardens of the drapers in London, he assured unto them and their successors twenty-three messuages and tenements, and eighteen garden-plots, in the parish of St. Olave in Hart street; with proviso, that if they perform not those points [1] above-mentioned, the said tenements and gardens to remain to the mayor and commonalty of the city of London.

Next to these alms houses is the Lord Lumley's house, built

---

[1] " These poyntes not performed. The Drapers have unlawfully solde these tenements and garden plots, and the poore be wronged."—*Stow*.

in the time of King Henry VIII. by Sir Thomas Wiat the father, upon one plot of ground of late pertaining to the foresaid Crossed friars, where part of their house stood: and this is the farthest part of Aldgate ward towards the south, and joineth to the Tower hill. The other side of that line, over against the Lord Lumley's house, on the wall side of the city, is now for the most part (or altogether) built even to Aldgate.

Then have you on the south side of Fenchurch street, over against the well or pump, amongst other fair and large built houses, one that sometime belonged to the prior of Monte Joves, or Monastery Cornute, a cell to Monte Joves beyond the seas, in Essex: it was the prior's inn, when he repaired to this city. Then a lane that leadeth down by Northumberland house towards the Crossed friars, as is afore showed.

This Northumberland house, in the parish of St. Katherine Colman, belonged to Henry Percie, Earl of Northumberland, in the 33rd of Henry VI., but of late being left by the earls, the gardens thereof were made into bowling alleys, and other parts into dicing houses, common to all comers for their money, there to bowle and hazard; but now of late so many bowling alleys, and other houses for unlawful gaming, hath been raised in other parts of the city and suburbs, that this their ancient and only patron of misrule, is left and forsaken of her gamesters, and therefore turned into a number of great rents, small cottages, for strangers and others.

At the east end of this lane, in the way from Aldgate toward the Crossed friars, of old time were certain tenements called the poor Jurie, of Jews dwelling there.

Next unto this Northumberland house is the parish church of St. Katherine, called Coleman; which addition of Coleman was taken of a great haw-yard, or garden, of old time called Coleman haw, in the parish of the Trinity, now called Christ's church, and in the parish of St. Katherine and All Saints called Coleman church.

Then have you Blanch Apleton; whereof I read, in the 13th of Edward I., that a lane behind the said Blanch Apleton was granted by the king to be inclosed and shut up. This Blanch Apleton was a manor belonging to Sir Thomas Roos of Hamelake, knight, the 7th of Richard II., standing at the north-east corner of Mart lane, so called of a privilege sometime enjoined to keep a mart there, long since discontinued, and therefore forgotten, so as nothing remaineth for memory but the name of Mart lane, and that corruptly termed Marke lane. I read that, in the third of Edward IV., all basket-makers, wire-drawers, and other foreigners, were permitted to have shops in this manor of Blanch Apleton, and not elsewhere, within this city or suburbs thereof; and this also being the farthest west part of this ward on that south side, I leave it, with three parish churches, St Katherine Christ church, St. Andrew Undershaft, and St. Katherine Colemans; and three halls of companies, the Bricklayers' hall, the Fletchers' hall, and the Ironmongers' hall. It hath an alderman, his deputy, common councillors six, constables six, scavengers nine, wardmote men for inquest eighteen, and a beadle. It is taxed to the fifteen in London at five pounds.[1]

LIME STREET WARD

The next is Lime street ward, and taketh the name of Lime street of making or selling of lime there (as is supposed); the east side of this Lime street, from the north corner thereof to the midst, is of Aldgate ward, as is aforesaid; the west side, for the most part from the said north corner, southward, is of this Lime street ward; the south end on both sides is of Langborne ward; the body of this Lime street ward is of the high street called Cornehill street, which stretcheth from Lime street on the south side to the west corner of Leaden hall, and on the north side from the south-west corner of St. Mary street to another corner over against Leaden hall. Now for St. Mary street; the west side thereof is of this Lime street ward, and also the street which runneth by the north end of this St. Mary street, on both sides, from thence west to an house called the Wrestlers, a sign so called, almost to Bishopsgate. And these are the bounds of this small ward.

Monuments, or places notable, in this ward be these:—In Lime street are divers fair houses for merchants and others; there was sometime a mansion-house of the kings, called the King's Artirie, whereof I find record in the 14th of Edward I., but now grown out of knowledge. I read also of another great house in the west side of Lime street, having a chapel on the south and a garden on the west, then belonging to the Lord Nevill, which garden is now called the Green yard of the Leaden hall. This house, in the 9th of Richard II., pertained to Sir Simon Burley, and Sir John Burley his brother; and of late the

---

[1] " It is taxed to the fifteene in London at 46 *li*., and accounted in the Exchequer to £45 10s."—*1st edition*, p. 113.

said house was taken down, and the forefront thereof new built of timber by Hugh Offley, alderman. At the north-west corner of Lime street was of old time one great messuage called Benbrige's inn; Ralph Holland, draper, about the year 1452 gave it to John Gill, master, and to the wardens and fraternity of tailors and linen-armourers of St. John Baptist in London, and to their successors for ever. They did set up in place thereof a fair large frame of timber, containing in the high street one great house, and before it to the corner of Lime street three other tenements, the corner house being the largest, and then down Lime street divers proper tenements; all which the merchant-tailors, in the reign of Edward VI., sold to Stephen Kirton, merchant-tailor and alderman: he gave, with his daughter Grisild, to Nicholas Woodroffe the said great house, with two tenements before it, in lieu of a hundred pounds, and made it up in money £366 13s. 4d. This worshipful man, and the gentlewoman his widow after him, kept those houses down Lime street in good reparations, never put out but one tenant, took no fines, nor raised rents of them, which was ten shillings the piece yearly: but whether that favour did overlive her funeral, the tenants now can best declare the contrary.

Next unto this, on the high street, was the Lord Sowche's messuage or tenement, and other; in place whereof, Richard Wethell, merchant-tailor, built a fair house, with a high tower, the second in number, and first of timber, that ever I learnt to have been built to overlook neighbours in this city.

This Richard, then a young man, became in a short time so tormented with gouts in his joints, of the hands and legs, that he could neither feed himself nor go further than he was led; much less was he able to climb and take the pleasure of the height of his tower. Then is there another fair house, built by Stephen Kirton, alderman; Alderman Lee doth now possess it, and again new buildeth it.

Then is there a fair house of old time called the Green gate; by which name one Michael Pistoy Lumbard held it, with a tenement and nine shops in the reign of Richard II., who in the 15th of his reign gave it to Roger Crophull, and Thomas Bromeflet, esquires, by the name of the Green gate, in the parish of St. Andrew upon Cornhill, in Lime street ward; since the which time Philip Malpas, sometime alderman, and one of the sheriffs, dwelt therein, and was there robbed and spoiled of his goods to a great value by Jack Cade, and other rebels, in the year 1449. Afterwards, in the reign of Henry VII., it was seized into the

king's hands, and then granted, first, unto John Alston, after
that unto William de la Rivers, and since by Henry VIII. to
John Mutas, a Picarde or Frenchman, who dwelt there, and
harboured in his house many Frenchmen, that kalendred
wolsteds, and did other things contrary to the franchises of the
citizens; wherefore on evil May-day, which was in the year
1517, the apprentices and other spoiled his house; and if they
could have found Mutas, they would have stricken off his head.
Sir Peter Mutas, son to the said John Mutas, sold this house to
David Woodroffe, alderman, whose son, Sir Nicholas Woodroffe,
alderman, sold it over to John Moore, alderman, that now
possesseth it.

Next is a house called the Leaden porch, lately divided into
two tenements; whereof one is a tavern, and then one other
house for a merchant, likewise called the Leaden porch, but
now turned to a cook's house. Next is a fair house and a large,
wherein divers mayoralties have been kept, whereof twain in
my remembrance; to wit, Sir William Bowyar and Sir Henry
Huberthorne.

The next is Leaden hall, of which I read, that in the year
1309 it belonged to Sir Hugh Nevill, knight, and that the Lady
Alice his widow made a feoffment thereof, by the name of
Leaden hall, with the advowsons of the church of St. Peter upon
Cornhill, and other churches, to Richard, Earl of Arundell and
Surrey, 1362. More, in the year 1380, Alice Nevill, widow to
Sir John Nevill, knight, of Essex, confirmed to Thomas Gogshall
and others the said manor of Leaden hall, the advowsons, etc.
In the year 1384, Humfrey de Bohun, Earl of Hereford, had the
said manor. And in the year 1408, Robert Rikeden, of Essex,
and Margaret his wife, confirmed to Richard Whittington, and
other citizens of London, the said manor of Leaden hall, with
the appurtenances, the advowsons of St. Peter's church, St.
Margaret's Pattens, etc. And in the year 1411, the said Whittington and other confirmed the same to the mayor and commonalty of London, whereby it came to the possession of the
city. Then in the year 1443, the 21st of Henry VI., John
Hatherley, mayor, purchased license of the said king to
take up two hundred fother of lead, for the building of
water conduits, a common granary, and the cross in West
Cheape, more richly, for the honour of the city. In the year
next following, the parson and parish of St. Dunston, in
the east of London, seeing the famous and mighty man (for
the words be in the grant, *cum nobilis et potens vir*), Simon Eyre,

citizen of London, among other his works of piety, effectually
determined to erect and build a certain granary upon the soil
of the same city at Leaden hall, of his own charges, for the
common utility of the said city, to the amplifying and enlarging
of the said granary, granted to Henry Frowicke, then mayor,
the aldermen and commonalty, and their successors for ever,
all their tenements, with the appurtenances, sometime called
the Horsemill, in Grasse street, for the annual rent of four
pounds, etc. Also, certain evidences of an alley and tenements
pertaining to the Horsemill adjoining to the said Leaden hall
in Grasse street, given by William Kingstone, fishmonger, unto
the parish church of St. Peter upon Cornehill, do specify the
said granary to be built by the said honourable and famous
merchant, Simon Eyre, sometime an upholsterer, and then a
draper, in the year 1419. He built it of squared stone, in form
as now it showeth, with a fair and large chapel in the east side
of the quadrant, over the porch of which he caused to be written,
Dextra Domini exaltavit me (The Lord's right hand exalted me).
Within the said church, on the north wall, was written, *Honor-
andus famosus mercator Simon Eyre hujus operis*, etc. In
English thus:—" The honourable and famous merchant, Simon
Eyre, founder of this work, once mayor of this city, citizen and
draper of the same, departed out of this life, the 18th day of
September, the year from the Incarnation of Christ 1459, and
the 38th year of the reign of King Henry VI." He was buried
in the parish church of St. Mary Woolnoth, in Lombard street:
he gave by his testament, which I have read, to be distributed
to all prisons in London, or within a mile of that city, somewhat
to relieve them. More, he gave two thousand marks, upon a
condition, which not performed, was then to be distributed to
maids' marriages, and other deeds of charity; he also gave three
thousand marks to the drapers, upon condition they should,
within one year after his decease, establish perpetually a master
or warden, five secular priests, six clerks, and two choristers,
to sing daily Divine service by note for ever, in his chapel of the
Leaden hall; also,[1] one master, with an usher, for grammar, one
master for writing, and the third for song, with housing there
newly built for them for ever; the master to have for his salary
ten pounds, and every other priest eight pounds, every other
clerk five pounds six shillings and eight pence, and every other
chorister five marks; and if the drapers refused this to do,
within one year after his decease, then the three thousand

[1] " Three schoolemaisters, with an usher, to wit."—*1st edition*, p. 118.

marks to remain to the prior and convent of Christ's church in London, with condition to establish, as is aforesaid, within two years after his decease; and if they refused, then the three thousand marks to be disposed by his executors, as they best could devise, in works of charity. Thus much for his testament, not performed by establishing of Divine service in his chapel, or free schools for scholars; neither how the stock of three thousand marks, or rather five thousand marks, was employed by his executors, could I ever learn. He left issue, Thomas, who had issue, Thomas, etc. True it is, that in one year, 1464, the 3rd of Edward IV., it was agreed by the mayor, aldermen, and commonalty of London, that notwithstanding the king's letters patent, lately before granted unto them, touching the tronage or weighing of wares to be holden at the Leaden hall, yet suit should be made to the king for new letters patent to be granted to the mayor of the staple for the tronage of wools to be holden there, and order to be taken by the discretion of Thomas Cooke, then mayor, the counsel of the city, Geffrey Filding, then mayor of the staple at Westminster, and of the king's council, what should be paid to the mayor and aldermen of the city, for the laying and housing of the wools there, that so they might be brought forth and weighed, etc.

Touching the chapel there, I find, that in the year 1466, by license obtained of King Edward IV., in the 6th of his reign, a fraternity of the Trinity, of sixty priests, besides other brethren and sisters, in the same chapel, was founded by William Rouse, John Risbie, and Thomas Ashby priests, some of the which sixty priests, every market-day in the forenoon, did celebrate Divine service there to such market-people as repaired to prayer; and once every year they met all together and had solemn service, with procession of the brethren and sisters. This foundation was in the year 1512, by a common council, confirmed to the sixty Trinity priests, and to their successors, at the will of the mayor and commonalty.

In the year 1484, a great fire happened upon this Leaden hall, by what casualty I know not, but much housing was there destroyed, with all the stocks for guns, and other provision belonging to the city, which was a great loss, and no less charge to be repaired by them.

In the year 1503, the 18th of Henry VII., a request was made by the commons of the city, concerning the usage of the said Leaden hall, in form as followeth:—" Please it, the lord mayor, and common council, to enact, that all Frenchmen bringing canvass, linen cloth, and other wares to be sold, and all foreigners bringing wolsteds, sayes, staimus, coverings, nails, iron work, or any other wares, and also all manner of foreigners bringing lead to the city to be sold, shall bring all such their wares aforesaid to the open market of the Leaden hall, there and no where else to be sold and uttered, like as of old time it hath been used, upon pain of forfeiture of all the said wares showed or sold in any other place than aforesaid; the show of the said wares to be made three days in the week, that is to say, Monday, Tuesday, and Wednesday; it is also thought reasonable that the common beam be kept from henceforth in the Leaden hall, and the farmer to pay therefore reasonable rent to the chamber; for better it is that the chamber have advantage thereby than a foreign person; and also the said Leaden hall, which is more chargeable now by half than profitable, shall better bear out the charges thereof; also the common beam for wool at Leaden hall, may yearly pay a rent to the chamber of London, toward supportation and charges of the same place; for reason it is, that a common office, occupied upon a common ground, bear a charge to the use of the commonalty; also, that foreigners bringing wools, felts, or any other merchandises or wares to Leaden hall, to be kept there for the sale and market, may pay more largely for the keeping of their goods than free men." Thus much for the request of the commons at this time.

Now to set down some proof that the said hall hath been employed and used as a granary for corn and grain (as the same was first appointed), leaving all former examples, this one may suffice: Roger Achley, mayor of London in the year 1512, the 3rd of Henry VIII., when the said mayor entered the mayoralty, there was not found one hundred quarters of wheat in all the garners of the city, either within the liberties, or near adjoining; through the which scarcity, when the carts of Stratford came laden with bread to the city (as they had been accustomed) there was such press about them, that one man was ready to destroy another, in striving to be served for their money. But this scarcity did not last long; for the mayor in short time made such provision of wheat, that the bakers, both of London and Stratford, were weary of taking it up, and were forced to take up much more than they would, and for the rest the mayor laid out the money, and stored it up in Leaden hall, and other garners of the city. This mayor also kept the market so well, that he would be at the Leaden hall by four o'clock in the summer's mornings; and from thence he went to other markets, to the great comfort of the citizens.

I read also that in the year 1528, the 20th of Henry VIII., surveyors were appointed to view the garners of the city, namely, the Bridgehouse and the Leaden hall, how they were stored of grain for the service of the city. And because I have here before spoken of the bread carts coming from Stratford at the Bow, ye shall understand that of old time the bakers of bread at Stratford were allowed to bring daily (except Sabbath and principal feasts) divers long carts laden with bread, the same being two ounces in the penny wheat loaf heavier than the penny wheat loaf baked in the city, the same to be sold in Cheape, three or four carts standing there, between Gutheron's lane and Fauster's lane end, one cart on Cornhill, by the conduit, and one other in Grasse street. And I have read, that in the 4th year of Edward II., Richard Reffeham being mayor, a baker named John of Stratforde, for making bread less than the assize, was with a fool's hood on his head, and loaves of bread about his neck, drawn on a hurdle through the streets of this city. Moreover, in the 44th of Edward III., John Chichester being mayor of London, I read in the *Visions of Pierce Plowman*, a book so called, as followeth:

> There was a careful comune,
> Whan no carte come to toune
> With bake bred fro Stretforth;
> Tho gan beggeres wepe,
> And werkmen were agaste a litel:
> This wil be thoughte longe.
> In the date of owre drighte,
> In a drye Apprile,
> A thousand and thre hondreth
> Tweis thretty and ten,
> My wafres there were gesen
> Whan Chichestre was maire." [1]

I read also in the 20th of Henry VIII., Sir James Spencer being mayor, six bakers of Stratford were amerced in the Guildhall of London, for baking under the size appointed. These bakers of Stratford left serving of this city, I know not upon what occasion, about thirty years since.

[1] This passage is printed very incorrectly, and as prose, by Stow.

In the year 1519 a petition was exhibited by the commons to the common council, and was by them allowed, concerning the Leaden hall, how they would have it used, viz. "Meekly beseeching, showeth unto your good lordship and masterships, divers citizens of this city, which under correction think, that the great place called the Leaden hall should, nor ought not to be letten to farm to any person or persons, and in especial to any fellowship or company incorporate, to have and hold the same hall for term of years, for such inconveniences as thereby may ensue, and come to the hurt of the common weal of the said city in time to come, as somewhat more largely may appear in the articles following.

"First, If any assembly or hasty gathering of the commons of the said city, for suppressing or subduing of misruled people within the said city, hereafter shall happen to be called or commanded by the mayor, aldermen, and other governors and councillors of the said city for the time being, there is none so convenient, meet, and necessary a place, to assemble them in, within the said city, as the said Leaden hall, both for largeness of room, and their sure defence in time of their counselling together about the premises. Also, in that place hath been used the artillery, guns, and other armours of the said city, to be safely kept in a readiness for the safeguard, wealth, and defence of the said city, to be had and occupied at times when need required. As also the store of timber for the necessary reparations of the tenements belonging to the chamber of the said city, there commonly hath been kept. Item, If any triumph or nobleness were to be done, or shown by the commonalty of the city, for the honour of our sovereign lord the king and realm, and for the worship of the said city, the said Leaden hall is most meet and convenient place to prepare and order the said triumph therein, and from thence to issue forth to the places therefore appointed. Item, at any largess or dole of any money made unto the poor people of this city, it hath been used to be done and given in the said Leaden hall, for that the said place is most meet therefore. Item, the honourable father, that was maker of the said hall, had a special will, intent, and mind, that (as it is commonly said) the market men and women that came to the city with victuals and other things, should have their free standing within the said Leaden hall in wet weather, to keep themselves and their wares dry, and thereby to encourage them, and all other, to have the better will and desire the more plenteously to resort to the said city, to victual the same. And if the said hall should be letten to farm, the will of the said honourable father should never be fulfilled nor take effect. Item, if the said place, which is the chief fortress, and most necessary place within all the city, for the tuition and safeguard of the same, should be letten to farm out of the hands of the chief heads of the same city, and especially to another body politic, it might at length by likelihood be occasion of discord and debate between the said bodies politic, which God defend.

" For these and many other great and reasonable causes, which hereafter shall be showed to this honourable court, your said beseechers think it much necessary that the said hall be still in the hands of this city, and to be surely kept by sad and discreet officers, in such wise, that it may alway be ready to be used and occupied for the common weal of the said city when need shall require, and in no wise to be letten to any body politic."

Thus much for the petition.

About the year 1534, great means were made about the Leaden hall to have the same made a burse, for the assembly of merchants, as they had been accustomed in Lombard street; many common councils were called to that end: but in the year 1535, John Champneys being mayor, it was fully concluded that the burse should remain in Lombard street as afore, and Leaden hall no more to be spoken of concerning that matter.

The use of Leaden hall in my youth was thus:—In a part of the north quadrant, on the east side of the north gate, were the common beams for weighing of wool and other wares, as had been accustomed ; on the west side the gate were the scales to weight meal; the other three sides were reserved for the most part to the making and resting of the pageants showed at Midsummer in the watch; the remnant of the sides and quadrant was employed for the stowage of wool sacks, but not closed up; the lofts above were partly used by the painters in working for the decking of pageants and other devices, for beautifying of the watch and watchmen; the residue of the lofts were letten out to merchants, the wool winders and packers therein to wind and pack their wools. And thus much for Leaden hall may suffice.

Now on the north of Lime street ward in the high street are divers fair houses for merchants, and proper tenements for artificers, with an alley also called Shaft alley, of the shaft or May-pole sometime resting over the gate thereof, as I have declared in Aldgate ward. In the year 1576, partly at the charges of the parish of St. Andrew, and partly at the charges of the chamber of London, a water-pump was raised in Lime street ward, near unto Lime street corner; for the placing of the which pump, having broken up the ground, they were forced to dig more than two fathom deep [1] before they came to any main ground, where they found a hearth made of Britain, or rather Roman tile [2] every tile half a yard square, and about two inches thick; they found coal lying there also (for that lying whole will never consume); then digging one fathom into the main, they found water sufficient, made their prall, and set up the pump; which pump, with oft repairing and great charges to the parish, continued not four-and-twenty years, but being rotted, was taken up and a new set in place in the year 1600. Thus much for the high street.

In St. Marie street had ye of old time a parish church of St. Marie the Virgin, St. Ursula, and the eleven thousand Virgins, which church was commonly called St. Marie at the Axe, of the sign of an axe, over against the east end thereof, or St. Marie Pellipar, of a plot of ground lying on the north side thereof, pertaining to the Skinners in London. This parish, about the year 1565, was united to the parish church of St. Andrew Undershaft, and so was St. Mary at the Axe suppressed and letten out to be a warehouse for a merchant. Against the east end of this church was sometime a fair wall, now turned to a pump. Also against the north end of this St. Mary street, was sometime one other parish church of St. Augustine, called St. Augustine in the Wall, for that it stood adjoining to the wall of the city, and otherwise called St. Augustin's Papey, or the poor, as I have read in the reign of Edward III. About the year 1430, in the reign of Henry VI., the same church was allowed to the brethren of the Papey, the house of poor priests, whereof I have spoken in Aldgate ward. The parishioners of this church were appointed to the parish church of Allhallows in the wall, which is in Broad street ward, this brotherhood called Papey, being suppressed, the church of St Augustin was pulled down, and in place thereof one Grey an apothecary built a stable, hay-loft, etc. It is now a dwelling-house.[3] Those two parish churches, both lying in the ward of Lime street, being thus suppressed, there is not any one parish church or place for Divine service in that ward, but the

---

[1] " Cornhill street, in some place raysed two fadome higher than of olde time, as appeared by buildings found so deepe."—*Stow.*
[2] " As they call it."—*1st edition*, p. 123.
[3] " Reserving the churchyard for a garden plot."—*1st edition*, p. 124.

inhabitants thereof repair to St. Peter in Cornhill ward, St. Andrew in Aldgate ward, Alhallows in the wall in Broad street ward, and some to St. Denis in Langborne ward.

Now because of late there hath been some question, to what ward this church of St. Augustine Papey should of right belong, for the same hath been challenged by them of Aldgate ward, and without reason taken into Bishopsgate ward from Lime street ward, I am somewhat to touch it.   About thirty years since the chamber of London granted a lease of ground, in these words: " lying near London wall in the ward of Lime street, from the west of the said church or chapel of St. Augustine Papey towards Bishopsgate," etc.   On the which plot of ground the lease built three fair tenements, and placed tenants there; these were charged to bear scot and lot, and some of them to bear office in Lime street ward; all which they did willingly without grudging. And when any suspected or disordered persons were by the landlord placed there, the officers of Lime street ward fetched them out of their houses, committed them to ward, procured their due punishments, and banished them from thence; whereby in short time that place was reformed, and brought into good order; which thing being noted by them of Aldgate ward, they moved their alderman, Sir Thomas Offley, to call in those houses to be of his ward; but I myself showing a fair ledger book, sometimes pertaining to the late dissolved priory of the Holy Trinity whithin Aldgate, wherein were set down the just bounds of Aldgate ward, before Sir Thomas Offley, Sir Rowland Heyward, the common council, and wardmote inquest of the same Lime street ward, Sir Thomas Offley gave over his challenge, and so that matter rested in good quiet until the year 1579, that Sir Richard Pype being mayor, and alderman of Bishopsgate ward, challenged those houses to be of his ward, whereunto (without reason showed) Sir Rowland Heyward yielded.   And thus is that side of the street, from the north corner of St. Mary street almost to Bishopsgate, wherein is one plot of ground, letten by the chamberlain of London to the parish of St. Martin's Oteswich, to be a churchyard or burying place for the dead of that parish, etc., unjustly drawn and withholden from the ward of Lime street.   Divers other proofs I could set down, but this one following may suffice.—The mayor and aldermen of London made a grant to the fraternity of Papie in these words: " Be it remembered, that where now of late the master and wardens of the fraternity of the Papie have made a brick wall, closing in the chapel of St. Augustine called Papie chapel, situate in the parish of All Saints in the Wall, in the ward of Lime street, of the city of London; from the south-east corner of the which brick wall is a scutcheon of twenty-one feet of assize from the said corner eastward. And from the same scutcheon there to a messuage of fifty-five feet and a half westward, the said scutcheon breaketh out of line right southward betwixt the measures aforesaid three feet and five inches of assize, upon the common ground of the said city aforesaid, Ralph Verney, mayor, and the aldermen of the same city, the 22nd day of October, the 6th year of Edward IV., granted to John Hod, priest, and to Master John Bolte, and Thomas Pachet, priests, wardens of the fraternity of Papie aforesaid, and to their successors for ever, etc., yielding four pence sterling yearly at Michaelmas." And this is, saith my book,[1] enrolled in the Guild hall of London; which is a sufficient proof the same plot of ground to be of Lime street ward, and never otherwise accounted or challenged.

On the south side of this street, stretching west from St. Mary street towards Bishopsgate street, there was of old time one large messuage built of stone and timber, in the parish of St. Augustine in the Wall, now the parish of Allhallows in the same wall, belonging to the Earl of Oxford, for Richard de Vere, Earl of Oxford, possessed it in the 4th of Henry V.; but in process of time the lands of the earl fell to females, amongst the which, one being married to Wingfielde of Suffolke, this house with the appurtenances fell to his lot, and was by his heir, Sir Robert Wingfield, sold to Master Edward Coke, at this time the queen's attorney-general. This house being greatly ruinated of late time, for the most part hath been letten out to poulterers, for stabling of horses and stowage of poultry, but now lately new built into a number of small tenements, letten out to strangers, and other mean people.

One note more of this ward, and so an end. I find of record, that in the year 1371, the 45th of Edward III., a great subsidy of one hundred thousand pounds was granted towards the king's wars in France, whereof the clergy paid fifty thousand pounds, and the laity fifty thousand pounds, to be levied to thirty-nine shires of England, containing parishes eight thousand six hundred, of every parish five pounds sixteen shillings, the greater to help the lesser. This city, as one of the shires, then containing twenty-four wards, and in them one hundred and ten parishes, was therefore assessed to six hundred and thirty-

---

[1] Liber Papie. [*See* Bibliography.]

five pounds twelve shillings, whereof Lime street ward did bear thirty-four shillings and no more, so small a ward it was, and so accounted, as having no one whole parish therein, but small portions only of two parishes in that ward. This ward hath an alderman, his deputy, common councillors four, constables four, scavengers two, wardmote inquest sixteen, and a beadle; and is taxed to the fifteenth at one pound nineteen shillings and two pence three farthings.

BISHOPSGATE WARD

The next is Bishopsgate ward; whereof a part is without the gate and of the suburbs, from the bars by St. Mary Spittle to Bishopsgate, and a part of Houndsditch; almost half thereof, also without the wall, is of the same ward. Then within the gate is Bishopsgate street, so called of the gate, to a pump, where sometimes was a fair well, with two buckets, by the east end of the parish church of St. Martin Oteswich, and then winding by the west corner of Leaden hall down Grass street to the corner over against Grass church; and this is the bounds of that ward.

Monuments most to be noted are these: The parish church of St. Buttolph without Bishopsgate, in a fair churchyard, adjoining to the town ditch, upon the very bank thereof, but of old time inclosed with a comely wall of brick, lately repaired by Sir William Allen, mayor, in the year 1571, because he was born in that parish, where also he was buried. An anchoress received 40s. the year of the sheriffs of London.

Now without this churchyard wall is a causeye, leading to a quadrant, called Petty France, of Frenchmen dwelling there, and to other dwelling-houses, lately built on the bank of the said ditch by some citizens of London, that more regarded their own private gain than the common good of the city; for by means of this causeye raised on the bank, and soilage of houses, with other filthiness cast into the ditch, the same is now forced to a narrow channel, and almost filled up with unsavoury things, to the danger of impoisoning the whole city.

Next unto the parish church of St. Buttolph is a fair inn for receipt of travellers; then an hospital of St. Mary of Bethelem, founded by Simon Fitz Mary, one of the sheriffs of London, in the year 1246: he founded it to have been a priory of canons, with brethren and sisters; and King Edward III. granted a protection, which I have seen, for the brethren, *Miliciæ beatæ Mariæ*

de Bethlem, within the city of London, the 14th year of his reign.
It was an hospital for distracted people: Stephen Geninges,
merchant-tailor, gave £40 towards purchase of the patronage by
his testament, 1523; the mayor and commonalty purchased the
patronage thereof, with all the lands and tenements thereunto
belonging, in the year 1546: the same year King Henry VIII.
gave this hospital unto the city; the church and chapel whereof
were taken down in the reign of Queen Elizabeth, and houses
built there by the governors of Christ's hospital in London.   In
this place people that be distraight in wits are, by the suit of their
friends, received and kept as afore, but not without charges to
their bringers in.   In the year 1569, Sir Thomas Roe, merchant-
tailor, mayor, caused to be inclosed with a wall of brick about
one acre of ground, being part of the said hospital of Bethelem;
to wit, on the west, on the bank of Deep Ditch, so called, parting
the said hospital of Bethelem from the More field: this he did
for burial and ease of such parishes in London as wanted ground
convenient within their parishes.   The lady his wife was there
buried (by whose persuasion he inclosed it), but himself, born in
London, was buried in the parish church of Hackney.

From this hospital northward, upon the street's side, many
houses have been built with alleys backward, of late time too
much pestered with people (a great cause of infection) up to the
bars.

The other side of this high street from Bishopsgate and
Hounds ditch, the first building a large inn for receipt of
travellers, and is called the Dolphin, of such a sign.   In the year
1513, Margaret Ricroft, widow, gave this house, with the
gardens and appurtenances, unto William Gam, R. Clye, their
wives, her daughters, and to their heirs, with condition they
yearly do give to the warden or governors of the Grey friers
church within Newgate forty shillings, to find a student of
divinity in the University for ever.   Then is there a fair house,
of late built by John Powlet.   Next to that, a far more large and
beautiful house, with gardens of pleasure, bowling alleys, and
such like, built by Jasper Fisher, free of the goldsmiths, late
one of the six clerks of the chauncerie and a justice of the peace.
It hath since for a time been the Earl of Oxford's place.   The
queen's majesty Elizabeth hath lodged there.   It now belongeth
to Sir Roger Manars.[1]   This house, being so large and sumptuously built by a man of no greater calling, possessions, or wealth
(for he was indebted to many) was mockingly called Fisher's

[1] " To Master Cornewallos."—*1st edition*, p. 128.

folly, and a rhythm was made of it, and other the like, in this manner:

> " Kirkebyes Castell, and Fishers Follie,
>   Spinilas pleasure, and Megses glorie."

And so of other like buildings about the city by citizens, men have not letted to speak their pleasure.

From Fisher's Folly up to the west end of Berward's lane, of old time so called, but now Hogge lane, because it meeteth with Hogge lane, which cometh from the bars without Aldgate, as is afore showed, is a continual building of tenements, with alleys of cottages, pestered, etc. Then is there a large close, called Tasel close, sometime for that there were tassels planted for the use of cloth-workers, since letten to the cross-bow makers, wherein they used to shoot for games at the popinjay: now the same being inclosed with a brick wall, serveth to be an artillery yard, whereunto the gunners of the Tower do weekly repair, namely, every Thursday; and there levelling certain brass pieces of great artillery against a butt of earth, made for that purpose, they discharge them for their exercise.

Then have you the late dissolved priory and hospital,[1] commonly called St. Mary Spittle, founded by Walter Brune and Rosia his wife, for canons regular. Walter, archdeacon of London, laid the first stone in the year 1197, William, of St. Mary church, then bishop of London, dedicated to the honour of Jesus Christ and his mother, the perpetual Virgin Mary, by the name of *Domus Dei*, and *Beatæ Mariæ*, extra Bishopsgate, in the parish of St. Buttolph; the bounds whereof, as appeareth by composition betwixt the parson and prior of the said hospital concerning tithes, beginneth at Berward's lane toward the south, and extendeth in breadth to the parish of St. Leonard of Shoreditch towards the north; and in length, from the King's street on the west to the bishop of London's field, called Lollesworth, on the east. The prior of this St. Mary Spittle, for the emortising and propriation of Bikenacar, in Essex, to his said house of St. Mary Spittle, gave to Henry VII. £400 in the 22nd of his reign. This hospital, surrendered to Henry VIII., was valued to dispend £478; wherein was found, besides ornaments of the church, and other goods pertaining to the hospital, one hundred and eighty beds, well furnished, for receipt of the poor; for it was an hospital of great relief. Sir Henry Plesington, knight, was buried there 1452.

In place of this hospital, and near adjoining, are now many

[1] " Of our blessed lady."—*1st edition*, p. 129.

fair houses built for receipt and lodging of worshipful persons. A part of the large churchyard pertaining to this hospital, and severed from the rest with a brick wall, yet remaineth as of old time, with a pulpit cross therein, somewhat like to that in Paules churchyard. And against the said pulpit on the south side, before the charnel and chapel of St. Edmond the Bishop and Mary Magdalen, which chapel was founded about the year 1391 by William Eneshan, citizen and paperer of London, who was there buried, remaineth also one fair built house, of two stories in height, for the mayor and other honourable persons, with the aldermen and sheriffs to sit in, there to hear the sermons preached in the Easter holidays. In the loft over them stood the bishop of London, and other prelates; now the ladies and aldermen's wives do there stand at a fair window, or sit at their pleasure. And here is to be noted, that, time out of mind, it hath been a laudable custom, that on Good Friday, in the afternoon, some especial learned man, by appointment of the prelates, hath preached a sermon at Paules cross, treating of Christ's Passion; and upon the three next Easter holidays, Monday, Tuesday, and Wednesday, the like learned men, by the like appointment, have used to preach on the forenoons at the said Spittle, to persuade the article of Christ's Resurrection; and then on Low Sunday, one other learned man at Paules cross, to make rehearsal of those four former sermons, either commending or reproving them, as to him by judgment of the learned divines was thought convenient. And that done, he was to make a sermon of his own study, which in all were five sermons in one. At these sermons, so severally preached, the mayor, with his brethren the aldermen, were accustomed to be present in their violets at Paules on Good Friday, and in their scarlets at the Spittle in the holidays, except Wednesday in violet, and the mayor with his brethren on Low Sunday in scarlet, at Paules cross, continued until this day.

Touching the antiquity of this custom, I find, that in the year 1398, King Richard having procured from Rome confirmation of such statutes and ordinances as were made in the parliament, begun at Westminster and ended at Shrewsbury, he caused the same confirmation to be read and pronounced at Paules cross, and at St. Mary Spittle, in the sermons before all the people. Philip Malpas, one of the sheriffs in the year 1439, gave twenty shillings by the year to the three preachers at the Spittle. Stephen Forster, mayor in the year 1454, gave forty pounds to the preachers at Paules cross and Spittle. I find also

that the aforesaid house, wherein the mayor and aldermen do
sit at the Spittle, was built for that purpose of the goods and by
the executors of Richard Lawson, alderman, and Isabell his
wife, in the year 1488. In the year 1594, this pulpit being old
was taken down, and a new set up; the preacher's face
turned towards the south, which was before toward the west;
also a large house, on the east side of the said pulpit, was then
built for the governors and children of Christ's hospital to sit
in, and this was done of the goods of William Elkens, alderman,
late deceased; but within the first year the same house decaying,
and like to have fallen, was again with great cost repaired at the
city's charge.

On the east side of this churchyard lieth a large field, of old
time called Lolesworth, now Spittle field; which about the year
1576 was broken up for clay to make brick; in the digging
whereof many earthen pots, called *urnæ*, were found full of
ashes, and burnt bones of men, to wit, of the Romans that
inhabited here; for it was the custom of the Romans to burn
their dead, to put their ashes in an urn, and then bury the same,
with certain ceremonies, in some field appointed for that purpose
near unto their city. Every of these pots had in them with the
ashes of the dead one piece of copper money, with the inscription
of the emperor then reigning: some of them were of Claudius,
some of Vespasian, some of Nero, of Anthoninus Pius, of Trajanus,
and others. Besides those urns, many other pots were there
found, made of a white earth with long necks and handles, like
to our stone jugs: these were empty, but seemed to be buried
full of some liquid matter long since consumed and soked
through; for there were found divers phials and other fashioned
glasses, some most cunningly wrought, such as I have not seen
the like, and some of crystal; all which had water in them,
nothing differing in clearness, taste, or savour from common
spring water, whatsoever it was at the first: some of these
glasses had oil in them very thick, and earthy in savour; some
were supposed to have balm in them, but had lost the virtue;
many of those pots and glasses were broken in cutting of the
clay, so that few were taken up whole. There were also found
divers dishes and cups of a fine red-coloured earth, which showed
outwardly such a shining smoothness as if they had been of coral;
those had in the bottoms Roman letters printed: there were
also lamps of white earth and red, artificially wrought with
divers antiques about them, some three or four images made of
white earth, about a span long each of them: one I remember

was of Pallas, the rest I have forgotten. I myself have reserved,
among divers of those antiquities there, one urn, with the ashes
and bones, and one pot of white earth very small, not exceeding
the quantity of a quarter of a wine pint, made in shape of a hare
squatted upon her legs, and between her ears is the mouth of the
pot.   There hath also been found in the same field divers coffins
of stone, containing the bones of men: these I suppose to be the
burials of some especial persons in time of the Britons or
Saxons, after that the Romans had left to govern here.   Moreover, there were also found the skulls and bones of men without
coffins, or rather whose coffins (being of great timber) were consumed.   Divers great nails of iron were there found, such as are
used in the wheels of shod carts, being each of them as big as a
man's finger, and a quarter of a yard long, the heads two inches
over; those nails were more wondered at than the rest of things
there found, and many opinions of men were there uttered of
them; namely, that the men there buried were murdered by
driving those nails into their heads; a thing unlikely, for a
smaller nail would more aptly serve to so bad a purpose, and a
more secret place would likely be employed for their burial.   But
to set down what I have observed concerning this matter, I there
beheld the bones of a man lying (as I noted), the head north, the
feet south, and round about him, as thwart his head, along both
his sides, and thwart his feet, such nails were found, wherefore
I conceived them to be the nails of his coffin, which had been a
trough cut out of some great tree, and the same covered with a
plank, of a great thickness, fastened with such nails; and therefore I caused some of the nails to be reached up to me, and found
under the broad heads of them the old wood, skant turned into
earth, but still retaining both the grain and proper colour: of
these nails, with the wood under the head thereof, I reserved
one, as also the nether jaw-bone of the man, the teeth being
great, sound, and fast fixed, which, among other many monuments there found, I have yet to show; but the nail lying dry,
is by scaling greatly wasted. And thus much for this part of
Bishopsgate ward, without the gate; for I have in another place
spoken of the gate, and therefore I am to speak of that other
part of this ward which lieth within the gate.

And first to begin on the left hand of Bishopsgate street, from
the gate you have certain tenements of old time pertaining to
a brotherhood of St. Nicholas, granted to the parish clerks of
London, for two chaplains, to be kept in the chapel of St. Mary
Magdalen, near unto the Guildhall of London, in the 27th of

Henry VI. The first of these houses towards the north, and against the wall of the city, was sometime a large inn or court called the Wrestlers, of such a sign, and the last in the high street towards the south was sometime also a fair inn called the Angel, of such a sign. Among these said tenements was on the same street side a fair entry, or court, to the common hall of the said parish clerks, with proper alms houses, seven in number, adjoining, for poor parish clerks, and their wives and their widows, such as were in great years not able to labour. One of these, by the said brotherhood of parish clerks, was allowed sixteen pence the week; the other six had each of them nine pence the week, according to the patent thereof granted. This brotherhood, amongst other, being suppressed, in the reign of Edward VI. the said hall, with the other buildings there, was given to Sir Robert Chester, a knight of Cambridgeshire; against whom the parish clerks commencing suit, in the reign of Queen Mary, and being like to have prevailed, the said Sir Robert Chester pulled down the hall, sold the timber, stone, and lead, and thereupon the suit was ended. The alms houses remain in the queen's hands, and people are there placed, such as can make best friends; some of them, taking the pension appointed, have let forth their houses for great rent, giving occasion to the parson of the parish to challenge tithes of the poor, etc.

Next unto this is the small parish church of St. Ethelburge Virgin, and from thence some small distance is a large court called Little St. Helen's, because it pertained to the nuns of St. Helen's, and was their house: there are seven alms rooms or houses for the poor, belonging to the company of Leathersellers. Then, somewhat more west, is another court with a winding lane, which cometh out against the west end of St. Andrew Undershaft church. In this court standeth the church of St. Helen, sometime a priory of black nuns, and in the same a parish church of St. Helen. [*See* Additional Notes.]

This priory was founded before the reign of Henry III. William Basing, dean of Paules, was the first founder, and was there buried; and William Basing, one of the sheriffs of London, in the 2nd year of Edward II. was holden also to be a founder, or rather a helper there. This priory being valued at £314 2s. 6d. was surrendered the 25th of November, the 30th of Henry VIII.; the whole church, the partition betwixt the nuns' church and parish church being taken down, remaineth now to the parish, and is a fair parish church, but wanteth such a steeple as Sir Thomas Gresham promised to have built, in recompense of ground in their church filled up with his monument. The nuns' hall, and other houses thereunto appertaining, was since purchased by the company of the Leathersellers, and is their common hall; which company was incorporate in the 21st year of Richard II.

In the church of St. Helen have you these monuments of the dead:—Thomas Langton, chaplain, buried in the choir 1350; Adam Frances, mayor, 1354; Elizabeth Vennar, wife to William Vennar, alderman, one of the sheriffs of London, 1401; Joan, daughter to Henry Seamer, wife to Richard, son and heir to Robert Lord Poynings, died a virgin 1420; John Swinflat, 1420; Nicholas Marshall, ironmonger, alderman, 1474; Sir John Crosby, alderman, 1475, and Ann his wife; Thomas Williams, gentleman, 1495; Joan Cocken, wife to John Cocken, esquire, 1509; Marie Orrell, wife to Sir Lewes Orrell, knight; Henry Sommer, and Katherine his wife; Walter Huntington, esquire; John Langthorpe, esquire, 1510; John Gower, steward of St. Helen's, 1512; Robert Rochester, esquire, sergeant of the pantry to Henry VIII.; Sir William Sanctlo, and Sir William Sanctlo, father and son; Eleanor, daughter to Sir Thomas Butler; Lord Sudley; John Southworth; Nicholas Harpsfield, esquire; Thomas Sanderford, or Sommerford, alderman; Alexander Cheyney; Walter Dawbeney; George Fastolph, son to Hugh Fastolph; Robert Liade; Thomas Benolt, alias Clarenciaulx, king at arms, 1534; William Hollis, mayor, 1540; John Fauconbridge, esquire, 1545; Hacket, gentleman of the king's chapel; Sir Andrew Jud, mayor, 1551; Sir William Pickering, and Sir William Pickering, father and son; William Bond, alderman, 1567; Sir Thomas Gresham, mercer, 1579; William Skegges, sergeant poulter; Richard Gresham, son to Sir Thomas Gresham, 1564.

Then have you one great house called Crosby place, because the same was built by Sir John Crosby, grocer and woolman, in place of certain tenements, with their appurtenances, letten to him by Alice Ashfed, prioress of St. Helen's, and the convent for ninety-nine years, from the year 1466 unto the year 1565, for the annual rent of £11 6s. 8d. This house he built of stone and timber, very large and beautiful, and the highest at that time in London. He was one of the sheriffs, and an alderman in the year 1470, knighted by Edward IV. in the year 1471, and deceased in the year 1475; so short a time enjoyed he that his large and sumptuous building; he was buried in St. Helen's, the parish church; a fair monument of him and his lady is raised there. He gave towards the reforming of that church five hundred marks, which was bestowed with the better, as appeareth by his arms, both in the stone work, roof of timber, and glazing. I hold it a fable said of him to be named Crosbie, of being found by a cross, for I have read of other to have that name of Crosbie before him; namely, in the year 1406, the 7th of Henry IV., the said king gave to his servant John Crosbie the wardship of Joan, daughter and sole heir to John Jordaine, fishmonger, etc. This Crosbie might be the father or grandfather to Sir John Crosbie.

Richard, Duke of Gloucester, and lord protector, afterward king, by the name of Richard III., was lodged in this house; since the which time, among other, Anthonie Bonvice, a rich merchant of Italy, dwelt there; after him, Germain Cioll, then William Bond, alderman, increased this house in height, with building of a turret on the top thereof: he deceased in the year 1576, and was buried in St. Helen's church. Divers ambassadors have been lodged there; namely, in the year 1586, Henry Ramelius, chancellor of Denmark, ambassador unto the queen's majesty of England from Frederick II., the king of Denmark; an ambassador of France, etc. Sir John Spencer, alderman, lately purchased this house, made great reparations, kept his mayoralty there, and since built a most large warehouse near thereunto.

From this Crosbie place up to Leaden hall corner, and so down Grass street, amongst other tenements, are divers fair and large built houses for merchants, and such like.

Now for the other side of this ward, namely, the right hand, hard by within the gate, is one fair water conduit, which Thomas Knesworth, mayor, in the year 1505, founded: he gave £60, the rest was furnished at the common charges of the city. This conduit hath since been taken down and new built. David Woodrooffe, alderman, gave £20 towards the conveyance of more water thereunto. From this conduit have you, amongst many fair tenements, divers fair inns, large for receipt of travellers, and some houses for men of worship; namely, one most spacious of all other thereabout, built of brick and timber by Sir Thomas Gresham, knight, who deceased in the year 1579, and was buried in St. Helen's church, under a fair monument, by him prepared in his life: he appointed by his testament this house to be made a college of readers, as before is said in the chapter of schools and houses of learning.

Somewhat west from this house is one other very fair house,

wherein Sir William Hollies kept his mayoralty, and was buried
in the parish church of St. Helen. Sir Andrew Jud also kept his
mayoralty there, and was buried at St. Helen's: he built alms
houses for six poor alms people near to the said parish church,
and gave lands to the Skinners, out of the which they are to
give 4s. every week to the six poor alms people, 8d. the piece,
and 25s. 4d. the year, in coals amongst them for ever.

Alice Smith, of London, widow, late wife of Thomas Smith,
of the same city, esquire, and customer of the port of London,
in her last will and testament, bequeathed lands to the value
of £15 by the year for ever, to the company of Skinners, for the
augmenting of the pensions of certain poor, inhabiting in eight
alms houses, erected by Sir Andrew Jud, knight, her father,
in the parish of Great St. Helen's, in Bishopsgate street, in
London. She hath also given in her said last will and testament,
in other charitable uses, as to the hospitals and to the poor of
other parishes and good preachers, the sum of £300. As also
to the poor scholars in the two universities of Oxford and
Cambridge the sum of £200; of which, her last will and testament, she made her sons, Thomas Smith, late sheriff of London,
and Richard and Robert Smith, her executors, who have performed the same according to her godly and charitable mind.

Then in the very west corner, over against the east end of
St. Martin's Oteswich (from whence the street windeth towards
the south), you had of old time a fair well, with two buckets,
so fastened that the drawing up of the one let down the other;
but now of late that well is turned into a pump.

From this to the corner over against the Leaden hall, and so
down Grasse street, are many fair houses for merchants and
artificers, and many fair inns for travellers, even to the corner
where that ward endeth, over against Grasse church. And thus
much for this Bishopsgate ward shall suffice; which hath an
alderman, two deputies, one without the gate, another within,
common councillors six, constables seven, scavengers seven,
for wardmote inquest thirteen, and a beadle: it is taxed to the
fifteen at £13.[1]

BROAD STREET WARD

The next is Brode street ward, which beginneth within Bishopsgate, from the water conduit westward on both sides of the

---

[1] " At twenty-two pounds in London, and in the Exchequer twenty-one
pounds ten shillings."—*1st edition*, p. 136.

street, by Allhallows church, to an iron grate on the channel which runneth into the water-course of Walbrooke, before you come to the postern called Mooregate; and this is the farthest west part of that ward.

Then have you Brode street, whereof the ward taketh name, which stretcheth out of the former street from the east corner of Allhallows churchyard, somewhat south to the parish church of St. Peter the Poor on both sides, and then by the south gate of the Augustine friars west, down Throkmorton street by the Drapers' hall into Lothburie, to another grate of iron over the channel there, whereby the water runneth into the course of Walbrook, under the east end of St. Margaret's church, certain posts of timber are there set up; and this is also the farthest west part of this ward, in the said street. Out of the which street runneth up Bartholomew lane south to the north side of the Exchange; then more east, out of the former street from over against the Friars Augustine's church south gate, runneth up another part of Brode street south to a pump over against St. Bennet's church. Then have you one other street called Three needle street, beginning at the west, with two buckets, by St. Martin's Oteswich church wall. This street runneth down on both sides to Finkes lane, and half way up that lane to a gate of a merchant's house on the west side, but not so far on the east; then the foresaid street, from this Finkes lane, runneth down by the Royal Exchange to the Stocks, and to a place formerly called Scalding house, or Scalding wick, but now Scalding alley; by the west side whereof, under the parish church of St. Mildred, runneth the course of Walbrooke; and these be the bounds of this ward.

Special monuments therein are these:—First, the parish church of Allhallows in the wall, so called of standing close to the wall of the city, in which have been buried Thomas Durrem, esquire, and Margaret his wife; Robert Beele, esquire, 1601. On the other side of that street, amongst many proper houses possessed for the most part by curriers, is the Carpenters' hall, which company was incorporated in the 17th year of King Edward IV.

Then east from the Currier's row is a long and high wall of stone, inclosing the north side of a large garden adjoining to as large an house, built in the reign of King Henry VIII. and of Edward VI. by Sir William Powlet, lord treasurer of England. Through this garden, which of old time consisted of divers parts, now united, was sometimes a fair footway, leading by the west

end of the Augustine friars church straight north, and opened
somewhat west from Allhallows church against London wall
towards Moregate; which footway had gates at either end,
locked up every night; but now the same way being taken into
those gardens, the gates are closed up with stone, whereby the
people are forced to go about by St. Peter's church, and the
east end of the said Friars church, and all the said great place
and garden of Sir William Powlet to London wall, and so to
Moregate.

This great house, adjoining to the garden aforesaid, stretcheth
to the north corner of Brode street, and then turneth up Brode
street all that side to and beyond the east end of the said Friars
church. It was built by the said lord treasurer in place of
Augustine friars house, cloister, and gardens, etc. The Friars
church he pulled not down, but the west end thereof, inclosed
from the steeple and choir, was in the year 1550 granted to the
Dutch nation in London, to be their preaching place: the other
part, namely, the steeple, choir, and side aisles to the choir
adjoining, he reserved to household uses, as for stowage of corn,
coal, and other things; his son and heir, Marquis of Winchester,
sold the monuments of noblemen there buried in great number,
the paving-stone and whatsoever (which cost many thousands),
for one hundred pounds, and in place thereof made fair stabling
for horses. He caused the lead to be taken from the roofs, and
laid tile in place; which exchange proved not so profitable as
he looked for, but rather to his disadvantage.

On the east side of this Brode street, amongst other buildings,
on the back part of Gresham house, which is in Bishopsgate
street, be placed eight proper alms houses, built of brick and
timber by Sir Thomas Gresham, knight, for eight alms men,
which he now there placed rent free, and receive each of them
by his gift of £6 13s. 4d. yearly for ever.

Next unto Pawlet house is the parish church of St. Peter the
Poor, so called for a difference from other of that name, sometime peradventure a poor parish, but at this present there be
many fair houses, possessed by rich merchants and other.
Buried in this church: Richard Fitzwilliams, merchant-tailor,
1520; Sir William Roch, mayor, 1540; Martin Calthrope,
mayor, 1588.

Then next have you the Augustine Friars church and churchyard; the entering thereunto by a south gate to the west porch,
a large church, having a most fine spired steeple, small, high,
and straight, I have not seen the like: founded by Humfrey

Bohun, Earl of Hereford and Essex, in the year 1253. Reginald Cobham gave his messuage in London to the enlarging thereof, in the year 1344. Humfrey Bohun, Earl of Hereford and Essex, re-edified this church in the year 1354, whose body was there buried in the choir. The small spired steeple of this church was overthrown by a tempest of wind in the year 1362, but was raised of new, as now it standeth, to the beautifying of the city. This house was valued at £57, and was surrendered the 12th of November, the 30th of Henry VIII.

There lie buried in this Friars church, amongst others, Edward, first son to Joan, mother to King Richard II.; Guy de Mericke, Earl of St. Paule; Lucie, Countess of Kent, and one of the heirs of Barnabie Lord of Millaine, with an epitaph; Dame Ide, wife to Sir Thomas West; Dame Margaret West; Stephen Lindericle, esquire; Sir Humfrey Bohun, Earl of Hereford and Essex, Lord of Brekenake; [1] Richard, the great Earl of Arundell, Surrey, and Warren, beheaded, 1397; Sir Edward Arundell, and Dame Elizabeth his wife; Sir Francis Atcourt, [2] Earl of Pembrooke, which married Alice, sister to the Earl of Oxford; Dame Lucie Knowles, of Kent; Sir Peter Garinsers, of France; the Lord John Vere, Earl of Oxford, beheaded on the Tower hill 1463; Aubrey de Vere, son and heir to the Earl of Oxford; Sir Thomas Tudnam, knight; William Bourser, Lord Fitz Warren; Sir Thomas de la Lande, knight; Dame Joan Norris, the Lady of Bedforde; Anne, daughter to John Viscount Welles; Walter Nevell, esquire; Sir John Manners, knight; the wife of Sir David Cradocke, knight; the mother to the Lord Spencer's wife; Sir Bartlemew Rodlegate; John, son to Sir John Wingfield; Sir Walter Mewes; Robert Newenton, esquire; Philip Spencer, son to Sir Hugh Spencer; Dame Isabell, daughter to Sir Hugh; the Lord Barons slain at Barnet field, buried there 1471. In the body of the church: Dame Julian, wife to Sir Richard Lacie; Sir Thomas Courtney, son to the Earl of Devonshire, and by him, his sister, wedded to Cheverstone; the daughter of the Lord Beaumont; two sons of Sir Thomas Morley, to wit, William and Ralph; Sir William Talmage, knight; Nicholas Blondell, esquire; Sir Richard Chamberlaine; John Halton, gentleman; Sir John Gifford, knight; Thomas Manningham, esquire; Sir William Kenude, knight; Sir William, son to Sir Thomas Terill; John Surell, gentleman. In the east wing: Margaret Barentin, gentlewoman; John Spicer, esquire, and Letis his wife; John le Percers, esquire; Roger Chibary,

[1] " Pembroke."—1st edition, p. 136.   [2] " Courtney."—1st edition, ibid.

esquire; Peter Morens, esquire; Thomas, son to Sir William Beckland; James Cuthing, esquire; John Chorner, esquire; William Kenley, esquire; Margery, wife to Thomas Band, and daughter to John Hutch; the Lord William, Marquis of Barkeley and Earl of Nottingham, and Dame Joan his wife. In the west wing: Sir John Tirrill, and Dame Katherine his wife; Sir Walter of Powle, knight; Sir John Blanckwell, and his wife Dame Jane Sayne, daughter to Sir John Lee; Sir John Dawbeney, son and heir to Sir Giles Dawbeney; William, son to Sir Roger Scroope; Dame Joan Dawbeney, wife to Sir William Dawbeney; Thomas Charles, esquire; Sir John Dawbeney, knight, and his son Robert; Sir James Bell, knight; Sir Oliver Manny, knight; Henry Deskie, esquire; Sir Diones Mordaske; Sir Bernard Rolingcort; Sir Peter Kayor; Sir William Tirell; Sir William, his brother knights; William Collingborne, esquire, beheaded 1484; Sir Roger Clifford, knight; Sir Thomas Coke, mayor in the year 1462; William Edward, mayor, 1471; Sir James Tirell, Sir John Windany, knights, beheaded 1502; Sir John Dawtrie, knight, 1519; Dame Margaret Rede, 1510; Edward, Duke of Buckingham, beheaded 1521; Gwiskard, Earl of Huntington.

On the south side, and at the west end of this church, many fair houses are built; namely, in Throgmorton street, one very large and spacious, built in the place of old and small tenements by Thomas Cromwell, master of the king's jewel-house, after that master of the rolls, then Lord Cromwell, knight, lord privy seal, vicar-general, Earl of Essex, high chamberlain of England, etc. This house being finished, and having some reasonable plot of ground left for a garden, he caused the pales of the gardens adjoining to the north part thereof on a sudden to be taken down; twenty-two feet to be measured forth right into the north of every man's ground; a line there to be drawn, a trench to be cast, a foundation laid, and a high brick wall to be built. My father had a garden there, and a house standing close to his south pale; this house they loosed from the ground, and bare upon rollers into my father's garden twenty-two feet, ere my father heard thereof; no warning was given him, nor other answer, when he spake to the surveyors of that work, but that their master Sir Thomas commanded them so to do; no man durst go to argue the matter, but each man lost his land, and my father paid his whole rent, which was 6s. 6d. the year, for that half which was left. Thus much of mine own knowledge have I thought good to note, that the sudden rising of some men causeth them [1] to forget themselves.

The company of the Drapers in London bought this house, and now the same is their common hall. This company obtained of King Henry VI., in the 17th of his reign, to be incorporate: John Gidney was chosen to be their first master, and the four wardens were, J. Wotton, J. Darbie, Robert Breton, and T. Cooke. The arms granted to the said company by Sir William Bridges, knight, first garter king at arms, in blason, are thus: Three sunbeams issuing out of three clouds of flame, crowned with three crowns imperial of gold, upon a shield azure. From this hall, on the same side down to the grates and course of Walbrook, have ye divers fair houses for merchants and other; from the which grates back again on the other side in Lethbury, so called in record of Edward III., the 38th year, and now corruptly called Lothbury, are candlestick founders placed, till ye come to Bartholomew lane, so called of St. Bartholomew's church, at the south-east corner thereof. In this lane also are divers fair built houses on both sides, and so likewise have ye in the other street, which stretcheth from the Friars Augustine's south gate to the corner over against St. Bennet's church. In this street, amongst other fair buildings, the most ancient was of old time a house pertaining to the abbot of St. Albans; John Catcher, alderman, now dwelleth there; then is the free school pertaining to the late dissolved hospital of St. Anthony, whereof more shall be shown in another place, and so up to Threeneedle street. On the south part of which street, beginning at the east, by the well with two buckets, now turned to a pump, is the parish church of St. Martin called Oteswich, of Martin de Oteswich, Nicholas de Oteswich, William Oteswich, and John Oteswich, founders thereof. There be monuments in this church of William Constantine, alderman, and Emme his wife; Katherine, wife to Benedick Augustine; Sir William Drifield, knight; John Oteswich, and his wife, under a fair monument on the south side; John Churchman, one of the sheriffs, in the year 1385; Richard Naylor, tailor, alderman, 1483; James Falleron; John Melchborne; Thomas Hey, and Hellis his wife; William Clitherow, and Margaret his wife; Oliver and William, sons to John Woodroffe, esquire; Hugh Pemberton, tailor, alderman, 1500, and Katherine his wife; Matthew Pemberton, merchant-tailor, about 1514: he gave £50 to the repairing of St. Lawrence chapel. The aforesaid

[1] " In some matters."—1st edition, p. 141.

John Churchman, for William and John Oteswich, by license of Henry IV., the 6th of his reign, gave the advowson or patronage of this church, four messuages, and seventeen shops, with the appurtenances in the parish of St. Martin's Oteswich, etc., to the master and wardens of tailors and linen-armourers, keepers of the guild and fraternity of St. John Baptist in London, and to their successors, in perpetual alms, to be employed on the poor brethren and sisters; whereupon, adjoining unto the west end of this parish church, the said master and wardens built about a proper quadrant or squared court, seven alms houses, wherein they placed seven alms men of that company, and their wives (if they had wives); each of these seven of old time had 13*d*. the week, but now of later time their stipend by the said master and wardens hath been augmented to the sum of 26*s*. the quarter, which is £5 4*s*. the year to each of them, besides coals; more, to each of them 20*s*. the year, by gift of Walter Fish, sometime master of that company, and tailor to her majesty.

Some small distance from thence is the Merchant-tailors'-hall, pertaining to the guild and fraternity of St. John Baptist, time out of mind called of tailors and linen-armourers of London; for I find that Edward I., in the 28th of his reign, confirmed this guild by the name of Tailors and Linen-armourers, and also gave to the brethren thereof authority every year at Midsummer to hold a feast, and to choose unto them a governor, or master, with wardens; whereupon the same year, 1300, on the feast day of the nativity of St. John Baptist, they chose Henry de Ryall to be their pilgrim for the master of this mystery (as one that travelled for the whole company was then so called) until the 11th of Richard II.; and the four wardens were then called purveyors of alms (now called quarterage) of the said fraternity. This merchant-tailors' hall, sometime pertaining to a worshipful gentleman named Edmond Creping (Dominus Creping after some record), he in the year of Christ 1331, the first of Edward III., for a certain sum of money to him paid, made his grant thereof by the name of his principal messuage in the wards of Cornehill and Brode street, which Sir Oliver Ingham, knight, did then hold, to John of Yakley, the king's pavilion maker. This was called the new hall, or tailors' inn, for a difference from their old hall, which was about the back side of the Red Lion in Basing lane, and in the ward of Cordwayner street.

The 21st of Edward IV., Thomas Holme, *alias* Clarenciaulx king of arms for the south part of England, granted by his patents to the said fraternity and guild of St. John Baptist, of tailors and linen-armourers, to bear in a field silver, a pavilion between two mantels imperial purple garnished with gold, in a chief azure an holy Lamb, set within a sun, the crest upon the helm, a pavilion purple garnished with gold, etc. After this King Henry VII. being himself a brother of this fraternity or guild of St. John Baptist, of tailors or linen-armourers (as divers other his predecessors kings before him had been, to wit, Richard III., Edward IV., Henry V., Henry IV., and Richard II.); and for that divers of that fraternity had, time out of mind, been great merchants, and had frequented all sorts of merchandises into most parts of the world, to the honour of the king's realm, and to the great profit of his subjects, and of his progenitors; and the men of the said mystery, during the time aforesaid, had exercised the buying and selling of all wares and merchandises, especially of woollen cloth, as well in gross, as by retail, throughout all this realm of England, and chiefly within the said city; therefore he, of his especial grace, did change, transfer, and translate the guild aforesaid, and did incorporate them into the name of the Master and Wardens of the Merchant-tailors of the fraternity of St. John Baptist, in the city of London.

Some distance west from this the Merchant-tailors' hall is Finke's lane, so called of Robert Finke, and Robert Finke his son, James Finke, and Rosamond Finke. Robert Finke the elder new built the parish church of St. Bennet, commonly called Fink, of the founder; his tenements were both of St. Bennet's parish and St. Martin's Oteswich parish. The one half of this Finke lane is of Brode street ward, to wit, on the west side up to the great and principal house wherein the said Finke dwelt; but on the other side, namely the east, not so much towards Cornhill. Then without this lane in the aforesaid Threeneedle street is the said parish church of St. Bennet, a proper church, in which are these monuments of the dead:— Robert Simson, and Elizabeth his wife; Roger Strange, esquire; Trerisse; William Coolby; John Frey; Thomas Briar, plumber, 1410, etc.

Some distance west is the Royal Exchange, whereof more shall be spoken in the ward of Cornhill, and so down to the little conduit, called the pissing conduit, by the Stockes market, and this is the south side of Threeneedle street.

On the north side of this street, from over against the east corner of St. Martin's Oteswich church, have ye divers fair and large houses till ye come to the hospital of St. Anthonie, sometime a cell to St. Anthonie's of Vienna. For I read that King Henry III. granted to the brotherhood of St. Anthonie of Vienna, a place amongst the Jews, which was sometime their synagogue, and had been built by them about the year 1231; but the Christians obtained of the king that it should be dedicated to our Blessed Lady; and since a hospital being there built, was called St. Anthonie's in London; it was founded in the parish of St. Bennet Finke, for a master, two priests, one schoolmaster, and twelve poor men: after which foundation, amongst other things, was given to this hospital, one messuage and garden, whereon was built the fair large free school, and one other parcel of ground, containing thirty-seven feet in length, and eighteen feet in breadth, whereon was built the alms houses of hard stone and timber, in the reign of Henry VI., which said Henry VI., in the 20th of his reign, gave unto John Carpenter, D.D., master of St. Anthonie's hospital, and to his brethren and their successors for ever, his manor of Ponington, with the appurtenances, with certain pensions and portions of Milburne, Burnworth, Charlton, and Up Wimborne, in the county of Southampton, towards the maintenance of five scholars in the university of Oxford, to be brought up in the faculty of arts, after the rate of ten pence the week for every scholar, so that the said scholars shall be first instructed in the rudiments of grammar at the college of Eaton, founded by the said king.

In the year 1474, Edward IV. granted to William Say, B.D., master of the said hospital, to have priests, clerks, scholars, poor men, and brethren of the same, clerks, or laymen, choristers, proctors, messengers, servants in household, and other things whatsoever, like as the prior and convent of St. Anthonie's of Vienna, etc. He also annexed, united, and appropriated the said hospital unto the collegiate church of St. George in Windsor.

The proctors of this house were to collect the benevolence of charitable persons towards the building and supporting thereof. And amongst other things observed in my youth, I remember that the officers charged with oversight of the markets in this city, did divers times take from the market people, pigs starved, or otherwise unwholesome for man's sustenance; these they slit in the ear. One of the proctors for St. Anthonie's tied a bell about the neck, and let it feed on the dunghills; no man would hurt or take them up, but if any gave to them bread, or other feeding, such would they know, watch for, and daily follow, whining till they had somewhat given them; whereupon was raised a proverb, "Such an one will follow such an one, and whine as it were an Anthonie pig;" but if such a pig grew to be fat, and came to good liking (as oft times they did), then the proctor would take him up to the use of the hospital.

In the year 1499, Sir John Tate, sometime ale-brewer, when a mercer, caused his brewhouse, called the Swan, near adjoining to the said free chapel, college, or hospital of St. Anthonie, to be taken down for the enlarging of the church, which was then new built, toward the building whereof the said Tate gave great sums of money, and finished in the year 1501. Sir John Tate deceased 1514, and was there buried under a fair monument by him prepared. Dr. Tayler, master of the rolls, and other.[1]

Walter Champion, draper, one of the sheriffs of London 1529, was buried there, and gave to the beadman twenty pounds. The lands by year of this hospital were valued in the 37th year of Henry VIII. to be fifty-five pounds six shillings and eight pence.

One Johnson (a schoolmaster of the famous free-school there) became a prebend of Windsor, and then by little and little followed the spoil of this hospital. He first dissolved the choir, conveyed the plate and ornaments, then the bells, and lastly put out the alms men from their houses, appointing them portions of twelve pence the week to each (but now I hear of no such matter performed), their houses with other be letten out for rent, and the church is a preaching place for the French nation.

This school was commended in the reign of Henry VI., and sithence commended above other, but now decayed, and come to nothing, by taking that from it what thereunto belonged.

Next is the parish church of St. Bartholomew, at the end of Bartholomew lane. Thomas Pike, alderman, with the assistance of Nicholas Yoo, one of the sheriffs of London, about the year 1438, new built this church. Sir John Fray, knight, was buried there, Margery his daughter and heir, wife to Sir John Lepington, knight, founded there a chantry the 21st of Edward IV. Alderban, a Gascoyne, was buried there; Sir Will. Capel, mayor 1509, added unto this church a proper chapel on the south side thereof, and was buried there; Sir Giles Cappell was

[1] "This goodly foundation having a free schoole and almes houses for poore men (builded of hard stone) adjoyning to the west end of the church, was of olde time confirmed by Henry the Sixt, in the year 1447. The outward work of this new church was finished in the year 1501, the said John Tate deceased about the year 1514, and was there buried in a monument by him prepared, as appeareth by an indenture tripartite made between the said John Tate, the Deane of Windsor, and William Milbourn, chamberlaine."—*1st edition*, p. 145.

also buried there; James Wilford, tailor, one of the sheriffs 1499, appointed by his testament a doctor of divinity, every Good Friday for ever, to preach there a sermon of Christ's Passion, from six of the clock till eight before noon, in the said church. John Wilford, merchant-tailor, alderman, 1544; Sir James Wilford, 1550; Sir George Barne, mayor 1552; John Dent; Miles Coverdale, Bishop of Excester; Thomas Dancer, and Anne his wife.

Then lower down towards the Stocks' market is the parish church of St. Christopher, but re-edified of new; for Richard Shore, one of the sheriffs 1506, gave money towards the building of the steeple. There lie buried Richard Sherington, 1392, who gave lands to that church; the Lady Margaret Norford, 1406; John Clavering, 1421, who gave lands thereunto; John Godnay, draper, mayor 1427. This Godnay, in the year 1444, wedded the widow of Robert Large, late mayor, which widow had taken the mantle and ring, and the vow to live chaste to God during the term of her life, for the breach whereof, the marriage done, they were troubled by the church, and put to penance, both he and she. William Hampton, mayor 1472, was a great benefactor, and glazed some of the church windows; Sir William Martin, mayor 1492; Roger Achley, mayor 1511, he dwelt in Cornehill ward, in a house belonging to Cobham college, rented by the year at twenty-six shillings and eight pence; Robert Thorne, merchant-tailor, a bachelor, 1532—he gave by his testament in charity more than four thousand four hundred and forty-five pounds; John Norryholme; Ralph Batte; Alice Percivall; Jane Drew; William Borresbie; John Broke; Richard Sutton; William Batte; James Well; Henry Beacher, alderman, 1570.

West from this church have ye Scalding alley, of old time called Scalding house, or Scalding wike, because that ground for the most part was then employed by poulterers that dwelt in the high street from the Stocks' market to the great conduit. Their poultry, which they sold at their stalls, were scalded there. The street doth yet bear the name of the Poultry, and the poulterers are but lately departed from thence into other streets, as into Grasse street, and the ends of St. Nicholas flesh shambles. This Scalding wike is the farthest west part of Brode street ward, and is by the water called Walbrook parted from Cheap ward. This Brode street ward hath an alderman, with his deputy, common councillors ten, constables ten, scavengers eight, wardmote inquest thirteen, and a beadle. It is taxed to the fifteenth in London at seven-and-twenty pounds, and accounted in the Exchequer after twenty-five pounds.

CORNEHILL WARD

The next ward to the south is Cornehill ward, so called of a corn market, time out of mind there holden, and is a part of the principal high street, beginning at the west end of Leaden hall, stretching down west on both the sides by the south end of Finks lane on the right hand, and by the north end of Birchovers lane; on the left part of which lanes, to wit, to the middle of them, is of this ward, and so down to the Stockes market; and this is the bounds.

The upper or east part of this ward, and also a part of Lime street ward, hath been (as I said) a market place, especially for corn, and since for all kind of victuals, as is partly showed in Lime street ward; yet it appeareth of record, that in the year 1522, the rippers of Rie and other places, sold their fresh fish in Leaden hall market upon Cornehill, but foreign butchers were not admitted there to sell flesh till the year 1533; and it was enacted, that butchers should sell [1] their beef not above a halfpenny the pound, and mutton a halfpenny half-farthing; which act being devised for the great commodity of the realm (as it was then thought) hath since proved far otherwise; for before that time a fat ox was sold in London for six-and-twenty shillings and eight pence at the most, a fat wether for three shillings and four pence, a fat calf the like price, a fat lamb for twelve pence, pieces of beef weighing two pounds and a half at the least, yea three pounds or better, for a penny, on every butcher's stall in this city, and of those pieces of beef thirteen or fourteen for twelve pence, fat mutton for eight pence the quarter, and one hundred weight of beef for four shillings and eight pence, at the dearest. What the price is now I need not to set down; many men thought the same act to rise in price, by mean that graziers knew or supposed what weight every their beasts contained, and so raising their price thereafter, the butcher could be no gainer, but by likewise raising his price.[2] The number of butchers then in the city and suburbs was accounted six score, of which every one killed six oxen a piece weekly, which is in forty-six weeks thirty-three thousand one hundred and twenty oxen, or seven hundred and twenty oxen weekly. The foreign butchers for a long time stood in the high street of Lime Street

---

[1] " Their beef and mutton by weight, to wit."—*1st edition*, p. 148.
[2] " But the true cause of enhanceing the prices both of those and other victuals are not to be disputed here."—*1st edition*, p. 148.

ward on the north side, twice every week, namely, Wednesday and Saturday, and were some gain to the tenants before whose doors they stood, and into whose houses they set their blocks and stalls; but that advantage being espied, they were taken into Leaden hall, there to pay for their standing to the chamber of London. Thus much for the market upon Cornhill.

The chief ornaments of Cornhill ward are these: first, at the east end thereof, in the middle of the high street, and at the parting of four ways, have ye a water standard, placed in the year 1582, in manner following. A certain German, named Peter Morris, having made an artificial forcier for that purpose, conveyed Thames water in pipes of lead over the steeple of St. Magnus church, at the north end of London Bridge, and from thence into divers men's houses in Thames street, New Fish street, and Grasse street, up to the north-west corner of Leaden hall, the highest ground of all the city, where the waste of the main pipe rising into this standard, provided at the charges of the city, with four spouts did at every tide run (according to covenant) four ways, plentifully serving to the commodity of the inhabitants near adjoining in their houses, and also cleansed the channels of the street towards Bishopsgate, Aldgate, the bridge, and the Stockes' market. But now no such matter, through whose default I know not.[1]

Then have ye a fair conduit of sweet water, castellated in the middest of that ward and street. This conduit was first built of stone in the year 1282, by Henry Walles, mayor of London, to be a prison for night-walkers, and other suspicious persons, and was called the Tun upon Cornehill, because the same was built somewhat in fashion of a tun standing on the one end.

To this prison the night watches of this city committed not only night walkers, but also other persons, as well spiritual as temporal, whom they suspected of incontinence, and punished them according to the customs of this city; but complaint thereof being made, about the year of Christ 1297, King Edward I. writeth to his citizens thus:—

" Edward, by the grace of God, etc. Whereas Richard Gravesend, bishop of London, hath showed unto us, that by the Great Charter of England, the Church hath a privilege, that no clerk should be imprisoned by a lay man without our command,

---

[1] It would seem, from the addition of these words, which are not in the first edition, that this conduit ceased so to run between the years 1598 and 1603.

and breach of peace, which notwithstanding some citizens of London, upon mere spite, do enter in their watches into clerks' chambers, and like felons carry them to the Tun, which Henry le Walleys, sometime mayor, built for night walkers; wherefore we will that this our commandment be proclaimed in full hustings, and that no watch hereafter enter into any clerk's chamber, under the forfeit of twenty pounds. Dated at Carlisle the 18th of March, the 25th of our reign."

More, I read about the year of Christ 1299, the 27th of Edward I., certain principal citizens of London, to wit, T. Romane, Richard Gloucester, Nicholas Faringdon, Adam Helingburie, T. Saly, John Dunstable, Richard Ashwy, John Wade, and William Stortford, brake up this prison called the Tun, and took out certain prisoners, for which they were sharply punished by long imprisonment and great fines. It cost the citizens (as some have written) more than twenty thousand marks, which they were amerced in, before William le March, treasurer of the king's exchequer, to purchase the king's favour, and confirmation of their liberties.

Also, that in the year 1383, the 7th of Richard II., the citizens of London, taking upon them the rights that belonged to their bishops, first imprisoned such women as were taken in fornication or adultery in the said Tun, and after bringing them forth to the sight of the world, they caused their heads to be shaven, after the manner of thieves, whom they named appellators, and so to be led about the city, in sight of all the inhabitants, with trumpets and pipes sounding before them, that their persons might be the more largely known. Neither did they spare such kind of men a whit the more, but used them as hardly, saying, they abhorred not only the negligence of their prelates, but also detested their avarice, that studying for money, omitted the punishment limited by law, and permitted those that were found guilty to live favourably in their sin. Wherefore, they would themselves, they said, purge their city from such filthiness, lest, through God's vengeance, either the pestilence or sword should happen to them, or that the earth should swallow them.

Last of all to be noted, I read in the charge of the wardmote inquest in every ward of the city, these words:—" If there be any priest in service within the ward, which before time hath been set in the Tun in Cornhill for his dishonesty, and hath forsworn the city, all such shall be presented."

Thus much for the Tun in Cornhill have I read. Now for the punishments of priests in my youth: one note and no more.

John Atwod, draper, dwelling in the parish of St. Michael upon Cornehill, directly against the church, having a proper woman to his wife, such an one as seemed the holiest among a thousand, had also a lusty chantry priest, of the said parish church, repairing to his house; with the which priest the said Atwod would sometimes after supper play a game at tables for a pint of ale: it chanced on a time, having haste of work, and his game proving long, he left his wife to play it out, and went down to his shop, but returning to fetch a pressing iron, he found such play to his misliking, that he forced the priest to jump out at a window over the penthouse into the street, and so to run to his lodging in the churchyard. Atwod and his wife were soon reconciled, so that he would not suffer her to be called in question; but the priest being apprehended and committed, I saw his punishment to be thus:—He was on three market days conveyed through the high street and markets of the city with a paper on his head, wherein was written his trespass. The first day he rode in a carry, the second on a horse, his face to the horse tail, the third led betwixt twain, and every day rung with basons, and proclamations made of his fact at every turning of the street, as also before John Atwod's stall, and the church door of his service, where he lost his chantry of twenty nobles the year, and was banished the city for ever.

By the west side of the foresaid prison, then called the Tun, was a fair well of spring water, curbed round with hard stone; but in the year 1401, the said prison house, called the Tun, was made a cistern for sweet water, conveyed by pipes of lead from Tiborne, and was from thenceforth called the Conduit upon Cornhill. Then was the well planked over, and a strong prison made of timber called a cage, with a pair of stocks therein set upon it, and this was for night walkers. On the top of which cage was placed a pillory, for the punishment of bakers offending in the assize of bread, for millers stealing of corn at the mill, for bawds, scolds, and other offenders. As in the year 1468, the 7th of Edward IV., divers persons being common jurors, such as at assizes were forsworn for rewards, or favour of parties, were judged to ride from Newgate to the pillory in Cornhill, with mitres of paper on their heads, there to stand, and from thence again to Newgate, and this judgment was given by the mayor of London. In the year 1509, the 1st of Henry VIII., Darby, Smith, and Simson, ringleaders of false inquests in London, rode about the city with their faces to the horse tails, and papers on their heads, and were set on the pillory in Cornhill, and after brought again to Newgate, where they died for very shame, saith Robert Fabian. A ringleader of inquests,[1] as I take it, is he that making a gainful occupation thereof, will appear on Nisi-priuses, or he be warned, or procure himself to be warned, to come on by a tales. He will also procure himself to be foreman when he can, and take upon him to overrule the rest to his opinion; such an one shall be laboured by plaintiffs and defendants, not without promise of rewards, and therefore to be suspected of a bad conscience. I would wish a more careful choice of jurors to be had; for I have known a man carted, rung with basons, and banished out of Bishopsgate ward, and afterward in Aldgate ward admitted to be a constable, a grand juryman, and foreman of the wardmote inquest: what I know of the like, or worse men, proffered to the like offices, I forbear to write, but wish to be reformed.

The foresaid conduit upon Cornhill, was in the year 1475 enlarged by Robert Drope, draper, mayor, that then dwelt in that ward; he increased the cistern of this conduit with an east end of stone, and castellated in comely manner.

In the year 1546, Sir Martin Bowes, mayor, dwelling in Lombard street, and having his back gate opening into Cornhill against the said conduit, minded to have enlarged the cistern thereof with a west end, like as Robert Drope before had done towards the east; view and measure of the plot was taken for this work; but the pillory and cage being removed, they found the ground planked, and the well aforesaid worn out of memory, which well they revived and restored to use—it is since made a pump; they set the pillory somewhat west from the well; and so this work ceased.

On the north side of the street, from the east unto the west, have ye divers fair houses for merchants and other, amongst the which one large house is called the Wey house, where merchandises brought from beyond the seas are to be weighed at the king's beam. This house hath a master, and under him four master porters, with porters under them: they have a strong cart, and four great horses, to draw and carry the wares from the merchants' houses to the beam and back again. Sir Thomas Lovell, knight, built this house, with a fair front of tenements towards the street; all which he gave to the Grocers of London, himself being free of the city, and a brother of that company.

---

[1] " Ringleaders of inquests will proffer their service, and bend every way for gain. Careful choice of jurors is to be had; a man detected, and that had sworn foolishly against his brother, is not to be admitted a common juror; neither butcher nor surgeon is to be admitted."—*Stow*.

Then have ye the said Finke's lane, the south end of which lane on both sides is in Cornehill ward.

Then next is the Royal Exchange, erected in the year 1566, after this order, namely, certain houses upon Cornehill, and the like upon the back thereof, in the ward of Brode street, with three alleys, the first called Swan alley, opening into Cornehill, the second New alley, passing throughout of Cornehill into Brode street ward, over against St. Bartholomew lane, the third St. Christopher's alley, opening into Brode street ward, and into St. Christopher's parish, containing in all fourscore households, were first purchased by the citizens of London, for more than three thousand five hundred and thirty-two pounds, and were sold for four hundred and seventy-eight pounds, to such persons as should take them down and carry them thence; also the ground or plot was made plain at the charges of the city; and then possession thereof was by certain aldermen, in name of the whole citizens, given to Sir Thomas Gresham, knight, agent to the queen's highness, thereupon to build a burse, or place for merchants to assemble, at his own proper charges. And he, on the 7th of June, laying the first stone of the foundation, being brick, accompanied with some aldermen, every of them laid a piece of gold, which the workmen took up, and forthwith followed upon the same with such diligence, that by the month of November, in the year 1567, the same was covered with slate, and shortly after fully finished.

In the year 1570, on the 23rd of January, the queen's majesty, attended with her nobility, came from her house at the Strand, called Somerset house, and entered the city by Temple Bar, through Fleet street, Cheape, and so by the north side of the burse, through Threeneedle street, to Sir Thomas Gresham's in Bishopsgate street, where she dined. After dinner her majesty returning through Cornehill, entered the burse on the south side; and after that she had viewed every part thereof above the ground, especially the pawn, which was richly furnished with all sorts of the finest wares in the city, she caused the same burse by an herald and trumpet to be proclaimed the Royal Exchange, and so to be called from thenceforth, and not otherwise.

Next adjoining this Royal Exchange remaineth one part of a large stone house, and is now called the Castle of such a sign; at a tavern door there is a passage through out of Cornehill into Threeneedle street; the other part of the said stone house was taken down for enlarging the Royal Exchange: this stone house was said of some to have been a church, whereof it had no proportion, of others a Jew's house, as though none but Jews had dwelt in stone houses; but that opinion is without warrant, for besides the strong building of stone houses against the invasion of thieves in the night, when no watches were kept, in the 1st year of Richard I., to prevent the casualties of fire, which often had happened in the city, when the houses were built of timber, and covered with reed or straw, Henry Fitz Alewine being mayor, it was decreed, that from henceforth no man should build within the city but of stone, until a certain height, and to cover the same building with slate or burnt tile; and this was the very cause of such stone buildings, whereof many have remained till our time, that for winning of ground they have been taken down, and in place of some one of them being low, as but two stories above the ground, many houses of four or five stories high are placed. From this stone house down to the Stocks are divers large houses, especially for height, for merchants and artificers.

On the south side of this high street is the parish church of St. Peter upon Cornehill, which seemeth to be of an ancient building, but not so ancient as fame reporteth, for it hath been lately repaired, if not all new built, expect the steeple, which is ancient. The roof of this church, and glazing, were finished in the reign of Edward IV., as appeareth by arms of noblemen and aldermen of London then living. There remaineth in this church a table whereon it is written, I know not by what authority, but of a late hand, that King Lucius founded the same church to be an archbishop's see metropolitan,[1] and chief church of his kingdom, and that it so endured the space of four hundred years, unto the coming of Augustin the monk.

Joceline of Furness writeth, that Thean, the first archbishop of London, in the reign of Lucius, built the said church by the aid of Ciran, chief butler to King Lucius; and also that Eluanus, the second archbishop, built a library to the same adjoining, and converted many of the Druids, learned men in the Pagan law, to Christianity. True it is, that a library there was pertaining to this parish church of old time, built of stone, and of late repaired with brick by the executors of Sir John Crosby, alderman, as his arms on the south end doth witness.

This library hath been of late time, to wit, within these fifty years, well furnished of books; John Leyland viewed and com-

[1] "Archbishops of London hard to be proved, and therefore not be affirmed."—*Stow*.

mended them; but now those books be gone, and the place is occupied by a schoolmaster and his usher, over a number of scholars learning their grammar rules, etc. Notwithstanding, before that time a grammar school had been kept in this parish, as appeareth in the year 1425, I read, that John Whitby was rector, and John Steward schoolmaster there; and in the 25th of Henry VI., it was enacted by parliament, that four grammar schools in London should be maintained, namely, in the parishes of Allhallows, in Thames street, St. Andrew in Oldbourne, St. Peter's upon Cornehill, and St. Thomas of Acars.

Monuments of the dead in this church defaced: I read, that Hugh Waltham, Nicholas Pricot, mercer, alderman, Richard Manhall, 1503; William Kingston, fishmonger, gave his tenements called the Horse mill in Grasse street to this church, and was there buried about the year 1298; John Unisburgh, poulterer, 1410; John Law. Also Peter Mason, tailor, gave to this church seven pounds sterling yearly for ever, out of his tenements in Colechurch parish, and deceased about the year 1416. John Foxton founded a chantry there. A brotherhood of St. Peter was in this church established by Henry IV., the 4th of his reign. William Brampton and William Askham, fishmongers and aldermen, were chief procurers thereof, for the fishmongers of late buried there; Sir William Bowyer, mayor 1543; Sir Henry Huberthorn, mayor 1546; Sir Christopher Morice, master-gunner of England to King Henry VIII.; Edward Elrington, esquire, chief-butler to Edward VI.; Thomas Gardener, grocer; and Justice Smith, and other.

Then have ye the parish church of St. Michael th' Archangel; for the antiquity whereof I find that Alnothus the priest gave it to the abbot and convent of Covesham, Reynold abbot, and the convent there did grant the same to Sperling the priest, in all measures as he and his predecessors before had held it; to the which Sperling also they granted all their lands which they there had, except certain lands which Orgar le Prowde had held of them, and paid two shilling yearly; for the which grant the said Sperling should yearly pay one mark of rent to the said abbot of Covesham, and find him and his lodging, salt, water, and fire, when he came to London. This was granted 1133, about the 34th of Henry I. Thus much for antiquity; of later time I find, that Elizabeth Peake, widow, gave the patronage or gift of this benefice to the Drapers in London; she lieth buried in the belfry, 1518: her monument yet remaineth.

This hath been a fair and beautiful church, but of late years,

since the surrender of their lands to Edward VI., greatly
blemished by the building of lower tenements on the north side
thereof towards the high street, in place of a green churchyard,
whereby the church is darkened, and other ways annoyed. The
fair new steeple, or bell tower of this church, was begun to be
built in the year 1421, which being finished, and a fair ring of
five bells therein placed, a sixth bell [1] was added, and given by
John Whitwell, Isabel his wife, and William Rus, alderman,
and goldsmith, about the year 1430, which bell, named "Rus,"
nightly at eight of the clock, and otherwise for knells, and in
peals, rung by one man, for the space of one hundred and sixty
years, of late overhauled by four or five at once, hath been thrice
broken, and new cast within the space of ten years, to the charges
of that parish more than one hundred marks.

And here a note of this steeple: as I have oft heard my father
report, upon St. James' night, certain men in the loft next under
the bells, ringing of a peal, a tempest of lightning and thunder
did arise, an ugly shapen sight appeared to them, coming in at
the south window, and lighted on the north, for fear whereof
they all fell down, and lay as dead for the time, letting the bells
ring and cease of their own accord; when the ringers came to
themselves, they found certain stones of the north window to be
razed and scratched, as if they had been so much butter, printed
with a lion's claw; the same stones were fastened there again,
and so remain till this day. I have seen them oft, and have put
a feather or small stick into the holes where the claws had entered
three or four inches deep. At the same time certain main
timber posts at Queene Hith were scratched and cleft from the
top to the bottom; and the pulpit cross in Powle's churchyard
was likewise scratched, cleft, and overturned. One of the
ringers lived in my youth, whom I have oft heard to verify the
same to be true.

But to return. William Rus was a special benefactor to this
church; his arms yet remain in the windows. William Comer-
ton, Symon Smith, Walter Belingham, were buried there, and
founded chantries there; John Grace, 1439; Robert Drope,
mayor, buried on the north side of the choir, under a fair tomb
of grey marble, 1485, he gave to poor maids' marriages of that
parish twenty pounds, to poor of that ward ten pounds, shirts
and smocks three hundred, and gowns of broad cloth one

---

[1] "This was accounted the best ring of six belles, to bee rung by six men,
that was in England, for harmonye, sweetness of sound, and tune."—
Stow.

hundred, etc.[1] Jane his wife, matching with Edward Gray, Viscount Lisle, was buried by her first husband, 1500; she gave ninety pounds in money to the beautifying of that church, and her great messuage, with the appurtenance, which was by her executors, W. Caple and other, 1517, the 9th of Henry VIII., assured to John Wardroper, parson, T. Clearke, W. Dixson, and John Murdon, wardens of the said church, and their successors for ever, they do keep yearly for her an obite, or anniversary, to be spent on the poor, and otherwise, in all three pounds, the rest of the profits to be employed in reparation of the church. In the 34th year of Henry VIII., Edward Stephan, parson, T. Spencer, P. Guntar, and G. Grouch, churchwardens, granted to T. Lodge a lease for sixty years of the said great messuage, with the appurtenance, which were called the Lady Lisle's lands, for the rent of eight pounds thirteen shillings and four pence the year. The parishioners since gave it up as chantry land, and wronged themselves. Also the said Robert Drope, and Lady Lisle, notwithstanding their liberality to that church and parish, their tomb is pulled down, no monument remaineth of them. Peter Hawton, late alderman, is laid in their vault, 1596. Robert Fabian, alderman, that wrote and published a Chronicle of England and of France, was buried there 1511, with this epitaph:—

> " Like as the day his course doth consume,
> And the new morrow springeth againe as fast,
> So man and woman, by Nature's custome,
> This life to pass, at last in earth are cast,
> In joy and sorrow, which here their time do wast,
> Never in one state, but in course transitory,
> So full of change is of this world the glory."

His monument is gone. Richard Garnam, 1527, buried there; Edmond Trindle and Robert Smith;[2] William Dickson and Margaret his wife,[3] buried in the cloister under a fair tomb now defaced; Thomas Stow, my grandfather, about the year 1526, and Thomas Stow, my father, 1559; John Tolus, alderman, 1548, he gave to John Willowby, parson of that church, to Thomas Lodge, G. Hind, P. Bolde, churchwardens, and to their successors, towards the reparation of that church, and relief of the poor for ever, his tenement with the appurtenances in the

---

[1] " To the poor at his burial sixteen pounds, to prisons, hospitals, and lazar houses, liberally; he also gave his house in Cornehill to be sold, and the price thereof to be spent on the amendment of highways."—1st edition, p. 153.

[2] " My godfathers."—1st edition, p. 153.

[3] " My godmother."—Ibid.

parish of St. Michael, which he had lately purchased of Alvery Randalph, of Badlesmeere in Kent; but the parish never had the gift, nor heard thereof by the space of forty years after; such was the conscience of G. Barne and other the executors, to conceal it to themselves; and such is the negligence of the parishioners, that being informed thereof, make no claim thereunto. Philip Gonter, that was alderman for a time, and gave four hundred pounds to be discharged thereof, was buried in the cloister about the year 1582, and Anne his wife, etc. Thomas Houghton, father to the said Peter Houghton, Francis Beneson, and William Towersan.

This parish church hath on the south side thereof a proper cloister, and a fair churchyard, with a pulpit cross, not much unlike to that in Paule's churchyard. Sir John Rudstone, mayor, caused the same pulpit cross in his lifetime to be built, the churchyard to be enlarged, by ground purchased of the next parish, and also proper houses to be raised for lodging of choir men, such as at that time were assistants to divine service, then daily sung by note in that church. The said John Rudstone deceased 1531, and was buried in a vault under the pulpit cross; he appointed sermons to be preached there, not now performed; his tomb before the pulpit cross is taken thence, with the tomb of Richard Yaxley, Doctor of Physic to King Henry VIII. and other. The choir of that church dissolved, the lodgings of choir men were by the grave fathers of that time charitably appointed for receipt of ancient decayed parishioners, namely, widows, such as were not able to bear the charge of greater rents abroad, which blessed work of harbouring the harbourless is promised to be rewarded in the kingdom of heaven.

Then have ye Birchover lane, so called of Birchover, the first builder and owner thereof, now corruptly called Birchin lane, the north half whereof is of the said Cornehill ward; the other part is of Langborne ward.

This lane, and the high street near adjoining, hath been inhabited for the most part with wealthy drapers, from Birchover's lane, on that side the street down to the stocks, in the reign of Henry VI., had ye for the most part dwelling Fripperers or Upholders, that sold old apparel and household stuff.

I have read of a countryman, that then having lost his hood in Westminster hall, found the same in Cornehill hanged out to be sold, which he challenged, but was forced to buy, or go without it, for their stall, they said, was their market. At that time also the wine drawer of the Pope's head tavern (standing without the door in the high street) took the same man by the sleeve, and said, "Sir, will you drink a pint of wine?" whereunto he answered, "A penny spend I may;" and so drank his pint, for bread nothing did he pay, for that was allowed free.[1]

This Pope's head tavern, with other houses adjoining, strongly built of stone, hath of old time been all in one, pertaining to some great estate, or rather to the king of this realm, as may be supposed, both by the largeness thereof, and by the arms, to wit, three leopards passant, gardant, which were the whole arms of England before the reign of Edward III., that quartered them with the arms of France, three fleur-de-lis.

These arms of England, supported between two angels, are fair and largely graven in stone on the fore front towards the high street, over the door or stall of one great house, lately for many years possessed by Mr. Philip Gunter. The Pope's head tavern is on the back part thereof towards the south, as also one other house called the stone house in Lombard street. Some say this was King John's house, which might so be; for I find in a written copy of Matthew Paris' History, that in the year 1232, Henry III. sent Hubert de Burgh, Earl of Kent, to Cornehill in London, there to answer all matters objected against him, where he wisely acquitted himself. The Pope's head tavern hath a footway through from Cornehill into Lombard street. And down lower on the high street of Cornehill, is there one other way through by the Cardinal's hat tavern into Lombard street. And so let this suffice for Cornhill ward. In which be governors:—an alderman, his deputy, common councillors four or six, constables four, scavengers four, wardmote inquest sixteen and a beadle. It is charged to the fifteen at sixteen pounds.

LANGBORNE WARD, AND FENNIE ABOUT

Langborne ward, so called of a long bourne of sweet water, which of old time breaking out into Fenchurch street, ran down the same street and Lombard street to the west end of St. Mary Woolnoth's church, where turning south, and breaking into small shares, rills, or streams, it left the name of Share borne lane, or South borne lane (as I have read), because it ran south to the river of Thames. This ward beginneth at the west end of Aldgate ward in Fenne church street, by the Ironmongers' hall, which is on the north side of that street, at a place called

[1] "Wine one pint for a pennie, and bread to drink it was given free in every tavern."—*Stow*.

Culver alley, where sometime was a lane, through the which men went into Lime street, but that being long since stopped up for suspicion of thieves that lurked there by night, as is shown in Lime street ward, there is now this said alley, a tennis-court, etc.

Fenne church street took that name of a fenny or moorish ground, so made by means of this borne which passed through it, and therefore until this day in the Guildhall of this city, that ward is called by the name of Langborne and Fennie about, and not otherwise; yet others be of opinion that it took that name of *Fœnum*, that is, hay sold there, as Grasse street took the name of grass, or herbs, there sold. [*See* Additional Notes.]

In the midst of this street standeth a small parish church called St. Gabriel Fen church, corruptly Fan church.

Helming Legget, esquire, by license of Edward III., in the 49th of his reign, gave one tenement, with a curtelage thereto belonging, and a garden, with an entry thereto leading, unto Sir John Hariot, parson of Fenchurch, and to his successors for ever; the house to be a parsonage-house, the garden to be a churchyard, or burying-place for the parish.

Then have ye Lombard street, so called of the Longobards, and other merchants, strangers of divers nations assembling there twice every day, of what original or continuance I have not read of record, more than that Edward II., in the 12th of his reign, confirmed a messuage, sometime belonging to Robert Turke, abutting on Lombard street toward the south, and toward Cornehill on the north, for the merchants of Florence, which proveth that street to have had the name of Lombard street before the reign of Edward II. The meeting of which merchants and others there continued until the 22nd of December, in the year 1568; on the which day the said merchants began to make their meetings at the burse, a place then new built for that purpose in the ward of Cornhill, and was since by her majesty, Queen Elizabeth, named the Royal Exchange.

On the north side of this ward is Lime street, one half whereof on both the sides is of this Langborne ward, and therein on the west side is the Pewterers' hall, which company were admitted to be a brotherhood in the 13th of Edward IV.

At the south-west corner of Lime street standeth a fair parish church of St. Dionys called Backe church, lately new built in the reign of Henry VI. John Bugge, esquire, was a great benefactor to that work, as appeareth by his arms, three water budgets, and his crest, a Morian's head, graven in the stone-work of the choir, the upper end on the north side, where he was buried. Also John Darby, alderman, added thereunto a fair aisle, or chapel, on the south side, and was there buried about the year 1466. He gave (besides sundry ornaments) his dwelling-house and others unto the said church. The Lady Wich, widow to Hugh Wich, sometime mayor of London, was there buried, and gave lands for sermons, etc. John Master, gentleman, was by his children buried there 1444; Thomas Britaine; Henry Travers, of Maidstone, in Kent, merchant, 1501; John Bond, about 1504; Robert Paget, merchant-tailor, one of the sheriffs, 1536; Sir Thomas Curteis, pewterer, then fishmonger, mayor, 1557; Sir James Harvie, ironmonger, mayor, 1581; William Peterson, esquire; William Sherington; Sir Edward Osborne, clothworker, mayor, etc.

Then by the four corners (so called of Fenchurch street in the east, Bridge street on the south, Grasse street on the north, and Lombard street on the west), in Lombard street is one fair parish church called Allhallows Grasse church, in Lombard street; I do so read it in evidences of record, for that the grass market went down that way, when that street was far broader than now it is, being straitened by incroachments.

This church was lately new built. John Warner, armourer, and then grocer, sheriff 1494, built the south aisle; his son, Robert Warner, esquire, finished it in the year 1516. The pewterers were benefactors towards the north aisle, etc. The steeple, or bell tower, thereof was finished in the year 1544, about the 36th of Henry VIII. The fair stone porch of this church was brought from the late dissolved priory of St. John of Jerusalem by Smithfield, so was the frame for their bells, but the bells being bought, were never brought thither, by reason that one old Warner, draper, of that parish deceasing, his son Marke Warner would not perform what his father had begun, and appointed, so that fair steeple hath but one bell, as friars were wont to use. The monuments of this church be these. The said Warners, and John Walden, draper.

Next is a common hostelry for travellers, called the George, of such a sign. This is said to have pertained to the Earl Ferrers, and was his London lodging in Lombard street, and that in the year 1175, a brother of the said earl, being there privily slain in the night, was there thrown down into the dirty street, as I have afore shown in the chapter of night watches.

Next to this is the parish church of St. Edmond, the king and martyr, in Lombard street, by the south corner of Birchover lane. This church is also called St. Edmond Grasse church, because the said grass market came down so low. The monuments in this church are these: Sir John Milborne, draper, mayor, deceased, 1535, buried there by Dame Joan and Dame Margaret his wives, under a tomb of touch; Humfrey Heyford, goldsmith, mayor 1477; Sir William Chester, draper, mayor 1560, with his wives, amongst his predecessors; Sir George Barne, mayor 1586; Matilde at Vine founded a chantry there, etc.

From this church down Lombard street, by Birchover's lane (the one half of which lane is of this ward), and so down, be divers fair houses, namely, one with a very fair fore front towards the street, built by Sir Martin Bowes, goldsmith, since mayor of London, and then one other, sometime belonging to William de la Pole, knight banneret, and yet the king's merchant,[1] in the 14th of Edward III., and after him to Michael de la Pole, Earl of Suffolk, in the 14th of Richard II., and was his merchant's house, and so down towards the Stocks market, lacking but some three houses thereof.

The south side of this ward beginneth in the east, at the chain to be drawn athwart Mart lane up into Fenchurch street, and so west by the north end of Minchen lane to St. Margaret Patten's street, or Roode lane, and down that street to the midway towards St. Margaret's church; then by Philpot lane (so called of Sir John Philpot that dwelt there, and was owner thereof), and down that lane some six or eight houses on each side, is all of this ward.

Then by Grasse church corner into Lombard street to St. Clement's lane, and down the same to St. Clement's church; then down St. Nicholas lane, and down the same to St. Nicholas church, and the same church is of this ward. Then to Abchurch church lane, and down some small portion thereof; then down Sherborne lane, a part thereof, and a part of Bearebinder lane, be of this ward; and then down Lombard street to the sign of the Angel, almost to the corner over against the Stocks market.

On the south side of this ward, somewhat within Mart lane, have you the parish church of Allhallows, commonly called Stane church (as may be supposed), for a difference from other churches of that name in this city, which of old time were built of timber, and since were built of stone. In this church have

[1] " Noblemen of this realm of old time, as also of late years, have dealt in merchandises."—*Stow.*

been divers fair monuments of the dead, namely, of John Costin, girdler, a great benefactor: he deceased 1244. His name remaineth painted in the church roof; if it had been set in brass, it would have been fetched down.[1] He gave out of certain tenements to the poor of that parish a hundred quarters of charcoals yearly for ever. Sir Robert Test, knight of the holy sepulchre, and Dame Joan his wife, about 1486; Robert Stone; Sir John Steward, and Dame Alice his wife;[2] John Bostocke, esquire; Christopher Holt, Sir Richard Tate, knight, ambassador to King Henry VIII. buried there 1554. His monument remaineth yet; the rest being all pulled down, and swept out of the church, the churchwardens were forced to make a large account; 12s. that year for brooms, besides the carriage away of stone and brass of their own charge. And here I am to note, that being informed of the Writhsleys to be buried there, I have since found them and other to be buried at St. Giles without Cripplegate, where I mind to leave them.

By this church sometime passed a lane, called Cradock's lane, from Mart lane, winding by the north side of the said church into Fenchurch street, the which lane being straitened by incroachments, is now called Church alley.

Then is the parish church of St. Nicholas Acon, or Hacon (for so have I read it in records), in Lombard street. Sir John Bridges, draper, mayor, 1520, newly repaired this church, and embattled it, and was there buried. Francis Boyer, grocer,

---

[1] " If it had been in brasse, it would not have remained there so long."
—1st edition, p. 159.

[2] In the first edition, p. 159, the following passage is here inserted:—

" Alice, William, and John, wife and sons to Thomas Clarell; Agnes, daughter to Thomas Niter, gent.; William Atwell; Felix, daughter to Sir Thomas Gisers, and wife to Travers Thomas Mason, esquire; Edmond Wartar, esquire; Joan, wife to John Chamberlaine, esquire, daughter to Roger Lewkner, esquire; William Frier; John Hamburger, esquire; Hugh Moresby; Gilbert Prince, alderman; Oliver Chorley, gentleman; Sir John Writh, or Writhesley, *alias* Garter principal king at arms, sometime laid under a fair tomb in the choir, now broken down and gone; Joan, wife to Thomas Writhesley, son to Sir John Writhesley, Garter, daughter and heir to William Hall, esquire; John Writhesley the younger, son to Sir John Writhesley, and Alienor, Eleanor, second wife to John Writhesley, daughter and heir to Thomas Arnalde, and Agnes his wife; John Writhesley, son of Thomas; Agnes Arnold, first married to William Writhesley, daughter of Richard Warmeforde; Barbara Hungerford, daughter to Sir John Writhesley, wife to Anthony Hungerford, son to Sir Thomas Hungerford, of Denmampney, in the county of Gloucester."

The cause for the omission of these names is explained at the close of the paragraph in the text; which is however so indistinctly expressed, that its meaning could not very well be ascertained except by a reference to what was originally written.

one of the sheriffs, was buried there 1580, with other of the Boyers: so was Julian, wife to John Lambart, alderman.[1]

Then is there in the high street a proper parish church of St. Mary Woolnoth, of the Nativity, the reason of which name I have not yet learnt. This church is lately new built. Sir Hugh Brice, goldsmith, mayor in the first year of Henry VII., keeper of the king's exchange at London, and one of the governors of the king's mint in the Tower of London, under William Lord Hastings, the 5th of Edward IV., deceased 1496. He built in this church a chapel called the Charnell, as also part of the body of the church and of the steeple, and gave money toward the finishing thereof, besides the stone which he had prepared: he was buried in the body of the church. Guy Brice, or Boys, was buried there. Dame Joan, wife to Sir William Peach;[2] Thomas Nocket, draper, 1396: he founded a chantry there. Simon Eyre, 1459: he gave the tavern called the Cardinal's Hat, in Lombard street, with a tenement annexed on the east part of the tavern, and a mansion behind the east tenement, together with an alley from Lombard street to Cornhill, with the appurtenances, all which were by him new built, toward a brotherhood of our Lady in St. Mary Woolnoth's church. John Moager, pewterer, and Emme his wife, in St. John's chapel; Sir John Percivall, merchant-tailor, mayor, about 1504; Thomas Roch, and Andrew Michael, vintners, and Joan their wife; William Hilton, merchant-tailor, and tailor to King Henry VIII., was buried there 1519, under the chapel of St. George, which chapel was built by George Lufken, sometime tailor to the prince; Robert Amades, goldsmith, master of the king's jewels; Sir Martin Bowes, mayor, buried about 1569: he gave lands for the discharge of that Langborn ward, of all fifteens to be granted to the king by parliament; George Hasken, Sir Thomas Ramsey, late mayor, etc. Thus have ye seven parishes in this ward, one hall of a company, divers fair houses for merchants, and other monuments none. It hath an alderman, his deputy, common councillors eight, constables fifteen, scavengers nine, men of the wardmote inquest seventeen, and a beadle. It is taxed to the fifteen,[3] in the exchequer, at £20 9s. 8d.

---

[1] " Mother of William Lambert, yet living."—1st edition, p. 160.
[2] " Hugh Acton, tailor."—Ibid.
[3] " In London at twenty-one pound."—Ibid.

BILLINGSGATE WARD

Billingsgate ward beginneth at the west end of Tower street ward in Thames street, about Smart's key, and runneth down along that street on the south side to St. Magnus church at the bridge foot, and on the north side of the said Thames street, from over against Smart's key, till over against the north-west corner of St. Magnus church aforesaid, on this north side of Thames street, is St. Marie hill lane, up to St. Margaret's church, and then part of St. Margaret Patten's street, at the end of St. Marie hill lane. Next out of Thames street is Lucas lane, and then Buttolph lane, and at the north end thereof Philpot lane; then is Rother lane, of old time so called, and thwart the same lane is Little Eastcheape; and these be the bounds of Billingsgate ward.

Touching the principal ornaments within this ward. On the south side of Thames street, beginning at the east end thereof, there is first the said Smart's key, so called of one Smart sometime owner thereof; the next is Belinsgate, whereof the whole ward taketh name; the which (leaving out of the fable, thereof feigning it to be built by King Beline, a Briton, long before the incarnation of Christ), is at this present a large water-gate, port, or harborough, for ships and boats, commonly arriving there with fish, both fresh and salt, shell-fishes, salt, oranges, onions, and other fruits and roots, wheat, rye, and grain of divers sorts, for service of the city and the parts of this realm adjoining. This gate is now more frequented than of old time, when the Queen's hithe was used, as being appointed by the kings of this realm, to be the special or only port for taking up of all such kind of merchandises brought to this city by strangers and foreigners, and the drawbridge of timber at London bridge was then to be raised or drawn up for passage of ships with tops thither.

Touching the ancient customs of Belinsgate in the reign of Edward III., every great ship landing there paid for standage two-pence, every little ship with orelockes a penny, the lesser boat called a Battle a halfpenny; of two quarters of corn measured the king was to have one farthing, of a combe of corn a penny, of every weight going out of the city a halfpenny, of two quarters of sea coal measured a farthing, and of every tun of ale going out of England beyond the seas, by merchant strangers, four-pence, of every thousand herrings a farthing, except franchises, etc.

Next to this is Sommer's key, which likewise took that name of one Sommer dwelling there, as did Lion key of one Lion, owner thereof, and since of the sign of a Lion.

Then is there a fair wharf, or key, called Buttolph's gate, by that name so called in the times of William the Conqueror, and of Edward the Confessor, as I have shown already in the description of the gates.

Next is the parish church of St. Buttolphs, a proper church, and hath had many fair monuments therein, now defaced and gone: notwithstanding I find, by testimonies abroad, that these were buried there; to wit, Roger Coggar, 1384; Andrew Pikeman, and Joan his wife, 1391; Nicholas James, ironmonger, one of the sheriffs, 1423; William Rainwell, fishmonger, and John Rainwell, his son, fishmonger, mayor 1426, and deceasing 1445, buried there with this epitaph:

> " Citizens of London, call to your remembrance,
> The famous John Rainwell, sometime your Maior.
> Of the staple of Callis, so was his chance.
> Here lieth now his corps; his soule bright and faire,
> Is taken to heaven's blisse, thereof is no dispaire.
> His acts beare witnes, by matters of recorde,
> How charitable he was, and of what accorde,
> No man hath beene so beneficiall as hee,
> Unto the Citie in giving liberallie," etc.

He gave a stone house to be a revestrie to that church for ever; more, he gave lands and tenements to the use of the commonalty, that the mayor and chamberlain should satisfy unto the discharge of all persons inhabiting the wards of Belinsgate, Downegate, and Aldgate, as oft as it shall happen any fifteen, by parliament of the king to be granted, also to the Exchequer, in discharge of the sheriffs, ten pounds yearly, which the sheriffs used to pay for the farm of Southwark, so that all men of the realm, coming or passing with carriage, should be free quitted and discharged of all toll and other payments, aforetime claimed by the sheriffs. Further, that the mayor and chamberlain shall pay yearly to the sheriffs eight pounds, so that the said sheriffs take no manner of toll or money of any person of this realm for their goods, merchandises, victuals, and carriages, for their passages at the great gate of the bridge of the city, nor at the gate called the Drawbridge, etc. The overplus of money coming of the said lands and tenements, divided into even portions; the one part to be employed to instore the granaries of the city with wheat for the release of the poor commonalty, and the other moiety to clear and cleanse the shelves, and other stoppages of the river of Thames, etc.

Stephen Forstar, fishmonger, mayor in the year 1454, and Dame Agnes his wife, lie buried there. William Bacon, haberdasher, one of the sheriffs 1480, was there buried, besides many other persons of good worship, whose monuments are all destroyed by bad and greedy men of spoil.

This parish of St. Buttolph is no great thing, notwithstanding divers strangers are there harboured, as may appear by a presentment, not many years since made of strangers, inhabitants in the ward of Billingsgate, in these words: " In Billingsgate ward were one and fifty households of strangers, whereof thirty of these households inhabited in the parish of St. Buttolph, in the chief and principal houses, where they give twenty pounds the year for a house lately letten for four marks; the nearer they dwell to the water-side the more they give for houses, and within thirty years before there was not in the whole ward above three Netherlanders; at which time there was within the said parish levied, for the help of the poor, seven and twenty pounds by the year; but since they came so plentifully thither, there cannot be gathered above eleven pounds, for the stranger will not contribute to such charges as other citizens do." Thus much for that south side of this ward.

On the north side is Bosse alley, so called of a boss of spring water continually running, which standeth by Billingsgate against this alley, and was sometime made by the executors of Richard Whittington.

Then is St. Marie hill lane, which runneth up north from Billingsgate to the end of St. Margaret Pattens, commonly called Roode lane, and the greatest half of that lane is also of Belinsgate ward. In this St. Marie hill lane is the fair parish church of St. Marie, called on the hill, because of the ascent from Billingsgate.

This church hath been lately built, as may appear by this that followeth. Richard Hackney, one of the sheriff's in the year 1322, and Alice his wife, were there buried, as Robert Fabian writeth, saying thus:—" In the year 1497, in the month of April, as labourers digged for the foundation of a wall, within the church of St. Marie hill, near unto Belinsgate, they found a coffin of rotten timber, and therein the corpse of a woman whole of skin, and of bones undissevered, and the joints of her arms pliable, without breaking of the skin, upon whose sepulchre this was engraven:—' Here lieth the bodies of Richard Hackney.

fishmonger, and Alice his wife.' "[1] The which Richard was
sheriff in the 15th of Edward II. Her body was kept above
ground three or four days without nuisance, but then it waxed
unsavoury, and so was again buried. John Mordand, stock-
fishmonger, was buried there, 1387; Nicholas Exton, fishmonger,
mayor 1387; William Cambridge, mayor, 1420; Richard Goslin,
sheriff, 1422; William Philip, sergeant-at-arms, 1473; Robert
Reuell, one of the sheriffs 1490, gave liberally toward the new
building of this church and steeple, and was there buried,
William Remington, mayor, 1500; Sir Thomas Blanke, mayor,
1582; William Holstocke, esquire, comptroller of the king's
ships; Sir Cuthbert Buckle, mayor, 1594.

This lane on both sides is furnished with many fair houses
for merchants; and hath at the north end thereof one other
lane, called St. Margaret Pattens, because of old time pattens
were there usually made and sold; but of latter time this is
called Roode lane, of a roode there placed in the churchyard
of St. Margaret, whilst the old church was taken down, and
again newly built; during which time the oblations made to
this rood were employed towards building of the church; but
in the year 1538, about the 23rd of May, in the morning, the
said rood was found to have been in the night preceding, by
people unknown, broken all to pieces, together with the tabernacle wherein it had been placed. Also, on the 27th of the
same month, in the same parish, amongst the basket makers, a
great and sudden fire happened in the night season, which within
the space of three hours consumed more than a dozen houses,
and nine persons were burnt to death there: and thus ceased
that work of this church, being at that time nigh finished to
the steeple. [*See* Additional Notes.]

The lane on both sides beyond the same church to the midway
towards Fenchurch street, is of Bellinsgate ward.

Then again out of Thames street, by the west end of St. Mary
hill church, runneth up one other lane, of old time called Roape
lane, since called Lucas lane, of one Lucas, owner of some part
thereof, and now corruptly called Love lane; it runneth up by
the east end of a parish church of St. Andrew Hubbert, or St.
Andrew in East Cheap. This church, and all the whole lane
called Lucas lane, is of this Belinsgate ward.

Then have ye one other lane out of Thames street, called
Buttolph lane, because it riseth over against the parish church

---

[1] " Alice Hackney found uncorrupted more than one hundred and
seventy yeres after she was buried."—*Stow.*

of St. Buttolph, and runneth up north by the east end of St. George's church to the west end of St. Andrew's church, and to the south end of Philpot lane.

This parish church of St. George in Buttolph lane is small, but the monuments for two hundred years past are well preserved from spoil, whereof one is of Adam Bamme, mayor 1397; Richard Bamme, esquire, his son, of Gillingham in Kent, 1452; John Walton, gentleman, 1401; Marpor, a gentleman, 1400; John St. John, merchant of Levant, and Agnes his wife, 1400; Hugh Spencer, esquire, 1424; William Combes, stock fishmonger, one of the sheriffs 1452, who gave forty pounds towards the works of that church; John Stokar, draper, one of the sheriffs, 1477; Richard Dryland, esquire, and Katherine his wife, daughter of Morrice Brune, knight, of Southuckenton in Essex, steward of household to Humfrey Duke of Glocester, 1487; Nicholas Patrich, one of the sheriffs, 1519. In the churchyard: William Forman, mayor, 1538; James Mumford, esquire, surgeon to King Henry VIII., buried 1544; Thomas Gayle, haberdasher, 1340; Nicholas Wilford, merchant-tailor, and Elizabeth his wife, about the year 1551; Edward Heyward, 1573, etc. Roger Delakere founded a chantry there.

Then have ye one other lane called Rother lane, or Red Rose lane, of such a sign there, now commonly called Pudding lane, because the butchers of Eastcheap have their scalding house for hogs there, and their puddings, with other filth of beasts, are voided down that way to their dung boats on the Thames.

This lane stretcheth from Thames street to Little East Cheape, chiefly inhabited by basket-makers, turners, and butchers, and is all of Billinsgate ward. The Garland in Little East Cheape, sometime a brewhouse, with a garden on the back side, adjoining to the garden of Sir John Philpot, was the chief house in this East Cheape; it is now divided into sundry small tenements, etc.

This ward hath an alderman, and his deputy, common councillors, constables eleven, scavengers six, for the wardmote inquest fourteen, and a beadle; it is taxed to the fifteen in London at thirty-two pounds, and in the Exchequer at thirty-one pounds ten shillings.

BRIDGE WARD WITHIN

Bridge ward within, so called of London bridge, which bridge is a principal part of that ward, and beginneth at the stulpes

on the south end by Southwark, runneth along the bridge, and
north up Bridge street, commonly called (of the fish market)
New Fish street, from Fish street hill, up Grasse street, to the
north corner of Grasse church; all the bridge is replenished on
both the sides with large, fair, and beautiful buildings, inhabitants for the most part rich merchants, and other wealthy
citizens, mercers, and haberdashers.

In New Fish street be fishmongers and fair taverns on Fish
street hill and Grasse street, men of divers trades, grocers and
haberdashers.

In Grasse street have ye one fair conduit of sweet water
castellated with crest and vent, made by the appointment of
Thomas Hill, mayor, 1484, who gave by his testament one hundred marks towards the conveyance of water to this place. It
was begun by his executors in the year 1491, and finished of
his goods whatsoever it cost.

On the east side of this bridge ward have ye the fair parish
church of St. Magnus; in the which church have been buried
many men of good worship, whose monuments are now for the
most part utterly defaced. I find John Blund, mayor, 1307;
Henry Yeuele, freemason to Edward III., Richard II., and
Henry IV., who deceased 1400; his monument yet remaineth;
William Brampton; John Michell, mayor, 1436; John French,
baker, yeoman of the crown to Henry VII., 1510; Robert
Clarke, fishmonger, 1521; Richard Turke, one of the sheriffs,
1549; William Steede, alderman; Richard Morgan, knight,
chief justice of the common pleas, 1556; Mauritius Griffeth,
Bishop of Rochester, 1559; Robert Blanch, girdler, 1567;
Robert Belgrave, girdler; William Brame, John Couper, fishmonger, alderman, who was put by his turn of mayoralty 1584;
Sir William Garrard, haberdasher, mayor 1555; a grave, wise,
and discreet citizen, equal with the best and inferior to none of
our time, deceased 1571 in the parish of St. Christopher, but was
buried in this church of St. Magnus as in the parish where he
was born; a fair monument is there raised on him; Robert
Harding, salter, one of the sheriffs, 1568; Simon Low, merchant-
tailor, esquire, etc.

Then is the parish church of St. Margaret on Fish street hill,
a proper church, but monuments it hath none: a footway
passeth by the south side of this church from Fish street hill
unto Rother lane.

Up higher on this hill is the parish church of St. Leonard,
Milke church, so termed of one William Melker, an especial

builder thereof, but commonly called St. Leonard's in East
Cheape, because it standeth at East Cheape corner. Monuments there be of the Doggets, namely, Walter Dogget, vintner,
one of the sheriffs, 1380; John Dogget, vintner, and Alice his
wife, about 1456; this John Dogget gave lands to that church;
William Dogget, etc.

This church, and from thence into Little East Cheape to the
east end of the said church, is of the Bridge ward.

Then higher in Grasse street is the parish church of St.
Bennet, called Grasse church, of the herb-market there kept:
this church also is of the Bridge ward, and the farthest north
end thereof. Some monuments remain there undefaced, as of
John Harding, salter, 1576; John Sturgeon, haberdasher,
chamberlain of London; Philip Cushen, Florentine, a famous
merchant, 1600.

The customs of Grass church market, in the reign of Edward
III., as I have read in a book of customs, were these: Every
foreign cart laden with corn or malt, coming thither to be sold,
was to pay one halfpenny, every foreign cart bringing cheese
two-pence, every cart of corn and cheese together (if the cheese
be more worth than the corn) two-pence, and if the corn be more
worth than the cheese, it was to pay a halfpenny; of two horses
laden with corn or malt the bailiff had one farthing; the cart of
the franchise of the Temple and of St. Martin le Grand paid a
farthing; the cart of the hospital of St. John of Jerusalem paid
nothing for their proper goods, and if the corn were brought by
merchants to sell again, the load paid a halfpenny, etc.

On the west side of this ward, at the north end of London
bridge, is a part of Thames street, which is also of this ward, to
wit, so much as of old time was called Stocke Fishmonger row,
of the stock fishmongers dwelling there, down west to a water-
gate, of old time called Ebgate, since Ebgate lane, and now the
Old Swan, which is a common stair on the Thames, but the
passage is very narrow by means of encroachments. On the
south side of Thames street, about the midway betwixt the
bridge foot and Ebgate lane, standeth the Fishmongers' hall,
and divers other fair houses for merchants.

These fishmongers were sometimes of two several companies,
to wit, Stock-fishmongers and Salt-fishmongers, of whose antiquity I read, that by the name of fishmongers of London, they
were, for forestalling, etc., contrary to the laws and constitutions of the city, fined to the king at five hundred marks, the
18th of King Edward I. More, that the said fishmongers,

hearing of the great victory obtained by the same king against the Scots, in the 26th of his reign, made a triumphant and solemn show through the city, with divers pageants, and more than one thousand horsemen, etc., as in the chapter of sports and pastimes. These two companies of stock-fishmongers and salt-fishmongers of old time had their several halls; to wit, in Thames street twain, in New Fish street twain, and in Old Fish street twain: in each place one for either company, in all six several halls, the company was so great, as I have read, and can prove by records. These fishmongers having been jolly citizens, and six mayors of their company in the space of twenty-four years; to wit, Walter Turke, 1350; John Lofkin, 1359; John Wroth, 1361; John Pechie, 1362; Simon Morden, 1369; and William Walworth, 1374. It followed that in the year 1382, through the counsel of John Northampton, draper, then being mayor, William Essex, John More, mercer, and Richard Northburie, the said fishmongers were greatly troubled, hindered of their liberties, and almost destroyed by congregations made against them, so that in a parliament at London the controversy depending between the mayor and aldermen of London, and the fishmongers there, Nicholas Exton, speaker for the fishmongers, prayeth the king to receive him and his company into his protection, for fear of corporal hurt: whereupon it was commanded, either part to keep the peace, on pain of losing all they had; hereupon, a fishmonger, starting up, replied that the complaint brought against them by the movers, etc., was but matter of malice, for that the fishmongers, in the reign of Edward III., being chief officers of the city, had for their misdemeanors then done, committed the chief exhibitors of those petitions to prison. In this parliament the fishmongers, by the king's charter patents, were restored to their liberties; notwithstanding in the year next following, to wit, 1383, John Cavendish, fishmonger, craveth the peace against the chancellor of England, which was granted, and he put in sureties the Earls of Stafford and Salisburie. Cavendish challengeth the chancellor for taking of a bribe of ten pounds for favour of his case, which the chancellor by oath upon the sacrament avoideth. In further trial it was found that the chancellor's man, without his master's privity, had taken it; whereupon Cavendish was adjudged to prison, and to pay the chancellor one thousand marks for slandering him.

After this, many of the nobles assembled at Reading to suppress the seditious stirs of the said John Northampton, or

Combarton, late mayor, that had attempted great and heinous enterprises, of the which he was convicted; and when he stood mute, nor would utter one word, it was decreed that he should be committed to perpetual prison, his goods confiscate to the king's use, and that he should not come within one hundred miles of London during his life. He was therefore sent to the castle of Tintegall in the confines of Cornewall, and in the mean space the king's servants spoiled his goods. John More, Richard Northbery, and other, were likewise there convicted, and condemned to perpetual prison, and their goods confiscate, for certain congregations by them made against the fishmongers in the city of London, as is aforesaid; but they obtained and had the king's pardon, in the 14th of his reign, as appeareth of record; and thus were all these troubles quieted. Those stock-fishmongers and salt-fishmongers were united in the year 1536, the 28th of Henry VIII.; their hall to be but one, in the house given unto them by Sir John Cornwall, Lord Fanhope, and of Ampthull, in the parish of St. Michael in Crooked lane, in the reign of Henry VI. Thus much have I thought good to note of the fishmongers, men ignorant of their antiquities, not able to show a reason why or when they were joined in amity with the goldsmiths, do give part of their arms, etc. Neither, to say aught of Sir William Walworth,[1] the glory of their company, more than that he slew Jack Straw, which is a mere fable, for the said Straw was after overthrowing of the rebels, taken, and by judgment of the mayor beheaded; whose confession at the gallows is extant in my *Annals*, where also is set down the most valiant and praiseworthy act of William Walworth against the principal rebel Waltar Tighlar. As in reproof of Walworth's monument in St. Michael's church, I have declared, and wished to be reformed there, as in other places.

On that south side of Thames street have ye Drinkwater wharf and Fish wharf, in the parish of St. Magnus. On the north side of Thames street is St. Martin's lane; a part of which lane is also of this ward, to wit, on the one side to a well of water, and on the other side as far up as against the said well. Then is St. Michael's lane, part whereof is also of this ward up to a well there, etc. Then at the upper end of New Fish street is a lane turning towards St. Michael's lane, and is called Crooked lane, of the crooked windings thereof.

Above this lane's end, upon Fish street hill, is one great house, for the most part built of stone, which pertained sometime to

[1] " W. Walworth slandered by a fable of Jack Straw."—*Stow.*

Edward the Black Prince, son to Edward III., who was in his lifetime lodged there. It is now altered to a common hostelry, having the Black Bell for a sign.

Above this house, at the top of Fish street hill, is a turning into Great Eastcheape, and so to the corner of Lombard street, over against the north-west corner of Grasse church; and these be the whole bounds of this Bridge ward within: the which hath an alderman and his deputy, for the common council sixteen, constables fifteen, scavengers six, for the wardmote inquest sixteen, and a beadle. It is taxed to the fifteen in London at forty-seven pounds.[1]

CANDLEWICK STREET WARD

Candlewick street, or Candlewright street ward, beginneth at the east end of Great Eastcheape; it passeth west through Eastcheape to Candlewright street, and through the same, down to the north end of Suffolk lane on the south side, and down that lane by the west end of St. Laurence churchyard, which is the farthest west part of that ward. The street of Great Eastcheape is so called of the market there kept in the east part of the city, as Westcheape is a market so called of being in the west.

This Eastcheape is now a flesh market of butchers there dwelling on both sides of the street: it had sometime also cooks mixed amongst the butchers, and such other as sold victuals ready dressed of all sorts. For of old time, when friends did meet, and were disposed to be merry, they went not to dine and sup in taverns, but to the cooks, where they called for meat what they liked, which they always found ready dressed at a reasonable rate, as I have before showed.

In the year 1410, the 11th of Henry IV., upon the even of St. John Baptist, the king's sons,[2] Thomas and John, being in Eastcheape at supper (or rather at breakfast, for it was after the watch was broken up, betwixt two and three of the clock after midnight), a great debate happened between their men and other of the court, which lasted one hour, till the mayor and sheriffs with other citizens, appeased the same; for the which afterwards the said mayor, aldermen, and sheriffs were

---

[1] " In London at fifty pounds, and in the Exchequer at forty-nine pounds ten shillings."—*1st edition*, p. 169.
[2] " The king's sons beaten to Eastcheape; there was no tavern then in Eastcheape."—*Stow*.

called to answer before the king, his sons, and divers lords, being highly moved against the city. At which time, William Gascoyne, chief justice, required the mayor and aldermen, for the citizens, to put them in the king's grace; whereunto they answered, that they had not offended, but (according to the law) had done their best in stinting debate and maintaining of the peace; upon which answer the king remitted all his ire, and dismissed them. And to prove this Eastcheape to be a place replenished with cooks, it may appear by a song called London Lickepennie, made by Lidgate, a monk of Berrie, in the reign of Henry V., in the person of a countryman coming to London, and travelling through the same. In Westcheape (saith the song) he was called on to buy fine lawn, Paris thread, cotton umble, and other linen clothes, and such like (he speaketh of no silks),[1] in Cornhill, to buy old apparel [2] and household stuff, where he was forced to buy his own hood, which he had lost in Westminster hall: in Candlewright street drapers proffered him cheap cloth, in Eastcheape the cooks cried hot ribs of beef roasted, pies well baked, and other victuals: there was clattering of pewter-pots, harp, pipe, and sawtry, yea by cock, nay by cock, for greater oaths were spared: some sang of Jenken, and Julian, etc.; all which melody liked well the passenger, but he wanted money to abide by it, and therefore gat him into Gravesend barge, and home into Kent.

Candlewright (so called in old records of the Guildhall, of St. Marie Overies, and other), or Candlewick street, took that name (as may be supposed) either of chandlers, or makers of candles, both of wax and tallow; for candlewright is a maker of candles, or of wick, which is the cotton or yarn thereof; or otherwise wike,[3] which is the place where they used to work them, as Scalding wike by the Stocks market was called of the poulterers scalding and dressing their poultry there; and in divers countries, dairy houses, or cottages, wherein they make butter and

[1] " In Westcheape linen cloth sold, but no silks spoken of."—*Stow*. But Lydgate does mention silk.

[2] " Fripparia, upholders upon Cornhill, sellers of old apparel and household stuff in Eastcheape."—*Stow*.
This is the stanza alluded to by Stow (see Lydgate's *Minor Poems*):

> " Then into Corn hyl anon I rode,
> Where was much stolen gere amonge;
> I saw where honge myne owne hoode,
> That I had lost amonge the thronge:
> To by my own hoode I thought it wronge;
> I knew it well as I did my crede,
> But for lack of money I could not spede."

[3] " Wike is a working place."—*Stow*.

cheese, are usually called wicks. There dwelt also of old time divers weavers of woollen clothes, brought in by Edward III. For I read, that in the 44th of his reign, the weavers, brought out of Flanders, were appointed their meetings to be in the churchyard of St. Laurence Poultney, and the weavers of Brabant in the churchyard of St. Mary Sommerset. There were then in this city weavers of divers sorts; to wit, of drapery, or tapery, and napery. These weavers of Candlewright street being in short time worn out, their place is now possessed by rich drapers, sellers of woollen cloth, etc.

On the north side of this ward, at the west end of Eastcheape, have ye St. Clement's lane; a part whereof on both sides is of Candlewick street ward, to wit, somewhat north beyond the parish church of St. Clement in Eastcheape. This is a small church, void of monuments, other than of Francis Barnam, alderman, who deceased 1575, and of Benedicke Barnam, his son, alderman also, 1598. William Chartney and William Overie founded a chantry there.

Next is St. Nicholas lane, for the most part on both sides of this ward, almost to St. Nicholas church. Then is Abchurch lane, which is on both the sides almost wholly of this ward, the parish church there (called of St. Marie Abchurch, Apechurch, or Upchurch, as I have read it), standeth somewhat near unto the south end thereof, on a rising ground: it is a fair church. Simon de Winchcomb founded a chantry there the 19th of Richard II.; John Littleton founded another, and Thomas Hondon another; and hath the monuments of J. Long, esquire, of Bedfordshire, 1442; William Wikenson, alderman, 1519; William Jawdrell, tailor, 1440; Sir James Hawes, mayor 1574; Sir John Branch, mayor 1580; John Miners; William Kettle, etc.

On the south side of this ward, beginning again at the east, is St. Michael's lane, which lane is almost wholly of this ward, on both sides down towards Thames street, to a well or pump there. On the east side of this lane is Crooked lane aforesaid, by St. Michael's church, towards New Fish street. One the most ancient house in this lane is called the Leaden porch, and belonged sometime to Sir John Merston, knight, the 1st of Edward IV. It is now called the Swan in Crooked lane, possessed of strangers, and selling of Rhenish wine. The parish church of this St. Michael's was sometime but a small and homely thing, standing upon part of that ground wherein now standeth the parsonage-house; and the ground there about was a filthy plot, by reason of the butchers in Eastcheape, who made the same their laystall. William de Burgo gave two messuages to that church in Candlewick street, 1317. John Lofkin, stock-fishmonger, four times mayor, built in the same ground this fair church of St. Michael, and was buried there in the choir, under a fair tomb, with the images of him and his wife, in alabaster. The said church hath been since increased with a new choir, and side chapels by Sir William Walworth, stock-fishmonger, mayor, sometime servant to the said John Lofkin: also the tomb of Lofkin was removed, and a flat stone of grey marble garnished with plates of copper laid on him, as it yet remaineth in the body of the church. This William Walworth is reported to have slain Jack Straw,[1] but Jack Straw being afterward taken, was first adjudged by the said mayor, and then executed by the loss of his head in Smithfield.

True it is that this William Walworth, being a man wise, learned, and of an incomparable manhood,[2] arrested Wat Tyler, a presumptuous rebel, upon whom no man durst lay hand, whereby he delivered the king and kingdom from most wicked tyranny of traitors. The mayor arrested him on the head with a sound blow, whereupon Wat Tyler, furiously struck the mayor with his dagger, but hurt him not, by reason he was well armed. The mayor, having received his stroke, drew his basiliard, and grievously wounded Wat in the neck, and withal gave him a great blow on the head; in the which conflict, an esquire of the king's house, called John Cavendish, drew his sword, and wounded Wat twice or thrice even to the death; and Wat, spurring his horse, cried to the commons to revenge him: the horse bare him about eighty feet from the place, and there he fell down half dead; and by and by they which attended on the king environed him about, so as he was not seen of his company: many of them thrust him in divers places of his body, and drew him into the hospital of St. Bartholomew, from whence again the mayor caused him to be drawn into Smithfield, and there to be beheaded. In reward of this service (the people being dispersed) the king commanded the mayor to put a bascinet on his head; and the mayor requesting why he should do so, the king answered, he being much bound unto him, would make him knight: the mayor answered, that he was

[1] " In Smithfield, and there to have been knighted by the king, but that is not true."—*1st edition*, p. 172.

[2] " Fable of William Walworth and Jack Straw reproved. Praise of W. Walworth for his manhood in arresting of Wat Tyler. The mayor was well armed, and had on his head a basonet."—*Stow.*

neither worthy nor able to take such estate upon him, for he was but a merchant, and had to live by his merchandise only; notwithstanding, the king bade him to put on his bascinet, and then with a sword in both his hands he strongly stroke him on the neck, as the manner was then; and the same day he made three other citizens knights for his sake in the same place; to wit, John Philpot, Nicholas Brember, and Robert Launde, alderman. The king gave to the mayor one hundred pounds land by year, and to each of the other forty pounds land yearly, to them and their heirs for ever.

After this, in the same year, the said Sir William Walworth, founded in the said parish church of St. Michael a college of a master and nine priests, or chaplains, and deceased 1385, was there buried in the north chapel by the choir; but his monument being amongst other by bad people defaced in the reign of Edward VI., and again since renewed by the fishmongers, for lack of knowledge of what before had been written in his epitaph, they followed a fabulous book, and wrote Jack Straw instead of Wat Tilar, a great error meet to be reformed there and elsewhere; and therefore have I the more at large discoursed of this matter.

It hath also been, and is now grown to a common opinion, that in reward of this service done by the said William Walworth against the rebel, King Richard added to the arms of this city (which was argent, a plain cross gules) a sword or dagger (for so they term it), whereof I have read no such record, but to the contrary. I find that in the 4th year of Richard II.,[1] in a full assembly made in the upper chamber of the Guildhall, summoned by this William Walworth, then mayor, as well of aldermen as of the common council, in every ward, for certain affairs concerning the king, it was there by common consent agreed and ordained, that the old seal of the office of the mayoralty of the city being very small, old, unapt, and uncomely for the honour of the city, should be broken, and one other new should be had, which the said mayor commanded to be made artificially, and honourable for the exercise of the said office thereafter, in place of the other; in which new seal, besides the images of Peter and Paul, which of old were rudely engraven, there should be under the feet of the said images a shield of the arms of the said city, perfectly graved,[2] with two lions sup-

---

[1] Dunthorne.

[2] "The armies of this citty were not altered, but remayne as afore; to witte, argent, a playne crosse gules, a sword of S. Paul in the first quarter, and no dagger of W. Walworth, as is fabuled."—*Stow*.

porting the same, with two sergeants of arms; another part, one, and two tabernacles, in which above should stand two angels; between whom, above the said images of Peter and Paul, shall be set the glorious Virgin. This being done, the old seal of the office was delivered to Richard Odiham, chamberlain, who brake it, and in place thereof was delivered the new seal to the said mayor, to use in his office of mayoralty, as occasion should require. This new seal seemeth to be made before William Walworth was knighted, for he is not here entitled Sir, as afterwards he was; and certain it is that the same new seal then made is now in use, and none other in that office of the mayoralty; which may suffice to answer the former fable, without showing of any evidence sealed with the old seal, which was the cross and sword of St. Paul, and not the dagger of William Walworth.

Now of other monuments in that church. Simon Mordon, mayor 1368, was buried there; John Olney, mayor 1446; Robert March, stock-fishmonger, gave two pieces of ground to be a churchyard; John Radwell, stock-fishmonger, buried 1415; George Gowre, esquire, son to Edward Gowre, stock-fishmonger, esquire, 1470; Alexander Purpoynt, stock-fishmonger, 1373; Andrew Burel, gentleman of Gray's-inn, 1487; John Shrow, stock-fishmonger, 1487, with this epitaph:

> " Farewell, my friends, the tide abideth no man,
> I am departed hence, and so shall ye.
> But in this passage the best song that I can,
> Is *requiem æternam*, now Jesus grant it me,
> When I have ended all mine adversitie,
> Grant me in Paradise to have a mansion,
> That sheddest thy blood for my redemption."

John Finkell, one of the sheriffs 1487, was knighted, and gave forty pounds to this church, the one half for his monument. John Pattesley, mayor 1441; Thomas Ewen, grocer, bare half the charges in building of the steeple, and was buried 1501; William Combes, gentleman, of Stoke, by Guilford in Surrey, 1502; Sir John Brudge, mayor 1530, gave fifty pounds for a house called the College in Crooked lane; he lieth buried in St. Nicholas Hacon. Waltar Faireford; Robert Barre; Alexander Heyban; John Motte; John Gramstone; John Brampton; John Wood, stock-fishmonger, 1531; Sir Henry Amcots, mayor 1548, etc. Hard by this St. Michael's church, on the south side thereof, in the year 1560, on the fifth of July, through the shooting of a gun, which brake in the house of one Adrian Arten, a Dutchman, and set fire on a firkin and barrel of gunpowder, four houses were blown up, and divers other sore shattered; eleven men and women were slain, and sixteen so hurt and bruised, that they hardly escaped with life.

West from this St. Michael's lane is St. Martin Orgar lane, by Candlewick street, which lane is on both sides down to a well, replenished with fair and large houses for merchants, and it is of this ward; one of which houses was sometime called Beachamp's inn, as pertaining unto them of that family. Thomas Arundel, archbishop of Canterbury, commonly for his time was lodged there.

The parish church of St. Martin Orgar is a small thing. William Crowmer, mayor, built a proper chapel on the south side thereof, and was buried there 1533; John Mathew, mayor 1490; Sir William Huet, mayor 1559, with his lady and daughter, wife to Sir Edward Osburne; Ralph Tabinham, alderman; Alice, wife to Thomas Winslow; Thorudon; Benedicke Reding; Thomas Harding; James Smith; Richard Gainford, esquire; John Bold, etc.

Then is there one other lane called St. Laurence, of the parish church there. This lane, down to the south side of the churchyard, is of Candlewick street ward. The parish church of St. Laurence was increased with a chapel of Jesus by Thomas Cole, for a master and chaplain; the which chapel and parish church was made a college of Jesus and of Corpus Christi, for a master and seven chaplains, by John Poultney, mayor, and was confirmed by Edward III., the 20th of his reign: of him was this church called St. Laurence Poultney, in Candlewick street; which college was valued at £79 17s. 11d., and was surrendered in the reign of Edward VI. Robert Ratcliffe, Earl of Essex, and Henry Ratcliffe, Earl of Sussex, was buried there; Alderman Beswicke was buried there; John Oliffe, alderman, Robert Browne, and others. Thus much for this ward, and the antiquities thereof. It hath now an alderman, his deputy, common councillors eight, constables eight, scavengers six, wardmote inquest men twelve, and a beadle. It is taxed to the fifteen at sixteen pounds.

WALBROOK WARD

Walbrook ward beginneth at the west end of Candlewick street ward. It runneth down Candlewick street west towards Budge row. It hath on the north side thereof St. Swithen's lane, so called of St. Swithen, a parish church by London stone.

This lane is replenished on both the sides with fair built houses, and is wholly of Walbrook ward.

The said parish church of St. Swithen standeth at the south-west corner of this lane. License was procured to new build and increase the said church and steeple in the year 1420. Sir John Hend, draper, mayor, was an especial benefactor thereunto, as appeareth by his arms in the glass windows, even in the tops of them, which is in a field silver, a chief azure, a lion passant silver, a cheveron azure, three escalops silver: he lieth buried in the body of this church, with a fair stone laid on him, but the plates and inscriptions are defaced. Roger Depham, alderman, Thomas Aylesbourgh, William Neve, and Matilda Caxton, founded chantries, and were buried there; John Butler, draper, one of the sheriffs, 1420; Ralph Jecoline, mayor, a benefactor, buried in a fair tomb; William White, draper, one of the sheriffs, 1482, and other.

On the north side of this church and churchyard is one fair and large built house, sometime pertaining to the prior of Tortington in Sussex, since to the earls of Oxford, and now to Sir John Hart, alderman; which house hath a fair garden belonging thereunto, lying on the west side thereof. On the back side of two other fair houses in Walbrook, in the reign of Henry VII., Sir Richard Empson, knight, chancellor of the duchy of Lancaster, dwelt in the one of them, and Edmond Dudley, esquire, in the other; either of them had a door of intercourse into this garden, wherein they met and consulted of matters at their pleasures. In this Oxford place Sir Ambrose Nicholas kept his mayoralty, and since him the said Sir John Hart.

On the south side of this high street, near unto the channel, is pitched upright a great stone called London stone, fixed in the ground very deep, fastened with bars of iron, and otherwise so strongly set, that if carts do run against it through negligence, the wheels be broken, and the stone itself unshaken.

The cause why this stone was set there, the time when, or other memory hereof, is none, but that the same hath long continued there is manifest, namely, since (or rather before) the Conquest; for in the end of a fair written Gospel book given to Christ's church in Canterburie, by Ethelstane, King of the West Saxons, I find noted of lands or rents in London belonging to the said church, whereof one parcel is described to lie near unto London stone. Of later time we read,[1] that in the year of Christ 1135, the 1st of King Stephen, a fire, which began

[1] Liber Trinitate.

in the house of one Ailward, near unto London stone, consumed all east to Aldgate, in the which fire the priory of the Holy Trinitie was burnt, and west to St. Erkenwald's shrine in Paule's church. And these be the eldest notes that I read thereof.

Some have said this stone to be set as a mark in the middle of the city within the walls; but in truth it standeth far nearer unto the river of Thames than to the wall of the city; some others have said the same to be set for the tendering and making of payment by debtors to their creditors at their appointed days and times, till of later time payments were more usually made at the font in Poules church, and now most commonly at the Royal Exchange; some again have imagined the same to be set up by one John or Thomas Londonstone dwelling there against; but more likely it is, that such men have taken name of the stone than the stone of them, as did John at Noke, Thomas at Stile, William at Wall, or at Well, etc.

Down west from this parish church, and from London stone, have ye Walbrooke corner; from whence runneth up a street, north to the Stocks, called Walbrook, because it standeth on the east side of the same brook, by the bank thereof, and the whole ward taketh the name of that street. On the east side of this street, and at the north corner thereof, is the Stocks market, which had this beginning. About the year of Christ 1282, Henry Wales, mayor, caused divers houses in this city to be built towards the maintenance of London bridge, namely, one void place near unto the parish church called Woole church, on the north side thereof, where sometime (the way being very large and broad) had stood a pair of stocks for punishment of offenders; this building took name of these stocks, and was appointed by him to be a market place for fish and flesh in the midst of the city. Other houses he built in other places, as by the patent of Edward I. it doth appear, dated the 10th of his reign. After this, in the year 1322, the 17th of Edward II., a decree was made by Hamond Chickwell, mayor, that none should sell fish or flesh out of the markets appointed, to wit, Bridge street, East Cheape, Old Fish street, St. Nicholas' shambles, and the said Stocks, upon pain to forfeit such fish or flesh as were sold, for the first time, and the second time to lose their freedom; which act was made by commandment of the king under his letters patent, dated at the Tower the 17th of his reign, and then was this stocks let to farm for £46 13s. 4d. by year. This Stocks market was again begun to be built in the year 1410, in the 11th of Henry IV., and was finished in the year next following. In the year 1507, the same was rented £56 19s. 10d. And in the year 1543, John Cotes being mayor, there were in this Stocks market for fishmongers twenty-five boards or stalls, rented yearly to £34 13s. 4d., there were for butchers eighteen boards or stalls, rented at £41 16s. 4d., and there were also chambers above, sixteen, rented at £5 13s. 4d., in all £82 3s.

Next unto this Stocks is the parish church of St. Mary Wool church, so called of a beam placed in the churchyard, which was thereof called Wool church haw, of the tronage, or weighing of wool there used; and to verify this, I find amongst the customs of London, written in French in the reign of Edward II., a chapter intituled *Les Customes de Wolchurch Haw*, wherein is set down what was there to be paid for every parcel of wool weighed. This tronage or weighing of wool, till the 6th of Richard II., was there continued; John Churchman then built the Customhouse upon Wool key, to serve for the said tronage, as is before showed in Tower street ward. This church is reasonable fair and large, and was lately new built by license granted in the 20th of Henry VI., with condition to be built fifteen foot from the Stocks market, for sparing of light to the same Stocks. The parson of this church is to have four marks the year for tithe of the said Stocks, paid him by the masters of the Bridge house, by special decree made the 2nd of Henry VII. John Winyar, grocer, mayor 1504, was a great helper to the building of this church, and was there buried 1505; he gave unto it by his testament two large basons of silver, and twenty pounds in money. Also Richard Shore, draper, one of the sheriffs 1505, was a great benefactor in his life, and by his testament gave twenty pounds to make a porch at the west end thereof, and was there buried; Richard Hatfield of Steplemorden in Cambridgeshire, lieth entombed there, 1467; Edward Deoly, esquire, 1467. John Handford, grocer, made the font of that church, very curiously wrought, painted, and gilded, and was there buried; John Archer, fishmonger, 1487; Anne Cawode founded a chantry there, etc.

From the Stocks' market and this parish church east up into Lombard street, some four or five houses on a side, and also on the south side of Wool church, have ye Bearbinder lane, a part whereof is of this Walbrooke ward; then lower down in the street called Walbrooke, is one other fair church of St. Stephen, lately built on the east side thereof, for the old church stood on the

west side, in place where now standeth the parsonage house,
and therefore so much nearer the brook, even on the bank.
Robert Chichley, mayor in the year 1428, the 6th of Henry VI.,
gave to this parish of St. Stephen one plot of ground, containing
two hundred and eight feet and a half in length, and sixty-six
feet in breadth, thereupon to build their new church, and for
their churchyard; and in the 7th of Henry VI. the said Robert,
one of the founders, laid the first stone for himself, the second
for William Stoddon, mayor, with whose goods the ground that
the church standeth on, and the housing, with the ground of
the churchyard, was bought by the said Chichley for two hundred marks from the Grocers, which had been letten before for
six-and-twenty marks the year; Robert Whittingham, draper,
laid the third stone, Henry Barton then mayor, etc. The said
Chichley gave more, one hundred pounds to the said work, and
bare the charges of all the timber work on the procession way,
and laid the lead upon it of his own cost; he also gave all the
timber for the roofing of the two side aisles, and paid for the
carriage thereof. This church was finished in the year 1439;
the breadth thereof is sixty-seven feet, and length one hundred
and twenty-five feet, the churchyard ninety feet in length, and
thirty-seven in breadth and more. Robert Whittingham (made
Knight of the Bath), in the year 1432, purchased the patronage
of this church from John Duke of Bedford, uncle to Henry VI.,
and Edward IV., in the 2nd of his reign, gave it to Richard Lee,
then mayor. There be monuments in this church of Thomas
Southwell, first parson of this new church, who lieth in the choir;
John Dunstable, master of astronomy and music, in the year
1453; Sir Richard Lee, mayor, who gave the said parsonage to
the Grocers; Rowland Hill, mayor 1549; Sir Thomas Pope,
first treasurer of the augmentations, with his wife Dame Margaret; Sir John Cootes, mayor 1542; Sir John Yorke, knight,
merchant-tailor, 1549; Edward Jackman, sheriff 1564; Richard
Achley, grocer; Dr. Owyn, physician to King Henry VIII.;
John Kirby, grocer, 1578; and others.

Lower down from this parish church be divers fair houses,
namely, one wherein of late Sir Richard Baker, a knight of Kent,
was lodged, and wherein dwelt Master Thomas Gore, a merchant
famous for hospitality. On the west side of this Walbrooke
street, over against the Stocks' market, is a part of the high
street called the Poultrie, on the south side west till over against
St. Mildrede's church, and the Skalding wike is of this ward.
Then down again Walbrooke street some small distance, is

Buckles bury, a street so called of Buckle, that sometime was owner thereof, part of which street on both sides, three or four houses, to the course of the brook, is of this ward, and so down Walbrooke street to the south corner; from thence west down Budge row some small distance, to an alley, and through that alley south by the west end of St. John's church upon Walbrooke, by the south side and east end of the same again to Walbrooke corner.

This parish church is called St. John upon Walbrooke, because the west end thereof is on the very bank of Walbrooke, by Horseshew bridge, in Horseshew bridge street. This church was also lately new built; for about the year 1412, license was granted by the mayor and commonalty to the parson and parish, for enlarging thereof, with a piece of ground on the north part of the choir, twenty-one feet in length, seventeen feet and three inches in breadth, and on the south side of the choir one foot of the common soil. There be no monuments in this church of any account, only I have learned, William Cobarton, skinner, who gave lands to that church, was there buried 1410, and John Stone, tailor, one of the sheriffs 1464, was likewise buried there.

On the south side of Walbrooke ward, from Candlewicke street, in the mid way betwixt London stone and Walbrooke corner, is a little lane with a turnpike in the midst thereof, and in the same a proper parish church, called St. Mary Bothaw, or Boatehaw by the Erber; this church being near unto the Downegate on the river of Thames, hath the addition of Boathaw or Boat haw, of near adjoining to a haw or yard, wherein of old time boats were made, and landed from Downegate to be mended, as may be supposed, for other reason I find none why it should be so called. Within this church, and the small cloister adjoining, divers noblemen and persons of worship have been buried, as appeareth by arms in the windows, the defaced tombs, and print of plates torn up and carried away: there remain only of John West, esquire, buried in the year 1408; Thomas Huytley, esquire, 1539, but his monument is defaced since; Lancelot Bathurst, etc.

The Erbar is an ancient place so called, but not of Walbrooke ward, and therefore out of that lane to Walbrooke corner, and then down till over against the south corner of St. John's church upon Walbrooke. And this is all that I can say of Walbrooke ward. It hath an alderman, and his deputy, common councillors eleven, constables nine, scavengers six, for the wardmote inquest thirteen, and a beadle. It is taxed to the fifteen in London to £33 5s.[1]

DOWNEGATE WARD

Downegate ward beginneth at the south end of Walbrooke ward over against the east corner of St. John's church upon Walbrooke, and descendeth on both the sides to Downegate on the Thames, and is so called of that down going or descending thereunto; and of this Downgate the ward taketh name. This ward turneth into Thames street westward, some ten houses on a side to the course of Walbrooke, but east in Thames street on both sides to Ebgate lane, or Old Swan, the land side whereof hath many lanes turning up, as shall be shown when I come to them.

But first to begin with the high street called Dowgate; at the upper end thereof is a fair conduit of Thames water, castellated, and made in the year 1568, at charges of the citizens, and is called the conduit upon Downegate. The descent of this street is such, that in the year 1574, on the 4th of September, in the afternoon, there fell a storm of rain, where through the channels suddenly arose, and ran with such a swift course towards the common shores, that a lad of eighteen years old, minding to have leapt over the channel near unto the said conduit, was taken with the stream, and carried from thence towards the Thames with such a violence, that no man with staves or otherwise could stay him, till he came against a cart wheel that stood in the said watergate, before which time he was drowned, and stark dead.

On the west side of this street is the Tallow-chandlers' hall, a proper house, which company was incorporated in the 2nd year of Edward IV.

Somewhat lower standeth the Skinners' hall, a fair house, which was sometime called Copped hall, by Downegate, in the parish of St. John upon Walbrooke. In the 19th year of Edward II., Ralph Cobham possessed it with five shops, etc.

This company of Skinners in London were incorporate by Edward III. in the 1st of his reign; they had two brotherhoods of Corpus Christi, viz. one at St. Mary Spittle, the other at St. Mary Bethlem without Bishopsgate. Richard II., in the 18th of his reign, granted them to make their two brotherhoods

[1] " In London to forty pound, and in the Exchequer to thirty-nine pound."—1st edition, p. 181.

one, by the name of the fraternity of Corpus Christi. Of Skinners, divers royal persons were named to be founders and brethren of this fraternity, to wit, kings six, dukes nine, earls two, lords one. Kings, Edward III., Richard II., Henry IV., Henry V., Henry VI., and Edward IV. This fraternity had also once every year, on Corpus Christi day afternoon, a procession passed through the principal streets of the city, wherein was borne more than one hundred torches of wax (costly garnished) burning light, and above two hundred clerks and priests, in surplices and copes, singing. After the which were the sheriffs' servants, the clerks of the compters, chaplains for the sheriffs, the mayor's sergeants, the counsel of the city, the mayor and aldermen in scarlet, and then the Skinners in their best liveries. Thus much to stop the tongues of unthankful men, such as used to ask, Why have ye not noted this, or that? and give no thanks for what is done.

Then lower down was a challenge of priests, called Jesus' Commons, a house well furnished with brass, pewter, napery, plate, etc., besides a fair library well stored with books, all which of old time was given to a number of priests that should keep commons there, and as one left his place, by death or otherwise, another should be admitted into his room, but this order within this thirty years being discontinued, the said house was dissolved and turned to tenements.

Down lower have ye Elbow lane; and at the corner thereof was one great stone house, called Olde hall; it is now taken down, and divers fair houses of timber placed there. This was sometime pertaining to William de Pont le Arch, and by him given to the priory of St. Mary Overy in Southwark, in the reign of Henry I. In this Elbow lane is the Innholders' hall, and other fair houses; this lane runneth west, and suddenly turneth south into Thames street, and therefore of that bending is called Elbow lane. On the east side of this Downegate street is the great old house before spoken of, called the Erber, near to the church of St. Mary Bothaw; Geffrey Scroope held it by the gift of Edward III., in the 14th of his reign; it belonged since to John Nevell, Lord of Rabie, then to Richard Nevell, Earl of Warwick; Nevell, Earl of Salisburie, was lodged there 1457; then it came to George Duke of Clarence, and his heirs male, by the gift of Edward IV., in the 14th of his reign. It was lately new built by Sir Thomas Pullison, mayor, and was afterward inhabited by Sir Francis Drake, that famous mariner. Next to this great house is a lane turning to Bush lane (of old

time called Carter lane, of carts and carmen having stables there),
and now called Chequer lane, or Chequer alley, of an inn called
the Chequer.

In Thames street, on the Thames side, west from Downegate,
is Greenewich lane, of old time so called, and now Frier lane, of
such a sign there set up. In this lane is the Joiners' hall, and
other fair houses.

Then is Grantham's lane, so called of John Grantham, sometime mayor, and owner thereof, whose house was very large and
strong, built of stone, as appeareth by gates arched, yet remaining. Ralph Dodmer, first a brewer, then a mercer, mayor
1529, dwelt there, and kept his mayoralty in that house; it is
now a brewhouse as it was afore.

Then is Dowgate, whereof is spoken in another place. East
from this Dowgate is Cosin lane, named of William Cosin that
dwelt there in the 4th of Richard II., as divers his predecessors,
father, grandfather, etc. had done before him. William Cosin
was one of the sheriffs in the year 1306. That house standeth
at the south end of the lane, having an old and artificial conveyance of Thames water into it, and is now a dyehouse called
Lambard's messuage. Adjoining to that house there was lately
erected an engine to convey Thames water unto Downegate
conduit aforesaid.

Next to this lane, on the east, is the Steelyard, as they term
it, a place for merchants of Almaine, that used to bring hither
as well wheat, rye, and other grain, as cables, ropes, masts,
pitch, tar, flax, hemp, linen cloth, wainscots, wax, steel, and
other profitable merchandises. Unto these merchants, in the
year 1259, Henry III., at the request of his brother Richard,
Earl of Cornewell, king of Almaine, granted that all and singular
the merchants, having a house in the city of London, commonly
called *Guilda Aula Theutonicorum*, should be maintained and
upholden through the whole realm, by all such freedoms, and
free usages, or liberties, as by the king and his noble progenitors'
time they had and enjoyed, etc. Edward I. renewed and
confirmed that charter of liberties granted by his father. And
in the 10th year of the same Edward, Henry Wales being mayor,
a great controversy did arise between the said mayor, and the
merchants of the Haunce of Almaine, about the reparations
of Bishopsgate, then likely to fall, for that the said merchants
enjoyed divers privileges in respect of maintaining the said gate,
which they now denied to repair; for the appeasing of which
controversy the king sent his writ to the treasurer and barons

of his Exchequer, commanding that they should make inquisition thereof; before whom the merchants being called, when they were not able to discharge themselves, sith they enjoyed the liberties to them granted for the same, a precept was sent to the mayor and sheriffs to distrain the said merchants to make reparations, namely, Gerard Marbod, alderman of the Haunce, Ralph de Cussarde, a citizen of Colen, Ludero de Denevar, a burgess of Trivar, John of Aras, a burgess of Trivon, Bartram of Hamburdge, Godestalke of Hundondale, a burgess of Trivon, John de Dele, a burgess of Munstar, then remaining in the said city of London, for themselves and all other merchants of the Haunce, and so they granted two hundred and ten marks sterling to the mayor and citizens, and undertook that they and their successors should from time to time repair the said gate, and bear the third part of the charges in money and men to defend it when need were. And for this agreement the said mayor and citizens granted to the said merchants their liberties, which till of late they have enjoyed, as namely, amongst other, that they might lay up their grain which they brought into this realm in inns, and sell it in their garners, by the space of forty days after they had laid it up, except by the mayor and citizens they were expressly forbidden, because of dearth, or other reasonable occasions. Also they might have their aldermen as they had been accustomed, foreseeing always that he were of the city, and presented to the mayor and aldermen of the city, so oft as any should be chosen, and should take an oath before them to maintain justice in their courts, and to behave themselves in their office according to law, and as it stood with the customs of the city. Thus much for their privileges; whereby it appeareth that they were great merchants of corn brought out of the east parts hither, insomuch that the occupiers of husbandry in this land were inforced to complain of them for bringing in such abundance when the corn of this realm was at such an easy price; whereupon it was ordained by parliament, that no person should bring into any part of this realm, by way of merchandise, wheat, rye, or barley, growing out of the said realm, when the quarter of wheat exceed not the price of 6s. 8d., rye 4s. the quarter, and barley 3s. the quarter, upon forfeiture the one half to the king, the other half to the seizor thereof. These merchants of Haunce had their Guildhall in Thames street in place aforesaid by the said Cosin lane. Their hall is large built of stone, with three arched gates towards the street, the middlemost whereof is far bigger than the other, and is seldom opened, the other two be mured up; the same is now called the old hall.

Of later time, to wit, in the 6th of Richard II., they hired one house next adjoining to their old hall, which sometime belonged to Richard Lions, a famous lapidary, one of the sheriffs of London in the 49th of Edward III., and in the 4th of Richard II., by the rebels of Kent, drawn out of that house and beheaded in West Cheap. This also was a great house with a large wharf on the Thames, and the way thereunto was called Windgoose, or Wild-goose lane, which is now called Windgoose alley, for that the same alley is for the most part built on by the stilyard merchants.

The abbot of St. Alban's had a messuage here with a key, given to him in the 34th of Henry VI. Then is one other great house, which sometime pertained to John Rainwell, stockfish-monger, mayor, and it was by him given to the mayor and commonalty, to the end that the profits thereof should be disposed in deeds of piety; which house, in the 15th of Edward IV., was confirmed unto the said merchants, in manner following, namely:—" It is ordayned by our soveraigne lord and his parliament, that the said marchants of Almaine, being of the companie called the *Guildhall Teutonicorum* (or the Flemish gild), that now be, or hereafter shall be, shall have, hold, and enjoy, to them and their successors for ever, the said place called the Steel house, yeelding to the said mayor and communaltie an annuall rent of £70 3s. 4d. etc."

In the year 1551, and the 5th of Edward VI., through complaint of the English merchants, the liberty of the steelyard merchants was seized into the king's hands, and so it resteth.

Then is Church lane, at the west end of Alhallowes church, called Alhallowes the More in Thames street, for a difference from Alhallowes the Less in the same street; it is also called Alhallowes *ad fœnum* in the Ropery, because hay sold near thereunto at Hay wharf, and ropes of old time made and sold in the high street. This is a fair church, with a large cloister on the south side thereof about their churchyard, but foully defaced and ruinated.

The church also hath had many fair monuments, but now defaced. There remaineth in the choir some plates on grave stones—namely, of William Lichfield, D.D., who deceased the year 1447: he was a great student, and compiled many books, both moral and divine, in prose and in verse, namely, one intituled *The Complaint of God unto Sinful Man*. He made in his time three thousand and eighty-three sermons, as appeared

by his own handwriting, and were found when he was dead.
One other plate there is of John Brickles, draper, who deceased
in the year 1451; he was a great benefactor to that church, and
gave by his testament certain tenements to the relief of the poor,
etc. Nicholas Loven and William Peston founded chantries
there.

At the east end of this church goeth down a lane called Hay
wharf lane, now lately a great brewhouse, built there by one
Pot; Henry Campion, esquire, a beer-brewer, used it, and
Abraham his son now possesseth it. Then was there one other
lane, sometime called Woolfe's gate, now out of use; for the
lower part thereof upon the bank of Thames is built by the late
Earl of Shrewsburie, and the other end is built on and stopped
up by the chamberlain of London. John Butler, draper, one
of the sheriffs in the year 1420, dwelt there; he appointed his
house to be sold, and the price thereof to be given to the poor:
it was of Alhallowes parish the less. Then is there the said
parish church of Alhallowes called the Less, and by some
Alhallowes on the Cellars, for it standeth on vaults; it is said
to be built by Sir John Poultney, sometime mayor. The steeple
and choir of this church standeth on an arched gate, being the
entry to a great house called Cold Harbrough. The choir of
late being fallen down, is now again at length, in the year 1594,
by the parishioners new built. Touching this Cold Harbrough,
I find, that in the 13th of Edward II., Sir John Abel, knight,
demised or let unto Henry Stow, draper, all that his capital
messuage called the Cold Harbrough, in the parish of All Saints
ad fœnum, and all the appurtenances within the gate, with the
key which Robert Hartford, citizen, son to William Hartford,
had, and ought; and the foresaid Robert paid for it the rent
of thirty-three shillings the year. This Robert Hartford being
owner thereof, as also of other lands in Surrey, deceasing without
issue male, left two daughters his coheirs, to wit, Idonia, married
to Sir Ralph Bigot, and Maude, married to Sir Stephen Cosenton,
knights, between whom the said house and lands were parted.
After the which, John Bigot, son to the said Sir Ralph, and Sir
John Cosenton, did sell their moieties of Cold Harbrough unto
John Poultney, son of Adam Poultney, the 8th of Edward III.
This Sir John Poultney dwelling in this house, and being four
times mayor, the said house took the name of Poultney's inn.
Notwithstanding this, Sir John Poultney, the 21st of Edward
III., by his charter, gave and confirmed to Humfrey de Bohun,
Earl of Hereford and Essex, his whole tenement called Cold

Harbrough, with all the tenements and key adjoining, and appurtenances, sometime pertaining to Robert de Hereford, on the way called Hay wharf lane, etc., for one rose at Midsummer, to him and to his heirs for all services, if the same were demanded. This Sir John Poultney, deceased 1349, and left issue, by Margaret his wife, William Poultney, who died without issue, and Margaret his mother was married to Sir Nicholas Lovel, knight, etc. Philip S. Cleare gave two messuages pertaining to this Cold Harbrough in the Roperie, towards the enlarging of the parish church and churchyard of All Saints, called the Less, in the 20th of Richard II. [*See* Additional Notes.]

In the year 1397, the 21st of Richard II., John Holland, Earl of Huntingdon, was lodged there, and Richard II., his brother dined with him: it was then counted a right fair and stately house; but in the next year following I find that Edmond, Earl of Cambridge, was there lodged, notwithstanding the said house still retained the name of Poultney's inn, in the reign of Henry VI., the 26th of his reign. It belonged since to H. Holland, Duke of Excester, and he was lodged there in the year 1472 [1471]. In the year 1485, Richard III., by his letters patent, granted and gave to John Writh, alias Garter, principal king of arms of Englishmen, and to the rest of the king's heralds and pursuivants of arms, all that messuage, with the appurtenances, called Cold Harbrough, in the parish of All Saints the Little in London, and their successors for ever. Dated at Westminster the 2nd of March, *anno regni primo*, without fine or fee. How the said heralds departed therewith I have not read; but in the reign of Henry VIII. the Bishop of Durham's house near Charing cross, being taken into the king's hand, Cuthbert Tunstal, Bishop of Durham, was lodged in this Cold Harbrough; since the which time it hath belonged to the Earls of Shrewsburie, by composition (as is supposed) from the said Cuthbert Tunstall. The last deceased earl took it down, and in place thereof built a great number of small tenements, now letten out for great rents to people of all sorts.

Then is the Dyers' hall, which company was made a brotherhood or guild, in the 4th of Henry VI., and appointed to consist of a guardian or warden, and a commonalty, the 12th of Edward IV. Then be there divers large brewhouses and others, till you come to Ebgate lane, where that ward endeth in the east. On the north side of Thames street be divers lanes also; the first is at the south end of Elbow lane, before spoken of, west from Downegate, over against Greenwich lane: then be divers fair houses for merchants and others all along that side. The next lane east from Downegate is called Bush lane, which turneth up to Candlewicke street, and is of Downegate ward. Next is Suffolke lane, likewise turning up to Candlewicke street. In this lane is one notable grammar school, founded in the year 1561 by the master, wardens, and assistants of the Merchant-Tailors, in the parish of St. Laurence Poultney; Richard Hilles, sometime master of that company, having before given £500 towards the purchase of a house, called the manor of the Rose, sometime belonging to the Duke of Buckingham, wherein the said school is kept. Then is there one other lane which turneth up to St. Laurence hill, and to the south-west corner of St. Laurence churchyard; then one other lane called Poultney lane, that goeth up of this ward to the south-east corner of St. Laurence churchyard, and so down again, and to the west corner of St. Martin Orgar lane, and over against Ebgate lane; and this is all of Downgate ward, the thirteenth in number lying east from the water-course of Walbrook, and hath not any one house on the west side of the said brook. It hath an alderman, his deputy, common councillors nine, constables eight, scavengers five, for the wardmote inquest fourteen, and a beadle. It is taxed to the fifteen eight-and-twenty pounds.[1]

WARDS ON THE WEST SIDE OF WALBROOKE, AND FIRST OF VINTRY WARD

Now I am to speak of the other wards, twelve in number, all lying on the west side of the course of Walbrooke. And first of Vintry ward, so called of vintners, and of the vintry, a part of the bank of the river of Thames, where the merchants of Burdeaux craned their wines out of lighters and other vessels, and there landed and made sale of them within forty days after, until the 28th of Edward I., at which time the said merchants complained that they could not sell their wines, paying poundage, neither hire houses or cellars to lay them in; and it was redressed by virtue of the king's writ, directed to the mayor and sheriffs of London, dated at Carlaveroke, or Carlisle, since the which time many fair and large houses, with vaults and cellars for stowage of wines, and lodging of the Burdeaux merchants have been built in place where before time were cooks' houses; for Fitzstephen, in the reign of Henry II., writeth, that upon the

---

[1] " In London at thirty-six pound, and in the Exchequer at thirty-four pound ten shillings."—*1st edition*, p. 189.

river's side, between the wine in ships, and the wine to be sold in taverns, was a common cookery or cooks' row, etc., as in another place I have set down; whereby it appeareth, that in those days (and till of late time) every man lived by his professed trade, not any one interrupting another: the cooks dressed meat, and sold no wine, and the taverner sold wine, but dressed no meat for sale, etc.

This ward beginneth in the east at the west end of Downegate ward, as the water-course of Walbrooke parteth them, to wit, at Grantham's lane, on the Thames side, and at Elbow lane on the land side; it runneth along in Thames street west some three houses beyond the Old Swanne, a brewhouse, and on the land side some three houses west beyond St. James' at Garlicke Hith. In breadth this ward stretcheth from the Vintry, north to the wall of the west gate of the Tower Royall; the other north part is of Cordwayner street ward. Out of this Royal street, by the south gate of Tower Royall, runneth a small street east to St. John's upon Walbrooke, which street is called Horshew bridge, of such a bridge sometime over the brook there, which is now vaulted over. Then from the said south gate west, runneth one other street, called Knightriders' street, by St. Thomas Apostle's church on the north side, and Wringwren lane by the said church, at the west end thereof, and to the east end of the Trinitie church in the said Knightriders' street, where this ward endeth on that south side the street; but on the north side it runneth no further than the corner against the new built tavern and other houses, in a plot of ground where sometime stood Ormond place; yet have ye one other lane lower down in Royall street, stretching from over against St. Michael's church, to, and by the north side of St. James' church by Garlicke Hith; this is called Kerion lane. And thus much for the bounds of Vintry ward. Now, on the Thames' side, west from Grantham's lane, have ye Herber lane, or Brikels' lane, so called of John Brikels, sometime owner thereof.

Then is Simpson's lane, of one Simpson, or Emperor's head lane, of such a sign. Then the Three Cranes' lane, so called not only of a sign of three cranes at a tavern door, but rather of three strong cranes of timber placed on the Vintry wharf by the Thames side, to crane up wines there, as is afore showed. This lane was of old time, to wit, the 9th of Richard II., called The Painted Tavern lane, of the tavern being painted.

Then next over against St. Martin's church, is a large house built of stone and timber, with vaults for the stowage of wines, and is called the Vintry. There dwelt John Gisers, vintner mayor of London, and constable of the Tower, and then was Henry Picard, vintner, mayor. In this house Henry Picard feasted four kings in one day (as in my *Summary* I have showed). Then next is Vanner's lane, so called of one Vanner that was owner thereof; it is now called Church lane, of the coming up from the wharf to St. Martin's church. Next is Brode lane, for that the same is broader for the passage of carts from the Vintrie wharf, than be the other lanes. At the north-west corner of this lane is the Parish Clerks' hall, lately by them purchased, since they lost their old hall in Bishopsgate street. Next is Spittle lane, of old time so called, since Stodie's lane, of the owner thereof named Stodie. Sir John Stodie, vintner, mayor in the year 1357, gave it with all the quadrant wherein Vintners' hall now standeth, with the tenements round about unto the Vintners; the Vintners built for themselves a fair hall, and also thirteen alms houses there for thirteen poor people, which are kept of charity rent free.

The Vintners in London were of old time called Merchant-vintners of Gascoyne; and so I read them in the records of Edward II., the 11th year, and Edward III., the 9th year: they were as well Englishmen as strangers born beyond the seas, but then subjects to the kings of England, great Burdeaux merchants of Gascoyne and French wines, divers of them were mayors of this city, namely John Adrian, vintner, Reginold at conduit, John Oxenford, Hen. Picard, that feasted the kings of England, France, Scotland, and Cypres, John Stodie, that gave Stodie's lane to the Vintners; which four last named were mayors in the reign of Edward III.; and yet Gascoyne wines were then to be sold at London not above four pence, nor Rhenish wine above six pence the gallon. I read of sweet wines, that in the 50th of Edward III., John Peachie, fishmonger, was accused, for that he procured a license for the only sale of them in London; which notwithstanding he justified by law, he was imprisoned and fined. More, I read, that in the 6th of Henry VI., the Lombards corrupting their sweet wines, when knowledge thereof came to John Rainwell, mayor of London, he in divers places of the city commanded the heads of the butts and other vessels in the open streets to be broken, to the number of one hundred and fifty, so that the liquor running forth, passed through the city like a stream of rain water, in the sight of all the people, from whence there issued a most loathsome savour.

I read, in the reign of Henry VII., that no sweet wines were brought into this realm but Malmesies by the Longabards, paying to the king for his license six shillings and eight pence of every butt, besides twelve pence for bottle large. I remember within this fifty-four years Malmsey not to be sold more than one penny halfpenny the pint. For proof whereof, it appeareth in the church book of St. Andrew Undershafte, that in the year 1547 I. G. and S. K., then churchwardens, for eighty pints of Malmsey spent in the church, after one penny halfpenny the pint, paid at the year's end for the same ten shillings. More, I remember that no sacks were sold but Rumney, and that for medicine more than for drink, but now many kinds of sacks are known and used. And so much for wines.

For the Vintry, to end therewith, I read, that in the reign of Henry IV., the young prince Henry, Thomas Duke of Clarence, John Duke of Bedford, and Humfrey Duke of Glocester, the king's sons, being at supper among the merchants of London in the Vintry, in the house of Lewes John, Henry Scogan sent to them a ballad beginning thus:—

> " My noble sonnes and eke my lords deare,
> I your father, called unworthily,
> Send unto you this ballad following here,
> Written with mine own hand full rudely,
> Although it be that I not reverently
> Have written to your estates, I you pray
> Mine uncunning, taketh benignely,
> For God's sake, and hearken what I say."

Then follow in like metre twenty-three staves, containing a persuasion from losing of time follily in lust and vice, but to spend the same in virtue and godliness, as ye may read in Geffrey Chawcer's works lately printed. The successors of those vintners and wine-drawers, that retailed by the gallons, pottle, quart, and pint, were all incorporated by the name of Wine-tunners [1] in the reign of Edward III., and confirmed in the 15th of Henry VI.

" [1] Having thus much, not without travail and some charges, noted for the antiquitie of the Vintners, about two years since or more I repayred to the common-hall of that company, and there showed and read it in a court of assistance, requiring them, as being one of the principal companies in the citie (of whom I meant therefore to write the more at large) that if they knew any more which might sound to their worship or commendation, at their leisure to send it me, and I would joyne it to my former collection; at which time I was answered by some that tooke upon them the speech, that they were none of the principall, but of the inferior companies; and so willing me to leave them, I departed, and never since heard from them, which hath somewhat discouraged me any farther to travail amongst the companies to learne ought at their handes."—1st edition, p. 192.

His comment (in a side note) is equally worth preserving: " The readiest to speake not alwaies the wisest men."

Next is Palmer's lane, now called Anchor lane; the Plumbers have their hall there, but are tenants to the Vintners. Then is Worcester house, sometime belonging to the Earls of Worcester, now divided into many tenements; the Fruiterers have their hall there. Then is the Old Swan, a great brewhouse. And this is all on the Thames' side that I can note in this ward.

On the land side is the Royall street and Paternoster lane, I think of old time called Arches; for I read that Robert de Suffolke gave to Walter Darford his tenement with the appurtenance in the lane called Les Arches, in the parish of St. Michael de Paternoster church, between the wall of the field called Winchester field on the east, and the same lane on the West, etc. More, I read of a stone house called Selde de Winton juxta Stenden bridge, which in that lane was over Walbrooke water.

Then is the fair parish church of St. Michael called Paternoster church in the Royall. This church was new built, and made a college of St. Spirit and St. Mary, founded by Richard Whitington, mercer, four times mayor, for a master, four fellows—masters of art, clerks, conducts, chorists, etc., and an alms house called God's house, or hospital, for thirteen poor men, one of them to be tutor, and to have sixteen pence the week; the other twelve, each of them to have fourteen pence the week for ever, with other necessary provisions, a hutch with three locks, a common seal, etc. These were bound to pray for the good estate of Richard Whitington and Alice his wife, their founders, and for Sir William Whitington, knight, and Dame Joan his wife, and for Hugh Fitzwaren, and Dame Molde his wife, the fathers and mothers of the said Richard Whitington and Alice his wife, for King Richard II., and Thomas of Woodstocke, Duke of Glocester, special lords and promoters of the said Richard Whitington, etc. The license for this foundation was granted by King Henry IV., the 11th of his reign, and in the 12th of the same king's reign, the mayor and commonalty of London granted to Richard Whitington a vacant piece of ground, thereon to build his college in the Royall, all which was confirmed by Henry VI., the 3rd of his reign, to John Coventrie, Jenkin Carpenter, and William Grove, executors to Richard Whitington. This foundation was again confirmed by parliament, the 10th of Henry VI., and was suppressed by the statute of Edward VI.

The alms houses, with the poor men, do remain, and are paid by the Mercers. This Richard Whitington was in this church three times buried: first by his executors under a fair monument;

then in the reign of Edward VI., the parson of that church, thinking some great riches (as he said) to be buried with him, caused his monument to be broken, his body to be spoiled of his leaden sheet, and again the second time to be buried; and in the reign of Queen Mary the parishioners were forced to take him up, to lap him in lead as afore, to bury him the third time, and to place his monument, or the like, over him again, which remaineth, and so he resteth. Thomas Windford, alderman, was buried in this church 1448; Arnold Macknam, vintner, a merchant of Burdeaux, 1457; Sir Heere Tanke, or Hartancleux, knight of the garter, born in Almayne, a noble warrior in Henry V. and Henry VI. days; Sir Edmond Mulshew, knight, near to Thomas Cokham, recorder of London; the Lady Kyme; Sir William Oldhall, knight, 1460; William Barnocke; Sir John Yong, grocer, mayor 1466; Agnes, daughter to Sir John Yong, first married to Robert Sherington, after to Robert Mulleneux, then to William Cheyney, esquire; John Having, gentleman; William Roswell, esquire; William Postar, clerk of the crown, 1520; Sir William Bayly, draper, mayor 1533, with Dame Katherine his wife, leaving sixteen children; John Haydon, mercer, sheriff 1582, who gave legacies to the thirteen alms men, and otherwise, for a lecture.

At the upper end of this street is the Tower Royall, whereof that street taketh name. This Tower and great place was so called of pertaining to the kings of this realm,[1] but by whom the same was first built, or of what antiquity continued, I have not read more than that in the reign of Edward I., the 2nd, 4th, and 7th years, it was the tenement of Symon Beawmes; also, that in the 36th of Edward III., the same was called the Royall, in the parish of St. Michael de Paternoster, and that in the 43rd of his reign, he gave it by the name of his inn, called the Royall, in the city of London, in value twenty pounds by year, unto his college of St. Stephen at Westminster; notwithstanding, in the reign of Richard II. it was called the Queen's Wardrobe, as appeareth by this that followeth:—King Richard having in Smithfield overcome and dispersed his rebels, he, his lords, and all his company, entered the city of London, with great joy, and went to the lady princess his mother, who was then lodged in the Tower Royall, called the Queen's Wardrobe, where she had remained three days and two nights, right sore abashed; but when she saw the king her son was greatly rejoiced, and said, " Ah, son! what great sorrow have I suffered for you this day! " The king answered and said, " Certainly, madam, I know it

[1] [*See* Additional Notes.]

well; but now rejoice, and thank God, for I have this day recovered mine heritage, and the realm of England, which I had near hand lost."

This tower seemeth to have been at that time of good defence; for when the rebels had beset the Tower of London, and got possession thereof, taking from thence whom they listed, as in my *Annals* I have shown, the princess being forced to fly, came to this Tower Royal, where she was lodged, and remained safe, as ye have heard; and it may be also supposed that the king himself was at that time lodged there. I read, that in the year 1386, Lyon King of Armonie, being chased out of his realm by the Tartarians, received innumerable gifts of the king and of his nobles, the king then lying in the Royall, where he also granted to the said king of Armonie, a charter of a thousand pounds by year during his life. This for proof may suffice that kings of England have been lodged in this tower, though the same of later time have been neglected, and turned into stabling for the king's horses, and now letten out to divers men, and divided into tenements.

In Horsebridge street is the Cutlars' hall. Richard de Wilehale, 1295, confirmed to Paul Butelar this house and edifices in the parish of St. Michael Paternoster church and St. John's upon Walbrooke, which sometime Lawrens Gisors and his son Peter Gisors did possess, and afterward Hugonis de Hingham, and lieth between the tenement of the said Richard towards the south, and the lane called Horseshew bridge towards the north, and between the way called Paternoster church on the west, and the course of Walbrooke on the east, paying yearly one clove of Gereflowers at Easter, and to the prior and convent of St. Mary Overy six shillings. This house sometime belonged to Simon Dolesly, grocer, mayor 1359. They of this company were of old time divided into three arts or sorts of workmen: to wit, the first were smiths, forgers of blades, and therefore called bladers, and divers of them proved wealthy men, as namely, Walter Nele, blader, one of the sheriffs the 12th of Edward III., deceased 1352, and buried in St. James' Garlicke Hith; he left lands to the mending of high ways about London, betwixt Newgate and Wicombe, Aldgate and Chelmesford, Bishopsgate and Ware, Southwark and Rochester, etc. The second were makers of hafts, and otherwise garnishers of blades. The third sort were sheathmakers, for swords, daggers, and knives. In the 10th of Henry IV. certain ordinances were made betwixt the bladers and the other cutlers; and in the 4th of Henry VI. they were all three companies drawn into one fraternity or brotherhood by the name of Cutlers.

Then is Knightriders' street, so called (as is supposed) of knights well armed and mounted at the Tower Royall, riding from thence through that street west to Creed lane, and so out at Ludgate towards Smithfield, when they were there to tourney, joust, or otherwise to show activities before the king and states of the realm.

In this street is the parish church of St. Thomas Apostle, by Wringwren lane, a proper church, but monuments of antiquity be there none, except some arms in the windows, as also in the stone work, which some suppose to be of John Barns, mercer, mayor of London in the year 1371, a great builder thereof; H. Causton, merchant, was a benefactor, and had a chantry there about 1396; T. Roman, mayor 1310, had also a chantry there 1319; Fitzwilliams, also a benefactor, had a chantry there. More, Sir William Littlesbery, *alias* Horne (for King Edward IV. so named him, because he was a most excellent blower in a horn); he was a salter and merchant of the staple, mayor of London in the year 1487, and was buried in this church, having appointed by his testament the bells to be changed for four new bells of good tune and sound, but that was not performed; he gave five hundred marks to the repairing of highways betwixt London and Cambridge; his dwelling-house, with a garden and appurtenances in the said parish to be sold, and bestowed in charitable actions, as his executors would answer before God; his house, called the George, in Bred street, he gave to the Salters, they to find a priest in the said church, to have £6 13s. 4d. the year, to every preacher at Paul's cross and at the Spittle four pence for ever; to the prisoners of Newgate, Ludgate, Marshalsey, and King's Bench, in victuals, ten shillings at Christmas, and ten shillings at Easter for ever; which legacies are not performed. William Shipton, William Champneis, and John de Burford, had chantries there; John Martin, butcher, one of the sheriffs, was buried there 1533; etc.   Then west from the said church, on the same side, was one great messuage, sometime called Ipres inn, of William Ipres, a Fleming, the first builder thereof.   This William was called out of Flanders, with a number of Flemings, to the aid of King Stephen against Maude the empress, in the year 1138, and grew in favour with the said king for his services, so far that he built this his house near Tower Royall, in the which tower it seemeth the king was then lodged, as in the heart of the city, for his more safety.

Robert, Earl of Gloucester, brother to the empress, being taken, was committed to the custody of this William, to be kept in the castle of Rochester, till King Stephen was also taken, and then the one was delivered in exchange for the other, and both set free. This William of Ipres gave Edredes hithe, now called the Queen's hithe, to the prior and canons of the Holy Trinity in London: he founded the abbey of Boxley in Kent, etc. In the first of Henry II., the said William, with all the other Flemings, fearing the indignation of the new king, departed the land; but it seemeth that the said William was shortly called back again, and restored both to the king's favour and to his old possessions here, so that the name and family continued long after in this realm, as may appear by this which followeth.

In the year 1377, the 51st of Edward III., the citizens of London, minding to have destroyed John of Gaunt, Duke of Lancaster, and Henry Percie, marshal (for cause shown in my *Annals*), sought up and down, and could not find them, for they were that day to dine with John of Ipres at his inn, which the Londoners wist not of, but thought the duke and marshal had been at the Savoy, and therefore posted thither; but one of the duke's knights seeing these things, came in great haste to the place where the duke was, and after that he had knocked and could not be let in, he said to Haveland the porter, "If thou love my lord and thy life, open the gate;" with which words he gat entry, and with great fear he tells the duke, that without the gate were infinite numbers of armed men, and unless he took great heed that day would be his last; with which words the duke leapt so hastily from his oisters, that he hurt both his legs against the form: wine was offered, but he could not drink for haste, and so fled with his fellow Henry Percie out at a back gate, and entering the Thames, never stayed rowing until they came to a house near the manor of Kennington, where at that time the princess lay with Richard the young prince, before whom he made his complaint, etc.

On the other side, I read of a messuage called Ringed hall. King Henry VIII., the 32nd of his reign, gave the same, with four tenements adjoining, unto Morgan Philip, *alias* Wolfe, in the parish of St. Thomas Apostles, in London, etc.

Over against Ipres inn, in Knight riders street, at the corner towards St. James at Garlicke hithe, was sometime a great house built of stone and called Ormond place, for that it sometimes belonged to the Earls of Ormond. King Edward IV., in the 5th of his reign, gave to Elizabeth his wife the manor of Greenwich, with the tower and park, in the county of Kent. He also gave this tenement called Ormond place, with all the appurtenances to the same, situate in the parish of St. Trinitie in Knight riders street, in London. This house is now lately taken down, and divers fair tenements are built there, the corner house whereof is a tavern. Then lower down in Royall street is Kerion lane, of one Kerion sometime dwelling there. In this lane be divers fair houses for merchants, and amongst others is the Glaziers' hall.

At the south corner of Royall street is the fair parish church of St. Martin called in the Vintry, sometime called St. Martin de Beremand church. This church was new built about the year 1399 by the executors of Mathew Columbars a stranger born, a Burdeaux merchant of Gascoyne and French wines; his arms remain yet in the east window, and are between a cheveron, three columbins. There lie buried in this church— Sir John Gisors, mayor 1311; Henry Gisors, his son, 1343, and John Gisors, his brother, 1350; he gave to his son Thomas his great mansion-house called Gisors hall, in the parish of St. Mildred, in Bread street. This Thomas had issue, John and Thomas; John made a feoffment, and sold Gisors hall and other his lands in London, about the year 1386; Thomas deceased 1395. Henry Vennar; Bartholomew de la Vauch; Thomas Cornwalles, one of the sheriffs 1384; John Cornwalles, esquire, 1436; John Mustrell, vintner, 1424; William Hodson; William Castleton; John Gray; Robert Dalusse, barber, in the reign of Edward IV., with this epitaph:

> " As flowers in the field thus passeth life,
> Naked, then clothed, feeble in the end,
> It sheweth by Robert Dalusse, and Alison his wife,
> Christ them save from the power of the fiend."

Sir Raph Austrie, fishmonger, new roofed this church with timber, covered it with lead, and beautifully glazed it: he deceased 1494, and was there buried with his two wives; Raph Austrie, his son, gentleman; William Austrie, and other of that name; Bartrand, wife to Grimond Descure, esquire, a Gascoyne and merchant of wines, 1494; Thomas Batson; Alice Fowler, daughter and heir to John Howton, wife to John Hulton; James Bartlet, and Alice his wife; William Fennor; Roger Cotton; Robert Stocker; John Pemberton; Philip de Plasse; John Stapleton; John Mortimer; William Lee; William Hamsteed; William Stoksbie, and Gilbert March, had chantries there.

Then is the parish church of St. James, called at Garlick

hithe, or Garlicke hive; for that of old time, on the bank of the river of Thames, near to this church, garlick was usually sold. This is a proper church, whereof Richard Rothing, one of the sheriffs 1326, is said to be the new builder, and lieth buried in the same: so was Waltar Nele, blader, one of the sheriffs 1337; John of Oxenford, vintner, mayor 1341. I read, in the 1st of Edward III., that this John of Oxenford gave to the priory of the Holy Trinity in London two tofts of land, one mill, fifty acres of land, two acres of wood, with the appurtenances, in Kentish town, in value 20s. 3d. by year. Richard Goodcheape, John de Cressingham, and John Whitthorne, and before them, Galfrid Moncley, 1281, founded a chantry there.

Monuments remaining there: Robert Gabeter, esquire, mayor of Newcastle-upon-Tyne, 1310; John Gisors; William Tiligham; John Stanley; Lord Strange, eldest son of the Earl of Derby, 1503; Nicholas Statham; Robert de Luton, 1361; Richard Lions, a famous merchant of wines, and a lapidary, sometime one of the sheriffs, beheaded in Cheape by Wat Tyler and other rebels in the year 1381; his picture on his gravestone, very fair and large, is with his hair rounded by his ears, and curled; a little beard forked; a gown, girt to him down to his feet, of branched damask, wrought with the likeness of flowers; a large purse on his right side, hanging in a belt from his left shoulder; a plain hood about his neck covering his shoulders, and hanging back behind him. Sir John Wrotch, fishmonger, mayor 1361, deceased 1407; Thomas Stonarde, of Oxfordshire; John Bromer, fishmonger, alderman 1474; the Lady Stanley, mother to the Lord Strange; the Countess of Huntingdon; the Lady Harbert; Sir George Stanley; Gilbert Bovet, 1398; a Countess of Worcester, and one of her children; William More, vintner, mayor 1395; William Venor, grocer, mayor 1389; Robert Chichley, mayor 1421; James Spencer, vintner, mayor 1543; Richard Plat, brewer, founded a free school there 1601.

And thus an end of Vintry ward, which hath an alderman, with a deputy, common councillors nine, constables nine, scavengers four, wardmote inquest fourteen, and a beadle. It is taxed to the fifteen [1] at £6 13s. 4d.

[1] " In London at six and thirty pounds, and in the Exchequer at thirty-five pounds five shillings."—1st edition, p. 195.

CORDWAINER STREET WARD

The next is Cordwainer street ward, taking that name of cordwainers, or shoemakers, curriers, and workers of leather, dwelling there; for it appeareth in the records of Henry VI., the 9th of his reign, that an order was taken then for cordwainers and curriers in Corney street and Sopars lane.

This ward beginneth in the east, on the west side of Walbrook, and turneth west through Budge row (a street so called of the Budge furre, and of skinners dwelling there), then up by St. Anthony's church through Aetheling (or Noble street), as Leland termeth it, commonly called Wathling street, to the Red Lion, a place so called of a great lion of timber placed there at a gate, entering a large court, wherein are divers fair and large shops, well furnished with broad cloths and other draperies of all sorts, to be sold: and this is the farthest west part of this ward.

On the south side of this street from Budge row lieth a lane turning down by the west gate of the Tower Royal, and to the south end of the stone wall beyond the said gate is of this ward, and is accounted a part of the Royal street: against this west gate of the Tower Royal is one other lane that runneth west to Cordwainer street, and this is called Turnebase lane; on the south side whereof is a piece of Wringwren lane, to the north-west corner of St. Thomas Church the Apostle. Then again, out of the high street called Wathling, is one other street, which runneth thwart the same; and this is Cordwainer street, whereof the whole ward taketh name. This street beginneth by West Cheape, and St. Mary Bow church is the head thereof on the west side, and it runneth down south through that part which of later time was called Hosier lane, now Bow lane, and then by the west end of Aldmary church to the new built houses, in place of Ormond house, and so to Garlicke hill, or hithe, to St. James' church. The upper part of this street towards Cheape was called Hosier lane, of hosiers dwelling there in place of shoemakers; but now those hosiers being worn out by men of other trades (as the hosiers had worn out the shoemakers), the same is called Bow lane of Bow church. On the west side of Cordewainers street is Basing lane, right over against Turnebasse lane. This Basing lane west to the back gate of the Red Lion, in Wathling street, is of this Cordwainers street ward.

Now again, on the north side of the high street in Budge row, by the east end of St. Anthonie's church, have ye St. Sithes lane, so called of St. Sithes church (which standeth against the north end of that lane), and this is wholly of Cordwainers street ward: also the south side of Needlers lane, which reacheth from the north end of St. Sithes lane west to Sopar's lane; then west from St. Anthonies church is the south end of Sopar's lane, which lane took that name, not of soap-making, as some have supposed, but of Alen le Sopar, in the 9th of Edward II.[1] I have not read or heard of soap-making in this city till within this fourscore years; that John Lame, dwelling in Grasse street, set up a boiling-house for this city, of former time, was served of white soap in hard cakes (called Castell soap, and other), from beyond the seas, and of grey soap,[2] speckled with white, very sweet and good, from Bristow, sold here for a penny the pound, and never above a penny farthing, and black soap for a halfpenny the pound. Then in Bow lane (as they now call it) is Goose lane, by Bow church. William Essex, mercer, had tenements there in the 26th of Edward III.

Then from the south end of Bow lane, by Wathling street, till over against the Red Lion: and these be the bounds of Cordwainer street ward.

Touching monuments therein, first you have the fair parish church of St. Anthonies in Budge row, on the north side thereof. This church was lately re-edified by Thomas Knowles, grocer, mayor, and by Thomas Knowles, his son, both buried there, with epitaphs, of the father thus:

> " Here lieth graven vnder this stone,
> Thomas Knowles, both flesh and bone;
> Grocer and alderman, yeares fortie,
> Shiriffe, and twice maior truly.
> And for he should not lie alone,
> Here lieth with him his good wife Joan.
> They were togither sixtie yeare,
> And ninteene children they had in feere," etc.

Thomas Holland, mercer, was there buried 1456; Thomas Windent, mercer, alderman, and Katherine his wife; Thomas Hind, mercer, 1528; he was a benefactor to this church, to Aldermarie church, and to Bow; Hugh Acton, merchant-tailor, buried 1520; he gave thirty-six pounds to the repairing of the steeple of this church. Simon Street, grocer, lieth in the church

---

[1] [*See* Additional Notes.]
[2] " Gray sope made in London dearer than bought from Bristol."—*Stow.*

wall toward the south; his arms be three colts, and his epitaph thus:

> " Such as I am, such shall you be,
> Grocer of London sometime was I,
> The king's wayer more then yeares twentie,
> Simon Streete called in my place,
> And good fellowship faine would trace;
> Therefore in heaven, everlasting life,
> Jesu send me, and Agnes my wife:
> Kerlie Merlie, my words were tho,
> And *Deo gratias* I coupled thereto:
> I passed to God in the yeare of grace,
> A thousand foure hundred it was," etc.

William Dauntsey, mercer, one of the sheriffs, buried 1542. Henry Collet, mercer, mayor, a great benefactor to this church; the pictures of him, his wife, ten sons, and ten daughters, remain in the glass window on the north side of the church; but the said Henry Collet was buried at Stebunhith. Henry Halton, grocer, one of the sheriffs, deceased 1415; Thomas Spight, merchant-tailor, 1533; and Roger Martin, mercer, mayor, deceased 1573. John Grantham and Nicholas Bull had chantries there.

Next on the south side of Budge row, by the west corner thereof, and on the east side of Cordwainer street, is one other fair church called Aldemarie church, because the same was very old, and elder than any church of St. Marie in the city, till of late years the foundation of a very fair new church was laid there by Henry Keble, grocer, mayor, who deceased 1518, and was there buried in a vault by him prepared, with a fair monument raised over him on the north side the choir, now destroyed and gone: he gave by his testament one thousand pounds towards the building up of that church, and yet not permitted a resting-place for his bones there. Thomas Roman, mayor 1310, had a chantry there. Richard Chawcer,[1] vintner, gave to that church his tenement and tavern, with the appurtenance, in the Royal street, the corner of Kerion lane, and was there buried 1348. John Briton; Ralph Holland, draper, one of the sheriffs, deceased 1452; William Taylor, grocer, mayor, deceased 1483: he discharged that ward of fifteens to be paid by the poor. Thomas Hinde, mercer, buried in St. Anthonies, gave ten fodder of lead to the covering of the middle aisle of this Aldemarie church. Charles Blunt, Lord Montjoy, was buried there about the year 1545; he made or glazed the east

[1] " Richard Chaucer, father to Geffrey Chaucer, the poet, as may be supposed."—*Stow.*

window, as appeareth by his arms: his epitaph, made by him
in his lifetime, thus:

> " Willingly have I fought, and willingly have I found
> The fatall end that wrought thither as dutie bound:
> Discharged I am of that I ought to my country by honest wound,
> My soule departed Christ hath bought, the end of man is ground."

Sir William Laxton, grocer, mayor, deceased 1556, and
Thomas Lodge, grocer, mayor 1583, were buried in the vault
of Henry Keble, whose bones were unkindly cast out, and his
monument pulled down;[1] in place whereof monuments are set
up of the later buried. William Blunt, Lord Mountjoy, buried
there 1594, etc.

At the upper end of Hosier lane, toward Westcheape, is the
fair parish church of St. Mary Bow. This church, in the reign
of William Conqueror, being the first in this city built on arches
of stone, was therefore called New Marie church, of St. Marie
de Arcubus,[2] or Le Bow, in West Cheaping; as Stratford bridge
being the first built (by Matilde the queen, wife to Henry I.)
with arches of stone, was called Stratford le Bow; which names
to the said church and bridge remaineth till this day. The
court of the Arches is kept in this church, and taketh name of
the place, not the place of the court; but of what antiquity or
continuation that court hath there continued I cannot learn.

This church is of Cordwainer street ward, and for divers
accidents happening there, hath been made more famous than
any other parish church of the whole city or suburbs. First,
we read, that in the year 1090, and the 3rd of William Rufus,
by tempest of wind, the roof of the church of St. Marie Bow, in
Cheape, was overturned, wherewith some persons were slain,
and four of the rafters, of twenty-six feet in length, with such
violence were pitched in the ground of the high street, that
scantly four feet of them remained above ground, which were

---

[1] " Sir William Laxton, grocer, mayor, deceased 1556, was buried in
the vault prepared by Henry Keble, principall founder of that church,
for himself, but now his bones are unkindly cast out, his monuments
pulled downe, and the bodies of the said Sir William Laxton, and of Sir
Thomas Lodge, grocer, mayor, are laid in place, with monuments over
them for the time, till an other give money for their place, and then away
with them."—1st edition, p. 199.

[2] " Called de Arcubus of the stone arches or bowes on the top of the
steeple or bell tower thereof, which arching was as well on the old steeple
as on the new, for no other part of the church seemeth to have been arched
at any time; yet hath the said church never been knowne by any other
name than St. Mary Bow, or le Bow; neither is that church so called of
the court there kept, but the said court taketh name of the place wherein
it is kept, and is called the Court of Arches."—1st edition, p. 203.

fain to be cut even with the ground, because they could not be plucked out (for the city of London was not then paved, and a marish ground).

In the year 1196, William Fitz Osbert, a seditious tailor, took the steeple of Bow, and fortified it with munitions and victuals, but it was assaulted, and William with his accomplices were taken, though not without bloodshed, for he was forced by fire and smoke to forsake the church; and then, by the judges condemned, he was by the heels drawn to the Elms in Smithfield, and there hanged with nine of his fellows; where, because his favourers came not to deliver him, he forsook Mary's son (as he termed Christ our Saviour), and called upon the devil to help and deliver him. Such was the end of this deceiver, a man of an evil life, a secret murderer, a filthy fornicator, a pollutor of concubines, and (amongst other his detestable facts) a false accuser of his elder brother,[1] who had in his youth brought him up in learning, and done many things for his preferment.

In the year 1271, a great part of the steeple of Bow fell down, and slew many people, men and women. In the year 1284, the 13th of Edward I., Laurence Ducket, goldsmith, having grievously wounded one Ralph Crepin in Westcheape, fled into Bow church; into the which in the night time entered certain evil persons, friends unto the said Ralph, and slew the said Laurence lying in the steeple, and then hanged him up, placing him so by the window as if he had hanged himself, and so was it found by inquisition; for the which fact Laurence Ducket, being drawn by the feet, was buried in a ditch without the city; but shortly after, by relation of a boy, who lay with the said Laurence at the time of his death, and had hid him there for fear, the truth of the matter was disclosed; for the which cause, Jordan Goodcheape, Ralph Crepin, Gilbert Clarke, and Geffrey Clarke, were attainted; a certain woman named Alice, that was chief causer of the said mischief, was burnt, and to the number of sixteen men were drawn and hanged, besides others that being richer, after long imprisonment, were hanged by the purse.

The church was interdicted, the doors and windows were stopped up with thorns, but Laurence was taken up, and honestly buried in the churchyard.

The parish church of St. Mary Bow, by mean of incroachment

---

[1] " A false accuser of his elder brother, in the end was hanged."—*Stow*. In his first edition, p. 203, this note is continued as follows: " God amend, or shortly send such an end to such false brethren."

and building of houses, wanting room in their churchyard for burial of the dead, John Rotham, or Rodham, citizen and tailor, by his testament, dated the year 1465, gave to the parson and churchwardens a certain garden in Hosier lane to be a churchyard, which so continued near a hundred years; but now is built on, and is a private man's house. The old steeple of this church was by little and little re-edified, and new built up, at the least so much as was fallen down, many men giving sums of money to the furtherance thereof; so that at length, to wit, in the year 1469, it was ordained by a common council that the Bow bell should be nightly rung at nine of the clock. Shortly after, John Donne, mercer, by his testament, dated 1472, according to the trust of Reginald Longdon, gave to the parson and churchwardens of St. Mary Bow two tenements, with the appurtenances, since made into one, in Hosier lane, then so called, to the maintenance of Bow bell, the same to be rung as aforesaid, and other things to be observed, as by the will appeareth.

This bell being usually rung somewhat late, as seemed to the young men 'prentices, and other in Cheape, they made and set up a rhyme against the clerk, as followeth:

> " Clarke of the Bow bell with the yellow lockes,
>   For thy late ringing thy head shall have knocks."

Whereunto the clerk replying, wrote,

> " Children of Cheape, hold you all still,
>   For you shall have the Bow bell rung at your will."

Robert Harding, goldsmith, one of the sheriffs 1478, gave to the new work of that steeple forty pounds; John Haw, mercer, ten pounds; Doctor Allen, four pounds; Thomas Baldry, four pounds, and other gave other sums, so that the said work of the steeple was finished in the year 1512. The arches or bowes thereupon, with the lanthorns, five in number, to wit, one at each corner, and one on the top in the middle upon the arches, were also afterward finished of stone, brought from Caen in Normandy, delivered at the Customers key for 4s. 8d. the ton; William Copland, tailor, the king's merchant, and Andrew Fuller, mercer, being churchwardens 1515 and 1516. It is said that this Copland gave the great bell, which made the fifth in the ring, to be rung nightly at nine of the clock. This bell was first rung as a knell at the burial of the same Copland. It appeareth that the lanthorns on the top of this steeple were meant to have been glazed, and lights in them placed nightly in the winter, whereby travellers to the city might have the better sight thereof, and not to miss of their ways.

In this parish also was a grammar school, by commandment of King Henry VI., which school was of old time kept in a house for that purpose prepared in the churchyard; but that school being decayed, as others about this city, the school-house was let out for rent, in the reign of Henry VIII., for four shillings the year, a cellar for two shillings the year, and two vaults under the church for fifteen shillings both.

The monuments in this church be these; namely, of Sir John Coventrie, mercer, mayor 1425; Richard Lambert, alderman; Nicholas Alwine, mercer, mayor 1499; Robert Harding, goldsmith, one of the sheriffs 1478; John Loke, one of the sheriffs 1461; Edward Bankes, alderman, haberdasher, 1566; John Warde; William Pierson, scrivener and attorney in the Common Pleas. In a proper chapel on the south side the church standeth a tomb, elevated and arched.[1] Ade de Buke, hatter, glazed the chapel and most part of the church, and was there buried. All other monuments be defaced. Hawley and Southam had chantries there.

Without the north side of this church of St. Mary Bow, towards West Cheape, standeth one fair building of stone, called in record Seldam, a shed, which greatly darkeneth the said church; for by means thereof all the windows and doors on that side are stopped up. King Edward III. upon occasion, as shall be shown in the ward of Cheape, caused this sild or shed to be made, and to be strongly built of stone, for himself, the queen, and other estates to stand in, there to behold the joustings and other shows at their pleasures. And this house for a long time after served to that use, namely, in the reign of Edward III. and Richard II.; but in the year 1410, Henry IV., in the 12th of his reign, confirmed the said shed or building to Stephen Spilman, William Marchford, and John Whateley, mercers, by the name of one New Seldam, shed, or building, with shops, cellars, and edifices whatsoever appertaining, called Crounsilde, or Tamersilde,[2] situate in the mercery in West Cheape, and in the parish of St. Mary de Arcubus in London, etc. Notwithstanding which grant, the kings of England, and other great estates, as well of foreign countries, repairing to this realm, as inhabitants of the same, have usually repaired to

---

[1] " Of some unknowne founder."—1st *edition*, p. 205.
[2] " And in the 8th of the same Henry called Tamarsilde."—1st *edition*, p. 206.

this place, therein to behold the shows of this city passing through West Cheape, namely, the great watches accustomed in the night, on the even of St. John Baptist, and St. Peter at Midsummer, the examples whereof were over long to recite, wherefore let it suffice briefly to touch one. In the year 1510, on St. John's even, at night, King Henry VIII. came to this place, then called the King's Head in Cheape, in the livery of a yeoman of the guard, with an halbert on his shoulder (and there beholding the watch) departed privily when the watch was done, and was not known to any but to whom it pleased him; but on St. Peter's night next following, he and the queen came royally riding to the said place, and there with their nobles beheld the watch of the city, and returned in the morning.

This church of St. Mary, with the said shed of stone, all the housing in or about Bow church yard, and without on that side the high street of Cheape to the Standard, be of Cordewainer street ward. These houses were of old time but sheds; for I read of no housing otherwise on that side the street, but of divers sheds from Sopar's lane to the Standard, etc. Amongst other, I read of three shops or sheds by Sopar's lane, pertaining to the priory of the Holy Trinity within Aldgate; the one was let out for twenty-eight shillings, one other for twenty shillings, and the third for twelve shillings, by the year. Moreover, that Richard Goodchepe, mercer, and Margery his wife, son to Jordaine Goodchepe, did let to John Dalinges the younger, mercer, their shed and chamber in West Cheape, in the parish of St. Mary de Arches for three shillings and four pence by the year. Also the men of Bread street ward contended with the men of Cordwayner street ward for a seld or shed opposite to the Standard, on the south side, and it was found to be of Cordwayner street ward; W. Waldorne being then mayor, the 1st of Henry VI. Thus much for Cordwainer street ward; which hath an alderman, his deputy, common councillors eight, constables eight, scavengers eight, wardmote inquest men fourteen, and a beadle. It standeth taxed to the fifteen in London at £52 16s., in the Exchequer at £52 6s.[1]

CHEAPE WARD

Next adjoining is Cheape ward, and taketh name of the market there kept, called West Cheping. This ward also beginneth in the east, on the course of Walbrooke in Buckles

[1] "In London at £72 16s., in the Exchequer at £72."—*1st edition*, p. 207.

bury, and runneth up on both the sides to the great conduit in Cheape. Also on the south side of Buckles bury, a lane turning up by St. Sithes church, and by St. Pancrates church, through Needler's lane, on the north side thereof, and then through a piece of Sopar's lane, on both sides up to Cheape, be all of Cheape ward.

Then to begin again in the east upon the said course of Walbrooke, is St. Mildred's church in the Poultrie, on the north side, and over against the said church gate, on the south, to pass up all that high street called the Poultrie, to the great conduit in Cheape, and then Cheape itself, which beginneth by the east end of the said conduit, and stretcheth up to the north-east corner of Bow lane on the south side, and to the Standard on the north side; and thus far to the west is of Cheape ward.

On the south side of this high street is no lane turning south out of this ward, more than some portion of Sopar's lane, whereof I have before written. But on the north side of this high street is Conyhope lane, about one quarter of Old Jury lane on the west side, and on the east side almost as much, to the sign of the Angel. Then is Ironmonger's lane, all wholly on both sides, and from the north end thereof through Catton street, west to the north end of St. Lawrence lane, and some four houses west beyond the same on that side, and over against Ironmonger's lane end on the north side of Catton street up by the Guildhall and St. Lawrence church in the Jurie, is altogether of Cheape ward. Then again in Cheape, more towards the west, is of St. Lawrence lane before named, which is all wholly of this ward. And last of all is Hony lane, and up to the Standard on the north side of Cheape. And so stand the bounds of Cheape ward.

Now for antiquities there. First is Buckles bury, so called of a manor and tenements pertaining to one Buckle, who there dwelt and kept his courts. This manor is supposed to be the great stone building, yet in part remaining on the south side of the street, which of late time hath been called the Old Barge, of such a sign hanged out near the gate thereof. This manor or great house hath of long time been divided and letten out into many tenements; and it hath been a common speech, that when Walbrooke did lie open, barges were rowed out of the Thames, or towed up so far, and therefore the place hath ever since been called the Old Barge.

Also on the north side of this street, directly over against the said Buckles bury, was one ancient and strong tower of stone, the which tower King Edward III., in the 18th of his reign, by the name of the king's house, called Cornette stoure in London, did appoint to be his Exchange of money there to be kept. In the 29th he granted it to Frydus Guynysane and Landus Bardoile, merchants of Luke, for twenty pounds the year. And in the 32nd he gave the same tower to his college or free chapel of St. Stephen at Westminster, by the name of Cernet's Tower at Buckles bury in London. This tower of late years was taken down by one Buckle, a grocer, meaning in place thereof to have set up and built a goodly frame of timber; but the said Buckle greedily labouring to pull down the old tower, a part thereof fell upon him, which so sore bruised him that his life was thereby shortened, and another that married his widow set up the new prepared frame of timber, and finished the work.

This whole street called Buckles bury on both the sides throughout is possessed of grocers and apothecaries towards the west end thereof: on the south side breaketh out one other short lane, called in records Peneritch street; it reacheth but to St. Sythe's lane, and St. Sythe's church is the farthest part thereof, for by the west end of the said church beginneth Needlar's lane, which reacheth to Sopar's lane, as is aforesaid. This small parish church of St. Sith hath also an addition of Bennet shorne (or Shrog or Shorehog), for by all these names have I read it, but the most ancient is Shorne, wherefore it seemeth to take that name of one Benedict Shorne, sometime a citizen and stock-fishmonger of London, a new builder, repairer, or benefactor thereof, in the reign of Edward II., so that Shorne is but corruptly called Shrog, and more corruptly Shorehog.

There lie buried in this church, John Froysh, mercer, mayor 1394; John Rochford and Robert Rochford; John Hold, alderman; Henry Froweke, mercer, mayor 1435; Edward Warrington; John Morrice; John Huntley; Richard Lincoln, fellmonger, 1546; Sir Ralph Warren, mercer, mayor 1553; Sir John Lion, grocer, mayor 1554: these two last have monuments, the rest are all defaced. Edward Hall, gentleman of Greyes inn, common sergeant of this city, and then under-sheriff of the same; he wrote the large chronicles from Richard II. till the end of Henry VIII., and was buried in this church.

Then in Needelars lane have ye the parish church of St. Pancrate, a proper small church, but divers rich parishioners therein, and hath had of old time many liberal benefactors, but of late such as (not regarding the order taken by her majesty), the least bell in their church being broken, have rather sold the

same [1] for half the value than put the parish to charge with
new casting; late experience hath proved this to be true, besides
the spoil of monuments there. In this church are buried Sir
Aker; John Aker; John Barens, mercer, mayor 1370; John
Beston and his wife; Robert Rayland; John Hamber; John
Gage; John Rowley; John Lambe; John Hadley, grocer,
mayor 1379; Richard Gardener, mercer, mayor 1478; John
Stockton, mercer, mayor 1470; John Dane, mercer; John
Parker; Robert Marshall, alderman, 1439; Robert Corcheforde;
Robert Hatfielde; and Robert Hatfield; Nicholas Wilfilde, and
Thomas his son; the monuments of all which be defaced and
gone. There do remain of Robert Burley, 1360; Richard
Wilson, 1525; Robert Packenton, mercer, slain with a gun shot
at him in a morning,[2] as he was going to morrow mass from his
house in Cheape to St. Thomas of Acars, in the year 1536; the
murderer was never discovered, but by his own confession made
when he came to the gallows at Banbury to be hanged for felony;
T. Wardbury, haberdasher, 1545; James Huish, grocer, 1590;
Ambrose Smith, etc. Then is a part of Soper's lane turning up
to Cheape.

By the assent of Stephen Abunden, mayor, the Pepperers in
Soper's lane were admitted to sell all such spices and other wares
as grocers now use to sell, retaining the old name of pepperers in
Soper's lane, till at length, in the reign of Henry VI., the same
Soper's lane was inhabited by cordwainers and curriers, after
that the pepperers or grocers had seated themselves in a more
open street, to wit, in Buckles bury, where they yet remain.
Thus much for the south wing of Cheape ward.

Now to begin again on the bank of the said Walbrooke, at
the east end of the high street called the Poultrie, on the north
side thereof, is the proper parish church of St. Mildred, which
church was new built upon Walbrooke in the year 1457. John
Saxton their parson gave thirty-two pounds towards the building of the new choir, which now standeth upon the course of
Walbrooke. Lovell and Puery, and Richard Keston, have their
arms in the east window as benefactors. The roofing of that
church is garnished with the arms of Thomas Archehull, one of
the churchwardens in the year 1455, who was there buried;
Thomas Morsted, esquire, and chirurgeon to King Henry IV.,
V., and VI., one of the sheriffs of London in the year 1436, gave

---

[1] "Justices charged to punish such as sel bels from their churches,
Elizabeth 14."—Stow.
[2] "The 13th of November."—1st edition, p. 210.

unto this church a parcel of ground, containing in length from
the course of Walbrooke toward the west forty-five feet, and in
breadth from the church toward the north thirty-five feet,
being within the gate called Scalding wike, in the said parish,
to make a churchyard wherein to bury their dead. Richard
Shore, draper, one of the sheriffs 1505, gave fifteen pounds for
making a porch to this church. Salomon Lanuare had a
chantry there in the 14th of Edward II. Hugh Game had one
other. Buried here, as appeareth by monuments, John Hildye,
poulter, 1416; John Kendall, 1468; John Garland, 1476;
Robert Bois, 1485, and Simon Lee, poulters, 1487; Thomas
Lee of Essex, gentleman; William Hallingridge; Christopher
Feliocke, 1494; Robert Draiton, skinner, 1484; John Christo-
pherson, doctor of physic, 1524; William Turner, skinner, 1536;
Blase White, grocer, 1558; Thomas Hobson, haberdasher, 1559;
William Hobson, haberdasher, 1581; Thomas Tusser, 1580,
with this epitaph:—

> " Here Thomas Tusser, clad in earth, doth lie,
> That sometime made the Poyntes of Husbandrie;
> By him then learne thou maist, here learne we must,
> When all is done we sleepe and turne to dust,
> And yet through Christ to heaven we hope to go,
> Who reades his bookes shall find his faith was so."

On the north side of the churchyard remain two tombs of
marble, but not known of whom, or otherwise than by tradition
it is said, they were of Thomas Monshampe and William,
brothers, about 1547, etc.

Some four houses west from this parish church of St. Mildred
is a prison house pertaining to one of the sheriffs of London,
and is called the Compter in the Poultrie. This hath been there
kept and continued time out of mind, for I have not read of the
original thereof. West from this compter was a proper chapel,
called of Corpus Christi, and St. Mary, at Conyhope lane end,
in the parish of St. Mildred, founded by one named Ion. Irunnes,
a citizen of London, in the reign of Edward III., in which chapel
was a guild or fraternity, that might dispend in lands better than
twenty pounds by year: it was suppressed by Henry VIII., and
purchased by one Thomas Hobson, haberdasher; he turned
this chapel into a fair warehouse and shops towards the street,
with lodgings over them.

Then is Conyhope lane, of old time so called of such a sign of
three conies hanging over a poulterer's stall at the lane's end.
Within this lane standeth the Grocers' hall, which company
being of old time called Pepperers, were first incorporated by

the name of Grocers in the year 1345, at which time they elected for custos, or guardian, of their fraternity, Richard Oswin and Laurence Haliwell, and twenty brethren were then taken in to be of their society. In the year 1411, the custos, or guardian, and the brethren of this company, purchased of the Lord Ro. Fitzwaters one plot of ground, with the building thereupon, in the said Conyhope lane, for three hundred and twenty marks, and then laid the foundation of their new common hall.

About the year 1429, the Grocers had license to purchase five hundred marks land, since the which time, near adjoining unto the Grocers' hall, the said company had built seven proper houses for seven aged poor alms people. Thomas Knowles, grocer, mayor, gave his tenement in St. Anthonie's churchyard to the Grocers, towards the relief of the poor brethren in that company. Also H. Keeble, grocer, mayor, gave to the seven alms people six pence the piece weekly for ever; which pension is now increased by the masters, to some of them two shillings the piece weekly, and to some of them less, etc. Henry Adie, grocer, 1563, gave one thousand marks to the Grocers to purchase lands. And Sir John Pechie, knight banneret, free of that company, gave them five hundred pounds to certain uses; he built alms houses at Ludingstone in Kent, and was there buried.

West from this Conyhope lane is the Old Jurie, whereof some portion is of Cheape ward, as afore is showed: at the south end of this lane is the parish church of St. Mary Colechurch, named of one Cole that built it; this church is built upon a wall above ground, so that men are forced to go to ascend up thereunto by certain steps. I find no monuments of this church, more than that Henry IV. granted license to William Marshal and others, to found a brotherhood of St. Katherine therein, because Thomas Becket, and St. Edmond, the archbishop, were baptized there. More, I read of Bordhangly lane, to be in that parish. And thus much for the north side of the Poultrie. The south side of the said Poultrie, beginning on the bank of the said brook over against the parish church of St. Mildred, passing up to the great conduit, hath divers fair houses, which were sometimes inhabited by poulters, but now by grocers, haberdashers, and upholsters.

At the west end of this Poultrie, and also of Buckles bury, beginneth the large street of West Cheaping, a market place so called, which street stretcheth west till ye come to the little conduit by Paule's gate, but not all of Chepe ward. In the east part of this street standeth the great conduit of sweet water, conveyed by pipes of lead under ground from Paddington [1] for the service of this city, castellated with stone, and cisterned in lead, about the year 1285, and again new built and enlarged by Thomas Ilam, one of the sheriffs 1479.

About the midst of this street is the Standard in Cheape, of what antiquity the first foundation I have not read. But Henry VI. by his patent dated at Windsor the 21st of his reign, which patent was confirmed by parliament 1442, granted license to Thomas Knolles, John Chichle, and other, executors to John Wels, grocer, sometime mayor of London, with his goods to make new the highway which leadeth from the city of London towards the palace of Westminster, before and nigh the manor of Savoy, parcel of the Duchy of Lancaster, a way then very ruinous, and the pavement broken, to the hurt and mischief of the subjects, which old pavement then remaining in that way within the length of five hundred feet, and all the breadth of the same before and nigh the site of the manor aforesaid, they to break up, and with stone, gravel, and other stuff, one other good and sufficient way there to make for the commodity of the subjects.

And further, that the Standard in Cheape, where divers executions of the law before time had been performed, which Standard at the present was very ruinous with age, in which there was a conduit, should be taken down, and another competent standard of stone, together with a conduit in the same of new, strongly to be built, for the commodity and honour of the city, with the goods of the said testator, without interruption, etc.

Of executions at the Standard in Cheape, we read, that in the year 1293 three men had their right hands smitten off there, for rescuing of a prisoner arrested by an officer of the city. In the year 1326, the burgesses of London caused Walter Stapleton, Bishop of Excester, treasurer to Edward II., and other, to be beheaded at the standard in Cheape (but this was by Paul's gate); in the year 1351 [1340], the 26th of Edward III., two fishmongers were beheaded at the standard in Cheape, but I read not of their offence; 1381, Wat Tyler beheaded Richard Lions and other there. In the year 1399, Henry IV. caused the blanch charters made by Richard II. to be burnt there. In the year 1450, Jack Cade, captain of the Kentish rebels, beheaded the Lord Say there. In the year 1461, John Davy had his hand stricken off

---

[1] " This conduite was the first sweete water that was conveyed by pipes of lead under ground to this place in the citie from Paddington."
—1st edition, p. 210.

there, because he had stricken a man before the judges at Westminster, etc.

Then next is a great cross in West Cheape, which cross was there erected in the year 1290 by Edward I. upon occasion thus: —Queen Elianor his wife died at Hardeby (a town near unto the city of Lincoln), her body was brought from thence to Westminster; and the king, in memory of her, caused in every place where her body rested in the way, a stately cross of stone to be erected, with the queen's image and arms upon it, as at Grantham, Woborne, Northampton, Stony Stratford, Dunstable, St. Albones, Waltham, West Cheape, and at Charing, from whence she was conveyed to Westminster, and there buried.

This cross in West Cheape being like to those other which remain to this day, and being by length of time decayed, John Hatherly, mayor of London, procured, in the year 1441, license of King Henry VI. to re-edify the same in more beautiful manner for the honour of the city, and had license also to take up two hundred fodder of lead for the building thereof of certain conduits, and a common garnery. This cross was then curiously wrought at the charges of divers citizens: John Fisher, mercer, gave six hundred marks toward it; the same was begun to be set up 1484, and finished 1486, the 2nd of Henry VII. It was new gilt over in the year 1522, against the coming of Charles V., emperor; in the year 1553, against the coronation of Queen Anne;[1] new burnished against the coronation of Edward VI.; and again new gilt 1554, against the coming in of King Philip; since the which time the said cross having been presented by divers juries (or inquests of wardmote) to stand in the high way to the let of carriages (as they alleged), but could not have it removed, it followed that in the year 1581, the 21st of June, in the night, the lowest images round about the said cross (being of Christ's resurrection, of the Virgin Mary, King Edward the Confessor, and such like) were broken and defaced, proclamation was made, that who so would bewray the doers, should have forty crowns, but nothing came to light; the image of the Blessed Virgin, at that time robbed of her Son, and her arms broken, by which she stayed him on her knees; her whole body

---

[1] This is obviously an error. It occurs in the first edition, is repeated in that of 1603, and by Anthony Munday, in his edition of 1618. Strype (vol. i. book iii. p. 35), endeavours to correct it, by reading " Mary," who was crowned in 1553, instead of Anne. The error, however, is in the date, which should be 1533, the year of Anne Boleyn's coronation, as we learn from the description of that ceremony given by Stow in his *Annals*, " that she went forward by the crosse which was *newly gilt*."

also was haled with ropes, and left likely to fall, but in the year
1595 was again fastened and repaired; and in the year next
following a new misshapen son, as born out of time, all naked,
was laid in her arms, the other images remaining broke as afore.
But on the east side of the same cross, the steps taken thence,
under the image of Christ's resurrection defaced, was then set
up a curiously wrought tabernacle of grey marble, and in the
same an image alabaster of Diana, and water conveyed from
the Thames prilling from her naked breast for a time, but now
decayed.

In the year 1599, the timber of the cross at the top being
rotted within the lead, the arms thereof bending, were feared
to have fallen to the harming of some people, and therefore the
whole body of the cross was scaffolded about, and the top thereof
taken down, meaning in place thereof to have set up a piramis;
but some of her majesty's honourable councillors directed their
letters to Sir Nicholas Mosley, then mayor, by her highness'
express commandment concerning the cross, forthwith to be
repaired, and placed again as it formerly stood, etc.; notwithstanding the said cross stood headless more than a year after:
whereupon the said councillors, in greater number, meaning
not any longer to permit the continuance of such a contempt,
wrote to William Rider, then mayor, requiring him, by virtue
of her highness' said former direction and commandment, that
without any further delay to accomplish the same her majesty's
most princely care therein, respecting especially the antiquity
and continuance of that monument, an ancient ensign of
Christianity, etc. Dated the 24th of December, 1600. After
this a cross of timber was framed, set up, covered with lead,
and gilded, the body of the cross downward cleansed of dust, the
scaffold carried thence. About twelve nights following, the
image of Our Lady was again defaced, by plucking off her crown,
and almost her head, taking from her her naked child, and stab-
bing her in the breast, etc. Thus much for the cross in West
Cheape.

Then at the west end of West Cheape street, was sometime
a cross of stone, called the Old Cross. Raph Higden, in his
Policronicon, saith, that Waltar Stapleton, Bishop of Excester,
treasurer to Edward II., was by the burgesses of London beheaded at this cross called the Standard, without the north door
of St. Paul's church; and so is it noted in other writers that
then lived. This old cross stood and remained at the east end
of the parish church called St. Michael in the corner by Paule's

gate, near to the north end of the old Exchange, till the year 1390, the 13th of Richard II., in place of which old cross then taken down, the said church of St. Michael was enlarged, and also a fair water conduit built about the 9th of Henry VI.

In the reign of Edward III. divers joustings were made in this street, betwixt Sopar's lane and the great cross, namely, one in the year 1331, the 21st of September, as I find noted by divers writers of that time. In the middle of the city of London (say they), in a street called Cheape, the stone pavement being covered with sand, that the horses might not slide when they strongly set their feet to the ground, the king held a tournament three days together, with the nobility, valiant men of the realm, and other some strange knights. And to the end the beholders might with the better ease see the same, there was a wooden scaffold erected across the street, like unto a tower, wherein Queen Philippa, and many other ladies, richly attired, and assembled from all parts of the realm, did stand to behold the jousts; but the higher frame, in which the ladies were placed, brake in sunder, whereby they were with some shame forced to fall down, by reason whereof the knights, and such as were underneath, were grievously hurt; wherefore the queen took great care to save the carpenters from punishment, and through her prayers (which she made upon her knees) pacified the king and council, and thereby purchased great love of the people. After which time the king caused a shed to be strongly made of stone, for himself, the queen, and other estates to stand on, and there to behold the joustings, and other shows, at their pleasure, by the church of St. Mary Bow, as is showed in Cordwainer street ward. Thus much for the high street of Cheape.

Now let us return to the south side of Cheape ward. From the great conduit west be many fair and large houses, for the most part possessed of mercers up to the corner of Cordwainer street, corruptly called Bow lane, which houses in former times were but sheds or shops, with solers [1] over them, as of late one

---

[1] *Soler* is described by Tyrwhitt, in his edition of Chaucer's *Canterbury Tales*, as originally signifying an open gallery or balcony at the top of the house, though latterly used for any upper room, loft, or garret. Tyrwhitt refers in his Glossary, to the *Cook's Tale of Gamelyn*, for an authority for the use of the word in the latter sense—

> " He fleigh up until alofte,
> And shet the dore fast.
> .   .   .   .
> And saugh where he looked out
> At a *solere* window. "

The German *Söller* is used by Luther in his magnificent translation of of them remained at Sopar's lane end, wherein a woman sold seeds, roots, and herbs; but those sheds or shops, by encroachments on the high street, are now largely built on both sides outward, and also upward, some three, four, or five stories high.

Now of the north side of Cheape street and ward, beginning at the great conduit, and by St. Mary Cole church, where we left. Next thereunto westward is the Mercers' chapel, sometime an hospital, intituled of St. Thomas of Acon, or Acars, for a master and brethren, "*Militia hospitalis*," etc., saith the record of Edward III., the 14th year; it was founded by Thomas Fitzthebald de Heili, and Agnes his wife, sister to Thomas Becket, in the reign of Henry II.; they gave to the master and brethren the lands, with the appurtenances that sometimes were Gilbart Becket's, father to the said Thomas, in the which he was born, there to make a church. There was a charnel, and a chapel over it, of St. Nicholas and St. Stephen. This hospital was valued to dispend £277 3s. 4d., surrendered the 30th of Henry VIII., the 21st of October, and was since purchased by the Mercers, by means of Sir Richard Gresham, and was again set open on the eve of St. Michael, 1541, the 33rd of Henry VIII.: it is now called the Mercers' chapel; therein is kept a free grammar school, as of old time had been accustomed, commanded by parliament.[1] Here be many monuments remaining, but more have been defaced:—James Butler, Earl of Ormond, and Dame Joan his countess, 1428; John Norton, esquire; Stephen Cavendish, draper, mayor 1362; Thomas Cavendish; William Cavendish; Thomas Ganon, called Pike, one of the sheriffs 1410; Hungate, of Yorkshire; Ambrose Cresacre; John Chester, draper; John Trusbut, mercer, 1437; Tho. Norland, sheriff 1483; Sir Edmond Sha, goldsmith, mayor 1482; Sir Thomas Hill, mayor 1485; Thomas Ilam, sheriff 1479;[2] Lancelot Laken, esquire; Raph Tilney, sheriff 1488; Garth, esquire; John Rich; Thomas Butler, Earl of Ormond, 1515; Sir W. Butler, grocer, mayor 1515; W. Browne, mercer, mayor 1513; John Loke, 1519;[3] Sir T. Baldry, mercer, mayor 1523; Sir W. Locke, mercer, sheriff 1548; Sir John Allen, mercer, mayor 1525, deceased 1544; Sir Thomas Leigh, mercer,

the Bible in both senses:—" Peter went up upon the house-top to pray " —" *Stieg Petrus hinauf auf den* SÖLLER *zu beten.*" Acts x. 9. " And when they were come in, they went up into an upper room "—" *Und als sie hinein kamen, stiegen sie auf den* SÖLLER." Acts i. 13.

[1] " There is also a preaching in the Italian tongue to the Italians and others on the Sondaies."—*1st edition*, p. 214.

[2] " Henry Frowicke."—*Ibid.*

[3] " Locke his armes in the windowes."—*Stow.*

mayor 1558; Sir Richard Malory, mercer, mayor 1564; Humf.
Baskervile, mercer, sheriff 1561; Sir G. Bond, mayor 1587; etc.

Before this hospital, towards the street, was built a fair and
beautiful chapel, arched over with stone, and thereupon the
Mercers' hall, a most curious piece of work; Sir John Allen,
mercer, being founder of that chapel, was there buried; but
since his tomb is removed thence into the body of the hospital
church, and his chapel, divided into shops, is letten out for
rent.

These Mercers were enabled to be a company, and to purchase
lands to the value of twenty pounds the year, the 17th of
Richard II.; they had three messuages and shops in the parish
of St. Martin Oteswitch, in the ward of Bishopsgate, for the
sustentation of the poor, and a chantry of the 22nd of Richard II.
Henry IV., in the 12th of his reign, confirmed to Stephen Spilman, W. Marchford, and John Whatile, mercers, by the name
of one new seldam, shed, or building, with shops, cellars, and
edifices whatsoever appertaining called Crownsild, situate in the
Mercery in West Cheape, in the parish of St. Mary de Arcubus
in London, etc., to be holden in burgage, as all the city of London
is, and which were worth by year in all issues, according to the
true value of them, £7 13s. 4d., as found by inquisition before
T. Knolles, mayor, and escheator in the said city. Henry VI.,
in the 3rd of his reign, at the request of John Coventrie, John
Carpenter, and William Grove, granted to the Mercers to have
a chaplain and a brotherhood, for relief of such of their company
as came to decay by misfortune on the sea. In the year 1536,
on St. Peter's night, King Henry VIII. and Queen Jane his wife,
stood in this Mercers' hall, then new built, and beheld the marching watch of this city most bravely set out, Sir John Allen,
mercer, one of the king's council, being mayor.

Next beyond the Mercers' chapel, and their hall, is Ironmonger lane, so called of ironmongers dwelling there, whereof
I read, in the reign of Edward I., etc. In this lane is the small
parish church of St. Martin called Pomary, upon what occasion
I certainly know not. It is supposed to be of apples growing
where houses are now lately built; for myself have seen large
void places there. Monuments in that church none to be
accounted of.

Farther west is St. Laurence lane, so called of St. Laurence
church, which standeth directly over against the north end
thereof. Antiquities in this lane I find none other, than that
among many fair houses, there is one large inn for receipt of

travellers called Blossoms inn, but corruptly Bosoms inn, and hath to sign St. Laurence the Deacon, in a border of blossoms or flowers.

Then near to the Standard in Cheape is Honey lane, so called, not of sweetness thereof, being very narrow, and somewhat dark, but rather of often washing and sweeping, to keep it clean. In this lane is the small parish church called Alhallows in Honey lane; there be no monuments in this church worth the noting. I find that John Norman, draper, mayor 1453, was buried there; he gave to the Drapers his tenements on the north side the said church, they to allow for the beam light and lamp, 13s. 4d. yearly from this lane to the Standard. And thus much for Cheape ward in the high street of Cheape, for it stretcheth no farther.

Now for the north wing of Cheape ward have ye Catte street, corruptly called Catteten street, which beginneth at the north end of Ironmonger lane, and runneth to the west end of St. Lawrence church, as is afore showed.

On the north side of the street is the Guildhall, wherein the courts for the city be kept, namely, 1. The court of common council; 2. The court of the lord mayor and his brethren the aldermen; 3. The court of hustings; 4. The court of orphans; 5. The court of the sheriff; 6. The court of the wardmote; 7. The court of hallmote; 8. The court of requests, commonly called the court of conscience; 9. The chamberlain's court for apprentices, and making them free. This Guildhall, saith Robert Fabian, was begun to be built new in the year 1411, the 12th of Henry IV., by Thomas Knoles, then mayor, and his brethren the aldermen: the same was made, of a little cottage, a large and great house, as now it standeth; towards the charges whereof the companies gave large benevolences; also offences of men were pardoned for sums of money towards this work, extraordinary fees were raised, fines, amercements, and other things employed during seven years, with a continuation thereof three years more, all to be employed to this building.

The 1st year of Henry VI., John Coventrie and John Carpenter, executors to Richard Whitington, gave towards the paving of this great hall twenty pounds, and the next year fifteen pounds more, to the said pavement, with hard stone of Purbeck; they also glazed some windows thereof, and of the mayor's court; on every which windows the arms of Richard Whitington are placed. The foundation of the mayor's court was laid in the 3rd year of the reign of Henry VI., and of the porch on the south side of the mayor's court, in the 4th of the said king. Then was built the mayor's chamber, and the council chamber, with other rooms above the stairs; last of all a stately porch entering the great hall was erected, the front thereof towards the south being beautified with images of stone, such as is showed by these verses following, made about some thirty years since by William Elderton, at that time an attorney in the sheriffs' courts there:—

> " Though most of the images be pulled down,
> And none be thought remayne in towne,
> I am sure there be in London yet,
> Seven images in such and in such a place;
> And few or none I think will hit,
> Yet every day they show their face,
> And thousands see them every year,
> But few I thinke can tell me where,
> Where Jesu Christ aloft doth stand:
> Law and Learning on eyther hand,
> Discipline in the Devil's necke,
> And hard by her are three direct,
> There Justice, Fortitude, and Temperance stand,
> Where find ye the like in all this land? "

Divers aldermen glazed the great hall and other courts, as appeareth by their arms in each window. William Hariot, draper, mayor 1481, gave forty pounds to the making of two loovers in the said Guildhall, and towards the glazing thereof. The kitchens and other houses of office adjoining to this Guildhall, were built of later time, to wit, about the year 1501, by procurement of Sir John Sha, goldsmith, mayor (who was the first that kept his feast there); towards the charges of which work the mayor had of the fellowships of the city, by their own agreement, certain sums of money, as of the Mercers forty pounds, the Grocers twenty pounds, the Drapers thirty pounds, and so of the other fellowships through the city, as they were of power. Also widows and other well-disposed persons gave certain sums of money, as the Lady Hill ten pounds, the Lady Austrie ten pounds, and so of many other, till the work was finished, since the which time the mayor's feasts have been yearly kept there, which before time had been kept in the Tailors' hall, and in the Grocers' hall. Nicholas Alwyn, grocer, mayor 1499, deceased 1505, gave by his testament for a hanging of tapestry, to serve for principal days in the Guildhall, £73 6s. 8d. How this gift was performed I have not heard, for executors of our time having no conscience (I speak of my own knowledge) prove more testaments than they perform.

Now for the chapel or college of our Lady Mary Magdalen, and of All Saints, by the Guildhall, called London college, I

read that the same was built about the year 1299, and that
Peter Fanelore, Adam Frauncis, and Henry Frowike, citizens,
gave one messuage, with the appurtenances, in the parish of St.
Fawstar, to William Brampton, custos of the chantry, by them
founded in the said chapel with four chaplains, and one other
house in the parish of St. Giles without Cripplegate, in the 27th
of Edward III., was given to them. Moreover, I find that
Richard II., in the 20th of his reign, granted to Stephen Spilman,
mercer, license to give one messuage, three shops, and one
garden, with the appurtenances, being in the parish of St.
Andrew Hubbard, to the custos and chaplains of the said chapel,
and to their successors, for their better relief and maintenance
for ever.

King Henry VI., in the 8th of his reign, gave license to John
Barnard, custos, and the chaplains, to build of new the said
chapel or college of Guildhall; and the same Henry VI., in the
27th of his reign, granted to the parish clerks in London a guild
of St. Nicholas, for two chaplains by them to be kept in the said
chapel of St. Mary Magdalen, near unto the Guildhall, and
to keep seven alms people. Henry Barton, skinner, mayor,
founded a chaplaincy there; Roger Depham, mercer, and Sir
William Langford, knight, had also chaplaincies there. This
chapel or college had a custos, seven chaplains, three clerks,
and four choristers.

Monuments there have been sundry, as appeareth by the
tombs of marble yet remaining, seven in number, but all defaced.
The uppermost in the choir, on the south side thereof, above
the revestry door, was the tomb of John Wells, grocer, mayor
1451. The likeness of Wells are graven on the tomb on the
revestry door, and other places on that side the choir. Also in
the glass window over this tomb, and in the east window, is the
likeness of Wells, with hands elevated out of the same Wells,
holding scrolls, wherein is written "Mercy!"—the writing in
the east window being broken, yet remaineth Wells. I found
his arms also in the south glass window; all which do show that
the east end and south side the choir of this chapel, and the
revestry, were by him both built and glazed. On the north
side the choir the tomb of Thomas Knesworth, fishmonger,
mayor 1505, who deceased 1515, was defaced, and within these
forty-four years again renewed by the Fishmongers. Two other
tombs lower there are; the one of a draper, the other of a haberdasher, their names not known. Richard Stomine is written
in the window by the haberdasher. Under flat stones do lie

divers custos of the chapel, chaplains and officers to the chamber. Amongst others, John Clipstone, priest, sometime custos of the library of the Guildhall, 1457; another of Edmond Alison, priest, one of the custos of the library, 1510, etc. Sir John Langley, goldsmith, mayor 1576, lieth buried in the vault, under the tomb of John Wells before-named. This chapel, or college, valued to dispend £15 8s. 9d. by the year, was surrendered amongst other: the chapel remaineth to the mayor and commonalty, wherein they have service weekly, as also at the election of the mayor, and at the mayor's feast, etc.

Adjoining to this chapel, on the south side, was sometime a fair and large library, furnished with books, pertaining to the Guildhall and college. These books, as it is said, were in the reign of Edward VI. sent for by Edward, Duke of Somerset, lord protector, with promise to be restored: men laded from thence three carries with them, but they were never returned. This library was built by the executors of Richard Whittington, and by William Burie: the arms of Whittington are placed on the one side in the stone work, and two letters, to wit, W. and B., for William Bury, on the other side: it is now lofted through, and made a storehouse for clothes.

South-west from this Guildhall is the fair parish church of St. Laurence, called in the Jury, because of old time [1] many Jews inhabited thereabout. This church is fair and large, and hath some monuments, as shall be shown. I myself, more than seventy years since,[2] have seen in this church the shank-bone of a man (as it is taken), and also a tooth,[3] of a very great bigness, hanged up for show in chains of iron, upon a pillar of stone; the tooth (being about the bigness of a man's fist) is long since conveyed from thence: the thigh, or shank-bone, of twenty-five inches in length by the rule, remaineth yet fastened to a post of timber, and is not so much to be noted for the length as for the thickness, hardness, and strength thereof; for when it was hanged on the stone pillar it fretted with moving the said

[1] Because " of old time, since the raigne of William the Conqueror (that first brought Jewes from Roan into this realme), many Jewes inhabited thereabouts, until that in the year 1290, the 18th of Edw. I., they were wholly and for ever by the said king banished this realme, having of their owne goodes to beare their charges, till they were out of dominions. The number of the Jewes at that time banished were 15,060 persons, whose houses being sold, the king made of them a mightie masse of money."— 1st edition, p. 219.

[2] " Sixty years since."—Ibid.

[3] " The tooth of some monstrous fish, as I take it. A shank-bone, of twenty-five inches long, of a man, as is said, but might be of an oliphant." —Stow.

pillar, and was not itself fretted, nor, as seemeth, is not yet lightened by remaining dry; but where or when this bone was first found or discovered I have not heard, and therefore, rejecting the fables of some late writers, I overpass them. Walter Blundell had a chantry there, the 14th of Edward II. There lie buried in this church—Elizabeth, wife to John Fortescue; Katherine Stoketon; John Stratton; Philip Albert; John Fleming; Philip Agmondesham; William Skywith; John Norlong; John Baker; Thomas Alleyne; William Barton, mercer, 1410; William Melrith, mercer, one of the sheriffs, 1425; Simon Bartlet, mercer, 1428; Walter Chartsey, draper, one of the sheriffs 1430; Richard Rich, esquire, of London, the father, and Richard Rich, his son, mercer, one of the sheriffs 1442, deceased 1469, with this epitaph:

> " Respice quod opus est præsentis temporis æuum,
> Omne quod est, nihil est præter amare Deum."

This Richard was father to John, buried in St. Thomas Acars, which John was father to Thomas, father to Richard Lord Ritch, etc.; John Pickering, honourable for service of his prince and for the English merchants beyond the seas, who deceased 1448; Godfrey Bollen, mercer, mayor 1457; Thomas Bollen, his son, esquire, of Norfolk, 1471; John Atkenson, gentleman; Dame Mary St. Maure; John Waltham; Roger Bonifant; John Chayhee; John Abbot; Geffrey Filding, mayor 1452, and Angell his wife; Simon Benington, draper, and Joan his wife; John Marshal, mercer, mayor 1493; William Purchat, mayor 1498; Thomas Burgoyne, gentleman, mercer, 1517; the wife of a master of defence, servant to the Princess of Wales, Duchess of Cornwall, and Countess of Chester;[1] Sir Richard Gresham, mayor 1537: Sir Michell Dormer, mayor 1541; Robert Charsey, one of the sheriffs 1548; Sir William Row, ironmonger, mayor 1593; Samuel Thornhill, 1397. Thus much for Cheape ward, which hath an alderman, his deputy, common councillors eleven, constables eleven, scavengers nine, for the wardmote inquest twelve, and a beadle. It is taxed to the fifteen at £72 16s., and in the Exchequer at £52 11s.[2]

---

[1] " A Countess of Cornwall and Chester, but her name and time is not apparent."—1st edition, p. 220.
[2] " In the Exchequer at seventy-two pound."—Ibid.

COLEMAN STREET WARD

Next to Cheape ward, on the north side thereof, is Coleman street ward, and beginneth also in the east, on the course of Walbrook in Lothbury, and runneth west on the south side to the end of Ironmongers' lane, and on the north side to the west corner of Bassinges hall street.

On the south side of Lothbury is the street called the Old Jury; the one half, and better on both sides, towards Cheape, is of this ward. On the north side lieth Coleman street, whereof the ward taketh name, wholly on both sides north to London wall, and from that north end along by the wall, and Moregate east, to the course of Walbrook; and again from Coleman street west to the iron grates: and these be the bounds of this ward.

Antiquities to be noted therein are these: First, the street of Lothberie, Lathberie, or Loadberie (for by all these names have I read it), took the name (as it seemeth) of berie, or court of old time there kept, but by whom is grown out of memory. This street is possessed for the most part by founders, that cast candlesticks, chafing-dishes, spice mortars, and such like copper or laton works, and do afterward turn them with the foot, and not with the wheel, to make them smooth and bright with turning and scrating (as some do term it), making a loathsome noise to the by-passers that have not been used to the like, and therefore by them disdainfully called Lothberie.

On the south side of this street, amongst the founders, be some fair houses and large for merchants, namely, one that of old time was the Jews' synagogue, which was defaced by the citizens of London, after that they had slain seven hundred Jews, and spoiled the residue of their goods, in the year 1262, the 47th of Henry III. And not long after, in the year 1291, King Edward I. banished the remnant of the Jews out of England, as is afore showed. The said synagogue being so suppressed, certain friars got possession thereof; " for in the year 1257," saith Mathew Paris, " there were seen in London a new order of friars, called De Pœnitentia Jesu, or Fratres de Sacca, because they were apparelled in sackcloth, who had their house in London, near unto Aldersgate without the gate, and had license of Henry III., in the 54th of his reign, to remove from thence to any other place; and in the 56th he gave unto them this Jews' synagogue; after which time, Elianor the queen, wife to Edward I., took into her protection, and warranted unto the prior and brethren *De Penitentia Jesu Christi* of London, the said land and building in Colechurch street, in the parish of St. Olave in the Jury, and St. Margaret in Lothbery, by her granted, with consent of Stephen de Fulbourne, under-warden of the Bridge-house, and other brethren of that house, for sixty marks of silver, which they had received of the said prior and brethren of repentance, to the building of the said bridge." This order of friars gathered many good scholars, and multiplied in number exceedingly, until the council at Lyons, by the which it was decreed, that from that time forth there should be no more orders of begging friars permitted, but only the four orders; to wit, the Dominicke, or preachers, the Minorites, or grey friars, the Carmelites, or white friars, and the Augustines: and so from that time the begging friars deceased, and fell to nothing.

Now it followed, that in the year 1305, Robert Fitzwalter requested and obtained of the said King Edward I., that the same friars of the Sacke might assign to the said Robert their chapel or church, of old time called the Synagogue of the Jews, near adjoining to the then mansion place of the same Robert, which was in place where now standeth the Grocers' hall; and the said Synagogue was at the north corner of the Old Jury. Robert Large, mercer, mayor in the year 1439, kept his mayoralty in this house, and dwelt there until his dying day. This house standeth, and is of two parishes, as opening into Lothberie, of St. Margaret's parish, and opening into the Old Jury of St. Olave's parish. The said Robert Large gave liberally to both these parishes, but was buried at St. Olave's. Hugh Clopton, mercer, mayor 1492, dwelt in this house; and kept his mayoralty there: it is now a tavern, and hath to sign a windmill. And thus much for this house, sometime the Jews' synagogue, since a house of friars, then a nobleman's house, after that a merchant's house, wherein mayoralties have been kept, and now a wine tavern.

Then is the Old Jurie, a street so called of Jews sometime dwelling there, and near adjoining, in the parishes of St. Olave, St. Michael Basings hall, St. Martin Ironmonger lane, St. Lawrence, called the Jury, and so west to Wood street. William, Duke of Normandy, first brought them from Rouen to inhabit here.

William Rufus favoured them so far, that he sware by Luke's

face, his common oath, if they could overcome the Christians, he would be one of their sect.

Henry II. grievously punished them for corrupting his coin.

Richard I. forbad Jews and women to be present at his coronation, for fear of enchantments; for breaking of which commandment many Jews were slain, who being assembled to present the king with some gift, one of them was stricken by a Christian, which some unruly people perceiving, fell upon them, beat them to their houses, and burnt them therein, or slew them at their coming out. Also the Jews at Norwich, St. Edmondsbury, Lincoln, Stamford, and Lynne, were robbed and spoiled; and at York, to the number of five hundred, besides women and children, entered a tower of the castle, proffered money to be in surety of their lives, but the Christians would not take it, whereupon they cut the throats of their wives and children, and cast them over the walls on the Christians' heads, and then entering the king's lodging, they burnt both the house and themselves.

King John, in the 11th of his reign, commanded all the Jews, both men and women, to be imprisoned and grievously punished, because he would have all their money: some of them gave all they had, and promised more, to escape so many kinds of torments, for every one of them had one of their eyes at the least plucked out; amongst whom there was one, which being tormented many ways, would not ransom himself, till the king had caused every day one of his great teeth to be plucked out by the space of seven days, and then gave the king ten thousand marks of silver, to the end they should pull out no more: the said king at that time spoiled the Jews of sixty-six thousand marks.

The 17th of this king, the barons brake into the Jews' houses, rifled their coffers, and with the stone of their houses repaired the gates and walls of London.

King Henry III., in the 11th of his reign, granted to Semayne, or Balaster, the house of Benonye Mittun the Jew, in the parish of St. Michael Bassinghaughe, in which the said Benonye dwelt, with the fourth part of all his land, in that parish which William Elie held of the fee of Hugh Nevell, and all the land in Coleman street belonging to the said Benonye, and the fourth part of the land in the parish of St. Lawrence, which was the fee of T. Buckerell, and were escheated to the king for the murder which the said Benonye committed in the city of London, to hold to the said Semaine, and his heirs, of the king, paying at Easter a pair of gilt spurs, and to do the service thereof due unto the lord's court. In like manner, and for like services, the king granted to Guso for his homage the other part of the lands of the said Bononye in St. Michael's parish, which lands that Paynter held, and was the king's escheat, and the lands of the said Bononye in the said parish, which Waltar Turnar held, and fifteen feet of land, which Hugh Harman held, with fifteen iron ells of land, and half in the front of Ironmonger lane, in the parish of St. Martin, which were the said Bononies of the fee of the hospital of St. Giles, and which Adam the smith held, with two stone-houses, which were Moses', the Jew of Canterbury, in the parish of St. Olave, and which are of the fee of Arnold le Reus, and are the king's escheats as before said.

The 16th of the said Henry, the Jews in London built a synagogue, but the king commanded it should be dedicated to our Blessed Lady, and after gave it to the brethren of St. Anthonie of Vienna, and so was it called St. Anthonie's hospital: this Henry founded a church and house for converted Jews in New street, by the Temple, whereby it came to pass that in short time there was gathered a great number of converts. The 20th of this Henry, seven Jews were brought from Norwich, which had stolen a christened child, had circumcised, and minded to have crucified him at Easter, wherefore their bodies and goods were at the king's pleasure: the 26th, the Jews were constrained to pay to the king twenty thousand marks, at two terms in the year, or else to be kept in perpetual prison: the 35th, he taketh inestimable sums of money of all rich men, namely, of Aaron, a Jew, born at York, fourteen thousand marks for himself and ten thousand marks for the queen; and before he had taken of the same Jew as much as in all amounted to thirty thousand marks of silver, and two hundred marks of gold to the queen: in the 40th, were brought up to Westminster two hundred and two Jews from Lincoln, for crucifying of a child named Hugh; eighteen of them were hanged: the 43rd, a Jew at Tewkesbery fell into a privy on the Saturday, and would not that day be taken out for reverence of his Sabbath; wherefore Richard Clare, Earl of Gloucester, kept him there till Monday, that he was dead: the 47th, the barons slew the Jews at London seven hundred; the rest were spoiled, and their synagogue defaced, because one Jew would have forced a Christian to have paid more than two pence for the loan of twenty shillings a week.

The 3rd of Edward I., in a parliament at London, usury was forbidden to the Jews; and that all usurers might be known, the king commanded that every usurer should wear a table on his breast, the breadth of a paveline, or else to avoid the realm. The 6th of the said King Edward a reformation was made for clipping of the king's coin, for which offence two hundred and sixty-seven Jews were drawn and hanged; three were English Christians, and other were English Jews: the same year the Jews crucified a child at Northampton, for the which fact many Jews at London were drawn at horse-tails and hanged. The 11th of Edward I., John Perkham, Archbishop of Canterbury, commanded the Bishop of London to destroy all the Jews' synagogues in his diocese. The 16th of the said Edward, all the Jews in England were in one day apprehended by precept from the king, but they redeemed themselves for twelve thousand pounds of silver; notwithstanding, in the 19th of his reign, he banished them all out of England, giving them only to bear their charge, till they were out of his realm: the number of Jews then expulsed were fifteen thousand and sixty persons. The king made a mighty mass of money of their houses, which he sold, and yet the commons of England had granted and gave him a fifteenth of all their goods to banish them: and thus much for the Jews.

In this said street, called the Old Jury, is a proper parish church of St. Olave Upwell, so called in record, 1320. John Brian, parson of St. Olave Upwell, in the Jury, founded there a chantry, and gave two messuages to that parish, the 16th of Edward II., and was by the said king confirmed. In this church,[1] to the commendation of the parsons and parishioners, the monuments of the dead remain less defaced than in many other: first, of William Dikman, fereno or ironmonger, one of the sheriffs of London 1367; Robert Haveloke, ironmonger, 1390; John Organ, mercer, one of the sheriffs 1385; John Forest, vicar of St. Olave's, and of St. Stephen, at that time as a chapel annexed to St. Olave, 1399; H. Friole, tailor, 1400; T. Morsted, esquire, chirurgeon to Henry IV., V., and VI., one of the sheriffs, 1436: he built a fair new aisle to the enlargement of this church, on the north side thereof, wherein he lieth buried, 1450; Adam Breakspeare, chaplain, 1411; William Kerkbie, mercer, 1465; Robert Large, mercer, mayor 1440; he gave to that church two hundred pounds; John Belwine, founder, 1467; Gabriel Rave,

---

[1] " A well was under the east end of this church, late turned to a pumpe, but decayed."—*Stow.*

fuller, 1511; Wentworth, esquire, 1510; Thomas Michell, iron-monger, 1527; Giles Dewes, servant to Henry VII. and to Henry VIII., clerk of their libraries, and schoolmaster for the French tongue to Prince Arthur and to the Lady Mary, 1535; Richard Chamberlaine, ironmonger, one of the sheriffs, 1562; Edmond Burlacy, mercer, 1583; John Brian, etc.

From this parish church of St. Olave, to the north end of the Old Jewry, and from thence west to the north end of Iron-mongers' lane, and from the said corner into Ironmongers' lane, almost to the parish church of St. Martin, was of old time one large building of stone, very ancient, made in place of Jews' houses, but of what antiquity, or by whom the same was built, or for what use, I have not learnt, more than that King Henry VI., in the 16th of his reign, gave the office of being porter or keeper thereof unto John Stent for term of his life, by the name of his principal palace in the Old Jury: this was in my youth called the old Wardrobe, but of later time the out-ward stone wall hath been by little and little taken down, and divers fair houses built thereupon, even round about.

Now for the north side of this Lothburie, beginning again at the east end thereof, upon the water-course of Walbrooke, have ye a proper parish church called St. Margaret, which seemeth to be newly re-edified and built about the year 1440; for Robert Large gave to the choir of that church one hundred shillings and twenty pounds for ornaments; more, to the vaulting over the water-course of Walbrook by the said church, for the en-larging thereof two hundred marks.

There be monuments in this church—of Reginald Coleman, son to Robert Coleman, buried there 1483: this said Robert Coleman may be supposed the first builder or owner of Coleman street, and that St. Stephen's church, then built in Coleman street, was but a chapel belonging to the parish church of St. Olave in the Jury; for we read (as afore) that John Forest, vicar of St. Olave's, and of the chapel annexed of St. Stephen, deceased in the year 1399.[1] Hugh Clopton, mercer, mayor, deceased 1496; John Dimocke, Anselme Becker, John Julian, and William Ilford, chantries there; Sir Brian Tewke, knight, treasurer of the chamber to King Henry VIII., and Dame Grisilde his wife, that deceased after him, were there buried 1536; John Fetiplace, draper, esquire, 1464, and Joan his wife; Sir Hugh Witch, mercer, mayor, son to Richard Witch, entombed there 1466: he gave to his third wife three thousand

---

[1] " This may be some argument which I overpasse."—1st edition, p. 223.

pounds, and to maids' marriages five hundred marks; Sir John Leigh, 1564, with this epitaph:

> " No wealth, no prayse, no bright renowne, no skill,
> No force, no fame, no princes loue, no toyle,
> Though forraigne land by trauell search ye will,
> No faithfull seruice of the country soyle,
> Can life prolong one minute of an houre,
> But death at length will execute his power;
> For Sir John Leigh to sundry countries knowne,
> A worthy knight well of his prince esteemde,
> By seeing much, to great experience growne,
> Though safe on seas, though sure on land he seemde,
> Yet here he lyes too soone by death opprest,
> His fame yet liues, his soule in heauen doth rest."

By the west end of this parish church have ye a fair water conduit, built at the charges of the city in the year 1546. Sir Martin Bowes being mayor, two fifteens were levied of the citizens toward the charges thereof. This water is conveyed in great abundance from divers springs lying betwixt Hoxton and Iseldon.

Next is the Founders' hall, a proper house, and so to the south-west corner of Bassinges hall street, have ye fair and large houses for merchants; namely, the corner house at the end of Bassinges hall street; an old piece of work, built of stone, sometime belonging to a certain Jew named Mansere, the son of Aaron, the son of Coke the Jew, the 7th of Edward I.; since to Rahere de Sopar's lane, then to Simon Francis. Thomas Bradbery, mercer, kept his mayoralty there; deceased 1509. Part of this house hath been lately employed as a market-house for the sale of woollen bays, watmols, flannels, and such like. Alderman Bennet now possesseth it.

On this north side against the Old Jury is Coleman street, so called of Coleman, the first builder and owner thereof; as also of Colechurch, or Coleman church, against the great conduit in Cheape. This is a fair and large street, on both sides built with divers fair houses, besides alleys, with small tenements in great number. On the east side of this street, almost at the north end thereof, is the Armourers' hall, which company of armourers were made a fraternity or guild of St George, with a chantry in the chapel of St. Thomas in Paule's church, in the 1st of Henry VI. Also on the same side is King's alley and Love lane, both containing many tenements; and on the west side, towards the south end, is the parish church of St. Stephen, wherein the monuments are defaced: notwithstanding, I find that William Crayhag founded a chantry there in the reign of Edward II., and was buried there: [1] also John Essex, the 35th of Edward III.; Adam Goodman, the 37th of Edward III.; William King, draper, sometime owner of King's alley, the 18th of Richard II.; John Stokeling, the 10th of Henry VI.; John Arnold, leather-seller, the 17th of Henry VI.; Thomas Bradberie, mercer, mayor, the 1st of Henry VIII.; his tomb remaineth on the north side the choir; Richard Hamney, 1418; Kirnigham, 1468; Sir John Garme; Richard Colsel; Edmond Harbeke, currier; all these were benefactors, and buried there. This church was sometime a synagogue of the Jews, then a parish church, then a chapel to St. Olave's in the Jury, until the 7th of Edward IV., and was then incorporated a parish church.

By the east end of this church is placed a cock of sweet water, taken of the main pipe that goeth into Lothberie. Also in London wall, directly against the north end of Coleman street, is a conduit of water, made at the charges of Thomas Exmew, goldsmith, mayor 1517. And let here be the end of this ward, which hath an alderman, his deputy, common councillors four, constables four, scavengers four, of the wardmote inquest thirteen, and a beadle. It is taxed to the fifteen at £15 16s. 9d.[2]

BASSINGS HALL WARD

The next adjoining to Coleman street, on the west side thereof, is Bassings hall ward, a small thing, and consisteth of one street called Bassings hall street, of Bassings hall, the most principal house whereof the ward taketh name. It beginneth in the south by the late spoken market-house called the Bay hall, which is the last house of Coleman street ward. This street runneth from thence north down to London wall, and some little distance, both east and west, against the said hall; and this is the bound of Bassings hall ward.

Monuments on the east side thereof, amongst divers fair houses for merchants, have ye three halls of companies; namely, the Masons' hall for the first, but of what antiquity that company is I have not read. The next is the Weavers' hall, which company hath been of great antiquity in this city, as appeareth by a charter of Henry II., in these words, *Rex omnibus ad quos*, etc., to be Englished thus:—" Henrie, king of England, duke of

---

[1] " There is one tomb on the south side the quire, but without inscription."—*1st edition*, p. 225.

[2] " It is taxed to the fifteen in London at nineteen pound, and in the Exchequer at nineteen pound."—*Ibid*.

Normandie, and of Guian, Earl of Anjou, to the bishop, justices, shiriffes, barons, ministers, and all his true lieges of London, sendeth greeting: Know ye that we have granted to the weavers in London their guild, with all the freedomes and customes that they had in the time of King Henrie my grandfather, so that none but they intermit within the citie of their craft but he be of their guild, neither in Southwark, or other places pertaining to London, otherwise it was done in the time of King Henrie my grandfather; wherefore I will and straightly commaund that over all lawfully they may treate, and have all aforesaid, as well in peace, free, worshipfull, and wholy, as they had it, freer, better, worshipfullier, and wholier, than in the time of King Henrie my grandfather, so that they yeeld yearely to mee two markes of gold at the feast of St. Michaell; and I forbid that any man to them do any unright, or disseise, upon paine of ten pound. Witnes, Thomas of Canterburie, Warwicke fili Gar, Chamberlaine at Winchester." [1] Also I read, that the same Henry II., in the 31st of his reign, made a confirmation to the weavers that had a guild or fraternity in London, wherein it appeareth that the said weavers made woollen cloth, and that they had the correction thereof; but amongst other articles in that patent, it was decreed, that if any man made cloth of Spanish wool, mixed with English wool, the portgrave, or principal magistrate of London, ought to burn it, etc.

Moreover, in the year 1197,[2] King Richard I., at the instance of Hubert, Archbishop of Canterbury, and Justicier of England, ordained that the woollen cloths in every part of this realm should be in breadth two yards within the lists, and as good in the midst as in the sides, etc. King Henry III. granted that they should not be vexed, for the burels, or cloth listed, according to the constitution made for breadth of cloth the 9th of his reign, etc. Richard II., in the 3rd of his reign, granted an order of agreement between the weavers of London, Englishmen, and aliens, or strangers born, brought in by Edward III.

Lower down is the Girdlers'[3] hall, and this is all touching the east side of this ward.

On the west side, almost at the south end thereof, is Bakewell

---

[1] Patent [*Liber Custum.*]   [2] Matthew Paris.
[3] The Girdlers were incorporated by letters patent of 27th Henry VI. 6th Aug. 1449, which were confirmed by Elizabeth in 1568, when the pinners and wire-drawers were incorporated with them. Strype says they seem to have been a fraternity of St. Lawrence, because of the three gridirons their arms; but those north country readers, who know what a *girdle iron* is, will probably agree with me in thinking the gridirons or girdle irons are borne with reference to the name of the company.

hall, corruptly called Blackewall hall: concerning the original whereof I have heard divers opinions, which I overpass as fables without colour of truth; for though the same seemed a building of great antiquity, yet in mine opinion the foundation thereof was first laid since the conquest of William, Duke of Normandie; for the same was built upon vaults of stone, which stone was brought from Caen in Normandie, the like of that of Paule's church, built by Mauritius and his successors, bishops of London; but that this house hath been a temple or Jewish synagogue (as some have fantasied) I allow not, seeing that it had no such form of roundness, or other likeness, neither had it the form of a church, for the assembly of Christians, which are built east and west, but contrariwise the same was built north and south, and in form of a nobleman's house; and therefore the best opinion in my judgment is, that it was of old time belonging to the family of the Bassings, which was in this realm a name of great antiquity and renown, and that it bare also the name of that family, and was called therefore Bassings haugh, or hall; whereunto I am the rather induced, for that the arms of that family were of old time so abundantly placed in sundry parts of that house, even in the stone-work, but more especially on the walls of the hall, which carried a continual painting of them on every side, so close together as one escutcheon could be placed by another, which I myself have often seen and noted before the old building was taken down: these arms were a gyronny of twelve points, gold and azure. Of the Bassinges therefore, builders of this house and owners of the ground near adjoining, that ward taketh the name, as Coleman street ward of Coleman, and Faringden ward of William and Nicholas Faringden, men that were principal owners of those places.

And of old time the most noble persons that inhabited this city were appointed to be principal magistrates there, as was Godfrey de Magun (or Magnavile), portgrave, or sheriff, in the reign of William Conqueror, and of William Rufus; Hugh de Buch, in the reign of Henry I.; Auberie de Vere, Earl of Oxford; after him, Gilbert Becket, in the reign of King Stephen; after that, Godfrey de Magnavile, the son of William, the son of Godfrey de Magnavile, Earls of Essex, were portgraves or sheriffs of London and Middlesex. In the reign of Henry II., Peter Fitzwalter; after him, John Fitznigel, etc.; so likewise in the reign of King John, the 16th of his reign, a time of great troubles, in the year 1214, Salomon Bassing and Hugh Bassing, barons of this realm, as may be supposed, were sheriffs; and the said Salomon Bassing was mayor in the year 1216, which was the 1st of Henry III. Also Adam Bassing, son to Salomon (as it seemeth), was one of the sheriffs in the year 1243, the 28th of Henry III.

Unto this Adam de Bassing King Henry III., in the 31st of his reign, gave and confirmed certain messuages in Aldermanbury, and in Milke street (places not far from Bassinges hall), the advowson of the church at Bassinges hall, with sundry liberties and privileges.

This man was afterwards mayor in the year 1251, the 36th of Henry III.; moreover, Thomas Bassing was one of the sheriffs 1269; Robert Bassing, sheriff, 1279; and William Bassing was sheriff 1308, etc.; for more of the Bassings in this city I need not note, only I read of this family of Bassinges in Cambridgeshire,[1] called Bassing at the bourn, and more shortly Bassing bourn, and gave arms, as is afore showed, and was painted about this old hall. But this family is worn out, and hath left the name to the place where they dwelt. Thus much for this Bassings hall.

Now how Blakewell hall took that name is another question; for which I read that Thomas Bakewell dwelt in this house in the 36th of Edward III.; and that in the 20th of Richard II., the said king, for the sum of fifty pounds, which the mayor and commonalty had paid into the hanaper, granted licence so much as was in him to John Frosh, William Parker, and Stephen Spilman (citizens and mercers), that they, the said messuage called Bakewell hall, and one garden, with the appurtenances, in the parish of St. Michael of Bassings haugh, and of St. Laurence in the Jurie of London, and one messuage, two shops, and one garden, in the said parish of St. Michael, which they held of the king in burghage, might give and assign to the mayor and commonalty for ever. This Bakewell hall, thus established, hath been long since employed as a weekly market-place for all sorts of woollen cloths, broad and narrow, brought from all parts of this realm, there to be sold. In the 21st of Richard II., R. Whittington, mayor, and in the 22nd, Drengh Barringtine being mayor, it was decreed that no foreigner or stranger should sell any woollen cloth but in the Bakewell hall, upon pain of forfeiture thereof.

---

[1] " Only I read of a branch of this family of Bassinges to have spread itself into Cambridgeshire, near unto a water or bourne, and was therefore, for a difference from other of that name, called Bassing at the bourn, and more shortly Bassing borne. But this family is also worne out, and hath left the name to the place where they dwell."—*1st edition*, p. 228.

This house of late years growing ruinous, and in danger of falling, Richard May, merchant-tailor, at his decease gave towards the new building of the outward part thereof three hundred pounds, upon condition that the same should be performed within three years after his decease; whereupon the old Bakewell hall was taken down, and in the month of February next following, the foundation of a new, strong, and beautiful storehouse being laid, the work thereof was so diligently applied, that within the space of ten months after, to the charges of two thousand five hundred pounds, the same was finished in the year 1588.

Next beyond this house be placed divers fair houses for merchants and others, till ye come to the back gate of Guildhall, which gate and part of the building within the same is of this ward. Some small distance beyond this gate the coopers have their common hall. Then is the parish church of St. Michaell, called St. Michaell at Bassings hall, a proper church lately re-edified or new built, whereto John Barton, mercer, and Agnes his wife, were great benefactors, as appeareth by his mark placed throughout the whole roof of the choir and middle aisle of the church: he deceased in the year 1460, and was buried in the choir, with this epitaph:

> " John Barton lyeth vnder here,
> Sometimes of London, citizen and mercer,
> And Ienet his wife, with their progenie,
> Beene turned to earth as ye may see:
> Friends free what so ye bee,
> Pray for vs we you pray,
> As you see vs in this degree,
> So shall you be another day."

Frances Cooke, John Martin, Edward Bromflit, esquire, of Warwickshire, 1460; Richard Barnes, Sir Roger Roe, Roger Velden, 1479; Sir James Yarford, mercer, mayor, deceased 1526, buried under a fair tomb with his lady in a special chapel by him built on the north side of the choir; Sir John Gresham, mercer, mayor, deceased 1554; Sir John Ailife, chirurgeon, then a grocer, one of the sheriffs 1548; Nicholas Bakhurst, one of the sheriffs 1577; Wolston Dixi, skinner, mayor, 1585, etc. Thus have you noted one parish church of St. Michaell, Bakewell hall, a market-place for woollen cloths; the Masons' hall, Weavers' hall, Cordellers' hall, and Coopers' hall. And thus I end this ward, which hath an alderman, his deputy, for common council four, constables two, scavengers two, for the wardmote inquest seventeen, and a beadle. It is taxed to the fifteen in London at seven pounds, and likewise in the Exchequer at seven pounds.

CRIPPLESGATE WARD

The next ward is called of Cripplesgate, and consisteth of divers streets and lanes, lying as well without the gate and wall of the city as within: first within the wall, on the east part thereof, towards the north, it runneth to the west side of Bassings hall ward, and towards the south it joineth to the ward of Cheape. It beginneth at the west end of St. Laurence church in the Jurie, on the north side, and runneth west to a pump, where sometime was a well with two buckets, at the south corner of Aldermanburie street; which street runneth down north to Gayspurre lane, and so to London wall, which street and lane are wholly on both sides of this ward, and so be some few houses on both the sides from Gayspurre lane, by and against the wall of the city, east to the grates made for the water-course of the channels, and west to Cripplesgate. Now on the south side, from over against the west end of St. Laurence church to the pump, and then by Milke street south unto Cheape, which Milke street is wholly on both the sides of Cripplegate ward, as also without the south end of Milke street, a part of West Cheape, to wit, from the Standard to the Cross, is all of Cripplegate ward. Then down Great Wood street, which is wholly of this ward on both the sides thereof; so is Little Wood street, which runneth down to Cripplegate.

Out of this Wood street be divers lanes; namely, on the east side is Lad lane, which runneth east to Milke street corner; down lower in Wood street is Love lane, which lieth by the south side of St. Alban's church in Wood street, and runneth down to the Conduit in Aldermanburie street. Lower down in Wood street is Addle street, out of the which runneth Phillip lane down to London wall. These be the lanes on the east side.

On the west side of Wood street is Huggen lane, by the south side of St. Michael's church, and goeth through to Guthuruns lane. Then lower is Maiden lane, which runneth west to the north end of Gutherons lane, and up the said lane on the east side thereof, till against Kery lane, and back again: then the said Maiden lane, on the north side, goeth up to Staining lane, and up a part thereof, on the east side, to the farthest north part of Haberdashers' hall, and back again to Wood street;

and there lower down to Silver street, which is of this ward, till ye come to the east end of St. Olave's church, on the south side, and to Munkes well street on the north side; then down the said Munkes well street on the east side thereof, and so to Cripplegate, do make the bounds of this ward within the walls.

Without Cripplegate, Fore street runneth thwart before the gate, from against the north side of St. Giles church, along to More lane end, and to a Postern lane end, that runneth betwixt the town ditch on the south, and certain gardens on the north, almost to Moregate; at the east of which lane is a pot-maker's house, which house, with all other the gardens, houses, and alleys, on that side the Morefields, till ye come to a bridge and cow-house near unto Fensburie court, is all of Cripplegate ward; then to turn back again through the said Postern lane to More lane, which More lane, with all the alleys and buildings there, is of this ward; after that is Grub street, more than half thereof to the straitening of the street; next is Whitecrosse street, up to the end of Bech lane, and then Redcrosse street wholly, with a part of Golding lane, even to the posts there placed, as a bounder.

Then is Bech lane before spoken of, on the east side of the Red Crosse and the Barbican street, more than half thereof toward Aldersgate street; and so have you all the bounds of Cripplegate ward without the walls.

Now for antiquities and ornaments in this ward to be noted: I find first, at the meeting of the corners of the Old Jurie, Milke street, Lad lane, and Aldermanburie, there was of old time a fair well with two buckets, of late years converted to a pump. How Aldermanbury street took that name many fables have been bruited, all which I overpass as not worthy the counting; but to be short, I say, this street took the name of Alderman's burie (which is to say a court), there kept in their bery, or court, but now called the Guildhall; which hall of old time stood on the east side of the same street, not far from the west end of Guildhall, now used. Touching the antiquity of this old Alderman's burie or court, I have not read other than that Richard Renery, one of the sheriffs of London in the 1st of Richard I., which was in the year of Christ 1189, gave to the church of St. Mary at Osney, by Oxford, certain ground and rents in Aldermanbery of London, as appeareth by the register of that church, as is also entered into the hoistinges of the Guildhall in London. This old bery court or hall continued, and the courts of the mayor and aldermen were continually holden there,

until the new bery court, or Guildhall that now is, was built
and finished; which hall was first begun to be founded in the
year 1411, and was not fully finished in twenty years after.
I myself have seen the ruins of the old court hall in Aldermanbery street, which of late hath been employed as a carpenter's
yard, etc.

In this Aldermanbery street be divers fair houses on both the
sides, meet for merchants or men of worship, and in the midst
thereof is a fair conduit, made at the charges of William Eastfield, sometime mayor, who took order as well for water to be
conveyed from Teyborne, and for the building of this Conduit,
not far distant from his dwelling-house, as also for a Standard
of sweet water, to be erected in Fleet street, all which was done
by his executors, as in another place I have showed.

Then is the parish church of St. Mary Aldermanbury, a fair
church, with a churchyard, and cloister adjoining; in the which
cloister is hanged and fastened a shank-bone of a man (as is
said), very great, and larger by three inches and a half than
that which hangeth in St. Lawrence church in the Jury, for it
is in length twenty-eight inches and a half of assise, but not so
hard and steele-like as the other, for the same is light, and
somewhat pory and spongy. This bone is said to be found
amongst the bones of men removed from the charnel-house of
Powles, or rather from the cloister of Powles church; of both
which reports I doubt, for that the late Reyne Wolfe, stationer
(who paid for the carriage of those bones from the charnel to
the Morefields), told me of some thousands of carrie loads and
more to be conveyed, whereof he wondered, but never told me
of any such bone in either place to be found; neither would the
same have been easily gotten from him if he had heard thereof,
except he had reserved the like for himself, being the greatest
preserver of antiquities in those parts for his time.[1] True it is,
that this bone (from whence soever it came) being of a man
(as the form showeth), must needs be monstrous, and more than
after the proportion of five shank-bones of any man now living
amongst us.

[1] " Reyne Wolf, a grave antiquary, collected the great chronicles,
increased and published by his executors, under the name of Ralph Holons-
head."—*Stow.*

The first edition of Holinshed's *Chronicles of England, Scotland, and
Ireland,* was printed for John Harrison the elder in 1577. From Holinshed's dedicatory epistle to Lord Burleigh, it would seem that Reginald
Wolfe projected and even executed the greater part of the work, it having
" pleased God to call him to his mercie after xxv. years travail spent
therein." Wolfe, in fact, intended to make these Chronicles the foundation of " *An Universall Cosmographie of the Whole World.*"

There lie buried in this church—Simon Winchcombe, esquire, 1391; Robert Combarton, 1422; John Wheatley, mercer, 1428; Sir William Estfild, knight of the bath, mayor 1438, a great benefactor to that church, under a fair monument: he also built their steeple, changed their old bells into five tuneable bells, and gave one hundred pounds to other works of that church. Moreover, he caused the Conduit in Aldermanbury, which he had begun, to be performed at his charges, and water to be conveyed by pipes of lead from Tyborne to Fleet street, as I have said: and also from High Berie to the parish of St. Giles without Cripplegate, where the inhabitants of those parts incastellated the same in sufficient cisterns. John Midleton, mercer, mayor 1472; John Tomes, draper, 1486; William Bucke, tailor, 1501; Sir William Browne, mayor 1507; Dame Margaret Jeninges, wife to Stephen Jeninges, mayor 1515; a widow named Starkey, sometime wife to Modie; Raffe Woodcock, grocer, one of the sheriffs 1586; Dame Mary Gresham, wife to Sir John Gresham, 1538; Thomas Godfrey, remembrancer of the office of the first fruits, 1577.

Beneath this church have ye Gay spur lane, which runneth down to London wall, as is afore showed. In this lane, at the north end thereof, was of old time a house of nuns; which house being in great decay, William Elsing, mercer, in the year of Christ 1329, the 3rd of Edward III., began in place thereof the foundation of an hospital for sustentation of one hundred blind men; towards the erection whereof he gave his two houses in the parishes of St. Alphage, and our Blessed Lady in Aldermanbury, near Cripplegate.[1] This house was after called a priory, or hospital, of St. Mary the Virgin, founded in the year 1332 by W. Elsing, for canons regular; the which William became the first prior there. Robert Elsing, son to the said William, gave to the hospital twelve pounds by the year, for the finding of three priests: he also gave one hundred shillings towards the inclosing of the new churchyard without Aldgate, and one hundred shillings to the inclosing of the new churchyard without Aldersgate; to Thomas Elsing, his son, eighty pounds, the rest of his goods to be sold and given to the poor. This house, valued £193 15s. 5d., was surrendered the eleventh of May, the 22nd of Henry VIII.

The monuments that were in this church defaced:—Thomas Cheney, son to William Cheney; Thomas, John, and William

---

[1] " Obtaining first the king's licence of mortmain under the great seal of England."—1st *edition*, p. 234.

Cheney; John Northampton, draper, mayor 1381; Edmond Hungerford; Henry Frowike; Joan, daughter to Sir William Cheney, wife to William Stoke; Robert Eldarbroke, esquire, 1460; Dame Joan Ratcliffe; William Fowler; William Kingstone; Thomas Swineley, and Helen his wife, etc. The principal aisle of this church towards the north was pulled down, and a frame of four houses set up in place: the other part, from the steeple upward, was converted into a parish church of St. Alphage; and the parish church which stood near unto the wall of the city by Cripplesgate was pulled down, the plot thereof made a carpenter's yard, with saw-pits. The hospital itself, the prior and canons' house, with other lodgings, were made a dwelling-house; the churchyard is a garden plot, and a fair gallery on the cloister; the lodgings for the poor are translated into stabling for horses.

In the year 1541, Sir John Williams, master of the king's jewels, dwelling in this house on Christmas even at night, about seven of the clock, a great fire began in the gallery thereof, which burned so sore, that the flame firing the whole house, and consuming it, was seen all the city over, and was hardly quenched, whereby many of the king's jewels were burnt, and more embezzled (as was said).[1] Sir Rowland Heyward, mayor, dwelt in this Spittle, and was buried there 1593; Richard Lee, *alias* Clarenciaux king of arms, 1597.

Now to return to Milk street, so called of milk sold there,[2] there be many fair houses for wealthy merchants and other; amongst the which I read, that Gregory Rokesley, chief assay master of the king's mints, and mayor of London in the year 1275, dwelt in this Milk street, in a house belonging to the priory of Lewes in Sussex, whereof he was tenant at will, paying twenty shillings by the year, without [3] other charge: such were the rents of those times.

In this Milke street is a small parish church of St. Marie Magdalen, which hath of late years been repaired. William Browne, mayor 1513, gave to this church forty pounds, and was buried there; Thomas Exmew, mayor 1528, gave forty pounds, and was buried there; so was John Milford, one of the sheriffs, 1375; John Olney, mayor 1475; Richard Rawson, one of the sheriffs 1476; Henry Kelsey; Sir John Browne, mayor

---

[1] " The Lord William of Thame was buried in this church, and so was his successor in that house, Sir Rowlard Heyward."—*1st edition*, p. 235.
[2] " As is supposed."—*Ibid.*
[3] " Without being bounden to reparations or other charge."—*Ibid.*

1497; Thomas Muschampe, one of the sheriffs 1463; Sir William Cantilo, knight, mercer, 1462; Henry Cantlow, mercer, merchant of the Staple, who built a chapel, and was buried there 1495; John West, alderman, 1517; John Machell, alderman, 1558; Thomas Skinner, clothworker, mayor 1596.

Then next is Wood street, by what reason so called I know not. True it is, that of old time, according to a decree made in the reign of Richard I., the houses in London were built of stone for defence of fire; which kind of building was used for two hundred years or more, but of later time for the winning of ground taken down, and houses of timber set up in place. It seemeth therefore that this street hath been of the latter building, all of timber (for not one house of stone hath been known there), and therefore called Wood street; otherwise it might take the name of some builder or owner thereof.

Thomas Wood, one of the sheriffs in the year 1491, dwelt there; he was an especial benefactor towards the building of St. Peter's church at Wood street end; he also built the beautiful front of houses in Cheape over against Wood street end, which is called Goldsmiths' row, garnished with the likeness of woodmen; his predecessors might be the first builders, owners, and namers of this street after their own name.

On the east side of this street is one of the prison houses pertaining to the sheriffs of London, and is called the Compter in Wood street, which was prepared to be a prison house in the year 1555; and on the eve of St. Michael the Archangel, the prisoners that lay in the Compter in Bread street were removed to this Compter in Wood street. Beneath this Compter is Lad lane, or Ladle lane, for so I find it of record in the parish of St. Michaell Wood street; and beneath that is Love lane, so called of wantons.

By this lane is the parish church of St. Alban, which hath the monuments of Sir Richard Illingworth, baron of the exchequer; Thomas Chatworth, grocer, mayor 1443; John Woodcocke, mayor 1405; John Collet, and Alice his wife; Ralph Thomas; Ralph and Richard, sons of Ralph Illingworth, which was son to Sir Richard Illingworth, baron of the exchequer; Thomas, son of Sir Thomas Fitzwilliams; Thomas Halton, mercer, mayor 1450; Thomas Ostrich, haberdasher, 1483; Richard Swetenham, esquire; and William Dunthorne, townclerk of London, with this epitaph:

> " *Fœlix prima dies postquam mortalibus ævi*
> *Cesserit, hic morbus subit, atque repente senectus*

Tum mors, qua nostrum Dunthorn cecidisse Wilelmum.
Haud cuiquam latuisse reor, dignissimus (inquam),
Artibus hic Doctor, nec non celeberrimus hujus,
Clericus Urbis erat, primus, nullique secundus,
Moribus, ingenio, studio, nil dixeris illi,
Quin dederit natura boni, pius ipse modestus,
Longanimus, solers, patiens, super omnia gratus,
Quique sub immensas curas variosque labores,
Anxius atteritur vitæ, dum carpserit auras,
Hoc tetro in tumulo, compostus pace quiescit."

Simon Morsted; Thomas Pikehurst, esquire; Richard Take; Robert Ashcombe; Thomas Lovet, esquire, sheriff of Northamptonshire 1491; John Spare; Katheren, daughter to Sir Thomas Mirley, knight;[1] William Linchdale, mercer, 1392; John Penie, mercer, 1450; John Thomas, mercer, 1485; Christopher Hawse, mercer, one of the sheriffs 1503; William Skarborough, vintner; Simon de Berching; Sir John Cheke, knight, schoolmaster to King Edward VI., deceased 1557; do lie here.

Then is Adle street, the reason of which name I know not, for at this present it is replenished with fair buildings on both sides; amongst the which there was sometime the Pinners' hall, but that company being decayed, it is now the Plaisterers' hall.

Not far from thence is the Brewers' hall, a fair house, which company of Brewers was incorporated by King Henry VI., in the 16th of his reign, confirmed by the name of St. Mary and St. Thomas the Martyr, the 19th of Edward IV.

From the West end of this Adle street, Little Wood street runneth down to Cripplesgate: and somewhat east from the Sun tavern, against the wall of the city, is the Curriers' hall.

Now, on the west side of Wood street, have ye Huggen lane, so called of one Hugan that of old time dwelt there: he was called Hugan in the lane, as I have read in the 34th of Edward I. This lane runneth down by the south side of St. Michael's church in Wood street, and so growing very narrow by means of late encroachments to Guthuron's lane.

The parish church of St. Michael in Wood street is a proper thing, and lately well repaired. John Ive, parson of this church, John Forster, goldsmith, and Peter Fikelden, tailor, gave two messuages, and two shops, with solars, cellars, and other edifices, in the same parish and street, and in Ladle lane, to the reparations of the church, chancel, and other works of charity, the 16th of Richard II.

The monuments here be of William Bambrough, the son of Henry Bambrough of Skardborough, 1392; William Turner,

[1] " John Collet.' —*1st edition*, p. 257.

waxchandler, 1400; John Peke, goldsmith, 1441; William
Taverner, girdler, 1454; William Mancer, ironmonger, 1465:
John Nash, 1466, with an epitaph; John Allen, timbermonger,
1441; Robert Draper, 1500; John Lamberde, draper, alderman,
one of the sheriffs of London, who deceased 1554, and was
father to [1] William Lambarde, esquire, well known by sundry
learned books that he hath published; John Medley, chamberlain of London; John Marsh, esquire, mercer, and common
sergeant of London, etc.   There is also (but without any outward monument) the head of James, the fourth king of Scots
of that name, slain at Flodden field, and buried here by this
occasion: After the battle the body of the said king being found,
was enclosed in lead, and conveyed from thence to London, and
so to the monastery of Shene in Surrey, where it remained for
a time, in what order I am not certain; but since the dissolution
of that house, in the reign of Edward VI., Henry Grey, Duke
of Suffolk, being lodged, and keeping house there, I have been
shown the same body so lapped in lead, close to the head and
body, thrown into a waste room amongst the old timber, lead,
and other rubble.   Since the which time workmen there, for
their foolish pleasure, hewed off his head; and Launcelot
Young,[2] master glazier to her majesty, feeling a sweet savour
to come from thence, and seeing the same dried from all moisture,
and yet the form remaining, with the hair of the head, and beard
red, brought it to London to his house in Wood street, where
for a time he kept it for the sweetness, but in the end caused
the sexton of that church to bury it amongst other bones taken
out of their charnel, etc.

I read in divers records of a house in Wood street, then called
Black hall, but no man at this day can tell thereof.

On the north side of this St. Michael's church is Mayden lane,
now so called, but of old time Ingene lane, or Ing lane.   In this
lane the Waxchandlers have their common hall, on the south
side thereof; and the Haberdashers have their like hall on the
north side, at Stayning lane end.   This company of the Haberdashers, or Hurrers, of old time so called, were incorporated
a brotherhood of St. Katherine, the 26th of Henry VI., and so
confirmed by Henry VII., the 17th of his reign, the Cappers and
Hat merchants, or Hurrers, being one company of Haberdashers.

Down lower in Wood street is Silver street (I think of silver-
smiths dwelling there), in which be divers fair houses.

[1] " My loving friend."—1st edition, p. 238.
[2] " At this present."—Ibid.

And on the north side thereof is Monkeswell street, so called of a well at the north end thereof, where the Abbot of Garendon had a house, or cell, called St. James in the wall by Cripplesgate, and certain monks of their house were the chaplains there, wherefore the well (belonging to that cell, or hermitage) was called Monks' well, and the street, of the well, Monkswell street. [*See* Additional Notes.]

The east side of this street, down against London wall, and the south side thereof to Cripplesgate, be of Cripplesgate ward, as is afore shown. In this street, by the corner of Monkswell street, is the Bowyers' hall. On the east side of Monkswell street be proper alms houses, twelve in number founded by Sir Ambrose Nicholas, salter, mayor 1575, wherein be placed twelve poor and aged people rent free, having each of them seven pence the week, and once the year, each of them five sacks of charcoal, and one quarter of a hundred fagots, of his gift, for ever.

Then, in Little Wood street be seven proper chambers in an alley on the west side, founded for seven poor people therein to dwell rent free, by Henry Barton, skinner, mayor 1416. Thus much for the monuments of this ward within the walls.

Now, without the postern of Cripplesgate, first is the parish church of St. Giles, a very fair and large church, lately repaired, after that the same was burnt in the year 1545, the 37th of Henry VIII., by which mischance the monuments of the dead in this church are very few: notwithstanding I have read of these following:—Alice, William, and John, wife and sons to T. Clarell; Agnes, daughter to Thomas Niter, gentleman; William Atwell; Felix, daughter to Sir Thomas Gisors, and wife to Thomas Travars; Thomas Mason, esquire; Edmond Wartar, esquire; Joan, wife to John Chamberlaine, esquire, daughter to Roger Lewkner; William Fryer; John Hamberger, esquire; Hugh Moresbye; Gilbert Prince, alderman; Oliver Cherley, gentleman; Sir John Wright or Writhesley, *alias* Garter king-at-arms; Joan, wife to Thomas Writhesley, Garter, daughter and heir to William Hal, esquire; John Writhesley, the younger, son to Sir John Writhesley and Alianor; Alianor, second wife to John Writhesley, daughter and heir to Thomas Arnold, sister and heir to Richard Arnold, esquire; John, her son and heir; Margaret, with her daughter; John Brigget; Thomas Ruston, gentleman; John Talbot, esquire, and Katheren his wife; Thomas Warfle, and Isabel his wife; Thomas Lucie, gentleman, 1447; Ralph Rochford, knight, 1409; Edmond Watar, esquire; Elizabeth, wife to Richard Barnes, sister and heir to Richard Malgrave, esquire, of Essex; Richard Gowre, and John Gowre, esquires; John Baronie, of Millain, 1546: Sir Henry Grey, knight, son and heir to George Grey, Earl of Kent, 1562; Reginald Grey. Earl of Kent; Richard Choppin, tallowchandler, one of the sheriffs 1530; John Hamber, esquire, 1573; Thomas Hanley, *alias* Clarenciaux king-at-arms; Thomas Busby, cooper, who gave the Queen's Head tavern to the relief of the poor in the parish, 1575; John Whelar, goldsmith, 1575; Richard Bolene, 1563; William Bolene, 1575; W. Bolene, physician, 1587; Robert Crowley, vicar there—all these four under one old stone in the choir; the learned John Foxe, writer of the *Acts and Monuments of the English Church*, 1587; the skilful Robert Glover, *alias* Sommerset herald, 1588.

There was in this church of old time a fraternity, or brotherhood, of Our Blessed Lady, or Corpus Christi, and St. Giles, founded by John Belancer, in the reign of Edward III., the 35th year of his reign.

Some small distance from the east end of this church is a water conduit, brought in pipes of lead from Highbery, by John Middleton, one of the executors to Sir William Eastfield, and of his goods; the inhabitants adjoining castellated it of their own cost and charges about the year 1483.

There was also a bosse of clear water in the wall of the churchyard, made at the charges of Richard Whitington, sometimes mayor, and was like to that of Bilinsgate: of late the same was turned into an evil pump, and so is clean decayed.

There was also a fair pool of clear water near unto the parsonage, on the west side thereof, which was filled up in the reign of Henry VI., the spring was coped in, and arched over with hard stone, and stairs of stone to go down to the spring on the bank of the town ditch: and this was also done of the goods, and by the executors of Richard Whitington.

In White Crosse street King Henry V. built one fair house, and founded there a brotherhood of St. Giles, to be kept, which house had sometime been an hospital of the French order, by the name of St. Giles without Cripplesgate, in the reign of Edward I., the king having the jurisdiction, and appointing a custos thereof for the precinct of the parish of St. Giles, etc. patent Richard II., the 15th year; which hospital being suppressed, the lands were given to the brotherhood for the relief of the poor.

One alley of divers tenements over against the north wall of St. Giles' churchyard, was appointed to be alms houses for the poor, wherein they dwelt rent free, and otherwise were relieved; but the said brotherhood was suppressed by Henry VIII.; since which time Sir John Gresham, mayor, purchased the lands, and gave part thereof to the maintenance of a free school which he had founded at Holt, a market town in Norfolk.

In Red Cross street, on the west side from St. Giles' church-yard up to the said cross, be many fair houses built outward, with divers alleys turning into a large plot of ground, called the Jews' Garden, as being the only place appointed them in England, wherein to bury their dead, till the year 1177, the 24th of Henry II., that it was permitted to them (after long suit to the king and parliament at Oxford) to have a special place assigned them in every quarter where they dwelt. This plot of ground remained to the said Jews till the time of their final banishment out of England, and is now turned into fair garden plots and summer-houses for pleasure.

On the east side of this Red Cross street be also divers fair houses, up to the cross. And there is Beech lane, peradventure so called of Nicholas de la Beech, lieutenant of the Tower of London, put out of that office in the 13th of Edward III. This lane stretcheth from the Red Cross street to White Cross street, replenished, not with beech trees, but with beautiful houses of stone, brick, and timber. Amongst the which was of old time a great house, pertaining to the Abbot of Ramsey, for his lodging when he repaired to the city: it is now called Drewry house, of Sir Drewe Drewrie, a worshipful owner thereof.

On the north side of this Beech lane, towards White Cross street, the Drapers of London have lately built eight alms houses of brick and timber, for eight poor widows of their own company, whom they have placed there rent free, according to the gift of Lady Askew, widow to Sir Christopher Askew, sometime draper, and mayor 1533.

Then in Golding lane, Richard Gallard of Islington, esquire, citizen and painter-stainer of London, founded thirteen alms houses for so many poor people placed in them rent free; he gave to the poor of the same alms houses two pence the piece weekly, and a load of charcoal amongst them yearly for ever: he left fair lands about Islington to maintain his foundation. Thomas Hayes, sometime chamberlain of London, in the latter time of Henry VIII., married Elizabeth, his daughter and heir; which Hayes and Elizabeth had a daughter named Elizabeth, married to John Ironmonger, of London, mercer, who now hath the order of the alms people.

On the west side of the Red Cross is a street, called the Barbican, because sometime there stood, on the north side thereof, a burgh-kenin, or watch-tower, of the city, called in some language a barbican, as a bikening is called a beacon; this burgh-kenning, by the name of the Manor of Base court, was given by Edward III. to Robert Ufford, Earl of Suffolk, and was lately appertaining to Peregrine Bartie, Lord Willoughby of Ersby. [See Additional Notes.]

Next adjoining to this is one other great house, called Garter house, sometime built by Sir Thomas Writhe, or Writhesley, knight, *alias* Garter principal king-of-arms, second son of Sir John Writhe, knight, *alias* Garter, and was uncle to the first Thomas, Earl of Southampton, knight of the Garter, and chancellor of England; he built this house, and in the top thereof a chapel, which is dedicated by the name of St. Trinitatis in Alto.

Thus much for that part of Cripplegate ward without the wall, whereof more shall be spoken in the suburb of that part. This ward hath an alderman, and his deputy, within the gate, common council eight, constables nine, scavengers twelve, for wardmote inquest fifteen, and a beadle. Without the gate it hath also a deputy, common council two, constables four, scavengers four, wardmote inquest seventeen, and a beadle. It is taxed in London to the fifteen at forty pound.[1]

ALDERSGATE WARD

The next is Aldersgate ward, taking name of that north gate of the city. This ward also consisteth of divers streets and lanes, lying as well within the gate and wall as without. And first to speak of that part within the gate, thus it is.

The east part thereof joineth unto the west part of Cripplegate ward in Engain lane, or Maiden lane. It beginneth on the north side of that lane, at Stayning lane end, and runneth up from the Haberdashers' hall to St. Mary Staining church, and by the church, east, winding almost to Wood street; and west through Oate lane, and then by the south side of Bacon house in Noble street, back again by Lilipot lane, which is also of that ward, to Maiden lane, and so on that north side west to St. John Zacharies church, and to Foster lane.

Now on the south side of Engain or Maiden lane is the west

---

[1] " It is taxed in London to the fifteene at forty pound, and in the Exchequer at thirty-nine pound ten shillings."—*1st edition*, p. 242.

side of Guthuruns lane to Kery lane, and Kery lane itself (which is of this ward), and back again into Engain lane, by the north side of the Goldsmiths' hall to Foster lane: and this is the east wing of this ward. Then is Foster lane almost wholly of this ward, beginneth in the south toward Cheap, on the east side by the north side of St. Foster's church, and runneth down north-west by the west end of Engain lane, by Lilipot lane and Oate lane to Noble street, and through that by Shelly house (of old time so called, as belonging to the Shelleys); Sir Thomas Shelley, knight, was owner thereof in the 1st of Henry IV. It is now called Bacon house, because the same was new built by Sir Nicholas Bacon, lord keeper of the great seal. Down on that side, by Sergeant Fleetwood's house, recorder of London, who also new built it, to St. Olave's church in Silver street, which is by the north-west end of this Noble street.

Then again in Foster lane this ward beginneth on the west side thereof, over against the south-west corner of St. Foster's church, and runneth down by St. Leonard's church, by Pope lane end, and by St. Ann's lane end, which lane is also of this ward, north to the stone wall by the wall of the city, over against Bacon house, which stone wall, and so down north to Cripplegate on that side, is of Faringdon ward.

Then have ye the main street of this ward, which is called St. Martin's lane, including St. Martin, on the east side thereof, and so down on both the sides to Aldersgate. And these be the bounds of this ward within the wall and gate.

Without the gate the main street called Aldersgate street runneth up north on the east side to the west end of Howndes ditch, or Barbican street; a part of which street is also of this ward. And on the west side to Long lane, a part whereof is likewise of this ward. Beyond the which Aldersgate street is Goswell street up to the bars.

And on this west side of Aldersgate street, by St. Buttolph's church is Briton street, which runneth west to a pump, and then north to the gate which entereth the churchyard, sometime pertaining to the priory of St. Bartholomew on the east side; and on the west side towards St. Bartholomew's Spittle, to a pair of posts there fixed. And these be the bounds of this Aldersgate ward without.

The antiquities be these, first in Stayning lane, of old time so called, as may be supposed, of painter-stainers dwelling there.

On the east side thereof, adjoining to the Haberdashers' hall, be ten alms houses, pertaining to the Haberdashers, wherein be placed ten alms people of that company, every of them having eight pence the piece every Friday for ever, by the gift of Thomas Huntlow, haberdasher, one of the sheriffs in the year 1539. More, Sir George Baron gave them ten pounds by the year for ever.

Then is the small parish church of St. Mary, called Stayning, because it standeth at the north end of Stayning lane. In the which church, being but newly built, there remains no monument worth the noting.

Then is Engain lane, or Mayden lane, and at the north-west corner thereof the parish church of St. John Zachary; a fair church, with the monuments well preserved, of Thomas Lichfield, who founded a chantry there in the 14th of Edward II.; of Sir Nicholas Twiford, goldsmith, mayor 1388, and Dame Margery his wife, of whose goods the church was made and new built, with a tomb for them, and others of their race, 1390; Drugo Barentine, mayor 1398; he gave fair lands to the Goldsmiths; he dwelt right against the Goldsmiths' hall; between the which hall and his dwelling house he built a gallery thwarting the street, whereby he might go from one to the other; he was buried in this church, and Christian his wife, 1427; John Adis, goldsmith, 1400, and Margaret his wife; John Francis, goldsmith, mayor 1400, and Elizabeth his wife, 1450; I Sutton, goldsmith, one of the sheriffs 1413;[1] Bartholomew Seman, goldbeater, master of the king's mints within the Tower of London and the town of Calice, 1430;[2] John Hewet, esquire, 1500; William Breakespere, goldsmith, 1461; Christopher Eliot, goldsmith, 1505; Bartholomew Reade, goldsmith, mayor 1502, was buried in the Charterhouse, and gave to this, his parish church, one hundred pounds; his wife was buried here with a fair monument, her picture in habit of a widow; Thomas Keyton Lorimar, 1522; William Potken, esquire, 1537; John Cornish, with an epitaph, 1470; Robert Fenruther, goldsmith, one of the sheriffs in the year 1512.

On the east side of this Foster lane, at Engain lane end, is the Goldsmiths' hall, a proper house, but not large; and, therefore, to say that Bartholomew Read, goldsmith, mayor in the year 1502, kept such a feast in this hall, as some have fabuled,[3] is far incredible, and altogether impossible, considering the smallness of the hall, and number of the guests, which, as they say, were more than a hundred persons of great estate. For the messes and dishes of meats to them served, the paled park in

---

[1] [See Additional Notes.]
[2] "Thomas Leichfield."—1st edition, p. 244. [3] R. Grafton. [See Bibl.]

the same hall furnished with fruitful trees, beasts of venery, and other circumstances of that pretended feast, well weighed, Westminster hall would hardly have sufficed; and, therefore, I will overpass it, and note somewhat of principal goldsmiths.

First I read, that Leofstane, goldsmith, was provost of this city in the reign of Henry I. Also, that Henry Fitz Alewin Fitz Leafstane, goldsmith, was mayor of London in the 1st of Richard I., and continued mayor twenty-four years. Also that Gregory Rocksly, chief say-master of all the king's mints within England, (and therefore by my conjecture) a goldsmith, was mayor in the 3rd of Edward I., and continued mayor seven years together. Then, William Faringdon, goldsmith, alderman of Faringdon ward, one of the sheriffs 1281, the 9th of Edward I., who was a goldsmith, as appeareth in record, as shall be shown in Faringdon ward. Then Nicholas Faringdon his son, goldsmith, alderman of Faringdon ward, four times mayor in the reign of Edward II., etc. For the rest of latter time are more manifestly known, and therefore I leave them. The men of this mystery were incorporated or confirmed in the 16th of Richard II.

Then at the north end of Noble street is the parish church of St. Olave in Silver street, a small thing, and without any noteworthy monuments.

On the west side of Foster lane is the small parish church of St. Leonard's, for them of St. Martin's le Grand. A number of tenements being lately built in place of the great collegiate church of St. Martin, that parish is mightily increased. In this church remain these monuments. First, without the church is graven in stone on the east end, John Brokeitwell, an especial re-edifier, or new builder thereof. In the choir, graven in brass, Robert Purfet, grocer, 1507; Robert Trapis, goldsmith, 1526, with this epitaph:—

> " When the bels be merily roong,
> And the masse devoutly sung,
> And the meat merily eaten,
> Then shall Robert Trips, his wives
> And children be forgotten."

Then in Pope lane, so called of one Pope that was owner thereof, on the north side of the parish church of St. Anne in the Willows, so called, I know not upon what occasion, but some say of willows growing thereabouts; but now there is no such void place for willows to grow, more than the churchyard, wherein do grow some high ash trees.

This church, by casualty of fire in the year 1548, was burnt, so far as it was combustible, but since being newly repaired, there remain a few monuments of antiquity: of Thomas Beckhenton, clerk of the pipe, was buried there 1499; Raph Caldwell, gentleman, of Grays inn, 1527; John Lord Sheffelde; John Herenden, mercer, esquire, 1572, these verses on an old stone:—[1]

Qu	an	Tris	di	e	vul	stra
os	guis	ti	ro	um	nere	uit
h	san	Chris	mi	T	mu	la

William Gregory, skinner, mayor of London in the year 1451, was there buried, and founded a chantry, but no monument of him remaineth.

Then in St. Martin's lane was of old time a fair and large college of a dean and secular canons or priests, and was called St. Martin's le Grand, founded by Ingelricus and Edwardus his brother, in the year of Christ 1056, and confirmed by William the Conqueror, as appeareth by his charter dated 1068. This college claimed great privileges of sanctuary and otherwise, as appeareth in a book, written by a notary of that house about the year 1442, the 19th of Henry VI., wherein, amongst other things, is set down and declared, that on the 1st of September, in the year aforesaid, a soldier, prisoner in Newgate, as he was led by an officer towards the Guildhall of London, there came out of Panyer alley five of his fellowship, and took him from the officer, brought him into sanctuary at the west door of St. Martin's church, and took grithe of that place; but the same day Philip Malpas and Rob. Marshall, then sheriffs of London, with many other, entered the said church, and forcibly took out with them the said five men thither fled, led them fettered to the Compter, and from thence, chained by the necks, to Newgate; of which violent taking the dean and chapter in large manner complained to the king, and required him, as their patron, to defend their privileges, like as his predecessors had done, etc. All which complaint and suit the citizens by their counsel, Markam, sergeant at the law, John Carpenter, late common clerk of the city, and other, learnedly answered, offering to prove that the said place of St. Martin had no such immunity or liberty as was pretended; namely, Carpenter

---

[1] These disjointed syllables, it will be seen, may be so read as to form the following rhyming couplet:—

> "*Quos anguis tristi diro cum vulnere stravit,*
> *Hos sanguis Christi miro tum munere lavit.*"

offered to lose his livelihood, if that church had more immunity than the least church in London. Notwithstanding, after long debating of this controversy, by the king's commandment, and assent of his council in the starred chamber, the chancellor and treasurer sent a writ unto the sheriffs of London, charging them to bring the said five persons with the cause of their taking and withholding afore the king in his Chancery, on the vigil of Allhallows. On which day the said sheriffs, with the recorder and counsel of the city, brought and delivered them accordingly, afore the said lords; whereas the chancellor, after he had declared the king's commandment, sent them to St. Martin's, there to abide freely, as in a place having franchises, whiles them liked, etc.

Thus much out of that book have I noted concerning the privilege of that place challenged in these days, since the which time, to wit, in the year 1457, the 36th of the said Henry VI., an ordinance was made by the king and his council concerning the said sanctuary men in St. Martin's le Grand, whereof the articles are set down in the book of K., within the chamber of the Guildhall, in the lease 299.

This college was surrendered to King Edward VI., the 2nd of his reign, in the year of Christ 1548; and the same year the college church being pulled down, in the east part thereof a large wine tavern was built, and with all down to the west, and throughout the whole precinct of that college, many other houses were built and highly prized, letten to strangers born, and other such, as there claimed benefit of privileges granted to the canons serving God day and night (for so be the words in the charter of William the Conqueror), which may hardly be wrested to artificers, buyers and sellers, otherwise than is mentioned in the 21st of St. Matthew's Gospel.

Lower down on the west side of St. Martin's lane, in the parish of St. Anne, almost by Aldersgate, is one great house, commonly called Northumberland house; it belonged to H. Percy. King Henry IV., in the 7th of his reign, gave this house, with the tenements thereunto appertaining, to Queen Jane his wife, and then it was called her Wardrobe: it is now a printing house.

Without Aldersgate, on the east side of Aldersgate street, is the Cooks' hall; which Cooks (or Pastelars) were admitted to be a company, and to have a master and wardens, in the 22nd of Edward IV. From thence along into Houndsditch, or Barbican street, be many fair houses. On the west side also be the like fair buildings till ye come to Long lane, and so to Goswell street.

In Briton street, which took that name of the dukes of Brittany lodging there, is one proper parish church of St. Buttolph, in which church was sometime a brotherhood of St. Fabian and Sebastian, founded in the year 1377, the 51st of Edward III., and confirmed by Henry IV., in the 6th of his reign. Then Henry VI., in the 24th of his reign, to the honour of the Trinity, gave license to Dame Joan Astley, sometime his nurse, to R. Cawod and T. Smith, to found the same a fraternity, perpetually to have a master and two custoses, with brethren and sisters, etc. This brotherhood was endowed with lands more than thirty pounds by the year, and was suppressed by Edward VI. There lie buried, John de Bath, weaver, 1390; Philip at Vine, capper, 1396; Benet Gerard, brewer, 1403; Thomas Bilsington founded a chantry there, and gave to that church a house, called the Helmet upon Cornhill; John Bradmore, chirurgeon, Margaret and Katheren his wives, 1411; John Michaell, sergeant-at-arms, 1415; Allen Bret, carpenter, 1425; Robert Malton, 1426; John Trigilion, brewer, 1417; John Mason, brewer, 1431; Rob. Cawood, clerk of the pipe in the king's exchequer, 1466; Ri. Emmessey; John Walpole; I. Hartshorne, esquire, servant to the king, 1400, and other of that family, great benefactors to that church; W. Marrow, grocer, mayor, and Katherine his wife, were buried there about 1468. The Lady Ann Packington, widow, late wife to Jo. Packinton, knight, chirographer of the court of the common pleas; she founded alms houses near unto the White Fryers' church in Fleet street: the Clothworkers in London have oversight thereof.

And thus an end of this ward; which hath an alderman, his deputy, common councillors five, constables eight, scavengers nine, for the wardmote inquest fourteen, and a beadle. It is taxed to the fifteen in London seven pounds, and [1] in the exchequer six pounds nineteen shillings.

FARINGDON WARD INFRA, OR WITHIN

On the south side of Aldersgate ward lieth Faringdon ward, called *infra* or within, for a difference from another ward of that name, which lieth without the walls of the city, and is therefore called Faringdon *extra*. These two wards of old time were but one, and had also but one alderman, till the 17th of

[1] " Likewise in the exchequer."—*1st edition*, p. 247.

Richard II., at which time the said ward, for the greatness
thereof, was divided into twain, and by parliament ordered to
have two aldermen, and so it continueth till this day. The
whole great ward of Farindon, both *infra* and *extra*, took name
of W. Farindon, goldsmith, alderman of that ward, and one of
the sheriffs of London in the year 1281, the 9th of Edward I.
He purchased the Aldermanry of this ward, as by the abstract
of deeds, which I have read thereof, may appear.

"Thomas de Arderne, son and heir to Sir Ralph Arderne,
knight, granted to Ralph le Feure, citizen of London, one of
the sheriffs in the year 1277, all the aldermanry, with the appurtenances within the city of London, and the suburbs of the same
between Ludgate and Newgate, and also without the same
gates: which aldermanry, Ankerinus de Averne held during his
life, by the grant of the said Thomas de Arderna, to have and
to hold to the said Ralph, and to his heirs, freely without all
challenge, yielding therefore yearly to the said Thomas and his
heirs one clove [1] or slip of gilliflowers, at the feast of Easter,
for all secular service and customs, with warranty unto the said
Ralph le Fevre and his heirs, against all people, Christians and
Jews, in consideration of twenty marks, which the said Ralph
le Fevre did give beforehand, in name of a gersum [2] or fine, to
the said Thomas, etc., dated the 5th of Edward I. Witness,
G. de Rokesley, maior; R. Arrar, one of the shiriffes; H. Wales,
P. le Taylor, T. de Basing, I. Horne, N. Blackthorn, aldermen
of London." After this, John le Fevre, son and heir to the said
Ralph le Fevre, granted to William Farindon, citizen and goldsmith of London, and to his heirs, the said aldermanry, with
the appurtenances, for the service thereunto belonging, in the
7th of Edward I., in the year of Christ 1279. This aldermanry
descended to Nicholas Farindon, son to the said William, and
to his heirs; which Nicholas Farindon, also a goldsmith, was
four times mayor, and lived many years after; for I have read
divers deeds, whereunto he was a witness, dated the year 1360:

---

[1] The word *clove* is from the Anglo-Saxon *Clifian* (the low German *Klöven*,
and Dutch *Klooven*), to split, or *clufe*, an ear of corn or *clove* of garlic. In
this case the flower is the common Stock, or Stock Gilliflower, so long
a favourite in the gardens of England, and indeed a native of the cliffs by
the sea-side. "The old English name of Gilliflower," says the author of
the *Flora Domestica*, "which is now almost lost in the prefix Stock, is
corrupted from the French *Giroflier*. Chaucer writes it *Gylofre;* but, by
associating it with the nutmeg and other spices, appears to mean the clove-
tree, which is in fact the proper signification of that word. Turner calls
it *Gelover* and *Gelyflower*, Gerrarde and Parkinson *Gilloflower*."
[2] The Anglo-Saxon *Gærsuma*—treasure, riches, fine, etc.

he made his testament 1361, which was fifty-three years after
his first being mayor, and was buried in St. Peter's church in
Cheape. So this ward continued under the government of
William Faringdon the father, and Nicholas his son, by the space
of eighty-two years, and retaineth their name until this present
day. [*See* Additional Notes.]

This ward of Faringdon within the walls is bounded thus:
Beginning in the east, at the great cross in Westcheape, from
whence it runneth west. On the north side from the parish
church of St. Peter, which is at the south-west corner of Wood
street, on to Guthurun's lane, and down that lane to Hugon
lane on the east side, and to Kery lane on the west.

Then again into Cheape and to Foster lane, and down that
lane on the east side, to the north side of St. Foster's church, and
on the west, till over against the south-west corner of the said
church, from whence down Foster lane and Noble street is all
of Aldersgate street ward, till ye come to the stone wall, in the
west side of Noble street, as is afore showed. Which said wall,
down to Nevil's inn or Windsor house, and down Monkes well
street, on that west side, then by London wall to Cripplegate,
and the west side of that same gate is all of Faringdon ward.

Then back again into Cheape, and from Foster lane end to
St. Martin's lane end, and from thence through St. Nicholas
shambles, by Penticost lane and Butchers' alley, and by Stinking
lane through Newgate market to Newgate; all which is the
north side of Faringdon ward.

On the south, from against the said great cross in Cheape
west to Fridayes street, and down that street on the east side,
till over against the north-east corner of St. Mathew's church;
and on the west side, till the south corner of the said church.

Then again along Cheape to the old Exchange, and down
that lane (on the east side) to the parish church of St. Augustine,
which church, and one house next adjoining in Watheling street,
be of this ward, and on the west side of this lane, to the east arch
or gate by St. Augustine's church, which entereth the south
churchyard of St. Paules, which arch or gate was built by
Nicholas Faringdon about the year 1361, and within that gate,
on the said north side, to the gate that entereth the north
churchyard, and all the north churchyard is of this Faringdon
ward.

Then again into Cheape, and from the north end of the Old
Exchange, west by the north gate of Paules churchyard, by
Pater noster row, by the two lanes out of Paules church, and

to a sign of the Golden Lion, which is some twelve houses short
of Ave Mary lane; the west side of which lane is of this
ward.

Then at the south end of Ave Mary lane is Creed lane; the
west side whereof is also of this ward.

Now betwixt the south end of Ave Mary lane and the north
end of Creede lane, is the coming out of Paules churchyard on
the east, and the high street called Bowier row to Ludgate on
the west, which way to Ludgate is of this ward. On the north
side whereof is St. Martin's church, and on the south side a
turning into the Blacke friars.

Now to turn up again to the north end of Ave Mary lane,
there is a short lane which runneth west some small distance,
and is there closed up with a gate into a great house: and this
is called Amen lane.

Then on the north side of Pater noster row, beginning at the
Conduit over against the Old Exchange lane end, and going
west by St. Michael's church; at the west end of which church
is a small passage through towards the north: and beyond this
church some small distance is another passage, which is called
Paniar alley, and cometh out against St. Martin's lane end.

Then further west in Pater noster row is Ivie lane, which
runneth north to the west end of St. Nicholas shambles; and
then west Pater noster row, till over against the Golden Lion,
where the ward endeth for that street.

Then about some dozen houses (which is of Baynard's castle
ward) to Warwick lane end; which Warwick lane stretcheth
north to the high street of Newgate market. And the west
side of Warwick lane is of this Faringdon ward; for the east
side of Warwick lane, of Ave Marie lane, and of Creede lane,
with the west end of Pater noster row, are all of Baynardes
castle ward.

Yet to begin again at the said Conduit by the Old Exchange,
on the north side thereof is a large street that runneth up to
Newgate, as is aforesaid. The first part, or south side whereof,
from the Conduit to the shambles, is called Bladder street. Then
on the back side of the shambles be divers slaughter-houses, and
such like, pertaining to the shambles; and this is called Mount
Godard street. Then is the shambles itself, and then Newgate
market; and so the whole street, on both sides up to Newgate,
is of this ward; and thus it is wholly bounded.

Monuments in this ward be these: First, the great cross in
Westcheape street, but in the ward of Faringdon; the which

cross was first erected in that place by Edward I., as before is showed in Westcheape street.

At the south-west corner of Wood street is the parish church of St. Peter the Apostle by the said cross, a proper church lately new built. John Sha, goldsmith, mayor, deceased 1508, appointed by his testament the said church and steeple to be newly built of his goods, with a flat roof; notwithstanding, Thomas Wood, goldsmith, one of the sheriffs 1491, is accounted principal benefactor, because the roof of the middle aisle is supported by images of woodmen. I find to have been buried in this church—Nicholas Farendon, mayor; Richard Hadley, grocer, 1592; John Palmer, fishmonger, 1500; William Rus, goldsmith, sheriff 1429; T. Atkins, esquire, 1400; John Butler, sheriff 1420;[1] Henry Warley, alderman 1524; Sir John Monday, goldsmith, mayor, deceased 1537; Augustine Hinde, clothworker, one of the sheriffs in the year 1550, whose monument doth yet remain, the others be gone; Sir Alexander Auenon, mayor 1570.

The long shop, or shed, incroaching on the high street before this church wall was licensed to be made in the year 1401, yielding to the chamber of London thirty shillings and four pence yearly for the time, but since thirteen shillings and four pence. Also the same shop was letten by the parish for three pounds at the most many years since.

Then is Guthurun's lane, so called of Guthurun, sometime owner thereof. The inhabitants of this lane of old time were goldbeaters, as doth appear by records in the Exchequer; for the Easterling money was appointed to be made of fine silver, such as men made into foil, and was commonly called silver of Guthurun's lane, etc. The Embroiderers' hall is in this lane. John Throwstone, embroiderer, then goldsmith, sheriff, deceased 1519, gave forty pounds towards the purchase of this hall. Hugon lane on the east side, and Kery lane (called of one Kery) on the west.

Then in the high street on the same north side is the Saddlers' hall, and then Fauster lane (so called) of St. Fauster's, a fair church lately new built. Henry Coote, goldsmith, one of the sheriffs, deceased 1509, built St. Dunston's chapel there. John Throwstone, one of the sheriffs, gave to the building thereof one hundred pounds by his testament. John Browne, sergeant painter, alderman, deceased 1532, was a great benefactor, and was there buried. William Trist, cellarer to the king, 1425,

[1] " John Palmer."—_1st edition_, p. 252.

John Standelfe,[1] goldsmiths, lie buried there; Richard Galder, 1544; Agnes, wife to William Milborne, chamberlain of London, 1500, etc.

Then down Foster lane and Noble street, both of Aldersgate street ward, till ye come to the stone wall which incloseth a garden plot before the wall of the city, on the west side of Noble street, and is of this Faringdon ward. This garden-plot, containing ninety-five ells in length, nine ells and a half in breadth, was by Adam de Burie, mayor, the alderman, and citizens of London, letten to John de Nevill, Lord of Raby, Radulph and Thomas his sons, for sixty years, paying 6s. 8d. the year, dated the 48th of Edward III., having in a seal pendant on the one side, the figure of a walled city and of St. Paul, a sword in his right hand, and in the left a banner; three leopards about that seal, on the same side, written, *Sigillum Baronium Londoniarum*. On the other side, the like figure of a city, a bishop sitting on an arch; the inscription, *Me : que : te : peperi : ne : Cesses : Thoma : tueri*. Thus much for the barons of London, their common seal at that time. At the north end of this garden-plot is one great house built of stone and timber, now called the Lord Windsor's house, of old time belonging to the Nevils; as in the 19th of Richard II. it was found by inquisition of a jury, that Elizabeth Nevil died, seised of a great messuage in the parish of St. Olave, in Monk's well street in London, holden of the king in free burgage, which she held of the gift of John Nevell of Raby her husband, and that John Latimer was next son and heir to the said Elizabeth.

In this west side is the Barbers-Chirurgeons' hall. This company was incorporated by means of Thomas Morestede, esquire, one of the sheriffs of London 1436, chirurgeon to the kings of England, Henry IV., V., and VI.: he deceased 1450. Then Jaques Fries, physician to Edward IV., and William Hobbs, physician and chirurgeon for the same king's body, continuing the suit the full time of twenty years, Edward IV., in the 2nd of his reign, and Richard, Duke of Gloucester, became founders of the same corporation in the name of St. Cosme and St. Damiane. The first assembly of that craft was Roger Strippe, W. Hobbs, T. Goddard, and Richard Kent; since the which time they built their hall in that street, etc.

At the north corner of this street, on the same side, was sometime an hermitage, or chapel of St. James, called in the wall, near Cripplegate: it belonged to the abbey and convent of

[1] " John Standelfe and John Standelfe."—*1st edition*, p. 253.

Garadon, as appeareth by a record, the 27th of Edward I., and also the 16th of Edward III. William de Lions was hermit there, and the abbot and convent of Geredon found two chaplains, Cistercian monks of their house, in this hermitage; one of them for Aymor de Valence, Earl of Pembroke, and Mary de Saint Paule, his countess.

Of these monks, and of a well pertaining to them, the street took that name, and is called Monks' well street. This hermitage, with the appurtenances, was in the reign of Edward VI. purchased from the said king by William Lambe, one of the gentlemen of the king's chapel, citizen and cloth-worker of London: he deceased in the year 1577, and then gave it to the clothworkers of London, with other tenements, to the value of fifty pounds the year, to the intent they shall hire a minister to say divine service there, etc.

Again to the high street of Cheape, from Fauster lane end to St. Martin's, and by that lane to the shambles or flesh-market, on the north side whereof is Penticost lane, containing divers slaughter-houses for the butchers.

Then was there of old time a proper parish church of St. Nicholas, whereof the said flesh-market took the name, and was called St. Nicholas' shambles. This church, with the tenements and ornaments, was by Henry VIII. given to the mayor and commonalty of the city, towards the maintenance of the new parish church then to be erected in the late dissolved church of the Grey Friars; so was this church dissolved and pulled down. In place whereof, and of the churchyard, many fair houses are now built in a court with a well, in the midst whereof the church stood.

Then is Stinking lane, so called, or Chick lane, at the east end of the Grey Friars church, and there is the Butchers' hall.

In the 3rd of Richard II. motion was made that no butcher should kill no flesh within London, but at Knightsbridge, or such like distance of place from the walls of the city.

Then the late dissolved church of the Grey Friars; the original whereof was this:

The first of this order of friars in England, nine in number, arrived at Dover; five of them remained at Canterburie, the other four came to London, were lodged at the preaching friars in Oldborne for the space of fifteen days, and then they hired a house in Cornhill of John Trevers, one of the sheriffs of London. They built there little cells, wherein they inhabited; but shortly after, the devotion of citizens towards them, and the number of the friars so increased, that they were by the citizens removed to a place in St. Nicholas' shambles; which John Ewin, mercer, appropriated unto the commonalty, to the use of the said friars, and himself became a lay brother amongst them. About the year 1225, William Joyner built their choir, Henry Walles the body of the church, Walter Potter, alderman, the chapter house, Gregorie Rokesley their dorter; Bartholomew of the Castle made the refectory, Peter de Heliland made the infirmitory, Bevis Bond, king of heralds, made the study, etc.

Margaret, queen, second wife to Edward I., began the choir of their new church in the year 1306; to the building whereof, in her lifetime, she gave two thousand marks, and one hundred marks by her testament. John Britaine, Earl of Richmond, built the body of the church to the charges of three hundred pounds, and gave many rich jewels and ornaments to be used in the same; Marie, Countess of Pembroke, seventy pounds. Gilbert de Clare, Earl of Gloucester, bestowed twenty great beams out of his forest of Tunbridge, and twenty pounds sterling. Lady Helianor le Spencer, Lady Elizabeth de Burgh, sister to Gilbert de Clare, gave sums of money; and so did divers citizens; as Arnald de Tolinea, one hundred pounds; Robert, Baron Lisle, who became a friar there, three hundred pounds; Bartholomew de Almaine, fifty pounds. Also Philippa, queen, wife to Edward III., gave sixty-two pounds; Isabell, queen, mother to Edward III., gave threescore and ten pounds. And so the work was done within the space of twenty-one years, 1337. This church was furnished with windows made at the charges of divers persons. The Lady Margaret Segrave, Countess of Norfolk, bare the charges of making the stalls in the choir, to the value of three hundred and fifty marks, about the year 1380. Richard Whittington, in the year 1429, founded the library, which was in length one hundred and twenty-nine feet, and in breadth thirty-one, all sealed with wainscot, having twenty-eight desks and eight double settles of wainscot; which in the next year following was altogether finished in building, and within three years after furnished with books, to the charges of five hundred and fifty-six pounds ten shillings; whereof Richard Whittington bare four hundred pounds; the rest was borne by Doctor Thomas Winchelsey, a friar there; and for the writing out of D. Nicholas de Lira, his works, in two volumes, to be chained there, one hundred marks, etc. The ceiling of the choir at divers men's charges, two hundred marks, and the painting at fifty marks; their conduit head and water-course given them by William Tailor, tailor to Henry III., etc.

This whole church containeth in length three hundred feet, of the feet of St. Paule; in breadth eighty-nine feet, and in height from the ground to the roof sixty-four feet and two inches, etc. It was consecrated 1325, and at the general suppression was valued at thirty-two pounds nineteen shillings, surrendered the 12th of November 1538, the 30th of Henry VIII., the ornaments and goods being taken to the king's use. The church was shut up for a time, and used as a storehouse for goods taken prizes from the French; but in the year 1546, on the 3rd of January, was again set open. On the which day preached at Paule's cross the Bishop of Rochester, where he declared the king's gift thereof to the city for the relieving of the poor. Which gift was by patent—of St. Bartholomew's Spittle, lately valued at three hundred and five pounds six shillings and seven pence, and surrendered to the king; of the said church of the Grey Friars, and of two parish churches, the one of St. Nicholas in the shambles, and the other of St. Ewines in Newgate market, which were to be made one parish church in the said Friars church; and in lands he gave for maintenance for the said church, with divine service, reparations, etc., five hundred marks by year for ever.

The 13th of January, the 38th of Henry VIII., an agreement was made betwixt the king and the mayor [1] and commonalty of London, dated the 27th of December, by which the said gift of the Grey Friars church, with all the edifices and ground, the fratry, the library, the dortor, and chapter-house, the great cloister and the lesser, tenements, gardens, and vacant grounds, lead, stone, iron, etc., the hospital of St. Bartholomew in West Smithfield, the church of the same, the lead, bells, and ornaments of the same hospital, with all the messuages, tenements, and appurtenances; the parishes of St. Nicholas and of St. Ewin, and so much of St. Sepulcher's parish as is within Newgate, were made one parish church in the Gray Friars church, and called Christ's church, founded by Henry VIII.

The vicar of Christ's church was to have twenty-six pounds thirteen shillings and four pence the year; the vicar of St. Bartholomew thirteen pounds six shillings and eight pence; the visitor of Newgate (being a priest), ten pounds; and other five priests in Christ's church, all to be helping in Divine service,

---

[1] " The maior and communalty of London, parsons of Christ's church, the vicar to be at their appointment."—*Stow.*

ministering the sacraments and sacramentals; the five priests to have eight pounds the piece, two clerks six pounds each, a sexton four pounds. Moreover, he gave them the hospital of Bethelem; with the laver of brass in the cloister, by estimation eighteen feet in length, and two feet and a half in depth; and the water-course of lead, to the said Friar house belonging, containing by estimation in length eighteen acres.

In the year 1552 began the repairing of the Grey Friars house for the poor fatherless children; and in the month of November the children were taken into the same, to the number of almost four hundred. On Christmas day, in the afternoon, while the lord mayor and aldermen rode to Paules, the children of Christ's hospital stood, from St. Lawrence lane end in Cheape towards Paules, all in one livery of russet cotton, three hundred and forty in number; and in Easter next they were in blue at the Spittle, and so have continued ever since.

The defaced monuments in this church were these; First in the choir, of the Lady Margaret, daughter to Philip, king of France, and wife to Edward I., foundress of this new church, 1317; of Isabel, queen, wife to Edward II., daughter to Philip, king of France, 1358; John of the Tower; Queen of Scots, wife to David Bruce, daughter to Edward II., died in Hartford castle, and was buried by Isabel her mother 1362; William Fitzwarren, baron, and Isabel his wife, sometime Queen of Man; Isabel, daughter to Edward III., wedded to the Lord Courcy of France, after created Earl of Bedford; Elianor, wife to John, Duke of Britaine: Beatrix, Duchess of Britaine, daughter to Henry III.; Sir Robert Lisle, baron; the Lady Lisle, and Margaret de Rivers, Countess of Devon, all under one stone; Roger Mortimer, Earl of March, beheaded 1329; Peter, Bishop of Carbon in Hungary, 1331; Gregory Rocksley, mayor, 1282; Sir John Devereux, knight, 1385; John Hastings, Earl of Pembroke, 1389; Margaret, daughter to Thomas Brotharton, Earl Marshal; she was Duchess of Norfolk, and Countess Marshal and Lady Segrave, 1389; Richard Havering, knight, 1388; Robert Trisilian, knight justice, 1308; Geffrey Lucy, son of Geffrey Lucy; John Anbry, son to John, mayor of Norwich, 1368; John Philpot, knight, mayor of London, and the Lady Jane Samford his wife, 1384; John, Duke of Bourbon and Anjou, Earl of Claremond, Montpensier, and Baron Beaujeu, who was taken prisoner at Agincourt, kept prisoner eighteen years, and deceased 1433; Robert Chalons, knight, 1439; John Chalons; Margaret, daughter to Sir John Philpot, first married to T. Santlor, esquire.

and after to John Neyband, esquire; Sir Nicholas Brimbar,
mayor of London, buried 1386; Elizabeth Nevel, wife to John,
son and heir to Ralph, Earl of Westmoreland, and mother to
Ralph, Earl of Westmoreland, and daughter to Thomas Holland,
Earl of Kent, 1423; Edward Burnell, son to the Lord Burnell.
In Allhallows chapel: James Fines, Lord Say, 1450, and Helinor
his wife, 1452; John Smith, Bishop of Landafe, 1478; John,
Baron Hilton; John, Baron Clinton; Richard Hastings, knight,
Lord of Willowby and Welles; Thomas Burdet, esquire,
beheaded 1477; Robert Lisle, son and heir to the Lord Lisle.
In our Lady's chapel: John Gisors, of London, knight; Hunfrey
Stafford, esquire, of Worcestershire, 1486; Robert Bartram,
Baron of Bothell; Ralph Barons, knight; William Apleton,
knight; Reynold de Cambrey, knight; Thomas Beaumont, son
and heir to Henry Lord Beaumont; John Butler, knight;
Adam de Howton, knight, 1417; Bartholomew Caster, knight
of London; Reinfride Arundele, knight, 1460; Thomas Covil,
esquire, 1422. In the 'Postles chapel: Walter Blunt, knight
of the Garter, and Lord Mountjoy, treasurer of England, son and
heir to T. Blunt, knight, treasurer of Normandy,[1] 1474; E.
Blunt, Lord Mountjoy, 1475; Alice Blunt Mountjoy, sometime
wife to William Brown, mayor of London, and daughter to
H. Kebel, mayor 1521; Anne Blunt, daughter to John Blunt,
knight; Lord Mountjoy, 1480; Sir Allen Cheinie, knight, and
Sir T. Greene, knight; William Blunt, esquire, son and heir to
Walter Blunt,[2] captain of Gwynes, 1492; Elizabeth Blunt,
wife to Robert Curson, knight, 1494; Bartholomew Burwashe,
and John Burwashe his son; John Blunt, Lord Mountjoy,
captain of Gwins and Hams, 1485; John Dinham, baron, some-
time treasurer of England, knight of the Garter, 1501; Elianor,
Duchess of Buckingham, 1530; John Blunt, knight, 1531;
Rowland Blunt, esquire, 1509; Robert Bradbury, 1489; Nicholas
Clifton, knight; Francis Chape; two sons of Allayne Lord
Cheiney, and John, son and heir to the same; Lord Allaine
Cheinie, knight; John Robsart, knight of the Garter, 1450;
Alleyne Cheiney, knight; Thomas Malory, knight, 1470;
Thomas Young, a justice of the bench, 1476; John Baldwin,
fellow of Gray's inn, and common sergeant of London, 1469;
Walter Wrotsley, knight of Warwickshire, 1473; Steven Jenins,
mayor, 1523; Thomas a Par, and John Wiltwater, slain at

---

[1] " Treasurer of England."—*1st edition*, p. 258.
[2] " And father to Edward Lord Hountjoy; James Blunt, knighte, son
to Walter Blunt, captain of Gwynes, 1492."—*Ibid.*

Barnet, 1471; Nicholas Poynes, esquire, 1512; Robert Elkenton, knight, 1460; John Water, alias Yorke herald, 1520; John More, alias Norroy king of arms, 1491; George Hopton, knight, 1489. Between the choir and the altar: Ralph Spiganel, knight; John Moyle, gentleman, of Gray's inn, 1495; William Huddy, knight, 1501; John Cobham, a baron of Kent; John Mortain, knight; John Deyncort, knight; John Norbery, esquire, high treasurer of England; Henry Norbery, his son, esquire; John Southlee, knight; Thomas Sakvile; Thomas Lucy, knight; 1525; Robert de la Rivar, son to Mauricius de la Rivar, Lord of Tormerton, 1457; John Malmaynas, esquire, and Thomas Malmaynas, knight; Hugh Acton, tailor, 1530; Nicholas Malmains; Hugh Parsal, knight, 1490; Alexander Kirketon, knight, etc. In the body of the church: William Paulet, esquire of Somersetshire, 1482; John Moyle, gentleman, 1530; Peter Champion, esquire, 1511; John Hart, gentleman, 1449; Alice Lat Hungerford, hanged at Tiborne for murdering her husband, 1523; Edward Hall, gentleman, of Gray's inn, 1470; Richard Churchyard, gentleman, fellow of Gray's inn, 1498; John Bramre, gentleman, of Gray's inn, 1498; John Mortimar, knight, beheaded 1423; Henry Frowike, alderman; Renauld Frowike; Philip Pats, 1518; William Porter, sergeant at arms, 1515; Thomas Grantham, gentleman, 1511; Edmond Rotheley, gentleman, 1470; Henry Roston, gentleman, of Gray's inn, 1485; Nicholas Montgomery, gentleman, son to John Montgomery, of Northamptonshire, 1485; Sir Bartholomew Emfield, knight; Sir Barnard St. Peter, knight; Sir Ralph Sandwich, knight, custos of London; Sir Andrew Sakevile, knight; John Treszawall, gentleman and tailor of London, 1520. All these and five times so many more have been buried there, whose monuments are wholly defaced; for there were nine tombs of alabaster and marble, environed with strikes of iron in the choir, and one tomb in the body of the church, also coped with iron, all pulled down, besides sevenscore grave-stones of marble, all sold for fifty pounds, or thereabouts, by Sir Martin Bowes, goldsmith and alderman of London. Of late time buried there, Walter Hadden, doctor, etc. From this church west to Newgate is of this ward.

Now for the south side of this ward, beginning again at the cross in Cheape, from thence to Friday street, and down that street on the west side, till over against the north-west corner of St. Matthew's church; and on the west side, to the south corner of the said church, which is wholly in the ward of Faringdon. This church hath these few monuments: Thomas Pole, goldsmith, 1395; Robert Johnson, goldsmith, alderman; John Twiselton, goldsmith, alderman, 1525; Ralph Allen, grocer, one of the sheriffs, deceased 1546; Anthony Gamage, ironmonger, one of the sheriffs, deceased 1579; Anthony Cage; John Mabbe, chamberlain of London, etc. Allen at Condit, and Thomas Warlingworth, founded a chantry there. Sir Nicholas Twiford, goldsmith, mayor, gave to that church a house, with the appurtenances, called the Griffon on the Hope, in the same street.[1]

From this Friday street, west to the Old Exchange, a street so called of the king's exchange there kept, which was for the receipt of bullion to be coined. For Henry III., in the 6th of his reign, wrote to the Scabines and men of Ipre, that he and his council had given prohibition, that none, Englishmen or other, should make change of plate or other mass of silver, but only in his Exchange at London, or at Canterbury. Andrew Buckerell then had to farm the Exchange of England, and was mayor of London in the reign of Henry III. John Somercote had the keeping of the king's Exchange over all England. In the 8th of Edward I., Gregory Rockesly was keeper of the said Exchange for the king. In the 5th of Edward II., William Hausted was keeper thereof; and in the 18th, Roger de Frowicke, etc.

These received the old stamps, or coining-irons, from time to time, as the same were worn, and delivered new to all the mints in London, as more at large in another place I have noted.

This street beginneth by West Cheape in the north, and runneth down south to Knightriders street; that part thereof which is called Old Fish street, but the very housing and office of the Exchange and coinage was about the midst thereof, south from the east gate that entereth Paules churchyard, and on the west side in Baynard's castle ward.

On the east side of this lane, betwixt West Cheape and the church of St. Augustine, Henry Walles, mayor (by license of Edward I.), built one row of houses, the profits rising of them to be employed on London bridge.

The parish church of St. Augustine, and one house next adjoining in Watheling street, is of this ward called Faringdon. This is a fair church, and lately well repaired, wherein be monuments remaining—of H. Reade, armourer, one of the sheriffs 1450; Robert Bellesdon, haberdasher, mayor 1491; Sir Townley William Dere, one of the sheriffs 1450; Robert Raven, haber-

---

[1] In the first edition, Sir Nicholas Twiford is described as having a monument in the church.

dasher, 1500; Thomas Apleyard, gentleman, 1515; William Moncaster, merchant-tailor, 1524; William Holte, merchant-tailor, 1544, etc.

Then is the north churchyard of Paules, in the which standeth the cathedral church, first founded by Ethelbert, king of Kent, about the year of Christ 610: he gave thereto lands as appeareth:

" *Ædelbertus Rex, Deo inspirante, pro animæ suæ remedio dedit episcopo Melito terram quæ appellatur Tillingeham ad monasterii sui solatium, scilicet monasterium Sancti Pauli : et ego Rex Æthelbertus ita firmiter concedo tibi presuli Melito potestatem ejus habendi & possidendi ut in perpetuum in monasterii utilitate permaneat,"* etc. Athelstan, Edgar, Edward the Confessor, and others, also gave lands thereunto. William the Conqueror gave to the church of St. Paule, and to Mauricius, then bishop, and his successors, the castle of Stortford, with the appurtenances, etc. He also confirmed the gifts of his predecessors in these words: " *W. Rex Angl. concedo Deo et S. Paulo in perpetuum,* 24 *Hidas quas Rex Æthelbert dedit S. Paulo juxta London,"* etc. The charter of King William the Conqueror, exemplified in the Tower, englished thus:

" William, by the grace of God, king of Englishmen, to all his welbeloued French and English people, greeting: Know ye that I do giue vnto God and the church of S. Paule of London, and to the rectors and seruitors of the same, in all their lands which the church hath, or shall have, within borough and without, sack and sock, thole and theam, infangthefe and grithbriche, and all freeships, by strand and by land, on tide and off tide, and all the rights that into them christendome byrath, on morth sprake, and on unright hamed, and on unright work, of all that bishoprick on mine land, and on each other man's land. For I will that the church in all things be as free as I would my soul to be in the day of judgement. Witnesses: Osmund, our Chancellor; Lanfrank, the Archbishop of Canterbury; and T. Archbishop of York; Roger, Earle of Shrewesbury; Alane, the county; Geffrey de Magnavilla; and Ralph Peuerel."

In the year 1087, this church of St. Paule was burnt with fire, and therewith the most part of the city; which fire began at the entry of the west gate, and consumed the east gate. Mauricius the bishop began therefore the foundation of a new church of St. Paule, a work that men of that time judged would never have been finished, it was to them so wonderful for length and breadth; and also the same was built upon arches (or vaults) of stone, for defence of fire, which was a manner of work before that time unknown to the people of this nation, and then brought in by the French; and the stone was fetched from Caen in Normandy.

This Mauricius deceased in the year 1107. Richard Beamor succeeded him in the bishopric, who did wonderfully increase the said church, purchasing of his own cost the large streets and lanes about it, wherein were wont to dwell many lay people; which ground he began to compass about with a strong wall of stone and gates. King Henry I. gave to the said Richard so much of the moat (or wall) of the castle, on the Thames side, to the south, as should be needful to make the said wall of the church, and so much as should suffice to make a wall without the way on the north side, etc.

It should seem that this Richard inclosed but two sides of the said church or cemetery of St. Paule, to wit, the south and north side; for King Edward II., in the 10th of his reign, granted that the said churchyard should be inclosed with a wall where it wanted, for the murders and robberies that were there committed. But the citizens then claimed the east part of the churchyard to be the place of assembly to their folkemotes, and that the great steeple there situate was to that use, their common bell, which being there rung, all the inhabitants of the city might hear and come together. They also claimed the west side, that they might there assemble themselves together, with the lord of Baynard's castle, for view of their armour, in defence of the city. This matter was in the Tower of London referred to Harvius de Stanton, and his fellow justices itinerants; but I find not the decision or judgment of that controversy.

True it is, that Edward III., in the 17th of his reign, gave commandment for the finishing of that wall, which was then performed, and to this day it continueth; although now on both the sides (to wit, within and without) it be hidden with dwelling-houses. Richard Beamer deceased in the year 1127, and his successors in process of time performed the work begun.

The steeple of this church was built and finished in the year 1222; the cross on the said steeple fell down, and a new was set up in the year 1314. The new work of Pauls (so called) at the east end above the choir, was begun in the year 1251.

Henry Lacy, Earl of Lincoln, constable of Chester, and custos of England, in his time was a great benefactor to this work, and was there buried in the year 1310. Also Ralph Baldocke, Bishop of London, in his lifetime gave two hundred marks to the building of the said new work, and left much by his testament towards the finishing thereof: he deceased in the year 1313, and was buried in the Lady chapel. Also the new work of Paules, to wit, the cross aisles, were begun to be new built in the year 1256.

The 1st of February, in the year 1444, about two of the clock in the afternoon, the steeple of Paules was fired by lightning, in the midst of the shaft or spire, both on the west side and on the south; but by labour of many well-disposed people the same to appearance was quenched with vinegar, so that all men withdrew themselves to their houses, praising God; but between eight and nine of the clock in the same night the fire burst out again more fervently than before, and did much hurt to the lead and timber, till by the great labour of the mayor and people that came thither, it was thoroughly quenched.

This steeple was repaired in the year 1462, and the weathercock again erected. Robert Godwin winding it up, the rope brake, and he was destroyed on the pinnacles, and the cock was sore bruised; but Burchwood (the king's plumber) set it up again: since the which time, needing reparation, it was both taken down and set up in the year 1553; at which time it was found to be of copper, gilt over; and the length from the bill to the tail being four feet, and the breadth over the wings three feet and a half, it weighed forty pounds; the cross from the bowl to the eagle (or cock) was fifteen feet and six inches, of assize; the length thereof overthwart was five feet and ten inches, and the compass of the bowl was nine feet and one inch.

The inner body of this cross was oak, the next cover was lead, and the uttermost was of copper, red varnished. The bowl and eagle, or cock, were of copper, and gilt also.

The height of the steeple was five hundred and twenty feet, whereof the stone-work is two hundred and sixty feet, and the spire was likewise two hundred and sixty feet: the length of the whole church is two hundred and forty tailors' yards, which make seven hundred and twenty feet; the breadth thereof is one hundred and thirty feet, and the height of the body of that church is one hundred and fifty feet. This church hath a bishop, a dean, a precentor, chancellor, treasurer, and five archdeacons; to wit, of London, Middlesex, Essex, Colchester, and St. Albans: it hath prebendaries thirty, canons twelve, vicars choral six, etc.

The college of petty canons there was founded by King Richard II. in honour of Queen Anne his wife, and of her progenitors, in the 17th of his reign. Their hall and lands were then given unto them, as appeareth by the patent; Master Robert Dokesworth then being master thereof. In the year 1408, the petty canons then building their college, the mayor and commonalty granted them their water-courses, and other easements.

There was also one great cloister, on the north side of this church, environing a plot of ground, of old time called Pardon churchyard; whereof Thomas More, dean of Paules, was either the first builder, or a most especial benefactor, and was buried there. About this cloister was artificially and richly painted the Dance of Machabray, or Dance of Death, commonly called the Dance of Paul's; the like whereof was painted about St. Innocent's cloister at Paris, in France. The metres, or poesy of this dance, were translated out of French into English by John Lidgate, monk of Bury,[1] and with the picture of death leading all estates, painted about the cloister, at the special request and at the dispence of Jenken Carpenter, in the reign of Henry VI. In this cloister were buried many persons, some of worship, and others of honour; the monuments of whom, in number and curious workmanship, passed all other that were in that church.

Over the east quadrant of this cloister was a fair library, built at the costs and charges of Walter Sherington, chancellor of the duchy of Lancaster, in the reign of Henry VI., which hath been well furnished with fair written books in vellum, but few of them now do remain there. In the midst of this Pardon churchyard was also a fair chapel, first founded by Gilbert Becket, port-grave and principal magistrate of this city, in the reign of King Stephen, who was there buried.

Thomas Moore, dean of Paul's before named, re-edified or new built this chapel, and founded three chaplains there, in the reign of Henry V.

In the year 1549, on the 10th of April, the said chapel, by commandment of the Duke of Somerset, was begun to be pulled down, with the whole cloister, the Dance of Death, the tombs and monuments; so that nothing thereof was left but the bare plot of ground, which is since converted into a garden for the petty canons. There was also a chapel at the north door of Paules, founded by the same Walter Sherrington, by license of Henry VI., for two, three, or four chaplains, endowed with forty

---

[1] Lydgate's verses were first printed at the end of Tottell's edition of the translation of his *Fall of Princes*, from Boccaccio, 1554, folio, and afterwards in Sir W. Dugdale's *History of St. Paul's Cathedral*.

pounds, by the year. This chapel also was pulled down in the reign of Edward VI., and in place thereof a fair house built.

There was furthermore a fair chapel of the Holy Ghost in Paules church, on the north side, founded in the year 1400 by Roger Holmes, chancellor and prebendary of Paules, for Adam Berie, alderman, mayor of London 1364, John Wingham and others, for seven chaplains, and called Holme's college. Their common hall was in Paul's churchyard, on the south side, near unto a carpenter's yard. This college was, with others, suppressed in the reign of Edward VI. Then under the choir of Paules is a large chapel, first dedicated to the name of Jesu, founded, or rather confirmed, the 37th of Henry VI., as appeareth by his patent thereof, dated at Croydone, to this effect: "Many liege men, and Christian people, having begun a fraternitie and guild, to the honour of the most glorious name of Jesus Christ our Saviour, in a place called the Crowdes of the cathedrall church of Paul's in London, which hath continued long time peaceably till now of late; whereupon they have made request, and we have taken upon us the name and charge of the foundation, to the laud of Almightie God, the Father, the Sonne, and the Holy Ghost, and especially to the honour of Jesu, in whose honour the fraternitie was begun," etc.

The king ordained William Say, then dean of Paules, to be the rector, and Richard Ford (a remembrancer in the Exchequer), and Henry Bennis (clerk of his privy seal), the guardians of those brothers and sisters; they and their successors to have a common seal, license to purchase lands or tenements to the value of forty pounds by the year, etc.

This foundation was confirmed by Henry VII., the 22nd of his reign, to Doctor Collet, then dean of Paules, rector there, etc.; and by Henry VIII., the 27th of his reign, to Richard Pace, then dean of Paules, etc.

At the west end of this Jesus chapel, under the choir of Paules, also was a parish church of St. Faith, commonly called St. Faith under Paul's, which served for the stationers and others dwelling in Paule's churchyard, Paternoster row, and the places near adjoining. The said chapel of Jesus being suppressed in the reign of Edward VI., the parishioners of St. Faith's church were removed into the same, as to a place more sufficient for largeness and lightsomeness, in the year 1551, and so it remaineth.

Then was there on the north side of this churchyard a large charnel house for the bones of the dead, and over it a chapel of an old foundation, such as followeth. In the year 1282, the

10th of Edward I., it was agreed, that Henry Walles, mayor, and the citizens, for the cause of shops by them built, without the wall of the churchyard, should assign to God and to the church of St. Paul ten marks of rent by the year for ever, towards the new building of a chapel of the Blessed Virgin Mary, and also to assign five marks of yearly rent to a chaplain to celebrate there.

Moreover, in the year 1430, the 8th of Henry VI., license was granted to Jenkin Carpenter (executor to Richard Whittington) to establish upon the said charnel a chaplain, to have eight marks by the year. Then was also in this chapel two brother-hoods. In this chapel were buried Robert Barton, Henry Barton, mayor, and Thomas Mirfin, mayor, all skinners, and were entombed with their images of alabaster over them, grated or coped about with iron before the said chapel, all which were pulled down in the year 1549: the bones of the dead, couched up in a charnel under the chapel, were conveyed from thence into Finsbery field (by report of him who paid for the carriage [1]), amounting to more than one thousand cart-loads, and there laid on a moorish ground; in short space after raised, by soilage of the city upon them, to bear three windmills. The chapel and charnel were converted into dwelling-houses, warehouses, and sheds before them, for stationers, in place of the tombs.

In the east part of this churchyard standeth Paules school, lately new built, and endowed in the year 1512 by John Collet, doctor of divinity and dean of Paules, for one hundred and fifty-three poor men's children, to be taught free in the same school; for which he appointed a master, a surmaster, or usher, and a chaplain, with large stipends for ever, committing the oversight thereof to the masters, wardens, and assistants of the mercers in London, because he was [2] son to Henry Collet, mercer, sometime mayor. He left to these mercers lands to the yearly value of one hundred and twenty pounds, or better.

Near unto this school, on the north side thereof, was of old time a great and high clochier, or bell-house, four square, built of stone, and in the same a most strong frame of timber, with four bells, the greatest that I have heard; these were called Jesus' bells, and belonged to Jesus' chapel, but I know not by whose gift: the same had a great spire of timber covered with lead, with the image of St. Paul on the top, but was pulled down by Sir Miles Partridge, knight, in the reign of Henry VIII. **The**

[1] Reign Wolfe.
[2] " Born in London, and son to Henry Collet."—*1st edition*, p. 267.

common speech then was, that he did set a hundred pounds upon a cast at dice against it, and so won the said clochiard and bells of the king; and then causing the bells to be broken as they hung, the rest was pulled down. This man was afterward executed on the Tower hill for matters concerning the Duke of Somerset, the 5th of Edward VI.

In place of this clochiard, of old times the common bell of the city was used to be rung for the assembly of the citizens to their folke motes, as I have before showed.

About the midst of this churchyard is a pulpit cross of timber, mounted upon steps of stone, and covered with lead, in which are sermons preached by learned divines every Sunday in the forenoon; the very antiquity of which cross is to me unknown. I read, that in the year 1259, King Henry III. commanded a general assembly to be made at this cross, where he in proper person commanded the mayor, that on the next day following, he should cause to be sworn before the alderman every stripling of twelve years of age or upward, to be true to the king and his heirs, kings of England. Also, in the year 1262, the same king caused to be read at Paul's cross a bull, obtained from Pope Urban IV., as an absolution for him, and for all that were sworn to maintain the articles made in parliament at Oxford. Also in the year 1299, the dean of Paules accursed at Paules cross all those which had searched in the church of St. Martin in the Field for a hoard of gold, etc. This pulpit cross was by tempest of lightning and thunder defaced. Thomas Kempe, Bishop of London, new built it in form as it now standeth.

In the year 1561, the 4th of June, betwixt the hours of three and four of the clock in the afternoon, the great spire of the steeple of St. Paule's church was fired by lightning, which brake forth (as it seemed) two or three yards beneath the foot of the cross; and from thence it went downward the spire to the battlements, stone-work, and bells, so furiously, that within the space of four hours the same steeple, with all the roofs of the church, were consumed, to the great sorrow and perpetual remembrance of the beholders. After this mischance, the queen's majesty directed her letters to the mayor, willing him to take order for the speedy repairing of the same: and she, of her gracious disposition, for the furtherance thereof, did presently give and deliver in gold one thousand marks, with a warrant for a thousand loads of timber, to be taken out of her woods or elsewhere.

The citizens also gave first a great benevolence, and after

that three fifteens, to be speedily paid. The clergy of England likewise, within the province of Canterbury, granted the fortieth part of the value of their benefices, charged with first fruits, the thirtieth part of such as were not so charged; but the clergy of London diocese granted the thirtieth part of all that paid first fruits, and the twentieth part of such as had paid their fruits.

Six citizens of London, and two petty canons of Paules church, had charge to further and oversee the work, wherein such expedition was used, that within one month next following the burning thereof, the church was covered with boards and lead, in manner of a false roof, against the weather; and before the end of the said year, all the said aisles of the church were framed out of new timber, covered with lead, and fully finished. The same year also the great roofs of the west and east ends were framed out of great timber in Yorkshire, brought thence to London by sea, and set up and covered with lead; the north and south ends were framed of timber, and covered with lead, before April 1566. Concerning the steeple, divers models were devised and made, but little else was done, through whose default, God knoweth; it was said that the money appointed for new building of the steeple was collected.[1]

Monuments in this church be these: first, as I read, of Erkenwalde, Bishop of London, buried in the old church about the year of Christ 700, whose body was translated into the new work in the year 1140, being richly shrined above the choir behind the high altar.

Sebba, or Seba, King of the East Saxons, first buried in the old church, since removed into the new, and laid in a coffin of stone, on the north side without the choirs; Ethelred, King of the West Saxons, was likewise buried and removed; William Norman, Bishop of London in the reigns of Edward the Confessor and of William the Conqueror, deceased 1070, and is new buried in the body of the church, with an epitaph, as in my *Summary* I have shown; Eustauchius de Fauconbridge, Bishop of London, 1228, buried in the south isle above the choir; Martin Pateshull, Dean of Powle's, 1239; W. Havarhul, canon; the king's treasurer, Hugh Pateshull, 1240; Roger Nigar, Bishop of London, 1241, buried in the north side of the choir; Fulco Basset, Bishop of London, 1259, and his brother, Philip Basset, knight, 1261; Henry Wingham, Bishop of London, buried in

[1] " And brought to the hands of Edmond Grendall, then Bishop of London."—*1st edition*, p. 269.

the south aisle above the choir, 1262; Geffrey de Arca, chaplain in the chapel of St. James, under the rood at north door, 1264; Alexander de Swarford, 1273; John Grantham, 1273; John Braynford, and Richard Umframuile, 1275; Roger de Iale, Archdeacon of Essex, 1280; Ralph Donion, canon, 1382; Godfrey S. Donstan, 1274; Fulke Lovell, 1298; William Harworth, clerk, 1302; Reginald Brandon, in the new Lady chapel, 1305; Richard Newporte, Archdeacon of Middlesex, 1309; Henry Lacie, Earl of Lincolne, in the new work of Paules betwixt the Lady chapel and St. Dunston's chapel, where a fair monument was raised for him, with his picture in armour, cross-legged, as one professed for defence of the Holy Land against the infidels, 1310, his monument is foully defaced; Ralph Baldoke, Bishop of London, 1313, in the said Lady chapel, whereof he was founder.

Some have noted,[1] that in digging the foundation of this new work, namely of a chapel on the south side of Paule's church, there were found more than a hundred scalps of oxen or kine, in the year 1316; which thing (say they) confirmed greatly the opinion of those which have reported, that of old time there had been a temple of Jupiter, and that there was daily sacrifice of beasts.

Othersome, both wise and learned, have thought the buck's head, borne before the procession of Paule's on St. Paul's day, to signify the like. But true it is, I have read an ancient deed to this effect.

Sir William Baud, knight, the 3rd of Edward I., in the year 1274, on Candlemas day, granted to Harvy de Borham, dean of Powle's, and to the chapter there, that in consideration of twenty-two acres of ground or land, by them granted, within their manor of Westley in Essex, to be inclosed into his park of Curingham, he would for ever, upon the feast day of the Conversion of St. Paul in winter, give unto them a good doe, seasonable and sweet, and upon the feast of the commemoration of St. Paul in summer, a good buck, and offer the same upon the high altar; the same to be spent amongst the canons residents. The doe to be brought by one man at the hour of procession, and through the procession to the high altar; and the bringer to have nothing: the buck to be brought by all his men in like manner, and they to have paid unto them by the chamberlain of the church twelve pence only, and no more to be required. This grant he made, and for performance bound

1 W. Paston. [*See* Bibliography.]

the lands of him and his heirs to be distrained on; and if the lands should be evicted, that yet he and his heirs should accomplish the gift. Witnesses: Richard Tilberie, William de Wockendon, Richard de Harlowe, knights, Peter of Stanforde, Thomas of Waldon, and some others.

Sir Walter Baude, son to William, confirmed this gift, in the 30th of the said king, and the witnesses thereunto were Nicholas de Wokendon, Richard de Rokeley, Thomas de Mandevile, John de Rochford, knights, Richard de Broniford, William de Markes, William de Fulham, and other. Thus much for the grant.

Now what I have heard by report, and have partly seen, it followeth. On the feast day of the commemoration of St. Paul, the buck being brought up to the steps of the high altar in Paul's church, at the hour of procession, the dean and chapter being apparelled in copes and vestments, with garlands of roses on their heads, they sent the body of the buck to baking, and had the head fixed on a pole, borne before the cross in their procession, until they issued out of the west door, where the keeper that brought it blowed the death of the buck, and then the horners that were about the city presently answered him in like manner; for the which pains they had each one of the dean and chapter, four pence in money, and their dinner, and the keeper that brought it, was allowed during his abode there, for that service, meat, drink, and lodging, at the dean and chapter's charges, and five shillings in money at his going away, together with a loaf of bread, having the picture of St. Paul upon it, etc.

There was belonging to the church of St. Paul, for both the days, two special suits of vestments, the one embroidered with bucks, the other with does, both given by the said Bauds (as I have heard). Thus much for the matter. Now to the residue of the monuments:—Sir Ralph Hingham, chief justice of both Benches successively, buried in the side of the north walk against the choir, 1308; Henry Guildford, clerk at the altar of the Apostles, 1313; Richard Newport, Bishop of London, 1318; William Chateslehunt, canon, in the new work, 1321, had a chantry there, Sir Nicholas Wokenden, knight, at the altar of St. Thomas in the new work, 1323; John Cheshull, Bishop of London, 1279; Roger Waltham, canon, 1325; Hamo Chikewell, six times mayor of London, 1328; Robert Monden, and John Monden his brother, canons, in the new work, 1332; Walter Thorpe, canon, in the new work, 1333;

John Fable, 1334; James Fisil, chaplain, 1341; William Mel-
ford, Archdeacon of Colchester, 1345; Richard de Placeto,
Archdeacon of Colchester, 1345, before St. Thomas' chapel;
Geffrey Eton, canon, 1345; Nicholas Husband, canon, 1347;
Sir John Poultney, mayor 1348, in a fair chapel by him built
on the north side of Paule's, wherein he founded three chaplains;
William Eversden, canon, in the crowds, 1349; Alan Hotham,
canon, in the new crowds, 1351; Henry Etesworth, under the
rood at north door, 1353; John Beauchampe, constable of
Dover, warden of the ports, knight of the Garter, son to Guy
Beauchampe, Earl of Warwick, and brother to Thomas Earl of
Warwick, in the body of the church, on the south side, 1358,
where a proper chapel and fair monument remaineth of him;
he is by ignorant people misnamed to be Humfrey, Duke of
Glocester, who lieth honourably buried at St. Albon's, twenty
miles from London, and therefore such as merrily or simply
profess themselves to serve Duke Humfrey in Paule's, are to be
punished here, and sent to St. Albon's, there again to be punished
for their absence from their lord and master, as they call him;
Michael Norborow, Bishop of London, 1361; Walter Nele,
blader, and Avis his wife, 1361; Gilbert Brewer, dean of Paule's,
1366; Richard Wendover, 1366; John Hiltoft, goldsmith, and
Alice his wife, in the new works, St. Dunston's chapel, 1368;
Adam de Bery, mayor in the year 1364, buried in a chapel of
St. Mary Magdalen, or of the Holy Ghost, called Holmes'
college, behind the rood at the north door of Paul's, 1390;
Roger Holmes, chancellor and prebend of Paul's, was buried
there 1400; John of Gaunt, Duke of Lancaster, 1399, buried on
the north side the choir, beside Blanch his first wife, who
deceased 1368; Sir Richard Burley, knight of the Garter, under
a fair monument in the side of the north walk against the choir,
a chantry was there founded for him, 1409; Beatrix his wife,
after his death, married to Thomas Lord Rouse, was buried
in the chapel of St. John Baptist (or Poultney's chapel) near
the north door of Paule's, 1409; Thomas Evers, dean of Paule's,
in St. Thomas' chapel, the new work, 1411; Thomas More, dean
of Paule's, in the chapel of St. Anne and St. Thomas, by him
new built in Pardon churchyard, 1419; Thomas Ston, dean of
Paule's, by the tomb of John Beauchampe, 1423; the Duchess
of Bedford, sister to Philip Duke of Burgoyne, 1433; Robert
Fitzhugh, Bishop of London, in the choir, 1435; Walter Sherington, in a chapel without the north door by him built, 1457;
John Drayton, goldsmith, in Alhallowes chapel, 1456; William

Say, dean of Paul's, in the Crowds, or Jesus' chapel, 1468; Margaret, Countess of Shrewsbury, in the Crowds, or Jesus' chapel, as appeareth by an inscription on a pillar there. [*See* Additional Notes.]

Here before the image of Jesu lieth the worshipful and right noble lady, Margaret Countess of Shrewsbury, late wife of the true and victorious knight and redoubtable warrior, John Talbot, Earl of Shrewsbury, which worship died in Guien for the right of this land. The first daughter, and one of the heirs of the right famous and renowned knight, Richard Beauchamp, late Earl of Warwick, which died in Rouen, and Dame Elizabeth his wife, the which Elizabeth was daughter and heir to Thomas, late Lord Berkeley, on his side, and of her mother's side, Lady Lisle and Tyes, which countess passed from this world the 14th day of June, in the year of our Lord 1468, on whose soul Jesu have mercy. Amen.

John Wenlocke, by his last will, dated 1477, appointed there should be dispended upon a mounment over the Lady of Shrewsbury where she is buried afore Jesus, one hundred pounds. He left Sir Humfrey Talbot his supervisor. This Sir Humfrey Talbot, knight, lord marshal of the town of Calais, made his will the year 1492. He was younger son of John Earl of Shrewsbury, and Margaret his wife; he appointed a stone to be put in a pillar before the grave of his lady mother in Paul's, of his portraiture and arms, according to the will of John Wenlocke, but for want of room and lightsomeness in that place, it was concluded, the image of Jesus to be curiously painted on the wall of Paul's church, over the door that entereth into the said chapel of Jesus, and the portraiture also of the said Lady Margaret, Countess of Shrewsbury, kneeling in her mantle of arms, with her progeny; all which was so performed, and remaineth till this day.

In the chapel of Jesus, Thomas Dowcrey, William Lambe, 1578, and many other, have been interred; John of London, under the north rood, 1266; John Lovell, clerk; John Romane; John of St. Olave; Waltar Bloxley; Sir Alen Boxhull, knight of the Garter, constable of the Tower, custos of the forest and park of Clarendon, the forest of Brokholt, Grovell, and Melchet, buried beside St. Erkenwald's shrine, and of later time Thomas Kempe, Bishop of London, in a proper chapel of the Trinity by him founded in the body of the church, on the north side, 1489; Thomas Linacre, doctor of physic; John Collet, dean of Paule's, on the south side without the choir, 1519; John Dowman, canon of Paule's, 1525; Richard Fitz-James, Bishop of

London, hard beneath the north-west pillar of Paule's steeple, under a fair tomb, and a chapel of St. Paul, built of timber, with stairs mounting thereunto over his tomb, of grey marble, 1521. His chapel was burned by fire falling from the steeple, his tomb was taken thence. John Stokesley, Bishop of London, in our Lady chapel, 1539; John Nevill, Lord Latimer, in a chapel by the north door of Paule's, about 1542; Sir John Mason, knight, in the north walk, against the choir, 1566; William Herbert, Earl of Pembroke, knight of the Garter, on the north side of the choir, 1569; Sir Nicholas Bacon, lord-keeper of the great seal, on the south side of the choir, 1578; Sir Philip Sidney, above the choir on the north side, 1586; Sir Frances Walsingham, knight, principal secretary, and chancellor of the duchy of Lancaster, 1590; Sir Christopher Hatton, lord chancellor of England, knight of the Garter, above the choir, 1591, under a most sumptuous monument, where a merry poet wrote thus:—

> " Philip and Francis have no tombe,
> For *great* Christopher takes all the roome."

John Elmer, Bishop of London, before St. Thomas' chapel, 1594; the Lady Heneage, and her husband, Sir Thomas Heneage, chancellor of the duchy, 1595; Richard Fletcher, Bishop of London, 1596. These, as the chief, have I noted to be buried there.

Without the north gate of Paule's church from the end of the Old Exchange, west up Paternoster row, by the two lanes out of Paule's church, the first out of the cross aisle of Paule's, the other out of the body of the church, about the midst thereof, and so west to the Golden Lion, be all of this ward, as is aforesaid. The houses in this street, from the first north gate of Paule's churchyard unto the next gate, was first built without the wall of the churchyard, by Henry Walles, mayor in the year 1282. The rents of those houses go to the maintenance of London bridge. This street is now called Pater Noster row, because of stationers or text writers that dwelt there, who wrote and sold all sorts of books then in use, namely, A. B. C. with the Pater Noster, Ave, Creed, Graces, etc.

There dwelt also turners of beads, and they were called Pater Noster makers, as I read in a record of one Robert Nikke, Pater Noster maker, and citizen, in the reign of Henry IV., and so of other. At the end of Pater Noster row is Ave Mary lane, so called upon the like occasion of text writers and bead makers then dwelling there; and at the end of that lane is likewise Creede lane, late so called, but sometime Spurrier row, of spurriers dwelling there; and Amen lane is added thereunto betwixt the south end of Warwicke lane and the north end of Ave Mary lane. At the north end of Ave Mary lane is one great house, built of stone and timber, of old time pertaining to John Duke of Britaine, Earl of Richmond, as appeareth by the records of Edward II., since that, it is called Pembrook's inn, near unto Ludgate, as belonging to the earls of Pembrook, in the times of Richard II., the 18th year, and of Henry VI., the 14th year. It is now called Burgaveny house, and belongeth to Henry, late Lord of Burgaveny.

Betwixt the south end of Ave Mary lane, and the north end of Creed lane, is the coming out of Paule's church yard on the east, and the high street on the west, towards Ludgate, and this is called Bowyer row, of bowyers dwelling there in old time, now worn out by mercers and others. In this street, on the north side, is the parish church of St. Martin, a proper church, and lately new built; for in the year 1437, John Michael, mayor, and the commonalty, granted to William Downe, parson of St. Martin's at Ludgate, a parcel of ground, containing in length twenty-eight feet, and in breadth four feet, to set and build their steeple upon, etc. The monuments here have been of William Sevenoake, mayor 1418; Henry Belwase and John Gest, 1458; William Taverner, gentleman, 1466; John Barton, esquire, 1439; Stephen Peacock, mayor 1533; Sir Roger Cholmley, John Went, and Roger Paine, had chantries there.

On the south side of this street is the turning into the Black Friers, which order sometime had their houses in Old borne, where they remained for the space of fifty-five years, and then in the year 1276, Gregorie Roksley, mayor, and the barons of this city, granted and gave to Robert Kilwarby, Archbishop of Canterbury, two lanes or ways next the street of Baynard's castle, and also the tower of Mountfitchit, to be destroyed; in place of which the said Robert built the late new church of the Black Friers, and placed them therein. King Edward I., and Elianor his wife, were great benefactors thereunto. This was a large church, and richly furnished with ornaments, wherein divers parliaments, and other great meetings, hath been holden; namely, in the year 1450, the 28th of Henry VI., a parliament was begun at Westminster, and adjourned to the Black Friers in London, and from thence to Leycester. In the year 1522, the Emperor Charles V. was lodged there. In the year 1524, the 15th of April, a parliament was begun at the Black Friers, wherein was demanded a subsidy of eight hundred thousand pounds to be raised of goods and lands, four shillings in every pound, and in the end was granted two shillings of the pound of goods or lands that were worth twenty pounds, or might dispend twenty pounds by the year, and so upward, to be paid in two years. This parliament was adjourned to Westminster amongst the black monks, and ended in the king's palace there, the 14th of August, at nine of the clock in the night, and was therefore called the Black parliament. In the year 1529, Cardinal Campeius, the legate, with Cardinal Woolsey, sat at the said Black Friars, where before them, as legates and judges, was brought in question the king's marriage with Queen Katherine, as unlawful, before whom the king and queen were cited and summoned to appear, etc. whereof more at large in my *Annals* I have touched.

The same year, in the month of October, began a parliament in the Black Friers, in the which Cardinal Woolsey was condemned in the premunire; this house, valued at £104 15s. 5d., was surrendered the 12th of November, the 30th of Henry VIII. There were buried in this church, Margaret Queen of Scots; Hubert de Burgh, Earl of Kent, translated from their old church by Oldborne; Robert de Attabeto, Earl of Bellimon; Dame Isabel, wife to Sir Roger Bygot, earl marshal; William and Jane Huse, children to Dame Ellis, Countess of Arundell; and by them lieth Dame Ellis, daughter to the Earl Warren, and after Countess of Arundell; Dame Ide, wife to Sir Waltar ——, daughter to Ferrers of Chartley; Richard de Brewes; Richard Strange, son to Roger Strange; Elizabeth, daughter to Sir Barthol. Badlesmere, wife to Sir William Bohun, Earl of Northampton; Marsh; the Earls of Marsh and Hereford; and Elizabeth Countess of Arundell; Dame Joan, daughter to Sir John Carne, first wife to Sir Gwide Brian; Hugh Clare, knight, 1295; the heart of Queen Helianor, the foundress; the heart of Alfonce, her son; the hearts of John and Margaret, children to W. Valence; Sir William Thorpe, justice; the Lord Lioth of Ireland; Maude, wife to Geffrey Say, daughter to the Earl of Warwick; Dame Sible, daughter to Wil. Pattehulle, wife to Roger Beauchampe; and by her Sir Richard or Roger Beauchampe; Lord St. Amand, and Dame Elizabeth his wife, daughter to the Duke of Lancaster; Sir Stephen Collington, knight; Sir William Peter, knight; the Countess of Huntington; Duchess of Excester, 1425; Sir John Cornwall; Lord Fanhope, died at Amphill in Bedfordshire, and was buried here in 1443; Sir John Triptoste, Earl of Worcester, beheaded 1470; and by him in his chapel, James Tuochet Lord Audley, beheaded 1497; William Paston, and Anne, daughter to Edmond Lancaster; the Lord Beamount; Sir Edmond Cornewall, Baron of Burford; the Lady Nevell, wedded to Lord Dowglas, daughter to the Duke of Excester; Richard Scrope, esquire; Dame Katheren Vaux, *alias* Cobham; Sir Thomas Browne, and Dame Elizabeth his wife; Jane Powell; Thomas Swinforth; John Mawsley, esquire, 1432; John De la Bere, Nicholas Eare, Geffrey Spring, William Clifford, esquires; Sir Thomas Brandon, knight of the Garter, 1509; William Stalworth, merchant-tailor, 1518; William Courtney, Earl of Devonshire nominate, but not created, the 3rd of Henry VIII., etc.

There is a parish of St. Anne within the precinct of the Black Friers, which was pulled down with the Friers' church, by Sir Thomas Carden; but in the reign of Queen Mary, he being forced to find a church to the inhabitants, allowed them a lodging chamber above a stair, which since that time, to wit, in the year 1597, fell down, and was again by collection therefore made, new built and enlarged in the same year, and was dedicated on the 11th of December.

Now to turn again out of the Black Friers through Bowyer row, Ave Mary lane, and Pater Noster row, to the church of St. Michael *ad Bladum*, or at the corne (corruptly at the querne), so called, because in place thereof was sometime a corn market, stretching by west to the shambles. It seemeth that the church was new built [1] about the reign of Edward III. Thomas Newton, first parson there, was buried in the choir the year 1461. At the east end of this church stood a cross, called the old cross in West Cheape, which was taken down in the year 1390; since the which time the said parish church was also taken down, but new built and enlarged in the year 1430, the 8th of Henry VI. William Eastfield, mayor, and the commonalty, granted of the common soil of the city three feet and a half in breadth on the north part, and four feet in breadth toward the east. This is now a proper church, and hath the monuments of Thomas Newton, first parson; Roger Woodcocke, hatter, 1475; Thomas Rossel, brewer, 1473; John Hulton, stationer, 1475; John Oxney; Roger North, merchant-haberdasher, 1509; John

---

[1] " Was first builded about the reigne of Edward III. Thomas Newton, the first parson there, was buried in the quire, the year 1361, which was the 35th of Edward the Thirde."—*1st edition*, p. 277.

Leiland, the famous antiquary; Henry Pranell, vintner, one of
the sheriffs 1585; William Erkin, one of the sheriffs 1586;
Thomas Bankes, barber-chirurgeon, 1598, etc.   John Mundham
had a chantry there in the reign of Edward II.

At the east end of this church, in place of the old cross, is now
a water-conduit placed.   W. Eastfield, mayor the 9th of Henry
VI., at the request of divers common councils, granted it so to be;
whereupon, in the 19th of the same Henry, one thousand marks
were granted by a common council towards the works of this
conduit, and the reparations of other: this is called the little
conduit in West Cheape by Paule's gate.   At the west end of
this parish church is a small passage for people on foot through
the same church; and west from the said church, some distance,
is another passage out of Pater Noster row, and is called, of
such a sign, Panyar alley, which cometh out into the north over
against St. Martin's lane.   Next is Ivie lane, so called of ivy
growing on the walls of the prebend [1] houses; but now the lane
is replenished on both sides with fair houses, and divers offices
be there kept by registers, namely, for the Prerogative Court
of the Archbishop of Canterbury, the probate of wills, and for
the lord treasurer's remembrance of the exchequer, etc.

This lane runneth north to the west end of St. Nicholas
shambles.   Of old time was one great house sometimes belonging
to the Earls of Britain, since that to the Lovels, and was called
Lovels' inn; for Mathild, wife to John Lovell, held it in the
1st of Henry VI.   Then is Eldenese lane, which stretcheth
north to the high street of Newgate market; the same is now
called Warwicke lane, of an ancient house there built by an
Earl of Warwicke, and was since called Warwicke inn.   It is
in record called a messuage in Eldenese lane, in the parish of
St. Sepulchre, the 28th of Henry the VI.   Cicille Duchess of
Warwicke possessed it.   Now again from the conduit by Paule's
gate on the north side is a large street running west to Newgate,
the first part whereof, from the conduit to the shambles, is of
selling bladders there, called Bladder street.   Then behind the
butchers' shops be now divers slaughter houses inward, and tippling houses outward.   This is called Mountgodard street of the
tippling houses there, and the goddards mounting from the tap
to the table, from the table to the mouth, and sometimes over
the head.   This street goeth up to the north end of Ivie lane.

Before this Mountgodard street stall boards were of old time
set up by the butchers to show and sell their flesh meat upon,

[1] " Prebend almes houses."—*1st edition*, p. 277.

over the which stallboards they first built sheds to keep off the weather; but since that, encroaching by little and little, they have made their stallboards and sheds fair houses, meet for the principal shambles. Next is Newgate market, first of corn and meal, and then of other victuals, which stretcheth almost to Eldenese lane. A fair, new, and strong frame of timber, covered with lead, was therefore set up at the charges of the city, near to the west corner of St. Nicholas' shambles, for the meal to be weighed, in the 1st of Edward VI., Sir John Gresham being then mayor. On this side the north corner of Eldenese lane stood sometime a proper parish church of St. Ewine, as is before said, given by Henry VIII., towards the erecting of Christ's church; it was taken down, and in place thereof a fair strong frame of timber erected, wherein dwell men of divers trades. And from this frame to Newgate is all of this ward, and so an end thereof.

It hath an alderman, his deputy, common council twelve, constables seventeen, scavengers eighteen, wardmote inquest eighteen, and a beadle. And is taxed to the fifteen fifty pounds.[1]

BREAD STREET WARD

Bred street ward beginneth in the high street of West Cheape, to wit, on the south side from the standard to the great cross. Then is also a part of Watheling street of this ward, to wit, from over against the Lion on the north side up almost to Paule's gate, for it lacketh but one house of St. Augustine's church. And on the south side, from the Red Lion gate to the Old Exchange, and down the same exchange on the east side by the west end of Mayden lane, or Distar lane, to Knightriders street, or, as they call that part thereof, Old Fish street. And all the north side of the said Old Fish street to the south end of Bread street, and by that still in Knightriders street till over against the Trinity church and Trinity lane. Then is Bread street itself, so called of bread in old time there sold; for it appeareth by records, that in the year 1302, which was the 30th of Edward I., the bakers of London were bound to sell no bread in their shops or houses, but in the market, and that they should have four hallmotes in the year, at four several terms, to determine of enormities belonging to the said company.

This street giving the name to the whole ward, beginneth in West Cheap, almost by the Standard, and runneth down south

---

[1] " In London at fifty-four pounds, and in the Exchequer at fifty-three pounds six shillings and eight pence."—*1st edition*, p. 345.

through or thwart Watheling street to Knightriders street aforesaid, where it endeth. This Bread street is wholly on both sides of this ward. Out of the which street, on the east side, is Basing lane, a piece whereof, to wit, to and over against the back gate of the Red Lion in Watheling street, is of this Bread street ward.

Then is Fryday street beginning also in West Cheap, and runneth down south through Watheling street to Knightriders street, or Old Fish street. This Friday street is of Bread street ward on the east side from over against the north-east corner of St. Matthew's church, and on the west side from the south corner of the said church, down as aforesaid.

In this Fryday street, on the west side thereof, is a lane, commonly called Mayden lane, or Distaffe lane, corruptly for Distar lane, which runneth west into the Old Exchange; and in this lane is also one other lane, on the south side thereof, likewise called Distar lane, which runneth down to Knightriders street, or Old Fish street; and so be the bounds of this whole ward.

Monuments to be noted here, first at Bread street corner, the north-east end, 1595, of Thomas Tomlinson, causing in the high street of Cheape a vault to be digged and made, there was found, at fifteen feet deep, a fair pavement like unto that above ground, and at the further end at the channel was found a tree sawed into five steps, which was to step over some brook running out of the west towards Walbrooke; and upon the edge of the said brook, as it seemeth, there were found lying along the bodies of two great trees, the ends whereof were then sawed off, and firm timber as at the first when they fell, part of the said trees remain yet in the ground undigged. It was all forced ground until they went past the trees aforesaid, which was about seventeen feet deep or better; thus much hath the ground of this city in that place been raised from the main.

Next to be noted, the most beautiful frame of fair houses and shops that be within the walls of London, or elsewhere in England, commonly called Goldsmith's row, betwixt Bread street end and the cross in Cheape, but is within this Bread street ward; the same was built by Thomas Wood, goldsmith, one of the sheriffs of London, in the year 1491. It containeth in number ten fair dwelling-houses and fourteen shops, all in one frame, uniformly built four stories high, beautified towards the street with the Goldsmiths' arms and the likeness of woodmen, in memory of his name, riding on monstrous beasts, all which is cast in lead, richly painted over and gilt: these he gave to the Goldsmiths, with stocks of money, to be lent to young men having those shops, etc. This said front was again new painted and gilt over in the year 1594; Sir Richard Martin being then mayor, and keeping his mayoralty in one of them, serving out the time of Cuthbert Buckle in that office from the 2nd of July till the 28th of October.

Then for Watheling street, which Leyland called Atheling or Noble street; but since he showeth no reason why, I rather take it to be so named of the great highway of the same calling. True it is, that at this present the inhabitants thereof are wealthy drapers, retailers of woollen cloths, both broad and narrow, of all sorts, more than in any one street of this city.

Of the Old Exchange, I have noted in Faringdon ward; wherefore I pass down to Knightriders street, whereof I have also spoken in Cordwainers street ward; but in this part of the said Knightriders street is a fish market kept, and therefore called Old Fish street for a difference from New Fish street.

In this Old Fish street is one row of small houses, placed along in the midst of Knightriders street, which row is also of Bread street ward: these houses, now possessed by fishmongers, were at the first but moveable boards (or stalls), set out on market-days, to show their fish there to be sold; but procuring license to set up sheds, they grew to shops, and by little and little to tall houses, of three or four stories in height, and now are called Fish street. Walter Turke, fishmonger, mayor 1349, had two shops in Old Fish street, over against St. Nicholas church; the one rented five shillings the year, the other four shillings.

Bread street, so called of bread sold there (as I said), is now wholly inhabited by rich merchants; and divers fair inns be there, for good receipt of carriers and other travellers to the city.

On the east side of this street, at the corner of Watheling street, is the proper church of Alhallowes in Bread street, wherein are the monuments—of James Thame, goldsmith; John Walpole, goldsmith, 1349; Thomas Beamount, alderman, one of the sheriffs 1442; Robert Basset, salter, mayor 1476; Sir Richard Chaury, salter, mayor 1509; Sir Thomas Pargitar, salter, mayor 1530; Henry Sucley, merchant-tailor, one of the sheriffs 1541; Richard Reade, alderman, that served and was taken prisoner in Scotland, 1542; Robert House, one of the sheriffs 1589; William Albany, Richard May, and Roger Abde, merchant-tailors.

In the 23rd of Henry VIII., the 17th of August, two priests of this church fell at variance, that the one drew blood of the other; wherefore the same church was suspended, and no service sung or said therein for the space of one month after: the priests were committed to prison, and the 15th of October, being enjoined penance, went before a general procession, bareheaded, bare-footed, and bare-legged, before the children, with beads and books in their hands, from Paules, through Cheape, Cornehill, etc.

More to be noted of this church, which had sometime a fair spired steeple of stone. In the year 1559, the 5th of September, about mid-day, fell a great tempest of lightning, with a terrible clap of thunder, which struck the said spire about nine or ten feet beneath the top; out of the which place fell a stone that slew a dog, and overthrew a man that was playing with the dog. The same spire being but little damnified thereby, was shortly after taken down, for sparing the charges of reparation.

On the same side is Salters' hall, with six alms houses in number, built for poor decayed brethren of that company. This hall was burnt in the year 1539, and again re-edified.

Lower down on the same side is the parish church of St. Mildred the Virgin. The monuments in this church be—of the Lord Trenchaunt of St. Alban's, knight, who was supposed to be either the new builder of this church, or best benefactor to the works thereof, about the year 1300 and odd;—Cornish, gentleman, 1312; William Palmer, blader, a great benefactor also, 1356; John Shadworth, mayor 1401, who gave the parsonage-hóuse, a re-vestry, and churchyard to that parish, in the year 1428; notwithstanding, his monument is pulled down; Stephen Bugge, gentleman; his arms be three water-bugs,[1] 1419; Henry Bugge founded a chantry there 1419; Roger Forde, vintner, 1440; Thomas Barnwell, fishmonger, one of the sheriffs 1434; Sir John Hawlen, clerk, parson of that church, who built the parsonage-house newly after the same had been burnt to the ground, together with the parson and his man also, burnt in that fire, 1485; John Parnell, 1510; William Hurstwaight, pewterer to the king, 1526; Christopher Turner, chirurgeon to King Henry VIII., 1530; Ralph Simonds, fishmonger, one of the sheriffs in the year 1527; Thomas Langham gave to the poor of that parish four tenements 1575; Thomas Hall, salter, 1582; Thomas Collins, salter, alderman; Sir

[1] Water Bougets—heraldic representations of the leathern bottles in which water was anciently carried.

Ambrose Nicholas, salter, mayor 1575, was buried in Sir John Shadworth's vault.

Out of this Bread street, on the same side, is Basing lane; a part whereof (as is afore showed) is of this ward, but how it took the name of Basing I have not read: in the 20th year of Richard II. the same was called the bakehouse, whether meant for the king's bakehouse, or of bakers dwelling there, and baking bread to serve the market in Bread street, where the bread was sold, I know not; but sure I am, I have not read of Basing, or of Gerrarde the giant, to have anything there to do.

On the south side of this lane is one great house, of old time built upon arched vaults, and with arched gates of stone, brought from Caen in Normandy. The same is now a common hostrey for receipt of travellers, commonly and corruptly called Gerrardes hall, of a giant said to have dwelt there. In the high-roofed hall of this house sometime stood a large fir pole, which reached to the roof thereof, and was said to be one of the staves [1] that Gerrarde the giant used in the wars to run withal. There stood also a ladder of the same length, which (as they say) served to ascend to the top of the staff. Of later years this hall is altered in building, and divers rooms are made in it. Notwithstanding, the pole is removed to one corner of the hall, and the ladder hanged broken upon a wall in the yard. The hostelar of that house said to me, " the pole lacketh half a foot of forty in length: " I measured the compass thereof, and found it fifteen inches. Reason of the pole could the master of the hostrey give me none, but bade me read the great Chronicles, for there he heard of it: which answer seemed to me insufficient, for he meant the description of Britaine, for the most part drawn out of John Leyland his commentaries (borrowed of myself), and placed before Reyne Wolfe's Chronicle,[2] as the labours of another (who was forced to confess he never travelled further than from London to the university of Oxford): he writing a chapter of giants or monstrous men, hath set down more matter than truth, as partly against my will I am enforced here to touch. R. G., in his brief collection of histories (as he termeth it) hath these words: " I, the writer hereof, did see,

[1] " A pole of forty foote long, and fifteen inches about, fabuled to be the iusting staffe of Gerrard a giant."—*Stow*.

[2] " Which aunswere seemed to me insufficient, for hee meant the description of Brittaine, before Reinwolfe's Chronicle, wherein the author writing a chapter of Gyaunts, and having been deceived by some authours, too much crediting their smoothe speeche, hath set down more matter than troth, as partly (and also against my will) I am enforced to touch." —*1st edition*, p. 283.

the 10th day of March, in the yeare of our Lord 1564, and had the same in my hand, the tooth of a man, which weighed ten ounces of troy weight; and the skull of the same man is extant, and to be seene, which will hold five pecks of wheat; and the shin-bone of the same man is six foote in length, and of a marvellous greatness." Thus far of R. G.[1] The error thereof is thus: He affirmeth a stone to be the tooth of a man, which stone (so proved) having no shape of a tooth, had neither skull or shin-bone. Notwithstanding, it is added in the said description, that by conjectural symetry of those parts the body to be twenty-eight feet long, or more. From this he goeth to another like matter, of a man with a mouth sixteen feet wide, and so to Gerrard the giant and his staff. But to leave these fables, and return where I left, I will note what myself hath observed concerning that house.

I read that John Gisors, mayor of London in the year 1245, was owner thereof, and that Sir John Gisors, knight, mayor of London, and constable of the Tower 1311, and divers others of that name and family, since that time owned it. William Gisors was one of the sheriffs 1329. More, John Gisors had issue, Henry and John; which John had issue, Thomas; which Thomas deceasing in the year 1350, left unto his son Thomas his messuage called Gisor's hall, in the parish of St. Mildred in Bread street; John Gisors made a feoffment thereof, 1386, etc. So it appeareth that this Gisor's hall, of late time by corruption hath been called Gerrard's hall [2] for Gisor's hall; as Bosom's inn for Blossom's inn, Bevis marks for Buries marks, Marke lane for Marte lane, Belliter lane for Belsetter's lane, Gutter lane for Guthuruns lane, Cry church for Christ's church, St. Mihel in the quorn for St. Mihel at corne, and sundry such others. Out of this Gisor's hall, at the first building thereof, were made divers arched doors, yet to be seen, which seem not sufficient for any great monster, or other than man of common stature to pass through, the pole in the hall might be used of old time (as then the custom was in every parish), to be set up in the summer as May-pole, before the principal house in the parish or street, and to stand in the hall before the screen, decked with holme and ivy, all the feast of Christmas.[3] The ladder served for the

[1] " R. G. saw a stone, and said the same to bee a tooth, but being by my selfe proued a stone, there fayled both scull and shank-bone, and followed a cluster of lies together, yet since increased by other."—*Stow*.

[2] " Gerrard's hall overthrowne with Gerrard the giant, and his great spear."—*Stow*.

[3] " Every man's house of old time was decked with holly and ivy in the winter, especially at Christmas."—*Stow*.

decking of the may-pole and roof of the hall. Thus much for Gisor's hall, and for that side of Bread street, may suffice.

Now on the west side of Bread street, amongst divers fair and large houses for merchants, and fair inns for passengers, had ye one prison-house pertaining to the sheriffs of London, called the compter in Bread street; but in the year 1555 the prisoners were removed from thence to one other new compter in Wood street, provided by the city's purchase, and built for that purpose; the cause of which remove was this: Richard Husband, pastelar, keeper of this compter in Bread street, being a wilful and head-strong man, dealt, for his own advantage, hard with the prisoners under his charge, having also servants such as himself liked best for their bad usage, and would not for any complaint be re-formed; whereupon, in the year 1550, Sir Rowland Hill being mayor, by the assent of a court of aldermen, he was sent to the gaol of Newgate, for the cruel handling of his prisoners; and it was commanded to the keeper to set those irons on his legs which are called the widow's alms. These he ware from Thursday to Sunday in the afternoon, and being by a court of aldermen released on the Tuesday, was bound in a hundred marks to observe from thenceforth an act made by the common council, for the ordering of prisoners in the compters; all which notwithstanding, he continued as afore, whereof myself am partly a witness; for being of a jury to inquire against a sessions of gaol delivery,[1] in the year 1552, we found the prisoners hardly dealt withal, for their achates and otherwise; as also that thieves and strumpets were there lodged for four pence the night, whereby they might be safe from searches that were made abroad; for the which enormities, and other not needful to be recited, he was indighted at that session, but did rub it out, and could not be reformed till this remove of prisoners, for the house in Bread street was his own by lease, or otherwise, so that he could not be put from it. Note, that gaolers buying their offices will deal hardly with pitiful prisoners.

Now in Friday street, so called of fishmongers dwelling there, and serving Friday's market, on the east side, is a small parish church, commonly called St. John Evangelist: the monuments therein be of John Dogget, merchant tailor, one of the sheriffs in the year 1509; Sir Christopher Askew, draper, mayor 1533; William de Avinger, farrier, was buried there in the 34th of Edward III. Then lower down, is one other parish church of

---

[1] "Quest of inquiry indight the keepers of the gayles for dealing hardly with their prisoners. They indighted the bowling alleys, etc."—*Stow.*

St. Margaret Moyses, so called (as seemeth) of one Moyses, that was founder or new builder thereof. The monuments there be of Sir Richard Dobbes, skinner, mayor 1551; William Dane, ironmonger, one of the sheriffs 1569; Sir John Allet, fishmonger, mayor 1591. There was of older time buried, Nicholas Stanes, and Nicholas Braye; they founded chantries there.

On the west side of this Friday street, is Mayden lane, so named of such a sign, or Distaffe lane, for Distar lane, as I read in the record of a brewhouse called the Lamb, in Distar lane, the 16th of Henry VI. In this Distar lane, on the north side thereof, is the Cordwainers, or Shoemakers' hall, which company were made a brotherhood or fraternity, in the 11th of Henry IV. Of these cordwainers I read, that since the fifth of Richard II. (when he took to wife Anne, daughter to Vesalaus, King of Boheme), by her example, the English people had used piked shoes, tied to their knees with silken laces, or chains of silver or gilt, wherefore in the 4th of Edward IV. it was ordained and proclaimed, that beaks of shoone and boots, should not pass the length of two inches, upon pain of cursing by the clergy, and by parliament to pay twenty shillings for every pair. And every cordwainer that shod any man or woman on the Sunday, to pay thirty shillings.

On the south side of this Distar lane, is also one other lane, called Distar lane, which runneth down to Knightriders' street, or Old Fish street, and this is the end of Bread street ward; which hath an alderman, his deputy, common council ten, constables ten, scavengers eight, wardmote inquest thirteen, and a beadle. It standeth taxed to the fifteen in London, at £37, and in the Exchequer at £36 18s. 2d.[1]

QUEENE HITHE WARD

Next unto Bread street ward, on the south side thereof, is Queene Hithe ward, so called of a water gate, or harbour for boats, lighters, and barges; and was of old time for ships, at what time the timber bridge of London was drawn up, for the passage of them to the said hithe, as to a principal strand for landing and unlading against the midst and heart of the city.

This ward beginneth in the east, in Knightriders' street, on the south side thereof, at the east end of the parish church called the Holy Trinity, and runneth west on the south side to

[1] " In the Exchequer thirty-six pounds, ten shillings."—*1st edition*, p. 285.

a lane called Lambert hill, which is the length of the ward in Knightriders' street, out of the which street are divers lanes, running south to Thames street, and are of this ward: the first is Trinity lane, which runneth down by the west end of Trinity church; then is Spuren lane, or Spooner's lane, now called Huggen lane; then Bread street hill; then St. Mary Mounthaunt, out of the which lane, on the east side thereof, is one other lane, turning east, through St. Nicholas Olave's churchyard to Bread street hill. This lane is called Finimore lane, or Fivefoot lane, because it is but five feet in breadth at the west end; in the midst of this lane runneth down one other lane broader, south to Thames street, I think the same to be called Desbourne lane, for I read of such a lane to have been in the parish of Mary Summerset, in the 22nd year of Edward III., where there is said to lie between the tenement of Edward de Montacute, knight, on the east part, and the tenement some time pertaining to William Gladwine on the west, one plot of ground, containing in length towards Thames street, twenty-five feet, etc.

Last of all, have you Lambart-hill lane, so called of one Lambart, owner thereof; and this is the furthest west part of this ward.

On the north side coming down from Knightriders' street, the east side of Lambart hill, is wholly of this ward; and the west side, from the north end of the Blackesmiths' hall (which is about the midst of this lane) unto Thames street; then part of Thames street is also of this ward, to wit, from a cook's house called the sign of King David, three houses west from the Old Swan brewhouse in the east, unto Huntington house, over against St. Peter's church in the west, near unto Paul's wharf; and on the land side, from a cook's house called the Blue Boar, to the west end of St. Peter's church, and up St. Peter's hill, two houses north above the said church. And these be the bounds of this ward, in which are parish churches seven, halls of companies two, and other ornaments as shall be shewed.

First in Knightriders' street, is the small parish church of the Holy Trinity, very old, and in danger of down falling: collections have been made for repairing thereof, but they will not stretch so far, and, therefore, it leaneth upon props or stilts. Monuments as followeth.

John Brian, alderman in the reign of Henry V., a great benefactor; John Chamber had a chantry there; Thomas Rishby, esquire, and Alice his wife, within the chancel; John Mirfin, auditor of the exchequer 1471; Sir Richard Fowler, of Ricks in

Oxfordshire, 1528; George Cope, second son to Sir John Cope of Copasashby in Northamptonshire, 1572.

Towards the west end of Knightriders' street is the parish church of St. Nicolas Cold Abbey, a proper church, somewhat ancient, as appeareth by the ways raised thereabout, so that men are forced to descend into the body of the church: it hath been called of many Golden Abbey, of some, Gold Abbey, or Cold Bey, and so hath the most ancient writings,[1] as standing in a cold place, as Cold harbour, and such like. The steeple or tall tower of this church, with the south aisle, have been of a later building: to wit, the 1st of Richard II., when it was meant the whole old church should have been new built, as appeareth by the arching begun on the east side the steeple, under the which, in the stone work, the arms of one Buckland, esquire, and his wife, daughter to Beaupere, are cut in stone, and also are in the glass windows, whereby it appeareth he was the builder of the steeple, and repairer of the residue. The 26th of Edward III., An. Aubrey being mayor,[2] T. Frere, fishmonger, gave one piece of ground to the said parish church of St. Nicholas, containing eighty-six feet in length, and forty-three feet at one end, and thirty-four at the other, in breadth, for a cemetery or church-yard. The 20th of Richard II., Thomas Barnard Castle, clerke, John Sonderash, clerke, and John Nouncy, gave to the parson and churchwardens of the said church and their successors, one messuage and one shop, with the appurtenances, in Distaffe lane and Old Fish street, for the reparation of the body of the said church, the belfry or steeple, and ornaments.

Buried in this church, John Calfe, and William Cogeshall, 1426; Waltar Turke, fishmonger, mayor 1349; Richarde Esastone, fishmonger, 1330; Nicholas Wolberge, fishmonger, 1407; Thomas Paddington, fishmonger, 1485; Robert Hary, fishmonger, John Suring, 1490; Roger Darlington, fish-monger, 1557; Richard Lacty, parson, under a fair tomb on the north side the choir, 1491; Richard Bradbrudge, 1497;

---

[1] " But I could never learne the cause why it should be so called, and therefore I will let it passe."—1st edition, p. 287.

[2] " There bee monumentes in this church of Andrew Awbery, grocer, mayor, and Thomas Fryar, fishmonger, in the yeare 1351, who gave to this church and parish one plot of ground, containing fiftie-six foote in length, and fortie-three foote in breadth at both endes, to be a buriall place for the dead of the said parish, the twenty-sixt of Edward the third. Also Thomas Madefry, clarke, and John Pylot, gave to the wardens of that parish one shop and a house in Distar lane, for the continual repairing of the body of that church, the belles and ornaments, the twentieth of Richard II."—1st edition, p. 287.

William Clarke, 1501; James Picman, 1507; Richard Farneford, 1525; Thomas Nicholas, fishmonger, 1527; William Barde, fishmonger, 1528.

On the north side of this church, in the wall thereof, was of late built a convenient cistern of stone and lead, for receipt of Thames water, conveyed in pipes of lead to that place, for the ease and commodity of the fishmongers and other inhabitants in and about Old Fish street. Barnard Randolph, common serjeant of the city of London, did in his lifetime deliver to the company of Fishmongers the sum of nine hundred pounds, to be employed towards the conducting of the said Thames water, and cisterning the same, etc.; in the parishes of St. Mary Magdalen, and St. Nicholas Colde Abbey, near unto Fish street, seven hundred pounds; and other two hundred pounds to charitable deeds: he deceased 1583, and shortly after this conduit with the other was made and finished.

In Trinity lane, on the west side thereof, is the Painterstainers' hall, for so of old time were they called, but now that workmanship of staining is departed out of use in England. Lower down in Trinity lane, on the east side thereof, was sometime a great messuage pertaining unto John, earl of Cornwall, in the 14th of Edward III. On Bread street hill, down to the Thames on both sides, be divers fair houses, inhabited by fishmongers, cheesemongers, and merchants of divers trades. On the west side whereof is the parish church of St. Nicholas Olive, a convenient church, having the monuments of W. Newport, fishmonger, one of the sheriffs 1375; Richard Willowes, parson, 1391; Richard Sturges, fishmonger, 1470; Thomas Lewen, ironmonger, one of the sheriffs 1537, who gave his messuage, with the appurtenances, wherein he dwelt, with fourteen tenements in the said parish of St. Nicholas, to be had after the decease of Agnes his wife, to the ironmongers, and they to give stipends appointed to almsmen, in five houses by them built in the churchyard of that parish, more to poor scholars in Oxford and Cambridge, etc. Blitheman, an excellent organist of the Queen's chapel, lieth buried there with an epitaph, 1591, etc.

The next is Old Fishstreet hill, a lane so called, which also runneth down to Thames street. In this lane, on the east side thereof, is the one end of Finimore, or Five foot lane. On the west side of this Old Fishstreet hill is the Bishop of Hereford's inn or lodging, an ancient house and large rooms, built of stone and timber, which sometime belonged to the Mounthauntes in Norfolk. Radulphus de Maydenstone, Bishop of Hereford, about 1234, bought it of the Mounthauntes, and gave it to the Bishops of Hereford, his successors. Charles, both Bishop of Hereford and Chancellor of the Marches, about the year 1517, repaired it, since the which time the same is greatly ruinated, and is now divided into many small tenements; the hall and principal rooms, are a house to make sugar-loaves, etc.

Next adjoining is the parish church of St. Mary de Monte Alto, or Mounthaunt; this is a very small church, and at the first built to be a chapel for the said house of the Mounthaunts, and for tenements thereunto belonging. The Bishop of Hereford is patron thereof. Monuments in this church of John Glocester, alderman 1345, who gave Salt wharf for two chantries there; John Skip, Bishop of Hereford, 1539, sate twelve years, died at London in time of parliament, and was buried in this church. There was sometime a fair house in the said parish of St. Mary Mounthaunt, belonging to Robert Belkenape, one of the king's justices, but the said Belkenape being banished this realm, King Richard II. in the twelfth of his reign, gave it to William Wickham, Bishop of Winchester.

On the east side of this Old Fishstreet hill, is one great house, now let out for rent, which house sometime was one of the halls, pertaining to the company of Fishmongers, at such time as they had six hallmotes or meeting places: namely, two in Bridge street, or New Fish street; two in Old Fish street, whereof this was one; and two in Stockfishmonger row, or Thames street, as appeareth by a record, the 22nd of Richard II.

Next westward is one other lane called Lambard hill, the east side whereof is wholly of this ward, and but half the west side, to wit, from the north end of the Blacksmiths' hall.

Then in Thames street of this ward, and on the north side over against the Queen's hith, is the parish church of St. Michaell, a convenient church, but all the monuments therein are defaced.

I find that Stephen Spilman, gentleman, of that family in Norfolk, sometime mercer, chamberlain of London, then one of the sheriffs, and alderman in the year 1404, deceasing without issue, gave his lands to his family the Spilmans, and his goods to the making or repairing of bridges and other like godly uses; and amongst others in this church he founded a chantry, and was buried in the choir.

Also Richard Marlowe, ironmonger, mayor 1409, gave twenty pounds to the poor of that ward, and ten marks to the church.

Richard Gray, ironmonger, one of the sheriffs 1515, gave forty pounds to that church, and was buried there. At the

west end of that church goeth up a lane, called Pyel lane. On
the same north side, at the south end of St. Mary Mounthaunt lane, is the parish church of St. Mary Summerset,
over against the Broken wharf; it is a proper church, but the
monuments are all defaced. I think the same to be of old time
called Summer's hith, of some man's name that was owner of the
ground near adjoining, as Edred's hithe was so called of Edred
owner thereof, and thence called Queene hithe, as pertaining to
the queen, etc.

Then is a small parish church of St. Peter, called *parva*, or
little, near unto Powle's wharf; in this church no monuments
do remain. At the west end thereof, is a lane called St. Peter's
hill, but two houses up that lane on the east side is of this ward,
and the rest is of Castle Baynarde ward.

On the south side of Thames street, beginning again in the
east, among the cooks, the first in this ward, is the sign of David
the King; then is Towne's end lane, turning down to the
Thames; then is Queene hithe, a large receptacle for ships,
lighters, barges, and such other vessels.

Touching the antiquity and use of this gate and hithe, first,
I find the same belongeth to one named Edred, and was then
called Edred's hithe, which since falling to the hands of King
Stephen, it was by his charter confirmed to William De Ypre; [1]
the farm thereof in fee and in heritage, William De Ypre gave
unto the prior and convent of the Holy Trinity within Aldgate,
as appeareth by this charter:—

'To Theobalde, by the grace of God, Archbishop of Canterbury, primate of England, and Legate Apostolike, to the Bishoppe
of London, and to all faithful people, clarkes and layemen,
William de Ypre sendeth greeting.

"Know ye me to have given and graunted to God, and to the
church of the Holy Trinitie of London, to the prior and canons
there serving God in perpetuall almes, Edred's hith, with the
appurtenances, with such devotion, that they shall send every
yeare twentie pound unto the maintenance of the hospital of
St. Katherens, which hospitall they have in their hands, and
one hundred shillinges to the monkes of Bermondsey, and sixty
shillinges to the brethren of the hospitall of St. Giles, and that
which remayneth, the said prior and canons shall enjoy to
themselves. Witnesses, Richard de Lucie, Raph Picot, etc."

This Edred's hithe, after the aforesaid grants, came again to
the king's hands, by what means I have not read, but it per-

[1] Liber Trinitate.

tained unto the queen, and, therefore, was called *Ripa reginæ*, the Queene's bank, or Queen's hithe, and great profit thereof was made to her use, as may appear by this which followeth.

King Henry III. in the 9th of his reign, commanded the constables of the Tower of London to arrest the ships of the Cinque Ports on the river of Thames, and to compel them to bring their corne to no other place, but to the Queen's hithe only. In the eleventh of his reign, he charged the said constable to distrain all fish offered to be sold in any place of this city, but at the Queene hithe. Moreover, in the 28th of the said king's reign, an inquisition was made before William of Yorke, provost of Beverley, Henry of Bath, and Hierome of Caxton, justices itinerant, sitting in the Tower of London, touching the customs of Queen hithe, observed in the year last before the wars between the king and his father, and the barons of England, and of old customs of other times, and what customs had been changed, at what time the tax and payment of all things coming together, and between Woore path and Anedehithe,[1] were found and ceased, according to the old order, as well corn and fish as other things: all which customs were as well to be observed in the part of Downegate, as in Queen hithe, for the king's use. When also it was found that the corn arriving between the gate of the Guildhall of the merchants of Cologne, and the soke of the Archbishop of Canterbury (for he had a house near unto the Blacke Fryers), was not to be measured by any other quarter, than by that of the Queene's soke.

After this, the bailiff of the said hithe complained that, since the said recognition, fourteen foreign ships laden with fish, arrived at Belinge's gate, which ships should have arrived at the same hithe; and, therefore, it was ordered, that if any foreign ship laden with fish, should in form aforesaid, arrive elsewhere than at this hithe, it should be at the king's pleasure to amerce them at forty shillings. Notwithstanding, the ships of the citizens of London were at liberty to arrive where the owners would appoint them.

After this, the said Henry III. confirmed the grant of Richard Earl of Cornwall for the farm of the Queen hithe unto John Gisors, then mayor, and to the commonalty of London, and their successors for ever, as by this his charter appeareth:

---

[1] It appears from Strype's *Stow* (i. p. 214, ed. 1720), that "Were path or Wore path, is in the east part of the Flete of Barking, about seven miles from London; and Anedeheth is near Westminster, on the west part of London."

" Henry, by the grace of God, King of England, Lord of
Ireland, Duke of Guien, and Earl of Anjou, to all archbishops,
etc. Be it known, that we have seen the covenant between our
brother, Richard Earl of Cornwall, on the one part, and the
mayor and commonalty on the other part, which was in this sort.
In the 30th year of Henry, the son of King John,[1] upon the
feast of the Translation of St. Edward, at Westminster, this
covenant was made between the honourable Lord Richard Earl
of Cornwall, and John Gisors, then mayor of London, and the
commons thereof, concerning certain exactions and demands
pertaining to the Queen hithe of London. The said earl granted
for himself and his heirs, that the said mayor, and all mayors
ensuing, and all the commons of the city, should have and hold
the Queen hithe, with all the liberties, customs, and other appurtenances, repaying yearly to the said earl, his heirs and assigns,
fifty pounds, at Clarkenwell, at two several terms; to wit, the
Sunday after Easter twenty-five pounds, and at Michaelmas
twenty-five pounds. And for more surety hereof the said earl
hath set thereunto his seal, and left it with the mayor, and the
mayor and commonalty have set to their seal, and left it with the
earl. Wherefore we confirm and establish the said covenant for
us, and for our heirs. Witnesses, Raph Fitz Nichol, Richard
Gray, John and Wil. Brithem, Paulin Painter, Raph Wancia,
John Cumbaud, and other, at Windsor, 26th of February, in
the 31st of our reign."

The charge of this Queen hithe was then committed to the
sheriffs, and so hath continued ever since; the profits whereof
are sore diminished, so that (as writeth Robert Fabian) it was
worth in his time little above twenty marks, or fifteen pounds,
one year with another. Now for customs of this Queen hithe.[2]
In the year 1302, the 30th of Edward I., it was found by the oath
of divers men, that bakers, brewers, and others, buying their
corn at Queen hithe, should pay for measuring, portage, and
carriage, for every quarter of corn whatsoever, from thence to
West Cheap, to St. Anthonie's church, to Horshew bridge, and
to Woolsey street, in the parish of Allhallowes the Less, and
such like distances, one halfpenny farthing; to Fleet bridge, to
Newgate, Cripplegate, to Bircheovers lane, to Eastcheape, and
Billingsgate, one penny. Also, that the measure (or the meter)
ought to have eight chief master-porters, every master to have
three porters under him, and every one of them to find one
horse, and seven sacks; and he that so did not, to lose his office.

---

[1] Liber Trinitate, Lon.   [2] Liber Constitut.

This hithe was then so frequented with vessels, bringing thither corn (besides fish, salt, fuel, and other merchandises), that all these men, to wit, the meter, and porters, thirty-seven in number, for all their charges of horses and sacks, and small stipend, lived well of their labours; but now [1] the bakers of London, and other citizens, travel into the countries, and buy their corn of the farmers, after the farmers' price.

King Edward II., in the 1st of his reign, gave to Margaret, wife to Piers de Gaveston, forty-three pounds twelve shillings and nine pence halfpenny farthing, out of the rent of London, to be received of the Queen's hithe. Certain impositions were set upon ships and other vessels coming thither, as upon corn, salt, and other things, toward the charge of cleansing Roomeland there, the 41st of Edward III.

The 3rd of Edward IV., the market at Queen hithe being hindered by the slackness of drawing up London bridge, it was ordained, that all manner of vessels, ships, or boats, great or small, resorting to the city with victual, should be sold by retail; and that if there came but one vessel at a time, were it salt, wheat, rye, or other corn, from beyond the seas, or other grains, garlic, onions, herrings, sprats, eels, whiting, plaice, cods, mackarel, etc., then that one vessel should come to Queen hithe, and there to make sale; but if two vessels come, the one should come to Queen hithe, the other to Billingsgate; if three, two of them should come to Queen hithe, the third to Billingsgate, etc., always the more to Queen hithe; if the vessel being great, coming with salt from the Bay, and could not come to these keys, then the same to be conveyed by lighters, as before is meant.

One large house for stowage of corn craned out of lighters and barges, is there lately built; Sir John Lion, grocer, mayor 1554, by his testament, gave a hundred pounds towards it; but since increased and made larger at the charges of the city, in the year 1565.

Against this Queen's hithe, on the river Thames, of late years, was placed a corn mill, upon or betwixt two barges or lighters, and there ground corn, as water mills in other places, to the wonder of many that had not seen the like; but this lasted not long without decay, such as caused the same barges and mill to be removed, taken asunder, and soon forgotten. I read of the like to have been in former time, as thus:—In the year 1525, the 16th of Henry VIII., Sir William Bayly being mayor, John

Cooke of Glocester, mercer, gave to the mayor and commonalty
of London, and theirs for ever, one great barge, in the which two
corn mills were made and placed, which barge and mills were
set in and upon the stream of the river of Thames, within the
jurisdiction and liberty of the said city of London.

And also he gave to the city all such timber, boards, stones,
iron, etc., provided for making, mending, and repairing of the
said barge and mills, in reward whereof the mayor gave him
fifty pounds presently, and fifty pounds yearly during his life;
and if the said Cooke deceased before Johan his wife, then she
to have forty marks the year during her life.

Next adjoining to this Queen hithe, on the west side thereof,
is Salt wharf, named of salt taken up, measured, and sold there.
The next is Stew lane, of a stew or hothouse there kept. After
that is Timber hithe, or Timber street, so called of timber or
boards there taken up and wharfed; it is in the parish of St.
Mary Somershithe, as I read in the 56th of Henry III., and in
the 9th of Edward II. Then is Brookes wharf, and Broken
wharf, a water gate or key, so called of being broken and fallen
down into the Thames. By this Broken wharf remaineth one
large old building of stone, with arched gates, which messuage,
as I find, in the reign of Henry III., the 43rd year, pertaining
unto Hugh de Bygot; and in the 11th of Edward III., to Thomas
Brotherton, the king's brother, Earl of Norfolk, Marshal of
England; in the 11th of Henry VI. to John Mowbray, Duke of
Norfolk, etc.

Within the gate of this house (now belonging to the city of
London) is lately, to wit, in the years 1594 and 1595, built one
large house of great height, called an engine, made by Bevis
Bulmar, gentleman, for the conveying and forcing of Thames
water to serve in the middle and west parts of the city. The
ancient great hall of this messuage is yet standing, and pertaining to a great brewhouse for beer. West from this is Trigge
lane, going down to Thames. Next is called Bosse lane, of a
bosse of water, like unto that of Billingsgate, there placed by
the executors of Richard Whittington. Then is one great
messuage, sometime belonging to the abbots of Chertsey in
Surrey, and was their inn, wherein they were lodged when they
repaired to the city; it is now called Sandie house, by what
reason I have not heard: I think the Lord Sands have been
lodged there.

And this is an end of this Queen hithe ward; which hath an
alderman and his deputy, common council six, constables nine,

scavengers eight, wardmote inquest thirteen, and a beadle. It is taxed to the fifteen in London twenty pounds, and in the Exchequer at nineteen pounds sixteen shillings and two pence.

The next is Castle Baynard ward, so named of an old castle there. This ward beginneth in the east on the Thames side, at a house called Huntingdon house, and runneth west by Paule's wharf, by Baynard's castle, Puddle wharf, and by the south side of Black Friers. Then turning by the east wall of the said Friers to the south-west end of Creed lane. Then, on the north side of Thames street, over against Huntington house, by St. Peter's church and lane, called Peter hill, along till over against Puddle wharf, and then north up by the great Wardrobe to the west end of Carter lane, then up Creed lane, Ave Mary lane, and a piece of Pater Noster row, to the sign of the Golden Lion, and back again up Warwicke lane, and all the east side thereof, to the sign of the Crown by Newgate market; and this is the farthest north part of this ward.

Then out of Thames street be lanes ascending north to Knight-riders street; the first is Peter hill lane, all of that ward (two houses excepted, adjoining to St. Peter's church). The next is Paule's wharf hill, which thwarting Knightriders street and Carter lane, goeth up to the south chain of Paule's churchyard.

Then in Adle street, over against the west part of Baynard's castle, going up by the west end of Knightriders street and to Carter lane. Thus much for lanes out of Thames street. The one half of the west side of Lambard hill lane being of this ward, at the north-west end thereof, on the south side, and at the west end of St. Mary Magdalen's church on the north side beginneth Knightriders street to be of this ward, and runneth west on both sides to the parish church of St. Andrew by the Wardrobe.

Then at the end of St. Mary Magdalen's church goeth up the Old Exchange, all the west side whereof up to the south-east gate of Paule's churchyard, and by St. Austen's church, is of this ward. About the midst of this Old Exchange, on the west side thereof is Carter lane, which runneth west to the east entry of the Blacke Friers, and to the south end of Creed lane, out of the which Carter lane descendeth a lane called Do-little lane, and cometh into Knightriders street by the Boar's head tavern; and more west is Sermon lane, by an inn called the Paule head. Then out of Carter lane, on the north side thereof, the south

chain of Paules churchyard, and the churchyard itself on that
south side of Paules church, and the church of St. Gregorie,
the bishop's palace, and the dean's lodging, be all of this
ward; and such be the bounds thereof. The ornaments in
this ward be parish churches four. Of old time a castle, divers
noblemen's houses, halls of companies twain, and such others,
as shall be shown.

In Thames street, at the south-east end, is an ancient messuage, of old time called Beaumount's inn, as belonging to that
family of noblemen of this realm in the 4th of Edward III.
Edward IV., in the 5th of his reign, gave it to W. Hastings, lord
chamberlain, master of his mints. It is now called Huntington
house, as belonging to the earls of Huntington. Next is Paul's
wharf, a large landing place, with a common stair upon the river
of Thames, at the end of a street called Paule's wharf hill, which
runneth down from Paule's chain. Next is a great messuage,
called Scropes inn, sometime belonging to Scropes, in the 31st of
Henry VI.

Then is one other great messuage, sometime belonging to the
abbey of Fiscampe, beyond the sea, and by reason of the wars,
it coming to the hands of King Edward III., the same was given
to Sir Simon Burley, knight of the Garter, and, therefore, called
Burley house in Thames street, between Baynard's castle and
Paule's wharf.

Then have you Baynard's castle, whereof this whole ward
taketh the name. This castle banketh on the river Thames,
and was called Baynard's castle, of Baynard, a nobleman that
came in with William the Conqueror, of the which castle, and of
Baynard himself, I have spoken in another place.

There was also another tower by Baynard's castle, built by
King Edward II. Edward III., in the 2nd of his reign, gave
it to William Duke of Hamelake, in the county of York, and his
heirs, for one rose yearly, to be paid for all service, the same
place (as seemeth to me) was since called Legate's inn, in the
7th of Edward IV., where be now divers wood wharfs in place.

Then is there a great brewhouse, and Puddle wharf, a water-
gate into the Thames, where horses use to water, and therefore
being defiled with their trampling, and made puddle, like as also
of one Puddle dwelling there, it is called Puddle wharf. Then
is there a lane between the Blacke Fryers and the Thames,
called in the 26th of Edward III. Castle lane.

In this lane also is one great messuage, of old time belonging
to the priory of Okeborne in Wiltshire, and was the prior's

lodging when he repaired to London. This priory being of the French order, was suppressed by Henry V., and with other lands and tenements pertaining to the said priory, was by Henry VI. given to his college in Cambridge, called now the King's college. About this castle lane was sometime a mill or mills belonging to the Templars of the New Temple, as appeareth of record; for King John, in the 1st year of his reign, granted a place in the Fleet, near unto Baynard's castle, to make a mill, and the whole course of water of the Fleet to serve the said mill.

I read also, that in the year 1247, the 2nd of Edward I., Ri. Raison, and Atheline his wife, did give to Nicho. de Musely, clerk, ten shillings of yearly free and quiet rent, out of all his tenements, with the houses thereupon built, and their appurtenances, which they had of the demise of the master and brethren of Knights Templars, in England, next to their mill of Fleet, over against the houses of Laurence de Brooke, in the parish of St. Andrew, next to Baynard's castle, which tenements lie between the way leading towards the said mill on the west part. Also in the rights belonging to Robert Fitzwater, and to his heirs, in the city of London, in the time of peace, it was declared in the year 1303, that the said Robert, castellan of London, and banner-bearer, had a soke (or ward) in the city, that was by the wall of St. Paule, as men go down the street before the brewhouse of St. Paule unto the Thames, and so to the side of the mill, which is in the water that cometh down from Fleet bridge, and goeth by London wall, betwixt Fryers preachers church and Ludgate; and so that ward turned back by the house of the said Fryers unto the said common wall of the said canonry of St. Paul; that is, all of the parish of St. Andrew, which is in the gift of his ancestors by seniority, as more I have shown in the Castles.

Now here is to be noted, that the wall of London at that time went straight south from Ludgate down to the river of Thames; but for building of the Blacke Fryers church, the said wall in that place was by commandment taken down, and a new wall made straight west from Ludgate to Fleet bridge, and then by the water of Fleet to the river of Thames, etc.

In the year 1307, the 35th of Edward I., in a parliament at Carlisle, Henry Lacie, Earl of Lincoln, complained of noyances done to the water of the Fleet; whereupon it was granted that the said mill should be removed and destroyed.

This ward ascendeth up by the east wall of the Black Fryers to the south-west end of Creed lane, where it endeth on that side.

Then to begin again on the north side of Thames street, over against Huntington house, by St. Peter's church and lane, called Peter hill, and so to St. Benet Hude (or Hithe) over against Powle's wharf, a proper parish church, which hath the monuments of Sir William Cheiny, knight, and Margaret his wife, 1442, buried there; Doctor Caldwell, physician; Sir Gilbert Dethik, knight, *alias* Garter king at arms. West from this church, by the south end of Adle street, almost against Pudle wharf, there is one ancient building of stone and timber, built by the lords of Barkley, and therefore called Barklies inn. This house is all in ruin, and letten out in several tenements, yet the arms of the Lord Barkley remain in the stone work of an arched gate, gules, between a cheveron, crosses ten—three, three, and four. Richard Beauchampe, Earl of Warwicke, was lodged in this house, then called Barklies inn, in the parish of St. Andrew, in the reign of Henry VI.

Then turning up towards the north is the parish church of St. Andrew in the Wardrobe, a proper church, but few monuments hath it. John Parnt founded a chantry there. Then is the king's Great Wardrobe: Sir John Beauchamp, knight of the Garter, Constable of Dover, Warden of the Sinke ports (son to Guido de Beauchampe, Earl of Warwicke), built this house, was lodged there, deceased in the year 1359, and was buried on the south side of the middle aisle of Paule's church. His executors sold the house to King Edward III., unto whom the parson of St. Andrewe's complaining that the said Beauchampe had pulled down divers houses, in their place to build the same house, where through he was hindered of his accustomed tithes, paid by the tenants of old time, granted him forty shillings by year out of that house for ever. King Richard III. was lodged there in the second of his reign.

In this house of late years is lodged Sir John Fortescue, knight, master of the wardrobe, chancellor and under-treasurer of the exchequer, and one of her majesty's most honourable privy council. The secret letters and writings touching the estate of the realm were wont to be enrolled in the king's wardrobe, and not in the chancery, as appeareth by the records. Claus. 18. E. 4. 1. Memb. 13. Claus. 33. E. 1. Memb. 3. Et liberat. 1. E. 2. Memb. 4, etc. From this wardrobe, by the west end of Carter lane, then up Creede lane, Ave Mary lane, a piece of Pater Noster row, up Warwick lane, all the east side, to a brewhouse called the Crown, as I said is of this ward. Touching lanes ascending out of Thames street to Knightriders' street, the first

is Peter's hill, wherein I find no matter of note, more than
certain alms houses, lately founded on the west side thereof, by
David Smith, embroiderer, for six poor widows, whereof each
to have twenty shillings by the year.

On the east side of this lane standeth a large house, of ancient
building, sometime belonging to the abbot of St. Mary in York,
and was his abiding house when he came to London; Thomas
Randolfe, esquire, hath lately augmented and repaired it.

At the upper end of this lane, towards the north, the corner-
houses there be called Peters key, but the reason thereof I have
not heard. Then is Paules wharf hill, on the east side whereof
is Woodmongers' hall. And next adjoining is Darby house,
sometime belonging to the Stanleys, for Thomas Stanley, first
Earl of Derby of that name, who married the Lady Margaret,
Countess of Richmond, mother to Henry VII., in his time
built it.

Queen Mary gave it to Gilbert Dethike, then Garter principal
king of arms of Englishmen; Thomas Hawley, Clarenceaux
king of arms of the south parts; William Harvy, *alias* Norroy
king of arms of the north parts, and the other heralds and pursuivants of arms, and to their successors, all the same capital
messuage or house called Derby house, with the appurtenances,
situate in the parish of St. Benet and St. Peter, then being in the
tenure of Sir Richard Sackvile, knight, and lately parcel of the
lands of Edward, Earl of Derby, etc., to the end that the said
kings of arms, heralds, and pursuivants of arms, and their
successors, might at their liking dwell together, and at meet
times to congregate, speak, confer, and agree among themselves,
for the good government of their faculty, and their records
might be more safely kept, etc. Dated the 18th of July, 1555,
Philip and Mary I., and third year.

Then higher up, near the south chain of Paules churchyard,
is the Paule Head tavern, which house, with the appurtenances,
was of old time called Paules brewhouse, for that the same was
so employed, but been since left off, and let out.

On the west side of this street, is one other great house, built
of stone, which belongeth to Paules church, and was sometime
let to the Blunts, Lords Mountjoy, but of latter time to a college
in Cambridge, and from them to the doctors of the civil law and
Arches, who keep a commons there; and many of them being
there lodged, it is called the Doctors' Commons. Above this,
on the same side, was one other great building over-against
Paules brewhouse, and this was called Paules bakehouse,

and was employed in baking of bread for the church of Paules.

In Addle street, or lane, I find no monuments.

In Lambart hill lane on the west side thereof, is the Blacksmiths' hall, and adjoining to the north side thereof have ye one plot of ground, inclosed with a brick wall for a churchyard, or burying-plot for the dead of St. Mary Magdalen's by Old Fish street, which was given to that use by John Iwarby, an officer in the receipt of the exchequer, in the 26th of King Henry VI., as appeareth by patent. John Iwarby, etc., gave a piece of land lying void in the parish of St. Mary Magdalen, nigh to Old Fish street, between the tenement of John Philpot on the south, and the tenement of Bartholomewe Burwash on the west, and the tenement pertaining to the convent of the Holy Well on the north, and the way upon Lambarde's hill on the east, for a churchyard, to the parson, and churchwardens, etc.

Over-against the north-west end of this Lambard hill lane in Knightriders' street, is the parish church of St. Mary Magdalen, a small church, having but few monuments, Richard Woodroffe, merchant tailor, 1519; Barnard Randolph, esquire, 1583.

On the west side of this church, by the porch thereof, is placed a conduit or cistern of lead, castellated with stone, for receipt of Thames water, conveyed at the charges of the before-named Barnard Randolph, esquire. By the east end of St. Mary Magdalen's church, runneth up the Old Exchange lane, by the west end of Carter lane, to the south-east gate or chain of Paule's churchyard, as is before shown. And in this part was the Exchange kept, and bullion was received for coinage, as is noted in Faringdon ward within.

In this parish church of St. Mary Magdalen, out of Knightriders' street up to Carter lane, be two small lanes, the one of them called Do Little lane, as a place not inhabited by artificers or open shopkeepers, but serving for a near passage from Knightriders' street to Carter lane.

The other, corruptly called Sermon lane, for Sheremoniers' lane, for I find it by that name recorded in the 14th of Edward I., and in that lane, a place to be called the Blacke loft (of melting silver) with four shops adjoining. It may, therefore, be well supposed that lane to take name of Sheremonyars, such as cut and rounded the plates to be coined or stamped into sterling pence; for the place of coining was the Old Exchange, near unto the said Sheremoniars' lane. Also I find that in the 13th of Richard II. William de la Pole had a house there.

In Knightriders' street is the College of Physicians, wherein was founded in the year 1582 a public lecture in surgery, to be read twice every week, etc., as is shown elsewhere.

In the south churchyard of Paules, is the south side and west end of the said church; in the which west end be three stately gates or entries, curiously wrought of stone: namely, the middle gate, in the midst whereof is placed a massy pillar of brass, whereunto the leaves of the said great gate are closed and fastened with locks, bolts, and bars of iron; all which, notwithstanding, on the 24th of December in the year 1565, by a tempest of wind then rising from the west, these gates were blown open, the bars, bolts, and locks broken in sunder, or greatly bended. Also on the 5th of January in the year 1589, by a like tempest of wind, then in the south-west, the lesser west gate of the said church, next to the bishop's palace, was broken, both bolts, bars, and locks, so that the same was blown over.

At either corner of this west end is, also of ancient building, a strong tower of stone, made for bell towers: the one of them, to wit, next to the palace, is at this present to the use of the same palace; the other, towards the south, is called the Lowlardes' tower,[1] and hath been used as the bishop's prison, for such as were detected for opinions in religion, contrary to the faith of the Church.

The last prisoner which I have known committed thereto, was in the year 1573, one Peter Burcher, gentleman, of the Middle Temple, for having desperately wounded, and minding to have murdered, a serviceable gentleman named John Hawkins, esquire, in the high street near unto the Strand, who being taken and examined, was found to hold certain opinions erroneous, and therefore committed thither, and convicted; but in the end, by persuasion, he promised to abjure his heresies; and was, by commandment of the council, removed from thence to the Tower of London, etc., where he committed as in my *Annales* I have expressed.

Adjoining to this Lowlardes' tower is the parish-church of St. Gregory, appointed to the petty canons of Paules. Monuments of note I know none there.

The rest of that south side of St. Paules church, with the chapter-house (a beautiful piece of work, built about the reign of Edward III.) is now defaced by means of licenses granted to cutlers, budget-makers, and others, first to build low sheds,

---

[1] For Lowlardes' Tower, read M. Foxe.—*Stow*.

but now high houses, which do hide that beautiful side of the church, save only the top and south gate.

On the north-west side of this churchyard is the bishop's palace, a large thing for receipt, wherein divers kings have been lodged, and great household hath been kept, as appeareth by the great hall, which of late years, since the rebatement of bishops' livings, hath not been furnished with household menie and guests, as was meant by the builders thereof, and was of old time used.

The dean's lodging on the other side, directly against the palace, is a fair old house, and also divers large houses are on the same side builded, which yet remain, and of old time were the lodgings of prebendaries and residentiaries, which kept great households and liberal hospitality, but now either decayed, or otherwise converted.

Then is the Stationers' hall on the same side, lately built for them in place of Peter College, where in the year 1549, the 4th of January, five men were slain by the fall of earth upon them, digging for a well. And let this be an end of Baynardes Castle ward, which hath an alderman, his deputy, common council nine, constables ten, scavengers seven, wardmote inquest fourteen, and a beadle. And to the fifteen is taxed at £12, in the exchequer £11 13s.

THE WARD OF FARINGDON EXTRA, OR WITHOUT

The farthest west ward of this city, being the twenty-fifth ward of London, but without the walls, is called Faringdon Without, and was of old time part of the other Faringdon Within, until the 17th of Richard II., that it was divided and made twain, by the names of Faringdon *infra* and Faringdon *extra*, as is afore shown.

The bounds of which ward without Newgate and Ludgate are these: first, on the east part thereof, is the whole precinct of the late priory of St. Bartholomew, and a part of Long lane on the north, towards Aldersgate street and Ducke lane, with the hospital of St. Bartholomew on the west, and all Smithfield to the bars in St. John Street. Then out of Smithfield, Chicke lane toward Turmile brook, and over that brook by a bridge of timber into the field, then back again by the pens (or folds) in Smithfield, by Smithfield pond to Cow lane, which turneth toward Oldborne, and then Hosiar lane out of Smithfield, also toward Oldborne, till it meet with a part of Cow lane. Then

Cocke lane out of Smithfield, over-against Pie corner, then also
is Giltspur street, out of Smithfield to Newgate, then from
Newgate west by St. Sepulchres church to Turnagaine lane, to
Oldborne conduit, on Snow hill, to Oldborne bridge, up Oldborne hill to the bars on both sides. On the right hand or
north side, at the bottom of Oldborne hill, is Gold lane, sometime a filthy passage into the fields, now both sides built with
small tenements. Then higher is Lither lane, turning also to the
field, lately replenished with houses built, and so to the bar.

Now on the left hand or south side from Newgate lieth a
street called the Old Bayly, or court of the chamberlain of this
city; this stretcheth down by the wall of the city unto Ludgate,
on the west side of which street breaketh out one other lane,
called St. Georges lane, till ye come to the south end of Seacole
lane, and then turning towards Fleet street it is called Fleet
lane. The next out of the high street from Newgate turning
down south, is called the Little Bayly, and runneth down to the
east of St. George's lane. Then is Seacole lane which turneth
down into Fleet lane; near unto this Seacole lane, in the turning
towards Oldborne conduit, is another lane, called in records
Wind Againe lane, it turneth down to Turnemill brook, and
from thence back again, for there is no way over. Then beyond
Oldborne bridge to Shoe lane, which runneth out of Oldborne
unto the Conduit in Fleet street. Then also is Fewtars lane,
which likewise stretcheth south into Fleet street by the east
end of St. Dunstans church, and from this lane to the bars be
the bounds without Newgate.

Now without Ludgate, this ward runneth by from the said
gate to Temple bar, and hath on the right hand or north side
the south end of the Old Bayly, then down Ludgate hill to the
Fleet lane over Fleet bridge, and by Shoe lane and Fewters
lane, and so to New street (or Chancery lane), and up that lane
to the house of the Rolles, which house is also of this ward, and
on the other side to a lane over against the Rolles, which entereth
Ficquets' field. [*See* Additional Notes.]

Then hard by the bar is one other lane called Shyre lane,
because it divideth the city from the shire, and this turneth
into Ficquets' field.

From Ludgate again on the left hand, or south side to Fleet
bridge, to Bride lane, which runneth south by Bridewell, then
to Water lane, which runneth down to the Thames.

Then by the White Fryers and by the Temple, even to the
bar aforesaid, be the bounds of this Faringdon Ward without.

Touching ornaments and antiquities in this ward, first betwixt the said Newgate and the parish church of St. Sepulchre's, is a way towards Smithfield, called Gilt Spurre, or Knightriders' street, of the knights and others riding that way into Smithfield, replenished with buildings on both sides up to Pie corner, a place so called of such a sign, sometimes a fair inn for receipt of travellers, but now divided into tenements, and over against the said Pie corner lieth Cocke lane, which runneth down to Oldborne conduit.

Beyond this Pie corner lieth West Smithfield, compassed about with buildings, as first on the south side following the right hand, standeth the fair parish church and large hospital of St. Bartilmew, founded by Rahere, the first prior of St. Bartilmewes thereto near adjoining, in the year 1102.

Alfune, that had not long before built the parish church of St. Giles without Criplegate, became the first hospitaller, or proctor, for the poor of the house, and went himself daily to the shambles and other markets, where he begged the charity of devout people for their relief, promising to the liberal givers (and that by alleging testimonies of the holy scripture) reward at the hands of God. Henry III. granted to Katherine, late wife to W. Hardell, twenty feet of land in length and breadth in Smithfield, next to the chapel of the hospital of St. Bartilmew, to build her a recluse or anchorage, commanding the mayor and sheriffs of London to assign the said twenty feet to the said Katherine, Carta 11 of Henry III. The foundation of this hospital, for the poor and diseased their special sustentation, was confirmed by Edward III. the 26th of his reign: it was governed by a master and eight brethren, being priests, for the church, and four sisters to see the poor served. The executors of R. Whitington, sometime mayor of London, of his goods repaired this hospital, about the year 1423.

Sir John Wakering, priest, master of this house in the year 1463, amongst other books, gave to their common library the fairest Bible that I have seen, written in large vellum by a brother of that house named John Coke, at the age of sixty-eight years, when he had been priest forty-three years: since the spoil of that library, I have seen this book in the custody of my worshipful friend, Master Walter Cope.

Monuments in this church of the dead, benefactors thereunto, be these: Elizabeth, wife to Adam Hone, gentleman; Bartilmew Bildington; Jane, wife to John Cooke; Dame Alis, wife to Sir Richarde Isham; Alice, wife to Nicholas Bayly; John Woodhouse, esquire; Robert Palmar, gentleman; Idona, wife to John Walden, lying by her husband on the north side, late newly built, 1424; Sir Thomas Malifant, or Nanfant, Baron of Winnow, Lord St. George in Glamorgan, and Lord Ockeneton and Pile in the county of Pembroke, 1438; Dame Margaret his wife, daughter to Thomas Astley, esquire, with Edmond and Henry his children; William Markeby, gentleman, 1438; Richard Shepley, and Alice his wife; Thomas Savill, serjeant-at-arms; Edward Beastby, gentleman, and Margaret his wife; Waltar Ingham, and Alienar his wife; Robert Warnar, and Alice Lady Carne; Robert Caldset, Johan and Agnes his wives; Sir Robert Danvars, and Dame Agnes his wife, daughter to Sir Richard Delaber; William Brookes, esquire; John Shirley, esquire, and Margaret his wife, having their pictures of brass, in the habit of pilgrims, on a fair flat stone, with an epitaph thus:—

> " Beholde how ended is our poore pilgrimage,
> Of John Shirley, esquier, with Margaret his wife,
> That xii. children had together in marriage,
> Eight sonnes and foure daughters withouten strife,
> That in honor, nurtur, and labour flowed in fame,
> His pen reporteth his lives occupation,
> Since Pier his life time, John Shirley by name,
> Of his degree, that was in Brutes Albion,
> That in the yeare of grace deceased from hen,
> Fourteene hundred winter, and sixe and fiftie,
> In the yeare of his age, fourescore and ten,
> Of October moneth, the day one and twenty."

This gentleman, a great traveller in divers countries, amongst other his labours, painfully collected the works of Geffrey Chaucer, John Lidgate, and other learned writers, which works he wrote in sundry volumes to remain for posterity; I have seen them, and partly do possess them. Jane, Lady Clinton, gave ten pounds to the poor of this house, was there buried, 1458; Agnes, daughter to Sir William St. George; John Rogerbrooke, esquire; Richard Sturgeon; Thomas Burgan, gentleman; Elizabeth, wife to Henry Skinard, daughter to Chincroft, esquire; William Mackley, gentleman, and Alice his wife; W. Fitzwater, gentleman, 1466.

This hospital was valued at the suppression in the year 1539, the 31st of Henry VIII., to thirty-five pounds five shillings and seven pence yearly. The church remaineth a parish church to the tenants dwelling in the precinct of the hospital; but in the year 1546, on the 13th of January, the bishop of Rochester, preaching at Paules cross, declared the gift of the said king to the citizens for relieving of the poor, which contained the church of the Gray Fryers, the church of St. Bartilmew, with the hospital, the messuages, and appurtenances in Giltspurre *alias* Knightriders' street, Breton street, Petar quay, in the parish of St. Mary Magdalen, in Old Fish street, and in the parish of St. Benet Buda, Lymehurst, or Limehost, in the parish of Stebunheth, etc. Then also were orders devised for relief of the poor, the inhabitants were all called to their parish churches, whereby Sir Richard Dobbes, then mayor, their several aldermen, or other grave citizens, they were by eloquent orations persuaded how great and how many commodities would ensue unto them and their city, if the poor of divers sorts, which they named, were taken from out their streets, lanes, and alleys, and were bestowed and provided for in hospitals abroad, etc. Therefore was every man moved liberally to grant, what they would impart towards the preparing and furnishing of such hospitals, and also what they would contribute weekly towards their maintenance for a time, which they said should not be past one year, or twain, until they were better furnished of endowment: to make short, every man granted liberally, according to his ability; books were drawn of the relief in every ward of the city, towards the new hospitals, and were delivered by the mayor to the king's commissioners, on the 17th of February, and order was taken therein; so as the 26th of July in the year 1552, the repairing of the Gray Fryers' house, for poor fatherless children, was taken in hand; and also in the latter end of the same month, began the repairing of this hospital of St. Bartilmew, and was of new endowed, and furnished at the charges of the citizens.

On the east side of this hospital lieth Ducke lane, which runneth out of Smithfield south to the north end of Little Britaine street. On the east side of this Ducke lane, and also of Smithfield, lieth the late dissolved priory of St. Bartilmew, founded also by Rahere, a pleasant witted gentleman, and therefore in his time called the king's minstrel, about the year of Christ 1102; he founded it in a part of the oft before-named morish ground, which was therefore a common laystall of all filth that was to be voided out of the city; he placed canons there, himself became their first prior, and so continued till his dying day, and was there buried in a fair monument,[1] of late renewed by Prior Bolton.

[1] With the following inscription: " *Hic jacet Raherus primus canonicus, et primus prior istius Ecclesiæ.*"

Amongst other memorable matters touching this priory, one is of an archbishop's visitation, which Matthew Paris hath thus:—Boniface (saith he) Archbishop of Canterbury, in his visitation came to this priory, where being received with procession in the most solemn wise, he said, that he passed not upon the honour, but came to visit them; to whom the canons answered, that they having a learned bishop, ought not in contempt of him to be visited by any other: which answer so much offended the archbishop, that he forthwith fell on the subprior, and smote him on the face, saying, "Indeed, indeed, doth it become you English traitors so to answer me." Thus raging, with oaths not to be recited, he rent in pieces the rich cope of the subprior, and trod it under his feet, and thrust him against a pillar of the chancel with such violence, that he had almost killed him; but the canons seeing their subprior thus almost slain, came and plucked off the archbishop with such force that they overthrew him backwards, whereby they might see that he was armed and prepared to fight; the archbishop's men seeing their master down, being all strangers, and their master's countrymen, born at Provence, fell upon the canons, beat them, tare them, and trod them under feet; at length the canons getting away as well as they could, ran bloody and miry, rent and torn, to the bishop of London to complain, who bade them go to the king at Westminster, and tell him thereof; whereupon four of them went thither, the rest were not able, they were so sore hurt; but when they came to Westminster, the king would neither hear nor see them, so they returned without redress. In the mean season the whole city was in an uproar, and ready to have rung the common bell, and to have hewn the archbishop into small pieces, who was secretly crept to Lambhith, where they sought him, and not knowing him by sight, said to themselves, Where is this ruffian? that cruel smiter! he is no winner of souls, but an exactor of money, whom neither God, nor any lawful or free election did bring to this promotion, but the king did unlawfully intrude him, being utterly unlearned, a stranger born, and having a wife, etc. But the archbishop conveyed himself over, and went to the king with a great complaint against the canons, whereas himself was guilty. This priory of St. Bartholomew was again new built in the year 1410.

Bolton was the last prior of this house, a great builder there; for he repaired the priory church, with the parish church adjoining, the offices and lodgings to the said priory belonging, and near adjoining; he built anew the manor of Canonbery at Islington, which belonged to the canons of this house, and is situate in a low ground, somewhat north from the parish church there; but he built no house at Harrow on the Hill, as Edward Hall hath written, following a fable then on foot. The people (saith he) being feared by prognostications, which declared, that in the year of Christ 1524 there should be such eclipses in watery signs, and such conjunctions, that by waters and floods many people should perish, people victualled themselves, and went to high grounds for fear of drowning, and especially one Bolton, which was prior of St. Bartholomewes in Smithfield, built him a house upon Harrow on the Hill, only for fear of this flood; thither he went, and made provision of all things necessary within him for the space of two months, etc.; but this was not so indeed, as I have been credibly informed. True it is, that this Bolton was also parson of Harrow, and therefore bestowed some small reparations on the parsonage-house, and built nothing there more than a dove-house, to serve him when he had forgone his priory.

To this priory King Henry II. granted the privilege of fair, to be kept yearly at Bartholomew tide for three days, to wit, the eve, the day, and next morrow, to the which the clothiers of all England, and drapers of London, repaired,[1] and had their booths and standings within the churchyard of this priory, closed in with walls, and gates locked every night, and watched, for safety of men's goods and wares; a court of pie powders was daily during the fair holden for debts and contracts. But now, notwithstanding all proclamations of the prince, and also the act of parliament, in place of booths within this churchyard (only let out in the fair-time, and closed up all the year after), be many large houses built, and the north wall towards Long lane taken down, a number of tenements are there erected for such as will give great rents.

Monuments of the dead in this priory are these: of Rahere, the first founder; Roger Walden, Bishop of London, 1406; John Wharton, gentleman, and Elizabeth his wife, daughter to William Scot, esquire; John Louth, gentleman; Robert Shikeld, gentleman; Sir —— Bacon, knight; John Ludlow and Alice his wife; W. Thirlewall, esquire; Richard Lancaster, herald-at-arms; Thomas Torald; John Royston; John Watforde; John Carleton; Robert, son to Sir Robert Willowby; Gilbert Hal-

---

[1] " The forrens were licensed for three dayes; the freemen so long as they would, which was sixe or seven dayes."—*Stow*.

stocke; Eleanor, wife to Sir Hugh Fen, mother to Margaret
Lady Burgavenie; William Essex, esquire; Richard Vancke,
baron of the exchequer, and Margaret his wife, daughter to
William de la Rivar; John Winderhall; John Duram, esquire,
and Elizabeth his wife; John Malwaine; Alice, wife to Balstred,
daughter to Kniffe; William Scarlet, esquire; John Golding;
Hugh Waltar, gentleman; and the late Sir Waltar Mildmay,
knight, chancellor of the exchequer, etc.

This priory at the late surrender, the 30th of Henry VIII.,
was valued at £653 15s. by year.

This church having in the bell-tower six bells in a tune, those
bells were sold to the parish of St. Sepulchre's; and then the
church being pulled down to the choir, the choir was, by the
king's order, annexed for the enlarging of the old parish church
thereto adjoining, and so was used till the reign of Queen Mary,
who gave the remnant of the priory church to the Friers
preachers, or Black Friers, and was used as their conventual
church until, the 1st of our sovereign lady Queen Elizabeth,
those friars were put out, and all the said church, with the old
parish church, was wholly as it stood in the last year of Edward
VI., given by parliament to remain for ever a parish church to
the inhabitants within the close called Great St. Bartholomewes.
Since the which time that old parish church is pulled down,
except the steeple of rotten timber ready to fall of itself. I have
oft heard it reported, that a new steeple should be built with
the stone, lead, and timber of the old parish church, but
no such thing was performed. The parish have lately repaired the old wooden steeple to serve their turn. On the
north side of this priory is the lane truly called Long, which
reacheth from Smithfield to Aldersgate street. This lane is
now lately built on both the sides with tenements for brokers,
tipplers, and such like; the rest of Smithfield from Long lane
end to the bars is enclosed with inns, brewhouses, and large
tenements; on the west side is Chicken lane down to Cowbridge.
Then be the pens or folds, so called, of sheep there parted, and
penned up to be sold on the market-days.

Then is Smithfield pond, which of old time in records was
called Horse-pool, for that men watered horses there, and was
a great water. In the 6th of Henry V. a new building was made
in this west part of Smithfield betwixt the said pool and the
river of the Wels, or Turnemill brooke, in a place then called
the Elmes, for that there grew many elm-trees; and this had
been the place of execution for offenders; since the which time

the building there hath been so increased, that now remaineth not one tree growing.

Amongst these new buildings is Cowbridge street, or Cow lane, which turneth toward Oldborne, in which lane the prior of Semperingham had his inn, or London lodging.

The rest of that west side of Smithfield hath divers fair inns, and other comely buildings, up to Hosiar lane, which also turneth down to Oldborne till it meet with Cowbridge street. From this lane to Cocke lane, over against Pie corner.

And thus much for encroachments and enclosure of this Smithfield, whereby remaineth but a small portion for the old uses; to wit, for markets of horses and cattle, neither for military exercises, as joustings, turnings, and great triumphs, which have been there performed before the princes and nobility both of this realm and foreign countries.

For example to note:—In the year 1357, the 31st of Edward III., great and royal jousts were there holden in Smithfield; there being present, the Kings of England, France, and Scotland, with many other nobles and great estates of divers lands.

1362, the 36th of Edward III., on the first five days of May, in Smithfield, were jousts holden, the king and queen being present, with the most part of the chivalry of England, and of France, and of other nations, to the which came Spaniards, Cyprians and Arminians, knightly requesting the king of England against the pagans that invaded their confines.

The 48th of Edward III., Dame Alice Perrers (the king's concubine), as Lady of the Sun, rode from the Tower of London, through Cheape, accompanied of many lords and ladies, every lady leading a lord by his horse-bridle, till they came into West Smithfield, and then began a great joust, which endured seven days after.

Also, the 9th of Richard II., was the like great riding from the Tower to Westminster, and every lord led a lady's horse-bridle; and on the morrow began the joust in Smithfield, which lasted two days: there bare them well, Henry of Darby, the Duke of Lankester's son, the Lord Beaumont, Sir Simon Burley, and Sir Paris Courtney.

In the 14th of Richard II., after Froisart, royal jousts and tournaments were proclaimed to be done in Smithfield, to begin on Sunday next after the feast of St. Michael. Many strangers came forth of other countries, namely, Valarian, Earl of St. Paul, that had married King Richard's sister, the Lady Maud Courtney, and William, the young Earl of Ostervant, son to Albart of

Baviere, Earl of Holland and Henault. At the day appointed there issued forth of the Tower, about the third hour of the day, sixty coursers, apparelled for the jousts, and upon every one an esquire of honour, riding a soft pace; then came forth sixty ladies of honour, mounted upon palfreys, riding on the one side, richly apparelled, and every lady led a knight with a chain of gold, those knights being on the king's party, had their harness and apparel garnished with white harts, and crowns of gold about the harts' necks, and so they came riding through the streets of London to Smithfield, with a great number of trumpets, and other instruments of music before them. The king and queen, who were lodged in the bishop's palace of London, were come from thence, with many great estates, and placed in chambers to see the jousts; the ladies that led the knights were taken down from their palfreys, and went up to chambers prepared for them. Then alighted the esquires of honour from their coursers, and the knights in good order mounted upon them; and after their helmets were set on their heads, and being ready in all points, proclamation made by the heralds, the jousts began, and many commendable courses were run, to the great pleasure of the beholders. These jousts continued many days, with great feasting, as ye may read in Froisart.

In the year 1393, the 17th of Richard II., certain lords of Scotland came into England to get worship by force of arms; the Earl of Mare challenged the Earl of Notingham to joust with him, and so they rode together certain courses, but not the full challenge, for the Earl of Mare was cast both horse and man, and two of his ribs broken with the fall, so that he was conveyed out of Smithfield, and so towards Scotland, but died by the way at Yorke. Sir William Darell, knight, the king's banner-bearer of Scotland, challenged Sir Percie Courtney, knight, the king's banner-bearer of England; and when they had run certain courses, gave over without conclusion of victory. Then Cookeborne, esquire, of Scotland, challenged Sir Nicholas Hawberke, knight, and rode five courses, but Cookeborne was borne over horse and man, etc.

In the year 1409, the 10th of Henry IV., a great play was played at the Skinners' well, which lasted eight days, where were to see the same the most part of the nobles and gentles in England. And forthwith began a royal jousting in Smithfield between the Earl of Somerset, and the Seneschal of Henalt, Sir John Cornwall, Sir Richard Arrundell, and the son of Sir John Cheiney, against certain Frenchmen. And the same year a battle was fought in Smithfield between two esquires, the one called Glaucester, appellant, and the other Arthure, defendant; they fought valiantly, but the king took up the quarrel into his hands, and pardoned them both.

In the year 1430, the 8th of Henry VI., the 14th of January, a battle was done in Smithfield, within the lists, before the king, between two men of Feversham in Kent, John Upton, notary, appellant, and John Downe, gentleman, defendant; John Upton put upon John Downe, that he and his compeers should imagine the king's death the day of his coronation. When these had fought long, the king took up the matter, and forgave both the parties.

In the year 1442, the 20th of Henry VI., the 30th of January, a challenge was done in Smithfield, within lists, before the king, there being Sir Philip la Beaufe of Aragon, knight, the other an esquire of the king's house, called John Ansley or Anstley; they came to the field all armed, the knight with his sword drawn, and the esquire with his spear, which spear he cast against the knight, but the knight avoided it with his sword, and cast it to the ground; then the esquire took his axe, and smote many blows on the knight, and made him let fall his axe, and brake up his uniber three times, and would have smote him on the face with his dagger, for to have slain him, but then the king cried hold, and so they were departed. The king made John Ansley, knight, and the knight of Aragon offered his harness at Windsor.

In the year 1446, the 24th of Henry VI., John David appeached his master, Wil. Catur, of treason, and a day being assigned them to fight in Smithfield; the master being well-beloved, was so cherished by his friends, and plied with wine, that being therewith overcome, was also unluckily slain by his servant; but that false servant (for he falsely accused his master) lived not long unpunished, for he was after hanged at Teyborne for felony. Let such false accusers note this for example,[1] and look for no better end without speedy repentance.

The same year Thomas Fitz-Thomas Prior of Kilmaine appeached Sir James Butlar, Earl of Ormond, of treasons; which had a day assigned them to fight in Smithfield, the lists were made, and the field prepared; but when it came to the point, the king commanded they should not fight, and took the quarrel into his hands.

In the year 1467, the 7th of Edward IV., the Bastard of

[1] "John Davy, a false accuser of his master, of him was raised the byword,—If ye serve me so, I will call you Davy."—*Stow.*

Burgoine challenged the Lord Scales, brother to the queen, to fight with him both on horseback and on foot; the king, therefore, caused lists to be prepared in Smithfield, the length of one hundred and twenty tailors' yards and ten feet, and in breadth eighty yards and twenty feet, double-barred, five feet between the bars, the timber-work whereof cost two hundred marks, besides the fair and costly galleries prepared for the ladies and other, at the which martial enterprise the king and nobility were present. The first day they ran together with spears, and departed with equal honour. The next day they tourneyed on horseback, the Lord Scales horse having on his chafron, a long spear pike of steel; and as the two champions coped together, the same horse thrust his pike into the nostrils of the Bastard's horse, so that for very pain he mounted so high that he fell on the one side with his master, and the Lord Scales rode about him with his sword drawn, till the king commanded the marshal to help up the Bastard, who said, I cannot hold me by the clouds; for though my horse fail me, I will not fail an encounter companion; but the king would not suffer them to do any more that day.

The next morrow they came into the lists on foot with two pole-axes, and fought valiantly; but at the last the point of the pole-axe of the Lord Scales entered into the side of the Bastard's helm, and by force might have placed him on his knees; but the king cast down his warder, and the marshal severed them. The Bastard required that he might perform his enterprise; but the king gave judgment as the Bastard relinquished his challenge, etc. And this may suffice for jousts in Smithfield.

Now to return through Giltspur street by Newgate, where I first began, there standeth the fair parish church called St. Sepulchers in the Bayly, or by Chamberlain gate, in a fair churchyard, though not so large as of old time, for the same is letten out for buildings and a garden-plot.

This church was newly re-edified or built about the reign of Henry VI. or of Edward IV. One of the Pophames was a great builder there, namely, of one fair chapel on the south side of the choir, as appeareth by his arms and other monuments in the glass windows thereof, and also the fair porch of the same church towards the south; his image, fair graven in stone, was fixed over the said porch, but defaced and beaten down; his title by offices was this, Chancellor of Normandy, Captain of Vernoyle, Pearch, Susan, and Bayon, and treasurer of the king's household: he died rich, leaving great treasure of strange coins, and was buried in the Charterhouse church by West Smithfield. The first nobilitating of these Pophames was by Matilda the empress, daughter to Henry I., and by Henry her son: one Pophame, gentleman, of very fair lands in Southamptonshire, died without issue male, about Henry VI., and leaving four daughters, they were married to Fostar, Barentine, Wodham, and Hamden. Popham Deane (distant three miles from Clarendon, and three miles from Mortisham) was sometime the chief lordship or manor-house of these Pophames.

There lie buried in this church, William Andrew, Stephen Clamparde, Lawrence Warcam, John Dagworth, William Porter, Robert Scarlet, esquires.

Next to this church is a fair and large inn for receipt of travellers, and hath to sign the Sarasen's head.

There lieth a street from Newgate west to the end of Turnagaine lane, and winding north to Oldborne conduit. This conduit by Oldborne cross was first built 1498. Thomasin, widow to John Percival, mayor, gave to the second making thereof twenty marks, Richard Shore ten pounds. Thomas Knesworth and others also did give towards it.

But of late a new conduit was there built in place of the old, namely, in the year 1577, by William Lamb, sometime a gentleman of the chapel to King Henry VIII., and afterward a citizen and clothworker of London; the water thereof he caused to be conveyed in lead, from divers springs to one head, and from thence to the said conduit, and waste of one cock at Oldborne bridge, more than two thousand yards in length; all of which was by him performed at his own charges, amounting to the sum of fifteen hundred pounds.

From the west side of this conduit is the high way, there called Snor hill; it stretcheth out by Oldborne bridge over the oft-named water of Turmill brook, and so up to Oldborne hill, all replenished with fair building.

Without Oldborne bridge, on the right hand, is Gold lane, as is before shown; up higher on the hill be certain inns, and other fair buildings, amongst the which of old time was a messuage called Scropes inn, for so I find the same recorded in the 37th of Henry VI.

This house was sometime letten out to serjeants-at-the-law, as appeareth, and was found by inquisition taken in the Guild hall of London, before William Purchase, mayor, and escheator for the king, Henry VII., in the 14th of his reign, after the death of John Lord Scrope, that he died deceased in his demesne of fee, by the feoffment of Guy Fairfax, knight, one of the king's justices, made in the 9th of the same king, unto the said John Scrope, knight, Lord Scrope of Bolton, and Robert Wingfield, esquire, of one house or tenement, late called Sergeants' inn, situate against the church of St. Andrew in Oldborne, in the city of London, with two gardens and two messuages to the same tenement belonging in the said city, to hold in burgage, valued by the year in all reprises ten shillings.

Then is the bishop of Elie's inn,[1] so called of belonging and pertaining to the bishops of Elie. William de Luda, bishop of Elie, deceased 1297, gave this house by the name of his manor, with the appurtenances in Oldborne, to his successors, with condition his next successor should pay one thousand marks to the finding of three chaplains in the chapel there. More, John Hotham, bishop of Elie, did give by the name of six messuages, two cellars, and forty acres of land, in the suburbs of London, in the parish of St. Andrew in Oldborne, to the prior and convent of Elie, as appeareth by patent, the 9th of Edward III.: this man was bishop of Elie twenty years, and deceased 1336.

Thomas Arundell, bishop of Elie, beautifully built of new his palace at Elie, and likewise his manors in divers places, especially this in Oldborne, which he did not only repair, but rather new-built, and augmented it with a large port, gate-house, or front, towards the street or highway; his arms are yet to be discerned in the stone-work thereof: he sat bishop of Elie fourteen years, and was translated to Yorke.

In this house, for the large and commodious rooms thereof, divers great and solemn feasts have been kept, especially by the serjeants-at-the-law, whereof twain are to be noted for posterity.

The first in the year 1464, the 4th of Edward IV., in Michaelmas term, the serjeants-at-law held their feast in this house, to the which, amongst other estates, Matthew Phillip, mayor of London, with the aldermen, sheriffs, and commons, of divers crafts, being invited, did repair; but when the mayor looked to keep the state in the hall, as it had been used in all places within the city and liberties (out of the king's presence), the Lord Gray of Ruthen, then lord treasurer of England, unwitting the serjeants, and against their wills (as they said), was first placed; whereupon the mayor, aldermen, and commons, departed home, and the mayor made the aldermen to dine with him; howbeit he and all the citizens were wonderfully displeased, that he was so

[1] " Commonly called Ely place."—1st *edition*, p. 323.

dealt with; and the new serjeants and others were right sorry therefore, and had rather then much good (as they said) it had not so happened.

One other feast was likewise there kept in the year 1531, the 23rd of King Henry VIII.: the serjeants then made were in number eleven; namely, Thomas Audeley, Walter Luke, I. Bawdwine, I. Hinde, Christopher Jennie, John Dowsell, Edward Mervine, Edmond Knightley, Roger Chomley, Edward Montague, and Robert Yorke.

These also held their feast in this Elie house for five days, to wit, Friday the 10th of November, Saturday, Sunday, Monday, and Tuesday. On Monday (which was their principal day) King Henry and Queen Katherine dined there (but in two chambers), and the foreign ambassadors in a third chamber. In the hall, at the high table, sat Sir Nicholas Lambard, Mayor of London, the judges, the barons of the exchequer, with certain aldermen of the city. At the board on the south side sat the master of the rolls, the master of the chancery, and worshipful citizens. On the north side of the hall certain aldermen began the board, and then followed merchants of the city; in the cloister, chapel, and gallery, knights, esquires, and gentlemen, were placed; in the halls the crafts of London; the serjeants-of-law and their wives, kept in their own chambers.

It were tedious to set down the preparation of fish, flesh, and other victuals, spent in this feast, and would seem almost incredible, and, as to me it seemeth, wanted little of a feast at a coronation; nevertheless, a little I will touch, for declaration of the change of prices. There were brought to the slaughter-house twenty-four great beefs at twenty-six shillings and eight pence the piece from the shambles, one carcass of an ox at twenty-four shillings, one hundred fat muttons, two shillings and ten pence the piece, fifty-one great veals at four shillings and eight pence the piece, thirty-four porks three shillings and eight pence the piece, ninety-one pigs, sixpence the piece, capons of grese, of one poulter (for they had three) ten dozens at twenty pence the piece, capons of Kent, nine dozens and six at twelve pence the piece, capons coarse, nineteen dozen at six pence the piece, cocks of grose, seven dozen and nine at eight pence the piece, cocks coarse, fourteen dozen and eight at three pence the piece, pullets, the best, two pence halfpenny, other pullets two pence, pigeons thirty-seven dozen at ten pence the dozen, swans fourteen dozen, larks three hundred and forty dozen at five pence the dozen, etc. Edward Nevill was seneschal or steward,

Thomas Ratcliffe, comptroller, Thomas Wildon, clerk of the kitchen.

Next beyond this manor of Ely house is Lither lane, turning into the field.   Then is Furnivalles inn, now an inn of chancery, but sometime belonging to Sir William Furnivall, knight, and Thomesin his wife, who had in Oldborne two messuages and thirteen shops, as appeareth by record of Richard II., in the 6th of his reign.

Then is the Earl of Bathes inn, now called Bath place, of late for the most part new built, and so to the bars.

Now again, from Newgate, on the left hand, or south side, lieth the Old Bayly, which runneth down by the wall upon the ditch of the city, called Houndes ditch, to Ludgate. I have not read how this street took that name, but is like to have risen of some court, of old time there kept; and I find, that in the year 1356, the 34th of Edward III., the tenement and ground upon Houndes ditch, between Ludgate on the south, and Newgate on the north, was appointed to John Cambridge, fishmonger, Chamberlain of London, whereby it seemeth that the chamberlains of London have there kept their courts, as now they do by the Guildhall, and till this day the mayor and justices of this city kept their sessions in a part thereof, now called the Sessions hall, both for the city of London and shire of Middlesex. Over against the which house, on the right hand, turneth down St. George's lane towards Fleet lane.

In this St. George's lane, on the north side thereof, remaineth yet an old wall of stone, enclosing a piece of ground up Seacole lane, wherein by report sometime stood an inn of chancery; which house being greatly decayed, and standing remote from other houses of that profession, the company removed to a common hostelry, called of the sign Our Lady inn, not far from Clement's inn, which they procured from Sir John Fineox, lord chief justice of the king's bench, and since have held it of the owners by the name of the New inn, paying therefore six pounds rent by the year, as tenants at their own will, for more (as is said) cannot be gotten of them, and much less will they be put from it.   Beneath this St. George's lane, the lane called Fleet lane, winding south by the prison of the Fleet into Fleet street by Fleet bridge.   Lower down in the Old Bayly is at this present a standard of timber, with a cock or cocks, delivering fair spring water to the inhabitants, and is the waste of the water serving the prisoners in Ludgate.

Next out of the high street turneth down a lane called the

Little Bayly, which runneth down to the east end of St. George's lane. The next is Seacole lane, I think called Limeburner's lane, of burning lime there with seacole. For I read in record of such a lane to have been in the parish of St. Sepulcher, and there yet remaineth in this lane an alley called Limeburner's alley. Near unto this Seacole lane, in the turning towards Oldborne conduit is Turnagain lane, or rather, as in a record of the 5th of Edward III., Windagain lane, for that it goeth down west to Fleet dike, from whence men must turn again the same way they came, for there it stopped. Then the high street turneth down Snore hill to Oldborne conduit, and from thence to Oldborne bridge, beyond the which bridge, on the left hand, is Shoe lane, by the which men pass from Oldborne to Fleet street, by the conduit there. In this Shoe lane, on the left hand, is one old house called Oldborne hall, it is now letten out into divers tenements.

On the other side, at the very corner, standeth the parish church of St. Andrew, in the which church, or near thereunto, was sometime kept a grammar school, as appeareth in another place by a patent made, as I have shown, for the erection of schools. There be monuments in this church of Thomas Lord Wriothesley, Earl of Southampton, buried 1550; Ralph Rokeby of Lincoln's inn, esquire, Master of St. Katherine's and one of the masters of requests to the queen's majesty, who deceased the 14th of June, 1596. He gave by his testament to Christ's Hospital in London one hundred pounds, to the college of the poor of Queen Elizabeth in East Greenwich one hundred pounds, to the poor scholars in Cambridge one hundred pounds, to the poor scholars in Oxford one hundred pounds, to the prisoners in the two compters in London two hundred pounds, to the prisoners in the Fleet one hundred pounds, to the prisoners in Ludgate one hundred pounds, to the prisoners in Newgate one hundred pounds, to the prisoners in the King's Bench one hundred pounds, to the prisoners in the Marshalsea one hundred pounds, to the prisoners in the White Lion twenty pounds, to the poor of St. Katherine's twenty pounds, and to every brother and sister there forty shillings; William Sydnam founded a chantry there. There was also of old time (as I have read in the 3rd of Henry V.) an hospital for the poor, which was a cell to the house of Cluny in France, and was, therefore, suppressed among the priories aliens.

From this church of St. Andrew, up Oldborne hill be divers fair built houses, amongst the which, on the left hand, there standeth three inns of Chancery, whereof the first adjoining unto Crookhorn alley is called Thaves inn, and standeth opposite, or over against the said Elyhouse. Then is Fewter lane, which stretcheth south into Fleet street, by the east end of St. Dunstone's church, and is so called of Fewters'[1] (or idle people) lying there, as in a way leading to gardens; but the same is now of latter years on both sides built through with many fair houses.

Beyond this Fewter lane is Barnard's inn, *alias* Mackworth's inn, which is of Chancery, belonging to the dean and chapter of Lincoln, as saith the record of Henry VI., the 32nd of his reign, and was founded by inquisition in the Guildhall of London, before John Norman, mayor, the king's escheator; the jury said, that it was not hurtful for the king to license T. Atkens, citizen of London, and one of the executors to John Mackworth, Dean of Lincoln, to give one messuage in Holborn in London, with the appurtenances called Mackworth's inn, but now commonly known by the name of Barnardes inn, to the dean and chapter of Lincoln, to find one sufficient chaplain to celebrate Divine service in the chapel of St. George, in the cathedral church of Lincoln, where the body of the said John is buried, to have and to hold the said messuage to the said dean and chapter, and to their successors for ever, in part of satisfaction of twenty pounds lands and rents, which Edward III. licensed the said dean and chapter to purchase to their own use, either of their own fee or tenor, or of any other, so the lands were not holden of the king *in capite*.

Then is Staple inn, also of Chancery, but whereof so named I am ignorant; the same of late is for a great part thereof fair built, and not a little augmented. And then at the bar endeth this ward without Newgate.

Without Ludgate, on the right hand, or north side from the said gate lieth the Old Bayly, as I said, then the high street called Ludgate hill down to Fleet lane, in which lane standeth the Fleet, a prison house so called of the Fleet or water running by it, and sometime flowing about it, but now vaulted over.

I read that Richard I., in the 1st of his reign, confirmed to Osbert, brother to William Longshampe, Chancellor of England and elect of Elie, and to his heirs for ever, the custody of his house or palace at Westminster, with the keeping of his gaol of the Fleet at London; also King John, by his patent, dated

---

[1] Fewters, idle people, probably from the old French *Fautier*, which Roquefort, *Glossaire de la Langue Romane*, defines "*Criminel Coupable*," or from *Fautteur*, "*rempli de défauts et de mauvaises habitudes*."

the 3rd of his reign, gave to the Archdeacon of Welles, the custody of the said king's house at Westminster, and of his gaol of the Fleet, together with the wardship of the daughter and heir of Robert Loveland, etc. Then is Fleet bridge pitched over the said water, whereof I have spoken in another place.

Then also against the south end of Shoe lane standeth a fair water-conduit, whereof William Eastfield, sometime mayor, was founder; for the mayor and commonalty of London being possessed of a conduit head, with divers springs of water gathered thereinto in the parish of Padington, and the water conveyed from thence by pipes of lead towards London unto Teyborne; where it had lain by the space of six years or more; the executors of Sir William Eastfield obtained licence of the mayor and commonalty for them, in the year 1453, with the goods of Sir William to convey the said waters, first in pipes of lead into a pipe begun to be laid beside the great conduit head at Maribone, which stretcheth from thence unto a separall, late before made against the chapel of Rounsevall by Charing cross, and no further, and then from thence to convey the said water into the city, and there to make receipt or receipts for the same unto the common weal of the commonalty, to wit, the poor to drink, the rich to dress their meats; which water was by them brought thus into Fleet street to a standard, which they had made and finished 1471.

The inhabitants of Fleet street, in the year 1478, obtained licence of the mayor, aldermen, and commonalty, to make at their own charges two cisterns, the one to be set at the said standard, the other at Fleet bridge, for the receipt of the waste water; this cistern at the standard they built, and on the same a fair tower of stone, garnished with images of St. Christopher on the top, and angels round about lower down, with sweet sounding bells before them, whereupon, by an engine placed in the tower, they divers hours of the day and night chimed such an hymn as was appointed.

This conduit, or standard, was again new built with a larger cistern, at the charges of the city, in the year 1582.

From this conduit up to Fewtars lane, and further, is the parish church of St. Dunstan called in the West (for difference from St. Dunstan in the East), here lieth buried T. Duke, skinner, in St. Katherin's chapel by him built, 1421; Nicholas Coningstone, John Knape, and other, founded chantries there; Ralph Bane, Bishop of Coventrie and Lichfield, 1559, and other.

Next beyond this church is Clifford's inn, sometime belonging to Robert Clifford, by gift of Edward II. in these words: "The king granteth to Robert Clifford that messuage, with the appurtenances, next the church of St. Dunstane in the West, in the suburbs of London, which messuage was sometime Malculines de Herley, and came to the hands of Edward I., by reason of certaine debts which the said Malculine was bound at the time of his death to our styde father, from the time that hee was escaetor on this side Trent; which house John, Earle of Richmount, did holde of our pleasure, and is now in our possession."— Patent, the 3rd of Edward II. After the death of this Robert Clifford, Isabel, his wife, let the same messuage to students of the law, as by the record following may appear:—

"*Isabel quæ fuit uxor Roberti Clifford, Messuagium unipartitum, quod Robertus Clifford habuit in parochia sci. Dunstonis West. in suburbio Londini, etc., tenuit, et illud dimisit post mortem dict. Roberti, Apprenticiis de banco, pro x. li. annuatium, etc. Anno 18 Eduardi Tertii, inquisitio post mortem Roberti Clifford.*"

This house hath since fallen into the king's hands, as I have heard, but returned again to the Cliffordes, and is now let to the said students for four pounds by the year.

Somewhat beyond this Clifford's inn is the south end of New street (or Chancelar lane), on the right hand whereof is Sergeantes' inn called in Chauncery lane. And then next was sometime the house of the converted Jewes, founded by King Henry III., in place of a Jewe's house to him forfeited, in the year 1233, and the 17th of his reign, who built there for them a fair church now used, and called the chapel for the custody of the Rolles and Records of Chancerie. It standeth not far from the Old Temple, but in the midway between the Old Temple and the New, in the which house all such Jewes and infidels, as were converted to the Christian faith, were ordained and appointed, under an honest rule of life, sufficient maintenance, whereby it came to pass, that in short time there were gathered a great number of converts, which were baptized, instructed in the doctrine of Christ, and there lived under a learned Christian appointed to govern them; since the which time, to wit, in the year 1290, all the Jews in England were banished out of the realm, whereby the number of converts in this place was decayed: and, therefore, in the year 1377, this house was annexed by patent to William Burstall Clearke, custos rotulorum, or keeper of the Rolles of the Chauncerie, by Edward III., in the 5th year of his reign; and this first Master of the Rolles was sworn in Westminster hall, at the table of marble stone; since the which time, that house hath been commonly called the Rolles in Chancerie lane.

Notwithstanding such of the Jewes, or other infidels, as have in this realm been converted to Christianity, and baptized, have been relieved there; for I find in record that one William Piers, a Jew that became a Christian, was baptised in the fifth of Richard II., and had two pence the day allowed him during his life by the said king.

On the west side was sometime a house pertaining to the prior of Necton Parke, a house of canons in Lincolnshire; this was commonly called Hereflete inn, and was a brewhouse, but now fair built for the five clerks of the Chancerie, and standeth over against the said house called the Rolles, and near unto the lane which now entereth Fickets croft, or Fickets field. Then is Shere lane, opening also into Fickets field, hard by the bars.

On this north side of Fleet street, in the year of Christ 1595, I observed, that when the labourers had broken up the pavement, from against Chancerie lane's end up towards St. Dunston's church, and had digged four feet deep, they found one other pavement of hard stone, more sufficient than the first, and, therefore, harder to be broken, under the which they found in the made ground, piles of timber driven very thick, and almost close together, the same being as black as pitch or coal, and many of them rotten as earth, which proveth that the ground there (as sundry other places of the city) have been a marish, or full of springs.

On the south side from Ludgate, before the wall of the city be fair built houses to Fleet bridge, on the which bridge a cistern for receipt of spring water was made by the men of Fleet street, but the watercourse is decayed, and not restored.

Next is Bride lane, and therein Bridewell, of old time the king's house, for the kings of this realm have been there lodged; and till the ninth of Henry III. the courts were kept in the king's house, wheresoever he was lodged, as may appear by ancient records, whereof I have seen many, but for example set forth one in the Chapter of Towers and Castles.

King Henry VIII. built there a stately and beautiful house of new, for receipt of the Emperor Charles V., who, in the year of Christ 1522, was lodged himself at the Blacke Friers, but his nobles in this new built Bridewell, a gallery being made out of the house over the water, and through the wall of the city, into the emperor's lodging at the Blacke Friers. King Henry himself oftentimes lodged there also, as, namely, in the year 1525, a parliament being then holden in the Black Friers, he created estates of nobility there, to wit, Henry Fitz Roy, a child (which he had by Elizabeth Blunt) to be Earl of Nottingham, Duke of Richmond and of Somerset, Lieutenant General from Trent northward, Warden of the East, Middle, and West Marches for anenst Scotland; Henry Courtney, Earl of Devonshire, cousin-german to the king, to be marquis of Exeter; Henry Brandon a child of two years old, son to the Earl of Suffolke, to be Earl of Lincolne; Sir Thomas Mannars, Lord Rose, to be Earl of Rutland; Sir Henry Clifford, to be Earl of Cumberland; Sir Robert Ratcliffe, to be Viscount Fitzwater; and Sir Thomas Boloine, treasurer of the king's household, to be Viscount Rochford.

In the year 1528, Cardinal Campeius was brought to the king's presence, being then at Bridewell, whither he had called all his nobility, judges, and councillors, etc. And there, the 8th of November, in his great chamber, he made unto them an oration touching his marriage with Queen Katherine, as ye may read in Edward Hall.

In the year 1529, the same King Henry and Queen Katherine were lodged there, whilst the question of their marriage was argued in the Blacke Friers, etc.

But now you shall hear how this house became a house of correction. In the year 1553, the 7th of King Edward VI., the 10th of April, Sir George Baron, being mayor of this city, was sent for to the court at Whitehall, and there at that time the king gave unto him for the commonalty and citizens to be a workhouse for the poor and idle persons of the city, his house of Bridewell, and seven hundred marks land, late of the posses-sions of the house of the Savoy, and all the bedding and other furniture of the said hospital of the Savoy, towards the main-tenance of the said workhouse of Bridewell, and the hospital of St. Thomas in Southwark.

This gift King Edward confirmed by his charter, dated the 26th of June next following; and in the year 1555, in the month of February, Sir William Gerarde, mayor, and the aldermen entered Bridewell, and took possession thereof according to the gift of the said King Edward, the same being confirmed by Queen Mary.

The Bishop of St. David's had his inn over against the north side of this Bridwell, as I have said.

Then is the parish church of St. Bridges, or Bride, of old time a small thing, which now remaineth to be the choir, but since increased with a large body and side aisles towards the west, at the charges of William Venor, esquire, warden of the Fleet, about the year 1480, all which he caused to be wrought about in the stone in the figure of a vine with grapes, and leaves, etc. The partition betwixt the old work and the new, sometime prepared as a screen to be set up in the hall of the Duke of Somerset's house at Strand, was brought for eight score pounds, and set up in the year 1557; one wilful body began to spoil and break the same in the year 1596, but was by the high commissioners forced to make it up again, and so it resteth. John Ulsthorpe, William Evesham, John Wigan, and other, found chantries there.

The next is Salisburie court, a place so called for that it belonged to the Bishops of Salisburie, and was their inn, or London house, at such time as they were summoned to come to the parliament, or came for other business; it hath of late time been the dwelling, first of Sir Richard Sackvile, and now of Sir Thomas Sackvile his son, Baron of Buckhurst, Lord Treasurer, who hath lately enlarged it with stately buildings.

Then is Water lane, running down, by the west side of a house called the Hanging Sword, to the Thames.

Then was the White Friers' church, called *Fratres beatæ Mariæ de Monte Carmeli*, first founded (saith John Bale) by Sir Richard Gray, knight, ancestor to the Lord Gray Codnor, in the year 1241. King Edward I. gave to the prior and brethren of that house a plot of ground in Fleet street, whereupon to build their house, which was since re-edified or new built, by Hugh Courtney, Earl of Devonshire, about the year 1350, the 24th of Edward III. John Lutken, mayor of London, and the commonalty of the city, granted a lane called Crockers lane, reaching from Fleet street to the Thames, to build in the west end of that church. Sir Robert Knoles, knight, was a great builder there also, in the reign of Richard II., and of Henry IV.; he deceased at his manor of Scone Thorpe, in Norffolke, in the year 1407, and was brought to London, and honourably buried by the Lady Constance his wife, in the body of the said White Friers' church, which he had newly built.

Robert Marshall, Bishop of Hereford, built the choir, presbytery, steeple, and many other parts, and was there buried, about the year 1420. There were buried also in the new choir, Sir John Mowbery, Earl of Nottingham, 1398; Sir Edwarde Cortney; Sir Hugh Montgomerie, and Sir John his brother;

John Wolle, son to Sir John Wolle; Thomas Bayholt, esquire; Elizabeth, Countess of Athole; Dame Johan, wife to Sir Thomas Say of Alden; Sir Pence Castle, Baron; John, Lord Gray, son to Reginald, Lord Gray of Wilton, 1418; Sir John Ludlow, knight; Sir Richard Derois, knight; Richarde Gray, knight; John Ashley, knight; Robert Bristow, esquire; Thomas Perry, esquire; Robert Tempest, esquire; William Call; William Neddow.

In the old choir were buried: Dame Margaret, etc.; Eleanor Gristles; Sir John Browne, knight, and John his son and heir; Sir Simon de Berforde, knight; Peter Wigus, esquire; Robert Mathew, esquire; Sir John Skargell, knight; Sir John Norice, knight; Sir Geffrey Roose, knight; Mathew Hadocke, esquire; William Clarell, esquire; John Aprichard, esquire; William Wentworth, esquire; Thomas Wicham, esquire; Sir Terwit, knight; Sir Stephen Popham, knight; Bastard de Scales; Henrie Blunt, esquire; Elizabeth Blunt; John Swan, esquire; Alice Foster, one of the heirs of Sir Stephen Popham; Sir Robert Brocket, knight; John Drayton, esquire; John, son to Robert Chanlowes, and his daughter Katherine; John Salvin, William Hampton, John Bampton, John Winter, Edmond Oldhall, William Appleyard, Thomas Dabby, esquires; Sir Hugh Courtney, knight; John Drury, son to Robert Drurie; Elizabeth Gemersey, gentlewoman; Sir Thomas Townsend, knight; Sir Richarde Greene, knight; William Scot, esquire; Thomas Federinghey, I. Fulforde, esquire; Edward Eldsmere, gentleman; W. Hart, gentleman; Dame Mary Senclare, daughter to Sir Thomas Talbot, knight; Ancher, esquire; Sir William Moris, knight, and Dame Christian his wife; Sir Peter de Mota, knight; Richard Hewton, esquire; Sir I. Heron, knight; Richard Eton, esquire; Hugh Stapleton, gentleman; William Copley, gentleman; Sir Ralph Saintowen, knight; Sir Hugh Bromeflete, knight; Lord Vessey, principal founder of that order, the 6th of Edward IV., etc.

This house was valued at £62 7s. 3d., and was surrendered the 10th of November, the 30th of Henry VIII.

In place of this Friers' church be now many fair houses built, lodgings for noblemen and others.

Then is the Sargeants' inn, so called, for that divers judges and sargeants at the law keep a commons, and are lodged there in term time.

Next is the New Temple, so called because the Templars, before the building of this house, had their Temple in Oldborne.

This house was founded by the Knights Templars in England, in the reign of Henry II., and the same was dedicated to God and our blessed Lady, by Heraclius, Patriarch of the church called the Holy Resurrection, in Jerusalem, in the year of Christ, 1185.

These Knights Templars took their beginning about the year 1118, in manner following. Certain noblemen, horsemen, religiously bent, bound by vow themselves in the hands of the Patriarch of Jerusalem, to serve Christ after the manner of regular canons in chastity and obedience, and to renounce their own proper wills for ever; the first of which order were Hugh Paganus, and Geffrey de S. Andromare. And whereas at the first they had no certain habitation, Baldwin, king of Jerusalem, granted unto them a dwelling place in his palace by the Temple, and the canons of the same Temple gave them the street thereby to build therein their houses of office, and the partiarch, the king, the nobles, and prelates gave unto them certain revenues out of their lordships.

Their first profession was for safeguard of the pilgrims coming to visit the sepulchre, and to keep the highways against the lying in wait of thieves, etc. About ten years after they had a rule appointed unto them, and a white habit, by Honorius II. then Pope; and whereas they had but nine in number, they began to increase greatly. Afterward, in Pope Eugenius' time, they bare crosses of red cloth on their uppermost garments, to be known from others; and in short time, because they had their first mansion hard by the Temple of our Lord in Jerusalem, they were called Knights of the Temple.

Many noble men in all parts of Christendom became brethren of this order, and built for themselves temples in every city or great town in England, but this at London was their chief house, which they built after the form of the temple near to the sepulchre of our Lord at Jerusalem; they had also other temples in Cambridge,[1] Bristow, Canterbury, Dover, Warwick.[2] This Temple in London, was often made a storehouse of men's treasure, I mean such as feared the spoil thereof in other places.

Matthew Paris noteth, that in the year 1232, Hubert de Burgh, Earl of Kent, being prisoner in the Tower of London, the king was informed that he had much treasure laid up in this New Temple, under the custody of the Templars; whereupon he sent for the master of the Temple, and examined him straitly, who confessed that money being delivered unto him and his brethren to be kept, he knew not how much there was

[1] Matthew Paris.　　[2] "And others in other places."—*1st edition*, p. 325.

of it; the king demanded to have the same delivered, but it was answered, that the money being committed unto their trust, could not be delivered without the licence of him that committed it to ecclesiastical protection, whereupon the king sent his Treasurer and Justiciar of the Exchequer unto Hubert, to require him to resign the money wholly into his hands, who answered that he would gladly submit himself, and all his, unto the king's pleasure; and thereupon desired the knights of the Temple, in his behalf, to present all the keys unto the king, to do his pleasure with the goods which he had committed unto them. Then the king commanded the money to be faithfully told and laid up in his treasury, by inventory, wherein was found (besides ready money) vessels of gold and silver unpriceable, and many precious stones, which would make all men wonder if they knew the worth of them.

This Temple was again dedicated 1240, belike also newly re-edified then.

These Templars at this time were in so great glory, that they entertained the nobility, foreign ambassadors, and the prince himself very often, insomuch that Matthew Paris crieth out on them for their pride, who being at the first so poor, as they had but one horse to serve two of them (in token whereof they gave in their seal two men riding of one horse), yet suddenly they waxed so insolent, that they disdained other orders, and sorted themselves with noblemen.

King Edward I. in the year 1283, taking with him Robert Waleran, and other, came to the Temple, where calling for the keeper of the treasure house, as if he meant to see his mother's-jewels, that were laid up there to be safely kept, he entered into the house, breaking the coffers of certain persons that had likewise brought their money thither, and he took away from thence to the value of a thousand pounds.

Many parliaments and great councils have been there kept, as may appear by our histories. In the year 1308, all the Templars in England, as also in other parts of Christendom, were apprehended and committed to divers prisons. In 1310, a provincial council was holden at London, against the Templars in England, upon heresy and other articles whereof they were accused, but denied all except one or two of them, notwithstanding they all did confess that they could not purge themselves fully as faultless, and so they were condemned to perpetual penance in several monasteries, where they behaved themselves modestly.

Philip, king of France, procured their overthrow throughout the whole world, and caused them to be condemned by a general council to his advantage, as he thought, for he believed to have had all their lands in France, and, therefore, seized the same in his hands (as I have read), and caused the Templars to the number of four and fifty (or after Fabian, threescore) to be burned at Paris.

Edward II. in the year 1313, gave unto Aimer de Valence, Earl of Pembroke, the whose place and houses called the New Temple at London, with the ground called Ficquetes Croft, and all the tenements and rents, with the appurtenances, that belonged to the Templars in the city of London and suburbs thereof.

After Aimer de Valence (sayeth some) Hugh Spencer, usurping the same, held it during his life, by whose death it came again to the hands of Edward III.; but in the meantime, to wit, 1324, by a council holden at Vienna, all the lands of the Templars (lest the same should be put to profane uses) were given to the knights hospitalers of the order of St. John Baptist, called St. John of Jerusalem, which knights had put the Turkes out of the Isle of Rhodes, and after won upon the said Turkes daily for a long time.

The said Edward III., therefore, granted the same to the said knights, who possessed it, and in the eighteenth year of the said king's reign, were forced to repair the bridge of the said Temple. These knights had their head house for England by West Smithfield, and they in the reign of the same Edward III. granted (for a certain rent of ten pounds by the year) the said Temple, with the appurtenances thereunto adjoining, to the students of the common laws of England, in whose possession the same hath ever since remained; and is now divided into two houses of several students, by the same of inns of court, to wit, the Inner Temple, and the Middle Temple, who kept two several halls, but they resort all to the said Temple church, in the round walk whereof (which is the west part without the choir) there remaineth monuments of noblemen buried, to the number of eleven, eight of them are images of armed knights, five lying cross-legged as men vowed to the Holy Land, against the infidels and unbelieving Jews; the other three straight-legged; the rest are coped stones all of grey marble; the first of the cross-legged was W. Marshall, the elder Earl of Pembroke, who died 1219; Will. Marshall his son, Earl of Pembroke, was the second, he died, 1231; and Gilbert Marshall his brother,

Earl of Pembroke, slain in a tournament at Hertford, beside Ware, in the year 1241.

After this Robert Rose, otherwise called Fursan, being made a Templar in the year 1245, died and was buried there, and these are all that I can remember to have read of. Sir Nicholas Hare, Master of the Rolls, was buried there in the year 1557.

In the year 1381, the rebels of Essex and of Kent destroyed and plucked down the houses and lodgings of this Temple, took out of the church the books and records that were in hutches of the apprentices of the law, carried them into the streets, and burnt them; the house they spoiled and burnt for wrath that they bare Sir Robert Halles, Lord-prior of St. John's in Smithfield; but it was since again at divers times repaired, namely, the gate-house of the Middle Temple, in the reign of Henry VIII., by Sir Amias Paulet, knight, upon occasion, as in my *Annales* I have shown. The great hall of the Middle Temple was newly built in the year 1572, in the reign of our Queen Elizabeth.

This Temple church hath a master and four stipendiary priests, with a clerk: these for the ministration of Divine service there have stipends allowed unto them out of the possessions and revenues of the late hospital and house of St. John's of Jerusalem in England, as it had been in the reign of Edward VI.; and thus much for the said new Temple, the farthest west part of this ward, and also of this city for the liberties thereof; which ward hath an alderman, and his deputies three. In Sepulchre's parish, common council six, constables four, scavengers four, wardmote inquest twelve; St. Bridgetes parish, common councillors eight, constables eight, scavengers eight, wardmote inquest twenty; in St. Andrewes, common council two, constables two, scavengers three, wardmote inquest twelve. It is taxed to the fifteen at thirty-five pounds one shilling.[1]

BRIDGE WARDE WITHOUT, THE TWENTY-SIXTH IN NUMBER; CONSISTING OF THE BOROUGH OF SOUTHWARKE, IN THE COUNTY OF SURREY.

Having treated of wards in London, on the north side of the Thames (in number twenty-five), I am now to cross over the said river into the borough of Southwark, which is also a ward of London without the walls, on the south side thereof, as is Portsoken on the east, and Farringdon extra on the west.

[1] " And in the Exchequer at thirty-four pounds."—*1st edition*, p. 338.

This borough being in the county of Surrey, consisteth of divers streets, ways, and winding lanes, all full of buildings, inhabited; and, first, to begin at the west part thereof, over against the west suburb of the city.

On the bank of the river Thames there is now a continual building of tenements, about half a mile in length to the bridge. Then from the bridge, straight towards the south, a continual street, called Long Southwark, built on both sides with divers lanes and alleys up to St. George's church, and beyond it through Blackman street towards New town (or Newington); the liberties of which borough extend almost to the parish church of New town aforesaid, distant one mile from London Bridge, and also south-west a continual building almost to Lambeth, more than one mile from the said bridge.

Then from the bridge along by the Thames eastward is St. Olave's street, having continual building on both the sides, with lanes and alleys, up to Battle bridge, to Horsedowne, and towards Rother hithe; also some good half mile in length from London Bridge.

So that I account the whole continual buildings on the bank of the said river, from the west towards the east, to be more than a large mile in length.

Then have ye, from the entering towards the said Horsedown, one other continual street called Bermondes high street, which stretcheth south, likewise furnished with buildings on both sides, almost half a mile in length, up to the late dissolved monastery of St. Saviour called Bermondsey. And from thence is one Long lane (so called of the length), turning west to St. George's church afore named. Out of the which lane mentioned Long lane breaketh one other street towards the south and by east, and this is called Kentish street, for that is the way leading into that country: and so have you the bounds of this borough.

The antiquities most notable in this borough are these: First, for ecclesiastical, there was Bermondsey, an abbey of black monks, St. Mary Overies, a priory of canons regular, St. Thomas, a college or hospital for the poor, and the Loke, a lazar house in Kent street. Parish churches there have been six, whereof five do remain; viz., St. Mary Magdalen, in the priory of St. Mary Overy, now the same St. Mary Overy is the parish church for the said Mary Magdalen, and for St. Margaret on the hill, and is called St. Saviour.

St. Margaret on the hill being put down is now a court for

justice; St. Thomas in the hospital serveth for a parish church as before; St. George a parish church as before it did; so doth St. Olave and St. Mary Magdalen, by the abbey of Bermondsey.

There be also these five prisons or gaols:

The Clinke on the Banke.
The Compter, in the late parish church of St. Margaret.
The Marshalsey.
The Kinges Bench.
And the White Lion, all in Long Southwarke.

Houses most notable be these:

The Bishop of Winchester's house.
The Bishop of Rochester's house.
The Duke of Suffolk's house, or Southwark place.
The Tabard, an hostery or inn.
The Abbot of Hyde, his house.
The Prior of Lewes, his house.
The Abbot of St. Augustine, his house.
The Bridge house.
The Abbot of Battaile, his house.
Battaile bridge.
The Stewes on the bank of Thames.
And the Bear gardens there.

Now, to return to the west bank, there be two bear gardens, the old and new places, wherein be kept bears, bulls, and other beasts, to be baited; as also mastiffs in several kennels, nourished to bait them. These bears and other beasts are there baited in plots of ground, scaffolded about for the beholders to stand safe.

Next on this bank was sometime the Bordello, or Stewes, a place so called of certain stew-houses privileged there, for the repair of incontinent men to the like women; of the which privilege I have read thus:

In a parliament holden at Westminster, the 8th of Henry II., it was ordained by the commons, and confirmed by the king and lords, that divers constitutions for ever should be kept within that lordship or franchise, according to the old customs that had been there used time out of mind: amongst the which these following were some, viz.

"That no stew-holder or his wife should let or stay any single woman, to go and come freely at all times when they listed.

"No stew-holder to keep any woman to board, but she to board abroad at her pleasure.

"To take no more for the woman's chamber in the week than fourteen pence.

"Not to keep open his doors upon the holidays.

"Not to keep any single woman in his house on the holidays, but the bailiff to see them voided out of the lordship.

"No single woman to be kept against her will that would leave her sin.

"No stew-holder to receive any woman of religion, or any man's wife.

"No single woman to take money to lie with any man, but she lie with him all night till the morrow.

"No man to be drawn or enticed into any stew-house.

"The constables, bailiff, and others, every week to search every stew-house.

"No stew-holder to keep any woman that hath the perilous infirmity of burning, not to sell bread, ale, flesh, fish, wood, coal, or any victuals, etc."

These and many more orders were to be observed upon great pain and punishment. I have also seen divers patents of confirmation, namely, one dated 1345, the 19th of Edward III.[1] Also I find, that in the 4th of Richard II., these stew-houses belonging to William Walworth, then mayor of London, were farmed by Froes of Flanders, and spoiled by Walter Tyler, and other rebels of Kent: notwithstanding, I find that ordinances for the same place and houses were again confirmed in the reign of Henry VI., to be continued as before. Also, Robert Fabian writeth, that in the year 1506, the 21st of Henry VII., the said stew-houses in Southwarke were for a season inhibited, and the doors closed up, but it was not long (saith he) ere the houses there were set open again, so many as were permitted, for (as it was said) whereas before were eighteen houses, from thenceforth were appointed to be used but twelve only. These allowed stew-houses had signs on their fronts, towards the Thames, not hanged out, but painted on the walls, as a Boar's head, the Cross keys, the Gun, the Castle, the Crane, the Cardinal's hat, the Bell, the Swan, etc. I have heard of ancient men, of good credit, report, that these single women were forbidden the rites of the church, so long as they continued that sinful life, and were excluded from Christian burial,

[1] "Li. St. Mary Eborum. English people disdayned to be baudes. Froes of Flaunders were women for that purpose."—*Stow*.

if they were not reconciled before their death. And therefore there was a plot of ground called the Single Woman's church-yard, appointed for them far from the parish church.

In the year of Christ 1546, the 37th of Henry VIII., this row of stews in Southwarke was put down by the king's command-ment, which was proclaimed by sound of trumpet, no more to be privileged, and used as a common brothel, but the inhabi-tants of the same to keep good and honest rule as in other places of this realm, etc.

Then next is the Clinke, a gaol or prison for the trespassers in those parts; namely, in old time, for such as should brabble, frey, or break the peace on the said bank, or in the brothel houses, they were by the inhabitants thereabout apprehended and committed to this gaol, where they were straitly imprisoned.

Next is the bishop of Winchester's house, or lodging, when he cometh to this city; which house was first built by William Gifford, bishop of Winchester, about the year 1107, the 7th of Henry I., upon a plot of ground pertaining to the prior of Bermondsey, as appeareth by a writ directed unto the barons of the Exchequer, in the year 1366, the 41st of Edward III. (the bishop's see being void), for eight pounds, due to the monks of Bermondsey for the bishop of Winchester's lodging in South-wark. This is a very fair house, well repaired, and hath a large wharf and landing-place, called the bishop of Winchester's stairs.

Adjoining to this, on the south side the roof, is the bishop of Rochester's inn or lodging, by whom first erected I do not now remember me to have read; but well I wot the same of long time hath not been frequented by any bishop, and lieth ruinous for any lack of reparations. The abbot of Maverley had a house there.

East from the bishop of Winchester's house, directly over against it, standeth a fair church called St. Mary over the Rie, or Overie, that is over the water. This church, or some other in place thereof, was of old time, long before the Conquest, a house of sisters, founded by a maiden named Mary; unto the which house and sisters she left (as was left to her by her parents) the oversight and profits of a cross ferry, or traverse ferry over the Thames, there kept before that any bridge was built. This house of sisters was after by Swithen, a noble lady, converted into a college of priests, who in place of the ferry built a bridge of timber, and from time to time kept the same in good repara-tions, but lastly the same bridge was built of stone; and then in the year 1106 was this church again founded for canons regulars by William Pont de la Arche and William Dauncy, knights, Normans. William Gifford, bishop of Winchester, was a good benefactor also, for he, as some have noted, built the body of that church in the year 1106, the 7th of Henry I.

The canons first entered the said church then; Algodus was the first prior.

King Henry I. by his charter gave them the church of St. Margaret in Southwarke.

King Stephen confirmed the gift of King Henry, and also gave the stone-house, which was William Pont de le Arche's, by Downegate.

This priory was burnt about the year 1207, wherefore the canons did found a hospital near unto their priory, where they celebrated until the priory was repaired; which hospital was after, by consent of Peter de la Roch, bishop of Winchester, removed into the land of Anicius, archdeacon of Surrey, in the year 1228, a place where the water was more plentiful, and the air more wholesome, and was dedicated to St. Thomas.

This Peter de Rupibus, or de la Roch, founded a large chapel of St. Mary Magdalen, in the said church of St. Mary Overie; which chapel was after appointed to be the parish church for the inhabitants near adjoining.

This church was again newly built in the reign of Richard II. and King Henry IV.

John Gower, esquire, a famous poet,[1] was then an especial benefactor to that work, and was there buried on the north side of the said church, in the chapel of St. John, where he founded a chantry: he lieth under a tomb of stone, with his image, also of stone, over him: the hair of his head, auburn, long to his shoulders, but curling up, and a small forked beard; on his head a chaplet, like a coronet of four roses; a habit of purple, damasked down to his feet; a collar of esses gold about his neck; under his head the likeness of three books, which he compiled. The first, named *Speculum Meditantis*, written in French; the second, *Vox Clamantis*, penned in Latin; the third, *Confessio Amantis*, written in English, and this last is printed. *Vox Clamantis*, with his *Cronica Tripartita*, and other, both in Latin and French, never printed, I have and do possess, but *Speculum Meditantis* I never saw,[2] though heard thereof to

---

[1] " John Gower was no knight, neither had he any garland of ivie and roses, but a chaplet of foure roses onely."—*Stow*.

[2] [*See* Additional Notes.]

be in Kent. Beside on the wall where he lieth, there was painted three virgins crowned; one of the which was named Charity, holding this device:

> " En toy qui es Fitz he dieu le pere,
> Sauve soit, que gist souz cest piere."

The second writing, Mercy, with this device:

> " O bone Jesu, fait ta mercie,
> Al alme, dont le corps gist icy."

The third writing, Pity, with this device:

> " Pur ta pité Jesu regarde,
> Et met cest alme en sauve garde."

His arms a field argent, on a cheveron azure, three leopards' heads gold, their tongues gules; two angels supporters, on the crest a talbot: his epitaph,

> " Armigeri scutum nihil a modo fert sibi tutum,
> Reddidit immolutum morti generale tributum,
> Spiritus exutum se gaudeat esse solutum,
> Est ubi virtutum regnum sine labe statutum,"

The roof of the middle west aisle fell down in the year 1469. This priory was surrendered to Henry VIII., the 31st of his reign, the 27th of October, the year of Christ 1539, valued at £624 6s. 6d. by the year.

About Christmas next following, the church of the said priory was purchased of the king by the inhabitants of the borough, Doctor Stephen Gardner, bishop of Winchester, putting to his helping hand; they made thereof a parish church for the parish church of St. Mary Magdalen, on the south side of the said choir, and of St. Margaret on the hill, which were made one parish of St. Saviour.

There be monuments in this church,—of Robert Liliarde, or Hiliarde, esquire; Margaret, daughter to the Lady Audley, wife to Sir Thomas Audley; William Grevill, esquire, and Margaret his wife; one of the heirs of William Spershut, esquire; Dame Katherine, wife to John Stoke, alderman; Robert Merfin, esquire; William Undall, esquire; Lord Ospay Ferar; Sir George Brewes, knight; John Browne; Lady Brandon, wife to Sir Thomas Brandon; William, Lord Scales; William, Earl Warren; Dame Maude, wife to Sir John Peach; Lewknor; Dame Margaret Elrington, one of the heirs of Sir Thomas Elrington; John Bowden, esquire; Robert St. Magil; John Sandhurst; John Gower; John Duncell, merchant-tailor, 1516; John Sturton, esquire; Robert Rouse; Thomas Tong, first

Norroy, and after Clarenceaux king of arms; William Wickham, translated from the see of Lincoln to the bishopric of Winchester in the month of March, 1595, deceased the 11th of June next following, and was buried here; Thomas Cure, esquire, saddler to King Edward VI., Queen Mary, and Queen Elizabeth, deceased the 24th of May, 1598, etc.

Now passing through St. Mary Over's close (in possession of the Lord Mountacute), and Pepper alley, into Long Southwark, on the right hand thereof the market-hill, where the leather is sold, there stood the late named parish church of St. Margaret, given to St. Mary Overies by Henry I., put down and joined with the parish of St. Mary Magdalen, and united to the late dissolved priory church of St. Mary Overy.

A part of this parish church of St. Margaret is now a court, wherein the assizes and sessions be kept, and the court of admiralty is also there kept. One other part of the same church is now a prison, called the Compter in Southwark, etc.

Farther up on that side, almost directly over against St. George's church, was sometime a large and most sumptuous house, built by Charles Brandon, late Duke of Suffolk, in the reign of Henry VIII., which was called Suffolk house, but coming afterwards into the king's hands, the same was called Southwarke place, and a mint of coinage was there kept for the king.

To this place came King Edward VI., in the second of his reign, from Hampton Court, and dined in it. He at that time made John Yorke, one of the sheriffs of London, knight, and then rode through the city to Westminster.

Queen Mary gave this house to Nicholas Heath, Archbishop of Yorke, and to his successors, for ever, to be their inn or lodging for their repair to London, in recompense of Yorke house near to Westminster, which King Henry her father had taken from Cardinal Wolsey, and from the see of Yorke.

Archbishop Heath sold the same house to a merchant, or to merchants, that pulled it down, sold the lead, stone, iron, etc.; and in place thereof built many small cottages of great rents, to the increasing of beggars in that borough. The archbishop bought Norwich house, or Suffolke place, near unto Charing cross, because it was near unto the court, and left it to his successors.

Now on the south side to return back again towards the bridge, over against this Suffolke place, is the parish church of St. George, sometime pertaining to the priory of Barmondsey, by the gift of Thomas Arderne and Thomas his son, in the year

1122. There lie buried in this church, William Kirton, esquire, and his wives, 1464.

Then is the White Lion, a gaol so called, for that the same was a common hosterie for the receipt of travellers by that sign. This house was first used as a gaol within these forty years last, since the which time the prisoners were once removed thence to a house in Newtowne, where they remained for a short time, and were returned back again to the foresaid White Lion, there to remain as in the appointed gaol for the county of Surrey.

Next is the gaol or prison of the King's Bench, but of what antiquity the same is I know not. For I have read that the courts of the King's Bench and Chancery have ofttimes been removed from London to other places, and so hath likewise the gaols that serve those courts; as in the year 1304, Edward I. commanded the courts of the King's Bench and the Exchequer, which had remained seven years at Yorke, to be removed to their old places at London. And in the year 1387, the 11th of Richard II., Robert Tresilian, chief justice, came to the city of Coventrie, and there sate by the space of a month, as justice of the Kinge's benches, and caused to be indited in that court, about the number of two thousand persons of that country, etc.

It seemeth, therefore, that for that time, the prison or gaol of that court was not far off. Also in the year 1392, the 16th of the same Richard, the Archbishop of York being Lord Chancellor, for good will that he bare to his city, caused the King's Bench and Chancery to be removed from London to York, but ere long they were returned to London.

Then is the Marshalsey, another gaol or prison, so called, as pertaining to the marshals of England. Of what continuance kept in Southwark I have not learned; but like it is, that the same hath been removable, at the pleasure of the marshals: for I find that in the year 1376, the 50th of Edward III., Henry Percie (being marshal) kept his prisoners in the city of London, where having committed one John Prendergast, of Norwich, contrary to the liberties of the city of London, the citizens, by persuasion of the Lord Fitzwalter their standard-bearer, took armour and ran with great rage to the marshal's inn, brake up the gates, brought out the prisoner, and conveyed him away, minding to have burnt the stocks in the midst of their city, but they first sought for Sir Henry Percy to have punished him, as I have noted in my *Annales*.

More about the feast of Easter next following, John, Duke of Lancaster, having caused all the whole navy of England to be gathered together at London: it chanced a certain esquire to kill one of the shipmen, which act the other shipmen taking in ill part, they brought their suit into the king's court of the Marshalsey, which then as chanced (saith mine author) was kept in Southwark: but when they perceived that court to be so favourable to the murderer, and further that the king's warrant was also gotten for his pardon, they in great fury ran to the house wherein the murderer was imprisoned, brake into it, and brought forth the prisoner with his gyves on his legs, they thrust a knife to his heart, and sticked him as if he had been a dog; after this they tied a rope to his gyves, and drew him to the gallows, where when they had hanged him, as though they had done a great act, they caused the trumpets to be sounded before them to their ships, and there in great triumph they spent the rest of the day.

Also the rebels of Kent, in the year 1381, brake down the houses of the Marshalsey and King's Bench in Southwark, took from thence the prisoners, brake down the house of Sir John Immorth, then marshal of the Marshalsey and King's Bench, etc. After this, in the year 1387, the 11th of Richard II., the morrow after Bartholomew day, the king kept a great council in the castle of Nottingham, and the Marshalsey of the king was then kept at Loughborrow by the space of five days or more. In the year 1443, Sir Walter Manny was marshal of the Marshalsey, the 22nd of Henry VI. William Brandon, esquire, was marshal in the 8th of Edward IV. In the year 1504 the prisoners of the Marshalsey, then in Southwark, brake out, and many of them being taken were executed, especially such as had been committed for felony or treason.

From thence towards London bridge, on the same side, be many fair inns, for recepit of travellers, by these signs, the Spurre, Christopher, Bull, Queene's Head, Tabarde, George, Hart, Kinge's Head, etc. Amongst the which, the most ancient is the Tabard, so called of the sign, which, as we now term it, is of a jacket, or sleeveless coat, whole before, open on both sides, with a square collar, winged at the shoulders; a stately garment of old time, commonly worn of noblemen and others, both at home and abroad in the wars, but then (to wit in the wars) their arms embroidered, or otherwise depict upon them, that every man by his coat of arms might be known from others: but now these tabards are only worn by the heralds, and be

called their coats of arms in service; for the inn of the tabard,
Geffrey Chaucer, esquire, the most famous poet of England,
in commendation thereof, writeth thus:—

> " Befell that in that season, on a day,
> In Southwarke at the Tabard, as I lay,
> Readie to wenden on my Pilgrimage
> To Canterburie with devout courage,
> At night was come into that hosterie,
> Well nine-and-twentie in a companie,
> Of sundrie folke, by adventure yfall,
> In fellowship, and pilgrimes were they all,
> That toward Canterburie woulden ride,
> The chambers and the stables weren wide,
> And well we weren eased at the best," etc.

Within this inn was also the lodging of the abbot of Hide (by
the city of Winchester), a fair house for him and his train, when
he came to that city to parliament, etc.

And then Theeves lane, by St. Thomas' hospital. The
hospital of St. Thomas, first founded by Richard Prior of
Bermondsey, in the Selerers ground against the wall of the
monastery, in the year 1213, he named it the Almerie, or house
of alms for converts and poor children; for the which ground the
prior ordained that the almoner should pay ten shillings and
four pence yearly to the Selerer at Michaelmas.

But Peter de Rupibus,[1] Bishop of Winchester, in the year
1215, founded the same again more fully for canons regular in
place of the first hospital; he increased the rent thereof to three
hundred and forty-four pounds in the year. Thus was this
hospital holden of the prior and abbot of Bermondsey till the
year 1428, at which time a composition was made between
Thomas Thetford, abbot of Bermondsey, and Nicholas Buckland, master of the said hospital of St. Thomas, for all the lands
and tenements which were holden of the said abbot and convent in Southwark, or elsewhere, for the old rent to be paid
unto the said abbot.

There be monuments in this hospital church of Sir Robert
Chamber, knight; William Fines, Lord Say; Richard Chaucer,
John Gloucester, Adam Atwood, John Ward, Michael Cambridge,
William West, John Golding, esquires; John Benham, George
Kirkes, Thomas Kninton, Thomas Baker, gentlemen; Robert,
son to Sir Thomas Fleming; Agnes, wife to Sir Walter Dennis,
knight, daughter, and one of the heirs of Sir Robert Danvars;
John Evarey, gentleman; etc.

This hospital was by the visitors, in the year 1538, valued at

[1] Lib. St. Marie Overy. [MS. lost.]

two hundred and sixty-six pounds seventeen shillings and six pence, and was surrendered to Henry VIII., in the 30th of his reign.

In the year 1552, the citizens of London having purchased the void suppressed hospital of St. Thomas in Southwark, in the month of July began the reparations thereof, for poor, impotent, lame, and diseased people, so that in the month of November next following, the sick and poor people were taken in. And in the year 1553, on the 10th of April, King Edward VI., in the 7th of his reign, gave to the mayor, commonalty, and citizens of London, to be a workhouse for the poor and idle persons of this city, his house of Bridewell, and seven hundred marks land of the Savoy rents, which hospital he had suppressed, with all the beds, bedding, and other furniture belonging to the same, towards the maintenance of the said workhouse of Bridewell, and of this hospital of St. Thomas in Southwark. This gift the king confirmed by his charter, dated the 26th of June next following, and willed it to be called the King's hospital in Southwark.

The church of this hospital, which of old time served for the tenements near adjoining, and pertaining to the said hospital, remaineth as a parish church.

But now to come to St. Olave's street. On the bank of the river of Thames, is the parish church of St. Olave, a fair and meet large church, but a far larger parish especially of aliens or strangers, and poor people; in which church there lieth entombed Sir John Burcettur, knight, 1466.

Over against this parish church, on the south side the street was sometime one great house built of stone, with arched gates, pertaining to the prior of Lewes in Sussex, and was his lodging when he came to London; it is now a common hosterie for travellers, and hath to sign the Walnut Tree.

Then east from the said parish church of St. Olave is a key. In the year 1330, by the license of Simon Swanlond, mayor of London, built by Isabel, widow to Hamond Goodchepe. And next thereunto was then a great house of stone and timber, belonging to the abbot of St. Augustine without the walls of Canterburie, which was an ancient piece of work, and seemeth to be one of the first built houses on that side the river over-against the city; it was called the abbot's inn of St. Augustine in Southwark, and was sometime holden of the Earls of Warren and Surrey, as appeareth by a deed made 1281, which I have read, and may be Englished thus:—

" To all whom this present writing shall come, John Earl

Warren sendeth greeting. Know ye, that we have altogether remised and quit-claimed for us and our heirs for ever, to Nicholas, abbot of St. Augustine's of Canterburie, and the convent of the same, and their successors, suit to our court of Southwarke, which they owe unto us, for all that messuage and houses thereon built, and all their appurtenances, which they have of our fee in Southwarke, situate upon the Thames, between the Bridge house and the church of St. Olave. And the said messuage, with the buildings thereon built, and all their appurtenances, to them and their successors, we have granted in perpetual alms, to hold of us and our heirs for the same, saving the service due to any other persons, if any such be, then to us; and for this remit and grant the said abbot and convent have given unto us five shillings of rent yearly in Southwarke, and have received us and our heirs in all benefices which shall be in their church for ever." This suit of court one William Graspeis was bound to do to the said earl for the said messuage, and heretofore to acquit in all things the church of St. Augustine against the said earl.

This house of late time belonged to Sir Anthony Sentlegar, then to Warham Sentlegar, etc., and is now called Sentlegar house, but divided into sundry tenements. Next is the Bridge-house, so called as being a storehouse for stone, timber, or whatsoever pertaining to the building or repairing of London bridge.

This house seemeth to have taken beginning with the first founding of the bridge either of stone or timber; it is a large plot of ground, on the bank of the river Thames, containing divers large buildings for stowage of things necessary towards reparation of the said bridge.

There are also divers garners, for laying up of wheat, and other grainers for service of the city, as need requireth. Moreover, there be certain ovens built, in number ten, of which six be very large, the other four being but half so big. These were purposely made to bake out the bread corn of the said grainers, to the best advantage for relief of the poor citizens, when need should require. Sir John Throstone, knight, sometime an embroiderer, then a goldsmith, one of the sheriffs 1516, gave by his testament towards the making of these ovens, two hundred pounds, which thing was performed by his executors. Sir John Munday, goldsmith, then being mayor, there was of late, for the enlarging of the said Bridge house, taken in an old brewhouse, called Goldings, which was given to the city by George Monex, sometime mayor, and in place thereof, is now a fair brewhouse new built, for service of the city with beer.

Next was the abbot of Battailes inn, betwixt the Bridge house and Battaile bridge, likewise on the bank of the river of Thames; the walks and gardens thereunto appertaining, on the other side of the way before the gate of the said house, and was called the Maze; there is now an inn, called the Flower de Luce, for that the sign is three Flower de Luces. Much other buildings of small tenements are thereon builded, replenished with strangers and other, for the most part poor people.

Then is Battaile bridge, so called of Battaile abbey, for that it standeth on the ground, and over a water-course (flowing out of Thames) pertaining to that abbey, and was, therefore, both built and repaired by the abbots of that house, as being hard adjoining to the abbot's lodging.

Beyond this bridge is Bermondsey street, turning south, in the south end whereof was sometime a priory or abbey of St. Saviour, called Bermond's Eye in Southwark, founded by Alwin Childe, a citizen of London, in the year 1081.

Peter, Richard, Obstert, and Umbalde, monks de Charitate, came unto Bermondsey, in the year 1089, and Peter was made first prior there, by appointment of the prior of the house, called Charity in France, by which means this priory of Bermondsey (being a cell to that in France) was accounted a priory of Aliens.

In the year 1094 deceased Alwin Childe, founder of this house. Then William Rufus gave to the monks his manor of Bermondsey, with the appurtenances, and built for them there a new great church.

Robert Blewet, Bishop of Lincolne (King William's chancellor), gave them the manor of Charlton, with the appurtenances. Also Geffrey Martell, by the grant of Geffrey Magnavile, gave them the land of Halingbury, and the tithe of Alferton, etc.

More, in the year 1122, Thomas of Arderne, and Thomas his son, gave to the monks of Bermond's Eye the church of St. George in Southwark, etc.

In the year 1165, King Henry II. confirmed to them the hyde or territory of Southwark, and Laygham Wadden, with the land of Coleman, etc.

In the year 1371, the priors of Aliens, throughout England, being seized into the king's hands, Richard Denton an Englishman was made prior of Bermondsey, to whom was committed the custody of the said priory, by the letters patents of King Edward III., saving to the king the advowsons of churches.

In the year 1380, the 4th of Richard II., this priory was made a denison (or free English) for the fine of two hundred marks paid to the king's Hanaper in the Chancery. In the year 1399 John Attelborough, prior of Bermondsey, was made the first abbot of that house by Pope Boniface IX., at the suit of King Richard II.

In the year 1417, Thomas Thetford, abbot of Bermondsey, held a plea in chancery against the king, for the manors of Preston, Bermondsey, and Stone, in the county of Somerset, in the which suit the abbot prevailed and recovered against the king.

In the year 1539 this abbey was valued to dispend by the year four hundred and seventy-four pounds fourteen shillings and four pence halfpenny, and was surrendered to Henry VIII., the 31st of his reign; the abbey church was then pulled down by Sir Thomas Pope, knight, and in place thereof a goodly house built of stone and timber, now pertaining to the earls of Sussex.

There are buried in that church, Leoftane, provost, shrive or domesman of London, 1115; Sir William Bowes, knight, and Dame Elizabeth his wife; Sir Thomas Pikeworth, knight; Dame Anne Audley; George, son to John Lord Audley; John Winkefield, esquire; Sir Nicholas Blonket, knight; Dame Bridget, wife to William Trussell; Holgrave, baron of the exchequer; etc.

Next unto this abbey church standeth a proper church of St. Mary Magdalen, built by the priors of Bermondsey, serving for resort of the inhabitants (tenants to the prior or abbots near adjoining) there to have their Divine service: this church remaineth, and serveth as afore, and is called a parish church.

Then in Kent street is a lazar house for leprous people, called the Loke in Southwark; the foundation whereof I find not. Now, having touched divers principal parts of this borough, I am to speak somewhat of its government, and so to end.

This borough, upon petition made by the citizens of London to Edward I., in the 1st year of his reign, was, for divers causes. by parliament granted to them for ever, yielding into the exchequer the fee-firm of ten pounds by the year; which grant was confirmed by Edward III., who, in the 3rd of his reign gave them license to take a toll towards the charge of paving the said borough with stone. Henry IV. confirmed the grant of his predecessors, so did Edward IV., etc.

But in the year 1550, King Edward VI., for the sum of six hundred and forty-seven pounds two shillings and one penny, paid into his court of augmentations and revenues of his crown, granted to the mayor and commonalty all his lands and tenements in Southwark, except, and reserved, the capital messuage, two mansions, called Southwark place, late the Duke of Suffolk's, and all the gardens and lands to the same appertaining, the park, and the messuage called the Antilope. Moreover, he gave them the lordship and manor of Southwark, with all members and rights thereof, late pertaining to the monastery of Bermondsey. And all messuages, places, buildings, rents, courts, waifs and strays, to the same appertaining, in the county of Surrey, except as is before excepted. He also granted unto them his manor and borough of Southwark, with all the members, rights, and appurtenances, late of the possession of the Archbishop of Canterbury and his see in Southwark. Moreover, for the sum of five hundred marks, he granted to the said mayor and commonalty, and their successors, in and through the borough and town of Southwark, and in all the parishes of St. Saviour, St. Olave, and St. George, and the parish of St. Thomas Hospital, now called the King's hospital, and elsewhere, in the said town and borough of Southwark, and Kentish street, Bermondsey street, in the parish of Newington, all waifs and strays, treasure trove, all felons' goods, etc., within the parishes and precinct aforesaid, etc.: the return of writs, processes, and warrants, etc.: together with a fair in the whole town for three days, to wit, the 7th, 8th, and 9th of September, yearly, with a court of pye powders. A view of franke pledge, with attachments, arrests, etc. Also to arrest all felons, and other malefactors, within their precinct, and send them to ward, and to Newgate. Provided that nothing in that grant should be prejudicial to the stewards and marshal of the king's house. The same premises to be holden of the manor of East Greenwich, in the county of Kent, by fealty in free forage. Dated at Westminster, the 23rd of April, in the 4th of his reign. All which was also confirmed by parliament, etc. And the same year, in the Whitsun week, in a court of aldermen, kept at the Guildhall of London, Sir John Aylophe, knight, was sworn the first alderman of Bridge ward without, and made up the number of twenty-six aldermen of London.

This borough at a subsidy to the king yieldeth about one thousand marks, or eight hundred pounds, which is more than any one city in England payeth, except the city of London. And also the muster of men in this borough doth likewise in number surpass all other cities, except London. And thus much for the borough of Southwark, one of the twenty-six wards of London, which hath an alderman, deputies three, and a bailiff, common-council none, constables sixteen, scavengers six, wardmote inquest twenty. And is taxed to the fifteen at seventeen pounds seventeen shillings and eight pence.

THE SUBURBS WITHOUT THE WALLS OF THE SAID CITY BRIEFLY TOUCHED. AS ALSO WITHOUT THE LIBERTIES MORE AT LARGE DESCRIBED.

Having spoken of this city, the original, and increase, by degrees: the walls, gates, ditch, castles, towers, bridges, the schools, and houses of learning: of the orders and customs, sports, and pastimes: of the honour of citizens, and worthiness of men: and last of all, how the same city is divided into parts and wards: and how the same be bounded: and what monuments of antiquity, or ornaments of building, in every of them, as also in the borough of Southwark: I am next to speak briefly of the suburbs, as well without the gates and walls as without the liberties, and of the monuments in them.

Concerning the estate of the suburbs of this city, in the reign of Henry II., Fitz Stephen hath these words:—" Upwards, on the west (saith he), is the king's palace, which is an incomparable building, rising with a vawmure and bulwark aloft upon the river, two miles from the wall of the city, but yet conjoined with a continual suburb. On all sides, without the houses of the suburbs, are the citizens' gardens and orchards, planted with trees, both large, sightly, and adjoining together. On the north side are pastures and plain meadows, with brooks running through them, turning water-mills with a pleasant noise. Not far off is a great forest, a well wooded chase, having good covert for harts, bucks, does, boars, and wild bulls. The corn fields are not of a hungry sandy mould, but as the fruitful fields of Asia, yielding plentiful increase, and filling the barns with corn. There are near London, on the north side, especial wells in the suburbs, sweet, wholesome, and clear. Amongst which, Holywell, Clarkenwell, and St. Clement's well, are most famous, and most frequented by scholars and youths of the city in summer evenings, when they walk forth to take the air." Thus far out of Fitz Stephen for the suburbs at that time.

The 2nd of King Henry III. the forest of Middlesex, and the warren of Staines, were disafforested; since the which time the suburbs about London hath been also mightily increased with buildings; for first, to begin in the East, by the Tower of London, is the hospital of St. Katherine, founded by Matilda the queen, wife to King Stephen, as is afore shown in Portsoken ward; from this precinct of St. Katherine to Wapping in the west,[1] the usual place of execution for hanging of pirates and sea rovers, at the low-water mark, and there to remain, till three tides had overflowed them, was never a house standing within these forty years; but since the gallows being after removed farther off, a continual street, or filthy strait passage, with alleys of small tenements, or cottages, built, inhabited by sailors' victuallers, along by the river of Thames, almost to Radcliff, a good mile from the Tower.

On the east side, and by north of the Tower, lieth East Smithfield, Hogs' street, and Tower hill; and east from them both, was the new abbey called Grace, founded by Edward III. From thence Radcliffe, up East Smithfield, by Nightingall lane (which runneth south to the hermitage, a brewhouse so called of a hermit sometime being there), beyond this lane to the manor of Bramley (called in record of Richard II. Villa East Smithfield, and Villa de Bramley), and to the manor of Shadwell, belonging to the Dean of Pauls, there hath been of late, in place of elm trees, many small tenements raised towards Radcliffe; and Radcliffe itself hath been also increased in building eastward (in place where I have known [2] a large highway, with fair elm trees on both the sides), that the same hath now taken hold of Lime hurst, or Lime host, corruptly called Lime house, sometime distant a mile from Ratcliffe.

Having said this much for building at Wapping, East Smithfield, Bramley, and Shadwell, all on the south side of the highway to Radcliffe, now one note on the north side, also concerning pirates. I read that in the year 1440, in the Lent season, certain persons, with six ships, brought from beyond the seas fish to victual the city of London, which fish, when they had delivered, and were returning homeward, a number of sea thieves, in a barge, in the night came upon them, when they were asleep in their vessels, riding at anchor on the river Thames, and slew them, cut their throats, cast them overboard, took their money, and drowned their ships, for that no man should espy or accuse them. Two of these thieves were after taken, and hanged in chains upon a gallows set upon a raised hill, for that purpose made, in the field beyond East Smithfield, so that they might be seen far into the river Thames. The first building at Radcliffe in my youth (not to be forgotten) was a fair free school and alms houses, founded by Avice Gibson, wife to Nicholas Gibson, grocer, as before I have noted: but of late years shipwrights, and (for the most part) other marine men, have built many large and strong houses for themselves, and smaller for sailors, from thence almost to Poplar, and so to Blake wall. Now for Tower hill; the plain there is likewise greatly diminished by merchants [1] for building of small tenements; from thence towards Aldgate was the Minories, whereof I have spoken.

From Aldgate east again lieth a large street, replenished with buildings; to wit, on the north side the parish church of St. Botolph, and so other buildings, to Hog lane, and to the bars on both sides.

Also without the bars both the sides of the street be pestered with cottages and alleys, even up to Whitechapel church, and almost half a mile beyond it, into the common field; all which ought to be open and free for all men. But this common field, I say, being sometime the beauty of this city on that part, is so encroached upon by building of filthy cottages, and with other purpressors, inclosures, and laystalls (notwithstanding all proclamations and acts of parliament made to the contrary), that in some places it scarce remaineth a sufficient highway for the meeting of carriages and droves of cattle; much less is there any fair, pleasant, or wholesome way for people to walk on foot; which is no small blemish to so famous a city to have so unsavoury and unseemly an entrance or passage thereunto.

Now of Whitechapel church somewhat, and then back again to Aldgate. This church is, as it were, a chapel of ease to the parish of Stebinhith, and the parson of Stebinhith hath the gift thereof; which being first dedicated to the name of God and the blessed Virgin, is now called St. Mary Matfellon. About the year 1428, the 6th of King Henry VI., a devout widow of that parish had long time cherished and brought up of alms a certain Frenchman, or Breton born, which most unkindly and cruelly in a night murdered the said widow sleeping in her bed,

[1] " By encroachments for building of small tenements, and taking in of garden-plots, timber-yards, or what they list. From this tower hill towards Aldgate (being a long continuous street), amongst other buildings, was that abbey of nunnes called the Minorities, or Minories, whereof I have spoken. And on the other side of that streete lyeth the ditche without the wall of the citie from the Tower unto Aldegate."—1st edition, pp. 347-8.

and after fled with such jewels and other stuff of her as he
might carry; but he was so freshly pursued, that for fear he
took the church of St. George in Southwark, and challenged
privilege of sanctuary there, and so abjured the king's land.
Then the constables (having charge of him) brought him into
London, intending to have conveyed him eastward; but so
soon as he was come into the parish, where before he had committed the murder, the wives cast upon him so much filth and
odour of the street, that (notwithstanding the best resistance
made by the constables) they slew him out of hand; and for
this feat, it hath been said, that parish to have purchased that
name of St. Mary Matfellon; but I find in record the same to be
called Villa beatæ Mariæ de Matfellon, in the 21st of Richard II.

More, we read, that in the year 1336, the 10th of Edward III.,
the bishop of Alba, cardinal and parson of Stebinhith, procurator
general in England, presented a clerk to be parson in the church
of the blessed Mary called Matfellon, without Aldgate of London,
etc.

Now again from Aldgate north-west to Bishopsgate, lieth
Houndsditch, and so to Bishopsgate.

North, and by east from Bishopsgate, lieth a large street or
highway, having on the west side thereof the parish church of
St. Buttolph.

Then is the hospital of St. Mary of Bethelem, founded by
a citizen of London, and as before is showed: up to the bars
without the which is Norton fall gate, a liberty so called, belonging to the dean of Pauls; thence up to the late dissolved priory
of St. John Baptist, called Holywell, a house of nuns, of old time
founded by a bishop of London. Stephen Grausend, bishop of
London, about the year 1318, was a benefactor thereunto;
re-edified by Sir Thomas Lovel,[1] knight of the garter, who
built much there in the reigns of Henry VII. and of Henry VIII.;
he endowed this house with fair lands, and was there buried
in a large chapel by him built for that purpose. This priory
was valued at the suppression to have of lands two hundred
and ninety-three pounds by year, and was surrendered 1539,
the 31st of Henry VIII. The church thereof being pulled down,
many houses have been built for the lodgings of noblemen, of
strangers born, and other.[2]

[1] " Brought up in Lincoln's inn."—*1st edition*, p. 349.
[2] " And neare thereunto are builded two publique houses for the acting
and shewe of comedies, tragedies, and histories, for recreation. Whereof
one is called the Courtein, the other the Theatre; both standing on the
south-west side towards the field."—*Ibid.*

From Holywell in the high street is a continual building of
tenements to Sewers ditch,[1] having one small side of a field,
already made a garden plot. Over against the north corner
of this field, between it and the church of St. Leonarde in Shoreditch, sometime stood a cross, now a smith's forge, dividing
three ways: forth right the highway is built upon either side,
more than a good flight shot, towards Kinges land, Newington,
Totanham, etc.

On the left hand is Ealde street, which reacheth west to a
stone cross, over against the north end of Golden lane,[2] and so
to the end of Goswell street. On the right hand of this Ealde
street, not far from Sowers ditch, but on the north side thereof,
is Hoxton, a large street with houses on both sides, and is a
prebend belonging to Pauls church in London, but of Soers
ditch parish.

On the right hand beyond Soers ditch church toward Hackney
are some late built houses upon the common soil, for it was
a leystall, but those houses belong to the parish of Stebunhith.

On the other side of the highway from Bishopsgate and
Houndsditch is the Dolphin, a common inn for receipt of
travellers; then a house built by the Lord John Powlet, then
Fisher's folly,[3] and so up to the west end of Berwardes lane, is
a continual building of small cottages, then the hospital called
St. Mary Spittle, hard within the bars, whereof I have spoken
in Bishopsgate ward.

From the which bars towards Soers ditch [4] on that side is all
along a continual building of small and base tenements, for the
most part lately erected.

Amongst the which (I mean of the ancientest building) was
one row of proper small houses, with gardens for poor decayed
people, there placed by the prior of the said hospital; every one
tenant whereof paid one penny rent by the year at Christmas,
and dined with the prior on Christmas day: but after the suppression of the hospital, these houses, for want of reparations,
in few years were so decayed, that it was called Rotten row,
and the poor worn out (for there came no new in their place)
houses, for a small portion of money, were sold from Goddard

[1] Shoreditch. In the first edition, it is called Sors ditch, or Sewers
ditch.

[2] " Over against the north end of Grub street."—*1st edition*, p. 349.

[3] " Next to that a large house, with gardens of pleasure, builded by
Jasper Fisher; from this up to the west end of Hog lane, etc."—*1st edition*,
p. 350.

[4] " Soerditch, so called more than four hundred yeares since, as I can
prove by record."—*Stow.*

to Russell, a draper, who new built them, and let them out for rent enough, taking also large fines of the tenants, near as much as the houses cost him purchase and building; for he made his bargains so hardly with all men, that both carpenter, bricklayer, and plasterer, were by that work undone: and yet, in honour of his name, it is now called Russell's row.

Now for the parish of St. Leonard at Soers ditch, the archdeacon of London is always parson thereof, and the cure is served by a vicar. In this church have been divers honourable persons buried, as appeareth by monuments yet remaining: Sir John Elrington, with Margaret his wife, daughter and heir to Thomas Lord Itchingham, widow to William Blount, son and heir to Walter Blount, the first Lord Mountjoy, which Margaret died 1481. Sir Humfrey Starkie, recorder of London, baron of the Exchequer; John Gadde, shereman of London, and Anne his wife, 1480; Sir Thomas Seymore, mayor of London, deceased 1535; Sir Thomas Ligh, doctor of law, 1545. Item, under one fair monument lieth buried the Lady Katherine, daughter to Edward, duke of Buckingham, wife to Ralph Nevell, Earl of Westmoreland, who died 1553; also Elianor, daughter to Sir William Paston, wife to Thomas Mannars, earl of Rutland, 1551; Margaret, daughter to Ralph Nevel, earl of Westmoreland, and wife to Henry Mannars, earl of Rutland, 1560; Katherine, daughter to Henry Nevel, earl of Westmoreland, and wife to Sir John Constable of Holderness, 1591; Anne, daughter to T. Mannars, earl of Rutland; Sir T. Mannars, fourth son to Thomas, earl of Rutland, 1591; Oliver Mannars, fifth son to Thomas, earl of Rutland, 1563, all under one monument; Richard and Harry Young, 1545.

Notwithstanding that of late one vicar there, for covetousness of the brass, which he converted into coined silver, plucking up many plates fixed on the graves, and left no memory of such as had been buried under them, a great injury both to the living and the dead, forbidden by public proclamation, in the reign of our sovereign lady Queen Elizabeth, but not forborne by many, that either of a preposterous zeal, or of a greedy mind, spare not to satisfy themselves by so wicked a means.

One note of Shoreditch, and so an end of that suburb. I read, that in the year 1440, the 18th of Henry VI. a fuller of Shoreditch appeached of treason many worthy esquires and gentlemen of Kent, but he being proved false, was attainted, condemned, and had judgment to be drawn, hanged, and quartered; which was done; his head set on London bridge, and his quarters on the gates. This justice was done according to the xvith of Deuteronomy: " The judges shall make diligent inquisition, and if the witness be found false, and to have given false witness against his brother, then shall they do unto him as he had thought to do unto his brother," etc. I read of the King's Manor vocatur Shoreditch-place, in the parish of Hackney, but how it took that name I know not, and therefore I will turn back from Shoreditch cross to Bethelem cross, and so pass through that hospital into the Morefield, which lieth without the postern called Moregate.

This field of old time was called the More, as appeareth by the charter of William the Conqueror to the college of St. Martin, declaring a running water to pass into the city from the same More. Also Fitzstephen writeth of this More, saying thus: " When the great fen, or moor, which watereth the walls on the north side, is frozen," etc. This fen, or moor field, stretching from the wall of the city betwixt Bishopsgate and the postern called Cripples gate, to Fensbery and to Holy well, continued a waste and unprofitable ground a long time, so that the same was all letten for four marks the year, in the reign of Edward II.; but in the year 1415, the 3rd of Henry V., Thomas Fawconer, mayor, as I have showed, caused the wall of the city to be broken toward the said moor, and built the postern called Moregate, for the ease of the citizens to walk that way upon causeys towards Iseldon and Hoxton: moreover, he caused the ditches of the city, and other the ditches from Soers ditch to Deepe ditch, by Bethelem, into the More ditch, to be new cast and cleansed; by means whereof the said fen or moor was greatly drained and dried; but shortly after, to wit, in 1477, Ralph Joceline, mayor, for repairing of the wall of the city, caused the said moor to be searched for clay, and brick to be burnt there, etc.; by which means this field was made the worse for a long time.

In the year 1498, all the gardens, which had continued time out of mind without Moregate, to wit, about and beyond the lordship of Finsbury, were destroyed; and of them was made a plain field for archers to shoot in. And in the year 1512, Roger Archley, mayor, caused divers dikes to be cast, and made to drain the waters of the said Morefielde, with bridges arched over them, and the grounds about to be levelled, whereby the said field was made somewhat more commodious, but yet it stood full of noisome waters; whereupon, in the year 1527, Sir Thomas Semor, mayor, caused divers sluices to be made to convey the said waters over the Town ditch, into the course of Walbrooke, and so into the Thames; and by these degrees was this fen or moor at length made main and hard ground, which before being overgrown with flags, sedges, and rushes, served to no use; since the which time also the further grounds beyond Finsbury court have been so overheightened with lay-stalls of dung, that now three windmills are thereon set; the ditches be filled up, and the bridges overwhelmed.

And now concerning the inclosures of common grounds about this city, whereof I mind not much to argue, Edward Hall setteth down a note of his time, to wit, in the 5th, or rather 6th of Henry VIII. " Before this time," saith he, " the inhabitants of the towns about London, as Iseldon, Hoxton, Shoreditch, and others, had so inclosed the common fields with hedges and ditches, that neither the young men of the city might shoot, nor the ancient persons walk for their pleasures in those fields, but that either their bows and arrows were taken away or broken, or the honest persons arrested or indicted; saying, ' that no Londoner ought to go out of the city, but in the highways.' This saying so grieved the Londoners, that suddenly this year a great number of the city assembled themselves in a morning, and a turner, in a fool's coat, came crying through the city, ' Shovels and spades! shovels and spades! ' so many of the people followed, that it was a wonder to behold; and within a short space all the hedges about the city were cast down, and the ditches filled up, and every thing made plain, such was the diligence of these workmen. The king's council hearing of this assembly, came to the Gray Friars and sent for the mayor and council of the city to know the cause, which declared to them the injury and annoying done to the citizens and to their liberties, which though they would not seek disorderly to redress, yet the commonalty and young persons could not be stayed thus to remedy the same. When the king's council had heard their answer, they dissimuled the matter, and commanded the mayor to see that no other thing were attempted, but that they should forthwith call home the younger sort; who having speedily achieved their desire, returned home before the king's council, and the mayor departed without more harm: after which time (saith Hall) these fields were never hedged, but now we see the thing in worse case than ever, by means of inclosure for gardens, wherein are built many fair summer-houses;[1] and, as in other places of the suburbs, some of them like Midsummer pageants, with towers, turrets, and

---

[1] " Banqueting houses like banqueroutes, bearing great shew and little worth."—*Stow*.

chimney-tops, not so much for use of profit as for show and pleasure, betraying the vanity of men's minds, much unlike to the disposition of the ancient citizens, who delighted in the building of hospitals and alms-houses for the poor, and therein both employed their wits, and spent their wealths in preferment of the common commodity of this our city.

But to come back again to Moregate, and from thence west through a narrow lane called the Postern, because it hath at either end a door to be shut in the night season, betwixt the More ditch inclosed with brick for tenter-yards, and the gardens of the said More field, to More lane; a part of the suburb without Cripplegate, without this postern, called Cripplegate, also lay a part of the said More even to the river of the Wells, as in another place I have showed; and no houses were there built till the latter end of the reign of William the Conqueror, and of his son William Rufus; about which times some few houses being there built along east and west, thwart before the said gate, one Alfune built for the inhabitants a parish church, which is of St. Giles, somewhat west from the said gate, and is now on the bank of the town ditch; and so was there a street, since called Fore street, as standing before the gate.

This Alfune, in the reign of Henry I., became the first hospitaller of St. Bartlemewe's hospital in Smithfield, as in another place I have noted. And this parish church of St. Giles being at the first a small thing, stood in place where now standeth the vicarage-house, but hath been since at divers times much enlarged, according as the parish hath increased, and was at the length newly built in place where now it standeth. But the same new church being large, strongly built, and richly furnished with ornaments, was in the year 1545, by casualty of fire, sore burnt and consumed, notwithstanding it was again within a short space of time repaired, as now it showeth.

Some little distance from the east end of this church standeth a fair conduit, castellated, in Fore street. Then have ye a boss of sweet water in the wall of the churchyard, lately made a pump, but already decayed.

Then have ye a fair pool of sweet water near to the church of St. Giles, wherein Anne of Lodbery was drowned, as I have before declared.

In the east end of Fore street is More lane: then next is Grub street; of late years inhabited, for the most part, by bowyers, fletchers, bow-string makers, and such like occupations, now little occupied; archery giving place to a number of bowling-alleys and dicing-houses, which in all places are increased, and too much frequented.

This street stretcheth north to Everards Well street, which thwarteth it to White cross street; the next from Fore street north is White cross street, likewise extending itself up to the west end of Everards Well street, and from the end thereof to Eald street.

From the west end of Fore street lieth Red cross street; from the which cross on the right hand east lieth Beech lane, and reacheth to the White cross street. From Red cross north lieth Golding lane, which stretcheth up to a cross in Ealde street, which Golding lane on both the sides is replenished with many tenements of poor people.

On the left hand, and west of the Red cross, lieth a street of old time called Houndes ditch, and of later time named Barbican, of such cause as I have before noted. And thus have you all the suburb without Cripplegate, being almost altogether in the parish of St. Giles, which hath more than eighteen hundred householders, and above four thousand communicants.

Without Aldersgate on the left hand is the parish church of St. Buttolph; on the north side of the which church lieth a way called Little Britane street, towards the priory of St. Bartholomew in Smithfield; but the highway without Aldersgate runneth straight north from the said gate unto Houndes ditch, or Barbican street, on the right hand, and Long lane on the left hand, which runneth into Smithfield.

Then from the farther end of Aldersgate street, straight north to the bar, is called Goswell street, replenished with small tenements, cottages, and alleys, gardens, banqueting-houses, and bowling-places.

Beyond these bars, leaving the Charter-house on the left hand, or the west side, the way stretcheth up towards Iseldon, and on the right hand, or east side, at a Red cross, turneth into Eald street, so called, for that it was the old highway from Aldersgate, for the north-east parts of England, before Bishopsgate was built, which street runneth east to a smith's forge, sometime a cross before Shoreditch church, from whence the passengers and carriages were to turn north to King's land, Tottenham, Waltham, Ware, etc.

There was sometime in this suburb without Aldersgate an hospital for the poor, but an alien of Clunie, a French order, and therefore suppressed by King Henry V., who gave the house, with lands and goods, to the parish of St. Buttolph, and a brotherhood of the Trinity was there founded, which was afterward suppressed by Henry VIII. or Edward VI.

There is at the farthest north corner of this suburb a windmill, which was sometime by a tempest of wind overthrown, and in place thereof a chapel was built by Queen Katherine (first wife to Henry VIII.), who named it the Mount of Calvary, because it was of Christ's passion, and was in the end of Henry VIII. pulled down, and a windmill newly set up as afore.

Without Newgate lieth the west and by north suburb; on the right hand, or north side whereof, betwixt the said gate and the parish of St. Sepulchre, turneth a way towards West Smithfield, called, as I have showed, Giltspurre street, or Knightriders street; then is Smithfield itself compassed about with buildings, as I have before declared, in Faringdon ward without.

And without the bar of West Smithfield lieth a large street or way, called of the house of St. John there St. John's street, and stretcheth toward Iseldon, on the right hand whereof stood the late dissolved monastery called the Charterhouse, founded by Sir Walter Manny, knight, a stranger born, lord of the town of Manny, in the diocese of Cambrey, beyond the seas, who for service done to King Edward III. was made knight of the garter: so his house he founded upon this occasion. A great pestilence entering this island, began first in Dorsetshire, then proceeded into Devonshire, Somersetshire, Gloucestershire, and Oxfordshire, and at length came to London, and overspread all England, so wasting the people, that scarce the tenth person of all sorts was left alive, and churchyards were not sufficient to receive the dead, but men were forced to choose out certain fields for burials; whereupon Ralph Stratford, bishop of London, in the year 1348, bought a piece of ground called No Man's Land, which he inclosed with a wall of brick, and dedicated for burial of the dead, building thereupon a proper chapel, which is now enlarged and made a dwelling-house; and this burying plot is become a fair garden, retaining the old name of Pardon churchyard.

About this, in the year 1349, the said Sir Walter Manny, in respect of danger that might befall in this time of so great a plague and infection, purchased thirteen acres and a rod of ground adjoining to the said No Man's Land, and lying in a place called Spittle croft, because it belonged to St. Bartilmewe's hospital, since that called the New church haw, and caused it to be consecrated by the said bishop of London to the use of burials.

In this plot of ground there were in that year more than fifty thousand persons buried, as I have read in the charters of

Edward III.: also, I have seen and read an inscription fixed on a stone cross, sometime standing in the same churchyard, and having these words:—" *Anno Domini* 1349, *regnante magna pestilentia consecratum fuit hoc Cœmiterium, in quo et infra septa presentis monasterii, sepulta fuerunt mortuorum corpora plusquam quinquaginta millia, præter alia multa abhinc usque ad presens, quorum animabus propitietur Deus. Amen.*"

In consideration of the number of Christian people here buried, the said Sir Walter Manny caused first a chapel to be built, where for the space of twenty-three years offerings were made; and it is to be noted, that above one hundred thousand bodies of Christian people had in that churchyard been buried; for the said knight had purchased that place for the burial of poor people, travellers, and other that were deceased, to remain for ever; whereupon an order was taken for the avoiding of contention between the parsons of churches and that house; to wit, that the bodies should be had unto the church where they were parishioners, or died, and, after the funeral service done, had to the place where they should be buried. And in the year 1371 he caused there to be founded a house of Carthusian monks, which he willed to be called the Salutation, and that one of the monks should be called prior; and he gave them the said place of thirteen acres and a rod of land, with the chapel and houses there built, for their habitation: he also gave them the three acres of land lying without the walls on the north part, betwixt the lands of the abbot of Westminster and the lands of the prior of St. John (which three acres were purchased, inclosed, and dedicated by Ralph Stratford, bishop of London, as is afore showed), and remained till our time by the name of Pardon churchyard, and served for burying of such as desperately ended their lives, or were executed for felonies, who were fetched thither usually in a close cart, bailed over and covered with black, having a plain white cross thwarting, and at the fore end a St. John's cross without, and within a bell ringing by shaking of the cart, whereby the same might be heard when it passed; and this was called the friary cart, which belonged to St. John's, and had the privilege of sanctuary.

In this charter-house were the monuments of the said Sir Walter Manny, and Margaret his wife; Marmaduke Lumley; Laurence Brumley, knight; Sir Edward Hederset, knight; Sir William Manny, knight; Dame Joan Borough; John Dore; Want Water, knight; Robert Olney, esquire; Katherine, daughter to Sir William Babington, knight; Blanch, daughter to Hugh Waterton; Katherine, wife to John at Poote, daughter and heir to Richard de Lacie; William Rawlin; Sir John Lenthaine, and Dame Margaret his wife, daughter to John Fray; John Peake, esquire; William Baron, and William Baron, esquire; Sir Thomas Thawites, knight; Philip Morgan, bishop of Ely, 1434.

In the cloister:—Bartholomew Rede, knight, mayor of London, buried 1505; Sir John Popham, etc.

This monastery, at the suppression in the 29th of Henry VIII., was valued at six hundred and forty-two pounds and four pence halfpenny yearly.

A little without the bars of West Smithfield is Charterhouse lane, so called, for that it leadeth to the said plot of the late dissolved monastery; in place whereof, first the Lord North, but since Thomas Howard, late Duke of Norfolk, have made large and sumptuous buildings both for lodging and pleasure. At the gate of this Charter-house is a fair water conduit, with two cocks, serving the use of the neighbours to their great commodity.

St. John's street, from the entering this lane, is also on both the sides replenished with buildings up to Clerkenwell. On the left hand of which street lieth a lane called Cow cross, of a cross sometime standing there; which lane turneth down to another lane called Turnemill street, which stretcheth up to the west of Clerkenwell, and was called Turnemill street, for such cause as is afore declared.

One other lane there is called St. Peter's lane, which turneth from St. John's street to Cow cross.

On the left hand also stood the late dissolved priory of St. John of Jerusalem in England, founded about the year of Christ 1100 by Jorden Briset, baron, and Muriell his wife, near unto Clarkes well besides West Smithfield; which Jorden having first founded the priory of nuns at Clarkes well, bought of them ten acres of land, giving them in exchange ten acres of land in his lordship of Welling hall, in the county of Kent. St. John's church was dedicated by Eraclius, patriarch of the holy resurrection of Christ at Jerusalem, in the year 1185, and was the chief seat in England of the religious knights of St. John of Jerusalem; whose profession was, besides their daily service of God, to defend Christians against pagans, and to fight for the church, using for their habit a black upper garment, with a white cross on the fore part thereof; and for their good service was so highly esteemed, that when the order of Templars was dissolved, their lands and possessions were by parliament granted unto these, who after the loss of Jerusalem recovered the isle of Rhodes from the Turks, and there placed themselves, being called thereof for many years knights of the Rhodes; but after the loss thereof, 1523, they removed to the isle of Malta, manfully opposing themselves against the Turkish invasions.

The rebels of Essex and of Kent, 1381, set fire on this house, causing it to burn by the space of seven days together, not suffering any to quench it; since the which time the priors of that house have new built both the church and houses thereunto appertaining; which church was finished by Thomas Docwrey, late lord prior there, about the year 1504, as appeareth by the inscription over the gate-house, yet remaining. This house, at the suppression in the 32nd of Henry VIII., was valued to dispend in lands three thousand three hundred and eighty-five pounds nineteen shillings and eight pence yearly. Sir W. Weston being then lord prior, died on the same seventh of May, on which the house was suppressed; so that great yearly pensions being granted to the knights by the king, and namely to the lord prior during his life one thousand pounds, he never received a penny.

The king took into his hands all the lands that belonged to that house and that order, wheresoever in England and Ireland, for the augmentation of his crown.

This priory church and house of St. John was preserved from spoil or down pulling, so long as King Henry VIII. reigned, and was employed as a store-house for the king's toils and tents, for hunting, and for the wars, etc.; but in the 3rd of King Edward VI., the church, for the most part, to wit, the body and side aisles, with the great bell tower (a most curious piece of workmanship, graven, gilt, and enamelled, to the great beautifying of the city, and passing all other that I have seen), was undermined and blown up with gunpowder; the stone thereof was employed in building of the lord protector's house at the Strand. That part of the choir which remaineth, with some side chapels, was by cardinal Pole, in the reign of Queen Mary, closed up at the west end, and otherwise repaired; and Sir Thomas Tresham, knight, was then made lord prior there, with restitution of some lands, but the same was again suppressed in the first year of Queen Elizabeth.

There were buried in this church brethren of that house and knights of that order: John Botell; William Bagecore; Richard

Barrow; John Vanclay; Thomas Launcelen; John Mallory;
William Turney; William Hulles, Hils, or Hayles; John
Weston; Redington; William Longstrother; John Long-
strother; William Tong; John Wakeline. Then of other:
Thomas Thornburgh, gentleman; William West, gentleman;
John Fulling, and Adam Gill, esquires; Sir John Mortimor,
and Dame Elianor his wife; Nicholas Silverston; William
Plompton, esquire; Margaret Tong, and Isabel Tong; Walter
Bellingham, alias Ireland, king of arms of Ireland; Thomas
Bedle, gentleman; Katherine, daughter of William Plompton,
esquire; Richard Turpin, gentleman; Joan, wife to Alexander
Dikes; John Bottle, and Richard Bottle, esquires; Rowland
Darcie; Richard Sutton, gentleman; Richard Bottill, gentle-
man; Sir W. Harpden, knight; Robert Kingston, esquire, and
Margery his wife; John Roch; Richard Cednor, gentleman;
Simon Mallory, 1442; William Mallory, Robert Longstrother,
Ralph Asteley, William Marshall, Robert Savage, Robert
Gondall, esquires, and Margery his wife; William Bapthorpe,
baron of the Exchequer, 1442.

North from the house of St. John's was the priory of Clarkenwell, so called of Clarkes well adjoining; which priory was also
founded about the year 1100 by Jorden Briset, baron, the son
of Ralph, the son of Brian Briset; who gave to Robert, a priest,
fourteen acres of land lying in the field next adjoining to the
said Clarkes well, thereupon to build a house of religious persons,
which he founded to the honour of God and the assumption
of our lady, and placed therein black nuns. This Jorden Briset
gave also to that house one piece of ground, thereby to build a
windmill upon, etc. He and Muriall his wife were buried in
the Chapter-house there. More buried in this church: John
Wikes, esquire, and Isabel his wife; Dame Agnes Clifford;
Ralph Timbleby, esquire; Dame Jahan, baroness of Grey-
stocke; Dame Jahan, Lady Ferrars. And of later time in the
parish church, Constances Bennet, a Greek born: he gave two
houses, the one in St. John's street, the other in Turnmill street;
the rents of them to be distributed in coals every year against
Christmas to the poor of that parish.

William Herne, a master of defence, and yeoman of the
guard, 1580, gave lands and tenements to the clothworkers in
London; they to pay yearly for ever fourteen pounds to the
churchwardens of Clarkenwell, and fourteen pounds to the
churchwardens of St. Sepulcher's, towards reparations of these
churches, and relief of the poor men; more he gave after the

death of one man, yet living, eight pounds the year for ever to the mending of highways.

Thomas Sackeford, esquire, one of the masters of requests, gave to the poor of that parish forty shillings the year for ever, out of his alms-house at Woodbridge in Suffolk, where he is buried. Henry Stoke, gardener, buried there, gave twenty shillings the year for ever, towards reparation of that church. This priory was valued to dispend two hundred and sixty-two pounds nine shillings by the year, and was surrendered the 31st of Henry VIII. Many fair houses are now built about the priory, namely, by the highway towards Iseldon.

So much of the church which remaineth (for one great aisle thereof fell down) serveth as a parish church of St. John, not only for the tenements and near inhabitants, but also (as is aforesaid) for all up to Highgate, Muswell, etc.

Near unto this church, beside Clarke's well lane, divers other wells, namely, Skinners well, Fags well, Tode well, Loder's well, Rede well, etc., now dammed up.

Now to return again to Giltspurre street, where I first began with this suburb, there standeth the parish church of St. Sepulchre in the Bayly, as is before showed; from this street to Turnagaine lane, by Hosiar lane, Cow lane, and Holdborn conduit, down Snore hill to Oldborne bridge, and up Oldborne hill, by Gold lane on the right hand, and Lither lane beyond it, to the bars; beyond the which bars on the same side is Porte pool, or Grayes inn lane, so called of the inn of court, named Grayes inn, a goodly house there situate, by whom built or first begun I have not yet learned, but seemeth to be since Edward III.'s time, and is a prebend to Paule's church in London.

This lane is furnished with fair buildings and many tenements on both the sides, leading to the fields towards Highgate and Hamsted.

On the high street have ye many fair houses built, and lodgings for gentlemen, inns for travellers, and such like up almost (for it lacketh but little) to St. Giles in the fields; amongst the which buildings, for the most part being very new, one passeth the rest in largeness of rooms, lately built by a widow, sometime wife to Richard Alington, esquire; which Richard Alington deceased in the year 1561. And thus much for that north side of Oldborne

Now from Newgate, on the left hand or south side, lieth the Old Bayly, and so down by Seacole lane end to Oldborne bridge, up Oldborne hill, by Shoe lane and Fewters lane, to the bars.

Beyond the bars had ye in old time a temple built by the Templars, whose order first began in the year of Christ 1118, in the 19th of Henry I. This temple was left and fell to ruin since the year 1184, when the Templars had built them a new temple in Fleet street, near to the river of Thames. A great part of this old temple was pulled down, but of late in the year 1595. Adjoining to this old Temple [1] was sometime the bishop of Lincolne's inn, wherein he lodged when he repaired to this city. Robert de Curars, bishop of Lincoln, built it about the year 1147. John Russell, bishop of Lincoln, chancellor of England, in the reign of Richard III., was lodged there. It hath of late years belonged to the earls of Southampton, and therefore called Southampton house. Master Ropar hath of late built much there; by means whereof part of the ruins of the old Temple were seen to remain built of Caen stone, round in form as the new Temple, by Temple bar, and other temples in England. Beyond this old Temple and the bishop of Lincoln's house [2] is New street, so called in the reign of Henry III., when he of a Jew's house founded the house of Converts, betwixt the old Temple and the new.

The same street hath since been called Chancery lane, by reason that King Edward III. annexed the house of Converts by patent to the office of Custos Rotulorum, or master of the rolls, in the 15th of his reign.

In this street the first fair building to be noted on the east side is called the Coursitors' office, built with divers fair lodgings for gentlemen, all of brick and timber, by Sir Nicholas Bacon, late lord keeper of the great seal.

Near unto this Coursitors' office be divers fair houses and large gardens, built and made in a ground sometime belonging to one great house on the other side the street, there made by Ralph Nevel, bishop of Chichester. This ground he had by the gift of Henry III., as appeareth. The king granteth to Ralph, bishop of Chichester, chancellor, that place, with the garden, which John Herlirum forfeited in that street, called New street, over against the land of the said bishop in the same street; which place, with the garden and appurtenance, was the king's escheat by the liberty of the city of London, as it was acknowledged before the king in his court at the Tower of London, in the last pleas of the crown of that city, cart. 11 Henry III.

---

[1] " The same was after the bishop of Lincoln's inn.—*1st edition*, p. 361
[2] " Beyond this Southampton house."—*Ibid*.

Then was the house of Converts, wherein now the rolls of Chancery be kept; then the Sergeants' inn, etc.

On the west side of New street, towards the north end thereof, was of old time the church and house of the Preaching Friers; concerning the which house I find, that in the year of Christ 1221, the friars' preachers, thirteen in number, came into England, and having to their prior one named Gilbert de Fraxineto, in company of Peter de la Roche, bishop of Winchester, came to Canterbury, where presenting themselves before the archbishop Steven, he commanded the said prior to preach, whose sermon he liked so well, that ever after he loved that order. These friars came to London, and had their first house without the wall of the city by Oldborne, near unto the old Temple.

Hubert de Burgh, earl of Kent, was a great benefactor unto these friars, and deceasing at his manor of Bansted in Surrey, or, after some writers, at his castle of Barkhamsted in Hartfordshire, in the year 1242, was buried in their church; unto the which church he had given his place at Westminster, which the said friars afterwards sold to Walter Grey, archbishop of York; and he left it to his successors in that see for ever, to be their house, when they should repair to the city of London. And therefore the same was called York place; which name so continued until the year 1529, that King Henry VIII. took it from Thomas Wolsey, cardinal and archbishop of York, and then gave it to name White hall.

Margaret, sister to the king of Scots, widow to Geffrey, earl marshal, deceased 1244, and was buried in this church.

In the year 1250, the friars of this order of preachers through Christendom and from Jerusalem, were by a convocation assembled together at this their house by Oldborne, to intreat of their estate, to the number of four hundred, having meat and drink found them of alms, because they had no possessions of their own. The first day, the king came to their chapter, found them meat and drink, and dined with them. Another day the queen found them meat and drink; afterward the bishop of London, then the abbot of Westminster, of St. Alban's, Waltham, and others. In the year 1276, Gregory Rokesley, mayor, and the barons of London, granted and gave to Robert Kilwarbie, archbishop of Canterbury, two lanes or ways next the street of Baynard's castle, and the tower of Mountfichet, to be destroyed. On the which place the said Robert built the late new church, with the rest of the stones that were left of the said tower: and thus the black friars left their church and house by Oldborne, and departed to their new. This old friar house (juxta Holborne, saith the patent) was by King Edward I., in the 16th of his reign, given to Henry Lacy, earl of Lincoln. [A. N.]

Next to this house of friars was one other great house, sometime belonging to the bishop of Chichester, whereof Matthew Paris writeth thus:—" Ralph de Nova Villa, or Nevill, bishop of Chichester and chancellor of England, sometime built a noble house, even from the ground, not far from the new Temple and house of Converts; in the which place he deceased in the year 1244. In this place, after the decease of the said bishop, and in place of the house of black friars before spoken of, Henry Lacy, earl of Lincoln, constable of Chester, and custos of England, built his inn, and for the most part was lodged there: he deceased in this house in the year 1310, and was buried in the new work (whereunto he had been a great benefactor) of St. Paul's church betwixt our Lady chapel and St. Dunstan's chapel. This Lincoln's inn, sometime pertaining to the bishops of Chichester, as a part of the said great house, is now an inn of court, retaining the name of Lincoln's inn as afore, but now lately increased with fair buildings, and replenished with gentlemen studious in the common laws. In the reign of Henry VIII. Sir Thomas Lovell was a great builder there; especially he built the gate-house and fore front towards the east, placing thereon as well the Lacies' arms as his own: he caused the Lacies' arms to be cast and wrought in lead, on the louer of the hall of that house, which was in the three escutcheons, a lion rampant for Lacie, seven mascules voided for Quincie, and three wheatsheafs for Chester. This louer being of late repaired, the said escutcheons were left out. The rest of that side, even to Fleet street, is replenished with fair buildings.

Now the High Oldborne street, from the north end of New street, stretcheth on the left hand in building lately framed, up to St. Giles in the field, which was an hospital founded by Matilda the queen, wife to Henry I., about the year 1117. This hospital, said the record of Edward III., the 19th year, was founded without the bar: *Veteris Templi London, et conversorum.*

This hospital was founded as a cell to Burton Lager of Jerusalem, as may appear by a deed dated the 24th of Henry VII. in these words:—" Thomas Norton, knight, master of Burton Lager of Jerusalem in England, and the brethren of the same place, keepers of the hospital of St. Giles, without the bars of the old Temple of London, have sold to Geffrey Kent, citizen and draper of London, a messuage or house, with two cellars above, edified in the parish of Alhallowes, Hony lane, in West Chepe, adjoining to the west part of a tenement called the Cote on the Hope, pertaining to the drapers of London, for thirty-one pounds."

At this hospital, the prisoners conveyed from the city of London towards Teyborne, there to be executed for treasons, felonies, or other trespasses, were presented with a great bowl of ale, thereof to drink at their pleasure, as to be their last refreshing in this life.

Now without Ludgate lieth the south end of the Old Bayly, then down Ludgate hill by Fleet lane, over Fleet bridge, up Fleet street, by Shoe lane, Fewtar's lane, New street, or Chauncerie lane, and to Shire lane, by the bar on the right hand; and from Ludgate on the left hand, or south side, by Bride lane, Water lane, Croker's lane, Sergeants' inn, and the new Temple, by the bar; all which is of Faringdon ward, as is afore showed.

LIBERTIES OF THE DUCHY OF LANCASTER

Next without the bar is the New Temple, and liberties of the city of London, in the suburbs, is a liberty pertaining to the duchy of Lancaster, which beginneth in the east, on the south side or left hand, by the river Thames, and stretcheth west to Ivie bridge, where it endeth; and again on the north side, or right hand, some small distance without Temple bar, in the high street, from a pair of stocks there standing, stretcheth one large Middle row, or troop of small tenements, partly opening to the south, partly towards the north, up west to a stone cross, now headless, over against the Strand; and this is the bounds to that liberty, which sometime belonged to Briane Lisle, since to Peter of Savoy, and then to the house of Lancaster, as shall be showed. Henry III., in the 30th year of his reign, did grant to his uncle Peter of Savoy all those houses upon the Thames, which sometimes pertained to Briane de Insula, or Lisle, without the walls of his city of London, in the way or street called the Strand, to hold to him and to his heirs, yielding yearly in the Exchequer, at the feast of St. Michaell the Archangell, three barbed arrows, for all services, dated at Reding, etc. This Peter of Savoy built the Savoy.

But first amongst other buildings memorable for greatness, on the river of Thames, Excester house, so called for that the same belonged to the bishops of Excester, and was their inn or London lodging: who was first builder thereof I have not read, but that Walter Stapleton was a great builder there in the reign of Edward II. is manifest; for the citizens of London, when they had beheaded him in Cheape, near unto the cathedral church of St. Paule, they buried him in a heap of sand or rubbish in his own house without Temple bar, where he had made great building. Edmond Lacie, bishop of Excester, built the great hall in the reign of Henry VI., etc. The same hath since been called Paget house, because William Lord Paget enlarged and possessed it. Then Leycester house, because Robert Dudley, earl of Leycester, of late new built there, and now Essex house, of the earl of Essex lodging there.

Then west was a chapel dedicated to the Holy Ghost, called St. Sprite, upon what occasion founded I have not read. Next is Milford lane down to the Thames, but why so called I have not read as yet.

Then was the bishop of Bathes inn, lately new built, for a great part thereof, by the Lord Thomas Seymour, admiral; which house came since to be possessed by the earl of Arundel, and thereof called Arundel house.

Next beyond the which, on the street side, was sometime a fair cemetery or churchyard, and in the same a parish church called of the Nativity of our Lady, and the Innocents of the Strand, and of some by means of a brotherhood kept there, called St. Ursula at the Strand. And near adjoining to the said church, betwixt it and the river of Thames, was an inn of Chancery commonly called Chester's inn (because it belonged to the bishop of Chester), by others, named of the situation, Strand inn.

Then was there a house belonging to the bishop of Landaff; for I find in record, the 4th of Edward II., that a vacant place lying near the church of our Lady at Strand, the said bishop procured it of Thomas, earl of Lancaster, for the enlarging of this house. Then had ye in the high street a fair bridge called Strand bridge, and under it a lane or way down to the landing-place on the bank of Thames.

Then was the bishop of Chester's (commonly called of Lichfield and Coventrie), his inn or London lodging: this house was first built by Walter Langton, bishop of Chester, treasurer of England in the reign of Edward I.

And next unto it adjoining was the bishop of Worcester's inn; all which, to wit, the parish of St. Mary at Strand, Strand inn, Strand bridge, with the lane under it, the bishop of Chester's inn, the bishop of Worcester's inn, with all the tenements adjoining, were by commandment of Edward, duke of Somerset, uncle to Edward VI., and lord protector, pulled down, and made level ground in the year 1549; in place whereof he built that large and goodly house, now called Somerset house.

In the high street, near unto the Strand, sometime stood a cross of stone against the bishop of Coventrie or Chester his house; whereof I read, that in the year 1294, and divers other times, the justices itinerants sate without London, at the stone cross over against the bishop of Coventrie's house, and sometime they sate in the Bishop's house, which was hard by the Strand, as is aforesaid.

Then next is the Savoy, so called of Peter, earl of Savoy, and Richmond, son to Thomas, earl of Savoy, brother to Boniface, archbishop of Canterbury, and uncle unto Eleanor, wife to King Henry III.

He first built this house in the year 1245; and here is occasion offered me for satisfying of some deniers thereof, to prove that this Peter of Savoy was also earl of Savoy: wherefore, out of a book of the genealogies of all the whole house of Savoy, compiled by Phillebert Pingonio, baron of Guzani, remaining in the hands of W. Smith, alias Rougedragon, officer of arms, I have gathered this:—Thomas, earl of Savoy, had issue by Beatrix, daughter to Aimon, earl of Geneva, nine sons and three daughters. Amades, his first son, succeeded earl of Savoy in the year 1253; Peter, his second son, earl of Savoy and of Richmond, in 1268; Philip, his third son, earl of Savoy and Burgundie, 1284; Thomas, the fourth, earl of Flanders and prince of Piemont; Boniface, the eighth, archbishop of Canterbury; Beatrix, his daughter, married to Raymond Beringarius of Aragon, earl of Province and Narbone, had issue, and was mother to five queens: the first, Margaret, wife to Lewes, king of France; the second, Eleanor, wife to Henry III. king of England; the third, Sanctia, wife to Richard, king of the Romans; the fourth, Beatrix, wife to Charles, king of Naples; the fifth, Johanna, wife to Philip, king of Navarre.

To return again to the house of Savoy: Queen Eleanor, wife to king Henry III., purchased this place afterwards of the fraternity or brethren of Montjoy; [1] unto whom Peter of Savoy, as it seemeth, had given it, for her son, Edmond earl of Lan-

---

[1] " Fratres de Monte Jovis, or Priory de Cornuto, by Havering at the Bower."—*Stow.*

caster (as M. Camden hath noted out of a register-book of the dukes of Lancaster). Henry, duke of Lancaster, repaired or rather new built it, with the charges of fifty-two thousand marks, which money he had gathered together at the town of Bridgerike. John, the French king, was lodged there in the year 1357, and also in the year 1363; for it was at that time the fairest manor in England.

In the year 1381, the rebels of Kent and Essex burnt this house; unto the which there was none in the realm to be compared in beauty and stateliness (saith mine author).[1] They set fire on it round about, and made proclamation that none, on pain to lose his head, should convert to his own use anything that there was, but that they should break such plate and vessels of gold and silver as was found in that house (which was in great plenty) into small pieces, and throw the same into the river of Thames: precious stones they should bruise in mortars, that the same might be to no use, and so it was done by them. One of their companions they burnt in the fire, because he minded to have reserved one goodly piece of plate.[2]

They found there certain barrels of gunpowder, which they thought had been gold or silver, and throwing them into the fire more suddenly than they thought, the hall was blown up, the houses destroyed, and themselves very hardly escaped away.

This house being thus defaced, and almost overthrown by these rebels for malice they bare to John of Gaunt, duke of Lancaster, of latter time came to the king's hands, and was again raised and beautifully built for an hospital of St. John Baptist by King Henry VII. about the year 1509, for the which hospital, retaining still the old name of Savoy, he purchased lands to be employed upon the relieving of a hundred poor people. This hospital being valued to dispend five hundred and twenty-nine pounds fifteen shillings, etc. by year, was suppressed the tenth of June, the 7th of Edward VI.: the beds, bedding, and other furniture belonging thereunto, with seven hundred marks of the said lands by year, he gave to the citizens of London, with his house of Bridewell, to the furnishing thereof, to be a workhouse for the poor and idle persons, and towards the furnishing of the hospital of St. Thomas in Southwark, lately suppressed.

---

[1] H. Knighton.—*Stow*.

[2] " Savoy brent: blown up with gunpowder. Rebels, more malitious then covetous, spoyle all before them."—*Stow*.

This hospital of Savoy was again new founded, erected, corporated, and endowed with lands by Queen Mary, the third of November: in the 4th of her reign, one Jackson took possession, and was made master thereof in the same month of November. The ladies of the court and maidens of honour (a thing not to be forgotten) stored the same of new with beds, bedding, and other furniture, in very ample manner, etc.; and it was by patent so confirmed at Westminster the 9th of May, the 4th and 5th of Philip and Mary. The chapel of this hospital serveth now as a parish church to the tenements thereof near adjoining, and others.

The next was sometime the bishop of Carlisle's inn, which now belongeth to the earl of Bedford, and is called Russell or Bedford house. It stretcheth from the hospital of Savoy, west to Ivie bridge, where Sir Robert Cecill, principal secretary to her majesty, hath lately raised a large and stately house of brick and timber, as also levelled and paved the highway near adjoining, to the great beautifying of that street and commodity of passengers. Richard II., in the 8th of his reign, granted license to pave with stone the highway called Strand street from Temple bar to the Savoy, and toll to be taken towards the charges; and again the like was granted in the 42nd of Henry VI.

Ivie bridge, in the high street, which had a way under it leading down to the Thames, the like as sometime had the Strand bridge, is now taken down, but the lane remaineth as afore, or better, and parteth the liberty of the duchy and the city of Westminster on that south side.

Now to begin again at Temple bar, over against it.[1] In the high street, as is afore showed, is one large Middle row of houses and small tenements built, partly opening to the south, partly towards the north; amongst the which standeth the parish church of St. Clement Danes, so called because Harold, a Danish king, and other Danes, were buried there. This Harold, whom king Canutus had by a concubine, reigned three years, and was buried at Westminster; but afterward Hardicanutus, the lawful son of Canutus, in revenge of a displeasure done to his mother, by expelling her out of the realm, and the murder of his brother Allured, commanded the body of Harold to be digged out of the earth, and to be thrown into the Thames, where it was by a fisherman taken up and buried in this churchyard; but out of a fair ledger-book, sometime belonging to the abbey of Chartsey, in the county of Surrey, is noted, as in Francis Thin, after this sort. In the reign of king Etheldred, the

[1] " In the high street standeth a pair of stocks."—*1st edition*, p. 369.

monastery of Chartsey was destroyed: ninety monks of that house were slain by the Danes, whose bodies were buried in a place next to the old monastery. William Malmseberie saith,— " They burnt the church, together with the monks and abbot; but the Danes continuing in their fury (throughout the whole land), desirous at the length to return home into Denmarke, were by the just judgment of God all slain at London in a place which is called the church of the Danes."

This said middle row of houses stretching west to a stone cross, now headless, by or against the Strand, including the said parish church of St. Clement, is also wholly of the liberty and duchy of Lancaster.

Thus much for the bounds and antiquities of this liberty, wherein I have noted parish churches twain, sometime three, houses of name six; to wit, the Savoy or Lancaster house, now a hospital, Somerset house, Essex house, Arundel house, Bedford or Russell house, and Sir Robert Cecil's house; besides of Chester's inn or Strand inn, sometime an inn of Chancery, etc. This liberty is governed by the chancellor of that duchy at this present, Sir Robert Cecil, knight, principal secretary to her majesty, and one of her majesty's most honourable privy councillors; there is under him a steward that keepeth court and leet for the queen; giveth the charge and taketh the oaths of every under officer: then is there four burgesses and four assistants, to take up controversies; a bailiff, which hath two or three under-bailiffs, that make arrests within that liberty; four constables; four wardens, that keep the lands and stock for the poor; four wardens for highways; a jury or inquest of fourteen or sixteen, to present defaults; four ale-conners, which look to assize of weights and measures, etc.; four scavengers and a beadle; and their common prison is Newgate. There is in this liberty fifty men, which is always to be at an hour's warning, with all necessary furniture to serve the queen, as occasion shall require. Their charge at a fifteen is thirteen shillings and four pence. Thus much for the suburb in the liberty of the duchy of Lancaster.

THE CITY OF WESTMINSTER, WITH THE ANTIQUITIES, BOUNDS, AND LIBERTIES THEREOF

Now touching the city of Westminster, I will begin at Temple bar, on the right hand or north side, and so pass up west through a back lane or street, wherein do stand three inns of chancery;

the first called Clement's inn, because it standeth near to St.
Clement's church, but nearer to the fair fountain called Clement's
well; the second, New inn, so called as latelier made, of a
common hostery, and the sign of Our Lady, an inn of chancery
for students than the other, to wit, about the beginning of the
reign of Henry VII., and not so late as some have supposed;
to wit, at the pulling down of Strand inn, in the reign of King
Edward VI.; for I read that Sir Thomas More, sometime lord
chancellor, was a student in this new inn, and went from thence
to Lincolne's inn, etc. The third is Lyon's inn, an inn of
chancery also.

This street stretcheth up unto Drury lane, so called, for that
there is a house belonging to the family of the Druries. This
lane turneth north toward St. Giles in the field: from the south
end of this lane in the high street are divers fair buildings,
hosteries, and houses for gentlemen and men of honour;
amongst the which Cicile house is one, which sometime belonged
to the parson of St. Martin's in the field, and by composition
came to Sir Thomas Palmer, knight, in the reign of Edward VI.,
who began to build the same of brick and timber, very large and
spacious, but of later time it hath been far more beautifully
increased by the late Sir William Cicile, baron of Burghley, lord
treasurer, and great councillor of the estate.

From thence is now a continual new building of divers fair
houses, even up to the earl of Bedford's house,[1] lately built nigh
to Ivy bridge, and so on the north side to a lane that turneth
to the parish church of St. Martin's in the field, in the liberty
of Westminster. Then had ye one house, wherein sometime
were distraught and lunatic people, of what antiquity founded
or by whom I have not read, neither of the suppression; but it
was said that sometime a king of England, not liking such a
kind of people to remain so near his palace, caused them to be
removed farther off, to Bethlem without Bishops gate of London,
and to that hospital: the said house by Charing cross doth yet
remain.

Then is the Mewse, so called of the king's falcons there kept
by the king's falconer, which of old time was an office of great
account, as appeareth by a record of Richard II., in the first

---

[1] " Which is a goodly house, lately builded nigh to Ivy bridge, over
against the old Bedforde house, namely, called Russell house and Dacres
house, now the house of Sir Thomas Cecile, Lorde Burghley; and so on
the north side to a lane that turneth to the parish church of St. Martin
in the Fielde, and stretcheth to St. Giles in the Fielde."—1st *edition*,
pp. 370-1.

year of his reign. Sir Simon Burley, knight, was made constable for the castles of Windsor, Wigmore, and Guilford, and of the manor of Kenington, and also master of the king's falcons at the Mewse, near unto Charing cross by Westminster; but in the year of Christ 1534, the 28th of Henry VIII., the king having fair stabling at Lomsbery (a manor in the farthest west part of Oldborne), the same was fired and burnt, with many great horses and great store of hay: after which time, the fore-named house, called the Mewse by Charing cross, was new built, and prepared for stabling of the king's horses, in the reign of Edward VI. and Queen Mary, and so remaineth to that use: and this is the farthest building west on the north side of that high street.

On the south side of the which street, in the liberties of Westminster (beginning at Ivie bridge), first is Durham house, built by Thomas Hatfielde, bishop of Durham, who was made bishop of that see in the year 1545, and sat bishop there thirty-six years.

Amongst matters memorable concerning this house, this is one:—In the year of Christ 1540, the 32nd of Henry VIII., on May-day, a great and triumphant justing was holden at Westminster, which had been formerly proclaimed in France, Flanders, Scotland, and Spain, for all comers that would undertake the challengers of England; which were, Sir John Dudley, Sir Thomas Seymour, Sir Thomas Ponings, and Sir George Carew, knights, and Anthonie Kingston and Richarde Cromwell, esquires; all which came into the lists that day richly apparelled, and their horses trapped all in white velvet. There came against them the said day forty-six defendants or undertakers, viz., the earl of Surrey, foremost, Lord William Howard, Lord Clinton, and Lord Cromwell, son and heir to Thomas Cromwell, earl of Essex, and chamberlain of England, with other; and that day, after the justs performed, the challengers rode unto this Durham house, where they kept open household, and feasted the king and queen, with her ladies, and all the court: the second day, Anthonie Kingston and Richard Cromwell were made knights there: the third day of May the said challengers did tournay on horseback with swords, and against them came forty-nine defendants; Sir John Dudley and the earl of Surrey running first, which at the first course lost their gauntlets; and that day Sir Richarde Cromwell overthrew master Palmer and his horse in the field, to the great honour of the challengers: the fifth of May the challengers fought on foot at the barriers, and against them came fifty defendants, which fought valiantly;

but Sir Richard Cromwell overthrew that day at the barriers master Culpepper in the field; and the sixth day the challengers brake up their household.

In this time of their housekeeping they had not only feasted the king, queen, ladies, and all the court, as is afore shewed; but also they cheered all the knights and burgesses of the common house in the parliament, and entertained the mayor of London, with the aldermen, and their wives, at a dinner, etc. The king gave to every of the said challengers, and their heirs for ever, in reward of their valiant activity, one hundred marks and a house to dwell in, of yearly revenue, out of the lands pertaining to the hospital of St. John of Jerusalem.

Next beyond this Durham house is another great house, sometime belonging to the bishop of Norwich, and was his London lodging, which now pertaineth to the archbishop of York by this occasion. In the year 1529, when Cardinal Wolsey, archbishop of Yorke, was indicted in the Premunire, whereby King Henry VIII. was entitled to his goods and possessions: he also seized into his hands the said archbishop's house, commonly called Yorke place, and changed the name thereof into White hall; whereby the archbishops of Yorke being dispossessed, and having no house of repair about London, Queen Mary gave unto Nicholas Heath, then archbishop of Yorke, and to his successors, Suffolke house in Southwark, lately built by Charles Brandon, duke of Suffolke, as I have showed.

This house the said archbishop sold, and bought the aforesaid house of old time belonging to the bishops of Norwich, which of this last purchase is now called Yorke house, the lord chancellors or lord keepers of the great seal of England, have been lately there lodged.

Then was there an hospital of St. Marie Rouncivall by Charing cross (a cell to the priory and covent of Rouncivall in Navar, in Pampelion diocese), where a fraternity was founded in the 15th of Edward IV., but now the same is suppressed and turned into tenements.

Near unto this hospital was a hermitage, with a chapel of St. Katherine, over against Charing cross; which cross, built of stone, was of old time a fair piece of work, there made by commandment of Edward I., in the 21st year of his reign, in memory of Eleanor, his deceased queen, as is before declared.

West from this cross stood sometime an hospital of St. James, consisting of two hides of land, with the appurtenances, in the parish of St. Margaret in Westminster, and founded by the citizens of London, before the time of any man's memory, for fourteen sisters, maidens, that were leprous, living chastely and honestly in divine service.

Afterwards divers citizens of London gave five-and-fifty pounds rent thereunto, and then were adjoined eight brethren to minister divine service there. After this, also, sundry devout men of London gave to this hospital four hides of land in the field of Westminster; and in Hendon, Calcote, and Hampsted, eighty acres of land and wood, etc. King Edward I. confirmed those gifts, and granted a fair to be kept on the eve of St. James, the day, the morrow, and four days following, in the 18th of his reign.

This hospital was surrendered to Henry VIII. the 23rd of his reign: the sisters being compounded with, were allowed pensions for the term of their lives; and the king built there a goodly manor, annexing thereunto a park, closed about with a wall of brick, now called St. James' park, serving indifferently to the said manor, and to the manor or palace of White hall.

South from Charing cross, on the right hand, are divers fair houses lately built before the park, then a large tilt-yard for noblemen, and other, to exercise themselves in justing, turning, and fighting at barriers.

On the left hand from Charing cross be also divers fair tenements lately built, till ye come to a large plot of ground inclosed with brick, and is called Scotland, where great buildings have been for receipt of the kings of Scotland, and other estates of that country; for Margaret, queen of Scots, and sister to King Henry VIII., had her abiding there, when she came into England after the death of her husband, as the kings of Scotland had in former times, when they came to the parliament of England.

Then is the said White hall, sometime belonging to Hubert de Burgh, earl of Kent, and justice of England, who gave it to the Black Friars in Oldborne, as I have before noted. King Henry VIII. ordained it to be called an honour, and built there a sumptuous gallery and a beautiful gate-house, thwart the high street to St. James' park, etc.

In this gallery the princes, with their nobility, used to stand or sit, and at windows, to behold all triumphant justings and other military exercises.

Beyond this gallery, on the left hand, is the garden or orchard belonging to the said White hall.

On the right hand be divers fair tennis-courts, bowling-alleys, and a cock-pit, all built by King Henry VIII.; and then one other arched gate, with a way over it, thwarting the street from the king's gardens to the said park.

From this gate up King's street to a bridge over Long ditch (so called for that the same almost insulateth the city of Westminster), near which bridge is a way leading to Chanon row, so called for that the same belonged to the dean and chanons of St. Stephen's chapel, who were there lodged, as now divers noblemen and gentlemen be; whereof one is belonging to Sir Edward Hobbey, one other to John Thine, esquire, one stately built by Ann Stanhope, duchess of Somerset, mother to the earl of Hartford, who now enjoyeth that house. Next a stately house, now in building by William earl of Darby; over against the which is a fair house, built by Henry Clinton, earl of Lincoln.

From this way up to the Woolestaple and to the high tower, or gate which entereth the palace court, all is replenished with buildings and inhabitants.

Touching this Woolestaple, I read, that in the reign of Edward I., the staple being at Westminster, the parishioners of St. Margaret and merchants of the staple built of new the said church, the great chancel excepted, which was lately before new built by the abbot of Westminster.

Moreover, that Edward III., in the 17th of his reign, decreed that no silver be carried out of the realm on pain of death; and that whosoever transporteth wool should bring over for every sack four nobles of silver bullion.

In the 25th of his reign, he appointed the staple of wool to be kept only at Canterbury, for the honour of St. Thomas; but in the 27th of the same King Edward, the staple of wool, before kept at Bruges in Flanders, was ordained by parliament to be kept in divers places of England, Wales, and Ireland, as at Newcastle, Yorke, Lincoln, Canterbury, Norwich, Westminster, Chichester, Winchester, Excester, Bristow, Carmardyn, etc., to the great benefit of the king and loss unto strangers and merchants: for there grew unto the king by this means (as it was said) the sum of one thousand one hundred and two pounds by the year, more than any his predecessors before had received; the staple at Westminster at that time began on the next morrow after the feast of St. Peter ad vincula. The next year was granted to the king by parliament, towards the recovery of his title in France, fifty shillings of every sack of wool transported over seas, for the space of six years next ensuing; by means whereof the king might dispend daily during those years more than a thousand marks sterling: for by the common opinion there were more than one hundred thousand sacks of wool yearly transported into foreign lands, so that during six years the said grant extended to fifteen hundred thousand pounds sterling.

In the 37th of Edward III., it was granted unto him for two years, to take five-and-twenty shillings and eight pence upon every sack of wool transported; and the same year the staple of wool (notwithstanding the king's oath and other great estates) was ordained to be kept at Callis, and six-and-twenty merchants, the best and wealthiest of all England, to be farmers there, both of the town and staple, for three years: every merchant to have six men of arms and four archers at the king's cost. He ordained there also two mayors, one for the town and one for the staple; and he took for *mala capta*, commonly called Maltorth,[1] twenty shillings, and of the said merchants' guardians of the town forty pence, upon every sack of wool.

In the 44th of Edward III., Quinborough, Kingston-upon-Hull, and Boston, were made staples of wool; which matter so much offended some, that in the 50th of his reign, in a parliament at London, it was complained that the staple of wool was so removed from Callis to divers towns in England, contrary to the statute, appointing that citizens and merchants should keep it there, and that the king might have the profits and customs, with the exchange of gold and silver, that was there made by all the merchants in Christindome (esteemed to amount to eight thousand pounds by year), the exchange only; and the citizens and merchants so ordered the matter, that the king spent nothing upon soldiers, neither upon defence of the town against the enemies; whereas now he spent eight thousand pounds by year.

In the 51st of Edward III., when the staple was sealed at Callis, the mayor of the staple did furnish the captain of the town upon any road with one hundred bilmen, twelve hundred archers of merchants and their servants, without any wages.

In the year 1388, the 12th of Richard II., in a parliament at Cambridge, it was ordained that the staple of wools should be brought from Middleborough in Holland to Callis.

In the 14th of his reign, there was granted forty shillings upon every sack of wool, and in the 21st was granted fifty shillings upon every sack transported by Englishmen, and three pounds by strangers, etc. It seemeth that the merchants of this staple be the most ancient merchants of this realm; and that all

[1] " I thinke custome."—1*st* *edition*, p. 376.

commodities of the realm are staple merchandises by law and charter as wools, leather, wool fells, lead, tin, cloth, etc.

King Henry VI. had six wool-houses within the staple at Westminster: those he granted to the dean and canons of St. Stephen at Westminster, and confirmed it the 21st of his reign. Thus much for the staple have I shortly noted.

And now to pass to the famous monastery of Westminster: at the very entrance of the close thereof, is a lane that leadeth toward the west, called Thieving lane, for that thieves were led that way to the gate-house, while the sanctuary continued in force.

This monastery was founded and built by Sebert,[1] king of the East Saxons, upon the persuasion of Ethelbert, king of Kent, how having embraced Christianity, and being baptised by Melitus, bishop of London, immediately (to show himself a Christian indeed) built a church to the honour of God and St. Peter, on the west side of the city of London, in a place which (because it was overgrown with thorns, and environed with water) the Saxons called Thorney, and now of the monastery and west situation thereof is called Westminster.

In this place (saith Sulcardus)[2] long before was a temple of Apollo, which being overthrown, King Lucius built therein a church of Christianity.

Sebert was buried in this church, with his wife Athelgoda; whose bodies many years after, to wit, in the reign of Richard II. (saith Walsingham), were translated from the old church to the new, and there entered.

Edgar, king of the West Saxons, repaired this monastery about the year of Christ 958; Edward the Confessor built it of new, whereupon T. Clifford writeth thus:

"Without the walls of London (saith he), upon the river of Thames, there was in times passed a little monastery, built to the honour of God and St. Peter, with a few Benedict monks in it, under an abbot, serving Christ: very poor they were, and little was given them for their relief. Here the king intended (for that it was near to the famous city of London and the river of Thames, that brought in all kinds of merchandises from all parts of the world) to make his sepulchre: he commanded, therefore, that of the tenths of all his rents the work should be begun in such sort as should become the prince of the Apostles.

"At this his commandment the work is nobly begun, even

[1] "Foundation of Westminster by Sebert, a Christian king, not onely in word, but in deed."—*Stow.*   [2] [*See* Bibliography.]

from the foundation, and happily proceedeth till the same was finished: the charges bestowed, or to be bestowed, are not regarded. He granted to this church great privileges, above all the churches in this land, as partly appeareth by this his charter:—

"Edwarde, king, greets William, bishop, and Leofstane, and Aelsie Portreves, and all my burgesses of London friendly, and I tell you, that I have this gift given and granted to Christ and St. Peter the holy Apostle, at Westminster, full freedome over all the land that belongeth to that holy place, etc."

He also caused the parish church of St. Margaret to be newly built without the abbey church of Westminster, for the ease and commodity of the monks, because before that time the parish church stood within the old abbey church in the south aisle, somewhat to their annoyance.

King Henry III., in the year of Christ 1220, and in the 5th of his reign, began the new work of our Lady's chapel, whereof he laid the first stone in the foundation; and in the year 1245, the walls and steeple of the old church (built by King Edward) were taken down, and enlarging the same church, caused them to be made more comely; for the furtherance whereof, in the year 1246, the same king (devising how to extort money from the citizens of London towards the charges) appointed a mart to be kept at Westminster, the same to last fifteen days, and in the mean space all trade of merchandise to cease in the city; which thing the citizens were fain to redeem with two thousand pounds of silver.

The work of this church, with the houses of office, was finished to the end of the choir, in the year 1285, the 14th of Edward I.: all which labour of sixty-six years was in the year 1299 defaced by a fire kindled in the lesser hall of the king's palace at Westminster; the same, with many other houses adjoining, and with the queen's chamber, were all consumed; the flame thereof also (being driven with the wind), fired the monastery, which was also with the palace consumed.

Then was this monastery again repaired by the abbots of that church; King Edward I. and his successors putting to their helping hands.

Edward II. appropriated unto this church the patronages of the churches of Kelveden and Sawbridgeworth in Essex, in the diocese of London.

Simon Langham, abbot (having been a great builder there

in the year 1362), gave forty pounds to the building of the body
of the church; but (amongst others) Abbot Islip was in his
time a great builder there, as may appear in the stonework and
glass windows of the church; since whose decease that work
hath staid as he left it, unperfected, the church and steeple
being all of one height.

King Henry VII., about the year of Christ 1502, caused the
chapel of our Lady, built by Henry III., with a tavern also,
called the White Rose, near adjoining, to be taken down: in
which plot of ground, on the 24th of January, the first stone of
the new chapel was laid by the hands of Abbot Islip, Sir Reginald
Bray, knight of the garter, Doctor Barnes, master of the Rolls,
Doctor Wall, chaplain to the king, Master Hugh Aldham,
chaplain to the countess of Darby and Richmond (the king's
mother), Sir Edward Stanhope, knight, and divers other: upon
the which stone was engraven the same day and year, etc.

The charges in building this chapel amounted to the sum of
fourteen thousand pounds. The stone for this work (as I have
been informed) was brought from Huddlestone quarry in
Yorkshire.

The altar and sepulture of the same King Henry VII., wherein
his body resteth in this his new chapel, was made and finished
in the year 1519 by one Peter, a painter of Florence; for the
which he received one thousand pounds sterling for the whole
stuff and workmanship at the hands of the king's executors;
Richard, Bishop of Winchester; Richard, bishop of London;
Thomas, bishop of Durham; John, bishop of Rochester;
Thomas, duke of Norfolk, treasurer of England; Charles, earl
of Worcester, the king's chamberlain; John Fineaux, knight,
chief justice of the King's bench; Robert Reade, knight, chief
justice of the Common Pleas.

This monastery being valued to dispend by the year three
thousand four hundred and seventy pounds, etc., was surrendered to Henry VIII. in the year 1539. Benson, then abbot,
was made the first dean, and not long after it was advanced to
a bishop's see in the year 1541. Thomas Thirlby being both
the first and last bishop there, who, when he had impoverished
the church, was translated to Norwich in the year 1550, the
4th of Edward VI., and from thence to Elie in the year 1554,
the 2nd of Queen Mary. Richard Cox, doctor in divinity (late
schoolmaster to King Edward VI.), was made dean of Westminster, whom Queen Mary put out, and made Doctor Wonest
dean until the year 1556, and then he being removed from thence

on the 21st of November, John Feckenham (late dean of Pauls) was made abbot of Westminster, and took possession of the same, being installed, and fourteen monks more received the habit with him that day of the order of St. Benedict; but the said John Feckenham, with his monks, enjoyed not that place fully three years, for in the year 1559, in the month of July, they were all put out, and Queen Elizabeth made the said monastery a college, instituting there a dean, twelve prebends, a schoolmaster, and usher, forty scholars, called commonly the Queen's scholars, twelve alms men; and so it was named the Collegiate church of Westminster, founded by Queen Elizabeth, who placed Doctor Bill,[1] first dean of that new erection; after whom succeeded Doctor Gabriel Goodman, who governed that church forty years, and after Doctor Lancelot Andrewes.

Kings and queens crowned in this church: William, surnamed the Conqueror, and Matilde his wife, were the first, and since them all other kings and queens of this realm have been there crowned.

Kings and queens buried in this church are these: Sebert, king of the East Saxons, with his wife Athelgede; Harold, surnamed Harefoot, king of the West Saxons; Edward the Simple, surnamed Confessor, sometime richly shrined in a tomb of silver and gold, curiously wrought by commandment of William the Conqueror; Egitha his wife was there buried also; Hugolyn, chamberlain to Edward the Confessor; King Henry III., whose sepulture was richly garnished with precious stones of jasper, which his son Edward I. brought out of France for that purpose; Eleanor, wife to Henry III.; Edward I., who offered to the shrine of Edward the Confessor the chair of marble, wherein the kings of Scotland were crowned, with the sceptre and crown, also to the same king belonging.

He gave also to that church lands to the value of one hundred pounds by the year; twenty pounds thereof yearly to be distributed to the poor for ever. Then there lieth Eleanor, his wife, daughter to Ferdinando, king of Castile, 1293; Edward III. by Queen Philippa of Henault his wife; Richard II. and Anne his wife, with their images upon them, which cost more than four hundred marks for the gilding; Henry V., with a royal image of silver and gilt, which Katherine his wife caused to be laid upon him, but the head of this image being of massy silver, is broken off, and conveyed away with the plates of silver and gilt that covered his body; Katherine, his wife, was buried

[1] " One of her majesties chaplens."—*1st edition*, p. 381.

in the old Lady chapel 1438, but her corpse being taken up in
the reign of Henry VII., when a new foundation was to be laid,
she was never since buried, but remaineth above ground in a
coffin of boards behind the east end of the presbytery; Henry
VII. in a sumptuous sepulture and chapel before specified, and
Elizabeth his wife; Edward VI. in the same chapel, without
any monument; Queen Mary, without any monument, in the
same chapel; Matilde, daughter to Malcolm, king of Scots, wife
to Henry I., died 1118, lieth in the revestry; Anne, wife to
Richard III.; Margaret, countess of Richmond and Darby,
mother to Henry VII.; Anne of Cleves, wife to Henry VIII.;
Edmond, second son to Henry III., first earl of Lancaster,
Darby, and Leycester, and Aveline his wife, daughter and heir
to William de Fortibus, earl of Albemarle. In St. Thomas'
chapel lie the bones of the children of Henry III. and of Edward
I., in number nine. In the chapter-house,—Elianor, countess
of Barre, daughter to Edward I.; William of Windsor, and
Blaunch his sister, children to Edward III.; John of Eltham,
earl of Cornewell, son to Edward II.; Elianor, wife to Thomas
of Woodstocke, duke of Gloucester; Thomas of Woodstocke by
King Edward III. his father; Margaret, daughter to Edward
IV.; Elizabeth, daughter to Henry VII.; William de Valence,
earl of Pembroke; Aymer de Valence, earl of Pembroke; Margaret and John, son and daughter to William de Valence; John
Waltham, bishop of Sarum, treasurer of England; Thomas
Ruthal, bishop of Durham, 1522; Giles, Lord Dawbeny,[1] lord
lieutenant of Callis, chamberlain to King Henry VII., 1508, and
Elizabeth his wife, of the family of the Arundels in Cornwal,
1500; John, Viscount Wells, 1498; the Lady Katherine,
daughter to the duchess of Norfolk; Sir Thomas Hungerford,
knight, father to Sir John Hungerford of Downampney, knight;
a son and daughter to Humfrey Bohun, earl of Hereford and
Essex, and Elizabeth his wife; Philippa, duchess of York,
daughter to the Lord Mohun, thrice married, to the Lord Fitzwalter, Sir John Golofer, and to the duke of Yorke; William
Dudley, bishop elect of Durham, son to John, baron of Dudley;
Nicholas, Baron Carew, 1470; Walter Hungerford, son to Edward Hungerford, knight; Sir John Burley, knight, and Anne
his wife, daughter to Alane Buxull, knight, 1416; Sir John
Golofer, knight, 1396; Humfrey Burcher, Lord Cromwell, son
to Bourchier, earl of Essex, slain at Barnet; Henry Bourchier,
son and heir to John Bourchier, Lord Barners, also slain at

---

[1] " Earle of Bridgewater."—*1st edition*, p. 382.

Barnet, 1471; Sir William Trussell, knight; Sir Thomas Vaughan, knight; Frances Brandon, duchess of Suffolke, 1560; Mary Gray, her daughter, 1578; Sir John Hampden, knight; Sir Lewis, Viscount Robsart, knight; Lord Bourchere of Henalt, 1430, and his wife, daughter and heir to the Lord Bourchere; Robert Brown, and William Browne, esquires; the Lady Johane Tokyne, daughter of Dabridge Court; George Mortimer, bastard; John Felbye, esquire; Ann, wife to John Watkins; William Southwike, esquire; William Southcot, esquire; Ralph Constantine, gentleman; Arthur Troffote, esquire; Robert Hawley, esquire, slain in that church; Sir Richarde Rouse, knight; Sir Geffrey Maundevile, earl of Essex, and Athelarde his wife; Sir Foulke of Newcastle; Sir James Barons, knight; Sir John Salisbury, knight; Margaret Dowglas, countess of Lennox, with Charles her son, earl of Lennox; Henrie Scogan, a learned poet, in the cloister; Geffrey Chaucer, the most famous poet of England, also in the cloister, 1400, but since Nicholas Brigham, gentleman, raised a monument for him in the south cross aisle of the church: his works were partly published in print by William Caxton, in the reign of Henry VI., increased by William Thinne, esquire, in the reign of Henry VIII.; corrected and twice increased, through mine own painful labours, in the reign of Queen Elizabeth, to wit, in the year 1561; and again beautified with notes by me, collected out of divers records and monuments, which I delivered to my loving friend, Thomas Speght; and he having drawn the same into a good form and method, as also explained the old and obscure words, etc., hath published them in anno 1597.

Anne Stanhope, duchess of Somerset, and Jane her daughter; Anne Cecill, countess of Oxford, daughter to the Lord Burghley, with Mildred Burghley her mother; Elizabeth Barkley, countess of Ormond; Frances Sidney, countess of Sussex; Francis Howard, countess of Hertford, 1598; Thomas, Baron Wentworth; Thomas, Baron Warton; John, Lord Russell; Sir Thomas Bromley, lord chancellor; Sir John Puckering, lord keeper; Sir Henry Cary, Lord Hunsdon, and lord chamberlain, 1596, to whose memory his son, Sir George Cary, Lord Hunsdon, and lord chamberlain, hath created a stately monument.

This church hath had great privilege of sanctuary within the precinct thereof, to wit, the church, churchyard, and close, etc.; from whence it hath not been lawful for any prince or other to take any person that fled thither for any cause: which privilege was first granted by Sebert, king of the East Saxons, since increased by Edgar, king of the West Saxons, renewed and confirmed by King Edward the Confessor, as appeareth by this his charter following:

"Edward, by the grace of God, king of Englishmen: I make it to be known to all generations of the world after me, that by speciall commandement of our holy father, Pope Leo, I have renewed and honored the holy church of the blessed apostle St. Peter, of Westminster; and I order and establish for ever, that what person, of what condition or estate soever he be, from whence soever he come, or for what offence or cause it be, either for his refuge into the said holy place, he be assured of his life, liberty, and limbs. And over this I forbid, under the paine of everlasting damnation, that no minister of mine, or of my successors, intermeddle them with any the goods, lands, or possessions of the said persons taking the said sanctuary; for I have taken their goodes and livelode into my special protection, and therefore I grant to every each of them, in as much as my terrestriall power may suffice, all maner freedom of joyous libertie; and whosoever presumes or doth contrary to this my graunt, I will hee lose his name, worship, dignity, and power, and that with the great traytor Judas that betraied our Saviour, he be in the everlasting fire of hell; and I will and ordayne that this my graunt endure as long as there remayneth in England eyther love or dread of Christian name."

More of this sanctuary ye may read in our histories, and also in the statute of Henry VIII., the 32nd year.

The parish church of St. Margaret, sometime within the abbey, was by Edward the Confessor removed, and built without, for ease of the monks. This church continued till the days of Edward I., at which time the merchants of the staple and parishioners of Westminster built it all of new, the great chancel excepted, which was built by the abbots of Westminster; and this remaineth now a fair parish church, though sometime in danger of down pulling. In the south aisle of this church is a fair marble monument of Dame Mary Billing, the heir of Robert Nesenham of Conington, in Huntingdonshire, first married to William Cotton, to whose issue her inheritance alone descended, remaining with Robert Cotton at this day, heir of her and her first husband's family; her second husband was Sir Thomas Billing, chief justice of England; and her last, whom likewise she buried, was Thomas Lacy; erecting this monument to the memory of her three husbands, with whose arms she hath garnished it, and for her own burial, wherein she was interred in the year 1499.

Next to this famous monastery is the king's principal palace, of what antiquity it is uncertain; but Edward the Confessor held his court there, as may appear by the testimony of sundry, and, namely, of Ingulphus, as I have before told you. The said king had his palace, and for the most part remained there; where he also so ended his life, and was buried in the monastery which he had built. It is not to be doubted but that King William I., as he was crowned there, so he built much at his palace, for he found it far inferior to the building of princely palaces in France: and it is manifest, by the testimony of many authors, that William Rufus built the great hall there about the year of Christ 1097. Amongst others, Roger of Wendover and Mathew Paris do write, that King William (being returned out of Normandy into England) kept his feast of Whitsontide very royally at Westminster, in the new hall which he had lately built; the length whereof (say some) was two hundred and seventy feet, and seventy-four feet in breadth; and when he heard men say that this hall was too great, he answered and said, "This hall is not big enough by the one half, and is but a bed-chamber in comparison of that I mean to make." A diligent searcher (saith Paris) might find out the foundation of the hall, which he was supposed to have built, stretching from the river of Thames, even to the common highway.

This palace was repaired about the year 1163 by Thomas Becket, chancellor of England, with exceeding great celerity and speed, which before was ready to have fallen down. This hath been the principal seat and palace of all the kings of England since the Conquest; for here have they in the great hall kept their feasts of coronation especially, and other solemn feasts, as at Christmas and such like, most commonly: for proof whereof, I find recorded, that in the year 1236, and the 20th of Henry III., on the 29th of December, William de Haverhull, the king's treasurer, is commanded, that upon the day of circumcision of our Lord, he caused six thousand poor people to be fed at Westminster, for the state of the king, the queen, and their children; the weak and aged to be placed in the great hall and in the lesser; those that were most strong, and in reasonable plight, in the king's chamber; the children in the queen's; and when the king knoweth the charge, he would allow it in the accounts.[1]

[1] In the first edition, the passage relative to Henry II.'s command to Hugh Gifford and William Browne, to distribute alms " according to the weight and measure of the king's children " (see ante, page 83), is inserted in this place.

In the year 1238, the same King Henry kept his feast of Christmas at Westminster in the great hall; so did he in the year 1241, where he placed the legate in the most honourable place of the table, to wit, in the midst, which the noblemen took in evil part: the king sat on the right hand, and the archbishop on the left, and then all the prelates and nobles according to their estates; for the king himself set the guests. The year 1242 he likewise kept his Christmas in the hall, etc. Also, in the year 1243, Richard, earl of Cornewall, the king's brother, married Cincia, daughter to Beatrice, countess of Province, and kept his marriage-feast in the great hall at Westminster, with great royalty and company of noblemen: insomuch that there were told (*triginta millia*) thirty thousand dishes of meats at that dinner.

In the year 1256, King Henry sate in the exchequer of this hall, and there set down order for the appearance of sheriffs, and bringing in of their accounts: there were five marks set on every sheriff's head for a fine, because they had not distrained every person that might dispend fifteen pounds land by the year to receive the order of knighthood, as the same sheriffs were commanded. Also, the mayor, aldermen, and sheriffs of London, being accused of oppression and wrongs done by them, and submitting themselves in this place before the king sitting in judgment upon that matter, they were condemned to pay their fines for their offences committed, and further, every one of them discharged of assise and ward.

In the years 1268 and 1269, the same king kept his Christmas feasts at Westminster as before; and also in the same 1269 he translated with great solemnity the body of King Edward the Confessor into a new chapel, at the back of the high altar: which chapel he had prepared of a marvellous workmanship, bestowing a new tomb or shrine of gold; and on the day of his translation he kept a royal feast in the great hall of the palace. Thus much for the feasts of old time in this hall.

We read also, that in the year 1236, the river of Thames overflowing the banks, caused the marshes about Woolwitch to be all on a sea, wherein boats and other vessels were carried with the stream; so that besides cattle, the greatest number of men, women, and children, inhabitants there, were drowned: and in the great palace of Westminster men did row with wherries in the midst of the hall, being forced to ride to their chambers.

Moreover, in the year 1242, the Thames overflowing the banks about Lambhithe, drowned houses and fields by the space of six miles, so that in the great hall at Westminster men took their horses, because the water ran over all. This palace was (in the year 1299, the 27th of Edward I.) burnt by a vehement fire, kindled in the lesser hall of the king's house: the same, with many other houses adjoining, and with the queen's chamber, were consumed, but after that repaired.

In the year 1313, the 31st of Edward I., the king's treasury at Westminster was robbed; for the which, Walter, abbot of Westminster, with forty-nine of his brethren and thirty-two other, were thrown into the Tower of London, and indicted of the robbery of a hundred thousand pounds; but they affirming themselves to be clear of the fact, and desiring the king of speedy justice, a commission was directed for inquiry of the truth, and they were freed.

In the year 1316, Edward II. did solemnize his feast of Penticost at Westminster, in the great hall; where sitting royally at the table, with his peers about him, there entered a woman adorned like a minstrel, sitting on a great horse, trapped as minstrels then used, who rode round about the tables, showing pastime, and at length came up to the king's table, and laid before him a letter, and forthwith turning her horse, saluted every one, and departed. The letter being opened, had these contents:—" Our soveraigne lord and king, hath nothing curteously respected his knights, that in his father's time, and also in his owne, have put forth their persons to divers perils, and have utterly lost, or greatly diminished their substance, for honor of the said king, and he hath inriched abundantly such as have not borne the waight as yet of the busines, etc."

This great hall was begun to be repaired in the year 1397 by Richard II., who caused the walls, windows, and roof, to be taken down, and new made, with a stately porch, and divers lodgings of a marvellous work, and with great costs; all which he levied of strangers banished or flying out of their countries, who obtained license to remain in this land, by the king's charters, which they had purchased with great sums of money; John Boterell being then clerk of the works.

This hall being finished in the year 1398, the same king kept a most royal Christmas there, with daily justings and runnings at tilt; whereunto resorted such a number of people, that there was every day spent twenty-eight or twenty-six oxen, and three hundred sheep, besides fowl without number: he caused a gown for himself to be made of gold, garnished with pearl and precious stones, to the value of three thousand marks: he was guarded by Cheshire men, and had about him commonly thirteen bishops, besides barons, knights, esquires, and other more than needed; insomuch, that to the household came every day to meat ten thousand people, as appeareth by the messes told out from the kitchen to three hundred servitors.

Thus was this great hall, for the honour of the prince, oftentimes furnished with guests, not only in this king's time (a prodigal prince), but in the time of other also, both before and since, though not so usually noted. For when it is said, the king held his feast of Christmas, or such a feast at Westminster, it may well be supposed to be kept in this great hall, as most sufficient to such a purpose.

I find noted by Robert Fabian (sometime an alderman of London), that King Henry VII., in the 9th of his reign (holding his royal feast of Christmas at Westminster), on the twelfth day, feasted Ralph Austry, then mayor of London, and his brethren the aldermen, with other commoners in great number, and after dinner dubbing the mayor knight, caused him with his brethren to stay and behold the disguisings and other disports in the night following, showed in the great hall, which was richly hanged with arras, and staged about on both sides; which disports being ended in the morning, the king, the queen, the ambassadors, and other estates, being set at a table of stone, sixty knights and esquires served sixty dishes to the king's mess, and as many to the queen's (neither flesh nor fish), and served the mayor with twenty-four dishes to his mess, of the same manner, with sundry wines in most plenteous wise: and finally, the king and queen being conveyed with great lights into the palace, the mayor with his company in barges returned and came to London by break of the next day. Thus much for building of this great hall, and feasting therein.

It moreover appeareth that many parliaments have been kept there; for I find noted, that in the year 1397, the great hall at Westminster being out of reparations, and therefore, as it were, new built by Richard II. (as is afore showed), the same Richard, in the mean time having occasion to hold a parliament, caused for that purpose a large house to be built in the midst of the palace-court, betwixt the clock tower and the gate of the old great hall. This house was very large and long, made of timber, covered with tile, open on both the sides and at both the ends, that all men might see and hear what was both said and done.

The king's archers (in number four thousand Cheshire men) compassed the house about with their bows bent, and arrows knocked in their hands, always ready to shoot: they had bouch of court (to wit, meat and drink), and great wages of six pence by the day.

The old great hall being new built, parliaments were again there kept as before: [1] namely, one in the year 1399, for the deposing of Richard II. A great part of this palace at Westminster was once again burnt in the year 1512, the 4th of Henry VIII.; since the which time it hath not been re-edified: only the great hall, with the offices near adjoining, are kept in good reparations, and serveth as afore for feasts at coronations, arraignments of great persons charged with treasons, keeping of the courts of justice, etc. But the princes have been lodged in other places about the city, as at Baynarde's castle, at Bridewell, and White hall, sometime called York place, and sometime at St. James'.

This great hall hath been the usual place of pleadings, and ministration of justice, whereof somewhat shortly I will note. In times past the courts and benches followed the king wheresoever he went, as well since the Conquest as before; which thing at length being thought cumbersome, painful, and chargeable to the people, it was in the year 1224, the 9th of Henry III., agreed that there should be a standing place appointed, where matters should be heard and judged, which was in the great hall at Westminster.

In this hall he ordained three judgment seats; to wit, at the entry on the right hand, the Common Pleas, where civil matters are to be pleaded, specially such as touch lands or contracts: at the upper end of the hall, on the right hand, or south-east corner, the King's Bench, where pleas of the crown have their hearing; and on the left hand, or south-west corner, sitteth the lord chancellor, accompanied with the master of the rolls, and other men, learned for the most part in the civil law, and called masters of the chancery, which have the king's fee. The times of pleading in these courts are four in the year, which are called terms: the first is Hillary term, which beginneth the 23rd of January, if it be not Sunday, and endeth the 12th of February; the second is Easter term, and beginneth seventeen days after Easter day, and endeth four days after Ascension day; the third term beginneth six or seven days after Trinity Sunday, and endeth the Wednesday fortnight after; the fourth is Michaelmas term, which

---

[1] " I find of record, the 50th of Edward III., that the chapter-house of the abbot of Westminster was then the usual house for the commons in parliament."—*Stow.*

beginneth the 9th of October, if it be not Sunday, and endeth the 28th of November.

And here it is to be noted, that the kings of this realm have used sometimes to sit in person in the King's Bench; namely, King Edward IV., in the year 1462, in Michaelmas term, sat in the King's Bench three days together, in the open court, to understand how his laws were ministered and executed.

Within the port, or entry into the hall, on either side are ascendings up into large chambers, without the hall adjoining thereunto, wherein certain courts be kept, namely, on the right hand, is the court of the Exchequer, a place of account for the revenues of the crown: the hearers of the account have auditors under them; but they which are the chief for accounts of the prince, are called barons of the Exchequer, whereof one is called the chief baron. The greatest officer of all is called the high treasurer.[1] In this court be heard those that are delators, or informers, in popular and penal actions, having thereby part of the profit by the law assigned unto them.

In this court, if any question be, it is determined after the order of the common law of England by twelve men, and all subsidies, taxes, and customs, by account; for in this office the sheriffs of the shire do attend upon the execution of the commandments of the judges, which the earl should do, if he were not attending upon the princes in the wars, or otherwise about him; for the chief office of the earl was to see the king's justice to have course, and to be well executed in the shire, and the prince's revenues to be well answered and brought into the treasury.

If any fines or amerciaments be extracted out of any of the said courts upon any man, or any arrerages of accounts of such things as is of customs, taxes, and subsidies, or other such like occasions, the same the sheriff of the shire doth gather, and is answerable therefore in the Exchequer: as for other ordinary rents of patrimonial lands, and most commonly of taxes, customs, and subsidies, there be particular receivers and collectors, which do answer it into the Exchequer. This court of the Exchequer hath of old time, and, as I think, since the Conquest, been kept at Westminster, notwithstanding sometimes removed thence by commandment of the king, and after restored again, as, namely, in the year 1209, King John commanded the Exchequer to be removed from Westminster to Northampton, etc.

[1] " Of England."—*1st edition*, p. 387.

On the left hand above the stair is the Duchy chamber, wherein is kept the court for the duchy of Lancaster by a chancellor of that duchy, and other officers under him. Then is there in another chamber the office of the receipts of the queen's revenues for the crown: then is there also the Star chamber, where in the term time, every week once at the least, which is commonly on Fridays and Wednesdays, and on the next day after the term endeth, the lord chancellor, and the lords, and other of the privy council, and the chief justices of England, from nine of the clock till it be eleven, do sit.

This place is called the Star chamber, because the roof thereof is decked with the likeness of stars gilt: there be plaints heard of riots, routs, and other misdemeanors; which if they be found by the king's council, the party offender shall be censured by these persons, which speak one after another, and he shall be both fined and commanded to prison.

Then at the upper end of the great hall, by the King's Bench, is a going up to a great chamber, called the White hall, wherein is now kept the court of Wards and Liveries, and adjoining thereunto is the Court of Requests. Then is St. Stephen's chapel, of old time founded by King Stephen. King John, in the 7th of his reign, granted to Baldwinus de London, clerk of his Exchequer, the chapelship of St. Stephen's at Westminster, etc. This chapel was again since, of a far more curious workmanship, new built by King Edward III. in the year 1347, for thirty-eight persons in that church to serve God; to wit, a dean, twelve secular canons, thirteen vicars, four clerks, five choristers, two servitors, to wit, a verger and a keeper of the chapel. He built for those from the house of Receipt, along nigh to the Thames, within the same palace, there to inhabit; and since that there was also built for them, betwixt the clock-house and the wool staple, called the Wey house. He also built to the use of this chapel (though out of the palace court), some distance west, in the little sanctuary, a strong clochard [Add. Notes] of stone and timber, covered with lead, and placed therein three great bells, since usually rung at coronations, triumphs, funeral of princes, and their obits. Of those bells men fabuled that their ringing soured all the drink in the town: more, that about the biggest bell was written,—

> " King Edward made me,
> Thirtie thousand and three;
> Take me downe and wey me,
> And more shall ye find me."

But these bells being taken down indeed, were found all three

not to weigh twenty thousand. True it is, that in the city of
Rouen, in Normandie, there is one great bell, that hath such
inscription as followeth:—

> " Je suis George de Ambois,
> Qui trente cinq mil a pois,
> Mes lui qui me pesera,
> Trente six mil me trouera.

> " I am George of Ambois,
> Thirty-five thousand in pois;
> But he that shall weigh me,
> Thirty-six thousand shall find me."

The said King Edward endowed this chapel with lands to the
yearly value of five hundred pounds. Doctor John Chambers,
the king's physician, the last dean of this college, built thereunto
a cloister of curious workmanship, to the charges of eleven
thousand marks. This chapel, or college, at the suppression,
was valued to dispend in lands by the year one thousand and
eighty-five pounds ten shillings and five pence, and was surrendered to Edward VI.; since the which time the same chapel
hath served as a parliament house.

By this chapel of St. Stephen was sometime one other smaller
chapel, called our Lady of the Pew, to the which lady great
offerings were used to be made: amongst other things, I have
read, that Richard II., after the overthrow of Wat Tyler and
other his rebels, in the 4th of his reign, went to Westminster, and
there giving thanks to God for his victory, made his offering in
this chapel; but as divers have noted, namely, John Piggot, in
the year 1252, on the 17th of February, by negligence of a
scholar appointed by his schoolmaster to put forth the lights of
this chapel, the image of our lady, richly decked with jewels,
precious stones, pearls, and rings, more than any jeweller could
judge the price for, so saith mine author, was, with all this
apparel, ornaments, and chapel itself, burnt; but since again
re-edified by Anthonie, Earl Rivers, Lord Scales, and of the Isle
of Wight, uncle and governor to the Prince of Wales, that should
have been King Edward V., etc.

The said palace, before the entry thereunto, hath a large court,
and in the same a tower of stone, containing a clock, which
striketh every hour on a great bell, to be heard into the hall in
sitting time of the courts, or otherwise; for the same clock, in
a calm, will be heard into the city of London. King Henry VI.
gave the keeping of this clock, with the tower called the clock-
house, and the appurtenances, unto William Walsby, dean of

St. Stephen's, with the wages of six pence the day out of his Exchequer. By this tower standeth a fountain, which at coronations and great triumphs is made to run with wine out of divers spouts.

On the east side of this court is an arched gate to the river of Thames, with a fair bridge and landing-place for all men that have occasion. On the north side is the south end of St. Stephen's alley, or Canon row, and also a way into the old wool staple; and on the west side is a very fair gate, begun by Richard III. in the year 1484, and was by him built a great height, and many fair lodgings in it, but left unfinished, and is called the high tower of Westminster. Thus much for the monastery and palace may suffice. And now will I speak of the gate-house, and of Totehill street, stretching from the west part of the close.

The gate-house is so called of two gates, the one out of the College court towards the north, on the east side whereof was the bishop of London's prison for clerks' convict; and the other gate, adjoining to the first, but towards the west, is a gaol or prison for offenders thither committed. Walter Warfield, cellarer to the monastery, caused both these gates, with the appurtenances, to be built in the reign of Edward III.

On the south side of this gate, King Henry VII. founded an alms-house for thirteen poor men; one of them to be a priest, aged forty-five years, a good grammarian, the other twelve to be aged fifty years, without wives: every Saturday the priest to receive of the abbot, or prior, four pence by the day, and each other two pence halfpenny by the day for ever, for their sustenance, and every year to each one a gown and a hood ready made; and to three women that dressed their meat, and kept them in their sickness, each to have every Saturday sixteen pence, and every year a gown ready made. More, to the thirteen poor men yearly eighty quarters of coal and one thousand of good faggots to their use, in the hall and kitchen of their mansion; a discreet monk to be overseer of them, and he to have forty shillings by the year, etc.; and hereunto was every abbot and prior sworn.

Near unto this house westward was an old chapel of St. Anne; over against the which the Lady Margaret, mother to King Henry VII., erected an alms-house for poor women, which is now turned into lodgings for the singing men of the college. The place wherein this chapel and alms-house standeth was called the Elemosinary, or Almonry, now corruptly the Ambry,[1] for that the alms of the abbey were there distributed to the poor. And therein Islip, abbot of Westminster, erected the first press of book printing that ever was in England, about the year of Christ 1471. William Caxton, citizen of London, mercer, brought it into England, and was the first that practised it in the said abbey; after which time, the like was practised in the abbeys of St. Augustine at Canterbury, St. Alban's, and other monasteries. [*See* Additional Notes.]

From the west gate runneth along Totehil street, wherein is a house of the Lord Gray of Wilton; and on the other side, at the entry into Totehill field, Stourton house, which Gyles, the last Lord Dacre of the south, purchased and built new, whose lady and wife Anne, sister to Thomas, the Lord Buckhurst, left money to her executors to build an hospital for twenty poor women, and so many children, to be brought up under them, for whose maintenance she assigned lands to the value of one hundred pounds by the year, which hospital her executors have new begun in the field adjoining. From the entry into Totehill field the street is called Petty France, in which, and upon St. Hermit's hill, on the south side thereof, Cornelius Van Dun (a Brabander born, yeoman of the guard to King Henry VIII., King Edward VI., Queen Mary, and Queen Elizabeth,) built twenty houses for poor women to dwell rent-free: and near hereunto was a chapel of Mary Magdalen, now wholly ruinated.

In the year of Christ 1256, the 40th of Henry III., John Mansell, the king's councillor and priest, did invite to a stately dinner the kings and queens of England and Scotland, Edward the king's son, earls, barons, and knights, the Bishop of London, and divers citizens, whereby his guests did grow to such a number, that his house at Totehill could not receive them, but that he was forced to set up tents and pavilions to receive his guests, whereof there was such a multitude that seven hundred messes of meat did not serve for the first dinner.

The city of Westminster for civil government is divided into twelve several wards; for the which the dean of the collegiate church of Westminster, or the high-steward, do elect twelve burgesses, and as many assistants; that is, one burgess, and one assistant, for every ward; out of the which twelve burgesses two are nominated yearly, upon Thursday in Easter week, for

---

[1] The corruption alluded to by Stow exists to the present day—the Almonry being styled by the lower classes in Westminster, the Ambry. The house said to have been Caxton's is also, we believe, still remaining, though in a state of great dilapidation.

chief burgesses to continue for one year next following, who have
authority given them by the act of parliament, 27th Elizabeth, to
hear, examine, determine, and punish, according to the laws of
the realm, and lawful customs of the city of London, matters of
incontinency, common scolds, inmates, and common annoyances;
and likewise, to commit such persons as shall offend against the
peace, and thereof to give knowledge within four-and-twenty
hours to some justice of peace, in the county of Middlesex.

GOVERNORS OF THE CITY OF LONDON; AND FIRST OF ECCLE-SIASTICAL BISHOPS AND OTHER MINISTERS THERE

Having thus run through the description of these cities of
London and Westminster, as well in their original foundations,
as in their increases of buildings and ornaments, together with
such incidents of sundry sorts as are before, both generally and
particularly discoursed, it remaineth that somewhat be noted
by me touching the policy and government, both ecclesiastical
and civil, of London, as I have already done for Westminster, the
order whereof is appointed by the late statute, even as that of
London is maintained by the customs thereof, most laudably
used before all the time of memory.

And first, to begin with the ecclesiastical jurisdiction: I read
that the Christian faith was first preached in this island (then
called Britaine) by Joseph of Arimathea, and his brethren,
disciples of Christ, in the time of Aruiragus, then governor
here under the Roman emperor; after which time, Lucius, king
of the Britaines, sent his ambassadors, Eluanus and Meduvanus,
two men learned in the Scriptures, with letters to Eleutherius,[1]
bishop of Rome, desiring him to send some devout and learned
men, by whose instruction he and his people might be taught
the faith and religion of Christ. Eleutherius baptised those
messengers, making Eluanus a bishop, and Meduvius a teacher,
and sent over with them into Britain two other famous clerks,
Faganus and Deruvianus, by whose diligence Lucius, and his
people of Britaine, were instructed in the faith of Christ, and
baptized, the temples of idols were converted into cathedral
churches, and bishops were placed where Flammines before had
been; at London, Yorke, and Carleon upon Uske, were placed
archbishops, saith some. The epistle said to be sent by
Eleutherius to king Lucius, for the establishing of the faith, ye

[1] " Eleutherius died in the yeare 186, when he had sitten bishop 15
yeares."—*Stow*.

may read in my *Annals, Summaries,* and *Chronicles,* truly translated and set down as mine author hath it, for some have
curtailed and corrupted it, and then fathered it upon reverend
Bede, who never wrote word thereof, or otherwise to that effect,
more than this as followeth.

In the year 156, Marcus Aurelius Verus, the fourteenth
emperor after Augustus, governed the empire with his brother
Aurelius Comodus; in whose time, Glutherius, a holy man,
being pope of the church of Rome, Lucius, king of Britaines,
wrote unto him, desiring that by his commandment he might be
made Christian; which his request was granted him; whereby
the Britaines receiving then the faith, kept it sound and unde-
filed in rest and peace until Dioclesian the emperor's time.
Thus far Bede, which may suffice to prove the Christian faith
there to be received here. And now of the London bishops as I
find them.

There remaineth in the parish church of St. Peter upon Cornhill in London a table, wherein is written, that Lucius founded
the same church to be an archbishop's see, and metropolitan or
chief church of his kingdom, and that it so endured the space of
four hundred years, until the coming of Augustine the monk, and
others, from Rome, in the reign of the Saxons. The archbishops' names I find only to be set down by Joceline of Furnes,
in his book of British bishops, and not elsewhere. Thean (saith
he) was the first archbishop of London, in the time of Lucius,
who built the said church of St. Peter, in a place called Cornhill
in London, by the aid of Ciran, chief butler to King Lucius.

2. Eluanus was the second, and he built a library to the same
church adjoining, and converted many of the Druids (learned
men in the Pagan law) to the Christian faith.

3. Cadar was the third; then followed,
4. Obinus.
5. Conan.
6. Paludius.
7. Stephen.
8. Iltute.
9. Dedwin.
10. Thedred.
11. Hillary.
12. Guidelium.
13. Vodimus, slain by the Saxons.
14. Theanus, the fourteenth, fled with the Britaines into
Wales, about the year of Christ 587.

Thus much out of Joceline of the archbishops; the credit whereof I leave to the judgment of the learned; for I read of a bishop of London (not before named) in the year of Christ 326, to be present at the second council, holden at Arles, in the time of Constantine the Great, who subscribed thereunto in these words: *Ex provinciæ Britaniæ Civitate Londiniensi Restitutus Episcopus*, as plainly appeareth in the first tome of the councils, he writeth not himself archbishop, and therefore maketh the matter of archbishops doubtful, or rather, over-throweth that opinion.

The Saxons being pagans, having chased the Britons, with the Christian preachers, into the mountains of Wales and Cornewall; and having divided this kingdom of the Britons amongst themselves, at the length, to wit, in the year 596, Pope Gregory, moved of a godly instinction (sayeth Bede), in the 147th year after the arrival of the Angles or Saxons in Britaine, sent Augustine, Miletus, Justus, and John, with other monks, to preach the Gospel to the said nation of the Angles: these landed in the isle of Thanet, and were first received by Ethelbert, king of Kent, whom they converted to the faith of Christ, with divers other of his people, in the 34th year of his reign, which Ethelbert gave unto Augustine the city of Canterbury.

This Augustine, in the year of Christ 604, consecrated Miletus and Justus bishops, appointing Miletus to preach unto the East Saxons, whose chief city was London; and there King Sebert, nephew to Ethelbert, by preaching of Miletus, received the Word of Life: and then Ethelbert king of Kent, built in the city of London St. Paul's church, wherein Miletus began to be bishop in the year 619, and sat five years. Ethelbert, by his charter, gave lands to this church of St. Paul, so did other kings after him. King Sebert, through the good life, and like preaching of Miletus, having received baptism, to show himself a Christian, built a church to the honour of God and St. Peter, on the west side of London, which church is called Westminster; but the successors of Sebert being pagans, expelled Miletus out of their kingdoms.

Justus, the second bishop for a time, and then Miletus again; after whose decease the seat was void for a time. At length Sigebert, son to Sigebert, brother to Sebert, ruled in Essex; he became a Christian, and took to him a holy man named Cedde, or Chadde, who won many by preaching, and good life, to the Christian religion.

Cedde, or Chad, was by Finan consecrated bishop of the East

Saxons, and he ordered priests and deacons in all the parts of Essex, but especially at Ithancaster and Tilberie.

This city of Ithancaster (saith Raph Cogshall) stood on the bank of the river Pante, that runneth by Maldun, in the hundred of Danesey, but now is drowned in Pante, so that nothing remaineth but the ruin of the city in the river. Tilberie (both the west and east) standeth on the Thames side, nigh over against Gravesend.

Wina, expelled from the church of Winchester by Cenewalche the king, was adopted to be the fourth bishop of London, in the reign of Wolferus king of Mercia, and sat nine years.

Erkenwalde, born in the castle or town of Stallingborough in Lindsey, first abbot of Crotesey, was by Theodore archbishop of Canterbury appointed to be bishop of the East Saxons, in the city of London. This Erkenwalde, in the year of Christ 677, before he was made bishop, had built two monasteries, one for himself, being a monk, in the isle of Crote in Surrey, by the river of Thames, and another for his sister Edilburge, being a nun, in a certain place called Berching in Essex; he deceased at Berching in the year 697, and was then buried in Paul's church, and translated into the new church of St. Paul in the year 1148.

Waldhere was bishop of London. Sebba king of the East Saxons at his hands received the habit of monk, for at that time there were monks in Paul's church, as writeth Radulphus de Diceto, and others. To this bishop he brought a great sum of money, to be bestowed and given to the poor, reserving nothing to himself, but rather desired to remain poor in goods as in spirit, for the kingdom of heaven. When he had reigned thirty years he deceased at Paul's, and was there buried, and lieth now in a coffin of stone, on the north side of the aisle next the choir.

Ingwaldus bishop of London was at the consecration of Tatwine archbishop of Canterbury; he confirmed the foundation of Crowland in the year 716, saith Ingulfus, and deceased in the year 744, as saith Hoveden.

746. Engulfe [Ecgwulf], bishop of London.

754. Wichet, or Wigerus [Sigheah], bishop of London.

761. Eaderightus, or Edbrithe [Aldberht], bishop of London.

768. Eadgain, or Eadgarus, bishop of London.

773. Kenewallth bishop of London.

784. Eadbaldus bishop of London.

795. Heatbright bishop of London, deceased 802, saith Hoveden.

813. Osmond bishop of London; he was witness to a [spurious] charter made to Crowland in the year 833, saith Ingulphus.

835. Ethelmothe bishop of London.

838. Elbertus, or Celbertus, bishop of London.

841. Caulfe bishop of London.

850. Swithulfus bishop of London; he likewise was witness to a [spurious] charter of Crowland 851.

860. Edstanus bishop of London; witness to a charter to Crowland 860. [See Additional Notes.]

870. Ulsius bishop of London.

878. Ethelwardus bishop of London.

886. Elstanus bishop of London, died in the year 900, saith Asser; and all these, saith the author of *Flores Historiarum*, were buried in the old church of St. Paul, but there remaineth now no memory of them.

900. Theodricus bishop of London; this man confirmed King Edred's charter made to Winchester in the year 947, whereby it seemeth that he was bishop of London of a later time than is here placed.

922. Welstanus bishop of London.

941. Brithelme bishop of London.

958. Dunstanus, abbot of Glastonberie, then bishop of Worcester, and then bishop of London; he was afterwards translated to Canterbury 960.

960. Ealfstanus bishop of London; the 28th in number.

981. Edgare bishop of London; he confirmed the grants made to Winchester and to Crowland 966, and again to Crowland 970, the charter of Ethelred, concerning Ulfrunhampton, 996.

1004. Elphinus bishop of London.

1010. Alwinus bishop of London; he was sent into Normandy in the year 1013, saith Asser. [See Additional Notes.]

1044. Robert, a monk of Gemerisins in Normandy, bishop of London seven years, afterwards translated from London to Canterbury.

1050. Specgasius, elected, but rejected by the king.

1051. William, a Norman chaplain to Edward the Confessor, was made bishop of London 1051, sate 17 years, and deceased 1070. He obtained of William the Conqueror the charter of liberties for the city of London, as I have set down in my *Summary*, and appeareth by his epitaph in Paul's church.

1070. Hugh de Orwell bishop of London; he died of a leprosy when he had sitten fifteen years.

1085. Maurice bishop of London; in whose time, to wit, in

the year 1086, the church of St. Paul was burnt, with the most part of this city; and therefore he laid the foundation of a new large church; and having sat twenty-two years he deceased 1107, saith Paris.

1108. Richard Beame, or Beamor, bishop of London, did wonderfully increase the work of this church begun, purchasing the streets and lanes adjoining with his own money; and he founded the monastery of St. Osyth in Essex. He sat bishop nineteen years, and deceased 1127.

1127. Gilbertus Universalis, a canon of Lyons, elected by Henry I.; he deceased 1141, when he had sat fourteen years.

1142. Robert de Sigillo, a monk of Reading, whom Mawde the empress made bishop of London, where he sat eleven years. Geffrey de Magnavile took him prisoner at Fulham, and he deceased 1152.

1153. Richard Beames, archdeacon of Essex, bishop of London ten years, who deceased 1162.

1163. Gilbert Foliot, bishop of Hereford, from whence translated to London, sat twenty-three years, and deceased 1186.

1189. Richard Fitz Nele, the king's treasurer, archdeacon of Essex, elected bishop of London at Pipwel, 1189. He sate nine years, and deceased 1198. This man also took great pains about the building of Paul's church, and raised many other goodly buildings in his diocese.

1199. William S. Mary Church, a Norman, bishop of London, who was one of the three bishops that, by the pope's commandment, executed his interdiction, or curse, upon the whole realm of England; but he was forced, with the other bishops, to flee the realm in 1208; and his castle at Stratford in Essex was by commandment of King John overthrown, 1210. This William, in company of the archbishop of Canterburie, and of the bishop of Elie, went to Rome, and there complained against the king, 1212, and returned, so as in the year 1215 King John, in the church of St. Paul, at the hands of this William, took upon him the cross for the Holy Land. He resigned his bishoprick of his own voluntary in the year 1221, saith Cogshall.

1221. Eustachius de Fauconbridge, treasurer of the exchequer (saith Paris), chancellor of the exchequer (saith Textor and Cogshall), bishop of London, 1223, whilst at Chelmesforde he was giving holy orders, a great tempest of wind and rain annoyed so many as came thither, whereof it was gathered how highly God was displeased with such as came to receive orders, to the end that they might live a more easy life of the stipend appointed to the churchmen, giving themselves to banquetting; and so with unclean and filthy bodies (but more unclean souls) presume to minister unto God, the author of purity and cleanness. Falcatius de Brent was delivered to his custody in the year 1224. This Eustachius deceased in the year 1228, and was buried in Paul's church, in the south side, without, or above, the choir.

1229. Roger Niger, archdeacon of Colchester, made bishop of London. In the year 1230 (saith Paris), upon the feast day of the Conversion of St. Paul, when he was at mass in the cathedral church of St. Paul, a great multitude of people being there present, suddenly the weather waxed dark, so as one could scantly see another, and a horrible thunder-clap lighted on the church, which so shook it, that it was like to have fallen, and therewithal out of a dark cloud proceeded a flash of lightning, that all the church seemed to be on fire, whereupon such a stench ensued, that all men thought they should have died; thousands of men and women ran out of the church, and being astonied, fell upon the ground void of all sense and understanding; none of all the multitude tarried in the church save the bishop and one deacon, which stood still before the high altar, awaiting the will of God. When the air was cleansed, the multitude returned into the church, and the bishop ended the service.

This Roger Niger is commended to have been a man of worthy life, excellently well-learned, a notable preacher, pleasant in talk, mild of countenance, and liberal at his table. He admonished the usurers of his time to leave such enormities as they tendered the salvation of their souls, and to do penance for that they had committed. But when he saw they laughed him to scorn, and also threatened him, the bishop generally excommunicated and accursed all such, and commanded straitly that such usurers should depart farther from the city of London, which hither towards had been ignorant of such mischief and wickedness, least his diocese should be infected therewithal. He fell sick and died at his manor of Bishops hall, in the lordship and parish of Stebunheth, in the year 1241, and was buried in Paul's church, on the north side of the presbytery, in a fair tomb, coped, of grey marble.

1241. Fulco Basset, dean of Yorke, by the death of Gilbert Basset, possessed his lands, and was then made bishop of London, deceased on the 21st of May, in the year 1259, as saith John Textor, and was buried in Paul's church.

1259. Henry Wingham, chancellor of England, made bishop

of London, deceased in the year 1262, saith Textor, and was buried in Paul's church, on the south side, without or above the choir, in a marble monument, close at the head of Fauconbridge.

1262. Richard Talbot, bishop of London, straightways after his consecration deceased, saith Eversden.

1262. Henry Sandwich, bishop of London, deceased in the year 1273, as the same author affirmeth.

1273. John Cheshul, dean of Paul's, treasurer of the Exchequer, and keeper of the great seal, was bishop of London, and deceased in the year 1279, saith Eversden.

1280. Fulco Lovel, archdeacon of Colchester, elected bishop of London, but refused that place.

1280. Richard Gravesend, archdeacon of Northampton, bishop of London. It appeareth by the charter-warren granted to this bishop, that in his time there were two woods in the parish of Stebunhith pertaining to the said bishop. I have since I kept house for myself known the one of them by Bishops hall; but now they are both made plain of wood, and not to be discerned from other grounds. Some have fabuled that this Richard Gravesend, bishop of London, in the year 1392, the 16th of Richard II., purchased the charter of liberties to this city; which thing hath no possibility of truth, as I have proved, for he deceased in the year 1303, almost ninety years before that time.

1307. Raph Baldocke, dean of Paul's, bishop of London, consecrated at Lyons by Peter, bishop of Alba, in the year 1307; he was a great furtherer of the new work of Paul's; to wit, the east end, called our Lady chapel, and other adjoining. This Raph deceased in the year 1313, and was buried in the said Lady chapel, under a flat stone.

1313. Gilbert Segrave was consecrated bishop of London, and sat three years.

1317. Richard Newport, bishop of London, sat two years, and was buried in Paul's church.

1318. Stephen Gravesend, bishop of London, sat twenty years.

1338. Richard Wentworth, bishop of London, and chancellor of England, and deceased the year 1339.

1339. Raph Stratford, bishop of London; he purchased the piece of ground called No Man's land, beside Smithfield, and dedicated it to the use of burial, as before hath appeared. He was born at Stratford upon Avon, and therefore built a chapel to St. Thomas there: he sat fourteen years, deceased at Stebunhith.

1354. Michael Norbroke, bishop of London, deceased in the year 1361, saith Mirimouth, sat seven years.

1362. Simon Sudbery, bishop of London, sat thirteen years, translated to be archbishop of Canterbury in the year 1375.

1375. William Courtney, translated from Hereford to the bishoprick of London, and after translated from thence to the archbishoprick of Canterbury in the year 1381.

1381. Robert Breybrook, canon of Lichfield, bishop of London, made chancellor in the 6th of Richard II., sat bishop twenty years, and deceased in the year 1404: he was buried in the said Lady chapel at Paul's.

1405. Roger Walden, treasurer of the exchequer, archbishop of Canterbury, was deposed, and after made bishop of London; he deceased in the year 1406, and was buried [1] in Paul's church, Allhallowes altar.

1406. Richard Bubwith, bishop of London, treasurer of the exchequer, translated to Salisbury, and from thence to Bathe, and lieth buried at Wels.

1407. Richard Clifford, removed from Worcester to London, deceased 1422, as saith Thomas Walsingham, and was buried in Paul's.

1422. John Kempe, fellow of Martin college in Oxford, was made bishop of Rochester, from whence removed to Chichester, and thence to London; he was made the king's chancellor in the year 1425, the 4th of Henry VI., and was removed from London to York in the year 1426: he sat archbishop there twenty-five years, and was translated to Canterbury; he was afterwards made cardinal in the year 1452. In the bishop of London's house at Fulham he received the cross, and the next day the pall, at the hands of Thomas Kempe, bishop of London. He deceased in the year 1454.

1426. William Gray, dean of York, consecrated bishop of London, who founded a college at Thele in Hartfordshire, for a master and four canons, and made it a cell to Elsing spittle in London; it had of old time been a college, decayed, and therefore newly-founded. He was translated to Lincoln 1431.

1431. Robert Fitzhugh, archdeacon of Northampton, consecrated bishop of London, sat five years, deceased 1435, and was buried on the south side of the choir of Paul's.

1435. Robert Gilbert, doctor of divinity, dean of York, consecrated bishop of London, sat twelve years, deceased 1448.

[1] " At Bartholomew's priory in Smithfield."—1st *edition*, p. 304.

1449. Thomas Kempe, archdeacon of Richmond, consecrated bishop of London at York house (now Whitehall), by the hands of his uncle John Kemp, archbishop of York, the 8th of February, 1449; he founded a chapel of the Trinity in the body of St. Paul's church, on the north side; he sat bishop of London thirty-nine years and forty-eight days, and then deceased in the year 1489, was there buried.

1489. John Marshal, bishop of London, deceased in the year 1493.

1493. Richard Hill, bishop of London, deceased 1495, and was buried in the body of St. Paul's church.

1496. Thomas Savage, first bishop of Rochester, then bishop of London five years, was translated to York 1501, where he sat archbishop seven years, and was there buried in the year 1507.

1502. William Warrham, bishop of London, made keeper of the great seal, sat two years, was translated to Canterbury.

1504. William Barons, bishop of London, sat ten months and eleven days, deceased in the year 1505.

1505. Richard Fitz James, fellow of Merton college in Oxford, in the reign of Henry VI., was made bishop of Rochester, after bishop of Chichester, then bishop of London; he deceased 1521, and lieth buried hard beneath the north-west pillar of the steeple in St. Paul's, under a fair tomb of marble, over the which was built a fair chapel of timber, with stairs mounting thereunto: this chapel was burned with fire from the steeple 1561, and the tomb was taken down.

1521. Cuthbert Tunstal, doctor of law, master of the rolls, lord privy seal, and bishop of London, was thence translated to the bishopric of Durham in the year 1529.

1529. John Stokeley, bishop of London, sat thirteen years, deceased in the year 1539, and was buried in the Lady chapel in Paul's.

1539. Edmond Boner, doctor of the civil law, archdeacon of Leycester, then bishop of Hereford, was elected to London in the year 1539, whilst he was beyond the seas, ambassador to King Henry VIII. On the 1st of September, 1549, he preached at Paul's cross; for the which sermon he was charged before the council of King Edward VI., by William Latimer, parson of St. Lawrence Poltney, and John Hooper, sometime a white monk, and being convented before certain commissioners at Lambith, was for his disobedience to the king's order, on the 20th day of the same month sent to the Marshalsey, and deprived from his bishopric.

1550. Nicholas Ridley, bishop of Rochester, elected bishop of London, was installed in Paul's church on the 12th of April. This man by his deed, dated the twelfth day after Christmas, in the 4th year of Edward VI., gave to the king the manors of Branketrie and Southminster, and the patronage of the church of Cogshall in Essex, the manors of Stebunheth and Hackney, in the county of Middlesex, and the marsh of Stebunheth, with all and singular messuages, lands, and tenements, to the said manors belonging, and also the advowson of the vicarage of the parish church of Cogshall in Essex aforesaid; which grant was confirmed by the dean and chapter of Paul's, the same day and year, with exception of such lands in Southminster, Stebunheth, and Hackney, as only pertained to them. The said King Edward, by his letters patents, dated the 16th of April, in the said 4th year of his reign, granted to Sir Thomas Wentworth, Lord Wentworth, lord chamberlain of the king's household, for, and in consideration of his good and faithful service before done, a part of the late received gift, to wit, the lordships of Stebunheth and Hackney, with all the members and appurtenances thereunto belonging, in Stebunheth, Hackney way, Shoreditch, Holiwell street, Whitechappell, Stratford at Bow, Poplar, North street, Limehouse, Ratliffe, Cleve street, Brock street, Mile end, Bleten hall green, Oldford, Westheth, Kingsland, Shakelwell, Newinton street *alias* Hackney street, Clopton, Church street, Wel street, Humbarton, Grove street, Gunston street, *alias* More street, in the county of Middlesex, together with the marsh of Stebunhith, etc. The manor of Hackney was valued at sixty-one pounds nine shillings and fourpence, and the manor Stebunhith at one hundred and forty pounds eight shillings and eleven pence, by year, to be holden in chief, by the service of the twentieth part of a knight's fee. This bishop, Nicholas Ridley, for preaching a sermon at Paul's cross, on the 16th of July, in the year 1553, was committed to the Tower of London, where he remained prisoner till the 10th of April, 1554, and was thence sent to Oxford, there to dispute with the divines and learned men of the contrary opinion; and on the 16th of October, 1555, he was burned at Oxford for opinions against the Romish order of sacraments, etc.

1553. Edmond Boner aforesaid, being released out of the Marshalsey, was restored to the bishoprick of London, by Queen Mary, on the 5th of August, in the year 1553, and again deposed by Queen Elizabeth, in the month of July 1559, and was eftsoones committed to the Marshalsey, where he died on the 5th of September, 1569, and was at midnight buried amongst other prisoners in St. George's churchyard.

1559. Edmond Grindal, bishop of London, being consecrated the 21st of December, 1559, was translated to York in the year 1570, and from thence removed to Canterbury in the year 1575. He died blind 1583 on the 6th of July, and was buried at Croydowne in Surrey.

1570. Edwine Stands, being translated from Worcester to the bishoprick of London, in the year 1570, was thence translated to Yorke in the year 1576, and died in the year 1588.

1576. John Elmere, bishop of London, deceased in the year 1594, on the 3rd of June at Fulham, and was buried in Paul's church, before St. Thomas chapel.

1594. Richard Fletcher, bishop of Worcester, was on the 30th of December in Paul's church elected bishop of London, and deceased on the 15th of June, 1596: he was buried in Paul's church without any solemn funeral.

1597. Richard Bancroft, doctor of divinity, consecrated at Lambeth on Sunday, the 8th of May, now sitteth bishop of London, in the year 1598 being installed there.

This much for the succession of the bishops of London, whose diocese containeth the city of London, the whole shires of Middlesex and Essex and part of Hartfordshire. These bishops have for assistants in the cathedral church of St. Paul, a dean, a chaunter, a chancellor, a treasurer, five archdeacons—to wit, London, Middlesex, Essex, Colchester, and St. Alban's, and thirty prebendaries; there appertaineth also to the said churches for furniture of the choir in Divine service, and ministration of the sacraments, a college of twelve petty canons, six vicars choral, and choristers, etc.

This diocese is divided into parishes, every parish having its parson, or vicar at the least, learned men for the most part, and sufficient preachers, to instruct the people. There were in this city, and within the suburbs thereof, in the reign of Henry II. (as writeth Fitz Stephens), thirteen great conventual churches, besides the lesser sort called parish churches, to the number of one hundred and twenty-six, all which conventual churches, and some others since that time founded, are now suppressed and gone, except the cathedral church of St. Paul in London, and the college of St. Peter at Westminster; of all which parish churches, though I have spoken, yet for more ease to the reader I will here again set them down in manner of a table, not by order of alphabet, but as they be placed in the wards and suburbs.

PARISH CHURCHES

1. *In Portsoken ward, parish churches, three.*

The hospital of St. Katherine, serveth for that liberty.

Trinity, in the Minories, for precinct thereof.

St. Bottolphe, by Aldegate, the only parish church for that ward.

2. *In Tower street ward, four.*

In the Tower, St. Peter, for the inhabitants there.

Alhallowes Barking, by the Tower.

St. Olave, in Hart street.

St. Dunstone in the East.

3. *In Aldgate ward, three.*

St. Katheren Christ's church.

St. Andrewes Undershafte.

St. Katheren Colman church.

4. *In Lime street ward none. There was St. Mary at the Axe, and St. Augustine in the Wall, both suppressed and united, the one to Alhallowes in the Wall in Brode street ward, the other to St. Andrewe Undershaft in Lime street ward.*

5. *In Bishopsgate ward, three.*

St. Bottolphes, without Bishopsgate.

St. Ethelburge, within the gate.

St. Helens', adjoining the nuns' priory.

6. *In Brode street ward, six.*

Alhallowes by the Wall.

St. Peter's the Poor.

St. Martin's Oteswitche.

St. Benet Fynke.

St. Bartilmew, by the Exchange.

St. Christopher, by the Stocks' market.

7. *In Cornhill ward, two.*

St. Peter, upon Cornehill.

St. Michaell, upon Cornehill.

8. *In Langborne ward, seven.*

St. Gabriel Fenchurch.

St. Dyones Backchurch.

Alhallowes, in Lombard street.

St. Edmond, in Lombard street.
Alhallowes Staning, at Mart lane end.
St. Nicholas Acon, in Lombard street.
St. Mary Wolnoth, in Lombard street.

9. *In Billingsgate ward, five.*

St. Buttolph, by Billingsgate.
St. Mary, on the hill.
St. Margaret Pattens.
St. Andrew Hubert, in Eastcheape.
St. George, in Buttolph lane.

10. *In Bridge ward within, four.*

St. Magnus, at the bridge foot.
St. Margaret, Bridge street.
St. Leonard Milkchurch, Fish street hill.
St. Benet Grasse church.

11. *In Candlewike street ward, five.*

St. Clement's, Eastcheape.
St. Mary Abchurch.
St. Michael, in Crooked lane, sometime a college.
St. Martin's Orgars.
St. Laurence Pountney, sometime a college.

12. *In Walbrooke ward, five.*

St. Swithen, by London stone.
St. Mary Woolchurch.
St. Stephen, by Walbrooke.
St. John, upon Walbrooke.
St. Mary Bothaw.

13. *In Downegate ward, two.*

Alhallowes, Hay wharf, in the Roperie.
Alhallowes the Less, in the Roperie.

14. *In the Vintry ward, four.*

St. Michael Paternoster, in the Royall, sometime a
   college.
St. Thomas Apostles.
St. Martin, in the Vintrie.
St. James, in Garlicke hith.

15. *In Cordwainer street ward, three.*

St. Anthonies, in Budge row.
Alde Mary church. New Mary church, or Mary le Bow.

16. *In Cheap ward, seven, and a chapel.*

St. Benet Sorhoge, or Syth.
St. Pancreate, by Sopar's lane.
St. Mildred, in the Poultrie.
St. Mary Colchurch.
St. Martin's Pomerie, in Ironmonger lane.
Alhallowes, Honie lane.
St. Laurence, in the Jury.
The Chapel in Guildhall, sometime a college.

17. *In Coleman street ward, three.*

St. Olave Upwell, in the Old Jurie.
St. Margaret, in Lothburie.
St. Stephen, in Coleman street.

18. *In Bassings hall ward, one.*

St. Michael, at Bassings hall.

19. *In Cripplegate ward, six.*

St. Mary Aldermanburie.
St. Alphage, sometime an hospital of Elsing.
St. Mary Magdalen, in Milk street.
St. Albon's, in Wood street.
St. Michael, in Hugen lane.
St. Giles, without Cripplegate.

20. *In Aldersgate ward, six.*

St. John Zachery.
St. Mary Staning.
St. Olave, in Silver street.
St. Leonard, in Foster Lane.
St. Anne, by Aldersgate.
St. Buttolph, without Aldersgate.

21. *In Faringdon ward within, the cathedral church of St. Paule, and parish churches nine.*

St. Peter's, at the Cross in Cheape.
St. Fauster, in Fauster lane.
Christ church, made a parish church of the Gray Friers church, and of two parish churches, St. Nicholas and St. Ewin, and also an hospital for poor children.
St. Mathew, in Fryday street.
St. Augustine, by Paules gate.
St. Faith, under Paules church.
St. Martin's, at Ludgate.

St. Anne, at the Blacke Friers.
St. Michael at Corne, by Paules.
Chapel of St. James, by Cripplegate.

22. *In Bread Street ward, four.*

Alhallowes, in Bread street.
St. Mildred's, in Bread street.
St. John Evangelist, in Fryday street.
St. Margaret Moses, in Fryday street.

23. *In Queene hithe ward, seven.*

St. Trinitie, in Trinity lane.
St. Nicholas, Cold abbey.
St. Nicholas, Olave.
St. Mary Mounthaunt.
St. Michael, at Queene hithe.
St. Mary, at Sommers hithe.
St. Peter's, at Paules wharf.

24. *In Castle Baynard's ward, four.*

St. Benet Hude, or hith, by Paules wharf.
St. Andrewe, by the Wardrobe.
St. Mary Magdalen, in Old Fish street.
St. Gregorie, by Paules church.

25. *In Faringdon ward without, seven.*

St. Sepulcher's, without Newgate.
St. Andrew, in Oldborne.
St. Dunstone in the West.
St. Bartlemew, by the priory.
St. Bartlemew, the hospital.
St. Briget, or Brides, in Fleet street.
St. Parnell, in the Temple, for the students there.

26. *In the borough of Southwark, and Bridge ward without, four.*

St. Saviour's in Southwark, made of
  twain, viz., St. Mary Magdalen, and   Diocese
  St. Margaret.   of
St. George the Martyr.   Winchester.
St. Thomas, the hospital.
St. Olave, in Southwark.

Thus have ye in the twenty-six wards of London and borough of Southwark parish churches to the number of one hundred and fourteen.

And in the suburbs adjoining, parish churches nine, as followeth :—

> St. Mary Magdalen, at Bermondsey, in the borough of Southwark, diocese of Winton.
> St. Mary Matfellon, Whitechapel.
> St. Leonard, Shoreditch.
> St. John Baptist, Clearken well.
> St. Giles in the Field, sometime an hospital.

In the duchy of Lancaster :

> St. Clement Danes, without Temple bar.
> St. John Baptist, Savoy, an hospital.

In the city of Westminster, that liberty, as followeth :

> The college of St. Peter, called Westminster.

Parish churches twain :

> St. Margaret, a parish church, by Westminster.
> St. Martin in the Field, by Charing cross.

Thus have ye in the wards of London, and in the suburbs of the same city, the borough of Southwark, and the city of Westminster, a cathedral church of St. Paul, a collegiate church of St. Peter in Westminster, and parish churches one hundred and twenty-three.

HOSPITALS IN THIS CITY, AND SUBURBS THEREOF, THAT HAVE BEEN OF OLD TIME, AND NOW PRESENTLY ARE, I READ OF THESE AS FOLLOWETH:

Hospital of St. Mary, in the parish of Barking church, that was provided for poor priests and others, men and women in the city of London, that were fallen into frenzy or loss of their memory, until such time as they should recover, was since suppressed and given to the hospital of St. Katherine, by the Tower.

St. Anthonies, an hospital of thirteen poor men, and college, with a free school for poor men's children, founded by citizens of London, lately by John Tate, first a brewer and then a mercer, in the ward of Broad street, suppressed in the reign of Edward VI., the school in some sort remaining, but sore decayed.

St. Bartlemew, in Smithfield, an hospital of great receipt and relief for the poor, was suppressed by Henry VIII., and again by him given to the city, and is endowed by the citizens' benevolence.

St. Giles in the Fields was an hospital for leprous people out of the city of London and shire of Middlesex, founded by Matilde the queen, wife to Henry I., and suppressed by King Henry VIII.

St. John of Jerusalem, by West Smithfield, an hospital of the Knights of the Rhodes, for maintenance of soldiers against the Turks and infidels, was suppressed by King Henry VIII.

St. James in the Field was an hospital for leprous virgins of the city of London, founded by citizens for that purpose, and suppressed by King Henry VIII.

St. John, at Savoy, an hospital for relief of one hundred poor people, founded by Henry VII., suppressed by Edward VI.: again new founded, endowed, and furnished by Queen Mary, and so remaineth.

St. Katherine, by the Tower of London, an hospital, with a master, brethren, and sisters, and alms women, founded by Matilde, wife to King Stephen; not suppressed, but in force as before.

St. Mary within Cripplegate, an hospital founded by William Elsing, for a hundred blind people of the city, was suppressed by King Henry VIII.

St. Mary Bethelem, without Bishopsgate, was an hospital, founded by Simon Fitzmary, a citizen of London, to have been a priory, and remaineth for lunatic people, being suppressed and given to Christ's hospital.

St. Mary, without Bishopsgate, was an hospital and priory, called St. Mary Spittle, founded by a citizen of London for relief of the poor, with provision of one hundred and eighty beds there for the poor: it was suppressed in the reign of King Henry VIII.

St. Mary Rouncevall, by Charing cross, was an hospital suppressed with the priories aliens in the reign of King Henry V.; then was it made a brotherhood in the 15th of Edward IV., and again suppressed by King Edward VI.

St. Thomas of Acres, in Cheape, was an hospital for a master and brethren (in the record called Militia); it was surrendered and sold to the mercers.

St. Thomas, in Southwark, being an hospital of great receipt for the poor, was suppressed, but again newly founded and endowed by the benevolence and charity of the citizens of London.

An hospital there was without Aldersgate, a cell to the house of Cluny, of the French order, suppressed by King Henry V.

An hospital without Cripplegate, also a like cell to the said house of Cluny, suppressed by King Henry V.

A third hospital in Oldborne, being also a cell to the said house of Cluny, suppressed by King Henry V.

The hospital, or alms-house, called God's house, for thirteen poor men, with a college, called Whitington college, founded by Richard Whitington, mercer, and suppressed; but the poor remain, and are paid their allowance by the mercers.

Christ's hospital, in Newgate market, of a new foundation in the Grey Fryers church by King Henry VIII.: poor fatherless children be there brought up and nourished at the charges of the citizens.

Bridewell, now an hospital (or house of correction), founded by King Edward VI., to be a workhouse for the poor and idle persons of the city, wherein a great number of vagrant persons be now set a-work, and relieved at the charges of the citizens. Of all these hospitals, being twenty in number, you may read before in their several places, as also of good and charitable provisions made for the poor by sundry well-disposed citizens.

NOW OF LEPROSE PEOPLE, AND LAZAR HOUSES

It is to be observed that leprous persons were always, for avoiding the danger of infection, to be separated from the sound, etc.; God himself commanding to put out of the host every leper.[1] Whereupon I read, that in a provincial synod holden at Westminster by Hubert, archbishop of Canterbury, in the year of Christ 1200, the 2nd of King John, it was decreed, according to the institution of the Lateran council, that when so many leprous people were assembled, that might be able to build a church, with a churchyard, for themselves, and to have one especial priest of their own, that they should be permitted to have the same without contradiction, so they be not injurious to the old churches, by that which was granted to them for pity's sake. And further, it was decreed that they be not compelled to give any tithes of their gardens or increase of cattle.

I have moreover heard, that there is a writ in our law, *de leproso amovendo ;* and I have read that King Edward III., in the 20th year of his reign, gave commandment to the mayor and sheriffs of London, to make proclamation in every ward of

[1] " Leviticus 13. Numbers 5. Leprose persons to be separated from the sound."—*Stow.*

the city and suburbs, that all leprous persons inhabiting there should avoid within fifteen days next, and that no man suffer any such leprous person to abide within his house, upon pain to forfeit his said house, and to incur the king's further displeasure; and that they should cause the said lepers to be removed into some out places of the fields, from the haunt or company of sound people: whereupon certain lazar-houses, as may be supposed, were then built without the city some good distance; to wit, the Locke without Southwark in Kent street; one other betwixt the Miles end and Stratford, Bow; one other at Kingsland, betwixt Shoreditch and Stoke Newington; and another at Knightes bridge, west from Charing cross. These four I have noted to be erected for the receipt of leprous people sent out of the city. At that time, also, the citizens required of the guardian of St. Giles' hospital to take from them, and to keep continually, the number of fourteen persons leprous, according to the foundation of Matilde the queen, which was for leprous persons of the city of London and the shire of Middlesex, which was granted. More, the wardens, or keepers of the ports, gates, or posterns of this city, were sworn in the mayor's court before the recorder, etc., that they should well and faithfully keep the same ports and posterns, and not to suffer any leprous person to enter the said city.

John Gardener, porter of the postern by the Tower, his oath before the mayor and recorder of London, on Monday, after the feast of St. Bartlemew, the 49th of Edward III.: That the gates and postern be well and faithfully kept in his office and baylywicke, and that he should not suffer any lepers or leper to enter the city, or to remain in the suburbs; and if any leper or lepers force themselves to enter by his gates or postern, he to bind them fast to horses, and send them to be examined of the superiors, etc.

Finally, I read that one William Pole, yeoman of the crown to King Edward IV., being stricken with a leprosy, was also desirous to build an hospital, with a chapel, to the honour of God and St. Anthony, for the relief and harbouring of such leprous persons as were destitute in the kingdom, to the end they should not be offensive to other in their passing to and fro: for the which cause Edward IV. did by his charter, dated the 12th of his reign, give unto the said William for ever a certain parcel of his land lying in his highway of Highgate and Haloway, within the county of Middlesex, containing sixty feet in length and thirty-four in breadth.

THE TEMPORAL GOVERNMENT OF THIS CITY, SOMEWHAT IN BRIEF MANNER

This city of London, being under the government of the Britons, Romans, and Saxons, the most ancient and famous city of the whole realm, was at length destroyed by the Danes, and left desolate, as may appear by our histories. But Aelfred, king of the West Saxons, having brought this whole realm (from many parts) into one monarchy, honourably repaired this city, and made it again habitable, and then committed the custody thereof to his son-in-law Adhered, earl of Mercia; after whose decease the city, with all other possessions pertaining to the said earl, returned to King Edward, surnamed the Elder, etc.: and so remained in the king's hands, being governed under him by portgraves (or portreves), which name is compounded of the two Saxon words, *porte* and *gerefe*, or *reve*. Porte betokeneth a town, and gerefe signifieth a guardian, ruler, or keeper of the town.

These governors of old time (saith Robert Fabian), with the laws and customs then used within this city, were registered in a book called the Dooms' day, written in the Saxon tongue; but of later days, when the said laws and customs were changed, and for that also the said book was of a small hand, sore defaced, and hard to be read or understood, it was less set by, so that it was embezzled and lost. Thus far Fabian.

Notwithstanding, I have found, by search of divers old registers and other records abroad, namely, in a book sometime appertaining to the monastery of St. Alban's, of the portgraves, and other governors of this city, as followeth:

First, that in the reign of King Edward, the last before the Conquest, Wolfegare was portgrave, as may appear by the charter of the same king, in these words: "Edward, king, greeteth Alfward, bishop, and Wolfegare, my portgrave, and all the burgesses in London." And afterward that, in another charter, "King Edward greeteth William, bishop, and Sweetman, my portgrave." And after, that in another charter to the abbey of Chertsey, to William, bishop, and Leofstane and Alsy, portgraves. In the reign of William the Conqueror, William, bishop of London, procured of the said Conqueror his charter of liberties, to the same William, bishop, and Godfrey, portgrave, in Saxon tongue, and corrected in English thus:

"William, king, greet William, bishop, and Godfrey, portgrave, and all the burgeses within London, French and English.

And I graunt that they be all their law worth, that they were in Edward's dayes the king. And I will that each child bee his father's heire. And I will not suffer that any man do you wrong, and God you keepe." And then in the reign of the said Conqueror and of William Rufus, Godfrey de Magnavile was portgrave (or sheriff), as may appear by their charters, and Richard de Par was provost.

In the reign of King Henry I., Hugh Buche was portgrave, and Leofstanus, goldsmith, provost, buried at Bermondsey.

After them Aubrey de Vere was portgrave, and Robert Bar Querel provost. This Aubrey de Vere was slain in the reign of King Stephen. It is to be noted, also, that King Henry I. granted to the citizens of London the shrivewick thereof, and of Middlesex, as in another place is showed.

In the reign of King Stephen, Gilbert Becket was portgrave, and Andrew Buchevet provost.

After him, Godfrey Magnavile, the son of William, the son of Godfrey Magnavile, by the gift of Maude, the empress, was portgrave, or sheriff of London and Middlesex, for the yearly farm of three hundred pounds, as appeareth by the charter.

In the time of King Henry II., Peter Fitzwalter was portgrave; after him John Fitznigel was portgrave; after him Ernulfus Buchel became portgrave; and after him William Fitz Isabel. These portgraves are also in divers records called vice-counties, vicounties, or sheriffs,[1] as being under an earl; for that they then, as since, used that office as the sheriffs of London do till this day. Some authors do call them domesmen, aldermen, or judges of the king's court.

William Fitz Stephen, noting the estate of this city, and government thereof in his time, under the reign of King Stephen and of Henry II., hath these words:

" This city (saith he), even as Rome, is divided into wards; it hath yearly sheriffs instead of consuls; it hath the dignity of senators and aldermen; it hath under officers, and, according to the quality of laws, it hath several courts and general assemblies upon appointed days." Thus much for the antiquity of sheriffs, and also of aldermen, in several wards of this city, may suffice. And now for the name of bailiffs, and after that of mayors, as followeth:

In the first year of King Richard I.,[2] the citizens of London

---

[1] " Since called shiriffes, and judges of the King's court, and have therefore under-shiriffes, men learned in the law, to sit in their courts. Domesmen, or judges of the King's court."—*Stow*.

[2] [*See* Additional Notes.]

obtained to be governed by two bailiffs, which bailiffs are in divers ancient deeds called sheriffs, according to the speech of the law, which called the shire Balliva, for that they, like as the portgraves, used the same office of shrivewicke, for the which the city paid to fee farm three hundred pounds yearly as before, since the reign of Henry I., which also is yet paid by the city into the Exchequer until this day.

They also obtained to have a mayor, to be their principal governor and lieutenant of the city, as of the king's chamber.

1180. The names of the first bailiffs, or officers, entering into their office at the feast of St. Michael the Archangel, in the year of Christ 1189, were named Henry Cornhill and Richard Reynere, bailiffs or sheriffs.

Their first mayor was Henry Fitz Alwin Fitz Liefstane, goldsmith, appointed by the said king, and continued mayor from the 1st of Richard I. until the 15th of King John, which was twenty-four years and more.

1190. The 2nd of Richard I., sheriffs, Wm. de Haverhill, John Bucuinte; mayor, Henry Fitz Alwin.

1191. The 3rd, sheriffs, Nicholas Duket, Peter Fitz Neuelon; mayor, Henry Fitz Alwin.

1192. The 4th, Roger le Duc, Roger Fitzalan; mayor, Henry Fitz Alwin.

1193. The 5th, Wm. Fitz Isabel, Wm. Fitz Alulf; mayor, Henry Fitz Alwin.

1194. The 6th, Robert Besaunt, Iukel; mayor, Henry Fitz Alwin.

1195. The 7th, Godard de Antioche, Robert Fitz Durand; mayor, Henry Fitz Alwin.

1196. The 8th, Nicholas Duket, Robert Blund; mayor, Henry Fitz Alwin.

1197. The 9th, Constantine Fitz Alulf, Robert de Bel; mayor, Henry Fitz Alwin.

1198. The 10th, Arnold Fitz Alulf, Richard Blunt; mayor, Henry Fitz Alwin.

King John began his reign the 6th of April, 1199.

1199. The 1st of King John, sheriffs, Roger de Deserto, James the Alderman; mayor, Henry Fitz Alwin.

King John granted the sheriffwicke of London and Middlesex to the citizens thereof, as King Henry I. before had done, for the sum of three hundred pounds year. Also he gave them authority to choose and deprive their sheriffs at their pleasure.

1200. The 2nd, sheriffs, Simon de Aldermanbury, Wm. Fitz Alis; mayor, Henry Fitz Alwin.

1201. The 3rd, Norman Blund, John de Cayo or Cay; mayor, Henry Fitz Alwin.

1202. The 4th, Walter Brun, Wm. Chamberleyn; mayor, Henry Fitz Alwin.

Walter Brune, and Rose his wife, founded the hospital of St. Mary without Bishopsgate, commonly called St. Mary Spittle.

1203. The 5th, Thomas Haverel, Hamon Brond; mayor, Henry Fitz Alwin.

1204. The 6th, John Walran, Richard Winchester; mayor, Henry Fitz Alwin.

1205. The 7th, John Fitz Elinand, Edmund Fitz Gerard; mayor, Henry Fitz Alwin.

1206. The 8th, Henry St. Albans, Serbo the Mercer; mayor, Henry Fitz Alwin.

1207. The 9th, William Hardel, Robert Winchester; mayor, Henry Fitz Alwin.

1208. The 10th, Peter Duke, Thomas Nele; mayor, Henry Fitz Alwin.

The king, by his letters patents, granted to the citizens of London liberty and authority yearly to choose to themselves a mayor. [See Additional Notes.]

1209. The 11th, Peter Neuelun, William Blund; mayor, Henry Fitz Alwin.

1210. The 12th, Adam de Withebi, Stephen le Grace; mayor, Henry Fitz Alwin.

1211. The 13th, Ioce Fitz Peter, John Garland; mayor, Henry Fitz Alwin.

This Henry Fitz Alwin deceased, and was buried in the priory of the Holy Trinity, near unto Aldgate.

1212. The 14th, Ralph Helyland, Constantine Fitz Alulf; mayor, Roger Fitz Alan.

1213. The 15th, Martin Fitz Alis, Peter Bate; mayor, Roger Fitz Alan.

This year the ditch about London was begun to be made, of two hundred and four feet broad, by the Londoners. [Additional Note.]

1214. The 16th, Salomon Basing, Hugh Basing; mayor, Serle Mercer.

1215. The 17th, John Travars, Andrew Neuelun; mayor William Hardel.

King Henry III. began his reign the 19th of October, 1216.

1216. The 1st, sheriffs, Benet Senturer, William Blund: mayor, James Alderman for part, and Salomon Basing for part.

1217. The 2nd, Thomas Bokerel, Ralph Eiland; mayor, Serle Mercer.

1218. The 3rd, John Viel, John le Spicer; mayor, Serle Mercer.

The forest of Middlesex and the warren of Staines were this year disafforested.

1219. The 4th, Richard Wimbledon, John Viel; mayor, Serle Mercer.

1220. The 5th, Richard Renger, Ioce le Iofne; mayor, Serle Mercer.

1221. The 6th, Richard Renger, Thomas Lambart; mayor, Serle Mercer.

Constantine Fitz Aluf raised great troubles in this city, and was hanged with his nephew and other.

1222. The 7th, William le Ioynour, Thomas Lambart; mayor, Richard Renger.

1223. The 8th, John Travars, Andrew Bokerel; mayor, Richard Renger.

1224. The 9th, John Travars, Andrew Bokerel; mayor Richard Renger.

The king granted to the commonalty of London to have a common seal.

1225. The 10th, Roger Duke, Martin Fitz William; mayor, Richard Renger.

1226. The 11th, Roger Duke, Martin Fitz William; mayor, Richard Renger.

This year the king confirmed to the citizens of London free warren or liberty to hunt a certain circuit about the city, in the warren of Staines, etc. And, also, that the citizens of London should pass toll-free throughout all England, and that the keddles, or wears, in the river of Thames and Medway should be plucked up and destroyed for ever, etc. Patent, 16th Henry III.

1227. The 12th, Stephen Bokerel, Henry Cocham; mayor, Roger Duke.

The liberties and franchises of London were ratified; and the king granted that either sheriff should have two clerks and two sergeants, also that the citizens should have a common seal.

1228. The 13th, Stephen Bokerell, Henry Cocham; mayor, Roger Duke.

1229. The 14th, William de Winchester, Robert Fitz John; mayor, Roger Duke.

1230. The 15th, Richard Walter, John de Woborne; mayor, Roger Duke.

1231. The 16th, Michael S. Helena, Walter le Bufle; mayor, Andrew Bokerel, pepperer.

1232. The 17th, Henry de Edmonton, Gerard Bat; mayor, Andrew Bokerel, pepperer.

1233. The 18th, Simon Fitz Mary, Roger Blunt; mayor, Andrew Bokerel, pepperer.

1234. The 19th, Raph Ashwye, John Norman; mayor, Andrew Bokerel, pepperer.

1235. The 20th, Gerard Bat, Richard Hardel; mayor, Andrew Bokerel, pepperer.

1236. The 21st, Henry Cocham, Jordan of Coventrie; mayor, Andrew Bokerel, pepperer.

1237. The 22nd, John Toloson, Gervais the Cordwainer; mayor, Andrew Bokerel, pepperer [and then Richard Renger].

1238. The 23rd, John de Codres, John de Wylhale; mayor, Richard Renger [and then William Ioyner].

This William Joyner built the choir of the Grey Friers church in London, and became a lay brother of that house.

1239. The 24th, Reiner de Bongey, Raph Ashwy; mayor, Gerard Bat.

1240. The 25th, John de Gisors, Michael Touy; mayor, Reginald Bungeye.

This year aldermen of London were chosen, and changed yearly, but that order lasted not long. Gerard Bat was again elected mayor for that year to come, but the king would not admit him, being charged with taking money of the victuallers in the precedent year.

1241. The 26th, Thomas Duresme, John Viel; mayor, Raph Ashwy.

1242. The 27th, Robert Fitzjohn, Raph Ashwye; mayor, Raph Ashwy.

1243. The 28th, Hugh Blunt, Adam Basing; mayor, Raph Ashwye.

1244. The 29th, Ralph de Arcubus, spicer, Nicholas Bat; mayor, Michael Touy.

1245. The 30th, Robert of Cornehil, Adam of Bentley; mayor, John Gisors, pepperer.

1246. The 31st, Simon Fitz Mary, Laurence Frowicke; mayor; Peter Fitz Alan.

Simon Fitz Mary founded the hospital of Mary, called Bethlem without Bishopsgate. Queene hithe let to farm to the citizens of London.

1247. The 32nd, John Viel, Nicholas Bat; mayor, Michael Touy.

1248. The 33rd, Nicholas Fitz Josey, Geffrey Winchester; mayor, Michael Touy.

1249. The 34th, Ralph Hardel, John de Tolesane; mayor, Roger Fitz Roger.

1250. The 35th, Humfrey le Feure, William Fitz Richard; mayor, John Norman.

1251. The 36th, Laurence Frowike, Nicholas Bat; mayor, Adam Basing.

1252. The 37th, William Durham, Thomas Wimborne; mayor, John Tolason, draper.

The king granted that the mayor should be presented to the barons of the exchequer, and they should admit him.

1253. The 38th, John Northampton, Richard Pickard; mayor, Nicholas Bat.

1254. The 39th, William Ashwy, Robert de Linton; mayor, Ralph Hardell, draper.

The liberties of this city were seized, the mayor charged that he looked not to the assise of bread.

1255. The 40th, Mathew Bukerel, John le Mynur; mayor, Ralph Hardel, draper.

1256. The 41st, Richard Ewel, William Ashwy; mayor, Ralph Hardel, draper.

The king caused the walls of this city to be repaired and made with bulwarks.

1257. The 42nd, Thomas Fitz Thomas, William Grapefige; mayor, William Fitz Richard, draper.

The mayors, divers aldermen, and the sheriffs of London, were deprived, and others placed in their rooms.

1258. The 43rd, John Adrian, Robert Cornhill; mayor, John Gisors, pepperer.

1259. The 44th, Adam Bruning, Henry de Coventry; mayor, John Gisors, William Fitz Richard.

1260. The 45th, John Northampton, Richard Picard; mayor, William Fitz Richard.

1261. The 46th, Philip le Taylor, Richard Walbrooke; mayor, Thomas Fitz Thomas.

1262. The 47th, Robert de Mountpiler, Osbert de Suffolk; mayor, Thomas Fitz Thomas.

1263. The 48th, Gregory Rokesley, Thomas de Ford; mayor, Thomas Fitz Thomas.

The citizens of London fortified the city with iron chains drawn thwart their streets.

1264. The 49th, Edward Blund, Peter Angar; mayor, Thomas Fitz Thomas.

1265. The 50th, John Adrian, Walter Hervi, till 28 Nov., and then Sir John de la Linde and John Walrauen; custos, Hugh Fitz Otho.

The chains and posts in London were plucked up, the mayor and principal citizens committed to ward, and Othon, constable of the tower, was made custos of the city, etc.

1266. The 51st, John Adrian, Lucas de Batencourt; custos, Alan de la Souche.

This Alen de la Souch, being a baron of this realm, and also chief justice, was in the year 1270 slain in Westminster hall by John Warren earl of Surrey.

The earl of Gloucester entered the city with an army, and therein builded bulwarks, cast trenches, etc.

1267. The 52nd, John Adrian, Lucas de Batencourt; custos, Alen de la Souch.

Thomas Fitz Theobald and Agnes his wife, founded the hospital of St. Thomas of Acon in Westcheap. [See Additional Notes.]

1268. The 53rd, Walter Harvy, William Duresme; custos, Sir Stephen de Edeworth.

A variance fell in London between the goldsmiths and the tailors, wherethrough many men were slain.

1269. The 54th, Thomas Basing, Robert Cornhill; custos, Hugh Fitz Ottonis, custos of London, and constable of the tower.

1270. The 55th, Gregory Rocksley, Henry Waleys; mayor, John Adrian, vintner.

The steple of Bow church in Cheap fell down, and slew many people.

1271. The 56th, Richard Paris, John de Bodele; mayor, Sir Walter Harry.

1272. The 57th, John Horne, Walter Potter; mayor, Sir Walter Harvy; custos, Henry Frowike, pepperer, for part of that year.

Edward I. began his reign the 16th of November, 1272.

1273. The first, sheriffs, Nicholas Winchester, Henry Coventry; mayor, Henry Waleys.

1274. The 2nd, Lucas Batencourt, Henry Frowicke; mayor, Gregory Rocksley: chief say-master of all the king's mints throughout England, and keeper of the king's exchange at London.

1275. The 3rd, John Horne, Ralph Blunt; mayor, Gregory Rocksley.

1276. The 4th, Robert de Araz, Ralph le Feure; mayor, Gregory Rocksley.

1277. The 5th, John Adrian, Walter Langley; mayor, Gregory Rocksley.

1278. The 6th, Robert Basing, William le Magerer; mayor, Gregory Rocksley.

1279. The 7th, Thomas Box, Ralph de la More; mayor, Gregory Rocksley.

1280. The 8th, William Farindon, Nicholas Winchester; mayor, Gregory Rocksley.

This W. Farindon, goldsmith, one of the sheriffs, was father to Nicholas Farindon: of these two, Farindon ward took that name.

1281. The 9th, William le Magerer, Richard Chigwel; mayor, Henry Waleys.

This Henry Walleis builded the tun upon Cornhill to be a prison, and the stocks to be a market house.

1282. The 10th, Anketel de Betevil, Walter le Blund; mayor, Henry Walleis.

1283. The 11th, Jordan Goodcheape, Martin Box; mayor, Henry Walleis.

Laurence Ducket, goldsmith, murdered in Bow church, and the murderers hanged.

1284. The 12th, Stephen Cornhill, Robert Rocksley: mayor, Gregory Rocksley, custos Ralph Sandwitch.

It was ordained, that millers should have but one halfpenny for a quarter of wheat grinding, and the great water conduit in Cheap was begun to be made.

1285. The 13th, Walter·le Blunt, John Wade; custos, Raph Sandwitch.

1286. The 14th, Walter Hawtoune, Thomas Cross; custos, Raph Sandwitch.

Wheat was sold at London for sixteen pence, and for twelve pence the quarter.

1287. The 15th, William Hereford, Thomas Stanes; custos, Raph Sandwitch.

1288. The 16th, William Betain, John Canterbury; custos, Raph Sandwitch, Raph Barnavars, and Sir John Breton.

1289. The 17th, Salomon le Cutiller, Folke S. Edmond; custos, Sir John Breton, knight.

This year a subsidy was granted, for the reparations of London bridge.

1290. The 18th, Thomas Romaine, William de Leyre; custos, Sir John Breton, knight.

1291. The 19th, Ralph Blunt, Hamo Box; custos, Raph Sandwitch.

1292. The 20th, Henry Bole, Elias Russel; custos, Raph Sandwitch.

Three men had their right hands cut off at the Standard in Cheape, for rescuing of a prisoner, arrested by a sergeant of London.

1293. The 21st, Robt. Rokesley the younger, Martin Amersbury; custos, Sir Raph Sandwitch.

1294. The 22nd, Henry Box, Richard Gloucester; custos, Sir John Breton.

1295. The 23rd, John Dunstable, Adam de Halingbery; custos, Sir John Breton.

1296. The 24th, Thomas of Suffolk, Adam of Fulham; custos, Sir John Breton.

This year all the liberties of the city were restored, the mayoralty excepted.

1297. The 25th, William de Storteford, John de Storteford; custos, Sir John Breton.

Certain citizens of London brake up the tun upon Cornhill, and took out prisoners, for the which they were grievously punished.

1298. The 26th, Richard Refham, Thomas Sely; mayor, Henry Walleis.

1299. The 27th, John Amenters, Henry de Fyngrye; mayor, Elias Russel.

1300. The 28th, Lucas de Havering, Richard Champs; mayor, Elias Russel.

1301. The 29th, Robert Callor, Peter de Bosenho; mayor, Sir John Blunt, knight.

1302. The 30th, Hugh Pourt, Simon Paris; mayor, Sir John Blunt.

1303. The 31st, W. Combmartin, John Bureford; custos, Sir John Blunt.

1304. The 32nd, Roger Paris, John de Lincolne; custos, Sir John Blunt.

Geffrey Hertilepole Alderman, was elected to be Recorder of London, and took his oath, and was appointed to wear his apparel as an Alderman.

1305. The 33rd, William Cosine, Reginald Thunderley; custos, Sir John Blunt.

1306. The 34th, Geffrey Cundute, Simon Bolet; custos, Sir John Blunt.

Seacoal was forbid to be burned in London, Southwark, etc.

Edward II. began his reign 7th of July, the year of Christ, 1307.

1307. The 1st, sheriffs, Nicholas Pigot, Nigellus Drury; mayor, Sir John Blunt.

1308. The 2nd, W. Basing, James le Boteler; mayor, Nicholas Farringdon, goldsmith.

1309. The 3rd, Roger le Paumer, James of St. Edmond; mayor, Thomas Romaine.

1310. The 4th, Simon de Corpe, Peter Blakeney; mayor, Richard Reffam, mercer.

The king commanded the mayor and commonality, to make the wall of London from Ludgate to Fleetbridge, and from thence to the Thames.

1311. The 5th, Simon Merwood, Richard Wilford; mayor, Sir John Gisors, pepperer.

Order was taken, that merchant strangers should sell their wares within forty days after their arrival, or else the same to be forfeited.

1312. The 6th, John Lambin, Adam Lutkin; mayor, Sir John Gisors, pepperer.

1313. The 7th, Robert Burdeyn, Hugh de Garton; mayor, Nicholas Farrindon, goldsmith.

Prices set on victuals:—a fat stalled ox, twenty-four shillings; a fat mutton, twenty pence; a fat goose, two pence halfpenny; a fat capon, two pence; a fat hen, one penny; two chickens, one penny; three pigeons, one penny; twenty-four eggs, one penny, etc.

1314. The 8th, Stephen Abingdon, Hamond Chigwel; mayor, Sir John Gisors, pepperer.

Famine and mortality of the people, so that the quick might unneath bury the dead; horse-flesh, and dogs-flesh, was good meat.

1315. The 9th, Hamond Goodcheap, William Bodelay; mayor, Stephen Abendon.

1316. The 10th, William Caustone, Raph Belancer; mayor, John Wingrave.

An early harvest, a bushel of wheat that had been sold for ten shillings, was now sold for ten pence, etc.

1317. The 11th, John Prior, W. Furneis; mayor, John Wingrave.

Such a murrain of kine, that dogs and ravens that fed on them were poisoned.

1318. The 12th, John Pontel, John Dalling; mayor, John Wingrave.

1319. 13th, Simon Abindon, J. Preston; mayor, Hamond Chickwel, pepperer.

John Gisors late mayor of London, and many other citizens, fled the city for things laid to their charge.

1320. The 14th, Renauld at Conduit, William Produn; mayor, Nicholas Farindon, goldsmith.

1321. The 15th, Richard Constantine, Richard Hackney; mayor, Hamond Chickwell, pepperer.

1322. The 16th, John Grantham, Richard Elie; mayor, Hamond Chickwell, pepperer.

Fish and flesh market established at the Stocks in the midst of the city.

1323. The 17th, Adam of Salisbury, John of Oxford; mayor, Nicholas Farindon, goldsmith.

Of this Nicholas Farindon, and of William Farindon, and of William Farindon his father, read more in Farindon ward.

1324. The 18th, Benet of Fulsham, John Cawson; mayor, Hamond Chickwell, pepperer.

1325. The 19th, Gilbert Mordon, John Cotton; mayor, Hamond Chickwell, pepperer.

The citizens of London took the bishop of Exeter, and cut off his head at the Standard in Cheape.

1326. The 20th, Richard Rothing, Roger Chaunteclere; mayor, Richard Betoyne, goldsmith.

This Richard Rothing is said to new build the parish church of St. James at Garlicke hith.

Edward III. began his reign the 25th of January, the year 1326.

This King Edward granted, that the mayor should be justice for the gaol delivery at Newgate, that the citizens of London should not be constrained to go out of the city of London to any war. More he granted, that the liberties and the franchises of the city should not after this time for any cause be taken into the king's hands, etc. More, he granted by his letters patents, dated the 6th of March, that no Escheater should be in the city, but the mayor for his time.

1327. The 1st, sheriffs, Henry Darcie, John Hauton; mayor, Hamond Chickwell, pepperer.

This year the walls of London were repaired.

1328. The 2nd, Simon Francis, Henry Combmartin; mayor, John Grantham.

1329. The 3rd, Richard Lacer, Henry Gisors; mayor, Richard Swandland.

This year, the king kept a great justing in Cheape, betwixt Sopars lane and the great Crosse.

1330. The 4th, Robert of Elie, Thomas Harewold; mayor, Sir John Pultney, draper.

1331. The 5th, John Mocking, Andrew Auberie; mayor, Sir John Pultney, draper.

1332. The 6th, Nicholas Pike, John Husbond; mayor, John Preston, draper.

This year was founded Elsinge's spittle, by W. Elsing, mercer, that became first prior of that hospital.

1333. The 7th, John Hamond, William Hansard; mayor, Sir John Pultney, draper.

1334. The 8th, John Hingstone, Walter Turke; mayor, Reginald at Conduit, vintner.

1335. The 9th, Walter Moredon, Ralph de Upton; mayor, Reginald at Conduit.

1336. The 10th, John Clarke, William Curtis; mayor, Sir John Pulteney, draper.

This Sir John Pultney founded a college in the parish church of St. Laurence, by Candlewicke street.

1337. The 11th, Walter Nele, Nicholas Crane; mayor, Henry Darcy.

Walter Nele, bladesmith, gave lands to the repairing of the high ways about London.

1338. The 12th, William Pomfret, Hugh Marberer; mayor, Henry Darcy.

The king granted that the sergeants of the mayor, and sheriffs of London, should bear maces of silver and gilt with the king's arms.

1339. The 13th, William Thorney, Roger Forsham; mayor, Andrew Aubery, grocer.

1340. The 14th, Adam Lucas, Bartlemew Deumars; mayor, Andrew Aubery, grocer.

1341. The 15th, Richard de Barking, John de Rokesley: mayor, John of Oxenford, vintner.

1342. The 16th, John Louekin, Richard Kyslyngbury; mayor, Simon Francis, mercer.

The price of Gascoyn wines at London, four pence, and Rhenish wine, six pence the gallon.

1343. The 17th, John Syward, John Aylesham; mayor, John Hamond.

1344. The 18th, Geffrey Wichingham, Thomas Leggy; mayor, John Hamond.

1345. The 19th, Edmond Hemenhall, John of Gloucester; mayor, Richard Leget.

1346. The 20th, John Croyden, William Claptus; mayor, Geffrey Wichingham.

1347. The 21st, Adam Brabasoun, Richard Basingstoke: mayor, Thomas Leggy, skinner.

King Edward won Calais from the French.

1348. The 22nd, Henry Picard, Simon Dolsely; mayor, John Louekin, fishmonger.

A great pest. Sir Walter Mannie, knight, founded the Charterhouse by Smithfield, to be a burial for the dead.

1349. The 23rd, Adam of Bury, Raph de Lenn; mayor, Walter Turk, fishmonger.

1350. The 24th, John Notte, W. Worcester; mayor, Richard Kyslyngbury.

1351. The 25th, John Wroth, Gilbert Stayndrop; mayor, Andrew Aubery, grocer.

1352. The 26th, John Peche, John Stodeye; mayor, Adam Francis, mercer.

This mayor procured an act of parliament, that no known whore should wear any hood or attire on her head, except red or striped cloth of divers colours, etc.

1353. The 27th, W. Weld, John Little; mayor, Adam Francis, mercer.

This Adam Francis was one of the founders of the college in Guildhall chapel, etc., Henry Frowicke was the other.

1354. The 28th, William Todinham, Richard Smelt; mayor, Thomas Leggy, skinner.

Aldermen of London were used to be changed yearly, but now it was ordained that they should not be removed without some special cause.

1355. The 29th, Walter Frester, Thomas Brandon; mayor, Simon Francis, mercer.

1356. The 30th, Richard Notingham, Thomas Dolsely; mayor, Henry Picard, vintner.

This Henry Picard feasted the kings of England, of France, Cypres, and Scots, with other great estates, all in one day.

1357. The 31st, Stephen Cavendish, Bartholomew Frestlynges; mayor, Sir John Stody, vintner.

This John Stody gave tenements to the vintners in London, for relief of the poor of that company.

1358. The 32nd, John Barnes, John Buris; mayor, John Louekin, stock-fishmonger.

1359. The 33rd, Simon of Benington, John of Chichester; mayor, Simon Dolsely, grocer.

1360. The 34th, John Denis, Walter Berny; mayor, John Wroth, fishmonger.

1361. The 35th, William Holbech, James Tame; mayor, John Peche, fishmonger.

1362. The 36th, John of St. Albans, James Andrew; mayor, Stephen Cavendish, draper.

1363. The 37th, Richard Croyden, John Hiltoft; mayor, John Not, pepperer.

1364. The 38th, John de Mitford, Simon de Mordon; mayor, Adam of Bury, skinner.

1365. The 39th, John Briklesworth, Thomas Ireland; mayor, John Louekin, fishmonger, and Adam of Bury, skinner.

1366. The 40th, John Warde, Thomas of Lee; mayor, John Lofkin, fishmonger.

This John Lofkin builded the parish church of St. Michael in Crooked lane.

1367. The 41st, John Turngold, William Dikeman; mayor, James Andrew, draper.

1368. The 42nd, Robert Girdelere, Adam Wimondham; mayor, Simon Mordon, stock-fishmonger.

This year wheat was sold for two shillings and six pence the bushel.

1369. The 43rd, John Piel, Hugh Holbech; mayor, John Chichester, goldsmith.

1370. The 44th, William Walworth, Robert Geyton; mayor, John Barnes, mercer.

1371. The 45th, Adam Stable, Robert Hatfield; mayor, John Barnes, mercer.

This John Barnes gave a chest with three locks, and one thousand marks to be lent to poor young men.

1372. The 46th, John Philpot, Nicholas Brembar; mayor, John Piel, mercer.

1373. The 47th, John Aubery, John Fifhyde; mayor, Adam of Bury, skinner.

1374. The 48th, Richard Lions, William Woodhouse; mayor, William Walworth, fishmonger.

1375. The 49th, John Hadley, William Newport; mayor, John Ward, grocer.

1376. The 50th, John Northampton, Robert Laund; mayor, Adam Stable, mercer.

The Londoners meant to have slain John duke of Lancaster: Adam Staple, mayor, put down, and Nicholas Brembar elected. Also the aldermen were deposed, and others set in their places.

Richard II. began his reign the 21st of June, in the year 1377.

1377. The 1st, sheriffs, Nicholas Twiford, Andrew Pikeman; mayor, Sir Nicholas Brembar, grocer.

John Philpot, a citizen of London, sent ships to the sea, and scoured it of pirates, taking many of them prisoners.

1378. The 2nd, John Boseham, Thomas Cornwalis; mayor, Sir John Philpot, grocer.

This Sir John Philpot gave to the city, lands for the finding of thirteen poor people for ever.

1379. The 3rd, John Helisdon, William Barrat; mayor, John Hadley, grocer.

1380. The 4th, Walter Doget, William Knightcoate; mayor, William Walworth, fishmonger.

This William Walworth arrested Wat Tyler the rebel, and was knighted. He increased the parish church of St. Michael in Crooked lane, and founded there a college. Other aldermen were also knighted for their service in the field.

1381. The 5th, John Rote, John Hend; mayor, John Northampton, draper.

1382. The 6th, Adam Bamme, John Sely; mayor, John Northampton, draper, or skinner, as I find in record.

1383. The 7th, Simon Winchcombe, John More; mayor, Sir Nicholas Brembar, grocer.

John Northampton, late mayor of London, was committed to perpetual prison, and his goods confiscated.

1384. The 8th, Nicholas Exton, John Fressh; mayor, Sir Nicholas Brembar, grocer, knighted with William Walworth.

1385. The 9th, John Organ, John Churchman; mayor, Sir Nicholas Brembar, grocer.

The foresaid John Churchman new-built the custom-house, near to the Tower of London, and did many other works for the commodity of this city.

1386. The 10th, W. Standone, W. More; mayor, Nicholas Exton, fishmonger.

This year the citizens of London, fearing the French, pulled down houses near about their city, repaired their walls, and cleansed their ditches, etc.

1387. The 11th, William Venor, Hugh Fastolf; mayor, Nicholas Exton, fishmonger.

Sir Nicholas Brembar, late mayor of London, was this year beheaded.

1388. The 12th, Thomas Austin, Adam Carlhul; mayor, Nicholas Tuiford, goldsmith, knighted with W. Walworth.

1389. The 13th, John Walcot, John Lovenay; mayor, William Venor, grocer.

1390. The 14th, John Francis, Thomas Vivent; mayor, Adam Bamme, goldsmith.

This Adam Bamme provided from beyond the seas corn in great abundance, so that the city was able to serve the country.

1391. The 15th, John Shadworth, Henry Vanner; mayor, John Hend, draper.

This mayor was for displeasure taken, sent to Windsor castle, and the king made wardens of the city, etc.

1392. The 16th, Gilbert Maghfield, Thomas Newton; mayor, William Stondon, grocer.

1393. The 17th, Drew Barintin, Richard Whitington; mayor, John Hadley, grocer.

Faringdon ward was by parliament appointed to be divided into two wards, to wit, infra and extra.

1394. The 18th, William Brampton, Thomas Knoles; mayor, John Froshe, mercer.

1395. The 19th, Roger Elles, William Shyryngham; mayor, William More, vintner.

1396. The 20th, Thomas Wilford, William Parker; mayor, Adam Bamme, goldsmith.

1397. The 21st, John Wodcoke, William Askam; mayor, Richard Whitington, mercer.

1398. The 22nd, John Wade, John Warnar; mayor, Drew Barentin, goldsmith.

Henry IV. began his reign the 29th of September, the year 1399.

1399. The 1st, sheriffs, William Waldern, William Hyde; mayor, Thomas Knoles, grocer.

1400. The 2nd, John Wakel, William Enote; mayor, John Francis, goldsmith.

1401. The 3rd, William Venor, John Fremelyngham; mayor, John Shadworth, mercer.

The conduit upon Cornhill was this year made of an old prison house called the Tun.

1402. The 4th, Richard Marlow, Robert Chicheley; mayor, I. Walcote, draper.

1403. The 5th, Thomas Falconer, Thomas Poole; mayor, W. Ascham, fishmonger.

1404. The 6th, William Louthe, Stephen Spilman; mayor, John Hend, draper.

This John Hend was a new builder of the parish church of St. Swithen, by London stone.

1405. The 7th, Henry Barton, William Crowmere; mayor, John Wodcocke, mercer.

This mayor caused all the weirs in the river of Thames, from Stanes to the river of Medway, to be destroyed, and the trinkes to be burned, etc.

1406. The 8th, Nicholas Wooton, Gefferey Brooke; mayor, Richard Whitington, mercer.

This year a great pestilence in London took away more than thirty thousand people.

1407. The 9th, Henry Pontfrackt, Henry Halton, mercer; mayor, William Stondon, grocer.

1408. The 10th, Thomas Duke, William Norton; mayor, Drew Barentine, goldsmith.

This Drew Barentine built a part of the Goldsmiths' hall, and gave them lands.

1409. The 11th, John Lane, William Chichley; mayor, Richard Marlow, ironmonger.

A great play at Skinners' well, which lasted eight days, and was of matter from the Creation of the world; the most part of all the great estates of England were there to behold it.

1410. The 12th, John Penne, Thomas Pike; mayor, Thomas Knoles, grocer.

This Thomas Knoles began anew to build the Guildhall in London, etc.

1411. The 13th, John Rainwel, William Cotton; mayor, Robert Chichley, grocer.

1412. The 14th, Raph Lobenham, William Sevenocke; mayor, William Waldren, mercer.

Henry V. began his reign, the 20th of March, the year 1412.

1413. The 1st, sheriffs, John Sutton, John Micholl; mayor, William Cromar, draper.

Sir John Oldcastle assembled a great power in Fickets field, by London, which power was overcome and taken by the king and his power.

1414. The 2nd, John Michell, Thomas Allen; mayor, Th. Falconer, mercer.

This mayor caused the postern called Moregate to be built, and he lent to the king ten thousand marks upon jewels, etc.

1415. The 3rd, William Cambridge, Alen Everard; mayor, Nicholas Wotton, draper.

1416. The 4th, Robert Whittington, John Coventrie; mayor, Henry Barton, skinner.

This Henry Barton ordained lanthorns with lights to be hanged out on the winter evening betwixt Hallontide [1] and Candlemasse.

1417. The 5th, H. Read, John Gidney; mayor, Richard Marlow, ironmonger.

1418. The 6th, John Brian, Raph Barton, John Parnesse; mayor, William Sevenoke.

This William Sevenoke, son to William Rumsched of Sevenoke in Kent, was by his father bound an apprentice with Hugh de Bois, citizen and ferrer of London, for a term of years, which being expired in the year 1394, the 18th of Richard II., John Hadley being mayor of London, and Stephen Spilman, chamberlain of the Guildhall, he alleged that his master had used the trade or mystery of a grocer, and not of a ferrer, and therefore required to be made free of the grocers' company, which was granted. This William Sevenoke founded in the town of Sevenoke a free school, and alms houses for the poor.

1419. The 7th, Robert Whytingham, John Butler; mayor, Richard Whittington, mercer.

This mayor founded Whittington college.

1420. The 8th, John Butler, John Wells; mayor, William Cambridge, grocer.

1421. The 9th, Richard Gosseline, William Weston; mayor, Robert Chichley, grocer.

---

[1] Hallontide,—or, as it was more generally designated, All Hallontide, —is the older designation of All Saints' day, the 1st of November.

This mayor gave one plot of ground, thereupon to build the parish church of St. Stephen upon Walbrooke.

Henry VI. began his reign the 31st of August, the year 1422.

1422. The 1st, sheriffs, William Eastfield, Robert Tatarsall; mayor, William Waldern, mercer.

This year the west gate of London was begun to be built by the executors of Richard Whitington.

1423. The 2nd, Nicholas James, Thomas Wandesford; mayor, William Cromer, draper.

1424. The 3rd, Simon Seman, John Bywater; mayor, John Michel, fishmonger.

1425. The 4th, William Melreth, John Brokle; mayor, John Coventrie, mercer.

1426. The 5th, John Arnold, John Higham; mayor, John Reinwell, fishmonger.

This mayor gave tenements to the city for the discharge of three wards in London for fifteens, etc.

1427. The 6th, Henry Frowicke, Robert Oteley; mayor, John Gidney, draper.

1428. The 7th, Thomas Duffehouse, John Abbot; mayor, Henry Barton, skinner.

1429. The 8th, William Russe, Raph Holland; mayor, William Eastfield, mercer.

Raph Holland gave to impotent poor, one hundred and twenty pounds, to prisoners eighty pounds, to hospitals forty pounds, etc.

1430. The 9th, Walter Chartesey, Robert Large; mayor, Nicholas Wotton, draper.

Walter Chartesey, draper, gave to the poor one hundred pounds, besides twenty pounds to the hospitals, etc.

1431. The 10th, John Hatherley, Stephen Browne; mayor, John Wels, grocer.

This John Wels, a great benefactor to the new building of the chapel by the Guildhall, and of his goods the standard in West Cheape was made.

1432. The 11th, John Olney, John Paddesley; mayor, John Parneis, fishmonger.

1433. The 12th, Thomas Chalton, John Ling; mayor, John Brokle, draper.

1434. The 13th, Thomas Barnewell, Simon Eyre; mayor, Robert Oteley, grocer.

1435. The 14th, Thomas Catworth, Robert Clopton; mayor, Henry Frowicke, mercer.

1436. The 15th, Thomas Morsted, William Gregorie; mayor, John Michel, fishmonger.

1437. The 16th, William Hales, William Chapman; mayor, Sir William Eastfield, mercer.

This Sir William Eastfield, knight of the Bath, a great benefactor to the water-conduits.

1438. The 17th, Hugh Dyke, Nicholas Yoo; mayor, Stephen Brown, grocer.

Wheat sold for three shillings the bushel; but this man sent into Prussia, and caused to be brought from thence certain ships laden with rye, which did great relief.

1439. The 18th, Philip Malpas, Robert Marshal; mayor, Robert Large, mercer.

Philip Malpas at his decease gave one hundred and twenty pounds to poor prisoners, and every year for five years four hundred and three shirts and smocks, forty pairs of sheets, and one hundred and fifty gowns of frieze to the poor, to poor maids' marriages one hundred marks, to highways one hundred marks, and to five hundred poor people in London every one six shillings and eight pence, etc.

1440. The 19th, John Sutton, William Wetinhale; mayor, John Paddesley, goldsmith, master of the works of money in the Tower of London.

1441. The 20th, William Combes, Richard Rich; mayor, Robert Clopton, draper.

1442. The 21st, Thomas Beamont, Richard Nordon; mayor, John Hatherley, ironmonger.

1443. The 22nd, Nicholas Wyfold, John Norman; mayor, Thomas Catworth, grocer.

1444. The 23rd, Stephen Forstar, Hugh Witch; mayor, Henry Frowicke, mercer.

This year Paul's steeple was fired with lightning, and hardly quenched.

1445. 24th, John Darby, Godfrey Filding; mayor, Simon Eyre, draper.

This Simon Eyre built the Leaden hall in London, to be a common garner for the city, etc.

1446. The 25th, Robert Horne, Godfrey Bolaine; mayor, John Olney, mercer.

1447. The 26th, William Abraham, Thomas Scot; mayor, John Gidney, draper.

1448. The 27th, William Cantelowe, William Marrow; mayor, Stephen Browne, grocer.

1449. The 28th, William Hulin, Thomas Caninges; mayor, Thomas Chalton, mercer.

This year Jack Cade, a rebel of Kent, came to London, entered the city, etc.

1450. The 29th, I. Middleton, William Deere; mayor, Nicholas Wyfold, grocer.

Soldiers made a fray against the mayor the same day he took his charge at Westminster.

1451. The 30th, Matthew Philip, Christopher Warter; mayor, William Gregory, skinner.

1452. The 31st, Richard Lee, Richard Alley; mayor, Godfrey Filding, mercer, of council to Henry VI. and Edward IV.

This year was a great fray at the wrestling.

1453. The 32nd, John Walden, Thomas Cooke; mayor, John Norman, draper.

This John Norman was the first mayor that was rowed to Westminster by water, for before that time they rode on horseback.

1454. The 33rd, John Field, W. Taylor; mayor, Stephen Forstar, fishmonger.

This Stephen Forstar enlarged Ludgate, for the ease of prisoners there, etc.

1455. The 34th, John Yong, Thomas Olgrave; mayor, William Marrow, grocer.

The mercers' servants made a riot upon the Lombards and other strangers.

1456. The 35th, John Styward, Raph Verney; mayor, Thomas Caning, grocer.

1457. The 36th, William Edwards, Thomas Reiner; mayor, Godfrey Boloine, mercer.

This Godfrey Boloine gave one thousand pounds to poor householders in London, etc.

1458. The 37th, Ralph Joceline, Richard Nedeham; mayor, Thomas Scot, draper.

1459. The 38th, John Plommar, John Stockar; mayor, William Hulin, fishmonger.

1460. 39th, Richard Fleming, John Lambard; mayor, Richard Lee, grocer.

Edward IV. began his reign the 4th of March, in the year 1460, after the account of the Church of England.

1461. The 1st, sheriffs, George Ireland, John Locke; mayor, Hugh Witch, mercer.

1462. The 2nd, William Hampton, Bartholomew James; mayor, Thomas Cooke, draper, made knight of the Bath in the 5th of Edward IV. and had great troubles after.

1463. The 3rd, Robert Basset, Thomas Muschampe; mayor, Matthew Philip, goldsmith, made knight of the Bath the 5th of Edward IV., and after in the field, the 10th of Edward IV.

1464. The 4th, John Tate, John Stone; mayor, Raph Joceline, draper, knight of the Bath, and also in the field.

1465. The 5th, Henry Waver, William Constantine; mayor, Raph Verney, mercer. Henry Waver, one of the sheriffs, made knight of the Bath.

1466. The 6th, John Bromer, Henry Brice; mayor, John Yong, grocer, made knight in the field.

This year began the troubles of Sir Thomas Cooke, and other aldermen, as ye may read in my *Summary*.

1467. The 7th, Thomas Stalbroke, Humfrey Heyford; mayor, Thomas Oldgrave, skinner.

1468. The 8th, Symon Smith, William Hariot; mayor, William Tayler, grocer.

This mayor gave tenements to discharge Cordwainer street ward of fifteens.

1469. The 9th, Richard Gardener, Robert Drope; mayor, Richard Lee, grocer.

This year the Tower of London being delivered to the mayor and his brethren, they delivered King Henry from thence.

1470. The 10th, Sir John Crosbie, John Ward; mayor, Sir John Stockton, mercer.

Thomas the Bastard Fauconbridge, with a riotous company, set upon this city at Aldgate, Bishopsgate, the Bridge, etc., and twelve aldermen, with the recorder, were knighted in the field by Edward IV., to wit, John Stockton, mayor, Raph Verney, late mayor, John Yong, later mayor, William Tayler, late mayor, Richard Lee, late mayor, Matthew Philips, late mayor, George Ireland, William Stoker, William Hampton, since mayor, Thomas Stolbroke, John Crosbie, and Bartlemew James, since mayor, with Thomas Urswike, recorder.

1471. The 11th, John Allin, John Shelley; mayor, William Edward, grocer.

The water-conduit at Aldermanburie, and the standard in Fleet street were finished.

1472. The 12th, John Browne, Thomas Bledlow; mayor, Sir William Hampton, fishmonger.

This Sir William Hampton punished strumpets, and caused stocks to be set in every ward to punish vagabonds.

1473. The 13th, Sir William Stokar, Robert Belisdon; mayor, John Tate, mercer.

This year the sheriffs of London were appointed each of them to have sixteen serjeants, every serjeant to have his yeoman, and six clerks, to wit, a secondary, a clerk of the papers, and four other clerks, besides the under-sheriff's clerks.

1474. The 14th, Edmond Shaw, Thomas Hill; mayor, Robert Drope, draper.

This Robert Drope increased the water-conduit upon Cornhill, etc.

1475. The 15th, Hugh Brice, Robert Colwich; mayor, Robert Basset, salter.

This Robert Basset corrected the bakers and other victuallers of this city.

1476. The 16th, Richard Rawson, William Horne; mayor, Sir Raph Joceline, draper, knight of the Bath.

By the diligence of this mayor the walls of the city were repaired.

1477. The 17th, Henry Collet, John Stoker; mayor, Humphrey Hayford, goldsmith.

1478. The 18th, Robert Harding, Robert Bifield; mayor, Richard Gardener, mercer.

Robert Bifield, sheriff, was fined by the mayor, and paid fifty pounds towards the water-conduits.

1479. The 19th, Thomas Ilam, John Warde; mayor, Sir Bartholomew James, draper, made knight in the field by Edward IV.

Thomas Ilam newly built the great conduit in West Cheape.

1480. The 20th, Thomas Daniel, William Bacon; mayor, John Browne, mercer.

1481. The 21st, Robert Tate, William Wiking; mayor, William Hariot, draper.

1482. The 22nd, William Whit, John Mathew; mayor, Edmond Sha, goldsmith.

This Edmond Sha caused the postern called Cripplesgate to be newly built, etc.

Edward V. began his reign the 9th of April, in the year 1483.

Richard III. began his reign the 22nd of June, in the year 1483.

1483. The 1st, sheriffs, Thomas Norland, William Martin; mayor, Robert Bilisden, haberdasher.

1484. The 2nd, Richard Chester, Thomas Brittaine, Raphe Austrie; mayor, Thomas Hill, grocer, Sir William Stocker, draper, John Ward, grocer.

Three sheriffs and three mayors this year by means of the sweating sickness, etc. Thomas Hill appointed by his testament the water-conduit in Grasse street to be built.

Henry VII. began his reign the 22nd of August, in the year 1485.

1485. The 1st, sheriffs, John Tate, John Swan; mayor, Hugh Brise, goldsmith.

This Hugh Brise was keeper of the king's mints at London.

1486. The 2nd, John Percivall, Hugh Clopton; mayor, Henry Collet, mercer.

The cross in Cheap was new built in beautiful manner.

1487. The 3rd, John Fenkell, William Remington; mayor, Sir William Horne, salter.

This William Horne made knight in the field by Henry VII., gave to the repairing of highways betwixt London and Cambridge five hundred marks, and to the preachers at Paul's cross, etc.

1488. The 4th, W. Isaack, Raph Tilney; mayor, Robert Tate, mercer.

1489. The 5th, William Caple, John Brocke; mayor, W. White, draper.

1490. The 6th, Henry Cote, Robert Revell, Hugh Pemberton; mayor, John Mathew, mercer.

1491. The 7th, Thomas Wood, William Browne; mayor, Hugh Clopton, mercer.

Hugh Clopton built the great stone bridge at Stratford upon Haven in Warwickshire.

1492. The 8th, William Purchase, William Welbecke; mayor, William Martin, skinner.

A riot made upon the Esterlings by the mercers' servants and other.

1493. The 9th, Robert Fabian, John Winger; mayor, Sir Raph Astrie, fishmonger, made knight by Henry VII.

Robert Fabian, alderman, made *Fabian's Chronicle*, a painful labour, to the honour of the city, and the whole realm.

1494. The 10th, Nicholas Alwine, John Warner; mayor, Richard Chawtry, salter.

1495. The 11th, Thomas Knesworth, Henry Somer; mayor, Henry Colet, mercer.

1496. The 12th, Sir John Sha, Sir Richard Haddon; mayor, Sir John Tate, the younger, mercer.

The king made this mayor, Robert Shefield, recorder, and both the sheriffs, knights, for their good service against the rebels at Black Hith field.

1497. The 13th, Bartlemew Read, Thomas Windout; mayor, W. Purchase, mercer.

All the gardens in the Morefield were destroyed, and made plain ground.

1498. Thomas Bradbury, Stephen Jeninges; mayor, Sir John Percevall, made knight in the field by King Henry VII.

1499. The 15th, James Wilford, Thomas Brond; mayor, Nicholas Alwin, mercer.

This Nicholas Alwin gave to three thousand poor people in London twelve pence the piece, and to three thousand in the town of Spalding, the like, etc.

1500. The 16th, John Hawes, William Steede; mayor, W. Remington, fishmonger.

1501. The 17th, Lawrence Ailmer, Henry Hede; mayor, Sir John Sha, goldsmith, made knight in the field by Henry VII.

This Sir John Sha caused his brethren the aldermen to ride from the Guildhall unto the water's side, where he took his barge to Westminster; he was sworn by the king's council: he commonly in the afternoons kept a court alone, called before him many matters, and redressed them.

1502. The 18th, Henry Kebel, Nicholas Nines; mayor, Bartlemew Reade, goldsmith.

1503. The 19th, Christopher Hawes, Robert Wats, Thomas Granger; mayor, Sir William Capell, draper, made knight by Henry VII.

This Sir William caused a cage in every ward to be set for punishing of vagabonds.

1504. The 20th, Roger Acheley, William Brown; mayor, John Winger, grocer.

1505. The 21st, Richard Shore, Roger Grove; mayor, Thomas Knesworth, fishmonger.

This Thomas Knesworth appointed the water-conduit at Bishopsgate to be built, etc.

1506. The 22nd, William Copenger, Thomas Johnson, William Fitzwilliams, merchant-tailor, after of council to Henry VIII.; mayor, Sir Richard Haddon, mercer.

1507. The 23rd, William Butler, John Kirkby; mayor, William Browne, mercer, for part, Lawrence Ailmer, draper.

1508. The 24th, Thomas Exmew, Richard Smith; mayor, Stephen Jeninges, merchant-tailor.

This Stephen Jeninges built the greatest part of St. Andrewes church called Undershaft. He built a free-school at Ulfrune-hampton in Staffordshire, etc.

Henry VIII. began his reign the 22nd of April, the year 1509.

1509. The 1st, sheriffs, George Monoxe, John Doget; mayor, Thomas Bradbury, mercer, for part, Sir William Caple, draper.

1510. The 2nd, John Milborne, John Rest; mayor, Henry Keble, grocer.

This Henry Keble gave one thousand pounds toward the new building of his parsh church of Aldermary.

1511. The 3rd, Nicholas Shelton, Thomas Mirfine; mayor, Roger Acheley, draper.

This Roger Acheley provided corn for service of this city in great plenty. He caused the same to be stowed up in the common garner called Leaden hall.

1512. The 4th, Robert Aldarnes, Robert Fenrother; mayor, Sir William Copinger, fishmonger, for part, Richard Haddon, mercer, for the rest.

Sir W. Copinger gave half his goods to his wife, and the other half to the poor that had most need.

1513. The 5th, John Dawes, John Bridges, Roger Basford; mayor, W. Browne, mercer, and John Tate, mercer.

This John Tate new built the church of St. Anthonies hospital in London.

1514. The 6th, James Yarford, John Monday; mayor, George Monoux, draper.

1515. The 7th, Henry Warley, Richard Grey, W. Bayly; mayor, Sir William Butler, grocer.

1516. The 8th, Thomas Seimer, John Thurstone; mayor, John Rest, grocer.

1517. The 9th, Thomas Baldrie, Raph Simondes; mayor, Sir Thomas Exmew, goldsmith.

Sir Thomas Exmew made the water-conduit in London wall by Mooregate, etc.

1518. The 10th, John Allen, James Spencer; mayor, Thomas Mirfin, skinner.

1519. The 11th, John Wilkenson, Nicholas Partrich; mayor, Sir James Yarford, mercer.

From this time the mayors of London, for the most part, have been knighted by courtesy of the kings, and not otherwise.

1520. The 12th, Sir John Skevington, John Kyme; mayor, Sir John Bruge, draper.

1521. The 13th, John Breton, Thomas Pargetor; mayor, Sir John Milborne, draper.

This Sir John Milborne founded fourteen alms houses by the Crossed Fryers church, etc.

1522. The 14th, John Rudstone, John Champneis; mayor, Sir John Mundy, goldsmith.

1523. The 15th, Michael English, Nicholas Jenines; mayor, Sir R. Baldry, mercer.

1524. The 16th, Raph Dodmer, William Roche; mayor, Sir W. Bayly, draper.

1525. The 17th, John Caunton, Christopher Askew; mayor, Sir John Allen, mercer.

1526. The 18th, Stephen Peacocke, Nicholas Lambert; mayor, Sir Thomas Seamer, mercer.

1527. The 19th, John Hardy, William Holles; mayor, Sir James Spencer, vintner.

1528. The 20th, Raph Warren, John Long; mayor, Sir John Rudstone, draper.

1529. The 21st, Michael Dormer, Walter Champion; mayor, Sir Raph Dodmer, mercer.

This year it was decreed that no man should be mayor of London more than one year.

1530. The 22nd, William Dauntsey, Richard Choppyn; mayor, Sir T. Pargitor, salter.

1531. The 23rd, Richard Gresham, Edward Altham; mayor, Sir Nicholas Lambard, grocer.

1532. The 24th, Richard Reynoldes, Nicholas Pinchon, John Martin, John Prest; mayor, Sir Stephen Pecocke, haberdasher,

1533. The 25th, William Forman, Sir T. Kitson; mayor, Sir Christopher Askew, draper.

1534. The 26th, Nicholas Levison, W. Denham; mayor, Sir John Champneis, skinner.

1535. The 27th, Humfrey Munmoth, John Cootes; mayor, Sir John Allen, mercer. By the king's appointment he was of his council. A man of great wisdom, and also of great charity.

The forenamed sheriffs, Munmouth and Cootes, put away twelve serjeants and twelve yeomen, but were by a common council forced to take them again.

1536. The 28th, Robert Paget, William Boyer; mayor, Sir Raph Waren, mercer.

1537. The 29th, Sir John Gresham, Thomas Lewen; mayor, Sir Richard Gresham, mercer.

1538. The 30th, William Wilkenson, Nicholas Gibson; mayor, William Forman, haberdasher.

1539. The 31st, John Feiry, Thomas Huntlow; mayor, Sir W. Holles, mercer.

1540. The 32nd, Sir William Laxton, Martin Bowes; mayor, Sir William Roch, draper.

1541. The 33rd, Rowland Hill, Henry Suckley; mayor, Sir Michael Dormer, mercer.

1542. The 34th, Henry Habberthorne, Henry Amcotes; mayor, John Cootes, salter.

1543. The 35th, John Toleus, Richard Dobbes; mayor, Sir W. Bowyer, draper, for part, Sir Raph Waren, mercer.

1544. The 36th, John Wilford, Andrew Jude; mayor, Sir W. Laxton, grocer.

1545. The 37th, George Barnes, Ralph Alley; mayor, Sir Martin Bowes, goldsmith.

1546. The 38th, Richard Jarveis, Thomas Curteis; mayor, Sir Henry Hubbarthorne, merchant-tailor.

Edward VI. began his reign the 28th of January, in the year 1546.

1547. The 1st, sheriffs, Thomas White, Robert Charsey; mayor, Sir John Gresham, mercer.

1548. The 2nd, William Locke, Sir John Ailife; mayor, Sir Henry Amcotes, fishmonger.

1549. The 3rd, Richard Turke, John Yorke; mayor, Rowland Hill, mercer.

1550. The 4th, Augustine Hind, John Lyon; mayor, Sir Andrew Judd, skinner.

1551. The 5th, John Lamberd, John Cowper; mayor, Sir Richard Dobbes, skinner.

1552. The 6th, William Gerard, John Maynard; mayor, Sir George Barnes, haberdasher.

Queen Mary began her reign, the 6th of July, the year 1553.

1553. The 1st, sheriffs, Thomas Ofley, William Huet; mayor, Sir Thomas White, merchant-tailor.

This Thomas White founded St. John's college, in Oxford. He gave to the city of Bristow two thousand pounds.

1554. The 2nd, David Woodrofe, William Chester; mayor, Sir John Lion, grocer.

1555. The 3rd, Thomas Leigh, John Machil; mayor, Sir William Gerard, haberdasher.

1556. The 4th, William Harper, John White; mayor, Sir Thomas Ofley, merchant-tailor.

1557. The 5th, Richard Malorie, James Aitham; mayor, Sir Thomas Curteis, fishmonger.

1558. The 6th, John Halse, Richard Champion; mayor, Sir Thomas Legh, mercer.

Queen Elizabeth began her reign, the 17th of November, in the year of Christ 1558.

1559. The 1st, sheriffs, Thomas Lodge, Roger Martin; mayor, Sir William Huet, clothworker.

1560. The 2nd, Christopher Draper, Thomas Row; mayor, Sir William Chester, draper.

This year the merchant-tailors founded their notable free-school for poor men's children, etc.

1561. The 3rd, Alexander Avenon, Humfrey Baskervile; mayor, Sir William Harper, merchant-tailor.

1562. The 4th, William Alin, Richard Chamberlaine; mayor, Sir Thomas Lodge, grocer.

1563. The 5th, Edward Bankes, Rowland Heyward; mayor, Sir John White, grocer.

1564. The 6th, Edward Jackeman, Lionel Ducket; mayor, Sir Richard Malorie, mercer.

1565. The 7th, John Rivers, James Hawes; mayor, Sir Richard Champion, draper.

1566. The 8th, Richard Lambert, Ambrose Nicholas, John Langley; mayor, Sir Christopher Draper, ironmonger.

1567. The 9th, Thomas Ramsey, William Bond; mayor, Sir Roger Martin, mercer.

1568. The 10th, John Oleph, Robert Harding, James Bacon; mayor, Sir Thomas Row, merchant-tailor.

1569. The 11th, Henry Becher, William Dane; mayor, Alexander Avenon, ironmonger.

1570. The 12th, Francis Bernam, William Box; mayor, Sir Rowland Heyward, clothworker.

1571. The 13th, Henry Miles, John Braunch; mayor, Sir William Allin, mercer.

1572. The 14th, Richard Pipe, Nicholas Woodrofe; mayor, Sir Lionel Ducket, mercer.

1573. The 15th, James Harvy, Thomas Pullison; mayor, Sir J. Rivers, grocer.

1574. The 16th, Thomas Blanke, Anthony Gamage; mayor, James Hawes, clothworker.

1575. The 17th, Edward Osborne, Wolstane Dixie; mayor, Ambrose Nicholas, salter.

1576. The 18th, William Kimpton, George Barne; mayor, Sir John Langley, goldsmith.

1577. The 19th, Nicholas Backhouse, Francis Bowyer; mayor, Sir Thomas Ramsey, grocer.

1578. The 20th, George Bond, Thomas Starkie; mayor, Sir Richard Pipe, draper.

1579. The 21st, Martin Calthrope, John Hart; mayor, Sir Nicholas Woodrofe, haberdasher.

1580. The 22nd, Ralph Woodcock, John Alate; mayor, Sir John Branch, draper.

1581. The 23rd, Richard Martin, William Webbe; mayor, Sir James Harvie, ironmonger.

1582. The 24th, William Roe, John Hayden, Cuthbert Buckle; mayor, Sir Thomas Blancke, haberdasher.

1583. The 25th, William Masham, John Spencer; mayor, Edward Osborne, clothworker.

1584. The 26th, Stephen Slany, Henry Billingsley; mayor, Sir Thomas Pullison, draper.

1585. The 27th, Anthony Radclife, Henry Pranell; mayor, Sir Wolstane Dixie, skinner.

1586. The 28th, Robert House, William Elkin; mayor, Sir George Barne, haberdasher.

1587. The 29th, Thomas Skinner, John Katcher; mayor, Sir George Bond, haberdasher.

1588. The 30th, Hugh Ofley, Richard Saltenstall; mayor, Sir Martin Calthrope, draper, for part, and Richard Martin, goldsmith, for the rest of that year.

1589. The 31st, Richard Gurney, Stephen Some; mayor, Sir John Hart, grocer.

1590. The 32nd, Nicholas Mosley, Robert Broke; mayor, John Allot, fishmonger, for part, Sir Rowland Heyward, clothworker, for the rest.

1591. The 33rd, William Rider, Benet Barnham; mayor, Sir William Webb, salter.

1592. The 34th, John Garrard, Robert Taylor; mayor, Sir William Roe, ironmonger.

1593. The 35th, Paule Banning, Peter Hauton; mayor, Sir

Cuthbert Buckie, vintner, for part, Sir Richard Martin, gold-smith, for the rest.

1594. The 36th, Robert Lee, Thomas Benet; mayor, Sir John Spencer, clothworker.

1595. The 37th, Thomas Low, Leonard Holiday; mayor, Sir Stephen Slany, skinner.

1596. The 38th, John Wattes, Richard Godard; mayor, Thomas Skinner, clothworker, for part, Sir Henry Billingsley, haberdasher.

1597. The 39th, Henry Roe, John More; mayor, Sir Richard Saltenstall, skinner.

1598. The 40th, Edward Holmeden, Robert Hampson; mayor, Sir Stephen Some, grocer.

1599. The 41st, Humfrey Welde, grocer, Roger Clarke, salter; mayor, Sir Nicholas Mosley, clothworker.

1600. The 42nd, Thomas Cambell, ironmonger, Thomas Smith, haberdasher, William Craven, merchant-tailor; mayor, Sir William Rider, haberdasher.

1601. The 43rd, Henry Anderson, girdler; William Glover, dyer; mayor, Sir John Garrard, haberdasher.

1602. The 44th, James Pemberton, goldsmith, John Swiner-ton, merchant-tailor; mayor, Robert Lee, merchant-tailor.

Thus much for the chief and principal governors of this famous city; of whose public government, with the assistance of inferior officers, their charges for keeping of the peace, service of the prince, and honour of this city, much might have been said, and I had thought to have touched more at large; but being informed that a learned gentleman (James Dalton, a citizen born), minded such a labour, and promised to perform it, I have forborne and left the same to his good leisure, but he being now lately deceased without finishing any such work (a common fault to promise more than to perform), and I hear not of any other that taketh it in hand, I have been divers times minded to add certain chapters to this book, but being (by the good pleasure of God) visited with sickness, such as my feet (which have borne me many a mile) have of late years refused, once in four or five months, to convey me from my bed to my study, and therefore could not do as I would.

At length, remembering I had long since gathered notes to have chaptered, am now forced to deliver them unperfected, and desire the readers to pardon me, that want not will to pleasure them.

ALDERMEN AND SHERIFFS OF LONDON

There be in this city, according to the number of wards, twenty-six aldermen; whereof yearly, on the feast day of St. Michael the Archangel, one of them is elected to be mayor for the year following, to begin on the 28th of October: the other aldermen, his brethren, are to him assistants in councils, courts, etc.

More, there is a recorder of London, a grave and learned lawyer, skilful in the customs of this city, also assistant to the lord mayor: he taketh place in councils and in courts before any man that hath not been mayor, and learnedly delivereth the sentences of the whole court.

The sheriffs of London, of old time chosen out of the commonalty, commoners, and oftentimes never came to be aldermen, as many aldermen were never sheriffs, and yet advanced to be mayor, but of late (by occasion) the sheriffs have been made aldermen before or presently after their election.

Nicholas Faringdon was never sheriff, yet four times mayor of this city, and so of other, which reproveth a bye word, such a one will be mayor, or he be sheriff, etc.

Then is there a chamberlain of London.

A common clerk, or town clerk.

A common sergeant.

OFFICERS BELONGING TO THE LORD MAYOR'S HOUSE

Sword-bearer,
Common hunt,
Common crier, } esquires, four.
Water bailiff.
Coroner of London.
Sergeant carvers, three.
Sergeants of the chamber, three.
Sergeant of the channel.
Yeoman of the channel.
Yeomen of the water side, four.
Under water-bailiff.
Yeomen of the chamber, two.
Meal weighers, three.
Yeomen of the wood wharfs, two.

The sword-bearer's man. ⎫
Common hunt's men, two. ⎪
Common crier's man. ⎬ gentlemen's men, seven.
Water-bailiffs' men, two. ⎪
The carver's man. ⎭

Whereof nine of these have liveries of the lord mayor, viz., the sword-bearer, and his man, the three carvers, and the four yeomen of the water side; all the rest have their liveries from the chamber of London.

Thus far after my notes delivered by an officer of the lord mayor's house, but unperfected; for I remember a crowner, an under-chamberlain, and four clerks of the mayor's court, and others.

THE SHERIFFS OF LONDON; THEIR OFFICERS

The sheriffs of London, in the year 1471, were appointed each of them to have sixteen sergeants, every sergeant to have his yeoman, and six clerks; to wit, a secondary, a clerk of the papers, and four other clerks, besides the under sheriffs' clerks, their stewards, butlers, porters, and other in household many.

OF THE MAYOR'S AND SHERIFFS' LIVERIES SOMEWHAT

To follow precedent of former time, the clerks of companies were to inquire for them of their companies that would have the mayor's livery, their money as a benevolence given, which must be twenty shillings at the least put in a purse, with their names that gave it, and the wardens to deliver it to the mayor by the first of December; for the which every man had then sent him four yards of broad cloth, rowed or striped athwart, with a different colour to make him a gown, and these were called ray gowns, which was then the livery of the mayor, and also of the sheriffs, but each differing from others in the colours.

Of older times I read, that the officers of this city wore gowns of party colours, as the right side of one colour and the left side of another; as, for example, I read in books of accounts in the Guildhall, that in the 19th year of Henry VI. there was bought for an officer's gown two yards of cloth, coloured mustard villars (a colour now out of use), and two yards of cloth, coloured blue, price two shillings the yard, in all eight shillings. More, paid to John Pope, draper, for two gown cloths, eight yards of two colours, *eux ombo deux de rouge* (or red), *medle bune*, and *porre* (or purple) colour, price the yard two shillings. These gowns were for Piers Rider and John Bukles, clerks of the chamber.

More, I read that in the year 1516, in the 7th of Henry VIII., it was agreed by a common council in the Guildhall that the sheriffs of London should (as they had been accustomed) give yearly rayed gowns to the recorder, chamberlain, common sergeant, and common clerk, the sword-bearer, common hunt, water-bailiff, common crier, like as to their own offices, etc.

1525. More, in the 16th of Henry VIII., Sir William Bayly, then being mayor, made a request, for that clothes of ray (as he alleged) were evil wrought, his officers might be permitted (contrary to custom) for that year to wear gowns of one colour; to the which, in a common council, one answered and said, " Yea, it might be permitted," and no man said, " Nay," and so it passed. Thus much for party coloured and ray gowns have I read: but for benevolence to the mayor, I find that of later time that each man giving forty shillings towards his charges, received four yards of broad cloth to make him a gown, for Thomas White performed it in the 1st of Queen Mary; but Sir Thomas Lodge gave instead of four yards of broad cloth, three yards of satin to make them doublets, and since that the three yards of satin is turned into a silver spoon, and so it holdeth.

The days of attendance that the fellowships do give to the mayor at his going to Paules were seven, as followeth:—

1. Alhallowen day.
2. Christmasse day.
3. St. Stephen's day.
4. St. John's day.
5. New Year's day.
6. Twelfth day.
7. Candlemasse day.

The 23rd of Henry VIII., these companies had place at the mayor's feast in the Guildhall, in order as followeth; I speak by precedent, for I was never feast-follower:—

1. Mercers, the wardens, and seventeen persons, five messes.
2. Grocers, the wardens, and sixteen persons, four messes.
3. Drapers, the wardens, and twelve persons, four messes.
4. Fishmongers, the wardens, and twelve persons, four messes.
5. Goldsmiths, the wardens, and ten persons, three messes.

6. Skinners, the wardens, and eight persons, three messes.

7. Merchant-tailors, the wardens, and nine persons, three messes.

8. Vintners, the wardens, and six persons, two messes.

9. Ironmongers, the wardens, and four persons, four messes and a half.

10. Merchant-haberdashers, the wardens, and fourteen persons, four messes and a half.

11. Salters, the wardens, and eight persons, two messes and a half.

12. Dyers, the wardens, and six persons, two messes.

13. Leathersellers, the wardens, and eight persons, three messes.

14. Pewterers, the wardens, and five persons, two messes.

15. Cutlers, the wardens and five persons, two messes.

16. Armourers, the wardens and three persons, one mess.

17. Waxchandlers, the wardens and six persons, two messes.

18. Tallow-chandlers, the wardens and three persons, two messes.

19. Shiremen, the wardens and five persons, two messes.

20. Fullers, the wardens and nine persons, two messes.

21. Sadlers, the wardens and four persons, two messes.

22. Brewers, the wardens and twelve persons, four messes.

23. Scriveners, the wardens and six persons, two messes.

24. Butchers, the wardens and seven persons, three messes.

25. Bakers, the wardens and four persons, two messes.

26. Poulterers, the wardens and one person, one mess.

27. Stationers, the wardens and two persons, one mess.

28. Inholders, the wardens and four persons, two messes.

29. Girdlers, the wardens and four persons, two messes.

30. Chirurgeons, the wardens and two persons, one mess.

31. Founders, the wardens and one person, one mess.

32. Barbers, the wardens and four persons, two messes.

No Clothing. Upholders, the wardens and two persons, one mess.

34. Broiderers, the wardens and two persons, one mess.

35. Bowyers, the wardens and two persons, one mess.

36. Fletchers, the wardens and two persons, one mess.

No Clothing. Turners, the wardens and two persons, one mess.

38. Cordwainers, the wardens and four persons, two messes.

39. Painters-stainers, the wardens and five persons, two messes.

40. Masons, the wardens and one person, one mess.
41. Plumbers, the wardens and two persons, one mess.
42. Carpenters, the wardens and four persons, two messes.
43. Pouch-makers, the wardens and two persons, one mess.
44. Joiners, the wardens and two persons, one mess.
45. Coopers, the wardens and one person, one mess.

No Clothing. Glaziers, the wardens and two persons, one mess.

No Clothing. Linendrapers, the wardens and two persons, one mess.

No Clothing. Woodmongers, the wardens and two persons, one mess.

49. Curriers, the wardens and two persons, one mess.

No Clothing. Foystors, the wardens and two persons, one mess.

No Clothing. Grey Tanners, the wardens and two persons, one mess.

52. Tilers, the wardens and one person, one mess.
53. Weavers, the wardens and one person, one mess.
54. Blacksmiths, the wardens, and one mess.

No Clothing. Lorimars, the wardens and two persons, one mess.

56. Spurriers, the wardens and two persons, one mess.
57. Wiresellers, the wardens and two persons, one mess.

No Clothing. Fruiterers, the wardens and two persons, one mess.

No Clothing. Farriers, the wardens and two persons, one mess.

60. Bladesmiths, the wardens and two persons, one mess.

These companies severally, at sundry times, purchased the king's favour and license by his letters patents, to associate themselves in brotherhoods, with master and wardens for their government: many also have procured corporations, with privileges, etc.; but I read not of license by them procured for liveries to be worn, but at their governor's discretion to appoint, as occasion asketh, some time in triumphant manner, some time more mourning like, and such liveries have they taken upon them, as well before, as since they were by license associated into brotherhoods, or corporations. For the first of these companies that I read of to be a guild, brotherhood, or fraternity, in this city, were the weavers, whose guild was confirmed by Henry II. The next fraternity, which was of St. John Baptist, time out of mind, called of tailors and linen-armourers of London; I find that King Edward I., in the 28th of his reign, confirmed that guild by the name of tailors and linen-armourers, and gave to the brethren there of authority yearly to choose unto them a governor, or master, with wardens, etc.   The other companies have since purchased license of societies, brotherhoods, or corporations, in the reigns of Edward III., Richard II., Henry IV., Henry V., Henry VI., and Edward IV., etc.

SOMEWHAT OF LIVERIES WORN BY CITIZENS OF LONDON, IN TIME OF TRIUMPHS AND OTHERWAYS

1236. The 20th of Henry III., the mayor, aldermen, sheriffs, and citizens of London, rode out to meet the king and his new wife, Queen Elianor, daughter to Reymond Beringarius of Aragon, earl of Provence and Narbone. The citizens were clothed in long garments, embroidered about with gold, and silk in divers colours, their horses finely trapped, to the number of three hundred and sixty, every man bearing a golden or silver cup in his hand, the king's trumpets before them sounding, etc., as ye may read in my *Annales*.

1300. The 29th of Edward I., the said king took to wife Margaret, sister to Philip Le Beau, king of France; they were married at Canterbury. The queen was conveyed to London, against whom the citizens to the number of six hundred rode in one livery of red and white, with the cognizances of their mysteries embroidered upon their sleeves, they received her four miles out of London, and so conveyed her to Westminster.

1415. The 3rd of Henry V., the said king arriving at Dover, the mayor of London with the aldermen and crafts-men riding in red, with hoods red and white, met with the king on the Blacke hith, coming from Eltham with his prisoners out of France.

1432. The 10th of Henry VI., he being crowned in France, returning into England, came to Eltham towards London, and the mayor of London, John Welles, the aldermen, with the commonalty, rode against him on horseback, the mayor in crimson velvet, a great velvet hat furred, a girdle of gold about his middle, and a bawdrike of gold about his neck trilling down behind him, his three henxmen, on three great coursers following him, in one suit of red, all spangled in silver, then the aldermen in gowns of scarlet, with sanguine hoods, and all the commonality of the city clothed in white gowns, and scarlet hoods, with divers cognizances embroidered on their sleeves, etc.

1485. The 1st of Henry VII., the mayor, aldermen, sheriffs, and commonality, all clothed in violet (as in a mourning colour), met the king at Shorditch, and conveyed him to Powles church, where he offered his banners.

Thus much for liveries of citizens in ancient times, both in triumphs and otherwise, may suffice, whereby may be observed, that the coverture of men's heads was then hoods, for neither cap nor hat is spoken of, except that John Welles mayor of London to wear a hat in time of triumph, but differing from the hats lately taken in use, and now commonly worn for noblemen's liveries. I read that Thomas earl of Lancaster in the reign of Edward II. gave at Christmas in liveries, to such as served him, a hundred and fifty-nine broad cloaths, allowing to every garment furs to fur their hoods: more near our time, there yet remaineth the counterfeits and pictures of aldermen, and others that lived in the reigns of Henry VI. and Edward IV., namely aldermen Darby dwelling in Fenchurch street, over against the parish church of St. Diones, left his picture, as of an alderman, in a gown of scarlet on his back, a hood on his head, etc., as is in that house (and elsewhere) to be seen: for a further monument of those late times, men may behold the glass windows of the mayor's court in the Guildhall above the stairs, the mayor is there pictured sitting in habit, party-coloured, and a hood on his head, his swordbearer before him with a hat or cap of maintenance: the common clerk, and other officers bare-headed, their hoods on their shoulders; and therefore I take it, that the use of square bonnets worn by noblemen, gentlemen, citizens, and others, took beginning in this realm by Henry VII. and in his time, and of further antiquity, I can see no counterfeit or other proof of use. Henry VIII. (towards his latter reign) wore a round flat cap of scarlet or of velvet, with a bruch or jewel, and a feather; divers gentlemen, courtiers, and others, did the like. The youthful citizens also took them to the new fashion of flat caps, knit of woollen yarn black, but so light, that they were obliged to tie them under their chins, for else the wind would be master over them. The use of these flat round caps so far increased (being of less price than the French bonnet) that in short time young aldermen took the wearing of them; Sir John White wore it in his mayoralty, and was the first that left example to his followers; but now the Spanish felt, or the like counterfeit, is most commonly of all men both spiritual and temporal taken to use, so that the French bonnet or square cap, and also the round or flat cap, have for the most part given place to the Spanish felt; but yet in London amongst the graver sort (I mean the liveries of companies), remaineth a memory of the hoods of old time worn by their predecessors: these hoods were worn, the roundlets upon their heads, the skirts to hang behind in their necks to keep them warm, the tippet to lie on their shoulder, or to wind about their necks, these hoods were of old time made in colours according to their gowns, which were of two colours, as red and blue, or red and purple, murrey, or as it pleased their masters and wardens to appoint to the companies; but now of late time, they have used their gowns to be all of one colour, and those of the saddest, but their hoods being made the one half of the same cloth their gowns be of, the other half remaineth red as of old time. And so I end, as wanting time to travel further in this work.

Now since that I have given you an outward view of this city, it shall not be impertinent to let you take an insight also of the same, such as a Londoner born discoursed about twenty years gone, for answer (as it seemeth) to some objections that then were made against the growing greatness thereof. The author gave it me, and therefore, howsoever I conceal his name (which itself pretendeth not), I think I may without his offence impart it to others, that they may take pleasure in the reading, as I doubt not but he did in the writing. Long may they (that list) envy, and long may we and our posterity enjoy the good estate of this city.

A DISCOURSE

OF THE

NAMES AND FIRST CAUSES OF THE INSTITUTION OF CITIES AND PEOPLED TOWNS

AND OF THE COMMODITIES THAT DO GROW BY THE SAME; AND, NAMELY, OF THE CITY OF LONDON

WRITTEN BY WAY OF AN APOLOGY (OR DEFENCE) AGAINST THE OPINION OF SOME MEN, WHICH THINK THAT THE GREATNESS OF THAT CITY STANDETH NOT WITH THE PROFIT AND SECURITY OF THIS REALM

CITIES and well-peopled places be called *Oppida*, in Latin; either *ab ope danda*, or *ab opibus*, or *ab opponendo se hostibus*. They be named also *Civitates a cöeundo*, and *urbes*, either of the word *urbare*, because the first inclosure of them was described with the draught of a plough, or else *ab orbe*, for the round compass that they at the first had.

In the Greek a city is termed πόλις, either of the word πολὺς, *multus*, or of πολεῖνω πολένεον,[1] *id est, habitare, alere, gubernare*.

In the Saxon (or old English) sometimes *Tun*, which we now call town, derived of the word *Tynan*, to inclose or tyne, as some yet speak. But forasmuch as that word was proper to every village and inclosed dwelling, therefore our ancestors called their walled towns *Burh* or *Byrg*, and we now Bury and Borough, of the Greek word πύργος (as I think), which signifieth a tower or a high building.

The walls of these towns had their name of *vallum*, because at the first they were but of that earth which was cast out of the trench, or ditch, wherewith they were environed. But afterward, being made of matter more fit for defence, they were named *a muniendo mænia*. By the etymology of these names, it may appear that common weals, cities, and towns, were at the first invented, to the end that men might lead a civil life amongst themselves, and be saved harmless against their

[1] Sic in Stow; Strype corrects it into πολεύω.

enemies; whereupon Plato saith, "*Civitates ab initio utilitatis causa constitutæ sunt.*" Aristotle, 1. Politicorum, 2. saith, "*Civitas a natura profecta est: homo enim animal aptum est ad cœtus, et proinde civitatis origo ad viuendum, institutio ad bene viuendum refertur.*" And Cicero, *lib. primo de Inventione*, in the beginning, saith, "*Fuit quoddam tempus cum in agris homines passim bestiarum more vagabantur, etc. quo quidem tempore, quidam (magnus, viz. vir et sapiens) dispersos homines in agris, et tectis silvestribus abditos, ratione quadam compulit in unum locum, atque eos in unamquamq; rem induxit utilem et honestam. Urbibus vero constitutis fidem colere, et justitiam retinere discebant, et aliis parere sua voluntate consuescebant,*" etc. The same man discourseth notably to the same effect in his Oration *Pro Sestio*, a little after the midst thereof, showing that in the life of men dispersed, *vis*, beareth all the sway; but in the civil life, *ars* is better maintained, etc. This thing well saw King William the Conqueror, who in his laws, fol. 125, saith, "*Burgi et civitates fundata, et edificata sunt, ad tuitionem gentium et populorum Regni, et idcirco observari debent cum omni libertate, integritate et ratione.*" And his predecessors, King Ethelstane and King Canutus, in their laws, fol. 62 and 106, had commanded thus: "*Oppida instaurantur,*" etc.

Seeing, therefore, that as Cicero, 2. *Officior.* saith, "*Proxime et secundum Deos, homines hominibus maxime utiles esse possunt;* " and that men are congregated into cities and common-wealths for honesty and utility's sake, these shortly be the commodities that do come by cities, commonalties, and corporations. First, men by this nearness of conversation are withdrawn from barbarous feritie and force to a certain mildness of manners, and to humanity and justice; whereby they are contented to give and take right, to and from their equals and inferiors, and to hear and obey their heads and superiors. Also the doctrine of God is more fitly delivered, and the discipline thereof more aptly to be executed, in peopled towns than abroad, by reason of the facility of common and often assembling; and consequently such inhabitants be better managed in order, and better instructed in wisdom: whereof it came to pass, that at the first, they that excelled others this way, were called *astuti*, of the Greek word ἄστυ, which signifieth a city, although the term be now declined to the worst part, and do betoken evil, even as *tyrannus, sophista,* and some such other originally good words are fallen; and hereof also good behaviour is yet called *urbanitas*, because it is rather found in cities than elsewhere. In some, by often hearing men be better persuaded in religion, and for that they live in the eyes of others, they be by example the more easily trained to justice, and by shamefastness restrained from injury.

And whereas commonwealths and kingdoms cannot have, next after God, any surer foundation than the love and good-will of one man towards another, that also is closely bred and maintained in cities, where men by mutual society and companying together, do grow to alliances, commonalties, and corporations.

The liberal sciences and learnings of all sorts, which be *lumina reipublicæ*, do flourish only in peopled towns; without the which a realm is in no better case than a man that lacketh both his eyes.

Manual arts, or handicrafts, as they have for the most part been invented in towns and cities, so they cannot anywhere else be either maintained or amended. The like is to be said of merchandise, under which name I comprehend all manner of buying, selling, bartering, exchanging, communicating of things that men need to and fro. Wealth and riches, which are truly called *subsidia belli, et ornamenta pacis*, are increased chiefly in towns and cities both to the prince and people.

The necessity of the poor and needy is in such places both sooner to be espied, and hath means to be more charitably relieved.

The places themselves be surer refuges in all extremities of foreign invasion, and the inhabitants be a ready hand and strength of men, with munition to oppress intestine sedition.

Moreover, forasmuch as the force of the wars of our time consisteth chiefly in shot, all other soldiers being either horsemen or footmen, armed on land, or mariners at the sea, it seemeth to me that citizens and townsmen be as fit to be employed in any of these services, that on horseback only excepted, as the inhabitants that be drawn out of the country.

Furthermore, even as these societies and assemblies of men in cities and great towns are a continual bridle against tyranny, which was the cause that Tarquin, Nero, Dionysius, and such others, have always sought to weaken them: so, being well tempered, they are a strong fort and bulwark, not only in the aristocracy, but also in the lawful kingdom or just royalty.

At once the propagation of religion, the execution of good policy, the exercise of charity, and the defence of the country, is best performed by towns and cities; and this civil life approacheth nearest to the shape of that mystical body whereof

Christ is the head, and men be the members; whereupon both at the first, that man of God Moses, in the commonwealth of the Israelites, and the governors of all countries, in all ages since, have continually maintained the same; and to change it were nothing else but to metamorphose the world, and to make wild beasts of reasonable men. To stand longer upon this it were, *in re non dubia, uti oratione non necessaria;* and therefore I will come to London.

THE SINGULARITIES OF THE CITY OF LONDON

Whatsoever is said of cities generally, maketh also for London specially; howbeit, these things are particularly for our purpose to be considered in it. The situation; the former estimation that it hath had; the service that it hath done; the present estate and government of it, and such benefits as do grow to the realm by the maintenance thereof.

This realm hath only three principal rivers, whereon a royal city may well be situated: Trent, in the north, Severn in the south-west, and Thames in the south-east; of the which Thames, both for the straight course in length reacheth furthest into the belly of the land, and for the breadth and stillness of the water is most navigable up and down the stream; by reason whereof London, standing almost in the middle of that course, is more commodiously served with provision of necessaries than any town standing upon the other two rivers can be, and doth also more easily communicate to the rest of the realm the commodities of her own intercourse and traffic.

This river openeth indifferently upon France and Flanders, our mightiest neighbours, to whose doings we ought to have a bent eye and special regard; and this city standeth thereon in such convenient distance from the sea, as it is not only near enough for intelligence of the affairs of those princes, and for the resistance of their attempts, but also sufficiently removed from the fear of any sudden dangers that may be offered by them; whereas for the prince of this realm to dwell upon Trent were to turn his back or blind side to his most dangerous borderers; and for him to rest and dwell upon Severn were to be shut up in a cumbersome corner, which openeth but upon Ireland only, a place of much less importance.

Neither could London be pitched so commodiously upon any other part of the same river of Thames as where it now standeth; for if it were removed more to the west it should lose the benefit of the ebbing and flowing, and if it were seated more towards the east it should be nearer to danger of the enemy, and further both from the good air and from doing good to the inner parts of the realm; neither may I omit that none other place is so plentifully watered with springs as London is.

And whereas, amongst other things, corn and cattle, hay and fuel, be of great necessity; of the which cattle may be driven from afar, and corn may easily be transported. But hay and fuel, being of greater bulk and burthen, must be at hand: only London, by the benefit of this situation and river, may be sufficiently served therewith. In which respect an alderman of London reasonably (as me thought) affirmed, that although London received great nourishment by the residence of the prince, the repair of the parliament and courts of justice, yet it stood principally by the advantage of the situation upon the river; for when, as on a time, it was told him by a courtier that Queen Mary, in her displeasure against London, had appointed to remove with the parliament and term to Oxford, this plain man demanded whether she meant also to divert the river of Thames from London, or no? and when the gentleman had answered " No," " Then," quoth the alderman, " by God's grace, we shall do well enough at London, whatsoever become of the term and parliament." I myself being then a young scholar at Oxford, did see great preparation made towards that term and parliament, and do well remember that the common opinion and voice was, that they were not holden there, because provision of hay could not be made in all the country to serve for ten whole days together, and yet is that quarter plentifully stored with hay for the proportion of the shire itself.

For proof of the ancient estimation of London, I will not use the authority of the British history, nor of such as follow it (although some hold it credible enough that London was first *Trinobantum civitas,* or *Troja nova,* that famous city in our histories, and then Ludstoune, and by corruption London, as they report), because they be not of sufficient force to draw the gainsayers. Neither will I stand much upon that honourable testimony which Gervas. Tilburiens. giveth to London in his book, *De Otiis Imperialibus,* saying thus, concerning the blessing of God towards it:—" *In Urbe London. exceptione habet divulgatum id per omnes æquè gentes Lucani proverbium:*

Invida fatorum series summisque negatum
Stare diu.

"*Nam ea annis* 354 *ante Romam condita nunquam amisit principatum, nec bello consumpta est.*"

But I will rather use the credit of one or two ancient foreign writers, and then descend to later histories. Cornel. Tacitus, lib. 4. Annal., saith, "*Londinum copia negociatorum, et comeatu maxime celebris,*" and Herodian, in the Life of Severus the emperor, saith, "*Londinum urbs magna et opulenta.*" Beda, lib. Ecclesiastic. 10. chap. 29, showeth that Pope Gregory appointed two archbishops' sees in England, the one at London, the other at York. King Ethelstane, in his laws, appointing how many mint-masters should be in each city, allotteth eight to London, and not so many to any other city. The penner of those laws, that are said to be made by Edward the Confessor, and confirmed by William the Conqueror, saith, "*London est caput Regni, et Legum.*" King Henry I., in the third chapter of his Laws, commandeth that no citizen of London should be amerced above one hundred shillings for any pecuniary pain. The great charter of England, that Helena for which there was so long and so great war and contention, in the ninth chapter, saith, "*Civitas London. habeat omnes suas Libertates antiquas,*" etc. About the time of King John London was reputed "*regni firmata Columna,*" as Alexander Neckham writeth; and in the beginning of the reign of Richard II. it was called "*Camera regis,*" as Thomas Walsingham reporteth. I pass over the recital of the Saxon charter of King William the Conqueror, the Latin charter of Henry I. and II., of Richard I., of John, and of Edward I., all which gave unto the citizens of London great privileges, and of Edward III., who reciting all the grants of his predecessors, not only confirmed but also increased the same, and of the latter kings, who have likewise added many things thereunto. Only I wish to be noted by them, that during all this time, all those wise and politic princes have thought it fit, not only to maintain London in such plight as they found it, but also to adorn, increase, and amplify it with singular tokens of their liberal favour and good liking. And whether there be not now the same or greater causes to draw the like, or better estimation and cherishing, let any man be judge, that will take the pains to compare the present estate of London, yet still growing to better, with the former condition of the same.

It were too much to recite particularly the martial services that this city hath done from time to time; neither do I think that they be all committed to writing; only for a taste, as it were, I will note these few following.

Almost sixty years before the Conquest a huge army of the Danes (whereof King Sweyne was the leader) besieged King Etheldred in London (than the which, as the story saith, then he had none other refuge), but they were manfully repulsed, and a great number of them slain.

After the death of this Sweyne, his son Canutus (afterward king of England) besieged London, both by land and water; but after much labour, finding it impregnable, he departed; and in the same year repairing his forces, he girded it with a new siege, in the which the citizens so defended themselves, and offended him, that in the end he went away with shame.

In the dissension that arose between King Edward the Confessor and his father-in-law, Earl Goodwin (which was the mightiest subject within this land that ever I have read of), the earl with a great army came to London, and was for all that by the countenance of the citizens resisted, till such time as the nobility made reconciliation between them. About seventy years after the Conquest, Maude, the empress, made war upon King Stephen for the right of the crown, and had taken his person prisoner; but, by the strength and assistance of the Londoners and Kentishmen, Maude was put to flight at Winchester, and her brother Robert, then earl of Gloucester, was taken, in exchange for whom King Stephen was delivered: I dispute not whose right was better, but I avouch the service, seeing Stephen was in possession.

The history of William Walworth, the mayor of London, is well known; by whose manhood and policy the person of King Richard II. was rescued, the city saved, Wat Tiler killed, and all his straglers discomfited; in reward of which service, the mayor and other aldermen were knighted.

Jack Cade also having discomfited the king's army that was sent against him, came to London, and was there manfully and with long fight resisted, until that by the good policy of the citizens his company was dispersed.

Finally, in the 10th year of the reign of King Edward IV., and not many days before the death of Henry VI., Thomas Nevill, commonly called the bastard of Fauconbridge, armed a great company against the king, and being denied passage through London, he assaulted it on divers parts; but he was repulsed by the citizens, and chased as far as Stratford, with the loss of a great many.

Thus much of certain their principal and personal services in war only, for it were infinite to repeat the particular aids of

men and money which London hath ministered; and I had
rather to leave it to be conjectured at, by comparison to be
made between it and other cities, whereof I will give you this
one note for an example. In the 12th year of the reign of King
Edward II., it was ordered by parliament that every city of the
realm should make out soldiers against the Scots; at which time
London was appointed to send two hundred men, and Canterbury, being then one of our best cities, forty, and no more: and
this proportion of five to one is now in our age increased, at the
least five to one, both in soldiers and subsidy. As for the other
services that London hath done in times of peace, they are to be
measured by consideration of the commodities, whereof I will
speak anon. In the mean season, let the estate and government
of this city be considered, to the end that it may appear that it
standeth well with the policy of the realm.

Cæsar, in his Commentaries, is witness, that in his time the
cities of Britain had large territories annexed unto them, and
were several estates of themselves, governed by particular kings,
or potentates, as in Italy and Germany yet be; and that Man-
dubratius was king of the Trinobants, whose chief city London
is taken to have been. And I find not that this government was
altered either by Cæsar or his successors, notwithstanding that
the country became tributary unto them: but that it continued
until at length the Britons themselves reduced all their peoples
into one monarchy; howbeit, that lasted not any long season,
for upon Vortiger their king came the Saxons our ancestors, and
they drave the Britons into Wales, Cornwall, and Bretagne in
France, and in process of war divided the country amongst
themselves into an heptarchy, or seven kingdoms; of the which
one was called the kingdom of the East Saxons, which having
in manner the same limits that the bishopric of London now
enjoyeth, contained Essex, Middlesex, and a part of Hertfordshire, and so included London. Again, it appeareth, that in
course of time, and about eight hundred years after Christ,
Egbert (then king of the West Saxons), *ut pisces sæpe minutos
magnus comest*, overcame the rest of the kings, and once more
erected a monarchy; the which till the coming in of the
Normans, and from thence even hitherto hath continued.

Now I doubt not (whatsoever London was in the time of
Cæsar), but that under the heptarchy and monarchy it hath been
a subject, and no free city, though happily endowed with some
large privileges, for King William the Conqueror found a
portreeve there, whose name was Godfrey (by which name he

greeteth him in his Saxon Charter), and his office was none other than the charge of a bailiff or reeve, as by the self-same name continuing yet in Gravesend, and certain other places, may well appear: but the Frenchmen, using their own language, called him sometimes a provost and sometime a bailiff: whatsoever his name and office were, he was *perpetuus magistratus*, given by the prince, and not chosen by the citizens, as it seemeth; for what time King Richard I. needed money towards his expedition in the Holy Land, they first purchased of him the liberty to choose yearly from amongst themselves two bailiffs; and King John, his successor, at their like suit, changed their bailiffs into a mayor and two sheriffs. To these Henry III. added aldermen, at the first eligible yearly, but afterward by King Edward III. made perpetual magistrates and justices of the peace within their wards, in which plight of government it presently standeth. This, shortly as I could, is the historical and outward estate of London; now come I to the inward pith and substance.

The estate of this city is to be examined by the quantity and by the quality.

The quantity therefore consisteth in the number of the citizens which is very great, and far exceedeth the proportion of Hippodamus, which appointed ten thousand, and of others which have set down other numbers, as meet stintes in their opinions to be well governed; but yet seeing both reason and experience have freed us from the law of any definite number, so that other things be observed, let that be admitted: neither is London, I fear me, so great as populous; for well saith one, " *Non idem est magna civitas et frequens, magna est enim quæ multos habet qui arma ferre possunt :* " whatsoever the number be, it breedeth no fear of sedition; forasmuch as the same consisteth not in the extremes, but in a very mediocrity of wealth and riches, as it shall better appear anon.

And if the causes of English rebellions be searched out, they shall be found in effect to be these twain, ambition and covetousness; of which the first reigneth in the minds of high and noble personages, or of such others as seek to be gracious and popular, and have robbed the hearts of the multitude; whereas in London, if any where in the world, *honos vere onus est*, and every man rather shunneth than seeketh the mayoralty, which is the best mark amongst them; neither hath there been any strong faction, nor any man more popular than the rest, forasmuch as the government is by a pattern, as it were, and always the same, how often soever they change their magistrate. Covetousness,

that other sire of sedition, possesseth the miserable and needy
sort, and such as be naughty packs, unthrifts, which although
it cannot be chosen, but that in a frequent city as London is,
there shall be found many, yet bear they not any great sway,
seeing the multitude and most part there is of a competent
wealth, and earnestly bent to honest labour. I confess that
London is a mighty arm and instrument to bring any great
desire to effect, if it may be known to a man's devotion; whereof
also there want not examples in the English history. But forasmuch as the same is, by the like reason, serviceable and meet to
impeach any disloyal attempt, let it rather be well governed
than evil liked therefore; for it shall appear anon, that as London
hath adhered to some rebellions, so hath it resisted many, and
was never the author of any one. The quality of this city consisteth either in the law and government thereof, or in the
degrees and condition of the citizens or in their strength and
riches.

It is besides the purpose to dispute, whether the estate of the
government here be a democracy or aristocracy; for whatever it
be, being considered in itself, certain it is, that in respect of the
whole realm, London is but a citizen and no city, a subject and
no free estate, an obedienciary and no place endowed with any
distinct or absolute power; for it is governed by the same law
that the rest of the realm is, both in causes criminal and civil, a
few customs only excepted, which also are to be adjudged or
forejudged by the common law. And in the assembly of the
estates of our realm (which we call parliament) they are but a
member of the commonalty, and send two burgesses for their city,
as every poor borough doth, and two knights for their county,
as every other shire doth; and are as straitly bound by such laws
as any part of the realm is, for if contribution in subsidy of
money to the prince be decreed, the Londoners have none
exemption; no, not so much as to assess themselves, for the
prince doth appoint the commissioners.

If soldiers must be mustered, Londoners have no law to keep
themselves at home; if provision for the prince's household be to
be made, their goods are not privileged. In sum, therefore, the
government of London differeth not in substance, but in ceremony, from the rest of the realm, as, namely, in the names and
choice of their officers, and in their guilds and fraternities, established for the maintenance of handicrafts and labourers, and for
equity and good order to be kept in buying and selling. And
yet in these also are they to be controlled by the general law;

for by the statutes, 28 Edward III. chap. 10, and 1 Henry IV. chap. 15, the points of their misgovernment are inquirable by the inhabitants of the foreign shires adjoining, and punishable by such justiciars as the prince shall thereunto depute: to conclude, therefore, the estate of London, for government, is so agreeable a symphony with the rest, that there is no fear of dangerous discord to ensue thereby.

The multitude (or whole body) of this populous city is two ways to be considered, generally and specially: generally, they be natural subjects, a part of the commons of this realm, and are by birth for the most part a mixture of all countries of the same; by blood gentlemen, yeomen, and of the basest sort, without distinction, and by profession busy bees, and travailers for their living in the hive of this commonwealth; but specially considered, they consist of these three parts,—merchants, handicraftsmen, and labourers.

Merchandise is also divided into these three sorts,—navigation, by the which merchandizes are brought, and carried in and out over the seas; invection, by the which commodities are gathered into the city, and dispersed from thence into the country by land and negotiation, which I may call the keeping of a retailing or standing shop. In common speech, they of the first sort be called merchants, and both the other retailers.

Handicraftsmen be those which do exercise such arts as require both labour and cunning, as goldsmiths, tailors, and haberdashers, skinners, etc.

Labourers and hirelings I call those *quorum operæ non artes emuntur*, as Tullie saith; of which sort be porters, carmen, watermen, etc.

Again, these three sorts may be considered, either in respect of their wealth or number: in wealth, merchants and some of the chief retailers have the first place; the most part of retailers and all artificers the second or mean place; and hirelings the lowest room: but in number they of the middle place be first, and do far exceed both the rest; hirelings be next, and merchants be the last. Now, out of this, that the estate of London, in the persons of the citizens, is so friendly interlaced, and knit in league with the rest of the realm, not only at their beginning by birth and blood, as I have showed, but also very commonly at their ending by life and conversation, for that merchants and rich men (being satisfied with gain) do for the most part marry their children into the country, and convey themselves, after Cicero's counsel, " *Veluti ex portu in agros et possessiones:* " I do infer that there is not only no danger towards the common quiet thereby, but also great occasion and cause of good love and amity. Out of this, that they be generally bent to travel, and do fly poverty, "*Per mare, per saxa, per ignes,*" as the poet saith: I draw hope that they shall escape the note of many vices which idle people do fall into. And out of this, that they be a great multitude, and that yet the greatest part of them be neither too rich nor too poor, but do live in the mediocrity, I conclude with Aristotle, that the prince needeth not to fear sedition by them, for thus saith he: "*Magnæ urbes magis sunt a seditione liberæ, quod in eis dominetur mediocritas; nam in parvis nihil medium est, sunt enim omnes vel pauperes vel opulenti.*" I am now to come to the strength and power of this city, which consisteth partly in the number of the citizens themselves, whereof I have spoken before, partly in their riches, and in their warlike furniture; for as touching the strength of the place itself, that is apparent to the eye, and therefore is not to be treated of.

The wealth and warlike furniture of London is either public or private, and no doubt the common treasure cannot be much there, seeing that the revenue which they have hardly sufficeth to maintain their bridge and conduits, and to pay their officers and servants. Their toll doth not any more than pay their fee farm, that they pay to the prince. Their issues for default of appearances be never levied, and the profits of their courts of justice do go to particular men's hands. Arguments hereof be these two: one, that they can do nothing of extraordinary charge without a general contribution; another, that they have suffered such as have borne the chief office amongst them, and were become bankrupt, to depart the city without relief, which I think they neither would nor could have done, if the common treasure had sufficed to cover their shame; hereof therefore we need not be afraid. The public armour and munition of this city remaineth in the halls of the companies, as it doth throughout the whole realm, for a great part in the parish churches; neither is that kept together, but only for obedience to the law, which commandeth it, and therefore if that threaten danger to the estate, it may by another law be taken from them, and committed to a more safe armoury.

The private riches of London resteth chiefly in the hands of the merchants and retailers, for artificers have not much to spare, and labourers have need that it were given unto them. Now how necessary and serviceable the estate of merchandise is to this realm, it may partly appear by the practice of that peaceable, politic, and rich prince, King Henry VII., of whom Polidore (writing his life) sayeth thus: "*Mercatores ille sæpenumero pecunia multa data gratuite juvabat, ut mercatura ars una omnium cunctis æque mortalibus tum commoda, tum necessaria, in suo regno copiosior esset.*" But chiefly by the inestimable commodities that grow thereby: for who knoweth not that we have extreme need of many things, whereof foreign countries have great store, and that we may spare many things whereof they have need: or who is ignorant of this, that we have no mines of silver or gold within our realm, so that the increase of our coin and bullion cometh from elsewhere; and yet nevertheless we be both fed, clad, and otherwise served with foreign commodities and delights, as plentiful as with our domestical; which thing cometh to pass by the mean of merchandise only, which importeth necessaries from other countries, and exporteth the superfluities of our own.

For seeing we have no way to increase our treasure by mines of gold or silver at home, and can have nothing without money or ware from other countries abroad, it followeth necessarily, that if we follow the counsel of that good old husband, Marcus Cato, saying, "*Oportet patrem familias vendacem esse, non emacem,*" and do carry more commodities in value over the seas than we bring hither from thence, that then the realm shall receive that overplus in money; but if we bring from beyond the seas merchandise of more value than that which we do send over may countervail, then the realm payeth for that overplus in ready money, and consequently is a loser by that ill husbandry; and therefore in this part great and heedful regard must be had that symmetry and due proportion be kept, lest otherwise either the realm be defrauded of her treasure, or the subjects corrupted in vanity, by excessive importation of superfluous and needless merchandise, or else that we feel penury, even in our greatest plenty and store, by immoderate exportation of our own needful commodities.

Other the benefits that merchandise bringeth shall hereafter appear in the general recital of the commodities that come by London; and therefore it resteth that I speak a word of retailers, and finally show that much good groweth by them both. The chief part of retailing is but a handmaid to merchandise, dispersing by piecemeal that which the merchant bringeth in gross; of which trade be mercers, vintners, haberdashers, ironmongers, milliners, and all such as sell wares growing or made beyond the

seas; and therefore so long as merchandise itself shall be profitable, and such proportion kept as neither we lose our treasure
thereby, nor be cloyed with unnecessary foreign wares, this
kind of retailing is to be retained also.

Now that merchants and retailers of London be very rich
and great, it is so far from any harm, that it is a thing both
praiseworthy and profitable; for " *Mercatura* (saith Cicero),
*si tenuis est, sordida putanda est ; sin magna est et copiosa, non
est vituperanda.*" And truly merchants and retailers do not
altogether *intus canere*, and profit themselves only, for the
prince and realm both are enriched by their riches: the
realm winneth treasure, if their trade be so moderated by
authority that it break not proportion, and they besides
bear a good fleece, which the prince may shear when he seeth
good.

But here, before I conclude this part, I have shortly to answer
the accusation of those men, which charge London with the
loss and decay of many (or most) of the ancient cities, corporate
towns, and markets within this realm, by drawing from them
to herself alone, say they, both all trade of traffic by sea, and the
retailing of wares and exercise of manual arts also. Touching
navigation, which I must confess is apparently decayed in
many port towns, and flourisheth only or chiefly at London,
I impute that partly to the fall of the Staple, the which being
long since a great trade, and bestowed sometimes at one town
and sometimes at another within the realm, did much enrich
the place where it was, and being now not only diminished in
force, but also translated over the seas, cannot but bring some
decay with it, partly to the impairing of havens, which in many
places have impoverished those towns, whose estate doth ebb
and flow with them, and partly to the dissolution of religious
houses, by whose wealth and haunt many of those places were
chiefly fed and nourished. I mean not to rehearse particular
examples of every sort, for the thing itself speaketh, and I
haste to an end.

As for retailers, therefore, and handicraftsmen, it is no marvel
if they abandon country towns, and resort to London; for not
only the court, which is now-a-days much greater and more
gallant than in former times, and which was wont to be contented to remain with a small company, sometimes at an abbey
or priory, sometimes at a bishop's house, and sometimes at some
mean manor of the king's own, is now for the most part either
abiding at London, or else so near unto it, that the provision

of things most fit for it may easily be fetched from thence; but also by occasion thereof, the gentlemen of all shires do fly and flock to this city; the younger sort of them to see and show vanity, and the elder to save the cost and charge of hospitality and house-keeping.

For hereby it cometh to pass, that the gentlemen being either for a good portion of the year out of the country, or playing the farmers, graziers, brewers, or such like, more than gentlemen were wont to do within the country, retailers and artificers, at the least of such things as pertain to the back or belly, do leave the country towns, where there is no vent, and do fly to London, where they be sure to find ready and quick market. And yet I wish, that even as many towns in the low countries of King Philip do stand, some by one handy art, and some by another; so also that it might be provided here that the making of some things might (by discreet dispensation) be allotted to some special towns, to the end, that although the daintiness of men cannot be restrained, which will needs seek those things at London, yet other places also might be relieved, at the least by the workmanship of them.

Thus much then of the estate of London, in the government thereof, in the condition of the citizens, and in their power and riches. Now follow the enumeration of such benefits as redound to the prince and this realm by this city: in which doing I profess not to rehearse all, but only to recite and run over the chief and principal of them.

Besides the commodities of the furtherance of religion and justice, the propagation of learning, the maintenance of arts, the increase of riches, and the defence of countries (all which are before showed to grow generally by cities, and be common to London with them), London bringeth singularly these good things following.

By advantage of the situation it disperseth foreign wares (as the stomach doth meat) to all the members most commodiously.

By the benefit of the river of Thames, and great trade of merchandise, it is the chief maker of mariners, and nurse of our navy; and ships (as men know) be the wooden walls for defence of our realm.

It maintaineth in flourishing estate the countries of Norfolk, Suffolk, Essex, Kent, and Sussex, which as they lie in the face of our most puissant neighbour, so ought they above others to be conserved in the greatest strength and riches; and these, as it is well known, stand not so much by the benefit of their own soil, as by the neighbourhood and nearness which they have to London.

It relieveth plentifully, and with good policy, not only her own poor people, a thing which scarcely any other town or shire doth, but also the poor that from each quarter of the realm do flock unto it, and it imparteth liberally to the necessity of the universities besides. It is an ornament to the realm by the beauty thereof, and a terror to other countries, by reason of the great wealth and frequency. It spreadeth the honour of our country far abroad by her long navigations, and maketh our power feared, even of barbarous princes. It only is stored with rich merchants, which sort only is tolerable; for beggarly merchants do bite too near, and will do more harm than good to the realm.

It only of any place in this realm is able to furnish the sudden necessity with a strong army. It availeth the prince in tronage, poundage, and other her customs, much more than all the rest of the realm.

It yieldeth a greater subsidy than any one part of the realm; I mean not for the proportion of the value of the goods only, but also for the faithful service there used, in making the assess, for no where else be men taxed so near to their just value as in London; yea, many are found there, that for their countenance and credit sake, refuse not to be rated above their ability, which thing never happeneth abroad in the country. I omit that in ancient time the inhabitants of London and other cities were accustomably taxed after the tenth of their goods, when the country was assessed at the fifteenth, and rated at the eighth; when the country was set at the twelfth, for that were to awake a sleeping dog; and I should be thought " *dicenda, tacenda, locutus*," as the poet said.

It only doth and is able to make the prince a ready present or loan of money.

It only is found fit and able to entertain strangers honourably, and to receive the prince of the realm worthily.

Almighty God (*qui nisi custodiat civitatem, frustrà vigilat custos*) grant that her majesty evermore rightly esteem and rule this city; and he give grace, that the citizens may answer duty, as well towards God and her majesty, as towards this whole realm and country. Amen.

AN APPENDIX, CONTAINING THE EXAMINATION OF SUCH CAUSES AS HAVE HERETOFORE MOVED THE PRINCES EITHER TO FINE AND RANSOM THE CITIZENS OF LONDON, OR TO SEIZE THE LIBERTIES OF THE CITY ITSELF.

These all may be reduced to these few heads; for either the citizens have adhered, in aid or arms, to such as have warred upon the prince, or they have made tumult, and broken the common peace at home; or they have misbehaved themselves in point of government and justice; or finally, and to speak the plain truth, the princes have taken hold of small matters, and coined good sums of money out of them.

To the first head I will refer whatsoever they have done, either in those wars that happened between King Stephen and Maude the empress, being competitors of the crown, or between King John and his nobles, assisting Lewis, the French king's son, when he invaded the realm; for it is apparent by all histories that the Londoners were not the movers of these wars, but were only used as instruments to maintain them. The like is to be said of all the offences that King Henry III., whose whole reign was a continual warfare, conceived against this city, concerning the bearing of armour against him; for the first part of his reign was spent in the continuation of those wars that his father had begun with Lewis; and the rest of his life he bestowed in that contention, which was commonly called the Barons' wars: in which tragedy London, as it could not be otherwise, had now and then a part, and had many a snub at the king's hand for it: but in the end, when he had triumphed over Simon Montford at Evesham, London felt it most tragical; for then he both seized their liberties and sucked themselves dry; and yet Edictum Kenilworth, made shortly after, hath an honourable testimony for London, saying, "*Te London laudamus,*" etc. As for the other offences that he took against the Londoners, they pertain to the other parts of my division.

Next after this, against whom the Londoners did put on arms, followeth King Edward II., who in the end was deprived of his kingdom, not by their means, but by a general defection both of his own wife and son, and almost of the whole nobility and realm besides. In which trouble, that furious assault and slaughter committed by them upon the bishop of Excester, then treasurer of the realm, is to be imputed partly to the sway of the time wherewith they were carried, and partly to a private displeasure which they had to the bishop.

Finally cometh to hand King Richard II.; for these three only, in all the catalogue of our kings, have been heavy lords to London, who also had much contention with his nobility, and was in the end deposed. But whatsoever countenance and aid the city of London brought to the wars and uproars of that time, it is notoriously true that London never led the dance, but ever followed the pipe of the nobility. To close up this first part, therefore, I affirm, that in all the troublesome actions during the reign of these three kings, as also in all that heaving in and hurling out that afterward happened between King Henry VI. and King Edward IV., the city of London was many times a friend and fautor, but never the first motive or author of any intestine war or sedition.

In the second room I place a couple of tumultuous affrays that chanced in the days of King Richard I.; the one upon the day of his coronation against the Jews, which, contrary to the king's own proclamation, would needs enter the church to see him sacred, and were therefore cruelly handled by the common people. The other was caused by William with the long beard, who after that he had inflamed the poor people against the richer sort, and was called to answer for his fault, took Bow church for sanctuary, and kept it, castle-like, till he was fired out.

Here is place also for the stoning to death of a gentleman, servant to the half-brother of King Henry III., which had before provoked the citizens to fury by wounding divers of them without any cause, 1257; for the riotous fray between the servants of the goldsmiths and the tailors, 1268; for the hurly burly and bloodshed between the Londoners and the men of Westminster, moved by the young men upon an occasion of a wrestling on St. James' day, 1221; and made worse by one Constantine, an ancient citizen, for the brawl and business that arose about a baker's loaf at Salisbury place, 1391; for the which, and some other misdemeanours, King Richard II. was so incensed by evil counsel against the Londoners, that he determined to destroy them and raze their city: and for the fight that was between the citizens and sanctuary men of St. Martin's, 1454, under King Henry VI.: and finally, for the misrule on evil May-day 1519, and for such other like, if there have been any.

To the third head may be referred the seizure of their liberties, for a false judgment given against a poor widow, called Margaret Viel, 1246; the two several seizures in one year, 1258, for false packing in collections of money and other enormities; and finally the seizure made by King Edward I. for taking of bribes of the bakers, 1285. But all this security in seizing and resuming of the liberties, which was in old time the only ordinary punishment, was at length mitigated by King Edward III. and King Henry IV., in their statutes before remembered.

In the last place stand those offences, which I repute rather taken than given, and do fall within the measure of the adage, "*Ut canem cædas, cito invenias baculum :*" for King John, in the 10th of his reign, deposed the bailiffs of London, because they had bought up the wheat in the market, so that there was not to serve his purveyors. King Henry III., his son, compelled the Londoners to pay him five thousand pounds, because they had lent to Lewis, the French king, the like sum, of a good mind to dispatch him out of their city and the realm, at such time as the protector and the whole nobility fell to composition with him for his departure. And the same king fined them at three thousand marks for the escape of a prisoner out of Newgate, of whom they took no charge; for he was a clerk, prisoner to the bishop of London, under the custody of his own servants; and as for the place, it was only borrowed of the Londoners to serve that turn. Hitherto of these things to this end, that whatsoever misdemeanour shall be objected out of history against London, the same may herein appear, both in its true place and proper colour.

FITZSTEPHEN'S DESCRIPTION OF LONDON

OF THE SITUATION OF THE SAME

AMONGST the noble and celebrated cities of the world, that of London, the capital of the kingdom of England, is one of the most renowned, possessing above all others abundant wealth, extensive commerce, great grandeur and magnificence. It is happy in the salubrity of its climate, in the profession of the Christian religion, in the strength of its fortresses, the nature of its situation, the honour of its citizens, and the chastity of its matrons; in its sports too it is most pleasant, and in the production of illustrious men most fortunate. All which things I wish separately to consider.

OF THE MILDNESS OF THE CLIMATE
There then

> " Men's minds are soft'ned by a temp'rate clime,"

not so however that they are addicted to licentiousness, but so that they are not savage and brutal, but rather kind and generous.

OF THE RELIGION

There is in St. Paul's church an episcopal see: it was formerly metropolitan, and, it is thought, will be so again, should the citizens return to the island: unless perhaps the archiepiscopal title of St. Thomas, and his bodily presence there, should always retain that dignity at Canterbury, where it now is. But as St. Thomas has ennobled both these cities, London by his birth, and Canterbury by his death, each of them, with respect to the saint, has much to allege against the other, and with justice too. As regards divine worship, there are also in London and in the suburbs thirteen larger conventual churches, besides one hundred and thirty-six lesser parochial ones.

OF THE STRENGTH OF THE CITY

On the east stands the Palatine tower, a fortress of great size and strength, the court and walls of which are erected upon a very deep foundation, the mortar used in the building being tempered with the blood of beasts. On the west are two castles strongly fortified; the wall of the city is high and thick, with seven double gates, having on the north side towers placed at proper intervals. London formerly had walls and towers in like manner on the south, but that most excellent river the Thames, which abounds with fish, and in which the tide ebbs and flows, runs on that side, and has in a long space of time washed down, undermined, and subverted the walls in that part. On the west also, higher up on the bank of the river, the royal palace rears its head, an incomparable structure, furnished with a breastwork and bastions, situated in a populous suburb, at a distance of two miles from the city.

OF THE GARDENS

Adjoining to the houses on all sides lie the gardens of those citizens that dwell in the suburbs, which are well furnished with trees, spacious and beautiful.

OF THE PASTURE AND TILLAGE LANDS

On the north side too are fields for pasture, and a delightful plain of meadow land, interspersed with flowing streams, on which stand mills, whose clack is very pleasing to the ear. Close by lies an immense forest, in which are densely wooded thickets, the coverts of game, stags, fallow-deer, boars, and wild bulls. The tillage lands of the city are not barren gravelly soils, but like the fertile plains of Asia, which produce abundant crops, and fill the barns of their cultivators with

" Ceres' plenteous sheaf."

OF THE SPRINGS

There are also round London, on the northern side, in the suburbs, excellent springs; the water of which is sweet, clear, and salubrious,

" 'Mid glistening pebbles gliding playfully: "

amongst which, Holywell, Clerkenwell, and St. Clement's well, are of most note, and most frequently visited, as well by the scholars from the schools, as by the youth of the city when they go out to take the air in the summer evenings. The city is delightful indeed, when it has a good governor.

OF THE HONOUR OF THE CITIZENS

This city is ennobled by her men, graced by her arms, and peopled by a multitude of inhabitants; so that in the wars under King Stephen there went out to a muster, of armed horsemen, esteemed fit for war, twenty thousand, and of infantry sixty thousand. The citizens of London are respected and noted above all other citizens for the elegance of their manners, dress, table, and discourse.

OF THE MATRONS

The matrons of the city are perfect Sabines.

OF THE SCHOOLS

The three principal churches possess, by privilege and ancient dignity, celebrated schools; yet often, by the favour of some person of note, or of some learned men eminently distinguished for their philosophy, other schools are permitted upon sufferance. On festival days the masters assemble their pupils at those churches where the feast of the patron saint is solemnised; and there the scholars dispute, some in the demonstrative way, and others logically; some again recite enthymemes, while others use the more perfect syllogism. Some, to show their abilities, engage in such disputation as is practised among persons contending for victory alone; others dispute upon a truth, which is the grace of perfection. The sophisters, who argue upon feigned topics, are deemed clever according to their fluency of speech and command of language. Others endeavour to impose by false conclusions. Sometimes certain orators in their rhetorical harangues employ all the powers of persuasion, taking care to observe the precepts of the art, and to omit nothing apposite to the subject. The boys of the different schools wrangle with each other in verse, and contend about the principles of grammar or the rules of the perfect and future tenses. There are some who in epigrams, rhymes, and verses, use that trivial raillery so much practised amongst the ancients, freely attacking their companions with Fescennine licence, but suppressing the names, discharging their scoffs and sarcasms against them, touching with Socratic wit the failings of their schoolfellows, or perhaps of greater personages, or biting them more keenly with a Theonine tooth.   The audience,

> " well disposed to laugh,
> With curling nose double the quivering peals."

OF THE MANNER IN WHICH THE AFFAIRS OF THE CITY ARE DISPOSED

The artizans of the several crafts, the vendors of the various commodities, and the labourers of every kind, have each their separate station, which they take every morning.   There is also in London, on the bank of the river, amongst the wine-shops which are kept in ships and cellars, a public eating-house: there every day, according to the season, may be found viands of all kinds, roast, fried, and boiled, fish large and small, coarser meat for the poor, and more delicate for the rich, such as venison, fowls, and small birds.   If friends, wearied with their journey, should unexpectedly come to a citizen's house, and, being hungry, should not like to wait till fresh meat be bought and cooked:

> " The canisters with bread are heap'd on high;
> The attendants water for their hands supply: "—DRYDEN.

Meanwhile some run to the river side, and there every thing that they could wish for is instantly procured.   However great the number of soldiers or strangers that enters or leaves the city at any hour of the day or night, they may turn in there if they please, and refresh themselves according to their inclination; so that the former have no occasion to fast too long, or the latter to leave the city without dining.   Those who wish to indulge themselves would not desire a sturgeon, or the bird of Africa, or the godwit of Ionia, when the delicacies that are to be found there are set before them.   This indeed is the public cookery, and is very convenient to the city, and a distinguishing mark of civilisation.   Hence we read in Plato's Gorgias, " Juxta medicinam esse coquorum officium, simulantium et adulationem quartæ particulæ civilitatis."   There is, without one of the gates, immediately in the suburb, a certain smooth field in name and in reality.   There every Friday, unless it be one of the more solemn festivals, is a noted show of well-bred horses exposed for sale.   The earls, barons, and knights, who are at

the time resident in the city, as well as most of the citizens, flock
thither either to look on or buy. It is pleasant to see the nags,
with their sleek and shining coats, smoothly ambling along,
raising and setting down alternately, as it were, their feet on
either side: in one part are horses better adapted to esquires;
these, whose pace is rougher but yet expeditious, lift up and set
down, as it were, the two opposite fore and hind feet together; in
another the young blood colts, not yet accustomed to the bridle,

> " Which upright walk on pasterns firm and straight,
>   Their motions easy, prancing in their gait."—DRYDEN.

in a third are the horses for burden, strong and stout-limbed;
and in a fourth, the more valuable chargers, of an elegant·shape
and noble height, with nimbly moving ears, erect necks, and
plump haunches. In the movements of these the purchasers
observe first their easy pace, and then their gallop, which is
when the fore-feet are raised from the ground and set down
together, and the hind ones in like manner, alternately. When
a race is to be run by such horses as these, and perhaps by others,
which in like manner, according to their breed, are strong for
carriage, and vigorous for the course, the people raise a shout,
and order the common horses to be withdrawn to another part of
the field. The jockeys, who are boys expert in the management
of horses, which they regulate by means of curb-bridles, sometimes by threes, and sometimes by twos, according as the
match is made, prepare themselves for the contest. Their
chief aim is to prevent a competitor getting before them. The
horses, too, after their manner, are eager for the race; their
limbs tremble, and, impatient of delay, they cannot stand still;
upon the signal being given, they stretch out their limbs, hurry
over the course, and are borne along with unremitting speed.
The riders, inspired with the love of praise and the hope of
victory, clap spurs to their flying horses, lashing them with their
whips, and inciting them by their shouts. You would think
with Heraclitus, that all things were in motion, and that Zeno's
opinion was altogether erroneous, when he said, that there was
no such thing as motion, and that it was impossible to reach the
goal. In another quarter, apart from the rest, stand the goods
of the peasants, implements of husbandry, swine with their long
sides, cows with distended udders,

> " Oxen of bulk immense, and woolly flocks."

There, too, stand the mares fitted for the plough, the dray, and
the cart, of which some are big with foal, others have their frolic-

some colts running close by their sides.   To this city, from every nation under heaven, merchants bring their commodities by sea,

> " Arabia's gold, Sabæa's spice and incense,
>   Scythia's keen weapons, and the oil of palms
>   From Babylon's rich soil, Nile's precious gems,
>   Norway's warm peltries, Russia's costly sables,
>   Sera's rich vestures, and the wines of Gaul,
>   Hither are sent."

According to the evidence of chroniclers London is more ancient than Rome: for, as both derive their origin from the same Trojan ancestors, this was founded by Brutus before that by Romulus and Remus.   Hence it is that, even to this day, both cities use the same ancient laws and ordinances.   This, like Rome, is divided into wards; it has annual sheriffs instead of consuls; it has an order of senators and inferior magistrates, and also sewers and aqueducts in its streets; each class of suits, whether of the deliberative, demonstrative, or judicial kind, has its appropriate place and proper court; on stated days it has its assemblies.   I think that there is no city in which more approved customs are observed—in attending churches, honouring God's ordinances, keeping festivals, giving alms, receiving strangers, confirming espousals, contracting marriages, celebrating weddings, preparing entertainments, welcoming guests, and also in the arrangement of the funeral ceremonies and the burial of the dead.   The only inconveniences of London are, the immoderate drinking of foolish persons, and the frequent fires. Moreover, almost all the bishops, abbots, and great men of England, are, in a manner, citizens and freemen of London; as they have magnificent houses there, to which they resort, spending large sums of money, whenever they are summoned thither to councils and assemblies by the king or their metropolitan, or are compelled to go there by their own business.

OF THE SPORTS

Let us now proceed to the sports of the city; since it is expedient that a city be not only an object of utility and importance, but also a source of pleasure and diversion.   Hence even in the seals of the chief pontiffs, up to the time of Pope Leo, there was engraved on one side of the Bull the figure of St. Peter as a fisherman, and above him a key stretched out to him, as it were, from heaven by the hand of God, and around him this verse—

> " For me thou left'st thy ship, receive the key."

On the obverse side was represented a city, with this inscription, GOLDEN ROME. It was also said in praise of Augustus Cæsar and the city of Rome,

> " All night it rains, the shows return with day,
>   Cæsar, thou bear'st with Jove alternate sway."

London, instead of theatrical shows and scenic entertainments, has dramatic performances of a more sacred kind, either representations of the miracles which holy confessors have wrought, or of the passions and sufferings in which the constancy of martyrs was signally displayed. Moreover, to begin with the sports of the boys (for we have all been boys), annually on the day which is called Shrovetide, the boys of the respective schools bring each a fighting cock to their master, and the whole of that forenoon is spent by the boys in seeing their cocks fight in the school-room. After dinner, all the young men of the city go out into the fields to play at the well-known game of foot-ball. The scholars belonging to the several schools have each their ball; and the city tradesmen, according to their respective crafts, have theirs. The more aged men, the fathers of the players, and the wealthy citizens, come on horseback to see the contests of the young men, with whom, after their manner, they participate, their natural heat seeming to be aroused by the sight of so much agility, and by their participation in the amusements of unrestrained youth. Every Sunday in Lent, after dinner, a company of young men enter the fields, mounted on warlike horses—

> " On coursers always foremost in the race; "

of which

> " Each steed's well-train'd to gallop in a ring."

The lay-sons of the citizens rush out of the gates in crowds, equipped with lances and shields, the younger sort with pikes from which the iron head has been taken off, and there they get up sham fights, and exercise themselves in military combat. When the king happens to be near the city, most of the courtiers attend, and the young men who form the households of the earls and barons, and have not yet attained the honour of knighthood, resort thither for the purpose of trying their skill. The hope of victory animates every one. The spirited horses neigh, their limbs tremble, they champ their bits, and, impatient of delay, cannot endure standing still. When at length

> " The charger's hoof seizes upon the course,"

the young riders having been divided into companies, some

pursue those that go before without being able to overtake them, whilst others throw their companions out of their course, and gallop beyond them. In the Easter holidays they play at a game resembling a naval engagement. A target is firmly fastened to the trunk of a tree which is fixed in the middle of the river, and in the prow of a boat driven along by oars and the current stands a young man who is to strike the target with his lance; if, in hitting it, he break his lance, and keep his position unmoved, he gains his point, and attains his desire: but if his lance be not shivered by the blow, he is tumbled into the river, and his boat passes by, driven along by its own motion. Two boats, however, are placed there, one on each side of the target, and in them a number of young men to take up the striker, when he first emerges from the stream, or when

> " A second time he rises from the wave."

On the bridge, and in balconies on the banks of the river, stand the spectators,

> " well disposed to laugh."

During the holydays in summer the young men exercise them-selves in the sports of leaping, archery, wrestling, stone-throwing, slinging javelins beyond a mark, and also fighting with bucklers. Cytherea leads the dances of the maidens, who merrily trip along the ground beneath the uprisen moon. Almost on every holyday in winter, before dinner, foaming boars, and huge-tusked hogs, intended for bacon, fight for their lives, or fat bulls or immense boars are baited with dogs. When that great marsh which washes the walls of the city on the north side is frozen over, the young men go out in crowds to divert them-selves upon the ice. Some, having increased their velocity by a run, placing their feet apart, and turning their bodies sideways, slide a great way: others make a seat of large pieces of ice like mill-stones, and a great number of them running before, and holding each other by the hand, draw one of their companions who is seated on the ice: if at any time they slip in moving so swiftly, all fall down headlong together. Others are more expert in their sports upon the ice; for fitting to, and binding under their feet the shinbones of some animal, and taking in their hands poles shod with iron, which at times they strike against the ice, they are carried along with as great rapidity as a bird flying or a bolt discharged from a cross-bow. Sometimes two of the skaters having placed themselves a great distance apart by mutual agreement, come together from opposite sides; they meet, raise their poles, and strike each other; either one or both of them fall, not without some bodily hurt: even after their fall they are carried along to a great distance from each other by the velocity of the motion; and whatever part of their heads comes in contact with the ice is laid bare to the very skull. Very frequently the leg or arm of the falling party, if he chance to light upon either of them, is broken. But youth is an age eager for glory and desirous of victory, and so young men engage in counterfeit battles, that they may conduct themselves more valiantly in real ones. Most of the citizens amuse themselves in sporting with merlins, hawks, and other birds of a like kind, and also with dogs that hunt in the woods. The citizens have the right of hunting in Middlesex, Hertfordshire, all the Chilterns, and Kent, as far as the river Cray. The Londoners, then called Trinovantes, repulsed Caius Julius Cæsar, a man who delighted to mark his path with blood. Whence Lucan says,

> "Britain he sought, but turn'd his back dismay'd."

The city of London has produced some men, who have subdued many kingdoms, and even the Roman empire; and very many others, whose virtue has exalted them to the skies, as was promised to Brutus by the oracle of Apollo:

> "Brutus, there lies beyond the Gallic bounds
> An island which the western sea surrounds:
> .   .   .   .
> To reach this happy shore thy sails employ:
> There fate decrees to raise a second Troy,
> And found an empire in thy royal line
> Which time shall ne'er destroy, nor bounds confine."

Since the planting of the Christian religion there, London has given birth to the noble emperor Constantine, who gave the city of Rome and all the insignia of the empire to God and St. Peter, and Pope Sylvester, whose stirrup he held, and chose rather to be called defender of the holy Roman church, than emperor: and that the peace of our lord the Pope might not, by reason of his presence, be disturbed by the turmoils consequent on secular business, he withdrew from the city which he had bestowed upon our lord the Pope, and built for himself the city of Byzantium. London also in modern times has produced illustrious and august princes, the empress Matilda, King Henry the Third, and St. Thomas, the archbishop and glorious martyr of Christ, than whom no man was more guileless or more devoted to all good men throughout the whole Roman world.

ADDITIONAL NOTES

P. 15, para. 2: The true derivation of " Langborne" is from Langburne (Lombard) Street; that of " Shareborne" for " Shitteborwe Lane." There was in fact no Langborne stream.

P. 16, para 1: The correct meaning of Oldborne, or Holeburne (= Holborn) is probably " the burn in the hollow."

P. 21, para. 3: Stow errs as to the site of old London Bridge. The medieval structure stood slightly to the east of the present bridge.

P. 28, l. 30: Aeldgate (Aldgate) is more probably derived from *Ealh,* an owner or builder.

P. 32, ll. 12–18: Stow is badly confused here. He is misquoting Lydgate (*Legend of St. Edmund and St. Fremund,* Bk. III, ll. 162–3), who says: " Off Burchardus folwe I shall the style, that of Seyn Fremund whilom was secretarye." Incidentally, Abbo of Fleury does not refer to the bringing of St. Edmund's body to London. Moreover, Cripplegate has nothing to do with cripples; it is derived from O.E. crepel (burrow), and means sunk (or narrow) gate.

P. 36, l. 28: " Ludgate " means simply a " postern."

P. 39, l. 10: Downegate (Dowgate) is from Douegate. Doue (Dove) may have been a woman's name.

Ibid., l. 36: "Wolfes " is almost certainly a misprint for " Wolses."

P. 60, l. 35: Stow's genealogy of the Lords Fitzwalter, as given in the next six lines, is erroneous. Robert died in 1325 (not 1305), and was succeeded not by Walter, but by Robert III. (*d.* 1328, not 1325). The latter's son John (not Robert) died in 1361.

P. 67, l. 16: The spurious fifteenth-century chronicle cited here is falsely ascribed to Ingulph. The story is without foundation.

P. 75, note 3: This quotation from " Thomas Clifford," and that on page 405, are taken from the *Life of Edward the Confessor* compiled for Queen Eadgyth soon after the king's death (1066). We may infer that Clifford supplied Stow with the two passages.

P. 76, note 2: W. Patten (living 1590) was a lawyer, antiquarian, and author of *The Expedition into Scotland* (1548); but it is not known to what work of his Stow refers in this place.

P. 112: Stow has erred in transcribing the copy from

Letter-Book C, 220–221, which reads "Gaufrido Cancellario" and refers to Geoffrey Rufus (chancellor 1124 ff.).

P. 120, l. 9: For "Thomas Pike," in the previous line, read "Thomas Pilk." The error is Stow's.

P. 126, l. 10: Belzettars (or Belzeters) means "bell-founders." It is not a proper name.

P. 130, l. 17: These lines occur nowhere in the accepted works of Chaucer. They occur (with some minor variations) in an anonymous poem entitled *Chance of the Dice* (Fairfax MS. 16, f. 194).

P. 132, note 2: "Oliver" should read "Cleve." Stow appears to have copied the misreading from Leland's *Collectanea*, i. 111.

P. 154, l. 33: Stow's information in the next chapter, as to the foundation of St. Helen's priory, is erroneous. It was established *circa* 1212; nor was there any dean of St. Paul's named William Basing.

P. 180, l. 12: The second derivation given by Stow is more probably correct.

P. 188, para. 2: The title St. Margaret Pattens is most probably derived from the name of a benefactor (? Patin).

P. 212, l. 11: For a more accurate account of Cold Harbour subsequent to Poultney's death, see *Archaeologia*, lvii, 257–84.

P. 218, l. 25: "Royal" here is a corruption of "Ryole," a name due to occupation by wine-merchants from La Réole in Gascony.

P. 225, l. 9: There is in fact no doubt that this name, which is found as early as 1259, *was* due to its having been inhabited by soap-makers.

P. 268, l. 6: The true derivation of "Monkswell Street" is "Mukewellestrate" which is found in documents of 1277.

P. 271, l. 8: The word "barbican" is from Low Latin *barbacana* (= an outwork), and is quite unconnected with "burghkenning."

P. 273, l. 24: Stow is in error here. This John Sutton's tomb bore the date July 6, 1450; which proves him to have been not the sheriff (1413), but an alderman of the same name who was killed in Cadn rebellion.

P. 279, l. 6: The account given above by Stow of the Farringdons is incorrect. William Farringdon died in 1294. Nicholas, the mayor, was his son-in-law (not son) and probably son of Ralph le Fevre. He died in 1334. His daughter's son Nicholas used the name Farringdon; he died in 1361, but was never an alderman.

P. 301, l. 3: There are several errors of date in the foregoing paragraph, as follows: p. 299, l. 33, Hingham *d.* 1311 (not 1308); ibid., l. 42, Monden *d.* 1338 (not 1332); p. 300, l. 1, Melford *d.* 1336 (not 1345); ibid., l. 21, Brewer *d.* 1353 (not 1366); ibid., Wendover *d.* 1252 (not 1366); ibid., l. 24, de Bery *d.* 1386 (not 1390); ibid., l. 26, Holmes *d.* 1395 (not 1400); ibid., l. 34, Evers *d.* 1400 (not 1411); ibid., l. 35, More *d.* 1421 (not 1419).

P. 332, l. 35: The foregoing paragraph errs in placing the Liberty of the Rolls in the City, where it has never been.

P. 363, last line: The *Speculum Meditantis* is identified with *Mirour de l'Omme* (Cambridge University Library, Add. MS. 1891), printed in G. C. Macaulay's edition of Gower's *Works*, i., 1–334.

P. 392, l. 4: Stow is almost certainly wrong in placing the first house of Black Friars outside the City boundary. It appears to have been in Shoe Lane, in the parish of St. Andrew, Holborn.

P. 418, l. 34: This clochard was built not by Edward III., but in 1249–53. It survived until 1750.

P. 421, l. 9: Stow is hopelessly confused. John Islip joined the community at Westminster in 1480 and was not elected abbot until 1500. Caxton's first book printed at Westminster was the *Dictes and Sayings of the Philosophers* (18th November 1477). He worked at the sign of the " Red Pale," a house rented from the Abbey and situated in the Almonry.

P. 426, l. 9: The dates to this point must be inaccurate; for it is known that Deorwulf was bishop as late as 862.

Ibid., l. 31: Stow's list from Swithulf to Robert is wrong. The succession was as follows: Aelfstan (*d.* 898); Wulfsige (898–910); Heahstan; Theodred (926–51); Wulfstan; Brihthelm (953–9); Dunstan (959–61); Aelfstan (961–95); Wulfstan (996–1003); Aelfwin (1004–12); Elfwig (1014–35); Elfweard (1035–44). Note also the following corrections to Stow's list (pp. 426 ff.): p. 426, ll. 36–8. William died in 1075, and therefore "sat" twenty-four (not seventeen) years. P. 427, ll. 10, 11. Gilbert Universalis was consecrated in 1128 (not 1127), died in 1134, and therefore "sat" six (not fourteen) years. Ibid., ll. 12–15. Robert de Sigillo, consecrated 1141 and died 1151, " sat " ten years. Ibid., l. 19. Gilbert Foliot died in 1187. P. 428, ll. 39–42. Fulco Basset was consecrated in 1244. Ibid., l. 43. Henry Wingham was consecrated in 1260. P. 429, l. 6. Henry Sandwich was consecrated in 1263. Ibid., ll. 8–10. John Chesul was consecrated in 1274 and died in 1280. Ibid., ll. 25, 26. For " 1307 " read " 1306." Ibid., l. 35. Stephen Gravesend was consecrated in 1319 and

" sat " for nineteen (not twenty) years. Ibid., ll. 38–43. Ralph Stratford was consecrated in 1340 and " sat " for thirteen years. P. 430, ll. 1, 2. Michael Norbroke (Northburgh) was consecrated in 1355. Ibid., ll. 8–11. Robert Breybrook was consecrated in 1382; he therefore " sat " twenty-two years. Ibid., ll. 40-2. Robert Gilbert was consecrated in 1436. P. 431, ll. 1–7. Thomas Kempe was consecrated in 1450. Ibid., ll. 8–11. There was no John Marshal, bishop of London. Richard Hill succeeded Kempe; he was consecrated in 1489 and died in 1496. Ibid., l. 21, for "1521" read "1522." Ibid., l. 27. Tunstal was consecrated in 1522. Ibid., l. 32. Boner was consecrated in 1540. P. 433, l. 11. John Elmere was consecrated in 1577.

P. 443, last line: This is erroneous; the privilege was extorted from John, brother of Richard, in 1191.

P. 445, ll. 22-4: There is no charter of this date; Stow is probably referring to that dated 9 May 1215.

Ibid., l. 36: Note, however, that elsewhere (p. 19) Stow gives 1211 as the year in which the ditch was begun.

P. 449, l. 22: Though placed here by Stow, the foundation was much earlier (see p. 241).

TOPOGRAPHICAL INDEX
OF LONDON

ff. after an entry implies that there are references to the same subject
on at least two immediately succeeding pages.

INDEX

EVERYMAN'S LIBRARY AND EVERYMAN PAPERBACKS: A Selection

indicates the volumes also in paperback: for their series numbers in Everyman Paperbacks add 1000 to the EML numbers given.
EUL stands for Everyman's University Library.
For copyright reasons some of the following titles are not available in the U.S.A.

BIOGRAPHY

ESSAYS AND CRITICISM

FICTION